THE LETTERS

OF

CHARLES DICKENS

EDITED BY

HIS SISTER-IN-LAW AND HIS ELDEST DAUGHTER

1833 TO 1870

𝕷𝖔𝖓𝖉𝖔𝖓

MACMILLAN AND CO., LIMITED

NEW YORK: THE MACMILLAN COMPANY.

1903

First Edition 1893
Reprinted 1903

PREFACE

IN publishing this New Edition of "The Letters of Charles Dickens" in a popular form, we have taken great pains to make our work complete. We have carefully revised and corrected the contents of our previous books, now condensed, chronologically, into two volumes.

With a view to making our selection as perfect as possible, we have collected together the letters from Charles Dickens which have already been published in various Biographies, and have chosen those which we consider to be of the greatest interest.

We intend this Collection of Letters to be a Supplement to the "Life of Charles Dickens," by John Forster. That work, admirable and exhaustive as a biography, is only incomplete as regards correspondence; the scheme of the book having made it impossible to include in its space any letters, or hardly any, besides those addressed to Mr. Forster. As no man ever expressed *himself* more in his letters than Charles Dickens, we believe that in publishing this careful selection from his general correspondence we are supplying a want which has been universally felt.

Our request for the loan of letters was so promptly and fully responded to, that we have been provided with more than sufficient material for our work. By arranging the letters in chronological order, we find that they very frequently explain themselves and form a narrative of the events of each year. Our collection dates from 1833, the commencement of Charles Dickens' literary life, just before the starting of the "Pickwick Papers," and is carried on up to the day before his death, in 1870.

We find some difficulty in being quite accurate in the

arrangements of letters up to the end of 1839, for he had a careless habit in those days about dating his letters, very frequently putting only the day of the week on which he wrote, curiously in contrast with the habit of his later life, when his dates were always of the very fullest.

A blank is made in Charles Dickens' correspondence with his family by the absence of any letters addressed to his daughter Kate (Mrs. Perugini), to her great regret and to ours. In 1873, her furniture and other possessions were stored in the warehouse of the Pantechnicon at the time of the great fire there. All her property was destroyed, and, among other things, a box of papers which included her letters from her father.

It was our intention as well as our desire to have thanked, individually, every one—both living friends and representatives of dead ones—for their readiness to give us every possible help. But the number of such friends, besides correspondents hitherto unknown, who have volunteered contributions of letters, make it impossible in our space to do otherwise than to express, collectively, our earnest and heartfelt thanks.

A separate word of gratitude, however, must be given by us to Mr. Wilkie Collins for the invaluable aid which we have received from his great knowledge and experience, in the technical part of our work, and for the deep interest which he has shown from the beginning, in our undertaking.

It is a great pleasure to us to have the name of Henry Fielding Dickens associated with this book. To him, for the very important assistance he has given in making our Index, we return our loving thanks.

In writing our explanatory notes we have, we hope, left nothing out which in any way requires explanation from us. But we have purposely made them as short as possible; our great desire being to give to the public another book from Charles Dickens' own hands—as it were, a portrait of himself by himself.

In publishing the more private letters, we do so with the view of showing him in his homely, domestic life—of showing how in the midst of his own constant and arduous work, no household matter was considered too trivial to claim his care and attention. He would take as much pains about the hanging of a picture, the choosing of furniture, the superintending any little improvement in the house, as he would about the more serious business of his life; thus carrying out to the very letter his favourite motto of "What is worth doing at all is worth doing well."

MAMIE DICKENS.
GEORGINA HOGARTH.

LONDON, *March*, 1882.

———

THERE is very little to say in addition to the original Preface to our book, except that this Edition, which is in a cheaper and more popular form than either of the previous Editions, has been again very carefully revised and corrected by us, and we hope it will help to make the "Letters of Charles Dickens" more widely known than they have hitherto been.

Since we published, in 1882, the Edition in two volumes to which the above Preface belongs, many of the dear friends to whom some of the most interesting and the brightest of these letters were addressed have passed away. This has added to the sadness of our task, but it adds also a new interest to the letters, which are so fresh and life-like that they seem to give graphic portraits both of the writer himself and of the friends to whom he wrote.

MAMIE DICKENS.
GEORGINA HOGARTH.

LONDON, *January*, 1893.

BOOK I.

1833 TO 1842.

THE LETTERS

OF

CHARLES DICKENS.

1833 OR 1834, AND 1835, 1836, 1837.

NARRATIVE.

WE have been able to procure so few early letters of any general interest that we put these first years together. Charles Dickens was then living, as a bachelor, in Furnival's Inn, and was engaged as a parliamentary reporter on *The Morning Chronicle*. The "Sketches by Boz" were written during these years, published first in "The Monthly Magazine" and continued in *The Evening Chronicle*. He was engaged to be married to Catherine Hogarth in 1835—the marriage took place on the 2nd April, 1836; and he continued to live in Furnival's Inn with his wife for more than a year after their marriage. They passed the summer months of that year in a lodging at Chalk, near Gravesend, in the neighbourhood associated with all his life, from his childhood to his death. The two letters which we publish, addressed to his wife as Miss Hogarth, have no date, but were written in 1835. The first of the two refers to the offer made to him by Messrs. Chapman and Hall to edit a monthly periodical, the "emolument" (which he calls "too tempting to resist!") to be fourteen pounds a month. The bargain was concluded, and this was the starting of "The Pickwick Papers." The first number was published in March, 1836. The second letter to Miss Hogarth was written after he had completed three numbers of "Pickwick," and the character who is to "make a decided hit" is "Jingle."

From the commencement of "The Pickwick Papers," and of Charles Dickens' married life, dates the commencement of his literary life and his sudden world-wide fame. And this year saw the beginning of many of those friendships which he most valued, and of which he had most reason to be proud, and which friendships were ended only by death. Most especially to be noted is his first letter to Mr. Macready.

In January, 1837, Charles Dickens was living in Furnival's Inn, where his first child, a son, was born. It was an eventful year to him in many ways. He removed from Furnival's Inn to Doughty Street in March, and here he sustained the first great grief of his life. His young sister-in-law, Mary Hogarth, to whom he was devotedly attached, died very suddenly, at his house, on the 7th May. In the Autumn of this year he took lodgings at Broadstairs. This was his first visit to that pleasant little watering-place, of which he became very fond, and whither he removed for the autumn months with all his household for many years in succession.

Besides the monthly numbers of "Pickwick," which were going on through this year until November, when the last number appeared, he had commenced "Oliver Twist," which was appearing also in monthly parts, in the magazine called "Bentley's Miscellany," long before "Pickwick" was completed. And during this year he had edited, for Mr. Bentley, "The Life of Grimaldi," the celebrated clown. To this book he wrote himself only the preface, and altered and rearranged the autobiographical MS., which was in Mr. Bentley's possession.

The first letter of this book is addressed to Henry Austin, a friend of Charles Dickens from his boyhood, who afterwards married his second sister Letitia. It bears no date, but must have been written in 1833 or 1834, during the early days of his reporting for *The Morning Chronicle;* the journey on which he was "ordered" being for that paper.

The first letter to his friend, Mr. J. P. Harley, the actor, which is undated, but must have been written about 1836, refers to a farce called "The Strange Gentleman," founded on one of the "Sketches," called "The Great Winglebury Duel," which Charles Dickens wrote expressly for Mr. Harley, and which was produced at the St. James's Theatre, under the management of Mr. Braham.

The letters which we give to Mr. John Hullah, the well-known composer, and a very early friend of Charles Dickens, are all on the subject of an operetta called "The Village Coquettes," written by him and the music by Mr. Hullah, which was also produced at the St. James's Theatre.

The "present" alluded to in the letter to Mrs. Hogarth was a chain made of Mary Hogarth's hair, sent on the first anniversary, after her death, of her birthday.

The letter to Mr. Thomas Tegg, the publisher, was upon the subject of a proposal to Charles Dickens to write for Mr. Tegg a work to be entitled "Serjeant Bell and his Raree Show." The terms were agreed upon and accepted, but for some reason the project fell through.

FURNIVAL'S INN, *Wednesday Night, past* 12.   Mr. Henry Austin.

DEAR HENRY,

I have just been ordered on a journey, the length of which is at present uncertain. I may be back on Sunday very probably, and start again on the following day. Should this be the case, you shall hear from me before.

Don't laugh. I am going (alone) in a gig; and, to quote the eloquent inducements which the proprietors of Hampstead *chays* hold out to Sunday riders—"the gen'l'm'n drives himself." I am going into Essex and Suffolk. It strikes me I shall be spilt before I pay a turnpike. I have a presentiment I shall run over an only child before I reach Chelmsford, my first stage.

Let the evident haste of this specimen of "The Polite Letter Writer" be its excuse, and

Believe me, dear Henry, most sincerely yours,

NOTE.—To avoid the monotony of a constant repetition, we propose to dispense with the signature at the close of each letter, excepting to the first and last letters of our collection. Charles Dickens' handwriting altered so much during the years of his life, that we have thought it advisable to give a facsimile of his autograph to this our first letter; and we reproduce in the same way his latest autograph.

* 13, FURNIVAL'S INN,   Mr. George Hogarth.
Tuesday Evening, Twentieth January, 1835.

MY DEAR SIR,

As you have begged me to write an original sketch for the first number of the new evening paper, and as I trust to your kindness to refer my application to the proper quarter, should I be unreasonably or improperly trespassing upon you, I beg to ask whether it is probable that if I commenced a series of articles,

* Printed in "Forty Years' Recollections of Life, Literature, and Public Affairs," by Charles Mackay.

written under some attractive title, for *The Evening Chronicle*, its conductors would think I had any claim to *some* additional remuneration (of course, of no great amount) for doing so?

Let me beg of you not to misunderstand my meaning. Whatever the reply may be, I promised you an article, and shall supply it with the utmost readiness, and with an anxious desire to do my best, which I honestly assure you would be the feeling with which I shall always receive any request coming personally from yourself. I merely wish to put it to the proprietors, first, whether a continuation of light papers in the style of my " Street Sketches " would be considered of use to the new paper ; and, secondly, if so, whether they do not think it fair and reasonable that, taking my share of the ordinary reporting business of *The Chronicle* besides, I should receive something for the papers beyond my ordinary salary as a reporter.

Begging you to excuse my troubling you, and taking this opportunity of acknowledging the numerous kindnesses I have already received at your hands since I have had the pleasure of acting under you,

I am, my dear Sir, very sincerely yours.

Miss Hogarth.

FURNIVAL'S INN, *Wednesday Evening*, 1835.

MY DEAREST KATE,

The House is up ; but I am very sorry to say that I must stay at home. I have had a visit from the publishers this morning, and the story cannot be any longer delayed ; it must be done to-morrow, as there are more important considerations than the mere payment for the story involved too. I must exercise a little self-denial, and set to work.

They (Chapman and Hall) have made me an offer of fourteen pounds a month, to write and edit a new publication they contemplate, entirely by myself, to be published monthly, and each number to contain four woodcuts. I am to make my estimate and calculation, and to give them a decisive answer on Friday morning. The work will be no joke, but the emolument is too tempting to resist.

*   *   *   *   *

The same.

Sunday Evening.

*   *   *   *   *

I have at this moment got Pickwick and his friends on the Rochester coach and they are going on swimmingly, in company with a very different character from any I have yet described, who

I flatter myself will make a decided hit. I want to get them from the ball to the inn before I go to bed; and I think that will take until one or two o'clock at the earliest. The publishers will be here in the morning, so you will readily suppose I have no alternative but to stick at my desk.

*   *   *   *   *

FURNIVAL'S INN, *Sunday Evening* (1836) (!).   Mr. John Hullah.

MY DEAR HULLAH,

Have you seen *The Examiner?* It is rather depreciatory of the opera; but, like all inveterate critiques against Braham, so well done that I cannot help laughing at it, for the life and soul of me. I have seen *The Sunday Times*, *The Dispatch*, and *The Satirist*, all of which blow their critic trumpets against unhappy me most lustily. Either I must have grievously awakened the ire of all the "adapters" and their friends, or the drama must be decidedly bad. I haven't made up my mind yet which of the two is the fact.

I have not seen the *John Bull* or any of the Sunday papers except *The Spectator*. If you have any of them, bring 'em with you on Tuesday. I am afraid that for "dirty Cummins'" allusion to Hogarth I shall be reduced to the necessity of being valorous the next time I meet him.

Believe me, most faithfully yours.

FURNIVAL'S INN, *Monday Afternoon*, 7 *o'clock* (1836).   The same.

MY DEAR HULLAH,

Mr. Hogarth has just been here, with news which I think you will be glad to hear. He was with Braham yesterday, who was *far more full* of the opera than he was; speaking highly of my works and "fame" (!), and expressing an earnest desire to be the first to introduce me to the public as a dramatic writer. He said that he intended opening at Michaelmas; and added (unasked) that it was his intention to produce the opera within *one month* of his first night. He wants a low comedy part introduced—without singing—thinking it will take with the audience; but he is desirous of explaining to me what he means and who he intends to play it. I am to see him on Sunday morning. Full particulars of the interview shall be duly announced.

Most faithfully yours.

Mr. John
Hullah.

PETERSHAM, *Monday Evening* (1836).

DEAR HULLAH,

Since I called on you this morning I have not had time to look over the words of "The Child and the Old Man." It occurs to me, as I shall see you on Wednesday morning, that the best plan will be for you to bring the music (if you possibly can) without the words, and we can put them in then. Of course this observation applies only to that particular song.

Braham having sent to me about the farce, I called on him this morning. Harley wrote, when he had read the whole of the opera, saying: "It's a sure card—nothing wrong there. Bet you ten pound it runs fifty nights. Come; don't be afraid. You'll be the gainer by it, and you mustn't mind betting; it's a capital custom." They tell the story with infinite relish. I saw the fair manageress,* who is fully of Harley's opinion, so is Braham. The only difference is, that they are far more enthusiastic than Harley—far more enthusiastic than ourselves even. That is a bold word, isn't it? It is a true one, nevertheless.

"Depend upon it, sir," said Braham to Hogarth yesterday when he went there to say I should be in town to-day, "depend upon it, sir, that there has been no such music since the days of Sheild, and no such piece since 'The Duenna.' Everybody is delighted with it," he added, to me to-day. "I played it to Stansbury, who is by no means an excitable person, and he was *charmed.*" This was said with great emphasis, but I have forgotten the grand point. It was not, "I played it to Stansbury," but "I sang it—*all through ! ! !*"

I begged him, as the choruses are to be put into rehearsal directly the company get together, to let us have, through Mrs. Braham, the necessary passports to the stage, which will be forwarded. He leaves town on the *Eighth of September*. He will be absent a month, and the first rehearsal will take place immediately on his return; previous to it (I mean the first rehearsal—not the return) I am to read the piece. His only remaining suggestion is, that Miss Rainforth will want another song when the piece is in rehearsal—"a bravura—something in 'The Soldier Tired' way." We must have a confab about this on Wednesday morning.

Harley called in Furnival's Inn, to express his high delight and gratification, but unfortunately we had left town.

Believe me, dear Hullah, most faithfully yours.

* Mrs. Braham.

48, DOUGHTY STREET, *Saturday Morning.*   Mr. J. P. Harley.

MY DEAR SIR,

I have considered the terms on which I could afford just now to sell Mr. Braham the acting copyright in London of an entirely new piece for the St. James's Theatre; and I could not sit down to write one in a single act of about one hour long, under a hundred pounds. For a new piece in two acts, a hundred and fifty pounds would be the sum I should require.

I do not know whether, with reference to arrangements that were made with any other writers, this may or may not appear a large item. I state it merely with regard to the value of my own time and writings at this moment; and in so doing I assure you I place the remuneration below the mark rather than above it.

As you begged me to give you my reply upon this point, perhaps you will lay it before Mr. Braham. If these terms exceed his inclination or the ability of the theatre, there is an end of the matter, and no harm done.

Believe me, ever faithfully yours.

48, DOUGHTY STREET, *Wednesday Evening.*   Mr. W. C. Macready.

MY DEAR SIR,

There is a semi-business, semi-pleasure little dinner which I intend to give at The Prince of Wales, in Leicester Place, Leicester Square, on Saturday, at five for half-past precisely, at which only Talfourd, Forster, Ainsworth, Jerdan, and the publishers will be present. It is to celebrate (that is too great a word, but I can think of no better) the conclusion of my "Pickwick" labours; and so I intend, before you take that roll upon the grass you spoke of, to beg your acceptance of one of the first complete copies of the work. I shall be much delighted if you would join us.

I know too well the many anxieties that press upon you just now to seek to persuade you to come if you would prefer a night's repose and quiet. Let me assure you, notwithstanding, most honestly and heartily that there is no one I should be more happy or gratified to see, and that among your brilliant circle of well-wishers and admirers you number none more unaffectedly and faithfully yours than,

My dear Sir, yours most truly.

* 15, FURNIVAL's INN, *Wednesday Morning,* 1837.   Mr. Thos. Tegg.

DEAR SIR,

I have made the nearest calculation in my power of the length of the little work you speak of; and guiding my own demand

* This Letter has been already printed in "Notes and Queries."

by the nature of the arrangements I am in the habit of making with other booksellers, I could not agree to do it for less than a hundred and twenty pounds.

I am not aware what the profit is upon this description of Book, or whether it would, or would not, justify you in such an outlay. If it would, I should be prepared to produce the whole by Christmas—the sale at that time of year, I apprehend, would be important.

For many reasons I should agree with you, in not wishing the name of "Boz" to be appended to the work.

I shall be happy to receive your answer before I leave town, which will most probably be on Wednesday next.

I am, dear Sir, your very obedient Servant.

Mrs.
Hogarth.

DOUGHTY STREET,
Thursday Night, Twenty-sixth October, 1837.

MY DEAR MRS. HOGARTH,

I need not thank you for your present of yesterday, for you know the sorrowful pleasure I shall take in wearing it, and the care with which I shall prize it, until—so far as relates to this life—I am like her.

I have never had her ring off my finger by day or night, except for an instant at a time, to wash my hands, since she died. I have never had her sweetness and excellence absent from my mind so long. I can solemnly say that, waking or sleeping, I have never lost the recollection of our hard trial and sorrow, and I feel that I never shall.

It will be a great relief to my heart when I find you sufficiently calm upon this sad subject to claim the promise I made you when she lay dead in this house, never to shrink from speaking of her, as if her memory must be avoided, but rather to take a melancholy pleasure in recalling the times when we were all so happy—so happy that increase of fame and prosperity has only widened the gap in my affections, by causing me to think how she would have shared and enhanced all our joys, and how proud I should have been (as God knows I always was) to possess the affections of the gentlest and purest creature that ever shed a light on earth. I wish you could know how I weary now for the three rooms in Furnival's Inn, and how I miss that pleasant smile and those sweet words which, bestowed upon our evening's work, in our merry banterings round the fire, were more precious to me than the applause of a whole world would be. I can recall everything she said and did in those happy days, and could show you every passage and line we read together.

I see *now* how you are capable of making great efforts, even against the afflictions you have to deplore, and I hope that, soon, our words may be where our thoughts are, and that we may call up those old memories, not as shadows of the bitter past, but as lights upon a happier future.

Believe me, my dear Mrs. Hogarth,

Ever truly and affectionately yours.

1838.

NARRATIVE.

IN February of this year Charles Dickens made an expedition with his friend, and the illustrator of most of his books, Mr. Hablot K. Browne ("Phiz"), to investigate for himself the real facts as to the condition of the Yorkshire schools, and it may be observed that portions of a letter to his wife, dated Greta Bridge, Yorkshire, which will be found among the following letters, were reproduced in "Nicholas Nickleby." In the early summer he had a cottage at Twickenham Park. In August and September he was again at Broadstairs; and in the late autumn he made another bachelor excursion—Mr. Browne being again his companion—in England, which included his first visit to Stratford-on-Avon and Kenilworth. In February appeared the first number of "Nicholas Nickleby," on which work he was engaged all through the year, writing each number ready for the following month, and never being in advance, as was his habit with all his other periodical works, until his very latest ones.

The first letter which appears under this date, from Twickenham Park, is addressed to Mr. Thomas Mitton, a schoolfellow at one of his earliest schools, and afterwards for some years his solicitor. The letter contains instructions for his first will; the friend of almost his whole life, Mr. John Forster, being appointed executor to this will as he was to the last, to which he was "called upon to act" only three years before his own death.

The letter which we give in this year to Mr. Justice Talfourd is, unfortunately, the only one we have been able to procure to that friend, who was, however, one with whom he was most intimately associated, and with whom he maintained a constant correspondence.

The letter beginning "Respected Sir" was an answer to a little boy (Master Hastings Hughes), who had written to him as "Nicholas Nickleby" approached completion, stating his views and wishes as to the rewards and punishments to be bestowed on the various characters in the book.   The letter was sent to him through the Rev. Thomas Barham, author of "The Ingoldsby Legends."

The two letters to Mr. Macready, at the end of this year, refer to a farce which Charles Dickens wrote, with an idea that it might be suitable for Covent Garden Theatre, then under Mr. Macready's management.

We commence the narrative for this year with a fragment of a diary, which was found amongst some papers which have only recently come to light.   We give only those paragraphs which are likely to be of any public interest.   The original manuscript has been added to "The Forster Collection" at the South Kensington Museum.

Monday, First January, 1838.

A sad New Year's Day in one respect, for at the opening of last year poor Mary was with us.   Very many things to be grateful for since then, however.   Increased reputation and means—good health and prospects.   We never know the full value of blessings till we lose them (we were not ignorant of this one when we had it, I hope).   But if she were with us now, the same winning, happy, amiable companion, sympathising with all my thoughts and feelings more than anyone I knew ever did or will, I think I should have nothing to wish for, but a continuance of such happiness.   But she is gone, and pray God I may one day, through His mercy, rejoin her.   I wrote to Mrs. Hogarth yesterday, taking advantage of the opportunity afforded me by her sending, as a New Year's token, a pen-wiper of poor Mary's, imploring her, as strongly as I could, to think of the many remaining claims upon her affection and exertions, and not to give way to unavailing grief.   Her answer came to-night, and she seems hurt at my doing so—protesting that in all useful respects she is the same as ever.   Meant it for the best, and still hope I did right.

Saturday, Sixth January, 1838.

Our boy's birthday—one year old.   A few people at night— only Forster, the De Gex's, John Ross, Mitton, and the Beards, besides our families—to twelfth-cake and forfeits.

This day last year, Mary and I wandered up and down Holborn and the streets about for hours, looking after a little table for Kate's bedroom, which we bought at last at the very first broker's which we had looked into, and which we had passed half-a-dozen times because *I didn't like* to ask the price.   I took her out to

Brompton at night, as we had no place for her to sleep in (the two mothers being with us); she came back again next day to keep house for me, and stopped nearly the rest of the month. I shall never be so happy again as in those chambers three storeys high —never if I roll in wealth and fame. I would hire them to keep empty, if I could afford it.

Monday, Eighth January, 1838.

I began the "Sketches of Young Gentlemen" to-day. One hundred and twenty-five pounds for such a little book, without my name to it, is pretty well. This and the "Sunday"* by-the-bye, are the only two things I have not done as Boz.

Tuesday, Ninth January, 1838.

Went to the Sun office to insure my life, where the Board seemed disposed to think I work too much. Made Forster and Pickthorn, my Doctor, the references—and after an interesting interview with the Board and the Board's Doctor, came away to work again.

Wednesday, Tenth January, 1838.

At work all day, and to a quadrille party at night. City people and rather dull. Intensely cold coming home, and vague reports of a fire somewhere. Frederick † says the Royal Exchange, at which I sneer most sagely; for——

Thursday, Eleventh January, 1838.

To-day the papers are full of it, and it *was* the Royal Exchange, Lloyd's, and all the shops round the building. Called on Browne and went with him to see the ruins, of which we saw as much as we should have done if we had stopped at home.

Sunday, Fourteenth January, 1838.

To church in the morning, and when I came home I wrote the preceding portion of this diary, which henceforth I make a stead-fast resolution not to neglect, or *paint.* I have not done it yet, nor will I; but say what rises to my lips—my mental lips at least —without reserve. No other eyes will see it, while mine are open in life, and although I daresay I shall be ashamed of a good deal in it, I should like to look over it at the year's end.

In Scott's diary, which I have been looking at this morning, there are thoughts which have been mine by day and by night, in good spirits and bad, since Mary died.

* "Sunday, under Three Heads," a small pamphlet published about this time.   † His brother.

"Another day, and a bright one to the external world again opens on us ; the air soft, and the flowers smiling, and the leaves glittering.   They cannot refresh her to whom mild weather was a natural enjoyment.   Cerements of lead and of wood already hold her ; cold earth must have her soon.   But it is not . . . (she) who will be laid among the ruins. . . . She is sentient and conscious of my emotions *somewhere*—where, we cannot tell, how, we cannot tell ; yet would I not at this moment renounce the mysterious yet certain hope that I shall see her in a better world, for all that this world can give me.

"I have seen her.   There is the same symmetry of form, though those limbs are rigid which were once so gracefully elastic ; but that yellow masque with pinched features, which seems to mock life rather than emulate it, can it be the face that was once so full of lively expression ?   I will not look upon it again."

I know but too well how true all this is.

Monday, Fifteenth January, 1838.

Here ends this brief attempt at a diary.   I grow sad over this checking off of days, and can't do it.

Mrs. Charles Dickens.

GRETA BRIDGE, *Thursday, First February*, 1838.

MY DEAREST KATE,

I am afraid you will receive this later than I could wish, as the mail does not come through this place until two o'clock to-morrow morning.   However I have availed myself of the very first opportunity of writing, so the fault is that mail's and not this.

We reached Grantham between nine and ten on Thursday night, and found everything prepared for our reception in the very best inn I have ever put up at.   It is odd enough that an old lady, who had been outside all day and came in towards dinner-time, turned out to be the mistress of a Yorkshire school returning from the holiday stay in London.   She was a very queer old lady, and showed us a long letter she was carrying to one of the boys from his father, containing a severe lecture (enforced and aided by many texts of Scripture) on his refusing to eat boiled meat.   She was very communicative, drank a great deal of brandy and water, and towards evening became insensible, in which state we left her.

Yesterday we were up again shortly after seven A.M., came on upon our journey by the Glasgow mail, which charged us the re-markably low sum of six pounds fare for two places inside.   We had a very droll male companion until seven o'clock in the evening, and a most delicious lady's-maid for twenty miles, who implored us to keep a sharp look-out at the coach windows, as she expected the carriage was coming to meet her and she was afraid of missing it. We had many delightful vauntings of the same kind; but in the end it is scarcely necessary to say that the coach did not come, but a very dirty girl did.

As we came further north the snow grew deeper. About eight o'clock it began to fall heavily, and, as we crossed the wild heaths hereabout, there was no vestige of a track. The mail kept on well, however, and at eleven we reached a bare place with a house, standing alone in the midst of a dreary moor, which the guard informed us was Greta Bridge. I was in a perfect agony of apprehension, for it was fearfully cold, and there were no outward signs of anybody being up in the house. But to our great joy we discovered a comfortable room, with drawn curtains and a most blazing fire. In half an hour they gave us a smoking supper and a bottle of mulled port (in which we drank your health), and then we retired to a couple of capital bedrooms, in each of which there was a rousing fire halfway up the chimney.

We have had for breakfast, toast, cakes, a Yorkshire pie, a piece of beef about the size and much the shape of my portmanteau, tea, coffee, ham and eggs; and are now going to look about us. Having finished our discoveries, we start in a postchaise for Barnard Castle, which is only four miles off, and there I deliver the letter given me by Mitton's friend. All the schools are round about that place, and a dozen old abbeys besides, which we shall visit by some means or other to-morrow. We shall reach York on Saturday I hope, and (God willing) I trust I shall be at home on Wednesday morning.

I wish you would call on Mrs. Bentley and thank her for the letter; you can tell her when I expect to be in York.

A thousand loves and kisses to the darling boy, whom I see in my mind's eye crawling about the floor of this Yorkshire inn. Bless his heart, I would give two sovereigns for a kiss. Remember me too to Frederick, who I hope is attentive to you.

Is it not extraordinary that the same dreams which have constantly visited me since poor Mary died follow me everywhere? After all the change of scene and fatigue, I have dreamt of her ever since I left home, and no doubt shall till I return. I should be sorry to lose such visions, for they are very happy ones, if it be only the seeing her in one's sleep. I would fain believe, too, sometimes, that her spirit may have some influence over them, but their perpetual repetition is extraordinary.

> Ever, my dear Kate,
> Your affectionate Husband.

TWICKENHAM PARK, *Tuesday Night.*

DEAR TOM,

I sat down this morning and put on paper my testamentary meaning. Whether it is sufficiently legal or not is another question, but I hope it is. The rough draft of the clauses which I enclose will be preceded by as much of the fair copy as I send you, and followed by the usual clause about the receipts of the trustees being a sufficient discharge. I also wish to provide that if all our children should die before twenty-one, and Kate married again, half the surplus should go to her and half to my surviving brothers and sisters, share and share alike.

This will be all, except a few lines I wish to add which there will be no occasion to consult you about, as they will merely bear reference to a few tokens of remembrance and one or two slight funeral directions. And so pray God that you may be gray, and Forster bald, long before you are called upon to act as my executors.

Ever yours.

TWICKENHAM PARK, *Sunday, Fifteenth July.* 1888.

MY DEAR TALFOURD,

I cannot tell you how much pleasure I have derived from the receipt of your letter. I have heard little of you, and seen less, for so long a time, that your handwriting came like the renewal of some old friendship, and gladdened my eyes like the face of some old friend.

If I hear from Lady Holland before you return, I shall, as in duty bound, present myself at her bidding; but between you and me and the general post, I hope she may not renew her invitation until I can visit her with you, as I would much rather avail myself of your personal introduction. However, whatever her ladyship may do I shall respond to, and anyway shall be only too happy to avail myself of what I am sure cannot fail to form a very pleasant and delightful introduction.

Your kind invitation and reminder of the subject of a pleasant conversation in one of our pleasant rides, has thrown a gloom over the brightness of Twickenham, for here I am chained. It is indispensably necessary that "Oliver Twist" should be published in three volumes, in September next. I have only just begun the last one, and, having the constant drawback of my monthly work, shall be sadly harassed to get it finished in time, especially as I have several important scenes (important to the story I mean) yet to write. Nothing would give me so much pleasure as to be with you for a week or so. I can only imperfectly console myself with the hope that when you see "Oliver" you will like the close of the book, and approve my self-denial in staying here to write it. I should like to know your address in Scotland when you leave town, so that I may send you the earliest copy if it be produced in the vacation, which I pray Heaven it may.

Meanwhile, believe that though my body is on the banks of the Thames, half my heart is going the Oxford circuit.

Mrs. Dickens and Charley desire their best remembrances (the latter expresses some anxiety, not unmixed with apprehension, relative to the Copyright Bill, in which he conceives himself interested), with hearty wishes that you may have a fine autumn, which is all you want, being sure of all other means of enjoyment that a man can have.

I am, my dear Talfourd,
Ever faithfully yours.

P.S.—You know, I suppose, that they elected me at the Athenæum? Pray thank Mr. Serjeant Storks for me.

LION HOTEL, SHREWSBURY,   Mrs. Charles
Thursday, First November, 1838.   Dickens.

MY DEAREST LOVE,

I received your welcome letter on arriving here last night, and am rejoiced to hear that the dear children are so much better. I hope that in your next, or your next but one, I shall learn that they are quite well. A thousand kisses to them. I wish I could convey them myself.

We found a roaring fire, an elegant dinner, a snug room, and capital beds all ready for us at Leamington, after a very agreeable (but very cold) ride. We started in a postchaise next morning for Kenilworth, with which we were both enraptured, and where I really think we MUST have lodgings next summer, please God that we are in good health and all goes well. You cannot conceive how delightful it is. To read among the ruins in fine weather would be perfect luxury. From here we went on to Warwick Castle, which is an ancient building, newly restored, and possessing no very great attraction beyond a fine view and some beautiful pictures; and thence to Stratford-upon-Avon, where we sat down in the room where Shakespeare was born, and left our autographs and read those of other people and so forth.

We remained at Stratford all night, and found to our unspeakable dismay that father's plan of proceeding by Bridgenorth was impracticable, as there were no coaches. So we were compelled to come here by way of Birmingham and Wolverhampton, starting at eight o'clock through a cold wet fog, and travelling, when the day had cleared up, through miles of cinder-paths, and blazing furnaces, and roaring steam-engines, and such a mass of dirt, gloom, and misery, as I never before witnessed. We got pretty well accommodated here when we arrived at half-past four, and are now going off in a postchaise to Llangollen—thirty miles—where we shall remain to-night, and where the Bangor mail will take us up to-morrow. Such are our movements up to this point, and when I have received your letter at Chester I shall write to you again and tell you when I shall be back. I can say positively that I shall not exceed the fortnight, and I think it very possible that I may return a day or two before it expires.

We were at the play last night. It was a bespeak—"The Love Chase," a ballet (with a phenomenon!), divers songs, and "A Roland for an Oliver." It is a good theatre, but the actors are very funny. Browne laughed with such indecent heartiness at one point of the entertainment, that an old gentleman in the next box suffered the most violent indignation. The bespeak party occupied two boxes, the ladies were full-dressed, and the gentlemen, to a man, in white gloves with flowers in their button-holes. It amused us mightily, and was really as like the Miss Snevellicci business as it could well be.

My side has been very bad since I left home, although I have been very careful, remaining to the full as abstemious as usual, and have not eaten any great quantity, having no appetite. I suffered such an ecstasy of pain all night at Stratford that I was half dead yesterday, and was obliged last night to take a dose of henbane. The effect was most delicious. I slept soundly, and without feeling the least uneasiness, and am a great deal better this morning; neither do I find that the henbane has affected my head, which, from the great effect it had upon me—exhilarating me to the most extraordinary degree, and yet keeping me sleepy— I feared it would. If I had not got better I should have turned back to Birmingham, and come straight home by the railroad. As it is, I hope I shall make out the trip.

God bless you, my darling. I long to be back with you again and to see the sweet Babs.

Your faithful and most affectionate Husband.

Master Hastings Hughes.

Doughty Street, London, *Twelfth December*, 1838.

Respected Sir,

I have given Squeers one cut on the neck and two on the head, at which he appeared much surprised and began to cry, which, being a cowardly thing, is just what I should have expected from him—wouldn't you?

I have carefully done what you told me in your letter about

the lamb and the two "sheeps" for the little boys. They have also had some good ale and porter, and some wine. I am sorry you didn't say *what* wine you would like them to have. I gave them some sherry which they liked very much, except one boy, who was a little sick and choked a good deal. He was rather greedy, and that's the truth, and I believe it went the wrong way, which I say served him right, and I hope you will say so too.

Nicholas had his roast lamb, as you said he was to, but he could not eat it all, and says if you do not mind his doing so he should like to have the rest hashed to-morrow with some greens, which he is very fond of, and so am I. He said he did not like to have his porter hot, for he thought it spoilt the flavour, so I let him have it cold. You should have seen him drink it. I thought he never would have left off. I also gave him three .pounds of money, all in sixpences, to make it seem more, and he said directly that he should give more than half to his mamma and .sister, and divide the rest with poor Smike. And I say he is a good fellow for saying so; and if anybody says he isn't I am ready to fight him whenever they like—there!

Fanny Squeers shall be attended to, depend upon it. Your drawing of her is very like, except that I don't think the hair is quite curly enough. The nose is particularly like hers, and so are the legs. She is a nasty disagreeable thing, and I know it will make her very cross when she sees it; and what I say is that I hope it may. You will say the same I know—at least I think you will.

I meant to have written you a long letter, but I cannot write very fast when I like the person I am writing to, because that makes me think about them, and I like you, and so I tell you. Besides, it is just eight o'clock at night, and I always go to bed at eight o'clock, except when it is my birthday, and then I sit up to supper. So I will not say anything more besides this—and that is my love to you and Neptune; and if you will drink my health every Christmas Day I will drink yours—come.

I am,
Respected Sir,
Your affectionate Friend.

P.S.—I don't write my name very plain, but you know what it is you know, so never mind.

DOUGHTY STREET, *Monday Morning.*   Mr. W. C. Macready.

MY DEAR MACREADY,

     I have not seen you for the past week, because I hoped when we next met to bring "The Lamplighter" in my hand. It would have been finished by this time, but I found myself compelled to set to work first at the "Nickleby," on which I am at present engaged, and which I regret to say—after my close and arduous application last month—I find I cannot write as quickly as usual. I must finish it, at latest, by the 24th (a doubtful comfort !), and the instant I have done so I will apply myself to the farce. I am afraid to name any particular day, but I pledge myself that you shall have it this month, and you may calculate on that promise. I send you with this a copy of a farce I wrote for Harley when he left Drury Lane, and in which he acted for some seventy nights. It is the best thing he does. It is barely possible you might like to try it. Any local or temporary allusions could be easily altered.

Believe me that I only feel gratified and flattered by your inquiry after the farce, and that if I had as much time as I have inclination, I would write on and on and on, farce after farce and comedy after comedy, until I wrote you something that would run. You do me justice when you give me credit for good intentions; but the extent of my good-will and strong and warm interest in you personally and your great undertaking, you cannot fathom nor express.

Believe me, my dear Macready,
Ever faithfully yours.

P.S.—For Heaven's sake don't fancy that I hold "The Strange Gentleman" in any estimation or have a wish upon the subject.

Mr. W. C.
Macready.

48, DOUGHTY STREET, Thirteenth December, 1838.

MY DEAR MACREADY,

I can have but one opinion on the subject—withdraw the farce at once, by all means.

I perfectly concur in all you say, and thank you most heartily and cordially for your kind and manly conduct, which is only what I should have expected from you; though, under such circumstances, I sincerely believe there are few but you—if any—who would have adopted it.

Believe me that I have no other feeling of disappointment connected with this matter but that arising from the not having been able to be of some use to you. And trust me that if the opportunity should ever arrive, my ardour will only be increased—not damped—by the result of this experiment.

Believe me always, my dear Macready,
Faithfully yours.

1839.

NARRATIVE.

CHARLES DICKENS was still living in Doughty Street, but he removed at the end of this year to 1, Devonshire Terrace, Regent's Park. He hired a cottage at Petersham for the summer months, and in the autumn took lodgings at Broadstairs.

The cottage at Alphington, near Exeter, mentioned in the letter to Mr. Mitton, was hired by Charles Dickens for his parents.

He was at work all through this year on "Nicholas Nickleby."

We have now the commencement of his correspondence with Mr. George Cattermole. His first letter was written immediately after Mr. Cattermole's marriage with Miss Elderton, a distant connection of Charles Dickens; hence the allusions to "cousin," which will be found in many of his letters to Mr. Cattermole. The bride and bridegroom were passing their honeymoon in the neighbourhood of Petersham, and the letter refers to a request from them for the loan of some books.

The first letter in this year to Mr. Macready is in answer to one from him, announcing his retirement from the management of Covent Garden Theatre.

We give in this year, two letters to Mr. Laman Blanchard, the well-known writer, for whom Charles Dickens had an affectionate regard. "Poor Chatfield" mentioned in the first of these letters was a promising young painter, who died very prematurely. It is, perhaps, hardly necessary to explain that "your son's play" alluded to in the same letter, was the production of a little boy.

The portrait by Mr. Maclise, mentioned to Mr. Harley, was the, now, well-known one, which appeared as a frontispiece to "Nicholas Nickleby."

The letter to Mr. Edward Chapman was written on the occasion of Charles Dickens having entered himself to "eat his dinners" at the Middle Temple, when Mr. Chapman was his "surety" according to the usual form. Charles Dickens, however, was never "called" to the Bar.

DOUGHTY STREET, *Sunday.* Mr. W. C. Macready.

MY DEAR MACREADY,

I ought not to be sorry to hear of your abdication, but I am, notwithstanding, most heartily and sincerely sorry, for my own sake and the sake of thousands, who may now go and whistle for a theatre—at least, such a theatre as you gave them; and I do now in my heart believe that for a long and dreary time that exquisite delight has passed away. If I may jest with my misfortunes, and quote the Portsmouth critic of Mr. Crummles's company, I say that: "As an exquisite embodiment of the poet's visions and a realisation of human intellectuality, gilding with refulgent light our dreamy moments, and laying open a new and magic world before the mental eye, the drama is gone—perfectly gone."

With the same perverse and unaccountable feeling which causes a heart-broken man at a dear friend's funeral to see something irresistibly comical in a red-nosed or one-eyed undertaker, I receive your communication with ghostly facetiousness; though on a moment's reflection I find better cause for consolation in the hope that, relieved from your most trying and painful duties, you will now have leisure to return to pursuits more congenial to your mind and to move more easily and pleasantly among your friends. In the long catalogue of the latter, I believe that there is not one prouder of the name, or more grateful for the store of delightful recollections you have enabled him to heap up from boyhood, than,

> My dear Macready,
> > Yours always faithfully.

* 48, DOUGHTY STREET, Sunday Morning.

Mr. Laman Blanchard.

MY DEAR BLANCHARD,

I have booked you—one inside—for the fly to Ainsworth's, wherein all available places are now secured. As we have one Mr. Lover,† of Charles Street, Middlesex Hospital, in the way-bill, and the gen'l'm'n is to be took up at his own door, I must trouble you to have your luggage ready at the "Courier Office" at a quarter-past five.

I am writing to you with a sad heart, for I have just indited a few lines to poor Chatfield, to whom I should have written long since but for Forster's assurance that it would be better not. I do not like to break in upon him without notice, but I have told him that you gave me reason to hope he would not be displeased to see me, and that if the changes of sickness leave him in the same mood I will see him on Christmas Morning (alas, poor fellow! a merry time to us), at two o'clock. I was very much obliged indeed to you for the paper. I was not aware of the quotation, and was greatly amused with the "leader." It seemed to me exceedingly happy, terse, pointed, smart, and quite an off (hand)

---

* Printed in "The Poetical Works of Laman Blanchard," with a Memoir, by Blanchard Jerrold.

† Mr. Samuel Lover, the Irish writer and composer.

leader in short. I have been amused beyond all telling with your son's play, in which the rival kings talk a great deal more common-sense than any stage-kings I have ever known. I suppose its excessive length is an insuperable objection to its representation at Covent Garden—even if the character of Stephen were not an insuperable objection with Macready, who could never stand Anderson in such a part as that.

My dear Blanchard, always faithfully yours.

48, DOUGHTY STREET, LONDON, *Thirty-first January*, 1839.   Mr. W. L.
                                                              Sammous.
SIR,
Circumstances have enabled me to relinquish my old con-nection with the "Miscellany"* at an earlier period than I had expected. I am no longer its editor, but I have referred your paper to my successor, and marked it as one "requiring attention." I have no doubt it will receive it.

With reference to your letter bearing date on the Eighth of last October, let me assure you that I have delayed answering it —not because a constant stream of similar epistles has rendered me callous to the anxieties of a beginner, in those doubtful paths in which I walk myself—but because you ask me to do that which I would scarce do, of my own unsupported opinion, for my own child, supposing I had one old enough to require such a service. To suppose that I could gravely take upon myself the responsibility of withdrawing you from pursuits you have already undertaken, or urging you on in a most uncertain and hazardous course of life, is really a compliment to my judgment and inflexi-bility which I cannot recognise and do not deserve (or desire). I hoped that a little reflection would show you how impossible it is that I could be expected to enter upon a task of so much delicacy, but as you have written to me since, and called (unfor-tunately at a period when I am obliged to seclude myself from all-comers), I am compelled at last to tell you that I can do nothing of the kind.

If it be any satisfaction to you to know that I have read what you sent me, and read it with great pleasure, though, as you treat of local matters, I am necessarily in the dark here and there, I can give you the assurance very sincerely. With this, and many thanks to you for your obliging expressions towards myself,

I am, Sir,
Your very obedient Servant.

* "Bentley's Miscellany."

Mr. J. P.
Harley.

DOUGHTY STREET, *Thursday Morning.**

MY DEAR HARLEY,

This is my birthday. Many happy returns of the day to you and me.

I took it into my head yesterday to get up an impromptu dinner on this auspicious occasion—only my own folks, Leigh Hunt, Ainsworth, and Forster. I know you can't dine here in consequence of the tempestuous weather on the Covent Garden shores, but if you will come in when you have done Trinculizing, you will delight me greatly, and add in no inconsiderable degree to the "conviviality" of the meeting.

Lord bless my soul! Twenty-seven years old. Who'd have thought it? I *never* did!

But I grow sentimental.

Always yours truly.

Mr. Thomas
Mitton.

NEW LONDON INN, EXETER,
Wednesday Morning, Sixth March, 1839.

DEAR TOM,

Perhaps you have heard from Kate that I succeeded yesterday in the very first walk, and took a cottage at a place called Alphington, one mile from Exeter, which contains, on the ground-floor, a good parlour and kitchen, and above, a full-sized country drawing-room and three bedrooms; in the yard behind, coal-holes, fowl-houses, and meat-safes out of number; in the kitchen, a neat little range; in the other rooms, good stoves and cupboards; and all for twenty pounds a year, taxes included. There is a good garden at the side well stocked with cabbages, beans, onions, celery, and some flowers. The stock belonging to the landlady (who lives in the adjoining cottage), there was some question whether she was not entitled to half the produce, but I settled the point by paying five shillings, and becoming absolute master of the whole!

I do assure you that I am charmed with the place and the beauty of the country round about, though I have not seen it under very favourable circumstances, for it snowed when I was there this morning, and blew bitterly from the east yesterday. It is really delightful, and when the house is to rights and the furniture all in, I shall be quite sorry to leave it. I have had some few things second-hand, but I take it seventy pounds will be the mark, even taking this into consideration. I include in that estimate glass and crockery, garden tools, and such like little

* No other date, but it must have been Seventh February, 1839.

things. There is a spare bedroom of course. That I have furnished too.

I am on terms of the closest intimacy with Mrs. Samuell, the landlady, and her brother and sister-in-law, who have a little farm hard by. They are capital specimens of country folks, and I really think the old woman herself will be a great comfort to my mother. Coals are dear just now—twenty-six shillings a ton. They found me a boy to go two miles out and back again to order some this morning. I was debating in my mind whether I should give him eighteenpence or two shillings, when his fee was announced—twopence!

The house is on the high-road to Plymouth, and, though in the very heart of Devonshire, there is as much long-stage and posting life as you would find in Piccadilly. The situation is charming. Meadows in front, an orchard running parallel to the garden hedge, richly-wooded hills closing in the prospect behind, and, away to the left, before a splendid view of the hill on which Exeter is situated, the cathedral towers rising up into the sky in the most picturesque manner possible. I don't think I ever saw so cheerful or pleasant a spot. The drawing-room is nearly, if not quite, as large as the outer room of my old chambers in Furnival's Inn. The paint and paper are new, and the place clean as the utmost excess of snowy cleanliness can be.

You would laugh if you could see me powdering away with the upholsterer, and endeavouring to bring about all sorts of impracticable reductions and wonderful arrangements. He has by him two second-hand carpets ; the important ceremony of trying the same comes off at three this afternoon. I am perpetually going backwards and forwards. It is two miles from here, so I have plenty of exercise, which so occupies me and prevents my being lonely that I stopped at home to read last night, and shall to-night, although the theatre is open. Charles Kean has been the star for the last two evenings. He was stopping in this house, and went away this morning. I have got his sitting-room now, which is smaller and more comfortable than the one I had before.

You will have heard perhaps that I wrote to my mother to come down to-morrow. There are so many things she can make comfortable at a much less expense than I could, that I thought it best. If I had not, I could not have returned on Monday, which I now hope to do, and to be in town at half-past eight.

Will you tell my father that if he could devise any means of bringing him down, I think it would be a great thing for him to have Dash, if it be only to keep down the trampers and beggars.

  * * * * *

Mr. George
Cattermole.

ELM COTTAGE, PETERSHAM, *Wednesday Morning.*

MY DEAR CATTERMOLE,

Why is "Peveril" lingering on my dusty shelves in town, while my fair cousin and your fair bride remains in blissful ignorance of his merits? There he is, I grieve to say, but there he shall not be long, for I shall be visiting my other home on Saturday morning, and will bring him bodily down and forward him the moment he arrives.

Not having many of my books here, I don't find any among them which I think more suitable to your purpose than a carpet-bagful sent herewith, containing the Italian and German novelists (convenient as being easily taken up and laid down again; and I suppose you won't read long at a sitting), Leigh Hunt's "Indicator" and "Companion" (which have the same merit), "Hood's Own" (complete), "A Legend of Montrose," and "Kenilworth," which I have just been reading with greater delight than ever, and so I suppose everybody else must be equally interested in. I have Goldsmith, Swift, Fielding, Smollett, and the British Essayists "handy;" and I need not say that you have them on hand too, if you like.

You know all I would say from my heart and soul on the auspicious event of yesterday; but you don't know what I could say about the delightful recollections I have of your "good lady's" charming looks and bearing, upon which I discoursed most eloquently here last evening, and at considerable length. As I am crippled in this respect, however, by the suspicion that possibly she may be looking over your shoulder while you read this note (I would lay a moderate wager that you have looked round twice or thrice already), I shall content myself with saying that I am ever heartily, my dear Cattermole,

Hers and yours.

Mr. J. P.
Harley.

ELM COTTAGE, PETERSHAM, NEAR RICHMOND,
Twenty-eighth June, 1839.

MY DEAR HARLEY,

I have "left my home," and been here ever since the end of April, and shall remain here most probably until the end of September, which is the reason that we have been such strangers of late.

I am very sorry to say that I cannot dine with you on Sunday, but some people are coming here, and I cannot get away, Better luck next time, I hope.

I was on the point of writing to you when your note came, to ask you if you would come down here next Saturday—to-morrow week, I mean—and stop till Monday. I will either call for you at the theatre, at any time you name, or send for you, "punctual," and have you brought down. Can you come if it's fine? Say yes, like a good fellow as you are, and say it per post.

I have countermanded that face. Maclise has made another face of me, which all people say is astonishing. The engraving will be ready soon, and I would rather you had that, as I am sure you would if you had seen it.

Faithfully yours.

DOUGHTY STREET, *Monday Morning.*   Mr. Wm. Longman.

MY DEAR SIR,

On Friday I have a family dinner at home—uncles, aunts, brothers, sisters, cousins—an annual gathering.

By what fatality is it that you always ask me to dine on the wrong day?

While you are tracing this non-consequence to its cause, I wish you would tell Mr. Sydney Smith that of all the men I ever heard of and never saw, I have the greatest curiosity to see and the greatest interest to know him.

Begging my best compliments at home,

I am, my dear Sir,
Faithfully yours.

ELM COTTAGE, PETERSHAM,   Mr. Laman
Thursday Night, Thirteenth July, 1889.   Blanchard.

MY DEAR BLANCHARD,

Living in these remote and distant parts, with the chain of mountains formed by Richmond Hill presenting an almost insurmountable barrier between me and the busy world, I know no more than that there *is* to be a dinner to Macready on Saturday week, and that I am a steward. But I shall be in town and at the theatre on Tuesday night. You will be there too, no doubt? In the proscenium-box on the Bow Street side I will hold further converse with you when the play is over; and if I have gained no further information by that time I will procure it for you next morning, and I have little doubt that I can "do your business" both ways. Macready has, as Talfourd remarked in one of his speeches, "cast a new grace round joy and gladness, and rendered mirth more holy!" Therefore are we preparing crowns and wreaths here, to shower upon the stage when that sad curtain falls and kivers up Shakespeare for years to come. I try to make a joke of it, but, upon my word, when the night comes I verily believe I shall cry.

I am very glad to read what you say about Nicholas. It is very difficult, indeed, to wind up so many people in "parts," and make each part tell by itself, but I hope to go out with flying colours notwithstanding. I have been at work all day, so if this note is illegible it's not my fault, but number seventeen's, which is yet an infant.

Always believe me,
My dear Blanchard,
Faithfully yours.

Mr. W. C.
Macready.   PETERSHAM, *Twenty-sixth July*, 1839.

MY DEAR MACREADY,

Fix your visit for whenever you please. It can never give us anything but delight to see you, and it is better to look forward to such a pleasure than to look back upon it, as the last gratification is enjoyable all our lives, and the first for a few short stages in the journey.

I feel more true and cordial pleasure than I can express to you in the request you have made. Anything which can serve to commemorate our friendship and to keep the recollection of it alive among our children is, believe me, and ever will be, most deeply prized by me. I accept the office with hearty and fervent satisfaction ; and, to render this pleasant bond between us the more complete, I must solicit you to become godfather to the last and final branch of a genteel small family of three which I am told may be looked for in that auspicious month when Lord Mayors are born and guys prevail. This I look upon as a bargain between us, and I have shaken hands with you in spirit upon it. Family topics remind me of Mr. Kenwigs. As the weather is wet, and he is about to make his last appearance on my little stage, I send Mrs. Macready an early proof of the next number, containing an account of his baby's progress.

I am going to send you something else on Monday—a tragedy. Don't be alarmed. I didn't write it, nor do I want it acted. A young Scotch lady whom I don't know (but she is evidently very intelligent and accomplished) has sent me a translation of a German play, soliciting my aid and advice in the matter of its publication. Among a crowd of Germanisms, there are many things in it which are so very striking, that I am sure it will amuse you very much. At least I think it will ; it has me. I am going to send it back to her—when I come to Elstree will be time enough ; and meantime, if you bestow a couple of hours upon it, you will not think them thrown away.

It's a large parcel, and I must keep it here till somebody goes up to town and can book it by the coach. I warrant it, large as it looks, readable in two hours ; and I very much want to know what you think of the first act, and especially the opening, which seems to me quite famous. The metre is very odd and rough, but now and then there's a wildness in it which helps the thing very much; and altogether it has left a something on my mind which I can't get rid of. My dear Macready,

Faithfully and truly yours.

40, Albion Street, Broadstairs,   Mr. W. C.
Twenty-first September, 1839.   Macready.

My dear Macready,

Let me prefix to the last number of "Nickleby," and to the book, a duplicate of the leaf which I now send you. Believe me that there will be no leaf in the volume which will afford me in times to come more true pleasure and gratification, than that in which I have written your name as foremost amongst those of the friends whom I love and honour. Believe me, there will be no one line in it conveying a more honest truth or a more sincere feeling than that which describes its dedication to you as a slight token of my admiration and regard.

So let me tell the world by this frail record that I was a friend of yours, and interested to no ordinary extent in your proceedings at that interesting time when you showed them such noble truths in such noble forms, and gave me a new interest in, and associations with, the labours of so many months.

I write to you very hastily and crudely, for I have been very hard at work, having only finished to-day, and my head spins yet. But you know what I mean. I am then always,

Believe me, my dear Macready,

Faithfully yours.

P.S.—(Proof of Dedication enclosed): "To W. C. Macready, Esq., the following pages are inscribed, as a slight token of admiration and regard, by his friend, the Author."

Doughty Street,   The same.
Friday Night, Twenty-fifth October, 1839.

My dear Macready,

The book, the whole book, and nothing but the book (except the binding, which is an important item), has arrived at last, and is forwarded herewith. The red represents my blushes at its gorgeous dress; the gilding, all those bright professions which I do not make to you; and the book itself, my whole heart for twenty months, which should be yours for so short a term, as you have it always. Believe me, my dear Macready,

Your faithful Friend.

Mr. W. C.
Macready.

DOUGHTY STREET,
Thursday, Fourteenth November, 1839.

MY DEAR MACREADY,

Tom Landseer—that is, the deaf one whom everybody quite loves for his sweet nature under a most deplorable infirmity—Tom Landseer asked me if I would present to you from him the accompanying engraving, which he has executed from a picture by his brother Edwin ; submitting it to you as a little tribute from an unknown but ardent admirer of your genius, which speaks to his heart, although it does not find its way there through his ears. I readily undertook the task and send it herewith.

I urged him to call upon you with me and proffer it boldly ; but he is a very modest and delicately-minded creature, and was shy of intruding. If you thank him through me, perhaps you will say something about my bringing him to call, and so gladden the gentle artist and make him happy.

You must come and see my new house when we have it to rights. By Christmas Day we shall be, I hope, your neighbours.

Ever believe me,
Dear Macready,
Faithfully yours.

Mr. Edward
Chapman.

1, DEVONSHIRE TERRACE,
Twenty-seventh December, 1839.

MY DEAR SIR,

The place where you pledge yourself to pay for my beef and mutton when I eat it, and my ale and wine when I drink it, is the Treasurer's Office of the Middle Temple, the new building at the bottom of Middle Temple Lane on the right-hand side. You walk up into the first-floor and say (boldly) that you come to sign Mr. Charles Dickens' bond—which is already signed by Mr. Serjeant Talfourd. I suppose I should formally acquaint you that I have paid the fees, and that the responsibility you incur is a very slight one—extending very little beyond my good behaviour, and honourable intentions to pay for all wine-glasses, tumblers, or other dinner-furniture that I may break or damage.

I wish you would do me another service, and that is to choose, at the place you told me of, a reasonable copy of "The Beauties of England and Wales." You can choose it quite as well as I can, or better, and I shall be much obliged to you. I should like you to send it at once, as I am diving into all kinds of matters at odd minutes with a view to our forthcoming operations.

The Brigand * is sleeping, but I suspect with one eye open.

* The baby.

Whether he is ogling the Vice-Chancellor with it, or not, time will show.

Will you mention to your book-keeper, that in case he should meet a Fair Copy of our accounts, walking about anywhere, I shall be glad if he will give her my compliments, and say she may rely upon a welcome, whenever she is disposed to come towards this end of the town?

Best remembrances to Mr. Hall.

Always faithfully yours.

1840.

NARRATIVE.

CHARLES DICKENS was at Broadstairs with his family for the autumn months.   During all this year he was busily engaged with the periodical entitled "Master Humphrey's Clock," in which the story of "The Old Curiosity Shop" subsequently appeared. Nearly all the letters to Mr. George Cattermole refer to the illustrations for this story.

The letter dated March 9th alludes to short papers written for "Master Humphrey's Clock" prior to the commencement of "The Old Curiosity Shop."

Mr. H. G. Adams was the Honorary Secretary of the Chatham Mechanics' Institute, which office he held for many years.   The "local magazine" mentioned in the letter to him was called "The Kentish Coronal."

We have in this year Charles Dickens' first letter to Mr. Daniel Maclise, this and one other being, unfortunately, the only letters we have been able to obtain addressed to this much-loved friend and most intimate companion.

Mr. Thompson was an intimate friend of Charles Dickens, and was afterwards the father of the celebrated artist, Elizabeth Thompson, now Lady Butler.

1, DEVONSHIRE TERRACE,
Monday, Thirteenth January, 1840.

Mr. George
Cattermole.

MY DEAR CATTERMOLE,

I am going to propound a mightily grave matter to you. My new periodical work appears—or I should rather say the first number does—on Saturday, the 28th of March; and as it has to be sent to America and Germany, and must therefore be considerably in advance, it is now in hand; I having in fact begun it on Saturday last.   Instead of being published in monthly parts at a shilling each only, it will be published in weekly parts at three-

pence and monthly parts at a shilling; my object being to baffle
the imitators and make it as novel as possible. The plan is a
new one—I mean the plan of the fiction—and it will comprehend.
a great variety of tales. The title is: "Master Humphrey's
Clock."

Now, among other improvements, I have turned my attention
to the illustrations, meaning to have woodcuts dropped into the
text and no separate plates. I want to know whether you would
object to make me a little sketch for a woodcut—in indian-ink
would be quite sufficient—about the size of the enclosed scrap;
the subject, an old quaint room with antique Elizabethan furniture,
and in the chimney-corner an extraordinary old clock—the clock
belonging to Master Humphrey, in fact, and no figures. This I
should drop into the text at the head of my opening page.

I want to know besides—as Chapman and Hall are my partners
in the matter, there need be no delicacy about my asking or your
answering the question—what would be your charge for such a
thing, and whether (if the work answers our expectations) you
would like to repeat the joke at regular intervals, and, if so, on
what terms? I should tell you that I intend to ask Maclise * to
join me likewise, and that the copying the drawing on wood and
the cutting will be done in first-rate style. We are justified by
past experience in supposing that the sale would be enormous, and
the popularity very great; and when I explain to you the notes I
have in my head, I think you will see that it opens a vast number
of very good subjects.

I want to talk the matter over with you, and wish you would
fix your own time and place—either here or at your house or at
the Athenæum, though this would be the best place, because I
have my papers about me. If you would take a chop with me,
for instance, on Tuesday or Wednesday, I could tell you more in
two minutes than in twenty letters, albeit I have endeavoured to
make this as businesslike and stupid as need be.

Of course all these tremendous arrangements are as yet a profound secret, or there would be fifty Humphreys in the field. So
send me a line like a worthy gentleman, and convey my best
remembrances to your worthy lady.

Believe me always, my dear Cattermole,
Faithfully yours.

---

* Mr. Maclise, however, did not join in this undertaking. Mr. Cattermole's
fellow-illustrator was Mr. Hablot K. Browne.

DEVONSHIRE TERRACE, *Tuesday Afternoon.*

MY DEAR CATTERMOLE,

I think the drawing most famous, and so do the publishers, to whom I sent it to-day. If Browne should suggest anything for the future which may enable him to do you justice, in copying (on which point he is very anxious), I will communicate it to you. It has occurred to me that perhaps you will like to see his copy on the block before it is cut, and I have therefore told Chapman and Hall to forward it to you.

In future, I will take care that you have the number to choose your subject from. I ought to have done so, perhaps, in this case; but I was very anxious that you should do the room.

Faithfully yours always.

1, DEVONSHIRE TERRACE, YORK GATE, REGENT'S PARK, *Saturday, Eighteenth January,* 1840.

DEAR SIR,

The pressure of other engagements will, I am compelled to say, prevent me from contributing a paper to your new local magazine. But I beg you to set me down as a subscriber to it, and foremost among those whose best wishes are enlisted in your cause. It will afford me real pleasure to hear of your success, for I have many happy recollections connected with Kent, and am scarcely less interested in it than if I had been a Kentish man bred and born, and had resided in the county all my life.

Faithfully yours.

1, DEVONSHIRE TERRACE, *Monday, Ninth March,* 1840.

MY DEAR CATTERMOLE,

I have been induced, on looking over the works of the " Clock," to make a slight alteration in their disposal, by virtue of which the story about " John Podgers " will stand over for some little time, and that short tale will occupy its place which you have already by you, and which treats of the assassination of a young gentleman under circumstances of peculiar aggravation. I shall be greatly obliged to you if you will turn your attention to the last morsel as the feature of No. 3. and still more if you will stretch a point with regard to time (which is of the last importance just now), and make a subject out of it, rather than find one in it. I would neither have made this alteration nor have troubled you about it, but for weighty and cogent reasons which I feel very strongly, and into the composition of which caprice or fastidiousness has no part.

D

I should tell you perhaps, with reference to Chapman and Hall, that they will never trouble you (as they never trouble me) but when there is real and pressing occasion, and that their representations in this respect, unlike those of most men of business, are to be relied upon.

I cannot tell you how admirably I think Master Humphrey's room comes out, or what glowing accounts I hear of the second design you have done. I had not the faintest anticipation of anything so good — taking into account the material and the despatch.

Believe me, dear Cattermole,
Heartily yours.

P.S.—The new (No. 3) tale begins : "I hold a lieutenant's commission in his Majesty's Army, and served abroad in the campaigns of 1677 and 1678." It has at present no title.

Mr. S. A.
Dietzman.

1, DEVONSHIRE TERRACE, YORK GATE, REGENT'S PARK,
LONDON, <i>Tenth March</i>, 1840.

MY DEAR SIR,

I will not attempt to tell you how much gratified I have been by the receipt of your first English letter; nor can I describe to you with what delight and gratification I learn that I am held in such high esteem by your great countrymen, whose favourable appreciation is flattering indeed.

To you, who have undertaken the laborious (and often, I fear, very irksome) task of clothing me in the German garb, I owe a long arrear of thanks. I wish you would come to England, and afford me an opportunity of slightly reducing the account.

It is with great regret that I have to inform you, in reply to the request contained in your pleasant communication, that my publishers have already made such arrangements and are in possession of such stipulations relative to the proof-sheets of my new works, that I have no power to send them out of England. If I had, I need not tell you what pleasure it would afford me to promote your views.

I am too sensible of the trouble you must have already had with my writings to impose upon you now a long letter. I will only add, therefore, that I am,

My dear Sir,
With great sincerity,
Faithfully yours.

BROADSTAIRS, *Second June*, 1840. Mr. Daniel
Maclise,
R.A.

MY DEAR MACLISE,

My foot is in the house,
My bath is on the sea,
And, before I take a souse,
Here's a single note to thee.

It merely says that the sea is in a state of extraordinary sublimity; that this place is, as the Guide Book most justly observes, "unsurpassed for the salubrity of the refreshing breezes, which are wafted on the ocean's pinions from far-distant shores." That we are all right after the perils and voyages of yesterday. That the sea is rolling away in front of the window at which I indite this epistle, and that everything is as fresh and glorious as fine weather and a splendid coast can make it. Bear these recommendations in mind, and shunning Talfourdian pledges, come to the bower which is shaded for you in the one-pair front, where no chair or table has four legs of the same length, and where no drawers will open till you have pulled the pegs off, and then they keep open and won't shut again.

COME!

I can no more.

Always faithfully yours.

DEVONSHIRE TERRACE, Mr. T. J.
Tuesday, Fifteenth December, 1840. Thompson.

MY DEAR THOMPSON,

I have received a most flattering message from the head turnkey of the jail this morning, intimating that "there warn't a genelman in all London he'd be gladder to show his babies to, than Muster Dickins, and let him come wenever he would to that shop he wos welcome." But as the Governor (who is a very nice fellow and a gentleman) is not at home this morning, and furthermore as the morning itself has rather gone out of town in respect of its poetical allurements, I think we had best postpone our visit for a day or two.

Faithfully yours.

DEVONSHIRE TERRACE, *Twenty-first December*. Mr. George
Cattermole.

MY DEAR GEORGE,

Kit, the single gentleman, and Mr. Garland go down to the place where the child is, and arrive there at night. There has been a fall of snow. Kit, leaving them behind, runs to the old house, and, with a lanthorn in one hand and the bird in its cage in the other, stops for a moment at a little distance with a natural hesitation before he goes up to make his presence known. In a window—supposed to be that of the child's little room—a light is burning, and in that room the child (unknown, of course, to her visitors, who are full of hope) lies dead.

If you have any difficulty about Kit, never mind about putting him in.

Faithfully always.

DEVONSHIRE TERRACE, *Friday Morning.*

Mr. George
Cattermole.

MY DEAR CATTERMOLE,

I sent the MS. of the enclosed proof, marked 2, up to Chapman and Hall, from Devonshire, mentioning a subject of an old gateway, which I had put in expressly with a view to your illustrious pencil. By a mistake, however, it went to Browne instead. Chapman is out of town, and such things have gone wrong in consequence.

The subject to which I wish to call your attention is in an unwritten number to follow this one, but it is a mere echo of what you will find at the conclusion of this proof marked 2. I want the cart, gaily decorated, going through the street of the old town with the wax brigand displayed to fierce advantage, and the child seated in it also dispersing bills. As many flags and inscriptions about Jarley's Wax Work fluttering from the cart as you please. You know the wax brigands, and how they contemplate small oval miniatures? That's the figure I want. I send you the scrap of MS. which contains the subject.

Will you, when you have done this, send it with all speed to Chapman and Hall, as we are mortally pressed for time, and I must go hard to work to make up for what I have lost by being dutiful and going to see my father.

I want to see you about a frontispiece to our first "Clock" volume, which will come out (I think) at the end of September, and about other matters. When shall we meet, and where?

Could you dine with us on Sunday, at six o'clock sharp? I'd come and fetch you in the morning, and we could take a ride and walk. We shall be quite alone, unless Macready comes. What say you?

Don't forget despatch, there's a dear fellow, and ever believe me,

Heartily yours.

The same.

Twenty-second December, 1840.

DEAR GEORGE,

The child lying dead in the little sleeping-room, which is behind the open screen. It is winter time, so there are no flowers;

but upon her breast and pillow, and about her bed, there may be strips of holly and berries, and such free green things. Window overgrown with ivy. The little boy who had that talk with her about angels may be by the bedside, if you like it so; but I think it will be quieter and more peaceful if she is quite alone. I want it to express the most beautiful repose and tranquillity, and to have something of a happy look, if death can.

2.

The child has been buried inside the church, and the old man, who cannot be made to understand that she is dead, repairs to the grave and sits there all day long, waiting for her arrival, to begin another journey. His staff and knapsack, her little bonnet and basket, etc., lie beside him. "She'll come to-morrow," he says when it gets dark, and goes sorrowfully home. I think an hour-glass running out would help the notion; perhaps her little things upon his knee, or in his hand.

I am breaking my heart over this story, and cannot bear to finish it.

Ever and always heartily.

1841.

NARRATIVE.

In the summer of this year Charles Dickens made, accompanied by Mrs. Dickens, his first visit to Scotland, and was received in Edinburgh with the greatest enthusiasm.

He was at Broadstairs with his family for the autumn, and at the close of the year he went to Windsor for change of air after a serious illness.

On the Seventeenth of January "The Old Curiosity Shop" was finished. In the following week the first number of his story of "Barnaby Rudge" appeared, in "Master Humphrey's Clock," and the last number of this story was written at Windsor, in November of this year.

We have the first letters to his dear and valued friends the Rev. William Harness and Mr. Harrison Ainsworth. Also his first letter to Mr. Monckton Milnes (now Lord Houghton).

The letter marked "Anonymous," on the character of Oliver Twist, was written to a dissenting minister, who had been himself a workhouse boy.

Of the letter to Mr. John Tomlin we can only remark, that it was published in an American magazine, edited by Mr. Edgar Poe, in the year 1842.

"The New First Rate" (first letter to Mr. Harrison Ainsworth) must, we think, be an allusion to the outside cover of "Bentley's Miscellany," which first appeared in this year, and of which Mr. Ainsworth was editor.

The two letters to Mr. Lovejoy are in answer to a requisition from the people of Reading that Charles Dickens would represent them in Parliament.

The letter to Mr. George Cattermole (Twenty-sixth June) refers to a dinner given to Charles Dickens by the people of Edinburgh, on his first visit to that city.

The "poor Overs" mentioned in the letter to Mr. Macready of Twenty-fourth August, was a carpenter dying of consumption, to whom Dr. Elliotson had shown extraordinary kindness. "When poor Overs was dying" (wrote Charles Dickens to Mr. Forster), "he suddenly asked for a pen and ink and some paper, and made up a little parcel for me, which it was his last conscious act to direct. She (his wife) told me this, and gave it me. I opened it last night. It was a copy of his little book, in which he had written my name, 'with his devotion.' I thought it simple and affecting of the poor fellow."

The letter to Mrs. Hogarth was written on the occasion of the sudden death of her son George.

"The Saloon," alluded to in the last letter of this year, was an institution at Drury Lane Theatre during Mr. Macready's management. The original purpose for which this saloon was established having become perverted and degraded, Charles Dickens had it much at heart to remodel and improve it. Hence this letter to Mr. Macready.

Rev.
William
Harness.

DEVONSHIRE TERRACE,
Saturday Morning, Second January, 1841.

MY DEAR HARNESS,

I should have been very glad to join your pleasant party, but all next week I shall be laid up with a broken heart, for I must occupy myself in finishing the "Curiosity Shop," and it is such a painful task to me that I must concentrate myself upon it tooth and nail, and go out nowhere until it is done.

I have delayed answering your kind note in a vague hope of being heart-whole again by the seventh. The present state of my work, however (Christmas not being a very favourable season for making progress in such doings), assures me that this cannot be, and that I must heroically deny myself the pleasure you offer.

Always believe me,
Faithfully yours.

DEVONSHIRE TERRACE,
Thursday, Fourteenth January, 1841.

MY DEAR CATTERMOLE,

I cannot tell you how much obliged I am to you for alter-ing the child, or how much I hope that my wish in that respect didn't go greatly against the grain.

I saw the old inn this morning. Words cannot say how good it is. I can't bear the thought of its being cut, and should like to frame and glaze it in *statu quo* for ever and ever.

Will you do a little tail-piece for the "Curiosity" story?—only one figure if you like—giving some notion of the etherealised spirit of the child; something like those little figures in the frontispiece. If you will, and can despatch it at once, you will make me happy.

I am, for the time being, nearly dead with work and grief for the loss of my child.

Always, my dear George,
Heartily yours.

DEVONSHIRE TERRACE,
Thursday Night, Twenty-eighth January, 1841.

MY DEAR GEORGE,

I sent to Chapman and Hall yesterday morning about the second subject for No. 2 of "Barnaby," but found they had sent it to Browne.

The first subject of No. 3 I will either send to you on Saturday, or, at latest, on Sunday morning. I have also directed Chapman and Hall to send you proofs of what has gone before, for reference, if you need it.

I want to know whether you feel ravens in general and would fancy Barnaby's raven in particular. Barnaby being an idiot, my notion is to have him always in company with a pet raven, who is immeasurably more knowing than himself. To this end I have been studying my bird, and think I could make a very queer character of him. Should you like the subject when this raven makes his first appearance?

Faithfully always.

DEVONSHIRE TERRACE,
Saturday Evening, Thirtieth January, 1841.

MY DEAR GEORGE,

I send you the first four slips of No. 48, containing the description of the locksmith's house, which I think will make a good subject, and one you will like. If you put the "'prentice" in it, show nothing more than his paper cap, because he will be an

·important character in the story, and you will need to know more about him as he is minutely described. I may as well say that he is very short. Should you wish to put the locksmith in, you will find him described in No. 2 of "Barnaby" (which I told Chapman and Hall to send you). Browne has done him in one little thing, but so very slightly that you will not require to see his sketch, I think.

Now, I must know what you think about the raven, my buck; I otherwise am in this fix. I have given Browne no subject for this number, and time is flying. If you would like to have the raven's first appearance, and don't object to having both subjects, so be it. I shall be delighted. If otherwise, I must feed that hero forthwith.

I cannot close this hasty note, my dear fellow, without saying that I have deeply felt your hearty and most invaluable co-operation in the beautiful illustrations you have made for the last story, that I look at them with a pleasure I cannot describe to you in words, and that it is impossible for me to say how sensible I am of your earnest and friendly aid. Believe me that this is the very first time any designs for what I have written have touched and moved me, and caused me to feel that they expressed the idea I had in my mind.

I am most sincerely and affectionately grateful to you, and am full of pleasure and delight.

Believe me, my dear Cattermole,

Always heartily yours.

Mr. George
Cattermole.

DEVONSHIRE TERRACE, *Tuesday, Ninth February.*

MY DEAR GEORGE,

My notes tread upon each other's heels. In my last I quite forgot business.

Will you, for No. 49, do the locksmith's house, which was described in No. 48? I mean the outside. If you can, without hurting the effect, shut up the shop as though it were night, so much the better. Should you want a figure, an ancient watchman in or out of his box, very sleepy, will be just the thing for me.

I have written to Chapman and requested him to send you a block of a long shape, so that the house may come upright as it were.

Faithfully ever.

1, DEVONSHIRE TERRACE, YORK GATE, REGENT'S PARK,   Mr. John
LONDON, *Tuesday, Twenty-third February*, 1841.   Tomlin.

DEAR SIR,

You are quite right in feeling assured that I should answer the letter you have addressed to me. If you had entertained a presentiment that it would afford me sincere pleasure and delight to hear from a warm-hearted and admiring reader of my books in the backwoods of America, you would not have been far wrong.

I thank you cordially and heartily both for your letter and its kind and courteous terms. To think that I have awakened a fellow-feeling and sympathy with the creatures of many thoughtful hours among the vast solitudes in which you dwell, is a source of the purest delight and pride to me; and believe me that your expressions of affectionate remembrance and approval, sounding from the green forests on the banks of the Mississippi, sink deeper into my heart and gratify it more than all the honorary distinctions that all the courts in Europe could confer.

It is such things as these that make one hope one does not live in vain, and that are the highest reward of an author's life. To be numbered among the household gods of one's distant countrymen, and associated with their homes and quiet pleasures; to be told that in each nook and corner of the world's great mass there lives one well-wisher who holds communion with one in the spirit, is a worthy fame indeed, and one which I would not barter for a mine of wealth.

That I may be happy enough to cheer some of your leisure hours for a very long time to come, and to hold a place in your pleasant thoughts, is the earnest wish of " Boz."

And, with all good wishes for yourself, and with a sincere reciprocation of all your kindly feeling,

I am, dear Sir,
Faithfully yours.

OLD SHIP HOTEL, BRIGHTON,   Mr. George
Twenty-sixth February, 1841.   Cattermole.

MY DEAR KITTENMOLES,

I passed your house on Wednesday, being then atop of the Brighton Era; but there was nobody at the door, saving a solitary poulterer, and all my warm-hearted aspirations lodged in the goods he was delivering. No doubt you observed a peculiar relish in your dinner. That was the cause.

I send you the MS. I fear you will have to read all the five slips; but the subject I think of is at the top of the last, when the guest, with his back towards the spectator, is looking out of window. I think, in your hands, it will be a very pretty one.

Then, my boy, when you have done it, turn your thoughts (as soon as other engagements will allow) first to the outside of The Warren—see No. 1; secondly, to the outside of the locksmith's house, by night—see No. 3. Put a penny pistol to Chapman's head and demand the blocks of him.

I have addled my head with writing all day, and have barely wit enough left to send my love to my cousin, and—there's a genealogical poser!—what relation of mine may the dear little child be? At present, I desire to be commended to her clear blue eyes.

Always, my dear George,
Faithfully yours,

DEVONSHIRE TERRACE,
Wednesday, Tenth March, 1841.

MY DEAR MILNES,

I thank you very much for the "Nickleby" correspondence, which I will keep for a day or two, and return when I see you. Poor fellow! The long letter is quite admirable, and most affecting.

I am not quite sure either of Friday or Saturday, for, independently of the "Clock" (which for ever wants winding), I am getting a young brother off to New Zealand just now, and have my mornings sadly cut up in consequence. But, knowing your ways, I know I may say that I will come if I can; and that if I can't I won't.

That Nellicide was the act of Heaven, as you may see any of these fine mornings when you look about you. If you knew the pain it gave me—but what am I talking of? if you don't know, nobody does. I am glad to shake you by the hand again autographically,

And am always,
Faithfully yours.

1, DEVONSHIRE TERRACE, YORK GATE, REGENT'S PARK,   *Anonymous.*
Thursday, Eighth April, 1841.

DEAR SIR,

I am much obliged to you for your interesting letter. Nor am I the less pleased to receive it, by reason that I cannot find it in my conscience to agree in many important respects with the body to which you belong.

In love of virtue and hatred of vice, in the detestation of cruelty and encouragement of gentleness and mercy, all men who endeavour to be acceptable to their Creator in any way, may freely agree. There are more roads to Heaven, I am inclined to think, than any sect believes; but there can be none which have not these flowers garnishing the way.

I feel it a great tribute, therefore, to receive your letter. It is most welcome and acceptable to me. I thank you for it heartily, and am proud of the approval of one who suffered in his youth, even more than my poor child.

While you teach in your walk of life the lessons of tenderness you have learnt in sorrow, trust me that in mine, I will pursue cruelty and oppression, the enemies of all God's creatures of all codes and creeds, so long as I have the energy of thought and the power of giving it utterance.   Faithfully yours.

DEVONSHIRE TERRACE, *Twenty-ninth April,* 1841.   Mr. William Harrison Ainsworth.

MY DEAR AINSWORTH,

With all imaginable pleasure. I quite look forward to the day. It is an age since we met, and it ought not to be.

The artist has just sent home your "Nickleby." He suggested variety, pleading his fancy and genius. As an artful binder must have his way, I put the best face on the matter, and gave him his. I will bring it together with the "Pickwick" to your house-warming with me.

The old *Royal George* went down in consequence of having too much weight on one side. I trust the new "First Rate" won't be heavy anywhere. There seems to me to be too much whisker for a shilling, but that's a matter of taste.   Faithfully yours always.

1, DEVONSHIRE TERRACE, YORK GATE, REGENT'S PARK,   Mr. G. Lovejoy.
Monday Evening, Thirty-first May, 1841.

SIR,

I am much obliged and flattered by the receipt of your letter, which I should have answered immediately on its arrival but for my absence from home at the moment.

My principles and inclinations would lead me to aspire to the distinction you invite me to seek, if there were any reasonable chance of success, and I hope I should do no discredit to such an honour if I won and wore it. But I am bound to add, and I have no hesitation in saying plainly, that I cannot afford the expense of a contested election. If I could, I would act on your suggestion instantly. I am not the less indebted to you and the friends to whom the thought occurred, for your good opinion and approval. I beg you to understand that I am restrained solely (and much against my will) by the consideration I have mentioned, and thank both you and them most warmly.

Yours faithfully.

The
Countess of
Blessington.
* DEVONSHIRE TERRACE, Second June, 1841.

DEAR LADY BLESSINGTON,

The year goes round so fast, that when anything occurs to remind me of its whirling, I lose my breath, and am bewildered. So your handwriting last night had as startling an effect upon me, as though you had sealed your note with one of your own eyes.

I remember my promise, as in cheerful duty bound, and with Heaven's grace will redeem it. At this moment, I have not the faintest idea how, but I am going into Scotland on the nineteenth to see Jeffrey, and while I am away (I shall return, please God, in about three weeks) will look out for some accident, incident, or subject for small description, to send you when I come home. You will take the will for the deed, I know; and, remembering that I have a "Clock" which always wants winding up, will not quarrel with me for being brief.

Have you seen Townshend's magnetic boy? . You heard of him, no doubt, from Count D'Orsay. If you get him to Gore House, don't, I entreat you, have more than eight people—four is a better number—to see him. He fails in a crowd, and is <i>marvellous</i> before a few.

I am told that down in Devonshire there are young ladies innumerable, who read crabbed manuscripts with the palms of their hands, and newspapers with their ankles, and so forth; and who are, so to speak, literary all over. I begin to understand what a blue-stocking means, and have not the smallest doubt that Lady —— (for instance) could write quite as entertaining a book with the sole of her foot as ever she did with her head. I am a believer in earnest, and I am sure you would be if you saw this boy, under

<hr>

* This, and all other Letters addressed to the Countess of Blessington, were printed in "The Literary Life and Correspondence of the Countess of Blessington."

moderately favourable circumstances, as I hope you will, before he leaves England.

Believe me, dear Lady Blessington,

Faithfully yours.

DEVONSHIRE TERRACE, *Tenth June*, 1841. Mr. G. Lovejoy.

DEAR SIR,

I am favoured with your note of yesterday's date, and lose no time in replying to it.

The sum you mention, though small I am aware in the abstract, is greater than I could afford for such a purpose; as the mere sitting in the House and attending to my duties, if I were a member, would oblige me to make many pecuniary sacrifices, consequent upon the very nature of my pursuits.

The course you suggest did occur to me when I received your first letter, and I have very little doubt indeed that the Government would support me—perhaps to the whole extent. But I cannot satisfy myself that to enter Parliament under such circumstances would enable me to pursue that honourable independence without which I could neither preserve my own respect nor that of my constituents. I confess therefore (it may be from not having considered the points sufficiently, or in the right light) that I cannot bring myself to propound the subject to any member of the administration whom I know. I am truly obliged to you nevertheless, and am,

Dear Sir,

Faithfully yours.

DEVONSHIRE TERRACE, *Wednesday Evening, Twenty-eighth July*, 1841. Mr. George Cattermole.

MY DEAR GEORGE,

Can you do for me by Saturday evening—I know the time is short, but I think the subject will suit you, and I am greatly pressed—a party of rioters (with Hugh and Simon Tappertit conspicuous among them) in old John Willet's bar, turning the liquor taps to their own advantage, smashing bottles, cutting down the grove of lemons, sitting astride on casks, drinking out of the best punch-bowls, eating the great cheese, smoking sacred pipes, etc. etc.; John Willet, fallen backward in his chair, regarding them with a stupid horror, and quite alone among them, with none of The Maypole customers at his back.

It's in your way, and you'll do it a hundred times better than I can suggest it to you, I know.

Faithfully always.

Mr. George
Cattermole.
BROADSTAIRS, *Friday, Sixth August*, 1841.

MY DEAR GEORGE,

Here is a subject for the next number; the next to that I
hope to send you the MS. of very early in the week, as the best
opportunities of illustration are all coming off now, and we are in
the thick of the story.

The rioters went, sir, from John Willet's bar (where you saw
them to such good purpose) straight to the Warren, which house
they plundered, sacked, burned, pulled down as much of as they could,
and greatly damaged and destroyed.   They are supposed to have
left it about half an hour.   It is night, and the ruins are here and
there flaming and smoking.   I want—if you understand—to show
one of the turrets laid open—the turret where the alarm-bell is,
mentioned in No. 1; and among the ruins (at some height if possible) Mr. Haredale just clutching our friend, the mysterious file,
who is passing over them like a spirit; Solomon Daisy, if you can
introduce him, looking on from the ground below.

Please to observe that the M.F. wears a large cloak and a slouched
hat.   This is important, because Browne will have him in the same
number, and he has not changed his dress meanwhile.   Mr. Haredale
is supposed to have come down here on horseback, pell-mell; to be
excited to the last degree.   I think it will make a queer picturesque
thing in your hands.   I have told Chapman and Hall that you may
like to have a block of a peculiar shape for it.   One of them will be
with you almost as soon as you receive this.

Always, dear Cattermole,

Heartily yours.

The same.
DEVONSHIRE TERRACE, *Thursday, Thirteenth August.*

MY DEAR CATTERMOLE,

Will you turn your attention to a frontispiece for our first
volume, to come upon the left-hand side of the book as you open
it, and to face a plain printed title?   My idea is, some scene from
the "Curiosity Shop," in a pretty border, or scroll-work, or architectural device; it matters not what, so that it be pretty.   The
scene even might be a fanciful thing, partaking of the character of
the story, but not reproducing any particular passage in it, if you
thought that better for the effect.

I ask you to think of this, because, although the volume is not
published until the end of September, there is no time to lose.
We wish to have it engraved with great care, and worked very
skilfully; and this cannot be done unless we get it on the stocks
soon.

They will give you every opportunity of correction, alteration, revision, and all other ations and isions connected with the fine arts.

Always believe me,

Faithfully yours.

BROADSTAIRS, *Nineteenth August,* 1841.   Mr. George Cattermole.

MY DEAR GEORGE,

When Hugh and a small body of the rioters cut off from The Warren beckoned to their pals, they forced into a very remarkable postchaise Dolly Varden and Emma Haredale, and bore them away with all possible rapidity; one of their company driving, and the rest running beside the chaise, climbing up behind, sitting on the top, lighting the way with their torches, etc. etc. If you can express the women inside without showing them—as by a fluttering veil, a delicate arm, or so forth appearing at the half-closed window—so much the better. Mr. Tappertit stands on the steps, which are partly down, and, hanging on to the window with one hand and extending the other with great majesty, addresses a few words of encouragement to the driver and attendants. Hugh sits upon the bar in front; the driver sitting postilion-wise, and turns round to look through the window behind him at the little doves within. The gentlemen behind are also anxious to catch a glimpse of the ladies. One of those who are running at the side may be gently rebuked for his curiosity by the cudgel of Hugh. So they cut away, sir, as fast as they can.

Always faithfully.

P.S.—John Willet's bar is noble.

BROADSTAIRS, *Tuesday, Twenty-fourth August,* 1841.   Mr. W. C. Macready.

MY DEAR MACREADY,

I must thank you most heartily and cordially, for your kind note relative to poor Overs. I can't tell you how glad I am to know that he thoroughly deserves such kindness.

What a good fellow Elliotson is. He kept him in his room a whole hour, and has gone into his case as if he were Prince Albert; laying down all manner of elaborate projects and determining to leave his friend Wood in town when he himself goes away, on purpose to attend to him. Then he writes me four sides of paper about the man, and says he can't go back to his old work, for that requires muscular exertion (and muscular exertion he mustn't make). What are we to do with him? He says: "Here's five pounds for the present."

I declare before God that I could almost bear the Jones's for five years out of the pleasure I feel in knowing such things, and

when I think that every dirty speck upon the fair face of the
Almighty's creation, who writes in a filthy, beastly newspaper;
every rotten-hearted pander who has been beaten, kicked, and
rolled in the kennel, yet struts it in the editorial "We," once
a week; every vagabond that an honest man's gorge must rise at;
every live emetic in that noxious drug-shop the press, can have
his fling at such men and call them knaves and fools and thieves,
I grow so vicious that, with bearing hard upon my pen, I break
the nib down, and, with keeping my teeth set, make my jaws ache.

I have put myself out of sorts for the day, and shall go and
walk, unless the direction of this sets me up again. On second
thoughts I think it will.

Always, my dear Macready,

Your faithful Friend.

Mr. George
Cattermole. BROADSTAIRS, *Sunday, Twelfth September*, 1841.

MY DEAR GEORGE,

Firstly. Will you design, upon a block of wood, Lord George
Gordon, alone and very solitary, in his prison in the Tower? The
chamber as ancient as you please, and after your own fancy; the
time, evening; the season, summer.

Secondly. Will you ditto upon a ditto, a sword duel between
Mr. Haredale and Mr. Chester, in a grove of trees? No one close
by. Mr. Haredale has just pierced his adversary, who has fallen,
dying, on the grass. He (that is, Chester) tries to staunch the
wound in his breast with his handkerchief; has his snuffbox on
the earth beside him, and looks at Mr. Haredale (who stands with
his sword in his hand, looking down on him) with most supercilious
hatred, but polite to the last. Mr. Haredale is more sorry than
triumphant.

Thirdly. Will you conceive and execute, after your own fashion,
a frontispiece for "Barnaby"?

Fourthly. Will you also devise a subject representing "Master
Humphrey's Clock" as stopped; his chair by the fireside, empty;
his crutch against the wall; his slippers on the cold hearth; his
hat upon the chair-back; the MSS. of "Barnaby" and the
"Curiosity Shop" heaped upon the table; and the flowers you
introduced in the first subject of all withered and dead? Master
Humphrey being supposed to be no more.

I have a fifthly, sixthly, seventhly, and eighthly; for I sorely
want you, as I approach the close of the tale, but I won't frighten
you, so we'll take breath.

Always, my dear Cattermole,

Heartily yours.

BROADSTAIRS, *Twenty-first September*, 1841. Mr. George Cattermole.

MY DEAR GEORGE,

Will you, before you go on with the other subjects I gave you, do one of Hugh, bareheaded, bound, tied on a horse, and escorted by horse-soldiers to jail? · If you can add an indication of old Fleet Market, and bodies of foot soldiers firing at people who have taken refuge on the tops of stalls, bulkheads, etc., it will be all the better.

Faithfully yours always.

Twenty-eighth September, 1841. Mr. L. Gaylord Clark. *

MY DEAR SIR,

I condole with you from my heart on the loss † you have sustained, and I feel proud of your permitting me to sympathise with your affliction. It is a great satisfaction to me to have been ·· addressed, under similar circumstances, by many of your country-men since the "Curiosity Shop" came to a close. Some simple and honest hearts in the remote wilds of America have written me letters on the loss of children—so numbering my little book, or rather heroine, with their household gods; and so pouring out their trials and sources of comfort in them, before me as a friend, that I have been inexpressibly moved, and am whenever I think of them, I do assure you. You have already all the comfort, that I could lay before you; all, I hope, that the affectionate spirit of your brother, now in happiness, can shed into your soul.

On the fourth of next January, if it please God, I am coming with my wife on a three or four months' visit to America. The British and North American packet will bring me, I hope, to Boston, and enable me, in the third week of the new year, to set my foot upon the soil I have trodden in my day-dreams many times and whose sons (and daughters) I yearn to know and to be among.

I hope you are surprised, and I hope not unpleasantly.

Faithfully yours.

DEVONSHIRE TERRACE, Mrs. Hogarth.
Sunday, Twenty-fourth October, 1841.

MY DEAR MRS. HOGARTH,

For God's sake be comforted, and bear this well, for the love of your remaining children.

I had always intended to keep poor Mary's grave for us and our dear children, and for you. But if it will be any comfort to you to have poor George buried there, I will cheerfully arrange to

* This letter was published in "Harper's New Monthly Magazine," in 1862.

† The death of his correspondent's twin-brother, Willis Gaylord Clark.

E

place the ground at your entire disposal.   Do not consider me in any way.   Consult only your own heart.   Mine seems to tell me that as they both died so young and so suddenly, they ought both to be buried together.

Try—do try—to think that they have but preceded you to happiness, and will meet you with joy in heaven.   There *is* consolation in the knowledge that you have treasure there, and that while you live on earth, there are creatures among the angels, who owed their being to you.   Always yours with true affection.

DEVONSHIRE TERRACE, *Sixteenth December*, 1841.

Miss Mary
Talfourd.

MY DEAR MARY,

I should be delighted to come and dine with you on your birthday, and to be as merry as I wish you to be always ; but as I am going, within a very few days afterwards, a very long distance from home, and I shall not see any of my children for six long months, I have made up my mind to pass all that week at home for their sakes ; just as you would like your papa and mamma to spend all the time they possibly could spare with you if they were about to make a dreary voyage to America ; which is what I am going to do myself.

But although I cannot come to see you on that day, you may be sure I shall not forget that it is your birthday, and that I shall drink your health and many happy returns, in a glass of wine, filled as full as it will hold.   And I shall dine at half-past five myself, so that we may both be drinking our wine at the same time ; and I shall tell my Mary (for I have got a daughter of that name but she is a very small one as yet) to drink your health too ; and we shall try and make believe that you are here, or that we are in Russell Square, which is the best thing we can do, I think, under the circumstances.

You are growing up so fast that by the time I come home again I expect you will be almost a woman ; and in a very few years we shall be saying to each other : "Don't you remember what the birthdays used to be in Russell Square ?" and "How strange it seems !" and "How quickly time passes !" and all that sort of thing, you know.   But I shall always be very glad to be asked on your birthday, and to come if you will let me, and to send my love to you, and to wish that you may live to be very old and very happy, which I do now with all my heart.

Believe me always,
My dear Mary,
Yours affectionately.

DEVONSHIRE TERRACE,
Tuesday, Twenty-eighth December, 1841.

MY DEAR MACREADY,

This note is about the saloon. I make it as brief as possible. Read it when you have time. As we were the first experimentalists last night you will be glad to know what it wants.

First, the refreshments are preposterously dear. A glass of wine is a shilling, and it ought to be sixpence.

Secondly, they were served out by the wrong sort of people—two most uncomfortable drabs of women, and a dirty man with his hat on.

Thirdly, there ought to be a box-keeper to ring a bell or give some other notice of the commencement of the overture to the after-piece. The promenaders were in a perpetual fret and worry to get back again.

And fourthly, and most important of all—if the plan is ever to succeed—you must have some notice up to the effect that as it is now a place of resort for ladies, gentlemen are requested not to lounge there in their hats and greatcoats. No ladies will go there, though the conveniences should be ten thousand times greater, while the sort of swells who have been used to kick their heels there do so in the old sort of way. I saw this expressed last night more strongly than I can tell you.

Hearty congratulations on the brilliant triumph. I have always expected one, as you know, but nobody could have imagined the reality.

Always, my dear Macready,
Affectionately yours.

MY DEAR SIR,[*]

There is no man in the world who could have given me the heartfelt pleasure you have, by your kind note of the thirteenth of last month. There is no living writer, and there are very few among the dead, whose approbation I should feel so proud to earn. And with everything you have written upon my shelves, and in my thoughts, and in my heart of hearts, I may honestly and truly say so. If you could know how earnestly I write this, you would be glad to read it—as I hope you will be, faintly guessing at the warmth of the hand I autobiographically hold out to you over the broad Atlantic.

I wish I could find in your welcome letter some hint of an intention to visit England. I can't. I have held it at arm's length,

. [*] This, and all other Letters addressed to Mr. Washington Irving, were printed in "The Life and Letters of Washington Irving," edited by his nephew, Mr. Pierre M. Irving.

and taken a bird's-eye view of it, after reading it a great many times, but there is no greater encouragement in it this way than on a microscopic inspection. I should love to go with you—as I have gone, God knows how often—into Little Britain, and Eastcheap, and Green Arbour Court, and Westminster Abbey. I should like to travel with you, outside the last of the coaches down to Bracebridge Hall. It would make my heart glad to compare notes with you about that shabby gentleman in the oilcloth hat and red nose, who sat in the nine-cornered back-parlour of the Masons' Arms; and about Robert Preston and the tallow-chandler's widow, whose sitting-room is second nature to me; and about all those delightful places and people that I used to walk about and dream of in the daytime, when a very small and not over-particularly-taken-care-of boy. I have a good deal to say, too, about that dashing Alonzo de Ojeda, that you can't help being fonder of than you ought to be; and much to hear concerning Moorish legend, and poor unhappy Boabdil. Diedrich Knickerbocker I have worn to death in my pocket, and yet I should show you his mutilated carcass with a joy past all expression.

I have been so accustomed to associate you with my pleasantest and happiest thoughts, and with my leisure hours, that I rush at once into full confidence with you, and fall, as it were naturally and by the very laws of gravity, into your open arms. Questions come thronging to my pen as to the lips of people who meet after long hoping to do so. I don't know what to say first or what to leave unsaid, and am constantly disposed to break off and tell you again how glad I am this moment has arrived.

My dear Washington Irving, I cannot thank you enough for your cordial and generous praise, or tell you what deep and lasting gratification it has given me. I hope to have many letters from you, and to exchange a frequent correspondence. I send this to say so. After the first two or three I shall settle down into a connected style, and become gradually rational.

You know what the feeling is, after having written a letter, sealed it, and sent it off. I shall picture your reading this, and answering it before it has lain one night in the post-office. Ten to one that before the fastest packet could reach New York I shall be writing again.

Do you suppose the post-office clerks care to receive letters? I have my doubts. They get into a dreadful habit of indifference. A postman, I imagine, is quite callous. Conceive his delivering one to himself, without being startled by a preliminary double knock!

Always your faithful Friend.

1842.

NARRATIVE.

In January of this year Charles Dickens went, with his wife, to America, the house in Devonshire Terrace being let for the term of their absence (six months), and the four children left in a furnished house in Osnaburgh Street, Regent's Park, under the care of Mr. and Mrs. Macready. They returned from America in July, and in August went to Broadstairs for the autumn months as usual, and in October Charles Dickens made an expedition to Cornwall, with Mr. Forster, Mr. Maclise, and Mr. Stanfield for his companions.

During his stay at Broadstairs he was engaged in writing his "American Notes," which book was published in October. At the end of the year he had written the first number of "Martin Chuzzlewit," which appeared in January, 1843.

An extract from a letter, addressed to Messrs. Chapman and Hall before his departure for America, is given as a testimony of the estimation in which Charles Dickens held the firm with whom he was connected for so many years.

His letters to Mr. H. P. Smith, for many years actuary of the Eagle Insurance Office, are a combination of business and friendship. Mr. Smith gives us, as an explanation of a note to him, dated 14th July, that Charles Dickens alluded to the stamp of the office upon the cheque, which was, as he described it, "almost a work of art"—a truculent-looking eagle seated on a rock and scattering rays over the whole sheet.

Charles Dickens made many life-long friendships during his first visit to America. Mr. Cornelius C. Felton, Greek Professor at the Cambridge University there, was one of the most heartily-loved of these friends, and we give in this year the first two letters to Mr. Felton which he wrote while he was in America. Besides these letters we give another to Mr. Washington Irving, and one to Mr. Halleck, the American poet, and one to Dr. F. H. Deane, of Cincinnati, complying with his request to write an epitaph for the tombstone of his little child, which has been kindly copied for us by Mrs. Fields, of Boston.

At the close of the voyage to America (a very bad and dangerous one), a meeting of the passengers, with Lord Mulgrave in the chair, took place, and a piece of plate was presented and a vote of thanks proposed to the captain of the *Britannia*, Captain Hewett. The vote of thanks, being drawn up by Charles Dickens, is given here. We have letters in this year to Mr. Thomas Hood,

Miss Pardoe, Mrs. Trollope, and Mr. W. P. Frith. The last-named artist—then a very young man—had made great success with several charming pictures of Dolly Varden. One of these was bought by Charles Dickens, who ordered a companion picture of Kate Nickleby from the young painter, whose acquaintance he made at the same time ; and the two letters to Mr. Frith have reference to the purchase of the one picture and the commission for the other.

The letter to Mr. Cattermole is an acknowledgment also of a completed commission of two water-colour drawings, from the subjects of two of Mr. Cattermole's illustrations to "The Old Curiosity Shop."

A note to Mr. Macready, at the close of this year, refers to the first representation of Mr. Westland Marston's play, "The Patrician's Daughter." Charles Dickens took great interest in the production of this work at Drury Lane. It was, to a certain extent, an experiment of the effect of a tragedy of modern times and in modern dress ; and the prologue, which Charles Dickens wrote and which we give, was intended to show that there need be no incongruity between plain clothes of this century and high tragedy. The play was quite successful.

Messrs.
Chapman
and Hall.

*   *   *   *   *

Having disposed of the business part of this letter, I should not feel at ease on leaving England if I did not tell you once more with my whole heart that your conduct to me on this and all other occasions has been honourable, manly, and generous, and that I have felt it a solemn duty, in the event of any accident happening to me while I am away, to place this testimony upon record. It forms part of a will I have made for the security of my children ; for I wish them to know it when they are capable of understanding your worth and my appreciation of it.

Always believe me,
Faithfully and truly yours.

Mr. Thomas
Mitton.

ADELPHI HOTEL, LIVERPOOL,
Monday, Third January, 1842.

MY DEAR MITTON,
This is a short note, but I will fulfil the adage and make it a merry one.

We came down in great comfort. Our luggage is now aboard. Anything so utterly and monstrously absurd as the size of our cabin, "no gentleman of England who lives at home at ease" can for a moment imagine. Neither of the portmanteaus would go into it. There !

These Cunard packets are not very big you know actually, but the quantity of sleeping-berths makes them much smaller, so that the saloon is not nearly as large as in one of the Ramsgate boats. The ladies' cabin is so close to ours that I could knock the door open without getting off something they call my bed, but which I believe to be a muffin beaten flat. This is a great comfort, for it is an excellent room (the only good one in the ship); and if there be only one other lady besides Kate, as the stewardess thinks, I hope I shall be able to sit there very often.

They talk of seventy passengers, but I can't think there will be so many; they talk besides (which is even more to the purpose) of a very fine passage, having had a noble one this time last year. God send it so! We are in the best spirits, and full of hope. I was dashed for a moment when I saw our "cabin," but I got over that directly, and laughed so much at its ludicrous proportions, that you might have heard me all over the ship.

God bless you! Write to me by the first opportunity. I will do the like to you. And always believe me,

Your old and faithful Friend.

At a meeting of the passengers on board the *Britannia* steamship, travelling from Liverpool to Boston, held in the saloon of that vessel, on Friday, the twenty-first January, 1842, it was moved and seconded :

"That the Earl of Mulgrave do take the chair."

The motion having been carried unanimously, the Earl of Mulgrave took the chair accordingly.

It was also moved and seconded, and carried unanimously :

"That Charles Dickens, Esq., be appointed secretary and treasurer to the meeting."

The three following resolutions were then proposed and carried *nem. con.* :

"First. That, gratefully recognising the blessing of Divine Providence by which we are brought nearly to the termination of our voyage, we have great pleasure in expressing our high appreciation of Captain Hewett's nautical skill and of his indefatigable attention to the management and safe conduct of the ship, during a more than ordinarily tempestuous passage.

"Secondly. That a subscription be opened for the purchase of a piece of silver plate, and that Captain Hewett be respectfully requested to accept it, as a sincere expression of the sentiments embodied in the foregoing resolution.

"Thirdly. That a committee be appointed to carry these resolutions into effect; and that the committee be composed of the following gentlemen : Charles Dickens, Esq., E. Dunbar, Esq., and Solomon Hopkins, Esq."

The committee having withdrawn and conferred with Captain Hewett, returned, and informed the meeting that Captain Hewett desired to attend and express his thanks, which he did.

The amount of the subscription was reported at fifty pounds, and the list was closed. It was then agreed that the following inscription should be placed upon the testimonial to Captain Hewett :

THIS PIECE OF PLATE
was presented to
CAPTAIN JOHN HEWETT,
of the BRITANNIA Steam-ship,
By the Passengers on board that vessel in a voyage from Liverpool
to Boston, in the month of January, 1842,
As a slight acknowledgment of his great ability and skill
under circumstances of much difficulty and danger,
And as a feeble token of their lasting gratitude.

Thanks were then voted to the chairman and to the secretary, and the meeting separated.

Mr. Thomas
Mitton.

TREMONT HOUSE, BOSTON,
Thirty-first January, 1842.

MY DEAR MITTON,

I am so exhausted with the life I am obliged to lead here, that I have had time to write but one letter which is at all deserving of the name, as giving any account of our movements. Forster has it in trust, to tell you all its news; and he has also some newspapers which I had an opportunity of sending him, in which you will find further particulars of our progress.

We had a dreadful passage, the worst, the officers all concur in saying, that they have ever known. We were eighteen days coming; experienced a dreadful storm which swept away our paddle-boxes and stove our lifeboats; and ran aground besides, near Halifax, among rocks and breakers, where we lay at anchor all night. After we left the English Channel we had only one fine day. And we had the additional discomfort of being eighty-six passengers. I was ill five days, Kate six; though, indeed, she had a swelled face and suffered the utmost terror all the way.

I can give you no conception of my welcome here. There never was a king or emperor upon the earth so cheered and followed by crowds, and entertained in public at splendid balls and dinners, and waited on by public bodies and deputations of all kinds. I have had one from the Far West—a journey of two thousand miles ! If I go out in a carriage, the crowd surround it and escort me home; if I go to the theatre, the whole house (crowded to the roof) rises as one man, and the timbers ring again. You cannot imagine what it is. I have five great public dinners on hand at this moment, and invitations from every town and village and city in the States.

There is a great deal afloat here in the way of subjects for description. I keep my eyes open pretty wide, and hope to have done so to some purpose by the time I come home.

Always your faithful Friend.

CARLTON HOUSE, Fourteenth February, 1842.

Mr. Fitz-
Greene
Halleck.

MY DEAR SIR,

Will you come and breakfast with me on Tuesday, the twenty-second, at half-past ten? Say yes. I should have been truly delighted to have a talk with you to-night (being quite alone), but the doctor says that if I talk to man, woman, or child this evening I shall be dumb to-morrow.

Believe me, with true regard,

Faithfully your Friend.

FULLER'S HOTEL, WASHINGTON,
Monday, Fourteenth March, 1842.

Professor
Felton.

MY DEAR FELTON,*

I was more delighted than I can possibly tell you, to receive (last Saturday night) your welcome letter. We and the oysters missed you terribly in New York. You carried away with you more than half the delight and pleasure of my New World; and I heartily wish you could bring it back again.

There are very interesting men in this place—highly interesting, of course—but it's not a comfortable place; is it? If spittle could wait at table we should be nobly attended, but as that property has not been imparted to it in the present state of mechanical science, we are rather lonely and orphan-like, in respect of "being looked arter." A blithe black was introduced on our arrival, as our peculiar and especial attendant. He is the only gentleman in the town who has a peculiar delicacy in intruding upon my valuable time. It usually takes seven rings and a threatening message from —— to produce him; and when he comes he goes to fetch something, and, forgetting it by the way, comes back no more.

* This, and all other Letters addressed to Professor Felton, were printed in Mr. Field's ."Yesterdays with Authors," originally published in "The Atlantic Monthly Magazine."

We have been in great distress, really in distress, at the non-arrival of the *Caledonia*. You may conceive what our joy was, when, while we were out dining yesterday, Putnam * arrived with the joyful intelligence of her safety. The very news of her having really arrived seemed to diminish the distance between ourselves and home, by one half at least.

And this morning (though we have not yet received our heap of despatches, for which we are looking eagerly forward to this night's mail)—this morning there reached us unexpectedly, through the Government bag (Heaven knows how they came there !), two of our many and long-looked-for letters, wherein was a circumstantial account of the whole conduct and behaviour of our pets ; with marvellous narrations of Charley's precocity at a Twelfth Night juvenile party at Macready's ; and tremendous predictions of the governess, dimly suggesting his having got out of pot-hooks and hangers, and darkly insinuating the possibility of his writing us a letter before long ; and many other workings of the same prophetic spirit, in reference to him and his sisters, very gladdening to their mother's heart, and not at all depressing to their father's. There was, also, the doctor's report, which was a clean bill ; and the nurse's report, which was perfectly electrifying ; showing as it did how Master Walter had been weaned, and had cut a double tooth, and done many other extraordinary things, quite worthy of his high descent. In short, we were made very happy and grateful ; and felt as if the prodigal father and mother had got home again.

What do you think of this incendiary card being left at my door last night ? "General G. sends compliments to Mr. Dickens, and called with two literary ladies. As the two L. L.'s are ambitious of the honour of a personal introduction to Mr. D., General G. requests the honour of an appointment for to-morrow." I draw a veil over my sufferings. They are sacred. We shall be in Buffalo, please Heaven, on the thirtieth of April. If I don't find a letter from you in the care of the postmaster at that place, I'll never write to you from England.

But if I *do* find one, my right hand shall forget its cunning, before I forget to be your truthful and constant correspondent ; not, dear Felton, because I promised it, nor because I have a natural tendency to correspond (which is far from being the case), nor because I am truly grateful to you for, and have been made truly proud by, that affectionate and elegant tribute which —— sent me, but because you are a man after my own heart, and I love you *well*. And for the love I bear you, and the pleasure with which I shall

---

* An American gentleman, who travelled with Charles Dickens, as his secretary, during this visit to America.

always think of you, and the glow I shall feel when I see your handwriting in my own home, I hereby enter into a solemn league and covenant to write as many letters to you as you write to me, at least. Amen.

Come to England! Come to England! Our oysters are small, I know; they are said by Americans to be coppery; but our hearts are of the largest size. We are thought to excel in shrimps, to be far from despicable in point of lobsters, and in periwinkles are considered to challenge the universe. Our oysters, small though they be, are not devoid of the refreshing influence which that species of fish is supposed to exercise in these latitudes. Try them and compare.

Affectionately yours.

WASHINGTON,   Mr. Washington Irving.
Monday Afternoon, Twenty-first March, 1842.

MY DEAR IRVING,

We passed through—literally passed through—this place again to-day. I did not come to see you, for I really have not the heart to say "good-bye" again, and felt more than I can tell you when we shook hands last Wednesday.

You will not be at Baltimore, I fear? I thought, at the time, that you only said you might be there, to make our parting the gayer.

Wherever you go, God bless you! What pleasure I have had in seeing and talking with you, I will not attempt to say. I shall never forget it as long as I live. What would I give, if we could have but a quiet week together! Spain is a lazy place, and its climate an indolent one. But if you have ever leisure under its sunny skies to think of a man who loves you, and holds communion with your spirit oftener, perhaps, than any other person alive—leisure from listlessness, I mean—and will write to me in London, you will give me an inexpressible amount of pleasure.

Your affectionate Friend.

BALTIMORE, *Twenty-second March*, 1842.   Mr. W. C. Macready.

MY DEAR FRIEND,

I beg your pardon, but you were speaking of rash leaps at hasty conclusions. Are you quite sure you designed that remark for me? Have you not, in the hurry of correspondence, slipped a paragraph into my letter which belongs of right to somebody else? When did you ever find me leap at wrong conclusions? I pause for a reply.

Pray, sir, did you ever find me admiring Mr. ——? On the

contrary, did you never hear of my protesting through good, better, and best report that he was not an open or a candid man, and would one day, beyond all doubt, displease you by not being so? I pause again for a reply.

Are you quite sure, Mr. Macready—and I address myself to you with the sternness of a man in the pit—are you quite sure, sir, that you do not view America through the pleasant mirage which often surrounds a thing that has been, but not a thing that is? Are you quite sure that when you were here you relished it as well as you do now when you look back upon it. The early spring birds, Mr. Macready, *do* sing in the groves that you were, very often, not over well pleased with many of the new country's social aspects. Are the birds to be trusted? Again I pause for a reply.

My dear Macready, I desire to be so honest and just to those who have so enthusiastically and earnestly welcomed me, that I burned the last letter I wrote to you—even to you to whom I would speak as to myself—rather than let it come with anything that might seem like an ill-considered word of disappointment. I preferred that you should think me neglectful (if you could imagine anything so wild) rather than I should do wrong in this respect. Still it is of no use. I *am* disappointed. This is not the republic I came to see; this is not the republic of my imagination. I infinitely prefer a liberal monarchy—even with its sickening accompaniments of court circulars—to such a government as this. The more I think of its use and strength, the poorer and more trifling in a thousand aspects it appears in my eyes. In everything of which it has made a boast—excepting its education of the people and its care for poor children—it sinks immeasurably below the level I had placed it upon; and England, even England, bad and faulty as the old land is, and miserable as millions of her people are, rises in the comparison.

You live here, Macready, as I have sometimes heard you imagining! *You!* Loving you with all my heart and soul, and knowing what your disposition really is, I would not condemn you to a year's residence on this side of the Atlantic for any money. Freedom of opinion! Where is it? I see a press more mean, and paltry, and silly, and disgraceful than any country I ever knew. If that is its standard, here it is. But I speak of Bancroft, and am advised to be silent on that subject, for he is "a black sheep—a Democrat." I speak of Bryant, and am entreated to be more careful, for the same reason. I speak of international copyright, and am implored not to ruin myself outright. I speak of Miss Martineau, and all parties—Slave Upholders and Abolitionists, Whigs, Tyler Whigs, and Democrats, shower down upon me a perfect cataract of abuse. "But what has she done? Surely she praised America enough!" "Yes, but she told us of some of our faults, and Americans can't bear to be told of their faults. Don't split on that rock, Mr. Dickens, don't write about America; we are so very suspicious."

Freedom of opinion! Macready, if I had been born here and had written my books in this country, producing them with no stamp of approval from any other land, it is my solemn belief that I should have lived and died poor, unnoticed, and a "black sheep" to boot. I never was more convinced of anything than I am of that.

The people are affectionate, generous, open-hearted, hospitable, enthusiastic, good-humoured, polite to women, frank and candid to all strangers, anxious to oblige, far less prejudiced than they have been described to be, frequently polished and refined, very seldom rude or disagreeable. I have made a great many friends here, even in public conveyances, whom I have been truly sorry to part from. In the towns I have formed perfect attachments. I have seen none of that greediness and indecorousness on which travellers have laid so much emphasis. I have returned frankness with frankness; met questions not intended to be rude, with answers meant to be satisfactory; and have not spoken to one man, woman, or child of any degree who has not grown positively affectionate before we parted. In the respects of not being left alone, and of being horribly disgusted by tobacco chewing and tobacco spittle, I have suffered considerably. The sight of slavery in Virginia, the hatred of British feeling upon the subject, and the miserable hints of the impotent indignation of the South, have pained me very much! on the last head, of course, I have felt nothing but a mingled pity and amusement; on the other, sheer distress. But however much I like the ingredients of this great dish, I cannot but come back to the point upon which I started, and say that the dish itself goes against the grain with me, and that I don't like it.

You know that I am truly a Liberal. I believe I have as little pride as most men, and I am conscious of not the smallest annoyance from being "hail fellow well met" with everybody. I have not had greater pleasure in the company of any set of men among the thousands I have received than in that of the carmen of Hertford, who presented themselves in a body in their blue frocks, among a crowd of well-dressed ladies and gentlemen, and bade me welcome through their spokesman. They had all read my books, and all perfectly understood them. It is not these things I have in my mind when I say that the man who comes to this country a

Radical and goes home again with his opinions unchanged, must
be a Radical on reason, sympathy, and reflection, and one who has
so well considered the subject that he has no chance of wavering.

We have been to Boston, Worcester, Hertford, New Haven,
New York, Philadelphia, Baltimore, Washington, Fredericksburgh,
Richmond, and back to Washington again.   The premature heat
of the weather (it was eighty yesterday in the shade) and Clay's
advice—how you would like Clay!—have made us determine not
to go to Charleston; but having got to Richmond, I think I should
have turned back under any circumstances.   We remain at Baltimore for two days, of which this is one; then we go to Harrisburgh.
Then by the canal boat and the railroad over the Alleghany
Mountains to Pittsburgh, then down the Ohio to Cincinnati, then
to Louisville, and then to St. Louis.   I have been invited to a
public entertainment in every town I have entered, and have
refused them; but I have excepted St. Louis as the farthest point
of my travels.   My friends there have passed some resolutions
which Forster has, and will show you.   From St. Louis we cross
to Chicago, traversing immense prairies.   Thence by the lakes and
Detroit to Buffalo, and so to Niagara.   A run into Canada follows
of course, and then—let me write the blessed word in capitals—
we turn towards HOME.

Kate has written to Mrs. Macready, and it is useless for me to
thank you, my dearest friend, or her, for your care of our dear
children, which is our constant theme of discourse.   Forster has
gladdened our hearts with his account of the triumph of ".Acis
and Galatea," and I am anxiously looking for news of the tragedy.
Forrest breakfasted with us at Richmond last Saturday—he was
acting there, and I invited him—and he spoke very gratefully,
and very like a man, of your kindness to him when he was in
London.

David Colden is as good a fellow as ever lived; and I am
deeply in love with his wife.   Indeed we have received the greatest
and most earnest and zealous kindness from the whole family, and
quite love them all.   Do you remember one Greenhow, whom you
invited to pass some days with you at the hotel on the Kaatskill
.Mountains?   He is translator to the State Office at Washington,
has a very pretty wife, and a little girl of five years old.   We
dined with them, and had a very pleasant day.   The President
invited me to dinner, but I couldn't stay for it.   I had a private
audience, however, and we attended the public drawing-room besides.

Now, don't you rush at the quick conclusion that I have rushed
at a quick conclusion.   Pray, be upon your guard.   If you can by
any process estimate the extent of my affectionate regard for you,

and the rush I shall make when I reach London to take you by your true right hand, I don't object. But let me entreat you to be very careful how you come down upon the sharpsighted individual who pens these words, which you seem to me to have done in what Willmott would call "one of Mr. Macready's rushes."

I am ever, my dear Macready,

Your faithful Friend.

BALTIMORE, UNITED STATES,   Mr. Thomas
Twenty-second March, 1842.   Mitton.

MY DEAR FRIEND,

We have been as far south as Richmond in Virginia (where they grow and manufacture tobacco, and where the labour is all performed by slaves), but the season in those latitudes is so intensely and prematurely hot, that it was considered a matter of doubtful expediency to go on to Charleston. We start for the Far West—which includes mountain travelling, and lake travelling, and prairie travelling—the day after to-morrow, at eight o'clock in the morning; and shall be in the West, and from there going northward again, until the thirtieth of April or first of May, when we shall halt for a week at Niagara, before going further into Canada. We have taken our passage home (God bless the word) in the *George Washington* packet-ship from New York. She sails on the seventh of June.

I have departed from my resolution not to accept any more public entertainments—they have been proposed in every town I have visited—in favour of the people of St. Louis, my utmost western point. That town is on the borders of the Indian territory, a trifling distance from this place—only two thousand miles! At my second halting-place I shall be able to write to fix the day; I suppose it will be somewhere about the twelfth of April. Think of my going so far towards the setting sun to dinner!

In every town where we stay, though it be only for a day, we hold a regular levee or drawing-room, where I shake hands on an average with five or six hundred people, who pass on from me to Kate, and are shaken again by her. Maclise's picture of our darlings stands upon a table or sideboard the while; and my travelling secretary, assisted very often by a committee belonging to the place, presents the people in due form. Think of two hours of this every day, and the people coming in by hundreds, all fresh, and piping hot, and full-of questions, when we are literally exhausted and can hardly stand! I really do believe that if I had not a lady with me, I should have been obliged to leave the country and go back to England. But for her they never would leave me alone by day or night, and as it is, a slave comes to me now and then in the middle of the night with a letter, and waits at the bedroom door for an answer.

It was so hot at Richmond that we could scarcely breathe, and the peach and other fruit trees were in full blossom; it was so cold at Washington next day that we were shivering; but even in the same town you might often wear nothing but a shirt and trousers in the morning, and two greatcoats at night, the thermometer very frequently taking a little trip of thirty degrees between sunrise and sunset.

They do lay it on at the hotels in such style! They charge by the day, so that whether one dines out or dines at home makes no manner of difference. T'other day I wrote to order our rooms at Philadelphia to be ready on a certain day, and was detained a week longer than I expected in New York. The Philadelphia landlord not only charged me half rent for the rooms during the whole of that time, but board for myself and Kate and Anne * during the whole time too, though we were actually boarding at the same expense during the same time in New York! What do you say to that? If I remonstrated, the whole virtue of the newspapers would be aroused directly.

Parties—parties—parties—of course, every day and night. But it's not all parties. I go into the prisons, the police-offices, the watch-houses, the hospitals, the workhouses. I was out half the night in New York with two of their most famous constables; started at midnight, and went into every brothel, thieves' house, murdering hovel, sailors' dancing place, and abode of villany, both black and white, in the town. I went *incog.* behind the scenes to the little theatre where Mitchell is making a fortune. He has been rearing a little dog for me, and has called him "Boz." † I am going to bring him home. In a word I go everywhere, and a hard life it is.

When I next write to you, I shall have begun, I hope, to turn my face homeward. I have a great store of oddity and whimsicality, and am going now into the oddest and most characteristic part of this most queer country.

And I am always.

* Mrs. Dickens' maid.

† The little dog—a white Havana spaniel—*was* brought home and renamed, after an incidental character in "Nicholas Nickleby," "Mr. Snittle Timbery." This was shortened to "Timber," and under that name the little dog lived to be very old, and accompanied the family in all its migrations, including the visits to Italy and Switzerland.

CINCINNATI, OHIO, *Fourth April*, 1842. Dr. F. H. Deane.

MY DEAR SIR,

I have not been unmindful of your request for a moment, but have not been able to think of it until now. I hope my good friends (for whose christian-names I have left blanks in the epitaph) may like what I have written, and that they will take comfort and be happy again. I sail on the seventh of June, and purpose being at the Carlton House, New York, about the first. It will make me easy to know that this letter has reached you.

Faithfully yours.

This is the Grave of a Little Child.

WHOM GOD IN HIS GOODNESS CALLED TO A BRIGHT ETERNITY
WHEN HE WAS VERY YOUNG.
HARD AS IT IS FOR HUMAN AFFECTION TO RECONCILE ITSELF TO DEATH
IN ANY SHAPE (AND MOST OF ALL, PERHAPS, AT FIRST, IN THIS),
HIS PARENTS CAN EVEN NOW BELIEVE THAT IT WILL BE A CONSOLATION
TO THEM THROUGHOUT THEIR LIVES,
AND WHEN THEY SHALL HAVE GROWN OLD AND GRAY,
Always to think of him as a Child in Heaven.
"*And Jesus called a little child unto Him, and set him in the midst of them.*"
HE WAS THE SON OF Q—— AND M—— THORNTON, CHRISTENED
CHARLES JERKING.
HE WAS BORN ON THE 20TH DAY OF JANUARY, 1841,
AND HE DIED ON THE 12TH DAY OF MARCH, 1842,
HAVING LIVED ONLY THIRTEEN MONTHS AND TWENTY DAYS.

NIAGARA FALLS (English Side),
Sunday, *First May*, 1842. Mr. Henry Austin.

MY DEAR HENRY,

We have had a blessed interval of quiet in this beautiful place, of which, as you may suppose, we stood greatly in need, not only by reason of our hard travelling for a long time, but on account of the incessant persecutions of the people, by land and water, on stage-coach, railway car, and steamer, which exceeds anything you can picture to yourself by the utmost stretch of your imagination. So far we have had this hotel nearly to ourselves. It is a large square house, standing on a bold height, with overhanging eaves like a Swiss cottage, and a wide handsome gallery outside every story. These colonnades make it look so very light, that it has exactly the appearance of a house built with a pack of cards; and I live in bodily terror lest any man should venture to step out of a little observatory on the roof, and crush the whole structure with one stamp of his foot.

Our sitting-room (which is large and low like a nursery) is on the second floor, and is so close to the Falls that the windows are

always wet and dim with spray.   Two bedrooms open out of it—
one our own ; one Anne's.   The secretary slumbers near at hand,
but without these sacred precincts.   From the three chambers, or
any part of them, you can see the Falls rolling and tumbling, and
roaring and leaping, all day long, with bright rainbows making
fiery arches down a hundred feet below us.   When the sun is on
them, they shine and glow like molten gold.   When the day is
gloomy, the water falls like snow, or sometimes it seems to crumble
away like the face of a great chalk cliff, or sometimes again to roll
along the front of the rock like white smoke.   But it all seems gay
or gloomy, dark or light, by sun or moon.   From the bottom of
both Falls, there is always rising up a solemn ghostly cloud, which
hides the boiling cauldron from human sight, and makes it in its
mystery a hundred times more grand than if you could see all the
secrets that lie hidden in its tremendous depth.   One Fall is as
close to us as York Gate is to No. 1, Devonshire Terrace.   The
other (the great Horse-shoe Fall) may be, perhaps, about half as
far off as " Creedy's." *   One circumstance in connection with them
is, in all the accounts, greatly exaggerated—I mean the noise.
Last night was perfectly still.   Kate and I could just hear them,
at the quiet time of sunset, a mile off.   Whereas, believing the
statements I had heard I began putting my ear to the ground,
like a savage or a bandit in a ballet, thirty miles off, when we
were coming here from Buffalo.

I was delighted to receive your famous letter, and to read your
account of our darlings, whom we long to see with an intensity it
is impossible to shadow forth, ever so faintly.   I do believe, though
I say it as shouldn't, that they are good 'uns—both to look at and
to go.   I roared out this morning, as soon as I was awake, " Next
month," which we have been longing to be able to say ever since
we have been here.   I really do not know how we shall ever
knock at the door, when that slowest of all impossibly slow
hackney-coaches shall pull up—at home.

I am glad you exult in the fight I have had about the copyright.
If you knew how they tried to stop me, you would have a still
greater interest in it.   The greatest men in England have sent me
out, through Forster, a very manly, and becoming, and spirited
memorial and address, backing me in all I have done.   I have
despatched it to Boston for publication, and am coolly prepared
for the storm it will raise.   But my best rod is in pickle.

Is it not a horrible thing that scoundrel booksellers should
grow rich here from publishing books, the authors of which do
not reap one farthing from their issue by scores of thousands ; and

* Mr. Macready's—so pronounced by one of Charles Dickens' little children.

that every vile, blackguard, and detestable newspaper, so filthy and bestial that no honest man would admit one into his house for a scullery door-mat, should be able to publish those same writings side by side, cheek by jowl, with the coarsest and most obscene companions with which they must become connected, in course of time, in people's minds? Is it tolerable that, besides being robbed and rifled, an author should be forced to appear in any form, in any vulgar dress, in any atrocious company; that he should have no choice of his audience, no control over his own distorted text, and that he should be compelled to jostle out of the course the best men in this country, who only ask to live by writing? I vow before high heaven that my blood so boils at these enormities, that when I speak about them I seem to grow twenty feet high, and to swell out in proportion. "Robbers that ye are," I think to myself when I get upon my legs, "here goes!"

The places we have lodged in, the roads we have gone over, the company we have been among, the tobacco-spittle we have wallowed in, the strange customs we have complied with, the packing-cases in which we have travelled, the woods, swamps, prairies, lakes, and mountains we have crossed, are all subjects for legends and tales at home; quires, reams, wouldn't hold them. I don't think Anne has so much as seen an American tree. She never looks at a prospect by any chance, or displays the smallest emotion at any sight whatever. She objects to Niagara that "it's nothing but water," and considers that "there is too much of that."

I suppose you have heard that I am going to act at the Montreal theatre with the officers? Farce-books being scarce, and the choice consequently limited, I have selected Keeley's part in "Two o'Clock in the Morning." I wrote yesterday to Mitchell, the actor and manager at New York, to get and send me a comic wig, light flaxen, with a small whisker halfway down the cheek; over this I mean to wear two night-caps, one with a tassel and one of flannel; a flannel wrapper, drab tights and slippers, will complete the costume.

I am very sorry to hear that business is so flat, but the proverb says it never rains but it pours, and it may be remarked with equal truth upon the other side, that it never *don't* rain but it holds up very much indeed. You will be busy again long before I come home, I have no doubt.

We purpose leaving this on Wednesday morning. Give my love to Letitia and to mother, and always believe me, my dear Henry,

Affectionately yours.

Professor
Felton.

MONTREAL, *Saturday, Twenty-first May*, 1842.

MY DEAR FELTON,

I was delighted to receive your letter yesterday, and was well pleased with its contents. I anticipated objection to Carlyle's letter.* I called particular attention to it for three reasons. Firstly, because he boldly *said* what all the others *think*, and therefore deserved to be manfully supported. Secondly, because it is my deliberate opinion that I have been assailed on this subject in a manner which no man with any pretensions to public respect or with the remotest right to express an opinion on a subject of universal literary interest would be assailed in any other country. . . .

I really cannot sufficiently thank you, dear Felton, for your warm and hearty interest in these proceedings. But it would be idle to pursue that theme, so let it pass.

The wig and whiskers are in a state of the highest preservation. The play comes off next Wednesday night, the twenty-fifth. What would I give to see you in the front row of the centre box, your spectacles gleaming not unlike those of my dear friend Pickwick, your face radiant with as broad a grin as a staid professor may indulge in, and your very coat, waistcoat, and shoulders expressive of what we should take together when the performance was over ! I would give something (not so much, but still a good round sum) if you could only stumble into that very dark and dusty theatre in the daytime (at any minute between twelve and three), and see me with my coat off, the stage manager and universal director, urging impracticable ladies and impossible gentlemen on to the very confines of insanity, shouting and driving about, in my own person, to an extent which would justify any philanthropic stranger in clapping me into a strait-waistcoat without further inquiry, endeavouring to goad Putnam into some dim and faint understanding of a prompter's duties, and struggling in such a vortex of noise, dirt, bustle, confusion, and inextricable entanglement of speech and action as you would grow giddy in contemplating. We perform "A Roland for an Oliver," "A Good Night's Rest," and "Deaf as a Post." This kind of voluntary hard labour used to be my great delight. The *furor* has come strong upon me again, and I begin to be once more of opinion that nature intended me for the lessee of a national theatre, and that pen, ink, and paper have spoiled a manager.

Oh, how I look forward across that rolling water to home and its small tenantry ! How I busy myself in thinking how my books

* On the subject of International Copyright.

look, and where the tables are, and in what positions the chairs stand relatively to the other furniture; and whether we shall get there in the night, or in the morning, or in the afternoon; and whether we shall be able to surprise them, or whether they will be too sharply looking out for us; and what our pets will say; and how they'll look, and who will be the first to come and shake hands, and so forth! If I could but tell you how I have set my heart on rushing into Forster's study (he is my great friend, and writes at the bottom of all his letters: "My love to Felton"), and into Maclise's painting-room, and into Macready's managerial ditto, without a moment's warning, and how I picture every little trait and circumstance of our arrival to myself, down to the very colour of the bow on the cook's cap, you would almost think I had changed places with my eldest son, and was still in pantaloons of the thinnest texture. I left all these things—God only knows what a love I have for them—as coolly and calmly as any animated cucumber; but when I come upon them again I shall have lost all power of self-restraint, and shall as certainly make a fool of myself (in the popular meaning of that expression) as ever Grimaldi did in his way, or George the Third in his.

And not the less so, dear Felton, for having found some warm hearts, and left some instalments of earnest and sincere affection, behind me on this continent. And whenever I turn my mental telescope hitherward, trust me that one of the first figures it will descry will wear spectacles so like yours that the maker couldn't tell the difference, and shall address a Greek class in such an exact imitation of your voice, that the very students hearing it should cry, "That's he! Three cheers. Hoo-ray-ay-ay-ay-ay!"

About those joints of yours, I think you are mistaken. They *can't* be stiff. At the worst they merely want the air of New York, which, being impregnated with the flavour of last year's oysters, has a surprising effect in rendering the human frame supple and flexible in all cases of rust.

A terrible idea occurred to me as I wrote those words. The oyster-cellars—what do they do when oysters are not in season? Is pickled salmon vended there? Do they sell crabs, shrimps, winkles, herrings? The oyster-openers—what do *they* do? Do they commit suicide in despair, or wrench open tight drawers and cupboards and hermetically-sealed bottles for practice? Perhaps they are dentists out of the oyster season. Who knows?

Affectionately yours.

Mr. Thomas
Longman.

MY DEAR SIR,

If I could possibly have attended the meeting yesterday I would most gladly have done so. But I have been up the whole night, and was too much exhausted even to write and say so before the proceedings came on.

I have fought the fight across the Atlantic with the utmost energy I could command; have never been turned aside by any consideration for an instant; am fresher for the fray than ever; will battle it to the death, and die game to the last.

I am happy to say that my boy is quite well again. From being in perfect health he fell into alarming convulsions with the surprise and joy of our return.

I beg my regards to Mrs. Longman,

And am always,

Faithfully yours.

Mr. H. P.
Smith.

DEVONSHIRE TERRACE,
Thursday, Fourteenth July, 1842.

MY DEAR SMITH,

The cheque safely received. As you say, it would be cheap at any money. My devotion to the fine arts renders it impossible for me to cash it. I have therefore ordered it to be framed and glazed.

I am really grateful to you for the interest you take in my proceedings. Next time I come into the City I will show you my introductory chapter to the American book. It may seem to prepare the reader for a much greater amount of slaughter than he will meet with; but it is honest and true. Therefore my hand does not shake.

Always faithfully your Friend.

Miss Pardoe.

DEVONSHIRE TERRACE, YORK GATE,
REGENT'S PARK, *Nineteenth July,* 1842.

DEAR MADAM,

I beg to set you right on one point in reference to the American robbers, which perhaps you do not quite understand.

The existing law allows them to reprint any English book, without any communication whatever with the author or anybody else. My books have all been reprinted on these agreeable terms.

But sometimes, when expectation is awakened there about a book before its publication, one firm of pirates will pay a trifle to procure early proofs of it, and get so much the start of the rest as they can obtain by the time necessarily consumed in printing it.

Directly it is printed it is common property, and may be reprinted a thousand times. My circular only referred to such bargains as these.

I should add that I have no hope of the States doing justice in this dishonest respect, and therefore do not expect to overtake these fellows; but we may cry "Stop thief!" nevertheless, especially as they wince and smart under it.

Faithfully yours always.

1, DEVONSHIRE TERRACE, YORK GATE, REGENT'S PARK,   Professor
    LONDON, *Sunday, Thirty-first July*, 1842.   Felton.

MY DEAR FELTON,

Of all the monstrous and incalculable amount of occupation that ever beset one unfortunate man, mine has been the most stupendous since I came home. The dinners I have had to eat, the places I have had to go to, the letters I have had to answer, the sea of business and of pleasure in which I have been plunged, not even the genius of an —— or the pen of a —— could describe.

Wherefore I indite a monstrously short and wildly uninteresting epistle to the American Dando; but perhaps you don't know who Dando was. He was an oyster-eater, my dear Felton. He used to go into oyster-shops, without a farthing of money, and stand at the counter eating natives, until the man who opened them grew pale, cast down his knife, staggered backward, struck his white forehead with his open hand, and cried, "You are Dando!!!" He has been known to eat twenty dozen at one sitting, and would have eaten forty, if the truth had not flashed upon the shopkeeper. For these offences he was constantly committed to the House of Correction. During his last imprisonment he was taken ill, got worse and worse, and at last began knocking violent double knocks at Death's door. The doctor stood beside his bed, with his fingers on his pulse. "He is going," says the doctor. "I see it in his eye. There is only one thing that would keep life in him for another hour, and that is—oysters." They were immediately brought. Dando swallowed eight, and feebly took a ninth. He held it in his mouth and looked round the bed strangely. "Not a bad one, is it?" says the doctor. The patient shook his head, rubbed his trembling hand upon his stomach, bolted the oyster, and fell back —dead. They buried him in the prison-yard, and paved his grave with oyster-shells.

We are all well and hearty, and have already begun to wonder what time next year you and Mrs. Felton and Dr. Howe will come across the briny sea together. To-morrow we go to the seaside for two months. I am looking out for news of Longfellow, and shall be delighted when I know that he is on his way to London and this house.

I am bent upon striking at the piratical newspapers with the sharpest edge I can put upon my small axe, and hope in the next session of Parliament to stop their entrance into Canada. For the first time within the memory of man, the professors of English literature seem disposed to act together on this question. It is a good thing to aggravate a scoundrel, if one can do nothing else, and I think we *can* make them smart a little in this way. . . .

I wish you had been at Greenwich the other day, where a party of friends gave me a private dinner; public ones I have refused. C—— was perfectly wild at the reunion, and, after singing all manner of marine songs, wound up the entertainment by coming home (six miles) in a little open phaeton of mine, *on his head*, to the mingled delight and indignation of the metropolitan police. We were very jovial indeed; and I assure you that I drank your health with fearful vigour and energy.

On board that ship coming home I established a club, called the United Vagabonds, to the large amusement of the rest of the passengers. This holy brotherhood committed all kinds of absurdities, and dined always, with a variety of solemn forms, at one end of the table, below the mast, away from all the rest. The captain being ill when we were three or four days out, I produced my medicine-chest and recovered him. We had a few more sick men after that, and I went round "the wards" every day in great state, accompanied by two Vagabonds, habited as Ben Allen and Bob Sawyer, bearing enormous rolls of plaster and huge pairs of scissors. We were really very merry all the way, breakfasted in one party at Liverpool, shook hands, and parted most cordially. . . .

Affectionately your faithful Friend.

P.S.—I have looked over my journal, and have decided to produce my American trip in two volumes. I have written about half the first since I came home, and hope to be out in October. This is " exclusive news," to be communicated to any friends to whom you may like to intrust it, my dear F——.

Professor
Felton.

1, DEVONSHIRE TERRACE, YORK GATE, REGENT'S PARK,
LONDON, *First September*, 1842.

MY DEAR FELTON,

Of course that letter in the papers was as foul a forgery as ever felon swung for. . . . I have not contradicted it publicly, nor shall I. When I tilt at such wringings out of the dirtiest mortality, I shall be another man—indeed, almost the creature they would make me.

I gave your message to Forster, who sends a despatch-box full of kind remembrances in return. He is in a great state of delight with the first volume of my American book (which I have just finished), and swears loudly by it. It is *True* and Honourable I know, and I shall hope to send it you, complete, by the first steamer in November.

Your description of the porter and the carpet-bags prepares me for a first-rate facetious novel, brimful of the richest humour, on which I have no doubt you are engaged. What is it called? Sometimes I imagine the title-page thus:

OYSTERS

IN

EVERY STYLE

OR

OPENINGS

OF

LIFE

BY

YOUNG DANDO.

As to the man putting the luggage on his head, as a sort of sign, I adopt it from this hour.

I date this from London, where I have come, as a good profligate, graceless bachelor, for a day or two; leaving my wife and babbies at the seaside. . . . Heavens! if you were but here at this minute! A piece of salmon and a steak are cooking in the kitchen; it's a very wet day, and I have had a fire lighted; the wine sparkles on a side-table; the room looks the more snug from being the only *un*dismantled one in the house; plates are warming for Forster and Maclise, whose knock I am momentarily expecting; that groom I told you of, who never comes into the house, except when we are all out of town, is walking about in his shirt-sleeves without the smallest consciousness of impropriety; a great mound of proofs are waiting to be read aloud, after dinner. With what a shout I would clap you down into the easiest chair, my genial Felton, if you could but appear, and order you a pair of slippers instantly!

Since I have written this, the aforesaid groom—a very small man (as the fashion is), with fiery red hair (as the fashion is *not*)—has looked very hard at me and fluttered about me at the same time, like a giant butterfly. After a pause, he says in a Sam Wellerish kind of way: "I vent to the club this mornin', sir. There vorn't no letters, sir." "Very good, Topping." "How's missis, sir?" "Pretty well, Topping." "Glad to hear it, sir.

My missis ain't wery well, sir." "No?" "No, sir, she's a goin', sir, to have an hincrease wery soon, and it makes her rather nervous, sir; and ven a young voman gets at all down at sich a time, sir, she goes down wery deep, sir." To this sentiment I replied affirmatively, and then he adds, as he stirs the fire (as if he were thinking out loud): "Wot a mystery it is! Wot a go is natur'!" With which scrap of philosophy, he gradually gets nearer to the door, and so fades out of the room.

This same man asked me one day, soon after I came home, what Sir John Wilson was. This is a friend of mine, who took our house and servants, and everything as it stood, during our absence in America. I told him an officer. "A wot, sir?" "An officer." And then, for fear he should think I meant a police-officer, I added, "An officer in the army." "I beg your pardon, sir," he said, touching his hat, "but the club as I always drove him to wos the United Servants."

The real name of this club is the United Service, but I have no doubt he thought it was a high-life-below-stairs kind of resort, and that this gentleman was a retired butler or superannuated footman.

There's the knock, and the *Great Western* sails, or steams rather, to-morrow. Write soon again, dear Felton, and ever believe me. . . .

Your affectionate Friend.

P.S.—All good angels prosper Dr. Howe! He, at least, will not like me the less, I hope, for what I shall say of Laura.

Mr. Henry
Austin.

BROADSTAIRS, *Sunday, Twenty-fifth September*, 1842.

MY DEAR HENRY,

Pray tell Mr. Chadwick that I am greatly obliged to him for his remembrance of me, and I heartily concur with him in the great importance and interest of the subject, though I do differ from him, to the death, on his crack topic—the New Poor-Law.

I have been turning my thoughts to this very item in the condition of American towns, and had put their present aspects strongly before the American people; therefore I shall read his report with the greater interest and attention.

I need scarcely say that I shall joyfully talk with you about the Metropolitan Improvement Society, then or at any time; and with love to Letitia, in which Kate and the babies join, I am always, my dear Henry,

Affectionately yours.

P.S.—The children's present names are as follows :

Katey (from a lurking propensity to fieryness), Lucifer Box.
Mamey (as generally descriptive of her bearing), Mild Glo'ster.
Charley (as a corruption of Master Toby), Flaster Floby.
Walter (suggested by his high cheek-bones), Young Skull.

Each is pronounced with a peculiar howl, which I shall have great pleasure in illustrating.

DEVONSHIRE TERRACE,   Mr. W. C.
Saturday, Twelfth November, 1842.   Macready.

MY DEAR MACREADY,

You pass this house every day on your way to or from the theatre. I wish you would call once as you go by, and soon, that you may have plenty of time to deliberate on what I wish to suggest to you. The more I think of Marston's play, the more sure I feel that a prologue to the purpose would help it materially, and almost decide the fate of any ticklish point on the first night. Now I have an idea (not easily explainable in writing but told in five words), that would take the prologue out of the conventional dress of prologues, quite. Get the curtain up with a dash, and begin the play with a sledge-hammer blow. If on consideration, you should think with me, I will write the prologue, heartily.

Faithfully yours ever.

PROLOGUE

TO MR. MARSTON'S PLAY OF "THE PATRICIAN'S DAUGHTER."

No tale of streaming plumes and harness bright
Dwells on the poet's maiden harp to-night ;
No trumpet's clamour and no battle's fire
Breathes in the trembling accents of his lyre ;
Enough for him, if in his lowly strain
He wakes one household echo not in vain ;
Enough for him, if in his boldest word
The beating heart of MAN be dimly heard.

Its solemn music which, like strains that sigh
Through charmèd gardens, all who hearing die ;
Its solemn music he does not pursue
To distant ages out of human view ;
Nor listen to its wild and mournful chime
In the dead caverns on the shore of Time ;
But musing with a calm and steady gaze
Before the crackling flames of living days,
He hears it whisper through the busy roar
Of what shall be and what has been before.
Awake the Present ! shall no scene display
The tragic passion of the passing day !

Is it with Man, as with some meaner things,
That out of death his single purpose springs ?
Can his eventful life no moral teach
Until he be, for aye, beyond its reach ?
Obscurely shall he suffer, act, and fade,
Dubb'd noble only by the sexton's spade !
Awake the Present ! Though the steel-clad age
Find life alone within its storied page,
Iron is worn, at heart, by many still—
The tyrant Custom binds the serf-like will ;
If the sharp rack, and screw, and chain be gone,
These later days have tortures of their own ;
The guiltless writhe, while Guilt is stretched in sleep,
And Virtue lies, too often, dungeon deep.
Awake the Present ! what the Past has sown
Be in its harvest garner'd, reap'd, and grown !
How pride breeds pride, and wrong engenders wrong,
Read in the volume Truth has held so long,
Assured that where life's flowers freshest blow,
The sharpest thorns·and keenest briars grow,
How social usage has the pow'r to change
Good thoughts to evil ; in its highest range
To cramp the noble soul, and turn to ruth
The kindling impulse of our glorious youth,
Crushing the spirit in its house of clay,
Learn from the lessons of the present day.
Not light its import and not poor its mien ;
Yourselves the actors, and your homes the scene.

Mr. W. C.
Macready.   *Saturday Morning.*

MY DEAR MACREADY,

One suggestion, though it be a late one. Do have upon the table, in the opening scene of the second act, something in a velvet case, or frame, that may look like a large miniature of Mabel, such as one of Ross's, and eschew that picture. It haunts me with a sense of danger. Even a titter at that critical time, with the whole of that act before you, would be a fatal thing. The picture is bad in itself, bad in its effect upon the beautiful room, bad in all its associations with the house. In case of your having nothing at hand, I send you by bearer what would be a million times better. Always, my dear Macready,

Faithfully yours.

P.S.—I need not remind you how common it is to have such pictures in cases lying about elegant rooms.

1, DEVONSHIRE TERRACE, YORK GATE, REGENT'S PARK,
Fifteenth November, 1842.

MY DEAR SIR,

I shall be very glad if you will do me the favour to paint me two little companion pictures; one, a Dolly Varden (whom you have so exquisitely done already), the other, a Kate Nickleby.

Faithfully yours always.

P.S.—I take it for granted that the original picture of Dolly with the bracelet is sold?

DEVONSHIRE TERRACE, *Seventeenth November*, 1842.

MY DEAR SIR,

Pray consult your own convenience in the matter of my little commission; whatever suits your engagements and prospects will best suit me.

I saw an unfinished proof of Dolly at Mitchell's some two or three months ago; I thought it was proceeding excellently well then. It will give me great pleasure to see her when completed.

Faithfully yours.

DEVONSHIRE TERRACE, *Thirtieth November*, 1842.

MY DEAR HOOD,

In asking your and Mrs. Hood's leave to bring Mrs. D.'s sister (who stays with us) on Tuesday, let me add that I should very much like to bring at the same time a very unaffected and ardent admirer of your genius, who has no small portion of that commodity in his own right, and is a very dear friend of mine and a very famous fellow; to wit, Maclise, the painter, who would be glad (as he has often told me) to know you better, and would be much pleased, I know, if I could say to him, "Hood wants me to bring you."

I use so little ceremony with you, in the conviction that you will use as little with me, and say, "My dear D.—Convenient;" or, "My dear D.—Ill-convenient," (as the popular phrase is), just as the case may be. Of course, I have said nothing to him.

Always heartily yours,

BOZ.

1, DEVONSHIRE TERRACE, YORK GATE, REGENT'S PARK,
Sixteenth December, 1842.

MY DEAR MRS. TROLLOPE,

Let me thank you most cordially for your kind note, in reference to my Notes, which has given me true pleasure and gratification.

As I never scrupled to say in America, so I can have no delicacy in saying to you, that, allowing for the change you worked in many social features of American society, and for the time that has passed since you wrote of the country, I am convinced that there is no writer who has so well and accurately (I need not add so entertainingly) described it, in many of its aspects, as you have done; and this renders your praise the more valuable to me. I do not recollect ever to have heard or seen the charge of exaggeration made against a feeble performance, though, in its feebleness, it may have been most untrue. It seems to me essentially natural, and quite inevitable, that common observers should accuse an uncommon one of this fault, and I have no doubt that you were long ago of this opinion; very much to your own comfort.

Faithfully yours.

Mr George
Cattermole

DEVONSHIRE TERRACE, *Twentieth December*, 1842.

MY DEAR GEORGE,

It is impossible for me to tell you how greatly I am charmed with those beautiful pictures, in which the whole feeling, and thought, and expression of the little story is rendered to the gratification of my inmost heart; and on which you have lavished those amazing resources of yours with a power at which I fairly wondered when I sat down yesterday before them.

I took them to Mac, straightway, in a cab, and it would have done you good if you could have seen and heard him. You can't think how moved he was by the old man in the church, or how pleased I was to have chosen it before he saw the drawings.

You are such a queer fellow and hold yourself so much aloof, that I am afraid to say half I would say touching my grateful admiration; so you shall imagine the rest.

Always, my dear Cattermole,

Faithfully yours.

Professor
Felton.

1, DEVONSHIRE TERRACE, YORK GATE, REGENT'S PARK,
LONDON, *Thirty-first December*, 1842.

MY DEAR FELTON,

Many and many happy New Years to you and yours! As many happy children as may be quite convenient (no more!), and as many happy meetings between them and our children, and between you and us, as the kind fates in their utmost kindness shall favourably decree!

The American book (to begin with that) has been a most complete and thorough-going success. Four large editions have now been sold *and paid for*, and it has won golden opinions from all sorts of men, except our friend in F——, who is a miserable creature; a disappointed man in great poverty, to whom I have ever been most kind and considerate (I need scarcely say that); and another friend in B——, no less a person than an illustrious gentleman named ——, who wrote a story called ——. They have done no harm, and have fallen short of their mark, which, of course, was to annoy me. Now I am perfectly free from any diseased curiosity in such respects, and whenever I hear of a notice of this kind, I never read it; whereby I always conceive (don't you?) that I get the victory. With regard to your slave-owners, they may cry, till they are as black in the face as their own slaves, that Dickens lies. Dickens does not write for their satisfaction, and Dickens will not explain for their comfort. Dickens has the name and date of every newspaper in which every one of those advertisements appeared, as they know perfectly well; but Dickens does not choose to give them, and will not at any time between this and the day of judgment. . . .

I have been hard at work on my new book, of which the first number has just appeared. The Paul Joneses who pursue happiness and profit at other men's cost will no doubt enable you to read it, almost as soon as you receive this. I hope you will like it. And I particularly commend, my dear Felton, one Mr. Pecksniff and his daughters to your tender regards. I have a kind of liking for them myself.

Blessed star of morning, such a trip as we had into Cornwall, just after Longfellow went away! The "we" means Forster, Maclise, Stanfield (the renowned marine painter), and the Inimitable Boz. We went down into Devonshire by the railroad, and there we hired an open carriage from an innkeeper, patriotic in all Pickwick matters, and went on with post-horses. Sometimes we travelled all night, sometimes all day, sometimes both. I kept the joint-stock purse, ordered all the dinners, paid all the turnpikes, conducted facetious conversations with the post-boys, and regulated the pace at which we travelled. Stanfield (an old sailor) consulted an enormous map on all disputed points of wayfaring; and referred, moreover, to a pocket-compass and other scientific instruments. The luggage was in Forster's department; and Maclise, having nothing particular to do, sang songs. Heavens! If you could have seen the necks of bottles—distracting in their immense varieties of shape—peering out of the carriage pockets! If you could have witnessed the deep devotion of the post-boys, the wild attachment of the hostlers, the maniac glee of the waiters! If you could have followed us into the earthy old churches we visited, and into the strange caverns on the gloomy sea-shore, and down into the depths of mines, and up to the tops of giddy heights where the unspeakably green water was roaring, I don't know how many hundred feet below! If you could have seen but one gleam of the bright fires by which we sat in the big rooms of ancient inns at night, until long after the small hours had come and gone, or smelt but one steam of the hot punch (not white, dear Felton, like that amazing compound I sent you a taste of, but a rich, genial, glowing brown) which came in every evening in a huge broad china bowl! I never laughed in my life as I did on this journey. It would have done you good to hear me. I was choking and gasping and bursting the buckle off the back of my stock, all the way. And Stanfield (who is very much of your figure and temperament, but fifteen years older) got into such apoplectic entanglements that we were often obliged to beat him on the back with portmanteaus before we could recover him. Seriously, I do believe there never was such a trip. And they made such sketches, those two men, in the most romantic of our halting-places, that you would have sworn we had the Spirit of Beauty with us, as well as the Spirit of Fun. But stop till you come to England—I say no more.

The actuary of the National Debt couldn't calculate the number of children who are coming here on Twelfth Night, in honour of Charley's birthday, for which occasion I have provided a magic-lantern and divers other tremendous engines of that nature. But the best of it is that Forster and I have purchased between us the entire stock-in-trade of a conjurer, the practice and display whereof is intrusted to me. And O my dear eyes, Felton, if you could see me conjuring the company's watches into impossible tea-caddies, and causing pieces of money to fly, and burning pocket-hand-kerchiefs without hurting 'em, and practising in my own room, without anybody to admire, you would never forget it as long as you live. In those tricks which require a confederate, I am assisted (by reason of his imperturbable good humour) by Stanfield, who always does his part exactly the wrong way, to the unspeakable delight of all beholders. We come out on a small scale, to-night, at Forster's, where we see the old year out and the new one in. Particulars shall be forwarded in my next.

I have quite made up my mind that Forster really believes he *does* know you personally, and has all his life. He talks to me about you with such gravity that I am afraid to grin, and feel it necessary to look quite serious. Sometimes he *tells* me things about you, doesn't ask me, you know, so that I am occasionally perplexed beyond all telling, and begin to think it was he, and not I, who went to America. It's the queerest thing in the world.

The book I was to have given Longfellow for you is not worth sending by itself, being only a Barnaby. But I will look up some manuscript for you (I think I have that of the "American Notes" complete), and will try to make the parcel better worth its long conveyance. With regard to Maclise's pictures, you certainly are quite right in your impression of them; but he is "such a discursive devil" (as he says about himself), and flies off at such odd tangents, that I feel it difficult to convey to you any general notion of his purpose. I will try to do so when I write again. I want very much to know about ——— and that charming girl. . . . Give me full particulars. Will you remember me cordially to Sumner, and say I thank him for his welcome letter? The like to Hillard, with many regards to himself and his wife, with whom I had one night a little conversation which I shall not readily forget. The like to Washington Allston, and all friends who care for me and have outlived my book. . . . Always, my dear Felton,

With true regard and affection, yours.

My DEAR HOOD,

Mr. Tom Hood.

I can't state in figures (not very well remembering how to get beyond a million) the number of candidates for the Sanatorium matronship, but if you will ask your little boy to trace figures in the beds of your garden, beginning at the front wall, going down to the cricket-ground, coming back to the wall again, and "carrying over" to the next door, and will then set a skilful accountant to add up the whole, the product, as the Tutor's Assistants say, will give you the amount required. I have pledged myself (being assured of her capability) to support a near relation of Miss E———'s; otherwise, I need not say how glad I should have been to forward any wish of yours.

Very faithfully yours.

BOOK II.

1843 TO 1857.

1843.

In this year we give the commencement of Charles Dickens correspondence with his beloved friends, Mr. Douglas Jerrold and Mr. Clarkson Stanfield; with Lord Morpeth (afterwards Lord Carlisle), for whom he always entertained the highest regard; and with Mr. Charles Babbage.

He was at work upon "Martin Chuzzlewit" until the end of the year, when he also wrote and published the first of his Christmas stories—"The Christmas Carol."

He was much distressed by the sad fate of Mr. Elton (a respected actor), who was lost in the wreck of the *Pegasus*, and was very eager and earnest in his endeavours to raise a fund on behalf of Mr. Elton's children.

The "complaint" alluded to in the letter to Mr. Macvey Napier was, that the reviewer of the "American Notes," in the number of *The Edinburgh Review* for January, 1843, had represented him as having gone to America as a missionary in the cause of international copyright—an allegation which Charles Dickens repudiated, and which was rectified in the way he himself suggested.

The letter beginning, "Unhappy Man," was addressed to Mr. Macready, who was presented with a testimonial by his friends and fellow-actors on the occasion of his retirement from the management of Drury Lane Theatre.

We are sorry to be unable to give any explanation as to the nature of the Cockspur Street Society, mentioned in this first letter to Mr. Charles Babbage; but we publish it notwithstanding, considering it to be one of general interest.

The "Little History of England" was never finished—that is to say, the one alluded to in the letter to Mr. Jerrold.

Mr. David Dickson kindly furnishes us with an explanation of the letter dated Tenth May. "It was," he says, "in answer to a letter from me, pointing out that the 'Shepherd' in 'Pickwick' was apparently reflecting on the scriptural doctrine of the new birth."

The beginning of the letter to Mr. Jerrold (Fifteenth June) is, as will be readily understood, an imaginary cast of a purely

imaginary play. It originated in a proposal of Mr. Webster's—
the manager of the Haymarket Theatre—to give five hundred
pounds for a prize comedy by an English author. A portion of
this letter and of most of the letters addressed to Mr. Jerrold
have already been published in Mr. Blanchard Jerrold's life of his
father.

Mr. Macvey
Napier.

* DEVONSHIRE TERRACE, LONDON,
Twenty-first January, 1843.

My DEAR SIR,

Let me hasten to say, in the fullest and most explicit
manner, that you have acted a most honourable, open, fair, and
manly part in the matter of my complaint, for which I beg you to
accept my best thanks, and the assurance of my friendship and
regard. I would on no account publish the letter you have sent
me for that purpose, as I conceive that by doing so, I should not
reciprocate the spirit in which you have written to me privately.
But if you should, upon consideration, think it not inexpedient to
set the *Review* right in regard to this point of fact, by a note in
the next number, I should be glad to see it there.

In reference to the article itself, it did, by repeating this statement, hurt my feelings excessively; and is, in this respect, I still
conceive, most unworthy of its author. I am at a loss to divine
who its author is. I *know* he read in some cut-throat American
paper, this and other monstrous statements, which I could at any
time have converted into sickening praise by the payment of some
fifty dollars. I know that he is perfectly aware that his statement
in the *Review* in corroboration of these lies, would be disseminated
through the whole of the United States; and that my contradiction
will never be heard of. And though I care very little for the
opinion of any person who will set the statement of an American
editor (almost invariably an atrocious scoundrel) against my
character and conduct, such as they may be; still, my sense of
justice does revolt from this most cavalier and careless exhibition
of me to a whole people, as a traveller under false pretences, and
a disappointed intriguer. The better the acquaintance with
America, the more defenceless and more inexcusable such conduct
is. For, I solemnly declare (and appeal to any man but the
writer of this paper, who has travelled in that country, for confirmation of my statement) that the source from which he drew
the "information" so recklessly put forth again in England, is

* This, and all other Letters addressed to Mr. Macvey Napier, were
printed in "Selection from the Correspondence of the late Macvey Napier,
Esq.," editor of *The Edinburgh Review*, edited by his son, Mr. Macvey
Napier.

infinitely more obscene, disgusting, and brutal than the very worst Sunday newspaper that has ever been printed in Great Britain. Conceive *The Edinburgh Review* quoting *The Satirist*, or *The Man about Town*, as an authority against a man with one grain of honour, or feather-weight of reputation.

With regard to yourself, let me say again that I thank you with all sincerity and heartiness, and fully acquit you of anything but kind and generous intentions towards me. In proof of which, I do assure you that I am even more desirous than before to write for the *Review*, and to find some topic which would at once please me and you.

Always faithfully yours.

1, DEVONSHIRE TERRACE, YORK GATE,
REGENT'S PARK, LONDON, *Second March*, 1843.

Professor Felton.

MY DEAR FELTON,

I don't know where to begin, but plunge headlong with a terrible splash into this letter, on the chance of turning up somewhere.

Hurrah! Up like a cork again, with *The North American Review* in my hand. Like you, my dear ——, and I can say no more in praise of it, though I go on to the end of the sheet. You cannot think how much notice it has attracted here. Brougham called the other day, with the number (thinking I might not have seen it), and I being out at the time, he left a note, speaking of it, and of the writer, in terms that warmed my heart. Lord Ashburton (one of whose people wrote a notice in the *Edinburgh* which they have since publicly contradicted) also wrote to me about it in just the same strain. And many others have done the like.

I am in great health and spirits and powdering away at Chuzzlewit, with all manner of facetiousness rising up before me as I go on. As to news, I have really none, saving that Forster has been laid up with rheumatism for weeks past, but is now, I hope, getting better. My little captain, as I call him—he who took me out, I mean, and with whom I had that adventure of the cork soles—has been in London too, and seeing all the lions under my escort. Good heavens! I wish you could have seen certain other mahogany-faced men (also captains) who used to call here for him in the morning, and bear him off to docks and rivers and all sorts of queer places, whence he always returned late at night, with rum-and-water tear-drops in his eyes, and a complication of punchy smells in his mouth! He was better than a comedy to us, having marvellous ways of tying his pocket-handkerchief round his neck at dinner-time in a kind of jolly embarrassment, and then forgetting what he had done with it; also of singing songs to wrong tunes, and calling land objects by sea names, and never knowing what o'clock it was, but taking midnight for seven in the evening; with many other sailor oddities, all full of honesty, manliness, and good temper. We took him to Drury Lane Theatre to see "Much Ado about Nothing." But I never could find out what he meant by turning round, after he had watched the first two scenes with great attention, and inquiring "whether it was a Polish piece." . . .

On the fourth of April I am going to preside at a public dinner for the benefit of the printers; and if you were a guest at that table, wouldn't I smite you on the shoulder, harder than ever I rapped the well-beloved back of Washington Irving at the City Hotel in New York!

You were asking me—I love to say asking, as if we could talk together—about Maclise. He is such a discursive fellow, and so eccentric in his might, that on a mental review of his pictures I can hardly tell you of them as leading to any one strong purpose. But the annual Exhibition of the Royal Academy comes off in May, and then I will endeavour to give you some notion of him. He is a tremendous creature, and might do anything. But, like all tremendous creatures, takes his own way, and flies off at unexpected breaches in the conventional wall.

You know H——'s book, I daresay. Ah! I saw a scene of mingled comicality and seriousness at his funeral some weeks ago, which has choked me at dinner-time ever since. C—— and I went as mourners; and as he lived, poor fellow, five miles out of town, I drove C—— down. It was such a day as I hope, for the credit of nature, is seldom seen in any parts but these—muddy, foggy, wet, dark, cold, and unutterably wretched in every possible respect. Now, C—— has enormous whiskers, which straggle all down his throat in such weather, and stick out in front of him, like a partially unravelled bird's-nest; so that he looks queer enough at the best, but when he is very wet, and in a state between jollity (he is always very jolly with me) and the deepest gravity (going to a funeral, you know), it is utterly impossible to resist him; especially as he makes the strangest remarks the mind of man can conceive, without any intention of being funny, but rather meaning to be philosophical. I really cried with an irresistible sense of his comicality all the way; but when he was dressed out in a black cloak and a very long black hat-band by an undertaker (who, as he whispered me with tears in his eyes—for he had known H—— many years—was a "character, and he would like to sketch him"), I thought I should have been obliged to go away. However, we went into a little parlour where the funeral party was, and God knows it was miserable enough, for the widow and children were crying bitterly in one corner, and the other mourners—mere people of ceremony, who cared no more for the dead man than the hearse did—were talking quite coolly and carelessly together in another; and the contrast was as painful and distressing as anything I ever saw. There was an Independent clergyman present, with his bands on and a bible under his arm, who, as soon as we were seated, addressed C—— thus, in a loud emphatic voice: "Mr. C——, have you seen a paragraph respecting our departed friend, which has gone the round of the morning papers?" "Yes, sir," says C——, "I have," looking very hard at me the while, for he had told me with some pride coming down that it was his composition. "Oh!" said the clergyman. "Then you will agree with me, Mr. C——, that it is not only an insult to me, who am the servant of the Almighty, but an insult to the Almighty, whose servant I am." "How is that, sir?" said C——. "It is stated, Mr. C——, in that paragraph," says the minister, "that when Mr. H—— failed in business as a bookseller, he was persuaded by *me* to try the pulpit; which is false, incorrect, unchristian, in a manner blasphemous, and in all respects contemptible. Let us pray." With which, my dear Felton, and in the same breath, I give you my word, he knelt down, as we all did, and began a very miserable jumble of an extemporary prayer. I was really penetrated with sorrow for the family, but when C—— (upon his knees, and sobbing for the loss of an old friend) whispered me, "that if that wasn't a clergyman, and it wasn't a funeral, he'd have punched his head," I felt as if nothing but convulsions could possibly relieve me. . . .

Faithfully always, my dear Felton.

DEVONSHIRE TERRACE, *Twenty-seventh April*, 1848.   Mr. Charles
                                                     Babbage.
MY DEAR SIR,

I write to you, *confidentially*, in answer to your note of last night, and the tenor of mine will tell you why.

You may suppose, from seeing my name in the printed letter you have received, that I am favourable to the proposed society. I am decidedly opposed to it. I went there on the day I was in the chair, after much solicitation; and being put into it, opened the proceedings by telling the meeting that I approved of the design in theory, but in practice considered it hopeless. I may tell you—I did not tell them—that the nature of the meeting, and the character and position of many of the men attending it, cried "Failure" trumpet-tongued in my ears. To quote an expression from Tennyson, I may say that if it were the best society in the world, the grossness of some natures in it would have weight to drag it down.

In the wisdom of all you urge in the notes you have sent me, taking them as statements of theory, I entirely concur. But in practice, I feel sure that the present publishing system cannot be overset until authors are different men. The first step to be taken is to move as a body in the question of copyright, enforce the existing laws, and try to obtain better. For that purpose I hold that the authors and publishers must unite, as the wealth, business, habits, and interests of that latter class are of great importance to such an end. The Longmans and Murray have been with me proposing such an association. That I shall support. But having seen the Cockspur Street Society, I am as well convinced of its invincible hopelessness as if I saw it written by a celestial penman in the Book of Fate.

My dear Sir,
Always faithfully yours.

Mr. Douglas
Jerrold.

DEVONSHIRE TERRACE, *Third May,* 1843.

MY DEAR JERROLD,

Let me thank you most cordially for your books, not only for their own sakes (and I have read them with perfect delight), but also for this hearty and most welcome mark of your recollection of the friendship we have established; in which light I know I may regard and prize them.

I am greatly pleased with your opening paper in the Illuminated. It is very wise, and capital; written with the finest end of that iron pen of yours; witty, much needed, and full of truth. I vow to God that I think the parrots of society are more intolerable and mischievous than its birds of prey. If ever I destroy myself, it will be in the bitterness of hearing those infernal and damnably good old times extolled. Once, in a fit of madness, after having been to a public dinner which took place just as this Ministry came in, I wrote the parody I send you enclosed, for Fonblanque. There is nothing in it but wrath; but that's wholesome, so I send it you.

I am writing a little history of England for my boy, which I will send you when it is printed for him, though your boys are too old to profit by it. It is curious that I have tried to impress upon him (writing, I daresay, at the same moment with you) the exact spirit of your paper, for I don't know what I should do if he were to get hold of any Conservative or High Church notions; and the best way of guarding against any such horrible result, is, I take it, to wring the parrots' necks in his very cradle.

Oh Heaven, if you could have been with me at a hospital dinner last Monday! There were men there who made such speeches and expressed such sentiments as any moderately intelligent dustman would have blushed through his cindery bloom to have thought of. Sleek, slobbering, bow-paunched, over-fed, apoplectic, snorting cattle, and the auditory leaping up in their delight! I never saw such an illustration of the power of purse, or felt so degraded and debased by its contemplation, since I have had eyes and ears. The absurdity of the thing was too horrible to laugh at. It was perfectly overwhelming. But if I could have partaken it with anybody who would have felt it as you would have done, it would have had quite another aspect; or would at least, like a "classic mask" (oh d—— that word!) have had one funny side to relieve its dismal features.

Supposing fifty families were to emigrate into the wilds of North America—yours, mine, and forty-eight others—picked for their concurrence of opinion on all important subjects and for their resolution to found a colony of common-sense, how soon would that devil, Cant, present itself among them in one shape or other? The day they landed do you say, or the day after?

That is a great mistake (almost the only one I know) in the "Arabian Nights," when the Princess restores people to their original beauty by sprinkling them with the golden water. It is quite clear that she must have made monsters of them by such a christening as that.

My dear Jerrold,
Faithfully your Friend.

DEVONSHIRE TERRACE, *Eighth May*, 1843.

Mrs. Hogarth.

MY DEAR MRS. HOGARTH,

I was dressing to go to church yesterday morning—thinking, very sadly, of that time six years—when your kind note and its accompanying packet were brought to me. The best portrait that was ever painted would be of little value to you and me, in comparison with that unfading picture we have within us; and of the worst (which ——'s really is) I can only say, that it has no interest in my eyes, beyond being something which she sat near in its progress, full of life and beauty. In that light, I set some store by the copy you have sent me; and as a mark of your affection, I need not say I value it very much. As any record of that dear face it is utterly worthless.

I trace in many respects a strong resemblance between her

mental features and Georgina's—so strange a one, at times, that when she and Kate and I are sitting together, I seem to think that what has happened is a melancholy dream from which I am just awakening. The perfect like of what she was, will never be again, but so much of her spirit shines out in this sister, that the old time comes back again at some seasons, and I can hardly separate it from the present.

After she died, I dreamed of her every night for many months —I think for the better part of a year—sometimes as a spirit, sometimes as a living creature, never with any of the bitterness of my real sorrow, but always with a kind of quiet happiness, which became so pleasant to me that I never lay down at night without a hope of the vision coming back in one shape or other. And so it did. I went down into Yorkshire, and finding it still present to me, in a strange scene and a strange bed, I could not help mentioning the circumstance in a note I wrote home to Kate. From that moment I have never dreamed of her once, though she is so much in my thoughts at all times (especially when I am successful, and have prospered in anything) that the recollection of her is an essential part of my being, and is as inseparable from my existence as the beating of my heart is.

Always affectionately.

Mr. David
Dickson.

1, DEVONSHIRE TERRACE, YORK GATE,
REGENT'S PARK, Tenth May, 1843.

SIR,

Permit me to say, in reply to your letter, that you do not understand the intention (I daresay the fault is mine) of that passage in the "Pickwick Papers" which has given you offence. The design of "the Shepherd" and of this and every other allusion to him is, to show how sacred things are degraded, vulgarised, and rendered absurd when persons who are utterly incompetent to teach the commonest things take upon themselves to expound such mysteries, and how, in making mere cant phrases of divine words, these persons miss the spirit in which they had their origin. I have seen a great deal of this sort of thing in many parts of England, and I never knew it lead to charity or good deeds.

Whether the great Creator of the world and the creature of his hands, moulded in his own image, be quite so opposite in character as you believe, is a question which it would profit us little to discuss. I like the frankness and candour of your letter, and thank you for it. That every man who seeks heaven must be born again, in good thoughts of his Maker, I sincerely believe. That it is expedient for every hound to say so in a snuffling form of words, to which he attaches no good meaning, I do not believe. I take it there is no difference between us.

Faithfully yours.

DEVONSHIRE TERRACE, *Thirteenth June*, 1843.   Mr. Douglas Jerrold.

MY DEAR JERROLD,

Yes, you have anticipated my occupation. Chuzzlewit be d—d. High comedy and five hundred pounds are the only matters I can think of. I call it "The One Thing Needful; or, A Part is Better than the Whole." Here are the characters:

Old Febrile	Mr. FARREN.
Young Febrile (his Son)	Mr. HOWE.
Jack Hessians (his Friend)	Mr. W. LACY.
Chalks (a Landlord)	Mr. GOUGH.
Hon. Harry Staggers	Mr. MELLON.
Sir Thomas Tip	Mr. BUCKSTONE.
Swig	Mr. WEBSTER.
The Duke of Leeds	Mr. COUTTS.
Sir Smivin Growler	Mr. MACREADY.
Servants, Gamblers, Visitors, etc.	
Mrs. Febrile	Mrs. GALLOT.
Lady Tip	Mrs. HUMBY.
Mrs. Sour	Mrs. W. CLIFFORD.
Fanny	Miss A. SMITH.

One scene, where Old Febrile tickles Lady Tip in the ribs, and afterwards dances out with his hat behind him, his stick before, and his eye on the pit, I expect will bring the house down. There is also another point, where Old Febrile, at the conclusion of his disclosure to Swig, rises and says: "And now, Swig, tell me, have I acted well?" And Swig says: "Well, Mr. Febrile, have you ever acted ill?" which will carry off the piece.

Herne Bay. Hum. I suppose it's no worse than any other place in this weather, but it is watery rather—isn't it? In my mind's eye, I have the sea in a perpetual state of smallpox; and the chalk running downhill like town milk. But I know the comfort of getting to work in a fresh place, and proposing pious projects to one's self, and having the more substantial advantage of going to bed early and getting up ditto, and walking about alone. I should like to deprive you of the last-named happiness, and to take a good long stroll, terminating in a public-house, and whatever they chanced to have in it. But fine days are over, I think. The horrible misery of London in this weather, with not even a fire to make it cheerful, is hideous.

But I have my comedy to fly to. My only comfort! I walk up and down the street at the back of the theatre every night, and peep in at the green-room window, thinking of the time when

"Dick—ins" will be called for by excited hundreds, and won't come till Mr. Webster (half Swig and half himself) shall enter from his dressing-room, and quelling the tempest with a smile, beseech that wizard, if he be in the house (here he looks up at my box), to accept the congratulations of the audience, and indulge them with a sight of the man who has got five hundred pounds in money, and it's impossible to say how much in laurel. Then I shall come forward, and bow once—twice—thrice—roars of approbation—Brayvo—brarvo—hooray—hoorar—hooroar—one cheer more ; and asking Webster home to supper, shall declare eternal friendship for that public-spirited individual.

I am always, my dear Jerrold,

Faithfully your Friend,

THE CONGREVE OF THE NINETEENTH CENTURY

(which I mean to be called in the Sunday papers).

P.S.—I shall dedicate it to Webster, beginning: "My dear Sir, —When you first proposed to stimulate the slumbering dramatic talent of England, I assure you I had not the least idea "—etc. etc. etc.

Mr. W. C. Macready.

Eighteenth June, 1843.

UNHAPPY MAN,

Yes. I am of opinion that in your miserable condition you might extend your remarks, so far, for instance, as to say what you had done in the theatre and tried to do. But whatever is easiest and most comfortable to yourself, will be the best course to take.

You will be expected on the scaffold at half-past twelve. Enquire for the Committee-room, or the Sheriff.

If you have anything on your mind, yet unrevealed, now is the time to throw the weight off your conscience, and make a clean breast.

Sympathetically yours,

THE ORDINARY.

From the Chapel of the Jail, Monday Morning.

Mr. Clarkson Stanfield, R.A.

1, DEVONSHIRE TERRACE, *Twenty-sixth July,* 1843.

My DEAR STANFIELD,

I am chairman of a committee, whose object is to open a subscription, and arrange a benefit for the relief of the seven destitute children of poor Elton the actor, who was drowned in the *Pegasus.* They are exceedingly anxious to have the great assistance of your name; and if you will allow yourself to be announced as one of the body, I do assure you you will help a very melancholy and distressful cause.

Faithfully always.

1, DEVONSHIRE TERRACE, YORK GATE,
REGENT'S PARK, *Third August*, 1843.

DEAR LORD MORPETH,

In acknowledging the safe receipt of your kind donation in behalf of poor Mr. Elton's orphan children, I hope you will suffer me to address you with little ceremony, as the best proof I can give you of my cordial reciprocation of all you say in your most welcome note. I have long esteemed you and been your distant but very truthful admirer; and trust me that it is a real pleasure and happiness to me to anticipate the time when we shall have a nearer intercourse.

Believe me, with sincere regard,
Faithfully your Servant.

BROADSTAIRS, KENT, *First September*, 1843.

MY DEAR FELTON,

If I thought it in the nature of things that you and I could ever agree on paper, touching a certain Chuzzlewitian question whereupon Forster tells me you have remarks to make, I should immediately walk into the same, tooth and nail. But as I don't, I won't. Contenting myself with this prediction, that one of these years and days, you will write or say to me: "My dear Dickens, you were right, though rough, and did a world of good, though you got most thoroughly hated for it." To which I shall reply: "My dear Felton, I looked a long way off and not immediately under my nose." . . . At which sentiment you will laugh, and I shall laugh; and then (for I foresee this will all happen in my land) we shall call for another pot of porter and two or three dozen of oysters.

Now, don't you in your own heart and soul quarrel with me for this long silence? Not half so much as I quarrel with myself, I know; but if you could read half the letters I write to you in imagination, you would swear by me for the best of correspondents. The truth is, that when I have done my morning's work, down goes my pen, and from that minute I feel it a positive impossibility to take it up again, until imaginary butchers and bakers wave me to my desk. I walk about brimful of letters, facetious descriptions, touching morsels, and pathetic friendships, but can't for the soul of me uncork myself. The post-office is my rock ahead. My average number of letters that *must* be written every day is, at the least, a dozen. And you could no more know what I was writing to you spiritually, from the perusal of the bodily thirteenth, than you could tell from my hat what was going on in my head, or could read my heart on the surface of my flannel waistcoat.

This is a little fishing-place; intensely quiet; built on a cliff, whereon—in the centre of a tiny semicircular bay—our house stands; the sea rolling and dashing under the windows. Seven miles out are the Goodwin Sands (you've heard of the Goodwin Sands?) whence floating lights perpetually wink after dark, as if they were carrying on intrigues with the servants. Also there is a big lighthouse called the North Foreland on a hill behind the village, a severe parsonic light, which reproves the young and giddy floaters, and stares grimly out upon the sea. Under the cliff are rare good sands, where all the children assemble every morning and throw up impossible fortifications, which the sea throws down again at high water. Old gentlemen and ancient ladies flirt after their own manner in two reading-rooms and on a great many scattered seats in the open air. Other old gentlemen look all day through telescopes and never see anything. In a bay-window in a one-pair sits, from nine o'clock to one, a gentleman with rather long hair and no neckcloth, who writes and grins as if he thought he were very funny indeed. His name is Boz. At one he disappears, and presently emerges from a bathing-machine, and may be seen—a kind of salmon-coloured porpoise—splashing about in the ocean. After that he may be seen in another bay-window on the ground-floor, eating a strong lunch; after that, walking a dozen miles or so, or lying on his back in the sand reading a book. Nobody bothers him unless they know he is disposed to be talked to; and I am told he is very comfortable indeed. He's as brown as a berry, and they *do* say is a small fortune to the innkeeper who sells beer and cold punch. But this is mere rumour. Sometimes he goes up to London (eighty miles, or so, away), and then I'm told there is a sound in Lincoln's Inn Fields at night, as of men laughing, together with a clinking of knives and forks and wine-glasses.

I never shall have been so near you since we parted aboard the *George Washington* as next Tuesday. Forster, Maclise, and I, and perhaps Stanfield, are then going aboard the Cunard steamer at Liverpool, to bid Macready good-bye, and bring his wife away. It will be a very hard parting. You will see and know him of course. We gave him a splendid dinner last Saturday at Richmond, whereat I presided with my accustomed grace. He is one of the noblest fellows in the world, and I would give a great deal that you and I should sit beside each other to see him play Virginius, Lear, or Werner, which I take to be, every way, the greatest piece of exquisite perfection that his lofty art is capable of attaining. His Macbeth, especially the last act, is a tremendous reality; but so indeed is almost everything he does. You recollect, perhaps, that he was the guardian of our children while we were away. I love him dearly. . . .

You asked me, long ago, about Maclise. He is such a wayward fellow in his subjects, that it would be next to impossible to write such an article as you were thinking of about him. I wish you could form an idea of his genius. One of these days a book will come out, "Moore's Irish Melodies," entirely illustrated by him, on every page. *When* it comes, I'll send it to you. You will have some notion of him then. He is in great favour with the Queen, and paints secret pictures for her to put upon her husband's table on the morning of his birthday, and the like. But if he has a care, he will leave his mark on more enduring things than palace walls.

And so Longfellow is married. I remember *her* well, and could draw her portrait, in words, to the life. A very beautiful and gentle creature, and a proper love for a poet. My cordial remembrances, and congratulations. Do they live in the house where we breakfasted? . . .

I very often dream I am in America again; but, strange to say, I never dream of you. I am always endeavouring to get home in disguise, and have a dreary sense of the distance. *A propos* of dreams, is it not a strange thing if writers of fiction never dream of their own creations; recollecting, I suppose, even in their dreams, that they have no real existence? *I* never dream of any of my own characters, and I feel it so impossible that I would wager Scott never did of his, real as they are. I had a good piece of absurdity in my head a night or two ago. I dreamed that somebody was dead. I don't know who, but it's not to the purpose. It was a private gentleman, and a particular friend; and I was greatly overcome when the news was broken to me (very delicately) by a gentleman in a cocked hat, top boots, and a sheet. Nothing else. "Good God!" I said, "is he dead?" "He is as dead, sir," rejoined the gentleman, "as a door-nail. But we must all die, Mr. Dickens, sooner or later, my dear sir." "Ah!" I said. "Yes, to be sure. Very true. But what did he die of?" The gentleman burst into a flood of tears, and said, in a voice broken by emotion: "He christened his youngest child, sir, with a toasting-fork." I never in my life was so affected as at his having fallen a victim to this complaint. It carried a conviction to my mind that he never could have recovered. I knew that it was the most interesting and fatal malady in the world; and I wrung the gentleman's hand in a convulsion of respectful admiration, for I felt that this explanation did equal honour to his head and heart.

H

What do you think of Mrs. Gamp? And how do you like the undertaker? I have a fancy that they are in your way. Oh heaven! such green woods as I was rambling among, down in Yorkshire, when I was getting that done last July! For days and weeks we never saw the sky but through green boughs; and all day long I cantered over such soft moss and turf, that the horse's feet scarcely made a sound upon it. We have some friends in that part of the country (close to Castle Howard, where Lord Morpeth's father dwells in state, *in* his park indeed), who are the jolliest of the jolly, keeping a big old country house, with an ale cellar something larger than a reasonable church, and everything, like Goldsmith's bear dances, "in a concatenation accordingly." Just the place for you, Felton! We performed some madnesses there in the way of forfeits, picnics, rustic games, inspections of ancient monasteries at midnight, when the moon was shining, that would have gone to your heart, and, as Mr. Weller says, "come out on the other side." . . .

Write soon, my dear Felton; and if I write to you less often than I would, believe that my affectionate heart is with you always. Loves and regards to all friends, from yours ever and ever.

Very faithfully yours.

Mr. Macvey
Napier. ·

BROADSTAIRS, *Sixteenth September*, 1843.

MY DEAR SIR,

I hinted, in a letter of introduction I gave Mr. Hood to you, that I had been thinking of a subject for the *Edinburgh*. Would it meet the purposes of the *Review* to come out strongly against any system of education based exclusively on the principles of the Established Church? If it would, I should like to show why such a thing as the Church Catechism is wholly inapplicable to the state of ignorance that now prevails; and why no system but one, so general in great religious principles as to include all creeds, can meet the wants and understandings of the dangerous classes of society. This is the only broad ground I could hold, consistently with what I feel and think on such a subject. But I could give, in taking it, a description of certain voluntary places of instruction, called "the ragged schools," now existing in London, and of the schools in jails, and of the ignorance presented in such places, which would make a very striking paper, especially if they were put in strong comparison with the effort making, by subscription, to maintain exclusive Church instruction. I could show these people in a state so miserable and so neglected, that their very nature rebels against the simplest religion, and that to convey to them. the faintest outlines of any system of distinction between right and wrong is in itself a giant's task, before which mysteries and squabbles for forms *must* give way. Would this be too much for the *Review?*

Faithfully yours.

DEVONSHIRE TERRACE, *Thirteenth October*, 1843.

Mr. William Harrison Ainsworth.

MY DEAR AINSWORTH,

I want very much to see you, not having had that old pleasure for a long time. I am at this moment deaf in the ears, hoarse in the throat, red in the nose, green in the gills, damp in the eyes, twitchy in the joints, and fractious in the temper from a most intolerable and oppressive cold, caught the other day, I suspect, at Liverpool, where I got exceedingly wet; but I will make prodigious efforts to get the better of it to-night by resorting to all conceivable remedies, and if I succeed so as to be only negatively disgusting to-morrow, I will joyfully present myself at six, and bring my womankind along with me.

Cordially yours.

DEVONSHIRE TERRACE, *November 13th*, 1843.

Mr. R. H. Horne.

*   *   *   *   *

Pray tell that besotted —— to let the opera sink into its native obscurity. I did it in a fit of d——ble good nature long ago, for Hullah, who wrote some very pretty music to it. I just put down for everybody what everybody at the St. James's Theatre wanted to say and do, and that they could say and do best, and I have been most sincerely repentant ever since. The farce I also did as a sort of practical joke, for Harley, whom I have known a long time. It was funny—adapted from one of the published sketches called "The Great Winglebury Duel," and was published by Chapman and Hall. But I have no copy of it now, nor should I think they have. But both these things were done without the least consideration or regard to reputation.

I wouldn't repeat them for a thousand pounds apiece, and devoutly wish them to be forgotten. If you will impress this on the waxy mind of —— I shall be truly and unaffectedly obliged to you.

Always faithfully yours.

1844.

NARRATIVE.

IN the summer of this year the house in Devonshire Terrace was let, and Charles Dickens started with his family for Italy, going first to a villa at Albaro, near Genoa, for a few months, and afterwards to the Palazzo Pescheire, Genoa. Towards the end of this year he made excursions to the many places of interest in this country, and was joined at Milan by his wife and sister-in-law, previous to his own departure alone on a business visit to England. He had written his Christmas story, "The Chimes," and was anxious to take it himself to England, and to read it to some of his most intimate friends there.

Mr. Macready went to America and returned in the autumn, and towards the end of the year he paid a professional visit to Paris.

Charles Dickens' letter to his wife (26th February) treats of a visit to Liverpool, where he went to take the chair on the opening of the Mechanics' Institution and to make a speech on education; he had also presided two evenings previously at a meeting of the Polytechnic Institution at Birmingham. The "Fanny" alluded to was his sister, Mrs. Burnett; the *Britannia*, the ship in which he and Mrs. Dickens made their outward trip to America; the "Mrs. Bean," the stewardess, and "Hewett," the captain of that same vessel.

The letter to Mr. Charles Knight was in acknowledgment of the receipt of a prospectus entitled "Book Clubs for all Readers." The attempt, which fortunately proved completely successful, was to establish a cheap book club. The scheme was, that a number of families should combine together, each contributing about three halfpennies a week; which contribution would enable them, by exchanging the volumes among them, to have sufficient reading to last the year. The publications, which were to be made as cheap as possible, could be purchased by families at the end of the year, on consideration of their putting by an extra penny a week for that purpose. Charles Dickens, who always had the comfort and happiness of the working-classes greatly at heart, was much interested in this scheme of Mr. Charles Knight's, and highly approved of it. Charles Dickens and this new correspondent became subsequently true and fast friends.

"Martin Chuzzlewit" was dramatised in the early autumn of this year, at the Lyceum Theatre, which was then under the management of Mr. and Mrs. Robert Keeley. Charles Dickens superintended some rehearsals, but had left England before the play was acted in public.

The man "Roche," alluded to in his letter to Mr. Maclise, was the French courier engaged to go with the family to Italy. He remained as servant there, and was with Charles Dickens through all his foreign travels. His many excellent qualities endeared him to the whole family, and his master never lost sight of this faithful servant until poor Roche's untimely death in 1849.

The Rev. Edward Tagart was a celebrated Unitarian·minister, and a very highly esteemed and valued friend.

The "Chickenstalker" (letter to Mrs. Dickens, November 8th) is an instance of the eccentric names Charles Dickens was constantly giving to his children, and these names he frequently made use of in his books.

In this year we have the first letter to Sir Edward Lytton Bulwer (afterwards Lord Lytton), and the first letter to Mr. (afterwards Sir Edwin) Landseer, for both of whom Charles Dickens had the highest admiration and personal regard.

DEVONSHIRE TERRACE, LONDON,   Professor
        Second January, 1844.   Felton.

MY VERY DEAR FELTON,

You are a prophet, and had best retire from business straightway. Yesterday morning, New Year's Day, when I walked into my little workroom after breakfast, and was looking out of window at the snow in the garden—not seeing it particularly well in consequence of some staggering suggestions of last night, whereby I was beset—the postman came to the door with a knock, for which I denounced him from my heart. Seeing your hand upon the cover of a letter which he brought, I immediately blessed him, presented him with a glass of whisky, inquired after his family (they are all well), and opened the dispatch with a moist and oystery twinkle in my eye. And on the very day from which the new year dates, I read your New Year congratulations as punctually as if you lived in the next house! Why don't you? .

Now, if instantly on the receipt of this you will send a free and independent citizen down to the Cunard wharf at Boston, you will find that Captain Hewett, of the *Britannia* steamship (my ship), has a small parcel for Professor Felton of Cambridge: and in that parcel you will find a Christmas Carol in prose; being a short story of Christmas by Charles Dickens. Over which Christmas Carol Charles Dickens wept and laughed and wept again, and excited himself in a most extraordinary manner in the composition;

and thinking whereof he walked about the black streets of London, fifteen and twenty miles many a night when all the sober folks had gone to bed. . . . Its success is most prodigious. And by every post all manner of strangers write all manner of letters to him about their homes and hearths, and how this same Carol is read aloud there, and kept on a little shelf by itself. Indeed, it is the greatest success, as I am told, that this ruffian and rascal has ever achieved.

Forster is out again; and if he don't go in again, after the manner in which we have been keeping Christmas, he must be very strong indeed. Such dinings, such dancings, such conjurings, such blindman's-buffings, such theatre-goings, such kissings-out of old years and kissings-in of new ones, never took place in these parts before. To keep the Chuzzlewit going, and do this little book, the Carol, in the odd times between two parts of it, was, as you may suppose, pretty tight work. But when it was done I broke out like a madman. And if you could have seen me at a children's party at Macready's the other night, going down a country dance with Mrs. M., you would have thought I was a country gentleman of independent property, residing on a tiptop farm, with the wind blowing straight in my face every day. . . .

Your friend, Mr. P——, dined with us one day (I don't know whether I told you this before), and pleased us very much. Mr. C—— has dined here once, and spent an evening here. I have not seen him lately, though he has called twice or thrice; for Kate being unwell and I busy, we have not been visible at our accustomed seasons. I wonder whether Putnam has fallen in your way. Poor Putnam! He was a good fellow, and has the most grateful heart I ever met with. Our journeyings seem to be a dream now. Talking of dreams, strange thoughts of Italy and France, and maybe Germany, are springing up within me as the Chuzzlewit clears off. It's a secret I have hardly breathed to anyone, but I "think" of leaving England for a year, next midsummer, bag and baggage, little ones and all——then coming out with *such* a story, Felton, all at once, no parts, sledge-hammer blow.

. I send you a Manchester paper, as you desire. The report is not exactly done, but very well done, notwithstanding. It was a very splendid sight, I assure you, and an awful-looking audience. I am going to preside at a similar meeting at Liverpool on the twenty-sixth of next month, and on my way home I may be obliged to preside at another at Birmingham. I will send you papers, if the reports be at all like the real thing.

I wrote to Prescott about his book, with which I was perfectly charmed. I think his descriptions masterly, his style brilliant, his purpose manly and gallant always. The introductory account of Aztec civilisation impressed me exactly as it impressed you. From beginning to end the whole history is enchanting and full of genius. I only wonder that, having such an opportunity of illustrating the doctrine of visible judgments, he never remarks, when Cortes and his men tumble the idols down the temple steps and call upon the people below to take notice that their gods are powerless to help themselves, that possibly, if some intelligent native had tumbled down the image of the Virgin or patron saint after them, nothing very remarkable might have ensued in consequence.

Of course you like Macready. Your name's Felton. I wish you could see him play Lear. It is stupendously terrible. But I suppose he would be slow to act it with the Boston company.

Hearty remembrances to Sumner, Longfellow, Prescott, and all whom you know I love to remember. Countless happy years to you and yours, my dear Felton, and some instalment of them, however slight, in England, in the loving company of

THE PROSCRIBED ONE.
Oh, breathe not his name!

DEVONSHIRE TERRACE, *Third January*, 1844.   Mr. W. C. Macready.

MY VERY DEAR MACREADY,

You know all the news, and you know I love you; so I no more know why I write than I do why I "come round" after the play to shake hands with you in your dressing-room. I say come, as if you were at this present moment the lessee of Drury Lane, and had —— with a long face on one hand, —— elaborately explaining that everything in creation is a joint-stock company on the other, the inimitable B. by the fire, in conversation with ——. Well-a-day! I see it all, and smell that extraordinary compound of odd scents peculiar to a theatre, which bursts upon me when I swing open the little door in the hall, accompanies me as I meet perspiring supers in the narrow passage, goes with me up the two steps, crosses the stage, winds round the third entrance P.S. as I wind, and escorts me safely into your presence, where I find you unwinding something slowly round and round your chest, which is so long that no man can see the end of it.

Oh that you had been at Clarence Terrace on Nina's birthday! Good God, how we missed you, talked of you, drank your health, and wondered what you were doing! Perhaps you are Falkland enough (I swear I suspect you of it) to feel rather sore—just a little bit, you know, the merest trifle in the world—on hearing that Mrs. Macready looked brilliant, blooming, young, and handsome, and that she danced a country dance with the writer hereof

(Acres to your Falkland) in a thorough spirit of becoming good humour and enjoyment. Now you don't like to be told that? Nor do you quite like to hear that Forster and I conjured bravely; that a plum-pudding was produced from an empty saucepan, held over a blazing fire kindled in Stanfield's hat without damage to the lining; that a box of bran was changed into a live guinea-pig, which ran between my godchild's feet, and was the cause of such a shrill uproar and clapping of hands that you might have heard it (and I daresay did) in America; that three half-crowns being taken from Major Burns and put into a tumbler-glass before his eyes, did then and there give jingling answers to the questions asked of them by me, and knew where you were and what you were doing, to the unspeakable admiration of the whole assembly. Neither do you quite like to be told that we are going to do it again next Saturday, with the addition of demoniacal dresses from the masquerade shop; nor that Mrs. Macready, for her gallant bearing always, and her best sort of best affection, is the best creature I know. Never mind; no man shall gag me, and those are my opinions.

My dear Macready, the lecturing proposition is not to be thought of. I have not the slightest doubt or hesitation in giving you my most strenuous and decided advice against it. Looking only to its effect at home, I am immovable in my conviction that the impression it would produce would be one of failure, and reduction of yourself to the level of those who do the like here. To us who know the Boston names and honour them, and who know Boston and like it (Boston is what I would have the whole United States to be), the Boston requisition would be a valuable document, of which you and your friends might be proud. But those names are perfectly unknown to the public here, and would produce not the least effect. The only thing known to the public here is, that they ask (when I say "they" I mean the people) everybody to lecture. It is one of the things I have ridiculed in "Chuzzlewit." Lecture you, and you fall into the roll of Lardners, Vandenhoffs, Eltons, Knowleses, Buckinghams. You are off your pedestal, have flung away your glass slipper, and changed your triumphal coach into a seedy old pumpkin. I am quite sure of it, and cannot express my strong conviction in language of sufficient force.

"Puff-ridden!" why to be sure they are. The nation is a miserable Sindbad, and its boasted press the loathsome, foul old man upon his back, and yet they will tell you, and proclaim to the four winds for repetition here, that they don't need their ignorant and brutal papers, as if the papers could exist if they didn't need them! Let any two of these vagabonds, in any town you go to, take it into their heads to make you an object of attack, or to direct the general attention elsewhere, and what avail those wonderful images of passion which you have been all your life perfecting!

I have sent you, to the charge of our trusty and well-beloved Colden, a little book I published on the 17th of December, and which has been a most prodigious success—the greatest, I think, I have ever achieved. It pleases me to think that it will bring you home for an hour or two, and I long to hear you have read it on some quiet morning. Do they allow you to be quiet, by-the-way? "Some of our most fashionable people, sir," denounced me awfully for liking to be alone sometimes.

Now that we have turned Christmas, I feel as if your face were directed homewards, Macready. The downhill part of the road is before us now, and we shall travel on to midsummer at a dashing pace; and, please Heaven, I will be at Liverpool when you come steaming up the Mersey, with that red funnel smoking out unutterable things, and your heart much fuller than your trunks, though something lighter! If I be not the first Englishman to shake hands with you on English ground, the man who gets before me will be a brisk and active fellow, and even then need put his best leg foremost. So I warn Forster to keep in the rear, or he'll be blown.

· If you shall have any leisure to project and put on paper the outline of a scheme for opening any theatre on your return, upon a certain list subscribed, and on certain understandings with the actors, it strikes me that it would be wise to break ground while you are still away. Of course I need not say that I will see anybody or do anything—even to the calling together of the actors— if you should ever deem it desirable. My opinion is that our respected and valued friend Mr. —— will stagger through another season, if he don't rot first. I understand he is in a partial state of decomposition at this minute. He was very ill, but got better. How is it that —— always do get better, and strong hearts are so easy to die?

Look homeward always, as we look abroad to you. God bless you, my dear Macready.

Ever your affectionate Friend.

Devonshire Terrace, Fourth January, 1844.   Mr. Laman
Blanchard.

My dear Blanchard,

I cannot thank you enough for the beautiful manner and the true spirit of friendship in which you have noticed my "Carol." But I *must* thank you because you have filled my heart up to the brim, and it is running over.

You meant to give me great pleasure, dear fellow, and you have done it. The tone of your elegant and fervent praise has touched me in the tenderest place. I cannot write about it, and as to talking of it, I could no more do that than a dumb man. I have derived inexpressible gratification from what I know was a labour of love on your part. And I can never forget it.

When I think it likely that I may meet you (perhaps at Ainsworth's on Friday?) I shall slip a "Carol" into my pocket and ask you to put it among your books for my sake. You will never like it the less for having made it the means of so much happiness to me.

Always, my dear Blanchard,

Faithfully your Friend.

Sir Edward
Lytton
Bulwer.

ATHENÆUM, *Thursday Afternoon,*
Twenty-fifth January, 1844.

MY DEAR SIR EDWARD,

I received your kind cheque yesterday, in behalf of the Elton family; and am much indebted to you on their behalf.

Pray do not believe that the least intentional neglect has prevented me from calling on you, or that I am not sincerely desirous to avail myself of any opportunity of cultivating your friendship. I venture to say this to you in an unaffected and earnest spirit, and I hope it will not be displeasing to you.

At the time when you called, and for many weeks afterwards, I was so closely occupied with my little Carol (the idea of which had just occurred to me), that I never left home before the owls went out, and led quite a solitary life. When I began to have a little time and to go abroad again, I knew that you were in affliction, and I then thought it better to wait, even before I left a card at your door, until the pressure of your distress had past.

I fancy a reproachful spirit in your note, possibly because I knew that I may appear to deserve it. But *do* let me say to you that it would give me real pain to retain the idea that there was any coldness between us, and that it would give me heartfelt satisfaction to know the reverse.

I shall make a personal descent upon you before Sunday, in the hope of telling you this myself. But I cannot rest easy without writing it also. And if this should lead to a better knowledge in each of us, of the other, believe me that I shall always look upon it as something I have long wished for.

Always faithfully yours.

LIVERPOOL, RADLEY'S HOTEL,
Monday, Twenty-sixth February, 1844.

Mrs. Charles
Dickens.

MY DEAR KATE,

I got down here last night (after a most intolerably wet journey) before seven, and found Thompson sitting by my fire. He had ordered dinner, and we ate it pleasantly enough, and went to bed in good time. This morning, Mr. Yates, the great man connected with the Institution (and a brother of Ashton Yates'), called. I went to look at it with him. It is an enormous place. The lecture-room, in which the celebration is held, will accommodate over thirteen hundred people. It was being fitted with gas after the manner of the ring at Astley's. I should think it an easy place to speak in, being a semicircle with seats rising one above another to the ceiling, and will have eight hundred ladies to-night, in full dress. I am rayther shaky just now, but shall pull up, I have no doubt. At dinner-time to-morrow you will receive, I hope, a facetious document hastily penned after I return to-night, telling you how it all went off.

When I came back here, I found Fanny and Hewett had picked me up just before. We all went off straight to the *Britannia,* which lay where she did when we went on board. We went into the old little cabin and the ladies' cabin, but Mrs. Bean had gone to Scotland, as the ship does not sail again before May. In the saloon we had some champagne and biscuits, and Hewett had set upon the table a block of Boston ice, weighing fifty pounds. Scott, of the *Caledonia,* lunched with us—a very nice fellow. He saw Macready play Macbeth in Boston, and gave me a tremendous account of the effect. Poor Burroughs, of the *George Washington,* died on board, on his last passage home. His little wife was with him.

Hewett dines with us to-day, and I have procured him admission to-night. I am very sorry indeed (and so was he) that you didn't see the old ship. It was the strangest thing in the world to go on board again.

I had Bacon with me as far as Watford yesterday, and very pleasant. Sheil was also in the train, on his way to Ireland.

Ever affectionately.

OUT OF THE COMMON—PLEASE.

DICKENS *against* THE WORLD.

CHARLES DICKENS, of No. 1, Devonshire Terrace, York Gate, Regent's Park, in the county of Middlesex, gentleman, the successful plaintiff in the above cause, maketh oath and saith : That on the day and date hereof, to wit at seven o'clock in the evening, he, this deponent, took the chair at a large assembly of the Mechanics' Institution at Liverpool, and that having been received with tremendous and enthusiastic plaudits, he, this deponent, did immediately dash into a vigorous, brilliant, humorous, pathetic, eloquent, fervid, and impassioned speech. That the said speech was enlivened by thirteen hundred persons, with frequent, vehement, uproarious, and deafening cheers, and to the best of this deponent's knowledge and belief, he, this deponent, did speak up like a man, and did, to the best of his knowledge and belief, considerably distinguish himself. That after the proceedings of the opening were over, and a vote of thanks was proposed to this deponent, he, this deponent, did again distinguish himself, and that the cheering at that time, accompanied with clapping of hands and stamping of feet, was in this deponent's case thundering and awful. And this deponent further saith, that his white-and-black or magpie waistcoat, did create a strong sensation, and that during the hours of promenading, this deponent heard from persons surrounding him such exclamations as, "What is it! *Is* it a waistcoat? No, it's a shirt"—and the like—all of which this deponent believes to have been complimentary and gratifying; but this deponent further saith that he is now going to supper, and wishes he may have an appetite to eat it.

CHARLES DICKENS.

Sworn before me, at the Adelphi }
   Hotel, Liverpool, on the Twenty-
   sixth of February, 1844.
                S. RADLEY.

Mr. T. J.
Thompson.

LIVERPOOL, Wednesday Night, Twenty-eighth February,
Half-past Ten at night.

MY DEAR THOMPSON,

     There never were such considerate people as they are here. After offering me unbounded hospitality and my declining it, they leave me to myself like gentlemen. They saved me from all sorts of intrusion at the Town Hall—brought me back—and left me to my quiet supper (now on the table) as they had left me to my quiet dinner.

     I wish you had come. It was really a splendid sight. The Town Hall was crammed to the roof by, I suppose, two thousand persons. The ladies were in full dress and immense numbers.; and when Dick showed himself, the whole assembly stood up, rustling like the leaves of a wood. Dick, with the heart of a lion, dashed in bravely. He introduced that about the genie in the casket with marvellous effect; and was applauded to the echo, which did applaud again. He was horribly nervous when he arrived at Birmingham, but when he stood upon the platform, I don't believe his pulse increased ten degrees. A better and quicker audience never listened to man.

The ladies had hung the hall (do you know what an immense place it is?) with artificial flowers all round. And on the front of the great gallery, immediately fronting this young gentleman, were the words in artificial flowers (you'll observe), "Welcome Boz," in letters about six feet high. Behind his head, and about the great organ, were immense transparencies representing several Fames crowning a corresponding number of Dicks, at which Victoria (taking out a poetic licence) was highly delighted.

*   *   *   *   *

I am going to bed. The landlady is not literary, and calls me Mr. Digzon. In other respects it is a good house.

My dear Thompson, always yours.

DEVONSHIRE TERRACE, *Tenth March*, 1844.   Countess of Blessington.

MY DEAR LADY BLESSINGTON,

I have made up my mind to "see the world," and mean to decamp, bag and baggage, next midsummer for a twelvemonth. I purpose establishing my family in some convenient place, from whence I can make personal ravages on the neighbouring country, and, somehow or other, have got it into my head that Nice would be a favourable spot for head-quarters. You are so well acquainted with these matters, that I am anxious to have the benefit of your kind advice. I do not doubt that you can tell me whether this same Nice be a healthy place the year through, whether it be reasonably cheap, pleasant to look at and to live in, and the like. If you will tell me, when you have ten minutes to spare for such a client, I shall be delighted to come to you, and guide myself by your opinion. I will not ask you to forgive me for troubling you, because I am sure beforehand that you will do so. I beg to be kindly remembered to Count D'Orsay and to your nieces—I was going to say "the Misses Power," but it looks so like the blue board at a ladies' school, that I stopped short.

Very faithfully yours.

DEVONSHIRE TERRACE, *Thirteenth March*, 1844.   Mr. T. J. Thompson.

MY DEAR THOMPSON,

Think of Italy! Don't give that up! Why, my house is entered at Phillips's and at Gillow's to be let for twelve months;

my letter of credit lies ready at Coutts'; my last number of Chuzzlewit comes out in June; and the first week, if not the first day in July, sees me, God willing, steaming off towards the sun.

Yes. We must have a few books, and everything that is idle, sauntering, and enjoyable. We must lie down at the bottom of those boats, and devise all kinds of engines for improving on that gallant holiday. I see myself in a striped shirt, moustache, blouse, red sash, straw hat, and white trousers, sitting astride a mule, and not caring for the clock, the day of the month, or the week. Tinkling bells upon the mule, I hope. I look forward to it day and night, and wish the time were come. Don't *you* give it up. That's all.

*   *   *   *   *

Always, my dear Thompson,
Faithfully your Friend.

Mr. T. J.
Thompson.

DEVONSHIRE TERRACE,
Sunday, Twenty-fourth March, 1844.

MY DEAR THOMPSON,

My study fireplace having been suddenly seized with symptoms of insanity, I have been in great affliction. The brick-layer was called in, and considered it necessary to perform an extensive operation without delay. I don't know whether you are aware of a peculiar bricky raggedness (not unaccompanied by pendent stalactites of mortar) which is exposed to view on the removal of a stove, or are acquainted with the suffocating properties of a kind of accidental snuff which flies out of the same cavernous region in great abundance. It is very distressing. I have been walking about the house after the manner of the dove before the waters subsided for some days, and have no pens or ink or paper. Hence this gap in our correspondence which I now repair.

What are you doing??? When are you coming away???? Why are you stopping there????? Do enlighten me, for I think of you constantly, and have a true and real interest in your proceedings.

D'Orsay, who knows Italy very well indeed, strenuously insists there is no such place for head-quarters as Pisa. Lady Blessington says so also. What do you say? On the first of July! The first of July! Dick turns his head towards the orange groves.

*   *   *   *   *

Daniel not having yet come to judgment, there is no news stirring. Every morning I proclaim: "At home to Mr. Thompson." Every evening I ejaculate with Monsieur Jacques * : "But he weel

<hr>

* A character in a Play, well known at this time.

come. I know he weel." After which I look vacantly at the boxes; put my hands to my gray wig, as if to make quite sure that it is still on my head, all safe : and go off, first entrance O.P. to soft music.

    *   *   *   *   *

Always faithfully your Friend.

DEVONSHIRE TERRACE, *Thirtieth April*, 1844.

Mr. Clarkson Stanfield, R.A.

MY DEAR STANFIELD,

The Sanatorium, or sick house for students, governesses, clerks, young artists, and so forth, who are above hospitals, and not rich enough to be well attended in illness in their own lodgings (you know its objects), is going to have a dinner at the London Tavern on Tuesday, the Fifth of June.

The Committee are very anxious to have you for a steward, as one of the heads of a large class; and I have told them that I have no doubt you will act. There is no steward's fee or collection whatever.

They are particularly anxious also to have Mr. Etty and Edwin Landseer. As you see them daily at the Academy, will you ask them or show them this note? Sir Martin * became one of the Committee some few years ago, at my solicitation, as recommending young artists, struggling alone in London, to the better knowledge of this establishment.

The dinner is to comprise the new feature of ladies dining at the tables with the gentlemen—not looking down upon them from the gallery. I hope in your reply you will not only book yourself, but Mrs. Stanfield and Mary. It will be very brilliant and cheerful I hope. Dick in the chair. Gentlemen's dinner-tickets a guinea, as usual; ladies', twelve shillings. I think this is all I have to say, except (which is nonsensical and needless) that I am always

Affectionately yours.

ATHENÆUM, *Monday Morning,*
Twenty-seventh May, 1844.

Mr. Edwin Landseer, R.A.

MY DEAR LANDSEER,

I have let my house with such delicious promptitude, or, as the Americans would say, "with sich everlass'in slickness and al-mity sprydom," that we turn out to-night ! in favour of a widow lady, who keeps it all the time we are away !

Wherefore if you, looking up into the sky this evening between five and six (as possibly you may be, in search of the spring), should see a speck in the air—a mere dot—which, growing larger

* Sir Martin Archer Shee, at this time President of the Royal Academy.

and larger by degrees, appears in course of time to be an eagle (chain and all) in a light cart, accompanied by a raven of uncommon sagacity, curse that good-nature which prompted you to say it—that you would give them house-room. And do it for the love of   Boz.

P.S.—The writer hereof may be heard on by personal enquiry at No. 9, Osnaburgh Terrace, New Road.

Mr. Charles Babbage.

9, Osnaburgh Terrace, New Road,
Twenty-eighth May, 1844.

My dear Sir,

I regret to say that we are placed in the preposterous situation of being obliged to postpone our little dinner-party on Saturday, by reason of having no house to dine in. We have not been burnt out; but a desirable widow (as a tenant, I mean) proposed, only last Saturday, to take our own house for the whole term of our intended absence abroad, on condition that she had possession of it to-day. We fled, and were driven into this place, which has no convenience for the production of any other banquet than a cold collation of plate and linen, the only comforts we have not left behind us.

My consolation lies in knowing what sort of dinner you would have had if you had come *here,* and in looking forward to claiming the fulfilment of your kind promise when we are again at home.

Always believe me, my dear Sir, faithfully yours.

Mr. Charles Knight.

9, Osnaburgh Terrace, *Fourth June,* 1844.

My dear Sir,

Many thanks for your proof, and for your truly gratifying mention of my name. I think the subject excellently chosen, the introduction exactly what it should be, the allusion to the International Copyright question most honourable and manly, and the whole scheme full of the highest interest. I had already seen your prospectus, and if I can be of the feeblest use in advancing a project so intimately connected with an end on which my heart is set—the liberal education of the people—I shall be sincerely glad. All good wishes and success attend you!

Believe me always,
Faithfully yours.

Mr. Robert Keeley.

9, Osnaburgh Terrace, *Monday Evening,*
Twenty-fourth June, 1844.

My dear Sir,

I cannot, consistently with the opinion I hold and have

always held, in reference to the principle of adapting novels for the stage, give you a prologue to "Chuzzlewit." But believe me to be quite sincere in saying that if I felt I could reasonably do such a thing for anyone, I would do it for you.

I start for Italy on Monday next, but if you have the piece on the stage, and rehearse on Friday, I will gladly come down at any time you may appoint on that morning, and go through it with you all. If you be not in a sufficiently forward state to render this proposal convenient to you, or likely to assist your preparations, do not take the trouble to answer this note.

I presume Mrs. Keeley will do Ruth Pinch. If so, I feel secure about her, and of Mrs. Gamp I am certain. But a queer sensation begins in my legs, and comes upward to my forehead, when I think of Tom.

Faithfully yours always.

VILLA DI BAGNARELLO, ALBARO,
Monday, Twenty-second July, 1844.

Mr. Daniel
Maclise,
R.A.

MY VERY DEAR MAC,

I address you with something of the lofty spirit of an exile —a banished commoner—a sort of Anglo-Pole. I don't exactly know what I have done for my country in coming away from it; but I feel it is something—something great—something virtuous and heroic. Lofty emotions rise within me, when I see the sun set on the blue Mediterranean. I am the limpet on the rock. My father's name is Turner, and my boots are green.

Apropos of blue. In a certain picture, called "The Serenade," you painted a sky. If you ever have occasion to paint the Mediterranean, let it be exactly of that colour. It lies before me now, as deeply and intensely blue. But no such colour is above me. Nothing like it. In the South of France—at Avignon, at Aix, at Marseilles—I saw deep blue skies (not *so* deep though—oh Lord, no!), and also in America; but the sky above me is familiar to my sight. Is it heresy to say that I have seen its twin-brother shining through the window of Jack Straw's *—that down in Devonshire I have seen a better sky? I daresay it is; but like a great many other heresies, it is true.

But such green—green—green—as flutters in the vineyard down below the windows, *that* I never saw; nor yet such lilac, and such purple as float between me and the distant hills; nor yet—in anything—picture, book, or verbal boredom—such awful, solemn, impenetrable blue, as is that same sea. It has such an absorbing, silent, deep, profound effect, that I can't help thinking it suggested

* The Jack Straw's Castle Inn, at Hampstead.

I

the idea of Styx. It looks as if a draught of it—only so much as you could scoop up on the beach, in the hollow of your hand—would wash out everything else, and make a great blue blank of your intellect.

When the sun sets clearly, then, by Heaven, it is majestic! From any one of eleven windows here, or from a terrace overgrown with grapes, you may behold the broad sea; villas, houses, mountains, forts, strewn with rose leaves—strewn with thorns—stifled in thorns! Dyed through and through and through. For a moment. No more. The sun is impatient and fierce, like everything else in these parts, and goes down headlong. Run to fetch your hat—and it's night. Wink at the right time of black night—and it's morning. Everything is in extremes. There is an insect here (I forget its name, and Fletcher and Roche are both out) that chirps all day. There is one outside the window now. The chirp is very loud, something like a Brobdingnagian grasshopper. The creature is born to chirp—to progress in chirping—to chirp louder, louder, louder—till it gives one tremendous chirp, and bursts itself. That is its life and death. Everything "is in a concatenation accordingly." The day gets brighter, brighter, brighter, till it's night. The summer gets hotter, hotter, hotter, till it bursts. The fruit gets riper, riper, riper, till it tumbles down and rots.

Ask me a question or two about fresco—will you be so good? All the houses are painted in fresco hereabout—the outside walls I mean; the fronts, and backs, and sides—and all the colour has run into damp and green seediness, and the very design has struggled away into the component atoms of the plaster. Sometimes (but not often) I can make out a virgin with a mildewed glory round her head; holding nothing, in an indiscernible lap, with invisible arms; and occasionally the leg or arms of a cherub, but it is very melancholy and dim. There are two old fresco-painted vases outside my own gate—one on either hand—which are so faint, that I never saw them till last night; and only then because I was looking over the wall after a lizard, who had come upon me while I was smoking a cigar above, and crawled over one of these embellishments to his retreat. There is a church here—the Church of the Annunciation—which they are now (by "they" I mean certain noble families) restoring at a vast expense, as a work of piety. It is a large church, with a great many little chapels in it, and a very high dome. Every inch of this edifice is painted, and every design is set in a great gold frame or border elaborately wrought. You can imagine nothing so splendid. It is worth coming the whole distance to see. But every sort of splendour is in perpetual enactment through the means of these churches.   Gorgeous processions in the streets, illuminations of windows on festa-nights ; lighting up of lamps and clustering of flowers before the shrines of saints ; all manner of show and display.   The doors of the churches stand wide open ; and in this hot weather great red curtains flutter and wave in their places ; and if you go and sit in one of these to get out of the sun, you see the queerest figures kneeling against pillars, and the strangest people passing in and out, and vast streams of women in veils (they don't wear bonnets), with great fans in their hands, coming and going, that you are never tired of looking on. Except in the churches, you would suppose the city (at this time of the year) to be deserted, the people keep so close within doors. Indeed it is next to impossible to get out into the heat.   I have only been into Genoa twice myself.   We are deliciously cool here, by comparison ; being high, and having the sea breeze.   There is always some shade in the vineyard, too ; and underneath the rocks on the sea-shore, so if I choose to saunter I can do it easily, even in the hot time of the day.   I am as lazy, however, as—as you are, and do little but eat and drink and read.

As I am going to transmit regular accounts of all sight-seeings and journeyings to Forster, who will show them to you, I will not bore you with descriptions, however.   I hardly think you allow enough for the great brightness and brilliancy of colour which is commonly achieved on the Continent, in that same fresco painting. I saw some—by a French artist and his pupil—in progress at the cathedral at Avignon, which was as bright and airy as anything can be,—nothing dull or dead about it ; and I have observed quite fierce and glaring colours elsewhere.

We have a piano now (there was none in the house), and have fallen into a pretty settled easy track.   We breakfast about half-past nine or ten, dine about four, and go to bed about eleven   We are much courted by the visiting people, of course, and I very much resort to my old habit of bolting from callers, and leaving their reception to Kate.   Green figs I have already learnt to like.   Green almonds (we have them at dessert every day) are the most delicious fruit in the world.   And green lemons, combined with some rare hollands that is to be got here, make prodigious punch, I assure you.   You ought to come over, Mac ; but I don't expect you, though I am sure it would be a very good move for you.   I have not the smallest doubt of that.   Fletcher has made a sketch of the house, and will copy it in pen-and-ink for transmission to you in my next letter.   I shall look out for a place in Genoa, between this and the winter time.   In the meantime, the people who come out here breathe delightedly, as if they had got into another climate.   Landing in the city, you would hardly suppose it possible that there could be such an air within two miles.

Write to me as often as you can, like a dear good fellow, and rely upon the punctuality of my correspondence.   Losing you and Forster is like losing my arms and legs, and dull and lame I am without you.   But at Broadstairs next year, please God, when it is all over, I shall be very glad to have laid up such a store of recollections and improvement.

I don't know what to do with Timber.   He is as ill-adapted to the climate at this time of year as a suit of fur.   I have had him made a lion dog; but the fleas flock in such crowds into the hair he has left, that they drive him nearly frantic, and render it absolutely necessary that he should be kept by himself.   Of all the miserable hideous little frights you ever saw, you never beheld such a devil.   Apropos, as we were crossing the Seine within two stages of Paris, Roche suddenly said to me, sitting by me on the box: "The littel dog 'ave got a great lip!"   I was thinking of things remote and very different, and couldn't comprehend why any peculiarity in this feature on the part of the dog should excite a man so much.   As I was musing upon it, my ears were attracted by shouts of "Hélo! holà! Hi, hi, hi! Le voilà! Regardez!" and the like.   And looking down among the oxen—we were in the centre of a numerous drove—I saw him, Timber, lying in the road, curled up—you know his way—like a lobster, only not so stiff, yelping dismally in the pain of his "lip" from the roof of the carriage; and between the aching of his bones, his horror of the oxen, and his dread of me (who he evidently took to be the immediate agent in and cause of the damage), singing out to an extent which I believe to be perfectly unprecedented; while every Frenchman and French boy within sight roared for company.   He wasn't hurt.

Kate and Georgina send their best loves; and the children add "theirs."   Katey, in particular, desires to be commended to "Mr. Teese."   She has a sore throat; from sitting in constant draughts, I suppose; but with that exception, we are all quite well.   Ever believe me, my dear Mac,

Your affectionate Friend.

Rev.
Edward
Tagart.

ALBARO, NEAR GENOA, *Friday, Ninth August,* 1844.

MY DEAR SIR,

I find that if I wait to write you a long letter (which has been the cause of my procrastination in fulfilling my part of our agreement), I am likely to wait some time longer.   And as I am very anxious to hear of you; not the less so, because I hear of you through my brother, who usually sees you once a week in my absence; I take pen in hand and stop a messenger who is going to Genoa. For my main object being to qualify myself for the receipt of a letter from you, I don't see why a ten-line qualification is not as good as one of a hundred lines.

You told me it was possible that you and Mrs. Tagart might wander into these latitudes in the autumn. I wish you would carry out that infant intention to the utmost. It would afford us the truest delight and pleasure to receive you. If you come in October, you will find us in the Palazzo Peschiere, in Genoa, which is surrounded by a delicious garden, and is a most charming habitation in all respects. If you come in September, you will find us less splendidly lodged, but on the margin of the sea, and in the midst of vineyards. The climate is delightful even now; the heat being not at all oppressive, except in the actual city, which is what the Americans would call considerable fiery, in the middle of the day. But the sea-breezes out here are refreshing and cool every day, and the bathing in the early morning is something more agreeable than you can easily imagine. The orange trees of the Peschiere shall give you their most fragrant salutations if you come to us at that time, and we have a dozen spare beds in that house that I know of! to say nothing of some vast chambers here and there with ancient iron chests in them, where Mrs. Tagart might enact Ginevra to perfection, and never be found out. To prevent which, I will engage to watch her closely if she will only come and see us.

The flies are incredibly numerous just now. The unsightly blot a little higher up was occasioned by a very fine one who fell into the inkstand, and came out, unexpectedly, on the nib of my pen. We are all quite well, thank Heaven, and had a very interesting journey here, of which, as well as of this place, I will not write a word, lest I should take the edge off those agreeable conversations with which we will beguile our walks.

Pray tell me about the presentation of the plate, and whether ——— was very slow, or trotted at all, and if so, when. He is an excellent creature, and I respect him very much, so I don't mind smiling when I think of him as he appeared when addressing you and pointing to the plate, with his head a little on one side, and one of his eyes turned up languidly.

Also let me know exactly how you are travelling, and when, and all about it; that I may meet you with open arms on the threshold of the city, if happily you bend your steps this way. You had better address me, "Poste Restante, Genoa," as the Albaro postman gets drunk, and when he has lost letters, and is sober, sheds tears—which is affecting, but hardly satisfactory.

As the messenger has just looked in at the door, and shedding on me a balmy gale of onions, has protested against being detained any longer, I will only say (which is not at all necessary) that I am ever,

Faithfully yours.

P.S.—There is a little to see here, in the church way, I assure you.

ALBARO, Saturday Night,
Twenty-fourth August, 1844.

Mr.
Clarkson
Stanfield,
R. A.

MY DEAR STANFIELD,

I love you so truly, and have such pride and joy of heart in your friendship, that I don't know how to begin writing to you. When I think how you are walking up and down London in that portly surtout, and can't receive proposals from Dick to go to the theatre, I fall into a state between laughing and crying, and want some friendly back to smite. "Je-im!" "Aye, aye, your honour," is in my ears every time I walk upon the sea-shore here; and the number of expeditions I make into Cornwall in my sleep, the springs of Flys I break, the songs I sing, and the bowls of punch I drink, would soften a heart of stone.

We have had weather here, since five o'clock this morning, after your own heart. Suppose yourself the Admiral in "Black-eyed Susan" after the acquittal of William, and when it was possible to be on friendly terms with him. I am T.P.* My trousers are very full at the ankles, my black neckerchief is tied in the regular style, the name of my ship is painted round my glazed hat, I have a red waistcoat on, and the seams of my blue jacket are "paid"—permit me to dig you in the ribs when I make use of this nautical expression —with white. In my hand I hold the very box connected with the story of Sandomingerbilly. I lift up my eyebrows as far as I can (on the T.P. model), take a quid from the box, screw the lid on again (chewing at the same time, and looking pleasantly at the pit), brush it with my right elbow, take up my right leg, scrape my right foot on the ground, hitch up my trousers, and in reply to a question of yours, namely, "Indeed, what weather, William?" I deliver myself as follows :

Lord love your honour! Weather! Such weather as would set all hands to the pumps aboard one of your fresh-water cockboats, and set the purser to his wits' ends to stow away, for the use of the ship's company, the casks and casks full of blue water as would come powering in over the gunnel! The dirtiest night, your honour, as ever you see 'atween Spithead at gun-fire and

---

* T. P. Cooke, the celebrated actor of William in Mr. Douglas Jerrold's play of "Black-eyed Susan."

the Bay of Biscay ! The wind sou'-west, and your house dead in the wind's eye ; the breakers running up high upon the rocky heads, the light'us no more looking through the fog than Davy Jones's sarser eye through the blue sky of heaven in a calm, or the blue toplights of your honour's lady cast down in a modest overhauling of her catheads : avast ! (*whistling*) my dear eyes ; here am I a-goin' head on to the breakers (*bowing*).

Admiral (*smiling*). No, William ! I admire plain speaking, as you know, and so does old England, William, and old England's Queen. But you were saying——

William. Aye, aye, your honour (*scratching his head*). I've lost my reckoning. Damme !—I ast pardon—but won't your honour throw a hencoop or any old end of towline to a man as is overboard !

Admiral (*smiling still*). You were saying, William, that the wind——

William (*again cocking his leg, and slapping the thighs very hard*). Avast heaving, your honour ! I see your honour's signal fluttering in the breeze, without a glass. As I was a-saying, your honour, the wind was blowin' from the sou'-west, due sou'-west, your honour, not a pint to larboard nor a pint to starboard ; the clouds a-gatherin' in the distance for all the world like Beachy Head in a fog, the sea a-rowling in, in heaps of foam, and making higher than the mainyard arm, the craft a-scuddin' by all taut and under storms'ils for the harbour ; not a blessed star a-twinklin' out aloft—aloft, your honour, in the little cherubs' native country—and the spray is flying like the white foam from the Jolly's lips when Poll of Portsea took him for a tailor ! (*laughs*).

Admiral (*laughing also*). You have described it well, William, and I thank you. But who are these ?

> *Enter Supers in calico jackets to look like cloth, some in brown holland petticoat-trousers and big boots, all with very large buckles. Last Super rolls on a cask, and pretends to keep it. Other Supers apply their mugs to the bunghole and drink, previously holding them upside down.*

William (*after shaking hands with everybody*). Who are these, your honour ! Messmates as staunch and true as ever broke biscuit. Ain't you, my lads ?

All. Aye aye, William. That we are ! that we are !

Admiral (*much affected*). Oh, England, what wonder that—— ! But I will no longer detain you from your sports, my humble friends (ADMIRAL *speaks very low, and looks hard at the orchestra, this being the cue for the dance*)— from your sports, my humble friends. Farewell !

All. Hurrah ! hurrah ! [*Exit* ADMIRAL.

Voice behind. Suppose the dance, Mr. Stanfield. Are you all ready ! Go, then !

My dear Stanfield, I wish you would come this way and see me in that Palazzo Peschiere ! Was ever man so welcome as I would make you ! What a truly gentlemanly action it would be to bring Mrs. Stanfield and the baby. And how Kate and her sister would wave pocket-handkerchiefs from the wharf in joyful welcome ! Ah, what a glorious proceeding !

Do you know this place ? Of course you do. I won't bore you with anything about it, for I know Forster reads my letters to you ; but what a place it is ! The views from the hills here, and the immense variety of prospects of the sea, are as striking, I think, as

such scenery can be. Above all, the approach to Genoa, by sea
from Marseilles, constitutes a picture which you ought to paint, for
nobody else can ever do it! William, you made that bridge at
Avignon better than it is. Beautiful as it undoubtedly is, you made
it fifty times better. And if I were Morrison, or one of that school
(bless the dear fellows one and all!), I wouldn't stand it, but would
insist on having another picture gratis, to atone for the imposition.

The night is like a seaside night in England towards the end of
September. They say it is the prelude to clear weather. But the
wind is roaring now, and the sea is raving, and the rain is driving
down, as if they had all set in for a real hearty picnic, and each had
brought its own relations to the general festivity. I don't know
whether you are acquainted with the coastguard men in these
parts? They are extremely civil fellows, of a very amiable manner
and appearance, but the most innocent men in matters you would
suppose them to be well acquainted with, in virtue of their office,
that I ever encountered. One of them asked me only yesterday, if
it would take a year to get to England in a ship? Which I thought
for a coastguardman was rather a tidy question. It would take a
long time to catch a ship going there if he were on board a pursuing
cutter though. I think he would scarcely do it in twelve months,
indeed.

So you were at Astley's t'other night. "Now, Mr. Stickney, sir,
what can I come for to go for to do for to bring for to fetch for to
carry for you, sir?" "He, he, he! Oh, I say, sir!" "Well, sir?"
"Miss Woolford knows me, sir. She laughed at me!" I see him
run away after this; not on his feet, but on his knees and the calves
of his legs alternately; and that smell of sawdusty horses, which
was never in any other place in the world, salutes my nose with
painful distinctness. What do you think of my suddenly finding
myself a swimmer? But I have really made the discovery, and
skim about a little blue bay just below the town here, like a fish in
high spirits. I hope to preserve my bathing-dress for your inspection and approval, or possibly to enrich your collection of Italian
costumes on my return. Do you recollect Yarnold in "Masaniello"?
I fear that I, unintentionally, "dress at him," before plunging into
the sea. I enhanced the likeness very much, last Friday morning,
by singing a barcarole on the rocks. I was a trifle too flesh-coloured
(the stage knowing no medium between bright salmon and dirty
yellow), but apart from that defect, not badly made up by any
means. I remain out here until the end of September, and send in
for my letters daily. There is a postman for this place, but he gets
drunk and loses the letters; after which he calls to say so, and to
fall upon his knees. About three weeks ago I caught him at a

wineshop near here, playing bowls in the garden. It was then about five o'clock in the afternoon, and he had been airing a newspaper addressed to me, since nine o'clock in the morning.

Kate and Georgina unite with me in most cordial remembrances to Mrs. and Miss Stanfield, and to all the children. They particularise all sorts of messages, but I tell them that they had better write themselves if they want to send any. Though I don't know that this writing would end in the safe deliverance of the commodities after all; for when I began this letter, I meant to give utterance to all kinds of heartiness, my dear Stanfield; and I come to the end of it without having said anything more than that I am —which is new to you—under every circumstance and everywhere,

Your most affectionate Friend.

PALAZZO PESCHIERE, GENOA,   Mr. W. C.
Fourteenth October, 1844.   Macready.

MY VERY DEAR MACREADY,

My whole heart is with you *at home.* I have not yet felt so far off as I do now, when I think of you there, and cannot fold you in my arms. This is only a shake of the hand. I couldn't *say* much to you, if I were home to greet you. Nor can I write much, when I think of you, safe and sound and happy, after all your wanderings.

My dear fellow, God bless you twenty thousand times. Happiness and joy be with you! I hope to see you soon. If I should be so unfortunate as to miss you in London, I will fall upon you, with a swoop of love, in Paris. Kate says all kind things in the language; and means more than are in the dictionary capacity of all the descendants of all the stonemasons that worked at Babel. Again and again and again, my own true friend, God bless you!

Ever yours affectionately.

PESCHIERE, GENOA,   Mr. Thomas
Tuesday, Fifth November, 1844.   Mitton.

MY DEAR MITTON,

The cause of my not having written to you is too obvious to need any explanation. I have worn myself to death in the month I have been at work. None of my usual reliefs have been at hand; I have not been able to divest myself of the story—have suffered very much in my sleep in consequence—and am so shaken by such work in this trying climate, that I am as nervous as a man who is dying of drink, and as haggard as a murderer.

I believe I have written a tremendous book, and knocked the

"Carol" out of the field. It will make a great uproar, I have no doubt.

I leave here to-morrow for Venice and many other places; and I shall certainly come to London to see my proofs, coming by new ground all the way, cutting through the snow in the valleys of Switzerland, and plunging through the mountains in the dead of winter. I would accept your hearty offer with right goodwill, but my visit being one of business and consultation, I see impediments in the way, and insurmountable reasons for not doing so. Therefore, I shall go to an hotel in Covent Garden, where they know me very well, and with the landlord of which I have already communicated. My orders are not upon a mighty scale, extending no further than a good bedroom and a cold shower-bath.

The house is *perfect*; the servants are as quiet and well-behaved as at home, which very rarely happens here, and Roche is my right hand. There never was such a fellow.

We have now got carpets down—burn fires at night—draw the curtains, and are quite wintry. We have a box at the opera, which is close by (for nothing), and sit there when we please, as in our own drawing-room. There have been three fine days in four weeks. On every other the water has been falling down in one continual sheet, and it has been thundering and lightening every day and night.

Ever faithfully.

P.S.—Charley has a writing master every day, and a French master. He and his sisters are to be waited on by a professor of the noble art of dancing, next week.

Mrs. Charles Dickens.

PARMA, ALBERGO DELLA POSTA,
Friday, Eighth November, 1844.

MY DEAREST KATE,

"If missis could see us to-night, what would she say?" That was the brave C.'s remark last night at midnight, and he had reason. We left Genoa, as you know, soon after five on the evening of my departure; and in company with the lady whom you saw, and the dog whom I don't think you did see, travelled all night at the rate of four miles an hour over bad roads without the least refreshment until daybreak, when the brave and myself escaped into a miserable café while they were changing horses, and got a cup of that drink hot. That same day, a few hours afterwards, between ten and eleven, we came to (I hope) the worst inn in the world, where, in a vast chamber, rendered still more desolate by the presence of a most offensive specimen of

what D'Israeli calls the Mosaic Arab (who had a beautiful girl
with him), I regaled upon a breakfast, almost as cold, and damp,
and cheerless as myself. Then, in another coach, much smaller
than a small Fly, I was packed up with an old padre, a young
Jesuit, a provincial avvocato, a private gentleman with a very red
nose and a very wet brown umbrella, and the brave C., and I went
on again at the same pace through the mud and rain until four in
the afternoon, when there was a place in the coupé (two indeed),
which I took, holding that select compartment in company with a
very ugly but very agreeable Tuscan "gent," who said "*gia*"
instead of "*si*," and rung some other changes in this changing
language, but with whom I got on very well, being extremely
conversational. We were bound, as you know, perhaps, for
Piacenza, but it was discovered that we couldn't get to Piacenza,
and about ten o'clock at night we halted at a place called Stradella,
where the inn was a series of queer galleries open to the night,
with a great courtyard full of waggons and horses, and "*velociferi*,"
and what not in the centre. It was bitter cold and very wet, and
we all walked into a bare room (mine!), with two immensely
broad beds on two deal dining-tables, a third great empty table,
the usual washing-stand tripod, with a slop-basin on it, and two
chairs. And then we walked up and down for three-quarters of
an hour or so, while dinner, or supper, or whatever it was, was
getting ready. This was set forth (by way of variety) in the old
priest's bedroom, which had two more immensely broad beds on
two more deal dining-tables in it. The first dish was a cabbage
boiled in a great quantity of rice and hot water, the whole
flavoured with cheese. I was so cold that I thought it comfortable, and so hungry that a bit of cabbage, when I found such
a thing floating my way, charmed me. After that we had a dish
of very little pieces of pork, fried with pigs' kidneys; after that
a fowl; after that something very red and stringy, which I think
was veal; and after that two tiny little new-born-baby-looking
turkeys, very red and very swollen. Fruit, of course, to wind up,
and garlic in one shape or another in every course. I made three
jokes at supper (to the immense delight of the company), and
retired early. The brave brought in a bush or two and made a
fire, and after that a glass of screeching hot brandy and water;
that bottle of his being full of brandy. I drank it at my leisure,
undressed before the fire, and went into one of the beds. The
brave reappeared about an hour afterwards and went into the
other; previously tying a pocket-handkerchief round and round
his head in a strange fashion, and giving utterance to the sentiment with which this letter begins. At five this morning we

resumed our journey, still through mud and rain, and at about eleven arrived at Piacenza; where we fellow-passengers took leave of one another in the most affectionate manner. As there was no coach on till six at night, and as it was a very grim despondent sort of place, and as I had had enough of diligences for one while, I posted forward here in the strangest carriages ever beheld, which we changed when we changed horses. We arrived here before six. The hotel is quite French. I have dined very well in my own room on the second floor; and it has two beds in it, screened off from the room by drapery. I only use one to-night, and that is already made.

It is dull work this travelling alone. My only comfort is in motion. I look forward with a sort of shudder to Sunday, when I shall have a day to myself in Bologna; and I think I must deliver my letters in Venice in sheer desperation. Never did anybody want a companion after dinner so much as I do.

There has been music on the landing outside my door to-night. Two violins and a violoncello. One of the violins played a solo, and the others struck in as an orchestra does now and then, very well. Then he came in with a small tin platter. "Bella musica," said I. "Bellissima musica, signore." "Mi piace moltissimo." "Sono felice, signore," said he. I gave him a franc. "O moltissimo generoso. Tanto generoso, signore."

It was a joke to laugh at when I was learning; but I swear, unless I could stagger on, Zoppa-wise, with the people, I verily believe I should have turned back this morning.

In all other respects I think the entire change has done me undoubted service already. I am free of the book, and am red-faced; and feel marvellously disposed to sleep.

So, for all the straggling qualities of this straggling letter, want of sleep must be responsible. Give my best love to Georgy, and my paternal blessing to

> Mamey,
> Katey,
> Charley,
> Wally,
> and
> Chickenstalker.

P.S.—Get things in their places. I can't bear to picture them otherwise.

P.P.S.—I think I saw Roche sleeping with his head on the lady's shoulder, in the coach. I couldn't swear it, and the light was deceptive. But I think I did.

CREMONA, *Saturday Night,*   Mr. Douglas
Sixteenth November, 1844.   Jerrold.

MY DEAR JERROLD,

As half a loaf is better than no bread, so I hope that half
a sheet of paper may be better than none at all, coming from one
who is anxious to live in your memory and friendship. I should
have redeemed the pledge I gave you in this regard long since, but
occupation at one time, and absence from pen and ink at another,
have prevented me.

Forster has told you, or will tell you, that I very much wish
you to hear my little Christmas book; and I hope you will meet
me, at his bidding, in Lincoln's Inn Fields. I have tried to strike
a blow upon that part of the brass countenance of wicked Cant,
when such a compliment is sorely needed at this time, and I trust
that the result of my training is at least the exhibition of a strong
desire to make it a staggerer. If *you* should think at the end of
the four rounds (there are no more) that the said Cant, in the
language of *Bell's Life,* "comes up piping," I shall be very much
the better for it.

I am now on my way to Milan; and from thence (after a day or
two's rest) I mean to come to England by the grandest Alpine pass
that the snow may leave open. You know this place as famous of
yore for fiddles. I don't see any here now. But there is a whole
street of coppersmiths not far from this inn, and they throb so
d——ably and fitfully, that I thought I had a palpitation of the
heart after dinner just now, and seldom was more relieved than
when I found the noise to be none of mine.

I was rather shocked yesterday (I am not strong in geographical
details) to find that Romeo was only banished twenty-five miles.
That is the distance between Mantua and Verona. The latter is a
quaint old place, with great houses in it that are now solitary and
shut up—exactly the place it ought to be. The former has a
great many apothecaries in it at this moment, who could play that
part to the life. For of all the stagnant ponds I ever beheld, it is
the greenest and weediest. I went to see the old palace of the
Capulets, which is still distinguished by their cognizance (a hat
carved in stone on the courtyard wall). It is a miserable inn.
The court was full of crazy coaches, carts, geese, and pigs, and
was ankle-deep in mud and dung. The garden is walled off and
built out. There was nothing to connect it with its old inhabitants, and a very unsentimental lady at the kitchen door.
The Montagues used to live some two or three miles off in the
country. It does not appear quite clear whether they ever inhabited Verona itself. But there is a village bearing their name

to this day, and traditions of the quarrels between the two families are still as nearly alive as anything can be, in such a drowsy neighbourhood.

It was very hearty and good of you, Jerrold, to make that affectionate mention of the "Carol" in *Punch*, and I assure you it was not lost on the distant object of your manly regard, but touched him as you wished and meant it should. I wish we had not lost so much time in improving our personal knowledge of each other. But I have so steadily read you, and so selfishly gratified myself in always expressing the admiration with which your gallant truths inspired me, that I must not call it time lost, either.

You rather entertained a notion, once, of coming to see me at Genoa. I shall return straight, on the ninth of December, limiting my stay in town to one week. Now couldn't you come back with me? The journey, that way, is very cheap, costing little more than twelve pounds; and I am sure the gratification to you would be high. I am lodged in quite a wonderful place, and would put you in a painted room, as big as a church and much more comfortable. There are pens and ink upon the premises; orange trees, gardens, battledores and shuttlecocks, rousing wood-fires for evenings, and a welcome worth having.

Come! Letter from a gentleman in Italy to Bradbury and Evans in London. Letter from a gentleman in a country gone to sleep to a gentleman in a country that would go to sleep too, and never wake again, if some people had their way. You can work in Genoa. The house is used to it. It is exactly a week's post. Have that portmanteau looked to, and when we meet, say, "I am coming."

I have never in my life been so struck by any place as by Venice. It is *the* wonder of the world. Dreamy, beautiful, inconsistent, impossible, wicked, shadowy, d——able old place. I entered it by night, and the sensation of that night and the bright morning that followed is a part of me for the rest of my existence. And, oh God! the cells below the water, underneath the Bridge of Sighs; the nook where the monk came at midnight to confess the political offender; the bench where he was strangled; the deadly little vault in which they tied him in a sack, and the stealthy crouching little door through which they hurried him into a boat, and bore him away to sink him where no fisherman dare cast his net—all shown by torches that blink and wink, as if they were ashamed to look upon the gloomy theatre of sad horrors; past and gone as they are, these things stir a man's blood, like a great wrong or passion of the instant. And with these in their minds, and with a museum there, having a chamber full of such frightful instruments of torture as the devil in a brain fever could scarcely invent, there are hundreds of parrots, who will declaim to you in speech and print, by the hour together, on the degeneracy of the times in which a railroad is building across the water at Venice; instead of going down on their knees, the drivellers, and thanking Heaven that they live in a time when iron makes roads, instead of prison bars and engines for driving screws into the skulls of innocent men. Before God, I could almost turn bloody-minded, and shoot the parrots of our island with as little compunction as Robinson Crusoe shot the parrots in his.

I have not been in bed, these ten days, after five in the morning, and have been travelling many hours every day. If this be the cause of my inflicting a very stupid and sleepy letter on you, my dear Jerrold, I hope it will be a kind of signal at the same time, of my wish to hail you lovingly even from this sleepy and unpromising state. And believe me as I am,

Always your Friend and Admirer.

MILAN, *Wednesday, Twentieth November*, 1844.   Countess of
    Blessington.

MY DEAR LADY BLESSINGTON,

Appearances are against me. Don't believe them. I have written you, in intention, fifty letters, and I can claim no credit for any one of them (though they were the best letters you ever read), for they all originated in my desire to live in your memory and regard. Since I heard from Count D'Orsay, I have been beset in I don't know how many ways. First of all, I went to Marseilles and came back to Genoa. Then I moved to the Peschiere. Then some people, who had been present at the Scientific Congress here, made a sudden inroad on that establishment, and overran it. Then they went away, and I shut myself up for a month, close and tight, over my little Christmas book, "The Chimes." All my affections and passions got twined and knotted up in it, and I became as haggard as a murderer, long before I wrote "The End." When I had done that, like "*The* man of Thessaly," who having scratched his eyes out in a quickset hedge, plunged into a bramble-bush to scratch them in again, I fled to Venice, to recover the composure I had disturbed. From thence I went to Verona and to Mantua. And now I am here—just come up from underground, and earthy all over, from seeing that extraordinary tomb in which the dead saint lies in an alabaster case, with sparkling jewels all about him to mock his dusty eyes, not to mention the twenty-franc pieces which devout votaries were ringing down upon a sort of skylight in the cathedral pavement above, as if it were the counter of his heavenly shop. You know Verona? You know everything in Italy, *I* know. The Roman Amphitheatre there delighted me beyond expression. I never saw anything so full of solemn ancient interest. There are the four-and-forty rows of seats, as fresh and perfect as if their occupants had vacated them but yesterday—the entrances, passages, dens, rooms, corridors, the numbers over some of the arches. An equestrian troop had been there some days before, and had scooped out a little ring at one end of the arena, and had their performances in that spot. I should like to have seen it, of all things, for its very dreariness. Fancy a handful of people sprinkled over one corner of the great place (the whole population of Verona wouldn't fill it now); and a spangled cavalier bowing to the echoes, and the grass-grown walls! I climbed to the topmost seat, and looked away at the beautiful view for some minutes; when I turned round, and looked down into the theatre again, it had exactly the appearance of an immense straw hat, to which the helmet in the Castle of Otranto was a baby; the rows of seats representing the different plaits of straw, and the arena the inside of the crown. I had great expectations of Venice, but they fell immeasurably short of the wonderful reality. The short time I passed there went by me like a dream. I hardly think it possible to exaggerate its beauties, its sources of interest, its uncommon novelty and freshness. A thousand and one realisations of the Thousand and one Nights, could scarcely captivate and enchant me more than Venice.

Your old house at Albaro—Il Paradiso—is spoken of as yours to this day. What a gallant place it is! I don't know the present inmate, but I hear that he bought and furnished it not long since, with great splendour, in the French style, and that he wishes to sell it. I wish I were rich and could buy it. There is a third-rate wine-shop below Byron's house, and the place looks dull and miserable and ruinous enough. Old —— is a trifle uglier than when I first arrived. He has periodical parties, at which there are a great many flower-pots and a few ices—no other refreshments. He goes about, constantly charged with extemporaneous poetry, and is always ready, like tavern dinners, on the shortest notice and the most reasonable terms. He keeps a gigantic harp in his bedroom, together with pen, ink, and paper, for fixing his ideas as they flow, a kind of profane King David, but truly good-natured and very harmless.

Pray say to Count D'Orsay everything that is cordial and loving from me. The travelling purse he gave me has been of immense service. It has been constantly opened. All Italy seems to yearn to put its hand in it. I think of hanging it, when I come back to

England, on a nail as a trophy, and of gashing the brim like the blade of an old sword, and saying to my son and heir, as they do upon the stage: "You see this notch, boy? Five hundred francs were laid low on that day, for post-horses. Where this gap is, a waiter charged your father treble the correct amount—and got it. This end, worn into teeth like the rasped edge of an old file, is sacred to the Custom Houses, boy, the passports, and the shabby soldiers at town-gates, who put an open hand and a dirty coat-cuff into the coach-windows of all 'Forestieri.' Take it, boy. Thy father has nothing else to give!"

My desk is cooling itself in a mail-coach, somewhere down at the back of the cathedral, and the pens and ink in this house are so detestable, that I have no hope of your ever getting to this portion of my letter. But I have the less misery in this state of mind, from knowing that it has nothing in it to repay you for the trouble of perusal.

Very faithfully yours.

FRIBOURG, Saturday Night,
Twenty-third November, 1844.

Mrs. Charles Dickens.

MY DEAREST KATE,

For the first time since I left you I am sitting in a room of my own hiring, with a fire and a bed in it. And I am happy to say that I have the best and fullest intentions of sleeping in the bed, having arrived here at half-past four this afternoon, without any cessation of travelling, night or day, since I parted from Mr. Bairr's cheap firewood.

The Alps appeared in sight very soon after we left Milan—by eight or nine o'clock in the morning; and the brave C. was so far wrong in his calculations that we began the ascent of the Simplon that same night, while you were travelling (as I would I were) towards the Peschiere. Most favourable state of circumstances for journeying up that tremendous pass! The brightest moon I ever saw, all night, and daybreak on the summit. The glory of which, making great wastes of snow a rosy red, exceeds all telling. We *sledged* through the snow on the summit for two hours or so. The weather was perfectly fair and bright, and there was neither difficulty nor danger—except the danger that there always must be, in such a place, of a horse stumbling on the brink of an immeasurable precipice. In which case no piece of the unfortunate traveller would be left large enough to tell his story in dumb show. You may imagine something of the rugged grandeur of such a scene as this great passage of these great mountains, and indeed Glencoe, well sprinkled with snow, would be very like the ascent. But the top itself, so wild, and bleak, and lonely, is a thing by itself, and not to be likened to any other sight. The cold was piercing; the north wind high and boisterous; and when it came driving in our faces, bringing a sharp shower of little points of snow and piercing it into our very blood, it really was, what it is often said to be, " cutting "— with a very sharp edge too. There are houses of refuge here— bleak, solitary places—for travellers overtaken by the snow to hurry to, as an escape from death; and one great house, called the Hospital, kept by monks, where wayfarers get supper and bed for nothing. We saw some coming out and pursuing their journey. If all monks devoted themselves to such uses, I should have little fault to find with them.

The cold in Switzerland, since, has been something quite indescribable. My eyes are tingling to-night as one may suppose cymbals to tingle when they have been lustily played. It is positive pain to me to write. The great organ which I was to have had " pleasure in hearing " don't play on a Sunday, at which the brave is inconsolable. But the town is picturesque and quaint, and worth seeing. And this inn (with a German bedstead in it about the size and shape of a baby's linen-basket) is perfectly clean and comfortable. Butter is so cheap hereabouts that they bring you a great mass like the squab of a sofa for tea. And of honey, which is most delicious, they set before you a proportionate allowance.

Swiss towns, and mountains, and the Lake of Geneva, and the famous suspension bridge at this place, and a great many other objects (with a very low thermometer conspicuous among them), are dancing up and down me, strangely. But I am quite collected enough, notwithstanding, to have still a very distinct idea that this hornpipe travelling is uncomfortable, and that I would gladly start for my palazzo out of hand without any previous rest, stupid as I am and much as I want it.

Ever, my dear love,
Affectionately yours.

P.S.—I hope the dancing lessons will be a success. Don't fail to let me know.

Mr. W. C. Macready.

HÔTEL BRISTOL, PARIS, Thursday Night,
Twenty-eighth November, 1844, Half-past Ten.

MY DEAREST MACREADY,

Since I wrote to you what would be called in law proceedings the exhibit marked A, I have been round to the Hôtel Brighton, and personally examined and cross-examined the attendants. It is painfully clear to me that I shall not see you to-night, nor until Tuesday, the Tenth of December, when, please God, I shall re-arrive here, on my way to my Italian bowers. I mean to stay all the Wednesday and all the Thursday in Paris. One night to see you act (my old delight when you little thought of such a being in existence), and one night to read to you and Mrs. Macready (if that scamp of Lincoln's Inn Fields has not anticipated me) my little Christmas book, in which I have endeavoured to plant an indignant right-hander on the eye of certain wicked Cant that makes my blood boil, which I hope will not only cloud that eye with black and blue, but many a gentle one with crystal of the finest sort. God forgive me, but I think there are good things in the little story !

I took it for granted you were, as your American friends say, "in full blast" here, and meant to have sent a card into your dressing-room, with "Mr. G. S. Hancock Muggridge, United States," upon it. But Paris looks coldly on me without your eye in its head, and not being able to shake your hand I shake my own head dolefully, which is but poor satisfaction.

My love to Mrs. Macready. I will swear to the death that it is truly hers, for her gallantry in your absence if for nothing else, and to you, my dear Macready, I am ever a devoted friend.

HÔTEL BRISTOL, PARIS, *Thursday Night,*
Twenty-eighth November, 1844.

Mrs. Charles
Dickens.

MY DEAREST KATE,

I got to Strasburg on Monday night, intending to go down the Rhine. But the weather being foggy, and the season quite over, they could not insure me getting on for certain beyond Mayence, or our not being detained by unpropitious weather. Therefore I resolved (the malle poste being full) to take the diligence hither next day in the afternoon. I arrived here at half-past five to-night, after fifty hours of it in a French coach. I was so beastly dirty when I got to this house, that I had quite lost all sense of my identity, and if anybody had said, "Are you Charles Dickens?" I should have unblushingly answered, "No; I never heard of him." A good wash, and a good dress, and a good dinner have revived me, however; and I can report of this house, concerning which the brave was so anxious when we were here before, that it is the best I ever was in. My little apartment, consisting of three rooms and other conveniences, is a perfect curiosity of completeness. You never saw such a charming little baby-house. It is infinitely smaller than those first rooms we had at Meurice's, but for elegance, compactness, comfort, and quietude, exceeds anything I ever met with at an inn.

The moment I arrived here, I enquired, of course, after Macready.

They said the English theatre had not begun yet, that they thought he was at Meurice's, where they knew some members of the company to be. I instantly despatched the porter with a note to say that if he were there, I would come round and hug him, as soon as I was clean. They referred the porter to the Hôtel Brighton. He came back and told me that the answer there was : " M. Macready's rooms were engaged, but he had not arrived. He was expected to-night !" If we meet to-night, I will add a postscript. Wouldn't it be odd if we met upon the road between this and Boulogne to-morrow ?

I mean, as a recompense for my late sufferings, to get a hackney-carriage if I can and post that journey, starting from here at eight to-morrow morning, getting to Boulogne sufficiently early next morning to cross at once, and dining with Forster that same day— to wit, Saturday. I have notions of taking you with me on my next journey (if you would like to go), and arranging for Georgy to come to us by steamer—under the protection of the English captain, for instance—to Naples ; there I would top and cap all our walks by taking her up to the crater of Vesuvius with me. But this is dependent on her ability to be perfectly happy for a fortnight or so in our stately palace with the children, and such foreign aid as the Simpsons. For I love her too dearly to think of any project which would involve her being uncomfortable for that space of time.

You can think this over, and talk it over ; and I will join you in doing so, please God, when I return to our Italian bowers, which I shall be heartily glad to do.

They tell us that the landlord of this house, going to London some week or so ago, was detained at Boulogne two days by a high sea, in which the packet could not put out. So I hope there is the greater chance of no such bedevilment happening to me.

Paris is better than ever. Oh dear, how grand it was when I came through it in that caravan to-night ! I hope we shall be very hearty here, and able to say with Wally, " Han't it pleasant !"

Ever, my dearest Kate,

Affectionately yours.

Mrs. Charles
Dickens.

PIAZZA COFFEE HOUSE, COVENT GARDEN,
Monday, Second December, 1844.

MY DEAREST KATE,

I received, with great delight, your *excellent* letter of this morning. Do not regard this as my answer to it. It is merely to say that I have been at Bradbury and Evans's all day, and have barely time to write more than that I *will* write to-morrow. I arrived about seven on Saturday evening, and rushed into the arms of Mac and Forster. Both of them send their best love to you and Georgy, with a heartiness not to be described.

The little book is now, as far as I am concerned, all ready. One cut of Doyle's and one of Leech's I found so unlike my ideas, that I had them both to breakfast with me this morning, and with that winning manner which you know of, got them with the highest good humour to do both afresh. They are now hard at it. Stanfield's readiness, delight, wonder at my being pleased with what he has done is delicious. Mac's frontispiece is charming. The book is quite splendid.

Anybody who has heard it has been moved in the most extraordinary manner. Forster read it (for dramatic purposes) to A'Beckett. He cried so much and so painfully, that Forster didn't know whether to go on or stop; and he called next day to say that any expression of his feeling was beyond his power. But that he believed it, and felt it to be—I won't say what.

Yours, with true affection.

P.S.—If you had seen Macready last night, undisguisedly sobbing and crying on the sofa as I read, you would have felt, as I did, what a thing it is to have power.

COVENT GARDEN,
Sunday, Noon (December, 1844).

Countess of Blessington

MY DEAR LADY BLESSINGTON,

Business for other people (and by no means of a pleasant kind) has held me prisoner during two whole days, and will so detain me to-day, in the very agony of my departure for Italy again, that I shall not even be able to reach Gore House once more, on which I had set my heart. I cannot bear the thought of going away without some sort of reference to the happy day you gave me on Monday, and the pleasure and delight I had in your earnest greeting. I shall never forget it, believe me. It would be worth going to China—it would be worth going to America, to come home again for the pleasure of such a meeting with you and Count D'Orsay—to whom my love, and something as near it to Miss Power and her sister as it is lawful to send. It will be an unspeakable satisfaction to me (though I am not maliciously disposed) to know under your own hand at Genoa that my little book made you cry. I hope to prove a better correspondent on my return to those shores. But better or worse, or any how, I am ever, my dear Lady Blessington, in no common degree, and not with an everyday regard, yours.

Very faithfully yours.

1845.

NARRATIVE.

AT the beginning of this year, Charles Dickens was still living at the Palazzo Peschiere, Genoa, with his family. In February, he went with his wife to Rome for the Carnival, leaving his sister-in-law and children at Genoa; Miss Hogarth joining them later on at Naples. They all returned to Rome for the Holy Week, and then went to Florence, and so back to Genoa. He continued his residence at Genoa until June of this year, when he returned to England by Switzerland and Belgium, the party being met at Brussels by Mr. Forster, Mr. Maclise, and Mr. Douglas Jerrold, and arriving at home at the end of June. The autumn months, until the First October, were again spent at Broadstairs. And in this September the first amateur play at Miss Kelly's theatre in Dean Street was given, under the management of Charles Dickens, with Messrs. Jerrold, Mark Lemon, John Leech, Gilbert A'Beckett, Leigh, Frank Stone, Forster, and others as his fellow-actors. The play selected was Ben Jonson's "Every Man in his Humour," in which Charles Dickens acted Captain Bobadil. The first performance was a private one, merely as an entertainment for the actors and their friends, but its success speedily led to a repetition of the same performance, and afterwards to many other performances for public and charitable objects. "Every Man in his Humour" was shortly after repeated, at the same little theatre, for a useful charity which needed help; and later in the year Beaumont and Fletcher's play of "The Elder Brother" was given by the same company, at the same place, for the benefit of Miss Kelly. There was a farce played after the comedy on each occasion—not always the same one—in which Charles Dickens and Mr. Mark Lemon were the principal actors.

The letters which we have for this year refer, with very few exceptions, to these theatricals, and therefore need no explanation.

Charles Dickens was at work at the end of this year on another Christmas book, "The Cricket on the Hearth," and was also much occupied with the project of *The Daily News* paper, of which he undertook the editorship at its starting, which took place in the beginning of the following year, 1846.

Miss
Hogarth.

ROME, *Tuesday, Fourth February*, 1845.

MY DEAREST GEORGY,

This is a very short note, but time is still shorter. Come by the first boat by all means. If there be a good one a day or two before it, come by that. Don't delay on any account. I am very sorry you are not here. The Carnival is a very remarkable and beautiful sight. I have been regretting the having left you at home all the way here.

Kate says will you take counsel with Charlotte about colour (I put in my word, as usual, for brightness), and have the darlings' bonnets made at once, by the same artist as before? Kate would have written, but is gone with Black to a day performance at the opera, to see Cerito dance. At two o'clock each day we sally forth in an open carriage, with a large sack of sugar-plums and at least five hundred little nosegays to pelt people with. I should think we threw away, yesterday, a thousand of the latter. We had the carriage filled with flowers three or four times. I wish you could have seen me catch a swell brigand on the nose with a handful of very large confetti every time we met him. It was the best thing I have ever done. "The Chimes" are nothing to it.

Anxiously expecting you, I am ever,

Dear Georgy,

Yours most affectionately.

NAPLES, *Monday, Seventeenth February,* 1845. Mr. Thomas Mitton.

MY DEAR MITTON,

This will be a hasty letter, for I am as badly off in this place as in America—beset by visitors at all times and seasons, and forced to dine out every day. I have found, however, an excellent man for me—an Englishman, who has lived here many years and is well acquainted with *the people,* whom he doctored in the bad time of the cholera, when the priests and everybody else fled in terror.

Under his auspices I have got to understand the low life of Naples (among the fishermen and idlers) almost as well as I understand the do. do. of my own country; always excepting the language, which is very peculiar and extremely difficult, and would require a year's constant practice at least. It is no more like Italian than English is to Welsh. And as they don't say half of what they mean, but make a wink or a kick stand for a whole sentence, it's a marvel to me how they comprehend each other. At Rome they speak beautiful Italian (I am pretty strong at that, I believe); but they are worse here than in Genoa, which I had previously thought impossible.

It is a fine place, but nothing like so beautiful as people make it out to be. The famous bay is, to my thinking, as a piece of scenery, immeasurably inferior to the Bay of Genoa, which is the most lovely thing I have ever seen. The city, in like manner, will bear no comparison with Genoa. But there is none in Italy that will, except Venice. As to houses, there is no palace like the Peschiere for architecture, situation, gardens, or rooms. It is a great triumph to me, too, to find how cheap it is. At Rome, the English people live in dirty little fourth, fifth, and sixth floors, with not one room as large as your own drawing-room, and pay, commonly, seven or eight pounds a week.

I was a week in Rome on my way here, and saw the Carnival, which is perfectly delirious, and a great scene for a description. All the ancient part of Rome is wonderful and impressive in the extreme, far beyond the possibility of exaggeration. As to the modern part, it might be anywhere or anything — Paris, Nice, Boulogne, Calais, or one of a thousand other places.

The weather is so atrocious (rain, snow, wind, darkness, hail, and cold) that I can't get over into Sicily. But I don't care very much about it, as I have planned out ten days of excursion into the neighbouring country. One thing of course — the ascent of Vesuvius. Herculaneum and Pompeii, are more full of interest and wonder than it is possible to imagine. I have heard of some ancient tombs (quite unknown to travellers) dug in the bowels of the earth, and extending for some miles underground. They are near a place called Viterbo, on the way from Rome to Florence. I shall lay in a small stock of torches, etc., and explore them when. I leave Rome. I return there on the first of March, and shall stay there nearly a month.

Saturday, February 22nd.—Since I left off as above, I have been away on an excursion of three days. Yesterday evening, at four o'clock, we began (a small party of six) the ascent of Mount Vesuvius, with six saddle-horses, an armed soldier for a guard, and twenty-two guides; the latter rendered necessary by the severity of the weather, which is greater than has been known for twenty years, and has covered the precipitous part of the mountain with deep snow, the surface of which is glazed with one smooth sheet of ice from the top of the cone to the bottom. By starting at that hour I intended to catch the sunset about halfway up, and night at the top, where the fire is raging. It was an inexpressibly lovely night without a cloud; and when the day was quite gone, the moon (within a few hours of the full) came proudly up, showing the sea, and the Bay of Naples, and the whole country in such majesty as no words can express. We rode to the beginning of the snow and then dismounted. Catherine and Georgina were put into two litters, just chairs with poles, like those in use in England on the 5th of November; and a fat Englishman, who was of the party, was hoisted into a third borne by eight men. I was accommodated with a tough stick, and we began to plough our way up. The ascent as steep as this line /—very nearly perpendicular. We were all tumbling at every step; and looking up and seeing the people in advance tumbling over one's very head, and looking down and seeing hundreds of feet of smooth ice below, was, I must confess, anything but agreeable. However, I knew there was little chance of another clear night before I leave this, and gave the word to get up somehow or other. So on we went, winding a little now and then, or we should not have got on at all. By prodigious exertious we passed the region of snow and came into that of fire—desolate and awful you may well suppose. It was like working one's way through a dry waterfall, with every mass of stone burnt and charred into enormous cinders, and smoke and sulphur bursting out of every chink and crevice, so that it was difficult to breathe. High before us, bursting out of a hill at the top of the mountain, shaped like this A, the fire was pouring out, reddening the night with flames, blackening it with smoke, and spotting it with red-hot stones and cinders that fell down again in showers. At every step everybody fell, now into a hot chink, now into a bed of ashes, now over a mass of cindered iron; and the confusion in the darkness (for the smoke obscured the moon in this part), and the quarrelling and shouting and roaring of the guides, and the waiting every now and then for somebody who was not to be found, and was supposed to have stumbled into some pit or other, made such a scene of it as I can give you no idea of. My ladies were now on foot, of course: but we dragged them on as well as we could (they were thorough game, and didn't make the least complaint), until we got to the foot of that topmost hill I have drawn so beautifully. Here we all stopped; but the head guide, an English gentleman of the name of Le Gros—who has been here many years, and has been up the mountain a hundred times—and your humble servant, resolved (like jackasses) to climb that hill to the brink and look into the crater itself. You may form some notion of what is going on inside it, when I tell you that it is a hundred feet higher than it was six weeks ago. The sensation of struggling up it, choked with the fire and smoke, and feeling at every step as if the crust of ground between one's feet and the gulf of fire would crumble in and swallow one up (which is the real danger), I shall remember for some little time, I think. But we did it. We looked down into the flaming bowels of the mountain and came back again, alight in half-a-dozen places, and burnt from head to foot. You never saw such devils. And *I* never saw anything so awful and terrible.

Roche had been tearing his hair like a madman, and crying that

we should all three be killed, which made the rest of the company
very comfortable, as you may suppose.   But we had some wine in
a basket, and all swallowed a little of that and a great deal of
sulphur before we began to descend.   The usual way, after the fiery
part is past—you will understand that to be all the flat top of the
mountain, in the centre of which, again, rises the little hill I have
drawn—is to slide down the ashes, which, slipping from under you,
make a gradually increasing ledge under your feet, and prevent
your going too fast.   But when we came to this steep place last
night, we found nothing there but one smooth solid sheet of ice.
The only way to get down was for the guides to make a chain,
holding by each other's hands, and beat a narrow track in it into
the snow below with their sticks.   My two unfortunate ladies were
taken out of their litters again, with half-a-dozen men hanging on to
each, to prevent their falling forward ; and we began to descend
this way.   It was like a tremendous dream.   It was impossible to
stand, and the only way to prevent oneself from going sheer down
the precipice, every time one fell, was to drive one's stick into one
of the holes the guides had made, and hold on by that.   Nobody
could pick one up, or stop one, or render one the least assistance.
Now, conceive my horror, when this Mr. Le Gros I have mentioned,
being on one side of Georgina and I on the other, suddenly staggers
away from the narrow path on to the smooth ice, gives us a jerk,
lets go, and plunges headforemost down the smooth ice into the
black night, five hundred feet below !   Almost at the same instant,
a man far behind, carrying a light basket on his head with some of
our spare cloaks in it, misses his footing and rolls down in another
place ; and after him, rolling over and over like a black bundle,
goes a boy, shrieking as nobody but an Italian can shriek, until
the breath is tumbled out of him.

The Englishman is in bed to-day, terribly bruised but without
any broken bones.   He was insensible at first and a mere heap of
rags ; but we got him before the fire, in a little hermitage there is
halfway down, and he so far recovered as to be able to take some
supper, which was waiting for us there.   The boy was brought in
with his head tied up in a bloody cloth, about half an hour after
the rest of us were assembled.   And the man who had had the
basket was not found when we left the mountain at midnight.
What became of the cloaks (mine was among them) I know as
little.   My ladies' clothes were so torn off their backs that they
would not have been decent, if there could have been any thought
of such things at such a time.   And when we got down to the
guides' house, we found a French surgeon (one of another party who
had been up before us) lying on a bed in a stable, with God knows what

horrible breakage about him, but suffering acutely and looking like death. A pretty unusual trip for a pleasure expedition, I think!

I am rather stiff to-day, but am quite unhurt, except a slight scrape on my right hand. My clothes are burnt to pieces. My ladies are the wonder of Naples, and everybody is open-mouthed.

Ever faithfully.

GENOA, Ninth May, 1845.

Countess of
Blessington.

MY DEAR LADY BLESSINGTON,

Once more in my old quarters, and with rather a tired sole to my foot, from having found such an immense number of different resting-places for it since I went away. I write you my last Italian letter for this bout, designing to leave here, please God, on the ninth of next month, and to be in London again by the end of June. I am looking forward with great delight to the pleasure of seeing you once more, and mean to come to Gore House with such a swoop as shall astonish the poodle, if, after being accustomed to his own size and sense, he retain the power of being astonished at anything in the wide world. You know where I have been, and every mile of ground I have travelled over, and every object I have seen. It is next to impossible, surely, to exaggerate the interest of Rome; though, I think, it <i>is</i> very possible to find the main source of interest in the wrong things. Naples disappointed me greatly. The weather was bad during a great part of my stay there. But if I had not had mud, I should have had dust, and though I had had sun, I must still have had the Lazzaroni. And they are so ragged, so dirty, so abject, so full of degradation, so sunken and steeped in the hopelessness of better things, that they would make heaven uncomfortable, if they could ever get there. I didn't expect to see a handsome city, but I expected something better than that long dull line of squalid houses, which stretches from the Chiaja to the quarter of the Porta Capuana; and while I was quite prepared for a miserable populace, I had some dim belief that there were bright rays among them, and dancing legs, and shining sun-browned faces. Whereas the honest truth is, that connected with Naples itself, I have not one solitary recollection. The country round it charmed me, I need not say. Who can forget Herculaneum and Pompeii?

As to Vesuvius, it burns away in my thoughts, beside the roaring waters of Niagara, and not a splash of the water extinguishes a spark of the fire; but there they go on, tumbling and flaming night and day, each in its fullest glory.

I have seen so many wonders, and each of them has such a voice of its own, that I sit all day long listening to the roar they make as if it were in a sea-shell, and have fallen into an idleness so complete, that I can't rouse myself sufficiently to go to Pisa on the twenty-fifth, when the triennial illumination of the Cathedral and Leaning Tower, and Bridges, and what not, takes place. But I have already been there ; and it cannot beat St. Peter's, I suppose. So I don't think I shall pluck myself up by the roots, and go aboard a steamer for Leghorn. Let me thank you heartily for the "Keepsake" and the "Book of Beauty." They reached me a week or two ago. I have been very much struck by two papers in them—one, Landor's "Conversations," among the most charming, profound, and delicate productions I have ever read ; the other, your lines on Byron's room at Venice. I am as sure that you wrote them from your heart, as I am that they found their way immediately to mine.

It delights me to receive such accounts of Maclise's fresco. If he will only give his magnificent genius fair play, there is not enough cant and dulness even in the criticism of art from which Sterne prayed kind heaven to defend him, as the worst of all the cants continually canted in this canting world—to keep the giant down an hour.

Our poor friend, the naval governor,* has lost his wife, I am sorry to hear, since you and I spoke of his pleasant face. Do not let your nieces forget me, if you can help it, and give my love to Count D'Orsay, with many thanks to him for his charming letter. I was greatly amused by his account of ——. There was a cold shade of aristocracy about it, and a dampness of cold water, which entertained me beyond measure.

Always faithfully yours.

Mr. Macvey
Napier.

1, DEVONSHIRE TERRACE, *Twenty-eighth July*, 1845.

MY DEAR SIR,

As my note is to bear reference to business, I will make it as short and plain as I can. I think I could write a pretty good and a well-timed article on the *Punishment of Death*, and sympathy with great criminals, instancing the gross and depraved curiosity that exists in reference to them, by some of the outrageous things that were written, done, and said in recent cases. But as I am not sure that my views would be yours, and as their statement would be quite inseparable from such a paper, I will briefly set down their purport that you may decide for yourself.

Society, having arrived at that state in which it spares bodily torture to the worst criminals, and having agreed, if criminals be

---

* Lieut. Tracey, R.N., who was at this time Governor of Tothill Fields Prison.

put to death at all, to kill them in the speediest way, I consider the question with reference to society, and not at all with reference to the criminal, holding that in a case of cruel and deliberate murder, he is already mercifully and sparingly treated. But, as a question for the deliberate consideration of all reflective persons, I put this view of the case. With such very repulsive and odious details before us, may it not be well to inquire whether the punishment of death be beneficial to society? I believe it to have a horrible fascination for many of those persons who render themselves liable to it, impelling them onward to the acquisition of a frightful notoriety; and (setting aside the strong confirmation of this idea afforded in individual instances) I presume this to be the case in very badly regulated minds, when I observe the strange fascination which everything connected with this punishment, or the object of it, possesses for tens of thousands of decent, virtuous, well-conducted people, who are quite unable to resist the published portraits, letters, anecdotes, smilings, snuff-takings, of the bloodiest and most unnatural scoundrel with the gallows before him. I observe that this strange interest does not prevail to anything like the same degree where death is not the penalty. Therefore I connect it with the dread and mystery surrounding death in any shape, but especially in this avenging form, and am disposed to come to the conclusion that it produces crime in the criminally disposed, and engenders a diseased sympathy—morbid and bad, but natural and often irresistible—among the well-conducted and gentle. Regarding it as doing harm to both these classes, it may even then be right to enquire, whether it has any salutary influence on those small knots and specks of people, mere bubbles in the living ocean, who actually behold its infliction with their proper eyes. On this head it is scarcely possible to entertain a doubt, for we know that robbery, and obscenity, and callous indifference are of no commoner occurrence anywhere than at the foot of the scaffold. Furthermore, we know that all exhibitions of agony and death have a tendency to brutalise and harden the feelings of men, and have always been the most rife among the fiercest people. Again, it is a great question whether ignorant and dissolute persons (ever the great body of spectators, as few others will attend), seeing *that* murder done, and not having seen the other, will not, almost of necessity, sympathise with the man who dies before them, especially as he is shown, a martyr to their fancy, tied and bound, alone among scores, with every kind of odds against him.

I should take all these threads up at the end by a vivid little sketch of the origin and progress of such a crime as Hocker's, stating a somewhat parallel case, but an imaginary one, pursuing its hero to his death, and showing what enormous harm he does *after* the crime for which he suffers. I should state none of these positions in a positive sledge-hammer way, but tempt and lure the reader into the discussion of them in his own mind ; and so we come to this at last—whether it be for the benefit of society to elevate even this crime to the awful dignity and notoriety of death ; and whether it would not be much more to its advantage to substitute a mean and shameful punishment, degrading the deed and the committer of the deed, and leaving the general compassion to expend itself upon the only theme at present quite forgotten in the history, that is to say, the murdered person.

I do not give you this as an outline of the paper, which I think I could make attractive. It is merely an exposition of the inferences to which its whole philosophy must tend.

Always faithfully yours.

Mr. W. C. Macready.

ALBION HOTEL, BROADSTAIRS, *Sunday, Seventeenth August,* 1845.

MY DEAR MACREADY,

In reference to Bruce Castle school, I think the question set at rest most probably by the fact of there being no vacancy (it is always full) until Christmas, when Howitt's two boys and Jerrold's one go in and fill it up again. But after going carefully through the school, a question would arise in my mind whether the system—a perfectly admirable one ; the only recognition of education as a broad system of moral and intellectual philosophy, that I have ever seen in practice—do not require so much preparation and progress in the mind of the boy, as that he shall have come there younger and less advanced than Willy ; * or at all events without that very different sort of school experience which he must have acquired at Brighton. I have no warrant for this doubt, beyond a vague uneasiness suggesting a suspicion of its great probability. On such slight ground I would not hint it to anyone but you, who I know will give it its due weight, and no more and no less.

I have the paper setting forth the nature of the higher classical studies, and the books they read. It is the usual course, and includes the great books in Greek and Latin. They have a miscellaneous library, under the management of the boys themselves, of some five or six thousand volumes, and every means of study and recreation, and every inducement to self-reliance and self-exertion that can easily be imagined. As there is no room just

* Mr. Macready's eldest son.

now, you can turn it over in your mind again.   And if you would like to see the place yourself, when you return to town, I shall be delighted to go there with you.   I come home on Wednesday.

Ever, my dear Macready,

Affectionately yours.

Twenty-seventh August, 1845.

Mr. George Cattermole.

MY DEAR GEORGE,

I write a line to tell you a project we have in view.   A little party of us have taken Miss Kelly's theatre for the night of the twentieth of next month, and we are going to act a play there, with correct and pretty costume, good orchestra, etc. etc.   The affair is strictly private.   The admission will be by cards of invitation ; every man will have from thirty to thirty-five.   Nobody can ask any person without the knowledge and sanction of the rest, my objection being final ; and the expense to each (exclusive of the dress, which every man finds for himself) will not exceed two guineas.   Forster plays, and Stone plays, and I play, and some of the *Punch* people play.   Stanfield, having the scenery and carpenters to attend to, cannot manage his part also.   It is Downright, in "Every Man in his Humour," not at all long, but very good ; he wants you to take it.   And so help me.   We shall have a brilliant audience.   The uphill part of the thing is already done, our next rehearsal is next Tuesday, and if you will come in you will find everything to your hand, and all very merry and pleasant.

Let me know what you decide, like a Kittenmolian Trojan.

Believe me ever,

Heartily yours.

DEVONSHIRE TERRACE, *Thursday,*
Eighteenth September, 1845.

Mr. W. C. Macready.

MY DEAR MACREADY,

We have a little supper, sir, after the farce, at No. 9, Powis Place, Great Ormond Street, in an empty house, belonging to one of the company.   There I am requested by my fellows to beg the favour of thy company and that of Mrs. Macready.   The guests are limited to the actors and their ladies—with the exception of yourselves, and D'Orsay, and George Cattermole, "or so"—that sounds like Bobadil a little.

I am going to adopt your reading of the fifth act with the worst grace in the world.   It seems to me that you don't allow enough for Bobadil having been frequently beaten before, as I have no doubt he had been.   The part goes down hideously on this construction, and the end is mere lees.   But never mind, sir, I intend bringing you up with the farce in the most brilliant manner.

Ever yours affectionately.

N.B.—Observe.   I think of changing my present mode of life, and am open to an engagement.

N.B. No. 2.—I will undertake not to play tragedy, though passion is my strength.

N.B. No. 3.—I consider myself a chained lion.*

DEVONSHIRE TERRACE, *Second October*, 1845.

Mr.
Clarkson
Stanfield,
R.A.

MY DEAR STANNY,

I send you the claret jug.   But for a mistake, you would have received the little remembrance almost immediately after my return from abroad.

I need not say how much I should value another little sketch from your extraordinary hand in this year's small volume, to which Mac again does the frontispiece.   But I cannot hear of it, and will not have it (though the gratification of such aid, to me, is really beyond all expression), unless you will so far consent to make it a matter of business as to receive, without asking any questions, a cheque in return from the publishers.   Do not misunderstand me— though I am not afraid there is much danger of your doing so, for between us misunderstanding is, I hope, not easy.   I know perfectly well that nothing can pay you for the devotion of any portion of your time to such a use of your art.   I know perfectly well that no terms would induce you to go out of your way, in such a regard, for perhaps anybody else.   I cannot, nor do I desire to, vanquish the friendly obligation which help from you imposes on me.   But I am not the sole proprietor of these little books; and it would be monstrous in you if you were to dream of putting a scratch into a second one without some shadowy reference to the other partners, ten thousand times more monstrous in me if any consideration on earth could induce me to permit it, which nothing will or shall.

So, see what it comes to.   If you will do me a favour on my terms it will be more acceptable to me, my dear Stanfield, than I can possibly tell you.   If you will not be so generous, you deprive me of the satisfaction of receiving it at your hands, and shut me out from that possibility altogether.   What a stony-hearted ruffian you must be in such a case !

Ever affectionately yours.

---

* This alludes to a theatrical story of a second-rate actor, who described himself as a " chained lion," in a theatre where he had to play inferior parts to Mr. Macready.

DEVONSHIRE TERRACE, *Seventeenth October*, 1845. Mr. T. J. Thompson.

MY DEAR THOMPSON,

    Roche has not returned; and from what I hear of your movements, I fear I cannot answer for his being here in time for you.

    I enclose you, lest I should forget it, the letter to the Peschiere agent. He is the Marquis Pallavicini's man of business, and speaks the most abominable Genoese ever heard. He is a rascal of course; but a more reliable villain, in his way, than the rest of his kind.

    You recollect what I told you of the Swiss banker's wife, the English lady?* If you would like Christiana † to have a friend at Genoa in the person of a most affectionate and excellent little woman, and if you would like to have a resource in the most elegant and comfortable family there, I need not say that I shall be delighted to give you a letter to those who would die to serve me.

Always yours.

DEVONSHIRE TERRACE, Mr. W. C. Macready.
Friday Evening, Seventeenth October, 1845.

MY DEAR MACREADY,

    You once—only once—gave the world assurance of a waistcoat. You wore it, sir, I think, in "Money." It was a remarkable and precious waistcoat, wherein certain broad stripes of blue or purple disported themselves as by a combination of extraordinary circumstances, too happy to occur again. I have seen it on your manly chest in private life. I saw it, sir, I think, the other day in the cold light of morning—with feelings easier to be imagined than described. Mr. Macready, sir, are you a father? If so, lend me that waistcoat for five minutes. I am bidden to a wedding (where fathers are made), and my artist cannot, I find (how should he?), imagine such a waistcoat. Let me show it to him as a sample of my tastes and wishes; and—ha, ha, ha, ha!—eclipse the bridegroom!

    I will send a trusty messenger at half-past nine precisely, in the morning. He is sworn to secrecy. He durst not for his life betray us, or swells in ambuscade would have the waistcoat at the cost of his heart's blood.

Thine,
THE UNWAISTCOATED ONE.

* Madame De la Rue.   † Mrs. Thompson.

Mr. H. P.
Smith.

DEVONSHIRE TERRACE, *Fourth November*, 1845.

MY DEAR SMITH,

My chickens and their little aunt will be delighted to do honour to the Lord Mayor on the ninth. So should I be, but I am hard at it, grinding my teeth.

I came down with Thompson the other day, hoping to see you. You were keeping it up, however, in some holiday region, and your glass-case looked like a large pantry, out of which some giant had stolen the meat.

Best regards to Mrs. Smith from all of us.

Always, my dear Smith, faithfully yours.

Mr. Macvey
Napier.

Tenth November, 1845.

MY DEAR SIR,

I write to you in great haste. I most bitterly regret the being obliged to disappoint and inconvenience you (as I fear I shall do), but I find it will be *impossible* for me to write the paper on Capital Punishment for your next number. The fault is really not mine. I have been involved for the last fortnight in one maze of distractions, which nothing could have enabled me to anticipate or prevent. Everything I have had to do has been interfered with and cast aside. I have never in my life had so many insuperable obstacles crowded into the way of my pursuits. It is as little my fault, believe me, as though I were ill and wrote to you from my bed. And pray bear as gently as you can with the vexation I occasion you, when I tell you how very heavily it falls upon myself.

Faithfully yours.

Viscount
Morpeth.

DEVONSHIRE TERRACE, *Twenty-eighth November*, 1845.

MY DEAR LORD MORPETH,

I have delayed writing to you until now, hoping I might have been able to tell you of our dramatic plans, and of the day on which we purpose playing. But as these matters are still in abeyance, I will give you that precious information when I come into the receipt of it myself. And let me heartily assure you, that I had at least as much pleasure in seeing you the other day as you can possibly have had in seeing me; and that I shall consider all opportunities of becoming better known to you among the most fortunate and desirable occasions of my life. And that I am with your conviction about the probability of our liking each other, and, as Lord Lyndhurst might say, with " something more."

Ever faithfully yours.

1846.

NARRATIVE.

In the spring of this year Charles Dickens gave up the editorship of *The Daily News*, and finally all connection with that journal, and went again abroad with his family; the house in Devonshire Terrace being let for twelve months. He made his summer residence at Lausanne, taking a villa (Rosemont) there, from May till November. Here he wrote "The Battle of Life," and the first number of "Dombey and Son." In November he removed to Paris, where he took a house in the Rue de Courcelles for the winter, and where he lived and was at work upon "Dombey" until March, 1847. Among the English residents that summer at Lausanne he made many friendships, in proof of which he dedicated the Christmas book written there to his "English friends at Lausanne." The especially intimate friendships which he formed were with M. De Cerjat, who was always a resident of Lausanne; with Mr. Haldimand, whose name was identified with the place; and with the Hon. Richard and Mrs. Watson, of Rockingham Castle. He maintained a constant correspondence with Mr. and Mrs. Watson, and afterwards dedicated to them his own favourite of all his books, "David Copperfield." M. De Cerjat, from the time of Charles Dickens' leaving Lausanne, began a custom, which he kept up almost without an interval to the time of his own death, of writing him a long letter every Christmas, to which Charles Dickens returned answers, which will be given in this and the following years.

In this year we have the commencement of his association and correspondence with Mr. W. H. Wills. Their connection began in the short term of his editorship of *The Daily News*, when he at once fully appreciated Mr. Wills' invaluable business qualities. And when, some time later, he started his own periodical, "Household Words," he thought himself very fortunate in being able to secure Mr. Wills' co-operation as editor of that journal, and afterwards of "All the Year Round," with which "Household Words" was incorporated. They worked together on terms of the most perfect mutual understanding, confidence, and affectionate regard, until Mr. Wills' health made it necessary for him to retire from the work in 1868.

Our first letters to the Rev. James White, Mr. Walter Savage Landor, and Miss Marion Ely (the niece of Lady Talfourd), all dear friends of Charles Dickens, are also given in this year.

We give also a note to Mr. W. J. Fox, afterwards M.P. for Oldham, well known for his eloquent advocacy of the Repeal of the Corn Laws, who was engaged to write the political articles in the first numbers of *The Daily News.*

Mr. W. J. Fox.

OFFICE OF "THE DAILY NEWS," WHITEFRIARS, *Twenty-first January,* 1846.

MY DEAR FOX,

The boy is in waiting. I need not tell you how our Printer failed us last night.* I hope for better things to-night, and am bent on a fight for it. If we can get a good paper to-morrow, I believe we are as safe as such a thing can be.

Your leader most excellent. I made bold to take out ——— for reasons that I hinted at the other day, and which I think have validity in them. He is unscrupulous and indiscreet. Cobden never so.

It didn't offend you?

Ever faithfully.

Mr. T. J. Thompson.

ROSEMONT, *Tuesday Morning.*

MY DEAR THOMPSON,

All kinds of hearty and cordial congratulations on the event.† We are all delighted that it is at last well over. There is an uncertainty attendant on angelic strangers (as Miss Tox says) which it is a great relief to have so happily disposed of.

Ever yours.

Mr. W. H. Wills.

DEVONSHIRE TERRACE, *Eighteenth February,* 1846.

MY DEAR MR. WILLS,

Do look at the enclosed from Mrs. What's-her-name. For a surprising audacity it is remarkable even to me, who am positively bullied, and all but beaten, by these people. I wish you would do me the favour to write to her (in your own name and from your own address), stating that you answered her letter as you did, because if I were the wealthiest nobleman in England I could not keep pace with one-twentieth part of the demands upon me, and because you saw no internal evidence in her application to induce you to single it out for any especial notice. That the tone of this letter renders you exceedingly glad you did so; and that you decline, from me, holding any correspondence with her. Something to that effect, after what flourish your nature will.

Faithfully yours always.

* The first issue of *The Daily News* was a sad failure, as to printing.
† The birth, at Lausanne, of Mr. Thompson's eldest daughter—now Mrs. Butler,

1, Devonshire Terrace, York Gate, Regent's Park,   Rev. James
Twenty-fourth February, 1846.   White.

I cannot help telling you, my dear White, for I can think of no formal use of Mister to such a writer as you, that I have just now read your tragedy, "The Earl of Gowrie," with a delight which I should in vain endeavour to express to you. Considered with reference to its story, or its characters, or its noble poetry, I honestly regard it as a work of most remarkable genius. It has impressed me powerfully and enduringly. I am proud to have received it from your hand. And if I have to tell you what complete possession it has taken of me—that is, if I *could* tell you —I do believe you would be glad to know it.

Always faithfully yours.

Devonshire Terrace, *Second March*, 1846.   Countess of
  Blessington.

Many thanks for the letters! I will take the greatest care of them, though I blush to find how little they deserve it.

It vexes me very much that I am going out on Friday, and cannot help it. I have no strength of mind, I am afraid. I am always making engagements in which there is no prospect of satisfaction.

Vague thoughts of a new book are rife within me just now; and I go wandering about at night into the strangest places, according to my usual propensity at such a time, seeking rest, and finding none. As an addition to my composure, I ran over a little dog in the Regent's Park yesterday (killing him on the spot), and gave his little mistress, a girl of thirteen or fourteen, such exquisite distress as I never saw the like of.

I must have some talk with you about those American singers.* They must never go back to their own country without your having heard them sing Hood's "Bridge of Sighs." My God, how sorrowful and pitiful it is!

Best regards to Count D'Orsay and the young ladies.

Devonshire Terrace, *Fourth March*, 1846.   Mr. W. H.
  Wills.
My dear Mr. Wills,

I assure you I am very truly and unaffectedly sensible of your earnest friendliness, and in proof of my feeling its worth I shall unhesitatingly trouble you sometimes, in the fullest reliance on your meaning what you say. The letter from Nelson Square is a very manly and touching one. But I am more helpless in

---

* The "Hutchinson Family," consisting of four brothers and a sister, who came to London to give a musical entertainment shortly after Charles Dickens' return from his first visit to America. He had a great interest in, and liking for, these young people.

such a case as that than in any other, having really fewer means of helping such a gentleman to employment than I have of firing off the guns in the Tower. Such appeals come to me here in scores upon scores.

The letter from Little White Lion Street does not impress me favourably. It is not written in a simple or truthful manner, I am afraid, and is *not* a good reference. Moreover, I think it probable that the writer may have deserted some pursuit for which he is qualified, for vague and laborious strivings which he has no pretensions to make. However, I will certainly act on your impression of him, whatever it may be. And if you could explain to the gentleman in Nelson Square, that I am not evading his request, but that I do not know of anything to which I can recommend him, it would be a great relief to me.

Tell Powell (with my regards) that he needn't " deal with " the American notices of the " Cricket." I never read one word of their abuse, and I should think it base to read their praises. It is something to know that one is righted so soon ; and knowing that, I can afford to know no more.

Ever faithfully yours.

Mr.
Clarkson
Stanfield,
R.A.

DEVONSHIRE TERRACE, *Sixth March*, 1846.

MY DEAR STANNY,

In reference to the damage of the candlesticks, I beg to quote (from " The Cricket on the Hearth," by the highly popular and deservedly so Dick) this reply :

"I'll damage you if you enquire:"

Ever yours,

My block-reeving,

Main-brace splicing,

Lead-heaving,

Ship-conning,

Stun'sail-bending,

Deck-swabbing

Son of a sea-cook,

HENRY BLUFF,

H.M.S. *Timber.*

Mr. Charles
Knight.

DEVONSHIRE TERRACE, *Saturday,*
Thirteenth April, 1846.

MY DEAR SIR,

Do you recollect sending me your biography of Shakespeare last autumn, and my not acknowledging its receipt ? I do, with remorse.

The truth is, that I took it out of town with me, read it with great pleasure as a charming piece of honest enthusiasm and perseverance, kept it by me, came home, meant to say all manner of things to you, suffered the time to go by, got ashamed, thought of speaking to you, never saw you, felt it heavy on my mind, and now fling off the load by thanking you heartily, and hoping you will not think it too late.

> Always believe me,
> Faithfully yours.

DEVONSHIRE TERRACE, *Sunday,*   Miss Ely.
Nineteenth April, 1846.

MY DEAR MISS ELY,

A mysterious emissary brought me a note in your always welcome handwriting at the Athenæum last night. I enquired of the servant in attendance whether the bearer of this letter was of my vast establishment. To which he replied, "Yezzir." "Then," said I, "tell him not to wait."

Maclise was with me. It was then half-past seven. We had been walking, and were splashed to the eyes. We debated upon the possibility of getting to Russell Square in reasonable time— decided that it would be in the worst taste to appear when the performance would be half over—and very reluctantly decided not to come. You may suppose how dirty and dismal we were when we went to the Thames Tunnel, of all places in the world, instead !

When I came home here at midnight I found another letter from you (I left off in this place to press it dutifully to my lips). Then my mind misgave me that *you* must have sent to the Athenæum. At the apparent rudeness of my reply, my face, as Hadji Baba says, was turned upside down, and fifty donkeys sat upon my father's grave—or would have done so, but for his not being dead yet.

Therefore I send this humble explanation—protesting, however, which I do most solemnly, against being invited under such untoward circumstances ; and claiming as your old friend and no less old admirer to be instantly invited to the next performance, if such a thing is ever contemplated.

> Ever, my dear Miss Ely,
> Faithfully yours.

GENEVA, *Saturday, Twenty-fourth October,* 1846.   Mr. W. C.
Macready.

MY DEAR MACREADY,

The welcome sight of your handwriting moves me (though I have nothing to say) to show you mine, and if I could recollect the passage in Virginius I would paraphrase it, and say, "Does it seem to tremble, boy? Is it a loving autograph? Does it beam with friendship and affection?" all of which I say, as I write, with—oh Heaven!—such a splendid imitation of you, and finally give you one of those grasps and shakes with which I have seen you make the young Icilius stagger again.

Here I am, running away from a bad headache as Tristram Shandy ran away from death, and lodging for a week in the Hôtel de l'Écu de Genève, wherein there is a large mirror shattered by a cannon-ball in the late revolution. A revolution, whatever its merits, achieved by free spirits, nobly generous and moderate, even in the first transports of victory, elevated by a splendid popular education, and bent on freedom from all tyrants, whether their crowns be shaven or golden. The newspapers may tell you what they please. I believe there is no country on earth but Switzerland in which a violent change could have been effected in the Christian spirit shown in this place, or in the same proud, independent, gallant style. Not one halfpennyworth of property was lost, stolen, or strayed. Not one atom of party malice survived the smoke of the last gun. Nothing is expressed in the government addresses to the citizens but a regard for the general happiness, and injunctions to forget all animosities; which they are practically obeying at every turn, though the late Government (of whose spirit I had some previous knowledge) did load the guns with such material as should occasion gangrene in the wounds, and though the wounded *do* die, consequently, every day, in the hospital, of sores that in themselves were nothing.

You a mountaineer! *You* examine (I have seen you do it) the point of your young son's bâton de montagne before he went up into the snow! And *you* talk of coming to Lausanne in March! Why, Lord love your heart, William Tell, times are changed since you lived at Altorf. There is not a mountain pass open until June. The snow is closing in on all the panorama already. I was at the Great St. Bernard two months ago, and it was bitter cold and frosty then. Do you think I could let you hazard your life by going up any pass worth seeing in bleak March? Never shall it be said that Dickens sacrificed his friend upon the altar of his hospitality! Onward! To Paris! (Cue for band. Dickens points off with truncheon, first entrance P.S. Page delivers gauntlets on one knee. Dickens puts 'em on and gradually falls into a fit of musing. Mrs. Dickens lays her hand upon his shoulder. Business. Procession. Curtain.)

It is a great pleasure to me, my dear Macready, to hear from yourself, as I had previously heard from Forster, that you are so well pleased with "Dombey," which is evidently a great success and a great hit, thank God! I felt that Mrs. Brown was strong, but I was not at all afraid of giving as heavy a blow as I could to a piece of hot iron that lay ready at my hand. For that is my principle always, and I hope to come down with some heavier sledge-hammers than that.

Your most affectionate Friend.

PARIS, November, 1846.   Mr. Haldimand.

*   *   *   *   *

Talking of which * reminds me to say, that I have written to my printers, and told them to prefix to "The Battle of Life" a dedication that is printed in illuminated capitals on my heart. It is only this:

"This Christmas book is cordially inscribed to my English friends in Switzerland."

I shall trouble you with a little parcel of three or four copies to distribute to those whose names will be found written in them, as soon as they can be made ready, and believe me, that there is no success or approval in the great world beyond the Jura that will be more precious and delightful to me, than the hope that I shall be remembered of an evening in the coming winter time, at one or two friends' I could mention near the Lake of Geneva. It runs with a spring tide, that will always flow and never ebb, through my memory; and nothing less than the waters of Lethe shall confuse the music of its running, until it loses itself in that great sea, for which all the currents of our life are desperately bent.

*   *   *   *   *

PARIS, Sunday, Twenty-second November, 1846.   Mr. Walter Savage Landor.

YOUNG MAN,

    I will not go there if I can help it. I have not the least confidence in the value of your introduction to the Devil. I can't help thinking that it would be of better use "the other way, the other way," but I won't try it there, either, at present, if I can help it. Your godson says is that your duty ! and he begs me to enclose a blush newly blushed for you.

As to writing, I have written to you twenty times and twenty more to that, if you only knew it. I have been writing a little Christmas book, besides, expressly for you. And if you don't like it, I shall go to the font of Marylebone Church as soon as I conveniently can and renounce you: I am not to be trifled with. I

* "The Battle of Life."

write from Paris.   I am getting up some French steam.   I intend to proceed upon the longing-for-a-lap-of-blood-at-last principle, and if you *do* offend me, look to it.

We are all well and happy, and they send loves to you by the bushel.   We are in the agonies of house-hunting.   The people are frightfully civil, and grotesquely extortionate.   One man (with a house to let) told me yesterday that he loved the Duke of Wellington like a brother.   The same gentleman wanted to hug me round the neck with one hand, and pick my pocket with the other.

Don't be hard upon the Swiss.   They are a thorn in the sides of European despots, and a good wholesome people to live near Jesuit-ridden kings on the brighter side of the mountains.   My hat shall ever be ready to be thrown up, and my glove ever be ready to be thrown down for Switzerland.   If you were the man I took you for, when I took you (as a godfather) for better and for worse, you would come to Paris and amaze the weak walls of the house I haven't found yet with that steady snore of yours, which I once heard piercing the door of your bedroom in Devonshire Terrace, reverberating along the bell-wire in the hall, so getting outside into the street, playing Eolian harps among the area railings, and going down the New Road like the blast of a trumpet.

I forgive you your reviling of me : there's a shovelful of live coals for your head—does it burn ?   And am, with true affection— does it burn now ?—

Ever yours.

Hon.
Richard
Watson.

PARIS, 48, RUE DE COURCELLES, ST. HONORÉ,
Friday, Twenty-seventh November, 1846.

MY DEAR WATSON,

We were housed only yesterday.   I lose no time in despatching this memorandum of our whereabouts, in order that you may not fail to write me a line before you come to Paris on your way towards England, letting me know on what day we are to expect you to dinner.

We arrived here quite happily and well.   I don't mean here, but at the Hôtel Brighton, in Paris, on Friday evening, between six and seven o'clock.   The agonies of house-hunting were frightfully severe.   It was one paroxysm for four mortal days.   I am proud to express my belief, that we are lodged at last in the most preposterous house in the world.   The like of it cannot, and so far as my knowledge goes does not, exist in any other part of the globe.   The bedrooms are like opera-boxes.   The dining-rooms, staircases, and passages, quite inexplicable. The dining-room is a sort of cavern, painted (ceiling and all) to represent a grove, with unaccountable bits of looking-glass sticking in among the branches of the trees. There is a gleam of reason in the drawing-room. But it is approached through a series of small chambers, like the joints in a telescope, which are hung with inscrutable drapery. The maddest man in Bedlam, having the materials given him, would be likely to devise such a suite, supposing his case to be hopeless and quite incurable.

Pray tell Mrs. Watson, with my best regards, that the dance of the two sisters in the little Christmas book is being done as an illustration by Maclise; and that Stanfield is doing the battle-ground and the outside of the Nutmeg Grater Inn. Maclise is also drawing some smaller subjects for the little story, and they write me that they hope it will be very pretty, and they think that I shall like it. I shall have been in London before I see you, probably, and I hope the book itself will then be on its road to Lausanne to speak for itself, and to speak a word for me too. I have never left so many friendly and cheerful recollections in any place; and to represent me in my absence, its tone should be very eloquent and affectionate indeed.

Well, if I don't turn up again next summer it shall not be my fault. In the meanwhile, I shall often and often look that way with my mind's eye, and hear the sweet, clear, bell-like voice of ———— with the ear of my imagination. In the event of there being any change—but it is not likely—in the appearance of ————'s cravat behind, where it goes up into his head, I mean, and frets against his wig—I hope some one of my English friends will apprise me of it, for the love of the great Saint Bernard.

I have not seen Lord Normanby yet. I have not seen anything up to this time but houses and lodgings. I saw the king the other day coming into Paris. His carriage was surrounded by guards on horseback, and he sat very far back in it, I thought, and drove at a great pace. It was strange to see the préfet of police on horseback some hundreds of yards in advance, looking to the right and left as he rode, like a man who suspected every twig in every tree in the long avenue.

Mrs. Dickens and her sister desire their best regards to be sent to you and their best loves to Mrs. Watson, in which I join, as nearly as I may. Believe me, with great truth,

Very sincerely yours.

M. De
Cerjat.

PARIS, RUE DE COURCELLES, ST. HONORÉ,
Friday, Twenty-seventh November, 1846.

MY DEAR CERJAT,

When we turned out of your view on that disconsolate
Monday, when you so kindly took horse and rode forth to say
good-bye, we went on in a very dull and drowsy manner, I can
assure you. I could have borne a world of punch in the rumble,
and been none the worse for it. There was an uncommonly cool
inn that night, and quite a monstrous establishment at Auxonne
the next night, full of flatulent passages and banging doors. The
next night we passed at Montbard, where there is one of the very
best little inns in all France. The next at Sens, and so we got
here. The roads were bad, but not very for French roads. There
was no deficiency of horses anywhere; and after Pontarlier the
weather was really not too cold for comfort. They weighed our
plate at the frontier custom-house, spoon by spoon, and fork by
fork, and we lingered about there, in a thick fog and a hard frost,
for three long hours and a half, during which the officials committed all manner of absurdities, and got into all sorts of disputes
with my brave courier. This was the only misery we encountered
—except leaving Lausanne, and that was enough to last us and
did last us all the way here. We are living on it now. I felt,
myself, much as I should think the murderer felt on that fair
morning when, with his gray-haired victim (those unconscious gray
hairs, soon to be bedabbled with blood), he went so far towards
heaven as the top of that mountain of St. Bernard without one
touch of remorse. A weight is on my breast. The only difference
between me and the murderer is, that his weight was guilt and
mine is regret.

I haven't a word of news to tell you. I shouldn't write at all
if I were not the vainest man in the world, impelled by a belief
that you will be glad to hear from me, even though you hear no
more than that I have nothing to say. "Dombey" is doing
wonders. Keeley and his wife are making great preparations for
producing the Christmas story, and I have made them (as an old
stage-manager) carry out one or two expensive notions of mine
about scenery and so forth—in particular a sudden change from
the inside of the doctor's house in the midst of the ball to the
orchard in the snow—which ought to tell very well. But actors
are so bad, in general, and the best are spread over so many
theatres, that the "cast" is black despair and moody madness.
There is no one to be got for Marion but a certain Miss ——
I am afraid—a pupil of Miss Kelly's, who acted in the private
theatricals I got up a year ago. Macready took her afterwards to

play Virginia to his Virginius, but she made nothing of it, great as the chance was. I have promised to show her what I mean, as near as I can, and if you will look into the English Opera House on the morning of the seventeenth, eighteenth, or ninteenth of next month, between the hours of eleven and four, you will find me in a very hot and dusty condition, playing all the parts of the piece, to the immense diversion of all the actors, actresses, scene-shifters, carpenters, musicians, chorus people, tailors, dress-makers, scene-painters, and general ragamuffins of the theatre.

Moore, the poet, is very ill—I fear dying. The last time I saw him was immediately before I left London, and I thought him sadly changed and tamed, but not much more so than such a man might be under the heavy hand of time. I believe he suffered severe grief in the death of a son some time ago. The first man I met in Paris was ——, who took hold of me as I was getting into a coach at the door of the hotel. He hadn't a button on his shirt (but I don't think he ever has), and you might have sown what boys call "mustard and cress" in the dust on his coat. There seems reason to fear that the growing dissensions between England and France, and the irritation of the French king, may lead to the withdrawal of the minister on each side of the Channel.

Have you cut down any more trees, played any more rubbers, propounded any more teasers to the players at the game of Yes and No? How is the old horse? How is the gray mare? How is Crab (to whom my respectful compliments)? Have you tried the punch yet; if yes, did it succeed; if no, why not? Is Mrs. Cerjat as happy and as well as I would have her, and all your house ditto ditto? Does Haldimand play whist with any science yet? Ha, ha, ha! the idea of his saying *I* hadn't any! And are those damask-cheeked virgins, the Miss ——, still sleeping on dewy rose leaves near the English church?

Remember me to all your house, and most of all to its other head, with all the regard and earnestness that a "numble individual" (as they always call it in the House of Commons) who once travelled with her in a car over a smooth country may charge you with. I have added two lines to the little Christmas book, that I hope both you and she may not dislike. Haldimand will tell you what they are. Kate and Georgy send their kindest loves. Believe me always, my dear Cerjat, full of cordial and hearty recollections of this past summer and autumn, and your part in my part of them,

Very faithfully your Friend.

48, Rue de Courcelles, St. Honoré, Paris,
Second December, 1846.

MY DEAR THOMPSON,

We got to Paris, in due course, on the Friday evening. We had a pleasant and prosperous journey, having rather cold weather in Switzerland and on the borders thereof, and a slight detention of three hours and a half at the frontier Custom House, atop of a mountain, in a hard frost and a dense fog. We came into this house last Thursday. It has a pretty drawing-room, approached through four most extraordinary chambers. It is the most ridiculous and preposterous house in the world, I should think. It belongs to a Marquis Castellane, but was fitted (so Paul Pry Poole said, who dined here yesterday) by —— in a fit of temporary insanity, I have no doubt. The dining-room is mere midsummer madness, and is designed to represent a bosky grove.

At this present writing, snow is falling in the street, and the weather is very cold, but not so cold as it was yesterday. I dined with Lord Normanby on Sunday last. Everything seems to be queer and uncomfortable in the diplomatic way, and he is rather bothered and worried, to my thinking. I found young Sheridan (Mrs. Norton's brother) the attaché. I know him very well, and he is a good man for my sight-seeing purposes. There are to be no theatricals unless the times should so adjust themselves as to admit of their being French, to which the Markis seems to incline, as a bit of conciliation and a popular move.

Lumley, of Italian opera notoriety, also dined here yesterday, and seems hugely afeard of the opposition opera at Covent Garden, who have already spirited away Grisi and Mario, which he affects to consider a great comfort and relief. I gave him some uncompromising information on the subject of his pit, and told him that if he didn't conciliate the middle classes, he might depend on being damaged, very decidedly. The danger of the Covent Garden enterprise seems to me to be that they are going in for ballet too, and I really don't think the house is large enough to repay the double expense.

Forster writes me that Mac has come out with tremendous vigour in the Christmas Book, and took off his coat at it with a burst of such alarming energy that he has done four subjects ! Stanfield has done three. Keeleys are making that "change"* I was so hot upon at Lausanne, and seem ready to spend money with bold hearts. Mr. Leigh Murray, from the Princess's, is to be the Alfred, and Forster says there is a Mrs. Gordon at Bolton's who must be got for Grace. I am horribly afraid —— will do

* In the dramatised "Battle of Life."

one of the lawyers, and there seems to be nobody but —— for Marion. I shall run over and carry consternation into the establishment, as soon as I have done the number. But I have not begun it yet, though I hope to do so to-night, having been quite put out by chopping and changing about, and by a vile touch of biliousness, that makes my eyes feel as if they were yellow bullets. "Dombey" has passed its thirty thousand already. Do you remember a mysterious man in a straw hat low-crowned, and a Petersham coat, who was a sort of manager or amateur man-servant at Miss Kelly's? Mr. Baynton Bolt, sir, came out, the other night, as Macbeth, at the Royal Surrey Theatre.

There's all my news for you! Let me know, in return, whether you have fought a duel yet with your milingtary landlord, and whether Lausanne is still that giddy world of dissipation it was wont to be, also full particulars of your fairer and better half, and of the baby. I will send a Christmas book to Clermont as soon as I get any copies. And so no more at present from yours ever.

58, LINCOLN'S INN FIELDS, *Saturday, Nineteenth December*, 1846.

Mrs. Charles Dickens.

MY DEAREST KATE,

I really am bothered to death by this confounded *dramatisation* of the Christmas book. They were in a state so horrible at Keeley's yesterday (as perhaps Forster told you when he wrote), that I was obliged to engage to read the book to them this morning. It struck me that Mr. Leigh Murray, Miss Daly, and Vining seemed to understand it best. Certainly Miss Daly knew best what she was about yesterday. At eight to-night we have a rehearsal with scenery and band, and everything but dresses. I see no possibility of escaping from it before one or two o'clock in the morning. And I was at the theatre all day yesterday. Unless I had come to London, I do not think there would have been much hope of the version being more than just tolerated, even that doubtful. All the actors bad, all the business frightfully behind-hand. The very words of the book confused in the copying into the densest and most insufferable nonsense. I must exempt, however, from the general slackness both the Keeleys. I hope they will be very good. I have never seen anything of its kind better than the manner in which they played the little supper scene between Clemency and Britain, yesterday. It was quite perfect, even to me.

The small manager, Forster, Talfourd, Stanny, and Mac dine with me at the Piazza to-day, before the rehearsal. I have already one or two uncommonly good stories of Mac. I reserve them for narration. I have also a dreadful cold, which I would not reserve if I could help it. I can hardly hold up my head, and fight through from hour to hour, but had serious thoughts just now of walking off to bed.

Christmas book published to-day—twenty-three thousand copies already gone ! ! !

Believe me, my love,
Most affectionately.

Mrs. Charles
Dickens.

PIAZZA COFFEE-HOUSE, COVENT GARDEN,
Monday, Twenty-first December, 1846.

MY DEAREST KATE,

In a quiet interval of half an hour before going to dine at Macready's, I sit down to write you a few words. But I shall reserve my letter for to-morrow's post, in order that you may hear what *I* hear of the "going" of the play to-night. Think of my being there on Saturday, with a really frightful cold, and working harder than ever I did at the amateur plays, until two in the morning. There was no supper to be got, either here or anywhere else, after coming out; and I was as hungry and thirsty as need be. The scenery and dresses are very good indeed, and they have spent money on it *liberally*. The great change from the ball-room to the snowy night is most effective, and both the departure and the return will tell, I think, strongly on an audience. I have made them very quick and excited in the passionate scenes, and so have infused some appearance of life into those parts of the play. But I can't make a Marion, and Miss —— is awfully bad. She is a mere nothing all through. I put Mr. Leigh Murray into such a state, by making him tear about, that the perspiration ran streaming down his face. They have a great let. I believe every place in the house is taken. Roche is going.

Tuesday Morning.—The play went, as well as I can make out —I hoped to have had Stanny's report of it, but he is ill—with great effect. There was immense enthusiasm at its close, and great uproar and shouting for me. Forster will go on Wednesday, and write you his account of it. I saw the Keeleys on the stage at eleven o'clock or so, and they were in prodigious spirits and delight.

Mr. John
Forster.

48, RUE DE COURCELLES, PARIS,
Sunday Night, Twenty-seventh December, 1846.

MY VERY DEAR FORSTER,

Amen, amen. Many merry Christmases, many happy new years, unbroken friendship, great accumulation of cheerful recollections, affection on earth, and heaven at last for all of us.

I enclose you a letter from Jeffrey, which you may like to read. *Bring it to me back when you come over.* I have told him all he wants to know. Is it not a strange example of the hazards of writing in numbers that a man like him should form his notion of Dombey and Miss Tox on three months' knowledge? I have asked him the same question, and advised him to keep his eye on both of them as time rolls on.

We had a cold journey here from Boulogne, but the roads were not very bad. The malle poste, however, now takes the trains at Amiens. We missed it by ten minutes, and had to wait three hours—from twelve o'clock until three, in which interval I drank brandy and water, and slept like a top. It is delightful travelling for its speed, that malle poste, and really for its comfort too. But on this occasion it was not remarkable for the last-named quality. The director of the post at Boulogne told me a lamentable story of his son at Paris being ill, and implored me to bring him on. The brave doubted the representations altogether, but I couldn't find it in my heart to say no; so we brought the director, bodkinwise, and being a large man, in a great number of greatcoats, he crushed us dismally until we got to the railroad. For two passengers (and it never carries more) it is capital. For three, excruciating.

Write to Poole what you have said to me. You need write no more. He is full of vicious fancies and wrong suspicions, even of Hardwick, and I would rather he heard it from you than from me, whom he is not likely to love much in his heart. I doubt it may be but a rusty instrument for want of use, the Pooleish heart.

My most important present news is that I am going to take a jorum of hot rum and egg in bed immediately, and to cover myself up with all the blankets in the house. I have a sensation in my head, as if it were "on edge." It is still very cold here, but the snow had disappeared on my return, both here and on the road, except within ten miles or so of Boulogne.

Ever affectionately.

1847.

NARRATIVE.

AT the beginning of the year Charles Dickens was still living in Paris—Rue de Courcelles. His stay there was cut shorter than he intended it to have been, by the illness from scarlet fever of his eldest son, who was at school in London. Consequent upon this, Charles Dickens and his wife went to London at the end of February, taking up their abode at the Victoria Hotel, Euston

Square, the Devonshire Terrace house being still occupied by its tenant, Sir James Duke. The sick boy was under the care of his grandmother, Mrs. Hogarth, in Albany Street. The children, with their aunt, remained in Paris, until a temporary house had been taken for the family in Chester Place, Regent's Park; and Roche was then sent back to take *all* home. In Chester Place another son was born—Sydney Smith Haldimand—his godfathers being Mr. Haldimand, of Lausanne, and Mr. H. P. Smith, of the Eagle Life Assurance office. He was christened at the same time as a daughter of Mr. Macready's, and the letters to Mr. Smith have reference to the postponement of the christening on Mr. Smith's account. In May, Charles Dickens had lodgings in Brighton for some weeks, for the recovery of Mrs. Dickens' health; going there first with his wife and sister-in-law and the eldest boy—now recovered from his fever—and being joined at the latter part of the time by his two little daughters, to whom there are some letters among those which follow here. He removed earlier than usual this summer to Broadstairs, which remained his head-quarters until October, with intervals of absence for amateur theatrical tours (which Mr. Forster calls "splendid strolling"), in which he was usually accompanied by his wife and sister-in-law. Several new recruits had been added to the theatrical company, from among distinguished literary men and artists, and it now included, besides those previously named, Mr. George Cruikshank, Mr. George Henry Lewes, and Mr. Augustus Egg; Charles Dickens being always the supreme manager of the company. "Every Man in his Humour" and farces were again played at Manchester and Liverpool, for the benefit of Mr. Leigh Hunt, and the dramatic author, Mr. John Poole.

By the end of the Broadstairs holiday, the house in Devonshire Terrace was vacant, and the family returned to it in October. All this year Charles Dickens had been at work upon the monthly numbers of "Dombey and Son," in spite of these many interruptions. He began at Broadstairs a Christmas book. But he found that the engrossing interest of his novel as it approached completion made it impossible for him to finish the other work in time. So he decided to let this Christmas pass without a story, and postponed the publication of "The Haunted Man" until the following year.

At the close of the year he went to Leeds, to take the chair at a meeting of the Mechanics' Institute, and on the Twenty-eighth December he presided at the opening of the Glasgow Athenæum; he and his wife being the guests of the historian—*then* Mr. Sheriff, afterwards Sir Archibald, Alison. From a letter to his sister-in-law, written from Edinburgh, it will be seen that Mrs. Dickens was prevented by sudden illness from being present at the "demonstration." At the end of this letter there is another illustration of the odd names he was in the habit of giving to his children, the last of the three, the "Hoshen Peck," being a corruption of "Ocean Spectre" —a name which had, afterwards, a sad significance, as the boy (Sydney Smith) became a sailor, and died and was buried at sea two years after his father's death.

The letters in this year need very little explanation. In the first letter to Mrs. Watson, Charles Dickens alludes to a sketch which she had made from "The Battle of Life," and had sent to him, as a remembrance, when her husband paid a short visit to Paris in this winter.

The letter to Mr. Sheridan Knowles was written after some slight misunderstanding, the cause of which is unknown to us.

The Dr. Hodgson, to whom we give a letter, was then Principal of the Liverpool Institute, and Principal of the Charlton High School, Manchester.

Mr. Alexander Ireland was manager and one of the proprietors of *The Manchester Examiner*. The "notice" mentioned in the third letter to Mr. Ireland refers to an essay on "The Genius and Writings of Leigh Hunt," contributed to *The Manchester Examiner*; and "The Working Man's Life," alluded to in this same letter, was the "Autobiography of a Working Man," by "One who has Whistled at the Plough" (Alex. Somerville), and originally appeared in *The Manchester Examiner*, and afterwards was published as a volume in 1848.

In this year we give the only letter we have been able to procure to the famous Danish writer, Hans Christian Andersen.

And there are two letters to Miss Marguerite Power, the niece of the Countess of Blessington—a lady for whom Charles Dickens had then, and until her death, a most affectionate friendship and respect, for the sake of her own admirable qualities, and in remembrance of her delightful association with Gore House, where he was a frequent visitor. For Lady Blessington he had a high admiration and great regard, and she was one of his earliest appreciators; and Alfred, Comte D'Orsay, was also a much-loved friend. His "own marchioness," alluded to in the second letter to Miss Power, was the younger and very charming sister of his correspondent.

We much regret having been unable to procure any letters addressed to Mr. Egg. His intimacy with Charles Dickens began first in the plays of this year; but Mr. Egg became, almost immediately, one of the friends for whom he had an especial affection, and was a regular visitor at his house and at his seaside places of resort for many years after this date.

The letter to Mr. William Sandys has reference to an intention which Charles Dickens *had* entertained, of laying the scene of a story in Cornwall; Mr. Sandys, himself a Cornishman, having proposed to send him some books to help him as to the dialect.

DEVONSHIRE TERRACE, *Twelfth January*, 1847.

MY DEAR SIR EDWARD,

The Committee of the General Theatrical Fund (who are all actors) are anxious to prefer a petition to you to preside at their next annual dinner at the London Tavern, and having no personal knowledge of you, have requested me as one of their Trustees, through their Secretary, Mr. Cullenford, to give them some kind of presentation to you.

I will only say that I have felt great interest in their design, which embraces all sorts and conditions of actors from the first, and it has been maintained by themselves with extraordinary perseverance and determination. It has been in existence some years, but it is only two years since they began to dine. At their first festival I presided, at their second, Macready. They very naturally hold that if they could prevail on you to reign over them now they would secure a most powerful and excellent advocate, whose aid would serve and grace their cause immensely. I sympathise with their feeling so cordially, and know so well that it would certainly be mine if I were in their case (as, indeed, it is, being their friend), that I comply with their request for an introduction. And I will not ask you to excuse my troubling you, feeling sure that I may use this liberty with you.

Believe me always, very faithfully yours.

48, RUE DE COURCELLES, PARIS,
Twenty-fourth January, 1847.

MY DEAR LADY BLESSINGTON,

I feel very wicked in beginning this note, and deeply remorseful for not having begun and ended it long ago. But *you* know how difficult it is to write letters in the midst of a writing life; and as you know too (I hope) how earnestly and affectionately I always think of you, wherever I am, I take heart, on a little consideration, and feel comparatively good again.

Forster has been cramming into the space of a fortnight every description of impossible and inconsistent occupation in the way of sight-seeing. He has been now at Versailles, now in the prisons, now at the opera, now at the hospitals, now at the Conservatoire, and now at the Morgue, with a dreadful insatiability. I begin to doubt whether I had anything to do with a book called "Dombey," or ever sat over number five (not finished a fortnight yet) day after day, until I half began, like the monk in poor Wilkie's story, to think it the only reality in life, and to mistake all the realities for shortlived shadows.

Among the multitude of sights, we saw our pleasant little bud of a friend, Rose Chéri, play Clarissa Harlowe the other night. I believe she does it in London just now, and perhaps you may have seen it. A most charming, intelligent, modest, affecting piece of acting it is, with a death superior to anything I ever saw on the stage, except Macready's Lear. The theatres are admirable just now. We saw "Gentil Bernard" at the Variétés last night, acted in a manner that was absolutely perfect. It was a little picture of Watteau, animated and talking from beginning to end. At the Cirque there is a new show-piece called "The French Revolution," in which there is a representation of the National Convention, and a series of battles (fought by some five hundred people, who look like five thousand) that are wonderful in their extraordinary vigour and truth. Gun-cotton gives its name to the general annual jocose review at the Palais Royal, which is dull enough, saving for the introduction of Alexandre Dumas, sitting in his study beside a pile of quarto volumes about five feet high, which he says is the first tableau of the first act of the first piece to be played on the first night of his new theatre. The revival of Molière's "Don Juan," at the Français, has drawn money. It is excellently played, and it is curious to observe how different *their* Don Juan and valet are from our English ideas of master and man. They are playing "Lucretia Borgia" again at the Porte St. Martin, but it is poorly performed and hangs fire drearily, though a very remarkable and striking play. We were at Victor Hugo's house last Sunday week, a most extraordinary place, looking like an old curiosity shop, or the property-room of some gloomy, vast, old theatre. I was much struck by Hugo himself, who looks like a genius as he is, every inch of him, and is very interesting and satisfactory from head to foot. His wife is a handsome woman, with flashing black eyes. There is also a charming ditto daughter of fifteen or sixteen, with ditto eyes. Sitting among old armour and old tapestry, and old coffers, and grim old chairs and tables, and old canopies of state from old palaces, and old golden lions going to play at skittles with ponderous old golden balls, they made a most romantic show, and looked like a chapter out of one of his own books.

*   *   *   *   *

The Hon
Mrs.
Watson.

PARIS, 48, RUE DE COURCELLES,
Twenty-fifth January, 1847.

MY DEAR MRS. WATSON,

I cannot allow your wandering lord to return to your—I suppose "arms" is not improper—arms, then, without thanking you in half-a-dozen words for your letter, and assuring you that I had great interest and pleasure in its receipt, and that I say Amen to all *you* say of our happy past and hopeful future. There is a picture of Lausanne—St. Bernard—the tavern by the little lake between Lausanne and Vevay, which is kept by that drunken dog whom Haldimand believes to be so sober—and of many other such scenes, within doors and without—that rises up to my mind very often, and in the quiet pleasure of its aspect rather daunts me, as compared with the reality of a stirring life; but, please God, we will have some more pleasant days, and go up some more mountains, somewhere, and laugh together, at somebody, and form the same delightful little circle again, somehow.

I quite agree with you about the illustrations to the little Christmas book. I was delighted with yours. Your good lord before-mentioned will inform you that it hangs up over my chair in the drawing-room here; and when you come to England (after I have seen you again in Lausanne) I will show it you in my little study at home, quietly thanking you on the bookcase. Then we will go and see some of Turner's recent pictures, and decide that question to Haldimand's utmost confusion.

You will find Watson looking wonderfully well, I think. When he was first here, on his way to England, he took an extraordinary bath, in which he was rubbed all over with chemical compounds, and had everything done to him that could be invented for seven francs. It *may* be the influence of this treatment that I see in his face, but I think it's the prospect of coming back to Elysée. All I can say is, that when *I* come that way, and find myself among those friends again, I expect to be perfectly lovely—a kind of Glorious Apollo, radiant and shining with joy.

* * * * *

Rev.
Edward
Tagart.

PARIS, 48, RUE DE COURCELLES, HONORÉ,
Thursday, Twenty-eighth January, 1847.

MY DEAR SIR,

Before you read any more, I wish you would take those tablets out of your drawer, in which you have put a black mark against my name, and erase it neatly. I don't deserve it, on my word I don't, though appearances are against me, I unwillingly confess.

I had gone to Geneva, to recover from an uncommon depression of spirits, consequent on too much sitting over "Dombey" and the little Christmas book, when I received your letter as I was going out walking, one sunshiny, windy day. I read it on the banks of the Rhone, where it runs, very blue and swift, between two high green hills, with ranges of snowy mountains filling up the distance. Its cordial and unaffected tone gave me the greatest pleasure—did me a world of good—set me up for the afternoon, and gave me an evening's subject of discourse. For I talked to "them" (that is Kate and Georgy) about those bright mornings at the Peschiere, until bedtime, and threatened to write you such a letter next day as would—I don't exactly know what it was to do, but it was to be a great letter, expressive of all kinds of pleasant things, and perhaps the most genial letter that ever was written.

From that hour to this, I have again and again and again said, "I'll write to-morrow," and here I am to-day full of penitence— really sorry and ashamed, and with no excuse but my writing-life, which makes me get up and go out, when my morning work is done, and look at pen and ink no more until I begin again.

Besides which, I have been seeing Paris—wandering into hospitals, prisons, dead-houses, operas, theatres, concert-rooms, burial-grounds, palaces, and wine-shops. In my unoccupied fortnight of each month, every description of gaudy and ghastly sight has been passing before me in a rapid panorama. Before that, I had come here from Switzerland, over frosty mountains in dense fogs, and through towns with walls and drawbridges, and without population, or anything else in particular but soldiers and mud. I took a flight to London for four days, and went and came back over one sheet of snow, sea excepted; and I wish that had been snow too. Then Forster (who is here now, and begs me to send his kindest regards) came to see Paris for himself, and in showing it to him, away I was borne again, like an enchanted rider. In short, I have had no rest in my play; and on Monday I am going to work again. A fortnight hence the play will begin once more; a fortnight after that the work will follow round, and so the letters that I care for go unwritten.

Do you care for French news? I hope not, because I don't know any. There is a melodrama, called "The French Revolution," now playing at the Cirque, in the first act of which there is the most tremendous representation of a *people* that can well be imagined. There are wonderful battles and so forth in the piece, but there is a power and massiveness in the mob which is positively awful. At another theatre "Clarissa Harlowe" is still the rage. There are some things in it rather calculated to astonish the ghost of Richardson, but Clarissa is very admirably played, and dies better than the original to my thinking; but Richardson is no great favourite of mine, and never seems to me to take his top-boots off, whatever he does. Several pieces are in course of representation, involving rare portraits of the English. In one, a servant, called "Tom Bob," who wears a particularly English waistcoat trimmed with gold lace and concealing his ankles, does very good things indeed. In another, a Prime Minister of England, who has ruined himself by railway speculations, hits off some of our national characteristics very happily, frequently making incidental mention of "Vishmingster," "Regeenstreet," and other places with which you are well acquainted. "Sir Fakson" is one of the characters in another play—"English to the Core;" and I saw a Lord Mayor of London at one of the small theatres the other night, looking uncommonly well in a stage-coachman's waistcoat, the order of the Garter, and a very low-crowned broad-brimmed hat, not unlike a dustman.

I was at Geneva at the time of the revolution. The moderation and mildness of the successful party were beyond all praise. Their appeals to the people of all parties—printed and pasted on the walls—have no parallel that I know of, in history, for their real good sterling Christianity and tendency to promote the happiness of mankind. My sympathy is strongly with the Swiss radicals. They know what Catholicity is; they see, in some of their own valleys, the poverty, ignorance, misery, and bigotry it always brings in its train wherever it is triumphant; and they would root it out of their children's way at any price. I fear the end of the struggle will be that some Catholic power will step in to crush the dangerously well-educated republics (very dangerous to such neighbours); but there is a spirit in the people, or I very much mistake them, that will trouble the Jesuits there many years, and shake their altar-steps for them.

This is a poor return (I look down and see the end of the paper) for your letter, but in its cordial spirit of reciprocal friendship, it is not so bad a one if you could read it as I do, and it eases my mind and discharges my conscience. We are coming home, please God, at the end of March. You will be glad, I know, to hear that "Dombey" is doing wonders, and that the Christmas book shot far ahead of its predecessors. I hope you will like *the last chapter of No. 5.* If you can spare me a scrap of your handwriting in token of forgiveness, do; if not, I'll come and beg your pardon on the thirty-first of March.

> Ever believe me,
>> Cordially and truly yours.

CHESTER PLACE, *Tuesday Night.* Miss Hogarth.

MY DEAREST GEORGY,

    *   *   *   *   *

So far from having "got through my agonies," as you benevolently hope, I have not yet begun them. Now, on this *ninth of the month* I have not yet written a single slip. What could I do; house-hunting at first, and beleaguered all day to-day and yesterday by furniture that must be altered, and things that must be put away? My wretchedness, just now, is inconceivable. Tell Anne, by-the-bye (not with reference to my wretchedness, but in connection with the arrangements generally), that I can't get on at all without her.

If Kate has not mentioned it, get Katey and Mamey to write and send a letter to Charley; of course not hinting at our being here. He wants to hear from them.

Poor little Hall * is dead, as you will have seen, I dare say, in the paper. This house is very cheerful on the drawing-room floor and above, looking into the park on one side and Albany Street on the other. Forster is mild. Maclise, exceedingly bald on the crown of his head. Roche has just come in to know if he may " blow datter light."

Ever affectionately.

Friday, Ninth April, 1847. Mr. John Forster.

MY DEAR FORSTER,

    Your messenger didn't wait, or cook, who took the note in, said I wasn't at home—or summat of that sort.

The dinner-hour is *six* to-morrow. I have only just begun. I have been trying for three or four days, but really have only just begun. I am particularly anxious not to anticipate in this No. what I design for the next, and consequently must invent and plan for it.

We got a box from Buckstone (Stanny, Mac, and I), and went to the Adelphi the night before last. I think that performance of Miss Woolgar's in "The Flowers of the Forest" the most remarkable and complete piece of melodrama I have ever seen upon the stage; and indeed I question whether I have ever seen anything better. It perfectly amazed me; it is so admirably considered and made out.

Jeffrey is coming here this afternoon at four. I received a note from him this morning. From what he says, I should infer that

---

* Mr. Hall, of the firm of Chapman and Hall.

they will be off with the sun—or wind—to-morrow, and that you won't see Empson * therefore if you don't see him to-day.

Deepest of despondency (as usual in commencing Nos.).

Ever affectionately.

Mr.
Edward
Chapman.

CHESTER PLACE, *Monday, Third May*, 1847.

MY DEAR SIR,

Here is a young lady—Miss Power, Lady Blessington's niece—has "gone and been" and translated a story by Georges Sand, the French writer, which she has printed, and got four woodcuts engraved for. She wants to get it published—something in the form of the Christmas books. I know the story, and it is a very fine one.

Will you do it for her? There is no other risk than putting a few covers on a few copies. Half-profits is what she expects and no loss. She has made appeal to me, and if there is to be a hard-hearted ogre in the business at all, I would rather that it should be you than I; so I have told her I would make proposals to your mightiness.

Answer this straightway, for I have no doubt the fair translator thinks I am tearing backwards and forwards in a cab all day to bring the momentous affair to a conclusion.

Faithfully yours.

Miss
Dickens and
Miss Katey
Dickens.

148, KING'S ROAD, BRIGHTON,
Monday, Twenty-fourth May, 1847.

MY DEAR MAMEY AND KATE,

I was very glad to receive your nice letter. I am going to tell you something that I hope will please you. It is this: I am coming to London on Thursday, and I mean to bring you both back here with me, to stay until we all come home together on the Saturday. I hope you like this.

Tell John to come with the carriage to the London Bridge Station, on Thursday morning at ten o'clock, and to wait there for me. I will then come home and fetch you.

Mamma and Auntey and Charley send their loves. I send mine too, to Walley, Spim, and Alfred, and Sydney.

Always, my dears,
Your affectionate Papa.

* Mr. Empson was the son-in-law of Lord Jeffrey.

148, King's Road, Brighton,
Twenty-sixth May, 1847.

My dear Knowles,

    I have learned, I hope, from the art we both profess (if you will forgive this classification of myself with you) to respect a man of genius in his mistakes, no less than in his triumphs. You have so often read the human heart well that I can readily forgive your reading mine ill, and gieatly wronging me by the supposition that any sentiment towards you but honour and respect has ever found a place in it.

    You write as few lines which, dying, you would wish to blot, as most men. But if you ever know me better, as I hope you may (the fault shall not be mine if you do not), I know you will be glad to have received the assurance that some part of your letter has been written on the sand and that the wind has already blown over it.

Faithfully yours always.

Regent's Park, London,
Friday, Fourth June, 1847.

My dear Sir,

    I have rarely, if ever, seen a more remarkable effort of what I may call intellectual memory than the enclosed. It is evidence, I think, of very uncommon power. I have read it with the greatest interest and surprise, and I am truly obliged to you for giving me the opportunity. If you should see no objection to telling the young lady herself this much, pray do so, as it is sincere praise.

    Your criticism of Coombe's pamphlet is as justly felt as it is earnestly and strongly written. I undergo more astonishment and disgust in connection with that question of education almost every day of my life than is awakened in me by any other member of the whole magazine of social monsters that are walking about in these times.

    You were in my thoughts when your letter arrived this morning, for we have a half-formed idea of reviving our old amateur theatrical company for a special purpose, and even of bringing it bodily to Manchester and Liverpool, on which your opinion would be very valuable. If we should decide on Monday, when we meet, to pursue our idea in this warm weather, I will explain it to you in detail, and ask counsel of you in regard of a performance in Liverpool. Meantime it is mentioned to no one.

    Your interest in " Dombey " gives me unaffected pleasure. I hope you will find no reason to think worse of it as it proceeds. There is a great deal to do—one or two things among the rest that society will not be the worse, I hope, for thinking about a little.

May I beg to be remembered to Mrs. Hodgson? You always remember me yourself, I hope, as one who has a hearty interest in all you do and in all you have so admirably done for the advancement of the best objects.

Always believe me very faithfully yours.

Dr.
Hodgson.

REGENT'S PARK, LONDON,
Twelfth June, 1847.

MY DEAR SIR,

I write to you in reference to a scheme to which you may, perhaps, already have seen some allusion in the London *Athenæum* of to-day.

The party of amateurs connected with literature and art, who acted in London two years ago, have resolved to play again at one of the large theatres here for the benefit of Leigh Hunt, and to make a great appeal to all classes of society in behalf of a writer who should have received long ago, but has not yet, some enduring return from his country for all he has undergone and all the good he has done. It is believed that such a demonstration by literature on behalf of literature, and such a mark of sympathy by authors and artists, for one who has written so well, would be of more service, present and prospective, to Hunt than almost any other means of help that could be devised. And we know, from himself, that it would be most gratifying to his own feelings.

The arrangements are, as yet, in an imperfect state; for the date of their being carried out depends on our being able to get one of the large theatres before the close of the present London season. In the event of our succeeding, we propose acting in London, on Wednesday the fourteenth of July, and on Monday the nineteenth. On the first occasion we shall play "Every Man in his Humour," and a farce; on the second, "The Merry Wives of Windsor," and a farce.

But we do not intend to stop here. Believing that Leigh Hunt has done more to instruct the young men of England, and to lend a helping hand to those who educate themselves, than any writer in England, we are resolved to come down, in a body, to Liverpool and Manchester, and to act one night at each place. And the object of my letter is, to ask you, as the representative of the great educational establishment of Liverpool, whether we can count on your active assistance; whether you will form a committee to advance our object; and whether, if we send you our circulars and addresses, you will endeavour to secure us a full theatre, and to enlist the general sympathy and interest in behalf of the cause we have at heart?

I address, by this post, a letter, which is almost the counterpart of the present, to the honorary secretaries of the Manchester Athenæum. If we find in both towns such a response as we confidently expect, I would propose, on behalf of my friends, that the Liverpool and Manchester Institutions should decide for us, at which town we shall first appear, and which play we shall act in each place.

I forbear entering into any more details, however, until I am favoured with your reply.

Always believe me, my dear Sir,

Faithfully your Friend.

1, DEVONSHIRE TERRACE, *Thirteenth June*, 1847.   Mr. William Sandys.

DEAR SIR,

Many thanks for your kind note. I shall hope to see you when we return to town, from which we shall now be absent (with a short interval in next month) until October. Your account of the Cornishmen gave me great pleasure; and if I were not sunk in engagements so far, that the crown of my head is invisible to my nearest friends, I should have asked you to make me known to them. The new dialogue I will ask you by-and-by to let me see. I have, for the present, abandoned the idea of sinking a shaft in Cornwall.

I have sent your Shakesperian extracts to Collier.* It is a great comfort, to my thinking, that so little is known concerning the poet. It is a fine mystery; and I tremble every day lest something should come out. If he had had a Boswell, society wouldn't have respected his grave, but would calmly have had his skull in the phrenological shop-windows.   Believe me,

Faithfully yours.

CHESTER PLACE, *Fourteenth June*, 1847.   Mr. H. P. Smith.

MY DEAR SMITH,

Haldimand stayed at No. 7, Connaught Place, Hyde Park, when I saw him yesterday. But he was going to cross to Boulogne to-day.

The young Pariah seems pretty comfortable. He is of a cosmopolitan spirit I hope, and stares with a kind of leaden satisfaction at his spoons, without afflicting himself much about the established church.   Affectionately yours.

P.S.—I think of bringing an action against you for a new sort

---

* Mr. John Payne Collier.

of breach of promise, and calling all the bishops to estimate the damage of having our christening postponed for a fortnight. It appears to me that I shall get a good deal of money in this way. If you have any compromise to offer, my solicitors are Dodson and Fogg.

Mr.
Alexander
Ireland.

REGENT'S PARK, LONDON,
Seventeenth June, 1847.

DEAR SIR,

In the hope that I may consider myself personally introduced to you by Dr. Hodgson, of Liverpool, I take the liberty of addressing you in this form.

I hear from that friend of ours, that you are greatly interested in all that relates to Mr. Leigh Hunt, and that you will be happy to promote our design in reference to him. Allow me to assure you of the gratification with which I have received this intelligence, and of the importance we shall attach to all your valuable co-operation.

I have received a letter from Mr. Langley, of the Athenæum, informing me that a committee is in course of formation, composed of directors of that institution (acting as private gentlemen) and others. May I hope to find that you are one of this body, and that I may soon hear of its proceedings, and be in communication with it?

Allow me to thank you beforehand for your interest in the cause, and to look forward to the pleasure of doing so in person, when I come to Manchester.

Dear Sir, very faithfully yours.

The same.

ATHENÆUM CLUB, LONDON,
Saturday, Twenty-sixth June, 1847.

MY DEAR SIR,

The news of Mr. Hunt's pension is quite true. We do not propose to act in London after this change in his affairs, but we DO still distinctly propose to act in Manchester and Liverpool. I have set forth the plain state of the case in a letter to Mr. Robinson by this post (a counterpart of which I have addressed to Liverpool), and to which, in the midst of a laborious correspondence on the subject, I beg to refer to you.

It will be a great satisfaction to us to believe that we shall still be successful in Manchester. There is great and urgent need why we should be so, I assure you.

If you can help to bring the matter speedily into a practical and plain shape, you will render Hunt the greatest service.

I fear, in respect to your kind invitation, that neither Jerrold nor I will feel at liberty to accept it. There was a pathetic proposal among us that we should "keep together"; and, as president of the society, I am bound, I fear, to stand by the brotherhood with particular constancy. Nor do I think that we shall have more than one very short evening in Manchester.

I write in great haste. The sooner I can know (at Broadstairs, in Kent) the Manchester and Liverpool nights, and what the managers say, the better (I hope) will be the entertainments.

My dear Sir, very faithfully yours.

P.S.—I enclose a copy of our London circular, issued before the granting of the pension.

BROADSTAIRS, KENT, *Second July*, 1847.   Miss Power.

MY DEAR MISS POWER,

Let me thank you, very sincerely, for your kind note and for the little book. I read the latter on my way down here with the greatest pleasure. It is a charming story gracefully told, and very gracefully and worthily translated. I have not been better pleased with a book for a long time.

I cannot say I take very kindly to the illustrations. They are a long way behind the tale to my thinking. The artist understands it very well, I dare say, but does not express his understanding of it, in the least degree, to any sense of mine.

Ah Rosherville!. That fated Rosherville, when shall we see it! Perhaps in one of those intervals when I am up to town from here, and suddenly appear at Gore House, somebody will propose an excursion there, next day. If anybody does, somebody else will be ready to go. So this deponent maketh oath and saith.

I am looking out upon a dark gray sea, with a keen north-east wind blowing it in shore. It is more like late autumn than midsummer, and there is a howling in the air as if the latter were in a very hopeless state indeed. The very Banshee of Midsummer is rattling the windows drearily while I write. There are no visitors in the place but children, and they (my own included) have all got the hooping-cough, and go about the beach choking incessantly. A miserable wanderer lectured in a library last night about astronomy; but being in utter solitude he snuffed out the transparent planets he had brought with him in a box and fled in disgust. A white mouse and a little tinkling box of music that stops at "come," in the melody of the Buffalo Gals, and can't play "out to-night," are the only amusements left.

I beg from my solitude to send my love to Lady Blessington, and your sister, and Count D'Orsay. I think of taming spiders, as Baron Trenck did. There is one in my cell (with a speckled body and twenty-two very decided knees) who seems to know me.

Dear Miss Power,

Faithfully yours ever.

Mr. H. P.
Smith.

BROADSTAIRS, *Ninth July*, 1847.

MY DEAR SMITH,

I am really more obliged to you for your kindness about "The Eagle" (as I always call your house) than I can say. But when I come to town to-morrow week, for the Liverpool and Manchester plays, I shall have Kate and Georgy with me. Moreover, I shall be continually going out and coming in at unholy hours. Item, the timid will come at impossible seasons to "go over" their parts with the manager. Item, two Jews with musty sacks of dresses will be constantly coming backwards and forwards. Item, sounds as of groans will be heard while the inimitable Boz is "getting" his words—which happens all day. Item, Forster will incessantly deliver an address by Bulwer. Item, one hundred letters per diem will arrive from Manchester and Liverpool; and five actresses, in very limp bonnets, with extraordinary veils attached to them, will be always calling, protected by five mothers.

No, no, my actuary. Some congenial tavern is the fitting scene for these things, if I don't get into Devonshire Terrace, whereof I have some spark of hope. Eagles couldn't look the sun in the face and have such enormities going on in their nests.

I am, for the time, that obscene thing, in short, now chronicled in the Marylebone Register of Births—

A PLAYER,

Though still yours.

Mr.
Alexander
Ireland.

BROADSTAIRS, KENT, *Eleventh July*, 1847.

MY DEAR SIR,

I am much indebted to you for the present of your notice of Hunt's books. I cannot praise it better or more appropriately than by saying it is in Hunt's own spirit, and most charmingly expressed. I had the most sincere and hearty pleasure in reading it.

Your announcement of "The Working Man's Life" had attracted my attention by reason of the title, which had a great interest for me. I hardly know if there is something wanting to my fancy in a certain genuine simple air I had looked for in the first part. But there is great promise in it, and I shall be earnest to know how it proceeds.

Now, to leave these pleasant matters, and resume my managerial character, which I shall be heartily glad (between ourselves) to lay down again, though I have none but pleasant correspondents, and the most easily governable company of actors on earth.

I have written to Mr. Robinson by this post that I wish these words, from our original London circular, to stand at top of the bills, after "For the benefit of Mr. Leigh Hunt":

"It is proposed to devote a portion of the proceeds of this benefit to the assistance of another celebrated writer, whose literary career is at an end, and who has no provision for the decline of his life."

I have also told him that there is no objection to its being known that this is Mr. Poole, the author of "Paul Pry," and "Little Pedlington," and many comic pieces of great merit, and whose farce of "Turning the Tables" we mean to finish with in Manchester. Beyond what he will get from these benefits, he has no resource in this wide world, *I know.* There are reasons which make it desirable to get this fact abroad, and if you see no objection to paragraphing it at your office (sending the paragraph round, if you should please, to the other Manchester papers), I should be much obliged to you.

You may like to know, as a means of engendering a more complete individual interest in our actors, who they are. Jerrold and myself you have heard of; Mr. George Cruikshank and Mr. Leech (the best caricaturists of any time perhaps) need no introduction. Mr. Frank Stone (a Manchester man) and Mr. Egg are artists of high reputation. Mr. Forster is the critic of *The Examiner*, the author of "The Lives of the Statesmen of the Commonwealth," and very distinguished as a writer in *The Edinburgh Review*. Mr. Lewes is also a man of great attainments in polite literature, and the author of a novel published not long since, called "Ranthorpe." Mr. Costello is a periodical writer, and a gentleman renowned as a tourist. Mr. Mark Lemon is a dramatic author, and the editor of *Punch*—a most excellent actor, as you will find. My brothers play small parts, for love, and have no greater note than the Treasury and the City confer on their disciples. Mr. Thompson is a private gentleman. You may know all this, but I thought it possible you might like to hold the key to our full company. Pray use it as you will. My dear Sir,

Faithfully yours always.

BROADSTAIRS, KENT, *Tuesday, Fourteenth July,* 1847. Miss Power.

MY DEAR MISS POWER,

Though I am hopeless of Rosherville until after the twenty-eighth—for am I not beckoned, by angels of charity and by local

N

committees, to Manchester and Liverpool, and to all sorts of bedevilments (if I may be allowed the expression) in the way of managerial miseries in the meantime—here I find myself falling into parenthesis within parenthesis, like Lord Brougham—yet will I joyfully come up to London on Friday, to dine at your house and meet the Dane,* whose Books I honour, and whose—to make the sentiment complete, I want something that would sound like "Bones, I love!" but I can't get anything that unites reason with beauty. You, who have genius and beauty in your own person, will supply the gap in your kindness.

An advertisement in the newspapers mentioning the dinner-time, will be esteemed a favour.

Some wild beasts (in cages) have come down here, and involved us in a whirl of dissipation. A young lady in complete armour—at least, in something that shines very much, and is exceedingly scaley—goes into the den of ferocious lions, tigers, leopards, etc., and pretends to go to sleep upon the principal lion, upon which a rustic keeper, who speaks through his nose, exclaims, "Behold the abazid power of woobad!" and we all applaud tumultuously.

Seriously, she beats Van Amburgh. And I think the Duke of Wellington must have her painted by Landseer.

My penitent regards to Lady Blessington, Count D'Orsay, and my own Marchioness.

Ever, dear Miss Power,
Very faithfully yours.

Miss
Dickens.

BROADSTAIRS, *Wednesday, Fourth August*, 1847.

MY DEAREST MAMEY,

I am delighted to hear that you are going to improve in your spelling, because nobody can write properly without spelling well. But I know you will learn whatever you are taught, because you are always good, industrious, and attentive. That is what I always say of my Mamey.

The note you sent me this morning is a very nice one, and the spelling is beautiful.

Always, my dear Mamey,
Your affectionate Papa.

Mr. W. C.
Macready.

DEVONSHIRE TERRACE,
Tuesday Morning, Twenty-third November, 1847.

MY DEAR MACREADY,

I am in the whirlwind of finishing a number with a crisis in it; but I can't fall to work without saying, in so many words, that

* Hans Christian Andersen.

I feel all words insufficient to tell you what I think of you after a night like last night. The multitudes of new tokens by which I know you for a great man, the swelling within me of my love for you, the pride I have in you, the majestic reflection I see in you of all the passions and affections that make up our mystery, throw me into a strange kind of transport that has no expression but in a mute sense of an attachment, which, in truth and fervency, is worthy of its subject.

What is this to say! Nothing, God knows, and yet I cannot leave it unsaid.

Ever affectionately yours.

P.S.—I never saw you more gallant and free than in the gallant and free scenes last night. It was perfectly captivating to behold you. However, it shall not interfere with my determination to address you as Old Parr in all future time.

EDINBURGH, *Thursday, Thirteenth December,* 1847.

Miss Hogarth.

MY DEAR GEORGY,

I "take up my pen," as the young ladies write, to let you know how we are getting on; and as I shall be obliged to put it down again very soon, here goes. We lived with very hospitable people in a very splendid house near Glasgow, and were perfectly comfortable. The meeting was the most stupendous thing as to numbers, and the most beautiful as to colours and decorations, I ever saw. The Inimitable did wonders. His grace, elegance, and eloquence enchanted all beholders. *Kate didn't go !* having been taken ill on the railroad between here and Glasgow.

It has been snowing, sleeting, thawing, and freezing, sometimes by turns and sometimes all together, since the night before last. Lord Jeffrey's household are in town here, not at Craigcrook, and jogging on in a cosy, old-fashioned, comfortable sort of way.

Kate sends her best love. She is a little poorly still, but nothing to speak of. She is frightfully anxious that her not having been to the great demonstration should be kept a secret. But I say that, like murder, it will out, and that to hope to veil such a tremendous disgrace from the general intelligence is out of the question. In one of the Glasgow papers she is elaborately described. I rather think Miss Alison, who is seventeen, was taken for her, and sat for the portrait.

Best love from both of us, to Charley, Mamey, Katey, Wally, Chickenstalker, Skittles, and the Hoshen Peck; last, and not least, to you. We talked of you at the Macreadys' party on Monday night. I hope ——— came out lively, also that ——— was truly amiable. Finally, that ——— took everybody to their carriages, and that ——— wept a good deal during the festivities ? God bless you. Take care of yourself, for the sake of mankind in general.

Ever affectionately, dear Georgy.

Hans
Christian
Andersen.

     * A thousand thanks, my dear Andersen, for your kind and very valuable recollection of me in your Christmas book. I am very proud of it, and feel deeply honoured by it ; I cannot tell you how much I value such a token of acknowledgment from a man with the genius which you are possessed of.

Your book made my Christmas hearth very happy. We are all enchanted by it. The little boy, the old man, and the tin soldier are especially my favourites. I have repeatedly read that story, and read it with the most unspeakable pleasure.

I was a few days ago at Edinburgh, where I saw some of your friends, who talked much about you. Come again to England, soon ! But whatever you do, do not stop writing, because we cannot bear to lose a single one of your thoughts. They are too true and simply beautiful to be kept safe only in your own head.

We returned some time since from the sea-coast, where I bade you adieu, and are now at our own house. My wife tells me that I must give you her kind greeting. Her sister tells me the same. The same say all my children. And as we have all the same sentiments, I beg you to receive the summary in an affectionate greeting from

Your sincere and admiring Friend.

1848.

NARRATIVE.

IN March of this year Charles Dickens went with his wife for two or three weeks to Brighton, accompanied by Mrs. Macready, who was in delicate health, and we give a letter to Mr. Macready from Brighton. Early in the year, "Dombey and Son" was finished, and Charles Dickens was again busy with an amateur play, with the same associates and some new adherents ; the proceeds being,

---

* Extracted from "The Story of my Life," by Hans Christian Andersen. This letter is not dated, but it would be written some time in the year 1847.

at first, intended to go towards the curatorship of Shakespeare's house, which post was to be given to Mr. Sheridan Knowles. The endowment was abandoned, upon the town and council of Stratford-on-Avon taking charge of the house; the large sum realised by the performances being handed over to Mr. Sheridan Knowles. The play selected was "The Merry Wives of Windsor;" the farce, "Love, Law, and Physic." There were two performances at the Haymarket in April, at one of which her Majesty and the Prince Consort were present; and in July there were performances at Manchester, Liverpool, Birmingham, Edinburgh, and Glasgow. Some ladies accompanied the "strollers" on this theatrical provincial tour, and Mrs. Dickens and her sister were of the party. Many of the following letters bear reference to these plays.

In this summer his eldest sister Fanny (Mrs. Burnett) died, and there are sorrowful allusions to her illness in several of the letters.

The autumn months were again spent at Broadstairs, where Charles Dickens wrote "The Haunted Man," which was illustrated by Mr. Frank Stone, Mr. Leech, and others. At the end of the year and at the end of his work, he took another short holiday at Brighton with his wife and sister-in-law; and the letters to Mr. Stone on the subject of his illustrations to "The Haunted Man" are written from Brighton. The first letters which we have to Mr. Mark Lemon come in this year. We regret to have been unable to procure any letters addressed to Mr. Leech, with whom, as with Mr. Lemon, Charles Dickens was very intimately associated for many years.

Also, we have the beginning of his correspondence with Mr. Charles Kent. He wrote (an unusual thing for him to do) to the editor of *The Sun* newspaper, begging him to thank the writer of a particularly sympathetic and earnest review of "Dombey and Son," which appeared in *The Sun* at the close of the book. Mr. Charles Kent replied in his proper person, and from that time dates a close friendship and constant correspondence.

With the letter to Mr. Forster we give, as a note, a letter which Baron Tauchnitz published in his edition of Mr. Forster's "Life of Oliver Goldsmith."

Mr. Peter Cunningham, as an important member of the "Shakespeare's House" committee, managed the *un*theatrical part of this Amateur Provincial Tour, and was always pleasantly connected with the plays.

The book alluded to in the last letter for this year, to be dedicated to Charles Dickens' daughters by Mr. Mark Lemon, was called "The Enchanted Doll."

Mr. Charles
Babbage.

DEVONSHIRE TERRACE,
Twenty-sixth February, 1848.

MY DEAR SIR,

Pray let me thank you for your pamphlet.

I confess that I am one of the unconvinced grumblers, and that I doubt the present or future, existence of any government in England, strong enough to convert the people to your income-tax principles. But I do not the less appreciate the ability with which you advocate them, nor am I the less gratified by any mark of your remembrance.

Faithfully yours always.

Mr. W. C.
Macready.

JUNCTION HOUSE, BRIGHTON, *Second March,* 1848.

MY DEAR MACREADY,

We have migrated from the Bedford and come here, where we are very comfortably (not to say gorgeously) accommodated. Mrs. Macready is certainly better already, and I really have very great hopes that she will come back in a condition so blooming, as to necessitate the presentation of a piece of plate to the undersigned trainer.

You mean to come down on Sunday and on Sunday week. If you don't, I shall immediately take the Victoria, and start Mr. ——, of the Theatre Royal, Haymarket, as a smashing tragedian. Pray don't impose upon me this cruel necessity.

I think Lamartine, so far, one of the best fellows in the world ; and I have lively hopes of that great people establishing a noble republic. Our court had best be careful not to overdo it in respect of sympathy with ex-royalty and ex-nobility. These are not times for such displays, as, it strikes me, the people in some of our great towns would be apt to express pretty plainly.

However, we'll talk of all this on these Sundays, and Mr. —— shall *not* be raised to the pinnacle of fame.

Ever affectionately yours,
My dear Macready.

Sir Edward
Bulwer
Lytton.

DEVONSHIRE TERRACE,
Monday Evening, Tenth April, 1848.

MY DEAR BULWER LYTTON,

I confess to small faith in any American profits having international copyright for their aim. But I will carefully consider Blackwood's letter (when I get it) and will call upon you and tell you what occurs to me in reference to it, before I communicate with that northern light.

I have been "going" to write to you for many a day past, to

thank you for your kindness to the General Theatrical Fund people, and for your note to me; but I have waited until I should hear of your being stationary somewhere. What you said of " The Battle of Life " gave me great pleasure. I was thoroughly wretched at having to use the idea for so short a story. I did not see its full capacity until it was too late to think of another subject, and I have always felt that I might have done a great deal better if I had taken it for the groundwork of a more extended book. But for an insuperable aversion I have to trying back in such a case, I should certainly forge that bit of metal again, as you suggest—one of these days perhaps.

I have not been special constable myself to-day—thinking there was rather an epidemic in that wise abroad. I walked over and looked at the preparations, without any baggage of staff, warrant, or affidavit.

Very faithfully yours.

DEVONSHIRE TERRACE, YORK GATE, REGENT'S PARK,   Editor of
    Friday, Fourteenth April, 1848.   *The Sun.*

Private.

Mr. Charles Dickens presents his compliments to the Editor of *The Sun*, and begs that gentleman will have the goodness to convey to the writer of the notice of "Dombey and Son," in last evening's paper, Mr. Dickens' warmest acknowledgments and thanks. The sympathy expressed in it is so very earnestly and unaffectedly stated, that it is particularly welcome and gratifying to Mr. Dickens, and he feels very desirous indeed to convey that assurance to the writer of that frank and genial farewell.

* DEVONSHIRE TERRACE, *Fourteenth April*, 1848.   Mrs.
                                                         Cowden
DEAR MRS. COWDEN CLARKE,   Clarke.

I did not understand, when I had the pleasure of conversing with you the other evening, that you had really considered the subject, and desired to play. But I am very glad to understand it now; and I am sure there will be a universal sense among us of the grace and appropriateness of such a proceeding. Falstaff (who depends very much on Mrs. Quickly) may have in his modesty, some timidity about acting with an amateur actress. But I have no question, as you have studied the part, and long wished to play it, that you will put him completely at his ease on the first night of your rehearsal. Will you, towards that end, receive this as a

----

* This and following letters to Mr. and Mrs. Cowden Clarke appeared in a volume entitled "Recollections of Writers."

solemn "call" to rehearsal of "The Merry Wives" at Miss Kelly's theatre, to-morrow (Saturday) *week*, at seven in the evening?

And will you let me suggest another point for your consideration? On the night when "The Merry Wives" will *not* be played, and when "Every Man in his Humour" *will* be, Kenny's farce of "Love, Law, and Physic" will be acted. In that farce there is a very good character (one Mrs. Hilary, which I have seen Mrs. Orger, I think, act to admiration), that would have been played by Mrs. C. Jones, if she had acted Dame Quickly, as we at first intended. If you find yourself quite comfortable and at ease among us in Mrs. Quickly, would you like to take this other part too? It is an excellent farce, and is safe, I hope, to be very well done.

We do not play to purchase the house (which may be positively considered as paid for), but towards endowing a perpetual curatorship of it, for some eminent literary veteran. And I think you will recognise in this even a higher and more gracious object than the securing, even, of the debt incurred for the house itself.

Believe me, very faithfully yours.

Mr.
Charles
Kent.

1, DEVONSHIRE TERRACE, YORK GATE, REGENT'S PARK,
Eighteenth April, 1848.

DEAR SIR,

Pray let me repeat to you personally what I expressed in my former note, and allow me to assure you, as an illustration of my sincerity, that I have never addressed a similar communication to anybody except on one occasion.

Faithfully yours.

Mr. John
Forster.

DEVONSHIRE TERRACE,
Saturday, Twenty-second April, 1848.

MY DEAR FORSTER,

I finished Goldsmith yesterday, after dinner, having read it from the first page to the last with the greatest care and attention.

As a picture of the time, I really think it impossible to give it too much praise. It seems to me to be the very essence of all about the time that I have ever seen in biography or fiction, presented in most wise and humane lights, and in a thousand new and just aspects. I have never liked Johnson half so well. Nobody's contempt for Boswell ought to be capable of increase, but I have never seen him in my mind's eye half so plainly. The introduction of him is quite a masterpiece. I should point to that, if I didn't know the author, as being done by somebody with a remarkably vivid conception of what he narrated, and a most admirable and fanciful power of communicating it to another. All about Reynolds is charming; and the first account of the Literary Club and of Beauclerc as excellent a piece of description as ever I read in my life. But to read the book is to be in the time. It lives again in as fresh and lively a manner as if it were presented on an impossibly good stage by the very best actors that ever lived, or by the real actors come out of their graves on purpose.

And as to Goldsmith himself, and *his* life, and the tracing of it out in his own writings, and the manful and dignified assertion of him without any sobs, whines, or convulsions of any sort, it is throughout a noble achievement, of which, apart from any private and personal affection for you, I think (and really believe) I should feel proud, as one who had no indifferent perception of these books of his—to the best of my remembrance—when little more than a child. I was a little afraid in the beginning, when he committed those very discouraging imprudences, that you were going to champion him somewhat indiscriminately; but I very soon got over that fear, and found reason in every page to admire the sense, calmness, and moderation with which you make the love and admiration of the reader cluster about him from his youth, and strengthen with his strength—and weakness too, which is better still.

I don't quite agree with you in two small respects. First, I question very much whether it would have been a good thing for every great man to have had his Boswell, inasmuch that I think that two Boswells, or three at most, would have made great men extraordinarily false, and would have set them on always playing a part, and would have made distinguished people about them for ever restless and distrustful. I can imagine a succession of Boswells bringing about a tremendous state of falsehood in society, and playing the very devil with confidence and friendship. Secondly, I cannot help objecting to that practice (begun, I think, or greatly enlarged by Hunt) of italicising lines and words and whole passages in extracts, without some very special reason indeed. It does appear to be a kind of assertion of the editor over the reader—almost over the author himself—which grates upon me. The author might almost as well do it himself to my thinking, as a disagreeable thing; and it is such a strong contrast to the modest, quiet, tranquil beauty of "The Deserted Village," for instance, that I would almost as soon hear "the town crier" speak the lines. The practice always reminds me of a man seeing a beautiful view, and not thinking how beautiful it is half so much as what he shall say about it.

In that picture at the close of the third book (a most beautiful one) of Goldsmith sitting looking out of window at the Temple trees, you speak of the "gray-eyed" rooks. Are you sure they are "gray-eyed"? The raven's eye is a deep lustrous black, and so, I suspect, is the rook's, except when the light shines full into it.

I have reserved for a closing word—though I *don't* mean to be eloquent about it, being far too much in earnest—the admirable manner in which the case of the literary man is stated throughout this book. It is splendid. I don't believe that any book was ever written, or anything ever done or said, half so conducive to the dignity and honour of literature as "The Life and Adventures of Oliver Goldsmith," by J. F., of the Inner Temple. The gratitude of every man who is content to rest his station and claims quietly on literature, and to make no feint of living by anything else, is your due for evermore. I have often said, here and there, when you have been at work upon the book, that I was sure it would be ; and I shall insist on that debt being due to you (though there will be no need for insisting about it) as long as I have any tediousness and obstinacy to bestow on anybody. Lastly, I never will hear the biography compared with Boswell's except under vigorous protest. For I do say that it is mere folly to put into opposite scales a book, however amusing and curious, written by an un-conscious coxcomb like that, and one which surveys and grandly understands the characters of all the illustrious company that move in it.

My dear Forster, I cannot sufficiently say how proud I am of what you have done, or how sensible I am of being so tenderly connected with it. When I look over this note, I feel as if I had said no part of what I think ; and yet if I were to write another I should say no more, for I can't get it out. I desire no better for my fame, when my personal dustiness shall be past the control of my love of order, than such a biographer and such a critic. And again I say, most solemnly, that literature in England has never had, and probably never will have, such a champion as you are, in right of this book.*   Ever affectionately.

* LETTER OF BARON TAÜCHNITZ.

Having had the privilege to see a letter which the late Mr. Charles Dickens wrote to the author of this work upon its first appearance, and which there was no intention to publish in England, it became my lively wish to make it known to the readers of my edition.

I therefore addressed an earnest request to Mr. Forster, that he would permit the letter to be prefixed to a reprint not designed for circulation in England, where I could understand his reluctance to sanction its publication. Its varied illustration of the subject of the book, and its striking passages of personal feeling and character, led me also to request that I might be allowed to present it in facsimile.

Mr. Forster complied ; and I am most happy to be thus enabled to give to

Rev. James White.

ATHENÆUM, *Thursday, Fourth May,* 1848.

MY DEAR WHITE,

I have not been able to write to you until now. I have lived in hope that Kate and I might be able to run down to see you and yours for a day, before our design for forcing the government to make Knowles the first custodian of the Shakespeare house should come off. But I am so perpetually engaged in drilling the forces, that I see no hope of making a pleasant expedition to the Isle of Wight until about the twentieth. Then I shall hope to do so for one day. But of this I will advise you further, in due course.

My doubts about the house you speak of are twofold. First, I could not leave town so soon as May, having affairs to arrange for a sick sister. And secondly, I fear Bonchurch is not sufficiently bracing for my chickens, who thrive best in breezy and cool places. This has set me thinking, sometimes of the Yorkshire coast, sometimes of Dover. I would not have the house at Bonchurch reserved for me, therefore. But if it should be empty, we will go and look at it in a body. I reserve the more serious part of my letter until the last, my dear White, because it comes from the bottom of my heart. None of your friends have thought and spoken oftener of you and Mrs. White than we have these many weeks past. I should have written to you, but was timid of intruding on your sorrow. What you say, and the manner in which you tell me I am connected with it in your recollection of your dear child, now among the angels of God, gives me courage to approach your grief—to say what sympathy we have felt with it, and how we have not been unimaginative of those deep sources of consolation to which you have had recourse. The traveller who journeyed in fancy from this world to the next was struck to the heart to find the child he had lost, many years before, building him a tower in heaven. Our blessed Christian hopes do not shut out the belief of love and remembrance still enduring there, but irradiate it and make it sacred. Who should know that better than you, or who more deeply feel the touching truths and comfort of that story in the older book, where, when the bereaved mother is asked, "Is it well with the child?" she answers, "It *is* well."

God be with you. Kate and her sister desire their kindest love to yourself and Mrs. White, in which I heartily join.

Being ever, my dear White,

Your affectionate Friend.

my public, on the following pages, so attractive and so interesting a letter, reproduced in the exact form in which it was written, by the most popular and admired of writers—too early gone.

TAÜCHNITZ.

Leipsic, *May* 23, 1873.

Mr. W. C.
Macready.

DEVONSHIRE TERRACE,
Wednesday, Tenth May, 1848.

MY DEAR MACREADY,

We are rehearsing at the Haymarket now, and Lemon mentioned to me yesterday that Webster had asked him if he would sound Forster or me as to your intention of having a farewell benefit before going to America, and whether you would like to have it at the Haymarket, and also as to its being preceded by a short engagement there. I don't know what your feelings may be on this latter head, but thinking it well that you may know how the land lies in these seas, send you this; the rather (excuse Elizabethan phrase, but you know how indispensable it is to me under existing circumstances)—the rather that I am thereto encouraged by thy consort, who has just come a-visiting here, with thy fair daughters, Mistress Nina and the little Kate. Wherefore most selected friend, perpend at thy leisure, and so God speed thee!

And no more at present from,

Thine ever.

From my tent in the garden.

ANOTHER "BOBADIL" NOTE.

I must tell you this, sir, I am no general man; but for William Shakespeare's sake (you may embrace it at what height of favour you please) I will communicate with you on the twenty-first, and do esteem you to be a gentleman of some parts—of a good many parts in truth. I love few words.

At Cobb's, a water-bearer,
Eleventh October.

DEVONSHIRE TERRACE, *Twenty-second May*, 1848.

MY DEAR SIR,

Mr.
Alexander
Ireland.

You very likely know that my company of amateurs have lately been playing, with a great reputation, in London here. The object is, " The endowment of a perpetual curatorship of Shakespeare's house, to be always held by some one distinguished in literature, and more especially in dramatic literature," and we have already a pledge from the Shakespeare House Committee that Sheridan Knowles shall be recommended to the Government as the first curator. This pledge, which is in the form of a minute, we intend to advertise in our country bills.

Now, on Monday, the Fifth of June, we are going to play at Liverpool, where we are assured of a warm reception, and where an active committee for the issuing of tickets is already formed. Do you think the Manchester people would be equally glad to see us again, and that the house could be filled, as before, at our old prices ? *If yes, would you and our other friends go, at once, to work in the cause ?* The only night on which we could play in Manchester would be Saturday, the Third of June. It is possible that the depression of the times may render a performance in Manchester unwise. In that case I would immediately abandon the idea. But what I want to know, *by return of post*, is, is it safe or unsafe ? If the former, here is the bill as it stood in London, with the addition, on the back, of a paragraph I would insert in Manchester, of which immediate use can be made. If the latter, my reason for wishing to settle the point immediately is that we may make another use of that Saturday night.

Assured of your generous feeling I make no apology for troubling you. A sum of money, got together by these means, will insure to literature (I will take good care of that) a proper expression of itself in the bestowal of an essentially literary appointment, not only now but henceforth. Much is to be done, time presses, and the least added the better.

I have addressed a counterpart of this letter to Mr. Francis Robinson, to whom perhaps you will communicate the bill.

Faithfully yours always.

DEVONSHIRE TERRACE,
Monday Evening, Twenty-second July, 1848.

Mrs.
Cowden
Clarke.

MY DEAR MRS. CLARKE,

I have no energy whatever, I am very miserable. I loathe domestic hearths. I yearn to be a vagabond. Why can't I marry Mary ? * Why have I seven children—not engaged at sixpence

* A character in " Used Up."

a-night apiece, and dismissable for ever, if they tumble down, not taken on for an indefinite time at a vast expense, and never,—no never, never,—wearing lighted candles round their heads.* I am deeply miserable. A real house like this is insupportable, after that canvas farm wherein I was so happy. What is a humdrum dinner at half-past five, with nobody (but John) to see me eat it, compared with *that* soup, and the hundreds of pairs of eyes that watched its disappearance? Forgive this tear.† It is weak and foolish, I know.

Pray let me divide the little excursional excesses of the journey among the gentlemen, as I have always done before, and pray believe that I have had the sincerest pleasure and gratification in your co-operation and society, valuable and interesting on all public accounts, and personally of no mean worth, nor held in slight regard.

You had a sister once, when we were young and happy—I think they called her Emma. If she remember a bright being who once flitted like a vision before her, entreat her to bestow a thought upon the " Gas " of departed joys. I can write no more.

Y. G.‡ THE (DARKENED) G. L. B.§

P.S.—"I am completely *blasé*—literally used up. I am dying for excitement. Is it possible that nobody can suggest anything to make my heart beat violently, my hair stand on end—but no ! "

Where did I hear those words (so truly applicable to my forlorn condition) pronounced by some delightful creature? In a previous state of existence, I believe.

Oh, Memory, Memory !

Ever yours faithfully.

Y—no C. G—no D. C. D. I think it is—but I don't know— " there's nothing in it."

The Hon.
Mrs.
Watson.

1, DEVONSHIRE TERRACE, REGENT'S PARK,
Twenty-seventh July, 1848.

MY DEAR MRS. WATSON,

I thought to have been at Rockingham long ago ! It seems a century since I, standing in big boots on the Haymarket stage, saw you come into a box upstairs and look down on the humbled Bobadil ; since then I have had the kindest of notes from you, since then the finest of venison, and yet I have not seen the Rockingham flowers, and they are withering I daresay.

---

* As fairies in " Merry Wives." † A huge blot of smeared ink.
‡ " Young Gas."
§ " Gas-Light Boy." } Names he had given himself.

But we have acted at Manchester, Liverpool, Birmingham, Edinburgh, and Glasgow; and the business of all this—and graver and heavier daily occupation in going to see a dying sister at Hornsey—has so worried me that I have hardly had an hour, far less a week. I shall never be quite happy, in a theatrical point of view, until you have seen me play in an English version of the French piece, "L'Homme Blasé," which fairly turned the head of Glasgow last Thursday night as ever was; neither shall I be quite happy, in a social point of view, until I have been to Rockingham again. When the first event will come about Heaven knows. The latter will happen about the end of the November fogs and wet weather. For am I not going to Broadstairs now, to walk about on the sea-shore (why don't you bring your rosy children there?) and think what is to be done for Christmas! An idea occurs to me all at once. I must come down and read you that book before it's published. Shall it be a bargain? Were you all in Switzerland? I don't believe *I* ever was. It is such a dream now. I wonder sometimes whether I ever disputed with Haldimand; whether I ever drank mulled wine on the top of the Great St. Bernard, or was jovial at the bottom with company that have stolen into my affection; whether I ever was merry and happy in that valley on the Lake of Geneva, or saw you one evening (when I didn't know you) walking down among the green trees outside Elysée, arm-in-arm with a gentleman in a white hat. I am quite clear that there is no foundation for these visions. But I should like to go somewhere, too, and try it all over again. I don't know how it is, but the ideal world in which my lot is cast has an odd effect on the real one, and makes it chiefly precious for such remembrances. I get quite melancholy over them sometimes, especially when, as now, those great piled-up semicircles of bright faces, at which I have lately been looking—all laughing, earnest and intent—have faded away like dead people. They seem a ghostly moral of everything in life to me.

Kate sends her best love, in which Georgy would as heartily unite, I know, but that she is already gone to Broadstairs with the children. We think of following on Saturday morning, but that depends on my poor sister. Pray give my most cordial remembrances to Watson, and tell him they include a great deal. I meant to have written you a letter. I don't know what this is. There is no word for it. So, if you will still let me owe you one, I will pay my debt, on the smallest encouragement, from the seaside. Here, there, and elsewhere, I am, with perfect truth, believe me,

> Very faithfully yours.

Mr. W. C.
Macready.

BROADSTAIRS, KENT,
Saturday, Twenty-sixth August, 1848.

MY DEAR MACREADY,

I was about to write to you when I received your welcome letter. You knew I should come from a somewhat longer distance than this to give you a hearty God-speed and farewell on the eve of your journey. What do you say to Monday, the fourth, or Saturday, the second? Fix either day, let me know which suits you best—at what hour you expect the Inimitable, and the Inimitable will come up to the scratch like a man and a brother.

Permit me, in conclusion, to nail my colours to the mast. Stars and stripes are so-so—showy, perhaps; but my colours is THE UNION JACK, which I am told has the remarkable property of having braved a thousand years the battle AND the breeze. Likewise, it is the flag of Albion—the standard of Britain; and Britons, as I am informed, never, never, never—will—be—slaves!

My sentiment is : Success to the United States as a golden campaigning ground, but blow the United States to 'tarnal smash as an Englishman's place of residence. Gentlemen, are you all charged?

Affectionately ever.

Miss
Dickens.

DEVONSHIRE TERRACE,
Friday, Eighth September, 1848.

MY DEAREST MAMEY,

We shall be very glad to see you all again, and we hope you will be very glad to see us. Give my best love to dear Katey, also to Frankey, Alley, and the Peck.

I have had a nice note from Charley just now. He says it is expected at school that when Walter puts on his jacket, all the Miss Kings will fall in love with him to desperation and faint away.

Ever, my dear Mamey,

Most affectionately yours.

Mr.
Effingham
William
Wilson.

1, DEVONSHIRE TERRACE, YORK GATE, REGENT'S PARK,
Seventh November, 1848.

"A NATIONAL THEATRE."

SIR,

I beg you to accept my best thanks for your pamphlet and your obliging note. That such a theatre as you describe would be but worthy of this nation, and would not stand low upon the list of its instructors, I have no kind of doubt. I wish I could cherish a stronger faith than I have in the probability of its establishment on a rational footing within fifty years.

Faithfully yours.

DEVONSHIRE TERRACE,
Tuesday, Twenty-first November, 1848.

MY DEAR STONE,

I send you herewith the second part of the book, which I hope may interest you. If you should prefer to have it read to you by the Inimitable rather than to read it, I shall be at home this evening (loin of mutton at half-past five), and happy to do it. The proofs are full of printers' errors, but with the few corrections I have scrawled upon it, you will be able to make out what they mean.

I send you, on the opposite side, a list of the subjects already in hand from this second part. If you should see no other in it that you like (I think it important that you should keep Milly, as you have begun with her), I will, in a day or two, describe you an unwritten subject for the third part of the book.

Ever faithfully.

SUBJECTS IN HAND FOR THE SECOND PART.

1. Illuminated page. Tenniel. Representing Redlaw going upstairs, and the Tetterby family below.

2. The Tetterby supper. Leech.

3. The boy in Redlaw's room, munching his food and staring at the fire.

BRIGHTON, *Thursday Night,*
Twenty-third November, 1848.

MY DEAR STONE,

We are unanimous.

The drawing of Milly on the chair is CHARMING. I cannot tell you how much the little composition and expression please me. Do that, by all means.

I fear she must have a little cap on. There is something coming in the last part, about her having had a dead child, which makes it yet more desirable than the existing text does that she should have that little matronly sign about her. Unless the artist is obdurate indeed, and then he'll do as he likes.

I am delighted to hear that you have your eye on her in the students' room. You will really, pictorially, make the little woman whom I love.

Ever, my dear Stone,
Faithfully yours.

BEDFORD HOTEL, BRIGHTON,
Monday Night, Twenty-seventh November, 1848.

MY DEAR STONE,

You are a TRUMP, emphatically a TRUMP, and such are my feelings towards you at this moment that I think (but I am not sure) that if I saw you about to place a card on a wrong pack at Bibeck * (?), I wouldn't breathe a word of objection.

Sir, there is a subject I have written to-day for the third part, that I think and hope will just suit you. Scene, Tetterby's. Time, morning. The power of bringing back people's memories of sorrow, wrong and trouble, has been given by the ghost to Milly, though she don't know it herself. As she comes along the street, Mr. and Mrs. Tetterby recover themselves, and are mutually affectionate again, and embrace, closing *rather* a good scene of quarrel and discontent. The moment they do so, Johnny (who has seen her in the distance and announced her before, from which moment they begin to recover) cries, "Here she is!" and she comes in, surrounded by the little Tetterbys, the very spirit of morning, gladness, innocence, hope, love, domesticity, etc. etc. etc. etc.

I would limit the illustration to her and the children, which will make a fitness between it and your other illustrations, and give them all a character of their own. The exact words of the passage I enclose on another slip of paper. Note. There are six boy Tetterbys present (young 'Dolphus is not there), including Johnny; and in Johnny's arms is Moloch, the baby, who is a girl. I hope to be back in town next Monday, and will lose no time in reporting myself to you. Don't wait to send me the drawing of this. I know how pretty she will be with the children in your hands, and should be a stupendous jackass if I had any distrust of it.

The Duke of Cambridge is staying in this house, and they are driving me mad by having Life Guards bands under our windows, playing *our* overtures! I have been at work all day, and am going to wander into the theatre, where (for the comic man's benefit) "two gentlemen of Brighton" are performing two Counts in a melodrama. I was quite addle-headed for the time being, and think an amateur or so would revive me. No 'Tone! I don't in the abstract approve of Brighton. I couldn't pass an autumn here; but it is a gay place for a week or so; and when one laughs and cries, and suffers the agitation that some men experience over their books, it's a bright change to look out of window, and see the gilt little toys on horseback going up and down before the mighty sea, and thinking nothing of it.

Kate's love and Georgy's. They say you'll contradict every word of this letter.

Faithfully ever.

* A round game of cards, often played at Broadstairs by the family and visitors. We do not know the correct spelling of it.

[SLIP OF PAPER ENCLOSED.]

"Hurrah! here's Mrs. William!" cried Johnny.

So she was, and all the Tetterby children with her; and as she came in, they kissed her and kissed one another, and kissed the baby and kissed their father and mother, and then ran back and flocked and danced about her, trooping on with her in triumph.

(After which, she is going to say: "What, are *you* all glad to see me too! Oh, how happy it makes me to find everyone so glad to see me this bright morning!")

BEDFORD HOTEL, BRIGHTON,   Mr. Mark
Twenty-eighth November, 1848.   Lemon.

MY DEAR MARK,

I assure you, most unaffectedly and cordially, that the dedication of that book to Mary and *Kate* (not Catherine) will be a real delight to me, and to all of us. I know well that you propose it in "affectionate regard," and value and esteem it, therefore, in a way not easy of expression.

You were talking of "coming" down, and now, in a mean and dodging way, you write about "sending" the second act! I have a propogician to make. Come down on Friday. There is a train leaves London Bridge at two—gets here at four. By that time I shall be ready to strike work. We can take a little walk, dine, discuss, and you can go back in good time next morning. I really think this ought to be done, and indeed MUST be done. Write and say it shall be done.

A little management will be required in dramatising the third part, where there are some things I *describe* (for effect's sake, and as a matter of art) which must be *said* on the stage. Redlaw is in a new condition of mind, which fact must be shot point-blank at the audience, I suppose, "as from the deadly level of a gun." By anybody who knew how to play Milly, I think it might be made very good. Its effect is very pleasant upon me. I have also given Mr. and Mrs. Tetterby another innings.

I went to the play last night—fifth act of Richard the Third. Richmond by a stout *lady*, with a particularly well-developed bust, who finished all the speeches with the soubrette simper. Also, at the end of the tragedy she came forward (still being Richmond) and said, "Ladies and gentlemen, on Wednesday next the entertainments will be for *My* benefit, when I hope to meet your approbation and support." Then, having bowed herself into the stage-door, she looked out of it, and said, winningly, "Won't you come?" which was enormously applauded.

Ever affectionately.

1849.

NARRATIVE.

IN the spring of this year Charles Dickens took another holiday at Brighton, accompanied by his wife and sister-in-law and two daughters, and they were joined in their lodgings by Mr. and Mrs. Leech. From Brighton he wrote the letter—as a song—to Mr. Mark Lemon, who had been ill, asking him to pay them a visit.

In the summer, Charles Dickens went with his family, for the first time, to Bonchurch, Isle of Wight, having hired for six months the charming villa, Winterbourne, belonging to the Rev. James White. And now began that close and loving intimacy which for the future was to exist between these two families. Mr. Leech also took a house at Bonchurch. All through this year Charles Dickens was at work upon "David Copperfield."

On the 14th November he witnessed the execution of a man and his wife—Mr. and Mrs. Manning—for the murder of their lodger. On this occasion he wrote the two letters to the Editor of *The Times*, which we give in their order, advocating the great reform in the mode of executions which he had always earnestly at heart and which has happily been carried out since that time.

A letter, on the same subject, addressed to Miss Joll, is explained to us by that lady as follows: "Soon after the appearance of his 'Household Words,' some friends were discussing an article in it on 'Private Executions.' They contended that it went to prove Mr. Dickens was an advocate of capital punishment. I, however, took a different view of the matter, and ventured to write and enquire his views on the subject, and to my letter he sent me a courteous reply."

Mr. Joseph Charles King, the friend of many artists and literary men, conducted a private school, at which the sons of Mr. Macready and of Charles Dickens were being educated at this time.

Mr. Dudley
Costello.

DEVONSHIRE TERRACE,
Friday Night, Twenty-sixth January, 1849.

MY DEAR COSTELLO,

I am desperate! Engaged in links of adamant to a "monster in human form"—a remarkable expression I think I remember to have once met with in a newspaper—whom I encountered at Franconi's, whence I have just returned, otherwise I would have done all three things right heartily, and with my accustomed sweetness. Think of me another time when chops are on the carpet (figuratively speaking), and see if I won't come and eat 'em !

Ever faithfully yours.

DEVONSHIRE TERRACE,
Twenty-third February, 1849.

MY DEAR SIR EDWARD,

I have not written sooner to thank you for "King Arthur" because I felt sure you would prefer my reading it before I should do so, and because I wished to have an opportunity of reading it with the sincerity and attention which such a composition demands.

This I have done. I do not write to express to you the measure of my gratification and pleasure (for I should find that very difficult to be accomplished to my own satisfaction), but simply to say that I have read the poem, and dwelt upon it with the deepest interest, admiration, and delight; and that I feel proud of it as a very good instance of the genius of a great writer of my own time. I should feel it as a kind of treason to what has been awakened in me by the book, if I were to try to set off my thanks to you, or if I were tempted into being diffuse in its praise. I am too earnest on the subject to have any misgiving but that I shall convey something of my earnestness to you, in the briefest and most unaffected flow of expression.

Accept it for what a genuine word of homage is worth, and believe me,

Faithfully yours.

DEVONSHIRE TERRACE,
Tuesday Night, Twenty-seventh February, 1849.

MY DEAREST MAMEY,

I am not engaged on the evening of your birthday. But even if I had an engagement of the most particular kind, I should excuse myself from keeping it, so that I might have the pleasure of celebrating at home, and among my children, the day that gave me such a dear and good daughter as you.

Ever affectionately yours.

DEVONSHIRE TERRACE, *Fifth May*, 1849.

MY DEAR SIR,

I am very sorry to say that my Orphan Working School vote is promised in behalf of an unfortunate young orphan, who, after being canvassed for, polled for, written for, quarrelled for, fought for, called for, and done all kinds of things for, by ladies who wouldn't go away and wouldn't be satisfied with anything anybody said or did for them, was floored at the last election and comes up to the scratch next morning, for the next election, fresher than ever. I devoutly hope he may get in, and be lost sight of for evermore.

Pray give my kindest regards to my quondam Quickly, and believe me,

Faithfully yours.

Mr.
Clarkson
Stanfield,
R.A.

DEVONSHIRE TERRACE, *Twenty-fifth May*, 1849.

MY DEAR STANFIELD,

No—no—no! Murder, murder! Madness and misconception! Any *one* of the subjects—not the whole. Oh, blessed star of early morning, what do you think I am made of, that I should, on the part of any man, prefer such a pig-headed, calf-eyed, donkey-eared, imp-hoofed request!

Says my friend to me, "Will you ask *your* friend, Mr. Stanfield, what the damage of a little picture of that size would be, that I may treat myself with the same, if I can afford it?" Says I, "I will." Says he, "Will you suggest that I should like it to be *one* of those subjects?" Says I, "I will."

I am beating my head against the door with grief and frenzy, and I shall continue to do so, until I receive your answer.

Ever heartily yours,

THE MISCONCEIVED ONE.

Mrs. Charles
Dickens.

SHANKLIN, ISLE OF WIGHT,
Monday Night, Sixteenth June, 1849.

MY DEAR KATE,

I have but a moment. Just got back and post going out. I have taken a most delightful and beautiful house, belonging to White, at Bonchurch; cool, airy, private bathing, everything delicious. I think it is the prettiest place I ever saw in my life, at home or abroad. Anne may begin to dismantle Devonshire Terrace. I have arranged for carriages, luggage, and everything.

The man with the post-bag is swearing in the passage.

Ever affectionately.

P.S.—A waterfall on the grounds, which I have arranged with a carpenter to convert into a perpetual shower-bath.

Mr. Mark
Lemon.

DEVONSHIRE TERRACE,
Monday, Twenty-fifth June, 1849.

MY DEAR LEMON,

I am very unwilling to deny Charley the pleasure you so kindly offer him. But as it is just the close of the half-year when they are getting together all the half-year's work—and as that day's pleasure would weaken the next day's duty, I think I must be "more like an ancient Roman than a ——" Sparkler, and that it will be wisest in me to say nothing about it.

Get a clean pocket-handkerchief ready for the close of " Copper-

field" No. 3; "simple and quiet, but very natural and touching."—
Evening Bore.

Ever affectionately.

NEW SONG.

TUNE—"Lesbia hath a beaming eye."

1.

Lemon is a little hipped,
  And this is Lemon's true position ;
He is not pale, he's not white-lipped,
  Yet wants a little fresh condition.
Sweeter 'tis to gaze upon
  Old ocean's rising, falling billows,
Than on the houses every one,
  That form the street called Saint Anne's Willers.
    Oh, my Lemon, round and fat,
      Oh, my bright, my right, my tight 'un,
    Think a little what you're at—
      Don't stay at home, but come to Brighton !

2.

Lemon has a coat of frieze,
  But all so seldom Lemon wears it,
That it is a prey to fleas,
  And ev'ry moth that's hungry tears it.
Oh, that coat's the coat for me,
  That braves the railway sparks and breezes,
Leaving every engine free
  To smoke it, till its owner sneezes !
    Then, my Lemon, round and fat,
      L., my bright, my right, my tight 'un,
    Think a little what you're at—
      On Tuesday first, come down to Brighton !

T. SPARKLER.

Also signed,
  CATHERINE DICKENS,
  ANNIE LEECH,
  GEORGINA HOGARTH,
  MARY DICKENS,
  KATIE DICKENS,
  JOHN LEECH.

WINTERBOURNE, Sunday Evening,   Rev. James
Twenty-third September, 1849.   White.

MY DEAR WHITE,

    I have a hundred times at least wanted to say to you how
good I thought those papers in "Blackwood"—how excellent their
purpose, and how delicately and charmingly worked out. Their

subtle and delightful humour, and their grasp of the whole question, were something more pleasant to me than I can possibly express.

"How comes this lumbering Inimitable to say this, on this Sunday night of all nights in the year?" you naturally ask. Now hear the Inimitable's honest avowal! I make so bold because I heard that Morning Service better read this morning than ever I have heard it read in my life. And because—for the soul of me— I cannot separate the two things, or help identifying the wise and genial man out of church with the earnest and unaffected man in it. Midsummer madness, perhaps, but a madness I hope that will hold us true friends for many and many a year to come. The madness is over as soon as you have burned this letter (see the history of the Gunpowder Plot), but let us be friends much longer for these reasons and many included in them not herein expressed.

Affectionately always.

The Editor
of The
Times.

DEVONSHIRE TERRACE, Tuesday,
Thirteenth November, 1849.

SIR,

I was a witness of the execution at Horsemonger Lane this morning. I went there with the intention of observing the crowd gathered to behold it, and I had excellent opportunities of doing so, at intervals all through the night, and continuously from day-break until after the spectacle was over. I do not address you on the subject with any intention of discussing the abstract question of capital punishment, or any of the arguments of its opponents or advocates. I simply wish to turn this dreadful experience to some account for the general good, by taking the readiest and most public means of adverting to an intimation given by Sir G. Grey in the last session of Parliament, that the Government might be induced to give its support to a measure making the infliction of capital punishment a private solemnity within the prison walls (with such guarantees for the last sentence of the law being inexorably and surely administered as should be satisfactory to the public at large), and of most earnestly beseeching Sir G. Grey, as a solemn duty which he owes to society, and a responsibility which he cannot for ever put away, to originate such a legislative change himself. I believe that a sight so inconceivably awful as the wickedness and levity of the immense crowd collected at that execution this morning could be imagined by no man, and could be presented in no heathen land under the sun. The horrors of the gibbet and of the crime which brought the wretched murderers to it faded in my mind before the atrocious bearing, looks, and language of the assembled spectators. When I came upon the scene at midnight, the *shrillness* of the cries and howls that were raised from time to time, denoting that they came from a concourse of boys and girls already assembled in the best places, made my blood run cold. As the night went on, screeching, and laughing, and yelling in strong chorus of parodies on negro melodies, with substitutions of "Mrs. Manning" for "Susannah," and the like, were added to these. When the day dawned, thieves, low prostitutes, ruffians, and vagabonds of every kind, flocked on to the ground, with every variety of offensive and foul behaviour. Fightings, faintings, whistlings, imitations of Punch, brutal jokes, tumultuous demonstrations of indecent delight when swooning women were dragged out of the crowd by the police, with their dresses disordered, gave a new zest to the general entertainment. When the sun rose brightly —as it did—it gilded thousands upon thousands of upturned faces, so inexpressibly odious in their brutal mirth or callousness, that a man had cause to feel ashamed of the shape he wore, and to shrink from himself, as fashioned in the image of the Devil. When the two miserable creatures who attracted all this ghastly sight about them were turned quivering into the air, there was no more emotion, no more pity, no more thought that two immortal souls had gone to judgment, no more restraint in any of the previous obscenities, than if the name of Christ had never been heard in this world, and there were no belief among men but that they perished like the beasts.

I have seen, habitually, some of the worst sources of general contamination and corruption in this country, and I think there are not many phases of London life that could surprise me. I am solemnly convinced that nothing that ingenuity could devise to be done in this city, in the same compass of time, could work such ruin as one public execution, and I stand astounded and appalled by the wickedness it exhibits. I do not believe that any community can prosper where such a scene of horror and demoralisation as was enacted this morning outside Horsemonger Lane Gaol is presented at the very doors of good citizens, and is passed by unknown or forgotten. And when in our prayers and thanksgivings for the season we are humbly expressing before God our desire to remove the moral evils of the land, I would ask your readers to consider whether it is not a time to think of this one, and to root it out.

I am, Sir, your faithful Servant.

The Editor
of *The
Times.*

DEVONSHIRE TERRACE, *Saturday, Seventeenth November,* 1849.

SIR,

When I wrote to you on Tuesday last I had no intention of troubling you again ; but as one of your correspondents has to-day expressed a reasonable desire that I would explain myself more clearly, and as I hope I may do no injury to the cause I would serve by stating my views upon it a little more in detail, I shall be glad to do so if you will allow me the opportunity.

My positions in reference to the demoralising nature of public executions are :

First, that they chiefly attract as spectators the lowest, the most depraved, the most abandoned of mankind, in whom they inspire no wholesome emotions whatever.

Second, that the public infliction of a violent death is not a salutary spectacle for any class of people ; but that it is in the nature of things that on the class by whom it is generally witnessed it should have a debasing and hardening influence.

On the first head I must appeal again to my own experience of the execution of last Tuesday morning ; to all the evidence that has ever been taken upon the subject, showing that executions have been the favourite sight of convicts of all descriptions ; to the knowledge possessed by the magistracy and police of the general character of such crowds ; to the police reports that are sure to follow their assemblage ; to the unvarying description of them given in the newspapers ; to the indisputable fact that no decent father is willing that his son, and no decent master is willing that his apprentices or servants, should mingle in them ; to the indisputable fact that all society, its dregs excepted, recoil from them as masses of abomination and brutality. That there were not more robberies committed at this last execution was not the fault of the assembled thieves, whose numbers on the occasion the Home Secretary may easily learn from the commissioners in Scotland Yard, but the merit of the police, whose vigilance was beyond all praise.

On the second head, after a passing allusion to the hardening influence which familiarity, even with natural death, produces on coarse minds, I must again refer to my own experience. Nothing would have been a greater comfort to me—nothing would have so much relieved in my mind the unspeakable terrors of the scene, as to have been enabled to believe that any portion of the immense crowd—that any grains of sand in the vast moral desert stretching away on every side—were moved to any sentiments of fear, repentance, pity, or natural horror by what they saw upon the drop.

It was impossible to look around and rest in any such belief. With every consideration and respect for your suggestion thát the concourse may have been belying their mental struggles by frantic exaggerations, I am confident that if you had been there beside me, seeing what I saw, and hearing what I heard, you could never have admitted the thought. Such a state of mind has its signs and tokens equally with any other, and no such signs and tokens were there. The mirth was not hysterical, the shoutings and fightings were not the efforts of a strained excitement seeking to vent itself in any relief. The whole was unmistakably callous and bad, as the ferocious woman who was charged on the same day with threatening to murder another in the midst of the multitude, proclaiming that she had a knife about her, and would have her heart's blood, and be hanged on the same gibbet with her namesake, Mrs. Manning, whose death she had come to see—as she had her evil passions excited to the utmost by the scene, so had all the crowd. I believe this was the whole and sole effect of what they had come to see, and I hold that no human being, not being the better for such a sight, could go away without being the worse for it.

To prevent such frightful spectacles in a Christian country, and all the incalculable evils they engender, I would have the last sentence of the law executed with comparative privacy within the prison walls. Before I state how, let me strengthen this proposal with some words of Fielding on this subject, to whose profound knowledge of human nature you, I know, will render full justice:

"The execution should be in some degree private. And here the poets will again assist us. Foreigners have found fault with the cruelty of the English drama, in representing frequent murders upon the stage. In fact, this is not only cruel, but highly injudicious: a murder behind the scenes, if the poet knows how to manage it, will affect the audience with greater terror than if it was acted before their eyes. Of this we have an instance in the murder of the king in Macbeth. Terror hath, I believe, been carried higher by this single instance than by all the blood which hath been spilt upon the stage. To the poets I may add the priests, whose politics have never been doubted. Those of Egypt in particular, where the sacred mysteries were first devised, well knew the use of hiding from the eyes of the vulgar what they intended should inspire them with the greatest awe and dread. The mind of man is so much more capable of magnifying than his eye, that I question whether every object is not lessened by being looked upon; and this more especially when the passions are concerned; for those are ever apt to fancy much more satisfaction in those objects which they affect, and much more of mischief in those

which they abhor, than are really to be found in either.   If executions, therefore, were so contrived that few could be present at
them, they would be much more shocking and terrible to the
crowd without doors than at present, as well as much more dreadful
to the criminals themselves."

From the moment of a murderer's being sentenced to death, I
would dismiss him to the dread obscurity to which the wisest judge
upon the bench consigned the murderer Rush.   I would allow no
curious visitors to hold any communication with him; I would
place every obstacle in the way of his sayings and doings being
served up in print on Sunday mornings for the perusal of families.
His execution within the walls of the prison should be conducted
with every terrible solemnity that careful consideration could
devise.   Mr. Calcraft, the hangman (of whom I have some information in reference to this last occasion), should be restrained in
his unseemly briskness, in his jokes, his oaths, and his brandy.
To attend the execution I would summon a jury of twenty-four, to
be called the witness jury, eight to be summoned on a low qualification, eight on a higher, eight on a higher still! so that it might
fairly represent all classes of society.   There should be present,
likewise, the governor of the gaol, the chaplain, the surgeon, and
other officers, the sheriff of the county or city, and two inspectors
of prisons.   All these should sign a grave and solemn form of
certificate (the same in every case) that on such a day, at such an
hour, in such a gaol, for such a crime, such a murderer was hanged
in their sight.   There should be another certificate from the officers
of the prison that the person hanged was that person, and no other;
a third, that that person was buried.   These should be posted on
the prison-gate for twenty-one days, printed in *The Gazette*, and
exhibited in other public places; and during the hour of the body's
hanging I would have the bells of all the churches in that town or
city tolled, and all the shops shut up, that all might be reminded
of what was being done.

I submit to you that, with the law so changed, the public would
(as is right) know much more of the infliction of this tremendous
punishment than they know of the infliction of any other.   There
are not many common subjects, I think, of which they know less
than transportation; and yet they never doubt that when a man is
ordered to be sent abroad he goes abroad.   The details of the
commonest prison in London are unknown to the public at large,
but they are quite satisfied that prisoners said to be in this or
that gaol are really there and really undergo its discipline.   The
"mystery" of private execution is objected to; but has not
mystery been the character of every improvement in convict treat-

ment and prison discipline effected within the last twenty years? From the police van to Norfolk Island, are not all the changes, changes that make the treatment of the prisoner mysterious? His seclusion in his conveyance hither and thither from the public sight, instead of his being walked through the streets, strung with twenty more to a chain, like the galley slaves in Don Quixote (as I remember to have seen in my school-days), makes a mystery of him. His being known by a number instead of by a name, and his being under the rigorous discipline of the associated silent system—to say nothing of the solitary, which I regard as a mistake —is all mysterious. I cannot understand that the mystery of such an execution as I propose would be other than a fitting climax to all these wise regulations, or why, if there be anything in this objection, we should not return to the days when ladies paid visits to highwaymen, drinking their punch in the condemned cells of Newgate; or Ned Ward, the London spy, went upon a certain regular day of the week to Bridewell to see the women whipped.

Another class of objectors I know there are, who, desiring the total abolition of capital punishment, will have nothing less, and who, not doubting the fearful influence of public executions, would have it protracted for an indefinite term, rather than spare the demoralisation they do not dispute, at the risk of losing sight for a while of their final end. But of these I say nothing, considering them, however good and pure in intention, unreasonable, and not to be argued with.

With many thanks to you for your courtesy, and begging most earnestly to assure you that I write in a deep conviction that I incurred a duty when I became a witness of the execution on Tuesday last, from which nothing ought to move me, and which every hour's reflection strengthens,

I am, Sir, your faithful Servant.

ROCKINGHAM CASTLE, NORTHAMPTONSHIRE,   Miss Joll.
Twenty-seventh November, 1849.

Mr. Charles Dickens presents his compliments to Miss Joll. He is, on principle, opposed to capital punishment, but believing that many earnest and sincere people who are favourable to its retention in extreme cases would unite in any temperate effort to abolish the evils of public executions, and that the consequences of public executions are disgraceful and horrible, he has taken the course with which Miss Joll is acquainted as the most hopeful, and as one undoubtedly calculated to benefit society at large.

DEVONSHIRE TERRACE, *Friday Night,*
Thirtieth November, 1849. *A Quarter-past Ten.*

MY DEAR MRS. WATSON,

Plunged in the deepest gloom, I write these few words to let you know that, just now, when the bell was striking ten, I drank to

H. E. R. !

and to all the rest of Rockingham; as the wine went down my throat, I felt distinctly that it was "changing those thoughts to madness."

On the way here I was a terror to my companions, and I am at present a blight and mildew on my home.

Think of me sometimes, as I shall long think of our glorious dance last night. Give my most affectionate regards to Watson, and my kind remembrances to all who remember me, and believe me,

Ever faithfully yours.

P.S.—I am in such an incapable state, that after executing the foregoing usual flourish I swooned, and remained for some time insensible. Ha, ha, ha! Why was I ever restored to consciousness ! ! !

P.P.S.—"Changing" those thoughts ought to be "driving." But my recollection is incoherent and my mind wanders.

DEVONSHIRE TERRACE,
Saturday, First December, 1849.

MY DEAR SIR,

I hasten to let you know what took place at Eton to-day. I found that I *did* stand in some sort committed to Mr. Evans, though not so much so but that I could with perfect ease have declined to place Charley in his house if I had desired to do so. I must say, however, that after seeing Mr. Cookesley (a most excellent man in his way) and seeing Mr. Evans, and Mr. Evans' house, I think I should, under any circumstances, have given the latter the preference as to the domestic part of Charley's life. I would certainly prefer to try it. I therefore thought it best to propose to have Mr. Cookesley for his tutor, and to place him as a boarder with Mr. Evans. Both gentlemen seemed satisfied with this arrangement, and Dr. Hawtrey expressed his approval of it also.

Mr. Cookesley, wishing to know what Charley could do, asked me if I would object to leaving him there for half-an-hour or so. As Charley appeared not at all afraid of this proposal, I left him then and there. On my return, Mr. Cookesley said, in high and unqualified terms, that he had been thoroughly well grounded and well taught—that he had examined him in Virgil and Herodotus, and that he not only knew what he was about perfectly well, but showed an intelligence in reference to those authors which did his tutor great credit. He really appeared most interested and pleased, and filled me with a grateful feeling towards you, to whom Charley owes so much.

He said there were certain verses in imitation of Horace (I really forget what sort of verses) to which Charley was unaccustomed, and which were a little matter enough in themselves, but were made a great point of at Eton, and could be got up well in a month "*from an Old Etonian.*" For this purpose he would desire Charley to be sent every day to a certain Mr. Hardisty, in Store Street, Bedford Square, to whom he had already (in my absence) prepared a note. Between ourselves, I must not hesitate to tell you plainly that this appeared to me to be a conventional way of bestowing a little patronage. But, of course, I had nothing for it but to say it should be done; upon which, Mr. Cookesley added that he was then certain that Charley, on coming after the Christmas holidays, would be placed at once in "the remove," which seemed to surprise Mr. Evans when I afterwards told him of it as a high station.

I will take him to this gentleman on Monday, and arrange for his going there every day; but, if you will not object, I should still like him to remain with you, and to have the advantage of preparing these amazing verses under your eye until the holidays. That Mr. Cookesley may have his own way thoroughly, I will send Charley to Mr. Hardisty daily until the school at Eton recommences.

Let me impress upon you in the strongest manner, not only that I was inexpressibly delighted myself by the readiness with which Charley went through this ordeal with a stranger, but that I also saw you would have been well pleased and much gratified if you could have seen Mr. Cookesley afterwards. He had evidently not expected such a result, and took it as not at all an ordinary one.

My dear Sir, yours faithfully and obliged.

[Private.]

Mr.
Alexander
Ireland.

DEVONSHIRE TERRACE, LONDON,
Twenty-fourth December, 1849.

MY DEAR SIR,

You will not be offended by my saying that (in common with many other men) I think "our London correspondent" one of the greatest nuisances of this kind, inasmuch as our London correspondent, seldom knowing anything, feels bound to know everything, and becomes in consequence a very reckless gentleman in respect of the truthfulness of his intelligence.

In your paper, sent to me this morning, I see the correspondent mentions one ——, and records how I was wont to feast in the house of the said ——. As I never was in the man's house in my life, or within five miles of it that I know of, I beg you will do me the favour to contradict this.

You will be the less surprised by my begging you to set this right, when I tell you that, hearing of his book, and knowing his history, I wrote to New York denouncing him as "a forger and a thief"; that he thereupon put the gentleman who published my letter into prison, and that having but one day before the sailing of the last steamer to collect the proofs printed in the accompanying sheet (which are but a small part of the villain's life), I got them together in short time, and sent them out to justify the character I gave him. It is not agreeable to me to be supposed to have sat at this amiable person's feasts.

Faithfully yours.

M. De Cerjat.

DEVONSHIRE TERRACE, *Saturday*,
Twenty-ninth December, 1849.

MY DEAR CERJAT,

I received your letter at breakfast-time this morning with a pleasure my eloquence is unable to express and your modesty unable to conceive. It is so delightful to be remembered at this time of the year in your house where we have been so happy, and in dear old Lausanne, that we always hope to see again, that I can't help pushing away the first page of "Copperfield" No. 10, now staring at me with what I may literally call a blank aspect, and plunging energetically into this reply.

What a strange coincidence that is about Blunderstone House! Of all the odd things I have ever heard (and their name is Legion), I think it is the oddest. I went down into that part of the country on the Seventh of January last year, when I was meditating the story, and chose Blunderstone for the sound of its name. I had previously observed much of what you say about the poor girls. In all you suggest with so much feeling about their return to virtue being cruelly cut off, I concur with a sore heart. I have been turning it over in my mind for some time, and hope, in the history of Little Em'ly (who *must* fall—there is no hope for her), to put it before the thoughts of people in a new and pathetic way, and perhaps to do some good. You will be glad to hear, I know, that " Copperfield " is a great success. I think it is better liked than any of my other books.

We had a most delightful time at Watsons' (for both of them we have preserved and strengthened a real affection), and were the gayest of the gay. There was a Miss Boyle staying in the house, who is an excellent amateur actress, and she and I got up some scenes from " The School for Scandal " and from " Nickleby," with immense success. We played in the old hall, with the audience filled up and running over with servants. The entertainments concluded with feats of legerdemain (for the performance of which I have a pretty good apparatus, collected at divers times and in divers places), and we then fell to country dances of a most frantic description, and danced all night. We often spoke of you and Mrs. Cerjat and of Haldimand, and wished you were all there. Watson and I have some fifty times "registered a vow" (like O'Connell) to come to Lausanne together, and have even settled in what month and week. Something or other has always interposed to prevent us; but I hope, please God, most certainly to see it again, when my labours-Copperfieldian shall have terminated.

You have no idea what that hanging of the Mannings really was. The conduct of the people was so indescribably frightful, that I felt for some time afterwards almost as if I were living in a city of devils. I feel, at this hour, as if I never could go near the place again. My letters have made a great to-do, and led to a great agitation of the subject; but I have not a confident belief in any change being made, mainly because the total abolitionists are utterly reckless and dishonest (generally speaking), and would play the deuce with any such proposition in Parliament, unless it were strongly supported by the Government, which it would certainly not be, the Whig motto (in office) being " *laissez aller.*" I think Peel might do it if he came in. Two points have occurred to me as being a good commentary to the objections to my idea. The first is that a most terrific uproar was made when the hanging processions were abolished, and the ceremony shrunk from Tyburn to the prison door. The second is that, at this very time, under the British Government in New South Wales, executions take place *within the prison walls*, with decidedly improved results. (I

am waiting to explode this fact on the first man of mark who gives
me the opportunity.)

Unlike you, we have had no marriages or giving in marriage
here. We might have had, but a certain young lady, whom you
know, is hard to please. The children are all well, thank God!
Charley is going to Eton the week after next, and has passed a
first-rate examination. Kate is quite well, and unites with me and
Georgina in love to you and Mrs. Cerjat and Haldimand, whom I
would give a good deal (tell him) to have several hours' contradiction of at his own table. Good heavens, how obstinate we would
both be! I see him leaning back in his chair, with his right forefinger out, and saying, "Good God!" in reply to some proposition
of mine, and then laughing.

All in a moment a feeling comes over me, as if you and I have
been still talking, smoking cigars outside the inn at Martigny, the
piano sounding inside, and Lady Mary Taylour singing. I look
into my garden (which is covered with snow) rather dolefully, but
take heart again, and look brightly forward to another expedition
to the Great St. Bernard, when Mrs. Cerjat and I shall laugh as I
fancy I have never laughed since, in one of those one-sided cars;
and when we shall again learn from Haldimand, in a little dingy
cabaret, at lunch-time, how to secure a door in travelling (do you
remember?) by balancing a chair against it on its two hind legs.

I do hope that we may all come together again once more, while
there is a head of hair left among us; and in this hope remain, my
dear Cerjat,

Your faithful Friend.

1850.

NARRATIVE.

IN the spring of this year Charles Dickens was again at Brighton,
from whence he wrote to Mr. Wills, on "Household Words"
business. The first number of this journal appeared on the 30th
March.

This autumn he succeeded, for the first time, in getting possession of the "Fort House," Broadstairs, on which he had always set
his affections. He was hard at work on the closing numbers of
"David Copperfield" during all the summer and autumn. The
family moved to Broadstairs in July, but as a third daughter was
born in August, they were not joined by Mrs. Dickens until the end
of September. "David Copperfield" was finished in October.

Charles Dickens began his correspondence with Mrs. Gaskell

by asking her to contribute to "Household Words," which she did from the first number, and very frequently afterwards both to "Household Words" and "All the Year Round."

The letter to Mr. David Roberts, R.A., is one thanking him for a remembrance of his (Mr. Roberts') travels in the East—a picture of a "Simoom in the Desert," which was one of Charles Dickens' most highly-prized possessions.

A letter to Mr. Sheridan Knowles contains allusions which we have no means of explaining, but we publish it, as it is characteristic, and addressed to a literary celebrity. Its being inscribed to "Daddy" Knowles illustrates a habit of Charles Dickens—as does a letter later in this year to Mr. Stone, beginning, "My dear P." —of giving nicknames to the friends with whom he was on the most affectionate and intimate terms. Mr. Stone—especially included in this category—was the subject of many such names; "Pump," or "Pumpion," being one by which he was frequently addressed. Charles Dickens did the same thing as regarded himself. In letters to his intimate friends he frequently called himself "the Inimitable," in remembrance of a joke dating from the time of "Pickwick," as to some newspaper notices, speaking of him as "the Inimitable Boz"; and the name of "Sparkler," which will be found in a note (also to Mr. Stone), was another name he often applied to himself.

There were no public amateur theatricals this year; but in November, the greater part of the amateur company played for three nights at Knebworth Park, as the guests of Sir Edward Bulwer Lytton (afterwards Lord Lytton), who entertained all his county neighbours to witness the performances. The play was "Every Man in his Humour," and farces, varied each night.

This year we have the first letter to Miss Mary Boyle, a cousin of Mrs. Watson, well known as an amateur actress and an accomplished lady. Miss Boyle was to have acted with the amateur company at Knebworth, but was prevented by domestic affliction. Early in the following year there was a private play at Rockingham Castle, when Miss Boyle acted with Charles Dickens, the play being "Used Up," in which Mrs. Dickens also acted; and the farce, "Animal Magnetism," in which Miss Boyle and Miss Hogarth played. The letters to Mrs. Watson in this year refer chiefly to the preparations for the play in her house.

The accident mentioned in the letter addressed to Mr. Henry Bicknell (son-in-law of Mr. David Roberts, R.A., and a much-esteemed friend of Charles Dickens) was one which happened to Mrs. Dickens, while rehearsing at a theatre. She fell through a trap-door, spraining her ankle so badly as to be incapacitated from taking her part in the theatricals at Knebworth.

Mr. David
Roberts,
R.A.

DEVONSHIRE TERRACE, *Third January*, 1850.

MY DEAR ROBERTS,

I am more obliged to you than I can tell you for the beautiful mark of your friendly remembrance which you have sent me this morning. I shall set it up among my household gods with pride. It gives me the highest gratification, and I beg you to accept my most cordial and sincere thanks. A little bit of the tissue paper was sticking to the surface of the picture, and has slightly marked it. It requires but a touch, as one would dot an " i " or cross a " t," to remove the blemish; but as I cannot think of a recollection so full of poetry being touched by any hand but yours, I have told Green the framer, whenever he shall be on his way with it, to call on you by the road. I enclose a note from Mrs. Dickens, which I hope will impress you into a country dance, with which we hope to dismiss Christmas merrily.

Ever, my dear Roberts,

Faithfully yours.

Mr. James
Sheridan
Knowles.

DEVONSHIRE TERRACE, *Third January*, 1850.

MY DEAR GOOD KNOWLES,

Many happy New Years to you, and to all who are near and dear to you. Your generous heart unconsciously exaggerates, I am sure, my merit in respect of that most honourable gentleman who has been the occasion of our recent correspondence. I cannot sufficiently admire the dignity of his conduct, and I really feel indebted to you for giving me the gratification of observing it.

As to that "cross note," which, rightly considered, was nothing of the sort, if ever you refer to it again, I'll do—I don't exactly know what, but something perfectly desperate and ferocious. If I have ever thought of it, it has only been to remember with delight how soon we came to a better understanding, and how heartily we confirmed it with a most expressive shake of the hand, one evening down in that mouldy little den of Miss Kelly's.

Heartily and faithfully yours.

" Daddy " Knowles.

Mrs.
Gaskell.

DEVONSHIRE TERRACE, *Thirty-first January*, 1850.

MY DEAR MRS. GASKELL,

You may perhaps have seen an announcement in the papers of my intention to start a new cheap weekly journal of general literature.

I do not know what your literary vows of temperance or abstinence may be, but as I do honestly know that there is no living English writer whose aid I would desire to enlist in preference to the authoress of "Mary Barton" (a book that most profoundly affected and impressed me), I venture to ask you whether you can give me any hope that you will write a short tale, or any number of tales, for the projected pages.

No writer's name will be used, neither my own nor any other; every paper will be published without any signature, and all will seem to express the general mind and purpose of the journal, which is the raising up of those that are down, and the general improvement of our social condition. I should set a value on your help which your modesty can hardly imagine; and I am perfectly sure that the least result of your reflection or observation in respect of the life around you, would attract attention and do good.

Of course I regard your time as valuable, and consider it so when I ask you if you could devote any of it to this purpose.

If you could and would prefer to speak to me on the subject, I should be very glad indeed to come to Manchester for a few hours and explain anything you might wish to know. My unaffected and great admiration of your book makes me very earnest in all relating to you. Forgive my troubling you for this reason, and believe me ever, Faithfully yours.

DEVONSHIRE TERRACE,
Tuesday, Fifth February, 1850.

Rev. James White.

MY DEAR WHITE,

I have been going to write to you for a long time, but have always had in my mind that you might come here with Lotty any day. As Lotty has come without you, however (witness a tremendous rampaging and ravaging now going on upstairs!), I despatch this note to say that I suppose you have seen the announcement of "the" new weekly thing, and that if you would ever write anything for it, you would please me better than I can tell you. We hope to do some solid good, and we mean to be as cheery and pleasant as we can. (And, putting our hands in our breeches pockets, we say complacently, that our money is as good as Blackwood's any day in the week.)

Now the murder's out!

Are you never coming to town any more? Must I come to Bonchurch? Am I born (for the eight-and-thirtieth time) next Thursday, at half-past five, and do you mean to say you are *not* coming to dinner? Well, well, I can always go over to Puseyism to spite my friends, and that's some comfort.

Poor dear Jeffrey! I had heard from him but a few days, and the unopened proof of No. 10 was lying on his table when he died.

I believe I have lost as affectionate a friend as I ever had, or ever shall have, in this world.

Ever heartily yours, my dear White.

Mr. Charles Knight.

DEVONSHIRE TERRACE, *Eighth February*, 1850.

MY DEAR KNIGHT,

Let me thank you in the heartiest manner for your most kind and gratifying mention of me in your able pamphlet. It gives me great pleasure, and I sincerely feel it.

I quite agree with you in all you say so well of the injustice and impolicy of this excessive taxation.* But when I think of the condition of the great mass of the people, I fear that I could hardly find the heart to press for justice in this respect, before the window-duty is removed. They cannot read without light. They cannot have an average chance of life and health without it. Much as we feel our wrong, I fear that they feel their wrong more, and that the things just done in this wise must bear a new physical existence.

I never see you, and begin to think we must have another play —say in Cornwall—expressly to bring us together.

Very faithfully yours.

SUGGESTIONS FOR TITLES OF "HOUSEHOLD WORDS."

THE FORGE:

A Weekly Journal,

Conducted by CHARLES DICKENS.

" Thus at the glowing Forge of Life our actions must be wrought,
Thus on its sounding anvil shaped
Each burning deed and thought."—*Longfellow.*

THE HEARTH.	HOME-MUSIC.
THE FORGE.	CHANGE.
THE CRUCIBLE.	TIME AND TIDE.
THE ANVIL OF THE TIME.	TWOPENCE.
CHARLES DICKENS' OWN.	ENGLISH BELLS.
SEASONABLE LEAVES.	WEEKLY BELLS.
EVERGREEN LEAVES.	THE ROCKET.
HOME.	GOOD HUMOUR.

Mr. W. H. Wills.

148, KING'S ROAD, BRIGHTON,
Tuesday Night, Twelfth March, 1850.

MY DEAR WILLS,

I have made a correction or two in my part of the post-office article. I still observe the top-heavy " Household Words " in the title. The title of " The Amusements of the People " has

---

* The duty on paper—since abolished.

to be altered as I have marked it. I would as soon have my hair cut off as an intolerable Scotch shortness put into my titles by the elision of little words. "The Seasons" wants a little punctuation. Will the "Incident in the Life of Mademoiselle Clairon" go into those two pages? I fear not, but one article would be infinitely better, I am quite certain, than two or three short ones. If it will go in, in with it.

I shall be back, please God, by dinner-time to-morrow week. I will be ready for Smithfield either on the following Monday morning at four, or any other morning you may arrange for.

Would it do to make up No. 2 on Wednesday, the twentieth, instead of Saturday? If so, it would be an immense convenience to me. But if it be distinctly necessary to make it up on Saturday, say by return, and I am to be relied upon. Don't fail in this.

I really *can't* promise to be comic. Indeed, your note put me out a little, for I had just sat down to begin, "It will last my time." I will shake my head a little, and see if I can shake a more comic substitute out of it.

As to *two* comic articles, or two any sort of articles, out of me, that is the intensest extreme of no-goism.

Ever faithfully.

DEVONSHIRE TERRACE, *Monday, Fourth June*, 1850. Mr. Frank Stone.

MY DEAR STONE,

Leech and Sparkler having promised their ladies to take them to Ascot, and having failed in their truths, propose to take them to Greenwich instead, next Wednesday. Will that alteration in the usual arrangements be agreeable to Gaffin, S.? If so, the place of meeting is the Sparkler's Bower, and the hour, one exactly.   Ever yours.

DEVONSHIRE TERRACE, Mr. W. C. Macready.
Tuesday Evening, Eleventh June, 1850.

MY DEAR MACREADY,

In next week, either Monday, Thursday, or Friday will suit us perfectly, and we shall be most heartily happy to talk over those trips that we mean to take into Devonshire. We don't at all take to the idea of your going away, and can't, as our American friends say, "realise" it. I shall forswear that side of the park ever after your departure.

Between "Copperfield" and "Household Words" I am as busy as a bee. I hope to go down to that old image of Eternity that I love so much, and finish the former to its hoarse music. May it be as good a book as I hope it will be, for your children's children's children to read.

With most affectionate loves,

Ever, my dear Friend,

Yours most sincerely.

Rev. James
White.

DEVONSHIRE TERRACE, *Thirteenth July*, 1850.

MY DEAR WHITE,

Being obliged (sorely against my will) to leave my work this morning and go out, and having a few spare minutes before I go, I write a hasty note, to hint how glad I am to have received yours, and how happy and tranquil we feel it to be for you all, that the end of that long illness has come.* Kate and Georgy send best loves to Mrs. White, and we hope she will take all needful rest and relief after those arduous, sad, and weary weeks. I have taken a house at Broadstairs, from early in August until the end of October, as I don't want to come back to London until I shall have finished "Copperfield." I am rejoiced at the idea of your going there. You will find it the healthiest and freshest of places; and there are Canterbury, and all varieties of what Leigh Hunt calls "greenery," within a few minutes' railroad ride. It is not very picturesque ashore, but extremely so seaward; all manner of ships continually passing close inshore. So come, and we'll have no end of sports, please God.

I am glad to say, as I know you will be to hear, that there seems a bright unanimity about "Copperfield." I am very much interested in it and pleased with it myself. I have carefully planned out the story, for some time past, to the end, and am making out my purposes with great care. I should like to know what you see from that tower of yours. I have little doubt you see the real objects in the prospect.

"Household Words" goes on *thoroughly well*. It is expensive, of course, and demands a large circulation; but it is taking a great and steady stand, and I have no doubt already yields a good round profit.

To-morrow week I shall expect you. You shall have a bottle of the "Twenty." I have kept a few last lingering caskets with the gem enshrined therein, expressly for you.

Ever, my dear White,

Cordially yours.

* The last illness of Mrs. White's mother.

HÔTEL WINDSOR, PARIS, *Thursday,*   Mr. W. H.
Twenty-seventh July, 1850. *After post-time.*   Wills.

MY DEAR WILLS,

I have had much ado to get to work; the heat here being so intense that I can do nothing but lie on the bare floor all day. I never felt it anything like so hot in Italy.

There is nothing doing in the theatres, and the atmosphere is so horribly oppressive there that one can hardly endure it. I came out of the Français last night half dead. I am writing at this moment with nothing on but a shirt and pair of white trousers, and have been sitting four hours at this paper, but am as faint with the heat as if I had been at some tremendous gymnastics; and yet we had a thunderstorm last night.

I hope we are doing pretty well in Wellington Street. My anxiety makes me feel as if I had been away a year. I hope to be home on Tuesday evening, or night at latest. I have picked up a very curious book of French statistics that will suit us, and an odd proposal for a company connected with the gambling in California, of which you will also be able to make something.

I saw a certain "Lord Spleen" mentioned in a playbill yesterday, and will look after that distinguished English nobleman to-night, if possible. Rachel played last night for the last time before going to London, and has not so much in her as some of our friends suppose.

The English people are perpetually squeezing themselves into courtyards, blind alleys, closed edifices, and other places where they have no sort of business. The French people, as usual, are making as much noise as possible about everything that is of no importance, but seem (as far as one can judge) pretty quiet and good-humoured. They made a mighty hullabaloo at the theatre last night, when Brutus (the play was "Lucretia") declaimed about liberty. Ever faithfully.

DEVONSHIRE TERRACE, *Ninth August,* 1850.   The same.

MY DEAR WILLS,

I shall be obliged to you if you will write to this man, and tell him that what he asks I never do—firstly, because I have no kind of connection with any manager or theatre; secondly, because I am asked to read so many manuscripts, that compliance is impossible, or I should have no other occupation or relaxation in the world.

☞ A foreign gentleman, with a beard, name unknown, but signing himself "A Fellow Man," and dating from nowhere, declined, twice yesterday, to leave this house for any less consideration than the insignificant one of "twenty pounds." I have had a policeman waiting for him all day.

Faithfully yours.

Mrs. Charles
Dickens.

BROADSTAIRS, *Tuesday, Third September,* 1850.

MY DEAREST KATE,

I enclose a few lines from Georgy, and write these to say that I purpose going home at some time on Thursday, but I cannot say precisely when, as it depends on what work I do to-morrow. Yesterday Charles Knight, White, Forster, Charley, and I walked to Richborough Castle and back. Knight dined with us afterwards; and the Whites, the Bicknells, and Mrs. Gibson came in in the evening and played vingt-et-un.

Having no news I must tell you a story of Sydney. The children, Georgy, and I were out in the garden on Sunday evening (by-the-bye, I made a beautiful passage down, and got to Margate a few minutes after one), when I asked Sydney if he would go to the railroad and see if Forster was coming. As he answered very boldly "Yes," I opened the garden gate, upon which he set off alone as fast as his legs would carry him; and being pursued, was not overtaken until he was through the Lawn House Archway, when he was still going on at full speed—I can't conceive where. Being brought back in triumph, he made a number of fictitious starts, for the sake of being overtaken again, and we made a regular game of it. At last, when he and Ally had run away, instead of running after them, we came into the garden, shut the gate, and crouched down on the ground. Presently we heard them come back and say to each other with some alarm, "Why, the gate's shut, and they're all gone!" Ally began in a dismayed way to cry out, but the Phenomenon shouting, "Open the gate!" sent an enormous stone flying into the garden (among our heads) by way of alarming the establishment. I thought it a wonderful piece of character, showing great readiness of resource. He would have fired a perfect battery of stones, or very likely have broken the pantry window, I think, if we hadn't let him in.

They are all in great force, and send their loves. They are all much excited with the expectation of receiving you on Friday, and would start me off to fetch you now if I would go.

Ever, my dearest Kate,

Most affectionately.

BROADSTAIRS, KENT,
Tuesday, Third September, 1850.

MY DEAR SIR EDWARD,

I have had the long-contemplated talk with Forster about the play, and write to assure you that I shall be delighted to come down to Knebworth and do Bobadil, or anything else, provided it would suit your convenience to hold the great dramatic festival in the last week of October. The concluding number of "Copperfield" will prevent me from leaving here until Saturday, the twenty-sixth of that month. If I were at my own disposal, I hope I need not say I should be at yours.

Forster will tell you with what men we must do the play, and what laurels we would propose to leave for the gathering of new aspirants; of whom I hope you have a reasonable stock in your part of the country.

Do you know Mary Boyle—daughter of the old Admiral? because she is the very best actress I ever saw off the stage, and immeasurably better than a great many I have seen on it. I have acted with her in a country house in Northamptonshire, and am going to do so again next November. If you know her, I think she would be more than pleased to play, and by giving her something good in a farce we could get her to do Mrs. Kitely. In that case my little sister-in-law would "go on" for the second lady, and you could do without actresses, besides giving the thing a particular grace and interest.

If we could get Mary Boyle, we would do "Used Up," which is a delightful piece, as the farce. But maybe you know nothing about the said Mary, and in that case I should like to know what you would think of doing.

You gratify me more than I can tell you by what you say about "Copperfield," the more so as I hope myself that some heretofore-deficient qualities are there. You are not likely to misunderstand me when I say that I like it very much, and am deeply interested in it, and that I have kept and am keeping my mind very steadily upon it.

Believe me always, very faithfully yours.

BROADSTAIRS, KENT,
Monday Night, Sixteenth September, 1850.

MY DEAR MISS BOYLE,

Your letter having arrived in time for me to write a line by the evening post, I came out of a paroxysm of "Copperfield," to say that I am *perfectly delighted* to read it, and to know that we are going to act together in that merry party. We dress

"Every Man" in Queen Elizabeth's time. The acting copy is much altered from the old play, but we still smooth down phrases when needful. I don't remember any one that is changed. Georgina says she can't describe the dress Mrs. Kitely used to wear. I shall be in town on Saturday, and will then get Maclise to make me a little sketch of it, carefully explained, which I will post to you. At the same time I will send you the book. After consideration of farces, it has occurred to me (old Ben being, I daresay, "rare"; but I *do* know rather heavy here and there) that Mrs. Inchbald's "Animal Magnetism," which we have often played, will "go" with a greater laugh than anything else. That book I will send you on Saturday too. You will find your part (Lisette, I think it is called, but it is a waiting-maid) a most admirable one; and I have seen people laugh at the piece until they have hung over the front of the boxes like ripe fruit. You may dress the part to please yourself after reading it. We wear powder. I will take care (bringing a theatrical hair-dresser for the company) of your wig! We will rehearse the two pieces when we go down, or at least anything with which you have to do, over and over again. You will find my company so well used to it, and so accustomed to consider it a grave matter of business, as to make it easy. I am now awaiting the French books with a view to Rockingham, and I hope to report of that too, when I write to you on Saturday.

My dear Miss Boyle, very faithfully yours.

Miss Mary
Boyle.

DEVONSHIRE TERRACE,
Friday, Twentieth September, 1850.

MY DEAR MISS BOYLE,

I enclose you the book of "Animal Magnetism," and the book of "Every Man in his Humour;" also a sketch by Mr. Maclise of a correct and picturesque Mrs. Kitely. Mr. Forster is Kitely; Mr. Lemon, Brainworm; Mr. Leech, Master Matthew; Mr. Jerrold, Master Stephen; Mr. Stone, Downright. Kitely's dress is a very plain purple gown, like a Bluecoat-boy's. Downright's dress is also very sober, chiefly brown and gray. All the rest of us are very bright. I am flaming red. Georgina will write you about your colour and hers in "Animal Magnetism;" the gayer the better. I am the Doctor, in black, with red stockings. Mr. Lemon (an excellent actor), the valet, as far as I can remember, in blue and yellow, and a chintz waistcoat. Mr. Leech is the Marquis, and Mr. Egg the one-eyed servant.

What do you think of doing "Animal Magnetism" as the last piece (we may play three in all, I think) at Rockingham? If so, we might make Quin the one-eyed servant, and beat up with Mrs. Watson for a Marquis. Will you tell me what you think of this, addressed to Broadstairs? I have not heard from Bulwer again. I daresay I have crossed a letter from him by coming up to-day; but I have every reason to believe that the last week in October is the time. *Ever very faithfully yours.*

P.S.—This is quite a managerial letter, which I write with all manner of appointments and business discussions going on about me, having my pen on the paper and my eye on "Household Words," my head on "Copperfield" and my ear nowhere particularly.

BROADSTAIRS, KENT, *Twenty-fourth September*, 1850. The Hon. Mrs. Watson.

MY DEAR MRS. WATSON,

Coming out of "Copperfield" into a condition of temporary and partial consciousness, I plunge into histrionic duties, and hold enormous correspondence with Miss Boyle, between whom and myself the most portentous packets are continually passing. I send you a piece we purpose playing last at Rockingham, which "my company" played in London, Scotland, Manchester, Liverpool, and I don't know where else. It is one of the most ridiculous things ever done. We purpose, as I have said, playing it last. Why do I send it to you? Because there is an excellent part (played in my troupe by George Cruikshank) for your brother in it—Jeffrey; with a black patch on his eye, and a lame leg, he would be charming—noble! If he is come home, give him my love and tell him so. If he is not come home, do me that favour when he does come. And add that I have a wig for him belonging to the part, which I have an idea of sending to the Exposition of '51, as a triumph of human ingenuity.

I am the Doctor; Miss Boyle, Lisette; Georgy, the other little woman. We have nearly arranged our "bill" for Rockingham. We shall want one more reasonably good actor, besides your brother and Miss Boyle's, to play the Marquis in this piece. Do you know a being endowed by nature with the requisite qualities?

There are some things in the next "Copperfield" that I think better than any that have gone before. After I have been believing such things with all my heart and soul, two results always ensue: first, I can't write plainly to the eye; secondly, I can't write sensibly to the mind. So "Copperfield" is to blame, and I am not, for this wandering note; and if you like it, you'll forgive me. Ever, my dear Mrs. Watson,

Very faithfully yours.

Miss Mary
Boyle.

DEVONSHIRE TERRACE, *Wednesday,*
Thirtieth October, 1850.

MY DEAR MISS BOYLE,

We are all extremely concerned and distressed to lose you. But we feel that it cannot be otherwise, and we do not, in our own expectation of amusement, forget the sad cause of your absence.

Bulwer was here yesterday; and if I were to tell you how earnestly he and all the other friends whom you don't know have looked forward to the projected association with you, and in what a friendly spirit they all express their disappointment, you would be quite moved by it, I think. Pray don't give yourself the least uneasiness on account of the blank in our arrangements. I did not write to you yesterday, in the hope that I might be able to tell you to-day that I had replaced you, in however poor a way. I cannot do that yet, but I am busily making out some means of filling the parts before we rehearse to-morrow night, and I trust to be able to do so in some out-of-the-way manner.

Mrs. Dickens and Bridget are bitterly disappointed at not seeing you to-day, but we all hope for a better time.

Dear Miss Boyle,

Faithfully yours always.

Sir Edward
Bulwer
Lytton.

DEVONSHIRE TERRACE,
Sunday Night, Third November, 1850.

MY DEAR BULWER LYTTON,

I should have waited at home to-day on the chance of your calling, but that I went over to look after Lemon; and I went for this reason: the surgeon opines that there is no possibility of Mrs. Dickens being able to play, although she is going on "as well as possible," which I sincerely believe.

Now, *when* the accident happened, Mrs. Lemon told my little sister-in-law that she would gladly undertake the part if it should become necessary. Going after her to-day, I found that she and Lemon had gone out of town, but will be back to-night. I have written to her, earnestly urging her to the redemption of her offer. I have no doubt of being able to see her well up in the characters; and I hope you approve of this remedy. If she once screws her courage to the sticking place, I have no fear of her whatever. This is what I would say to you. If I don't see you here, I will write to you at Forster's, reporting progress. Don't be discouraged, for I am full of confidence, and resolve to do the utmost that is in me—and I well know they all will—to make the nights at Kneb-worth *triumphant.* Once in a thing like this—once in everything, to my thinking—it must be carried out like a mighty enterprise, heart and soul.

Pray regard me as wholly at the disposal of the theatricals, until they shall be gloriously achieved.

My unfortunate other half (lying in bed) is very anxious that I should let you know that she means to break her heart if she should be prevented from coming as one of the audience, and that she has been devising means all day of being brought down in the brougham with her foot upon a T.

Ever faithfully yours.

OFFICE OF "HOUSEHOLD WORDS,"
Wednesday Evening, Thirteenth November, 1850.

Sir Edward Bulwer Lytton.

MY DEAR BULWER LYTTON,

On the principle of postponing nothing connected with the great scheme, I have been to Ollivier's, where I found our friend the Choremusicon in a very shattered state—his mouth wide open—the greater part of his teeth out—his bowels disclosed to the public eye—and his whole system frightfully disordered. In this condition he is speechless. I cannot, therefore, report touching his eloquence, but I find he is a piano as well as a Choremusicon—that he requires to pass through no intermediate stage between Choremusicon and piano, and therefore that he can easily and certainly accompany songs.

Now, will you have it? I am inclined to believe that on the whole, it is the best thing.

I have not heard of anything else having happened to anybody.

If I should not find you gone to Australia or elsewhere, and should not have occasion to advertise in the third column of *The Times*, I shall hope not to add to your misfortunes—I dare not say to afford you consolation—by shaking hands with you to-morrow night, and afterwards keeping every man connected with the theatrical department to his duty.

Ever faithfully yours.

DEVONSHIRE TERRACE, *Saturday Evening,*
Twenty-Third November, 1850.

The Hon. Mrs. Watson.

MY DEAR MRS. WATSON,

Being well home from Knebworth, where everything has gone off in a whirl of triumph and fired the whole length and breadth of the county of Hertfordshire, I write a short note to say that we are yours any time after Twelfth-night, and that we look forward to seeing you with the greatest pleasure. I should have made this reply to your last note sooner, but that I have been waiting to send you "Copperfield" in a new waistcoat.

His tailor is so slow that it has not yet appeared; but when the resplendent garment comes home it shall be forwarded.

I have not your note at hand, but I think you said "any time after Christmas." At all events, and whatever you said, we will conclude a treaty on any terms you may propose. And if it should include any of Charley's holidays, perhaps you would allow us to put a brass collar round his neck, and chain him up in the stable.

Kate and Georgina (who has covered herself with glory) join me in best remembrances and regards to Watson and you and all the house. I have stupendous proposals to make concerning Switzerland in the spring.

My dear Mrs. Watson,
Ever faithfully yours.

Mr. Henry Bicknell.

DEVONSHIRE TERRACE, *Twenty-eighth November*, 1850.

MY DEAR MR. BICKNELL,

If I ever did such a thing, believe me I would do it at your request. But I don't, and if you could see the ramparts of letters from similar institutions, with which my desk bristles every now and then, you would feel that nothing lies between total abstinence (in this regard) and utter bewilderment and lecturation.

Mrs. Dickens and her sister unite with me in kind regards to you and Mrs. Bicknell. The consequences of the accident are fast fading, I am happy to say. We all hope to hear shortly that Mrs. Bicknell has recovered that other little accident, which (as you and I know) will occasionally happen in well-regulated families.

Very faithfully yours.

Mr. Walter Savage Landor.

OFFICE OF "HOUSEHOLD WORDS,"
Wednesday, Fourth December, 1850.

MY DEAR LANDOR,

I have been (a strange thing for me) so very unwell since Sunday, that I have hardly been able to hold up my head. This, my dear friend, is the reason why I have not sooner written to you in reference to your noble letter, which I read in *The Examiner*, and for which—as it exalts me—I cannot, cannot thank you in words.

We had been following up the blow in Kinkel's* favour, and I

* Dr. Gottfried Kinkel, a distinguished scholar and Professor in the University of Bonn, who was at that time undergoing very rigorous State imprisonment in Prussia, for political reasons. Dr. Kinkel was afterwards well known as a teacher and lecturer on Art in London, where he resided for many years.

was growing sanguine, in the hope of getting him out (having enlisted strong and active sympathy in his behalf), when the news came of his escape. Since then we have heard nothing of him. I rather incline to the opinion that the damnable powers that be connived at his escape, but know nothing. Whether he be retaken or whether he appear (as I am not without hope he may) in the streets of London, I shall be a party to no step whatever without consulting you; and if any scrap of intelligence concerning him shall reach me, it shall be yours immediately.

Horne * wrote the article. I shall see him here to-night, and know how he will feel your sympathy and support. But I do not wait to see him before writing, lest you should think me slow to feel your generosity. We said at home, when we read your letter, that it was like the opening of your whole munificent and bare heart.

Ever most affectionately yours,
My dear Landor.

☞   THIS IS No. 2.

DEVONSHIRE TERRACE, *Monday Morning,*
Ninth December, 1850.

The Hon.
Mrs.
Watson.

MY DEAR MRS. WATSON,

Your note to me of Saturday has crossed mine to you, I find. If you open both of mine together, please to observe *this is No.* 2.

You may rely on Mr. Tucker's doing his work thoroughly well and charging a fair price. It is not possible for him to say aforehand, in such a case, what it will cost, I imagine, as he will have to adapt his work to the place. Nathan's stage knowledge may be stated in the following figures: 00000000000. Therefore, I think you had best refer Mr. Tucker to *me*, and I will apply all needful screws and tortures to him.

I have thought of one or two very ingenious (hem !) little contrivances for adapting the difficulties of "Used Up" to the small stage. They will require to be so exactly explained to your carpenter (though very easy little things in themselves), that I think I had better, before Christmas, send my servant down for an hour—he is quite an old stager now—to show him precisely what I mean. It is not a day's work, but it would be extremely difficult to explain in writing. I developed these wonderful ideas to the master carpenter at one of the theatres, and he shook his head with an intensely mournful air, and said, "Ah, sir, it's a

---

* Mr. B. H. Horne, the author of "Orion."

Q

universal observation in the profession, sir, that it was a great loss to the public when you took to writing books!" which I thought complimentary to "Copperfield."

Ever faithfully yours.

1, DEVONSHIRE TERRACE,
Saturday, Fourteenth December, 1850.

MY DEAR MRS. WATSON,

I shall be delighted to come on the seventh instead of the eighth. We consider it an engagement. Over and above the pleasure of a quiet day with you, I think I can greatly facilitate the preparations (that's the way, you see, in which we cheat ourselves into making duties of pleasures) by being at Rockingham a day earlier. So that's settled.

I was quite certain when that Child of Israel mentioned those dimensions, that he must be wrong. For which wooden-headedness the Child shall be taken to task on Monday morning, when I am going to look at his preparations, by appointment, about the door. Don't you observe, that the scenery not being made expressly for the room, it may be impossible to use it as you propose? There is a scene before that wall, and unless the door in the scene (supposing there to be one, which I am not sure of) should come exactly into the place of the door of the room, the door of the room might as well be in Africa. If it could be used it would still require to be backed (excuse professional technicality) by another scene in the passage. And if it be rather in the side of the bottom of the room (as I seem to remember it), it would be put out of sight, or partially, by the side scenes. Do you comprehend these stage managerial sagacities? That piece of additional room in so small a stage would be of immense service, if we could avail ourselves of it. If we can't, I have another means (I think) of discovering Leech, Saville, and Coldstream at table. I am constantly turning over in my mind the capacities of the place, and hope by one means or other to make something more than the best of it. As to the fireplace, you will never be able to use that. The heat of the lamp will be very great, and ventilation will be the thing wanted. Thirteen feet and a half of depth, diminished by stage fittings and furniture, is a small space. I think the doorway could be used in the last scene, with the castle steps and platform for the staircase running straight through it toward the hall. *Nous verrons.* I will write again about my visit of inspection, probably on Monday.

Will you let them know that Messrs. Nathan, of Titchborne

Street, Haymarket, will dress them, please, and that I will engage for their doing it thoroughly well ; also that Mr. Wilson, theatrical hairdresser, Strand, near St. Clement's Churchyard, will come down with wigs, etc., to "make up" everybody ; that he has a list of the pieces from me, and that he will be glad to measure the heads and consult the tastes of all concerned, if they will give him the opportunity beforehand ? I should like to see Sir Adonis Leech and the Hon. T. Saville if I can. For they ought to be wonderfully made up, and to be as unlike themselves as possible, and to contrast well with each other and with me. I rather grudge *caro sposo* coming into the company. I should like him so much to see the play. If we do it all well together it ought to be so very pleasant. I never saw a great mass of people so charmed with a little story as when we acted it at the Glasgow Theatre. But I have no other reason for faltering when I take him to my arms. I feel that he is the man for the part.* I see him with a blue bag, a flaxen wig, and green spectacles. I know what it will be. I foresee how all that sessional experience will come out. I reconcile myself to it, in spite of the selfish consideration of wanting him elsewhere ; and while I have a heavy sense of a light being snuffed out in the audience, perceive a new luminary shining on the stage !

Your brother would make a capital tiger,† too ! Very short tight surtout, doeskins, bright top-boots, white cravat, bouquet in button-hole, close wig—very good, ve—ry good. It clearly must be so. The thing is done. I told you we were opening a tremendous correspondence when we first began to write on such a long subject. But do let me tell you, once and for all, that I am in the business heart and soul, and that you cannot trouble me respecting it, and that I wouldn't willingly or knowingly leave the minutest detail unprovided for. It cannot possibly be a success if the smallest peppercorn of arrangement be omitted. And a success it must be ! I couldn't go into such a thing, or help to bring you poorly out of it, for any earthly consideration. Talking of forgetting, isn't it odd ? I doubt if I could forget words I had learned, so long as I wanted them. But the moment the necessity goes, they go. I know my place and everybody's place in this identical piece of "Used Up" perfectly, and could put every little object on its own square inches of room exactly where it ought to be. But I have no more recollection of my words now (I took the

---

* The part of the lawyer in "Used Up." It was *not* played by Mr. Watson, but by Mr. (afterwards Sir William) Boxall, R.A., a very old and intimate friend of Mr. and Mrs. Watson, and of Charles Dickens.

† This part, finally, was played by Charles Dickens, junior.

book up yesterday) than if I had only seen the play as one of the audience at a theatre.   Perhaps not so much.

Ever, dear Mrs. Watson,
Faithfully yours.

DEVONSHIRE TERRACE, *Nineteenth December*, 1850.

MY DEAR MRS. WATSON,

I am sorry to say that business ("Household Words" business) will keep me in town to-morrow.   But on Monday I propose coming down and returning the same day.   The train for my money appears to be the half-past six A.M. (horrible initials !), and to that invention for promoting early rising I design to commit myself.

I am shocked if I also made the mistake of confounding those two (and too) similar names.*   But I think Mr. S-T-A-F-F-O-R-D had better do the Marquis.   I am glad to find that we agree, but we always do.

I have closely overhauled the little theatre, and the carpenter and painter.   The whole has been entirely repainted (I mean the proscenium and scenery) for this especial purpose, and is extremely pretty.   I don't think, the scale considered, that anything better *could* be done.   It is very elegant.   I have brought "the Child" to this.   For the hire of the theatre, fifteen pounds.   The carriage to be extra.   The Child's fares and expenses (which will be very moderate) to be extra.   The stage-carpenter's wages to be extra— seven shillings a day.   I don't think, when you see the things, that you will consider this too much.   It is as good as the Queen's little theatre at Windsor, raised stage excepted.   I have had an extraction made, which will enable us to use the door.   I am at present breaking my man's heart, by teaching him how to imitate the sounds of the smashing of the windows and the breaking of the balcony in "Used Up."   In the event of his death from grief, I have promised to do something for his mother.   Thinking it possible that you might not see the enclosed until next month, and hoping that it is seasonable for Christmas, I send it.   Being, with cordial regards and all seasonable good wishes,

Ever, dear Mrs. Watson,
Faithfully yours.

P.S.—This [blot] is a tear over the devotion of Captain Boyle, who (as I learned from the Child of Israel this morning) would not decide upon Farmer Wurzel's coat, without referring the question of buttons to managerial approval.

* Mr. Stafford and Mr. Stopford, who both acted in the plays at Rockingham.

DEVONSHIRE TERRACE,
Tuesday Night, Christmas Eve, 1850.

MY DEAR POOLE,

On the Sunday when I last saw you, I went straight to Lord John's with the letter you read. He was out of town, and I left it with my card.

On the following Wednesday I received a note from him, saying that he did not bear in mind exactly what I had told him of you before, and asking me to tell it again. I immediately replied, of course, and gave him an exact description of you and your condition, and your way of life in Paris and everything else; a perfect diorama in little, with you pervading it. To-day I got a letter from him, announcing that you have a pension of *a hundred a year !* of which I heartily wish you joy.

He says : "I am happy to say that the Queen has approved of a pension of one hundred pounds a year to Mr. Poole.

"The Queen, in her gracious answer, informs me that she meant to have mentioned Mr. Poole to me, and that she had wished to place him in the Charter House, but found the society there was not such that he could associate with.

"Be so good as to inform Mr. Poole that directions are given for his pension, which will date from the end of June last."

I have lost no time in answering this, but you must brace up your energies to write him a short note too, and another for the Queen.

If you are in Paris, shall I ascertain what authority I shall need from you to receive the half-year, which I suppose will be shortly due ? I can receive it as usual.

With all good wishes and congratulations, seasonable and unseasonable,

Always faithfully yours.

DEVONSHIRE TERRACE, *Monday Morning,
Thirtieth December,* 1850.

MY DEAR MRS. WATSON,

As your letter is *decided,* the scaffolding shall be re-erected round Charley's boots (it has been taken down, and the workmen had retired to their respective homes in various parts of England and Wales) and his dressing proceeded with. I have been very much pleased with him in the matter, as he never made the least demonstration of disappointment or mortification, and was perfectly contented to give in. (*Here I break off to go to Boxall.*) (*Here I return much exhausted.*)

Your time shall be stated in the bills for both nights. I propose to rehearse on the day, on Thursday and Friday, and in the evening on Saturday, that we may try our lights.   Therefore :

NATHAN and STAGE CARPENTER	will come on Tuesday, Seventh January, as there must be a responsible person to anathematise, and as the company seem so slow about their dresses, that I foresee the strong probability of Nathan having a good deal to do at Rockingham in that respect.
WILSON	will come on Saturday, Eleventh January.
TUCKER	will come on Saturday, Eleventh January.

I shall be delighted to see your brother, and so no more at present from   Yours ever,

                    COLDSTREAM FREELOVE DOCTOR DICKENS.

P.S.—As Boxall (with his head very much on one side and his spectacles on) danced backward from the canvas incessantly with great nimbleness, and returned, and made little digs at it with his pencil, with a horrible grin on his countenance, I augur that he pleased himself this morning.

"Tag," added by Mr. Dickens to "Animal Magnetism," played at Rockingham Castle.

ANIMAL MAGNETISM.—TAG.

[After LA FLEUR says to the MARQUIS : "Sir return him the wand ; and the ladies, I daresay, will fall in love with him again."]

DOCTOR.   I'm cheated, robbed !   I don't believe !   I hate
            Wand, Marquis, Doctor, Ward, Lisette, and Fate !
LA FLEUR.   Not me !
DOCTOR.   *You* worse, you rascal, than the rest.
LA FLEUR (*bowing*).   To merit it, good sir, I've done my best.
LISETTE (*sharply*).   And I.
CONSTANCE.   I fear that I too have a claim
            Upon your anger.
LISETTE.   Anger, madam ?   Shame !
            He's justly treated, as he might have known.
            And if the wand were a divining one
            It would have turned, within his very hands,
            Point-blank to where your handsome husband stands.
CONSTANCE (*glancing at* DOCTOR).   I would it were the wand of Harlequin,
            To change his temper and his favour win.
JEFFREY (*peeping in*).   In that case, mistress, you might be so kind
            As wave me back the eye of which I'm blind.
MARQUIS (*laughing and examining it*).   'Tis nothing but a piece of
            senseless wood,
            And has no influence for harm or good.
            Yet stay !   It surely draws me towards those
            Indulgent, pleasant, smiling, beaming rows !
            It surely charms me.

ALL.   And us too.
MARQUIS.   To bend
Before their gen'rous efforts to commend ;
To cheer us on, through these few happy hours,
And strew our mimic way with real flowers.
                              [*All make obeisance.*

Stay yet again.   Among us all, I feel
One subtle, all-pervading influence steal,
Stirring one wish within one heart and head,
Bright be the path our host and hostess tread !
Blest be their children, happy be their race,
Long may they live, their ancient hall to grace ;
Long bear of English virtues noble fruit—
Green-hearted ROCKINGHAM ! strike deep thy root.

1851.

NARRATIVE.

IN February this year, Charles Dickens made a short bachelor
excursion with Mr. Leech and the Hon. Spencer Lyttelton to Paris,
from whence we give a letter to his wife.   She was at this time
in very bad health, and the little infant Dora had a serious illness
during the winter.   The child rallied for the time, but Mrs.
Dickens continued so ill that she was advised to try the air—and
water—of Malvern.   And early in March, she and her sister were
established in lodgings there, the children being left in London, and
Charles Dickens dividing his time between Devonshire Terrace and
Malvern.   He was busily occupied before this time in superintending the arrangements for Mr. Macready's last appearance on
the stage at Drury Lane, and for a great dinner which was given
to Mr. Macready after it on the First March, at which the chair
was taken by Sir Edward Bulwer Lytton.   With him Charles
Dickens was then engaged in maturing a scheme, which had been
projected at the time of the amateur play at Knebworth, of a
Guild of Literature and Art, which was to found a provident fund
for literary men and artists ; and to start which, a series of
dramatic performances by the amateur company was proposed.
Sir E. B. Lytton wrote a comedy, "Not so Bad as We Seem," for
the purpose, to be played in London and the provinces ; and the
Duke of Devonshire turned one of the splendid rooms in Devonshire House into a theatre, for the first occasion of its performance.
It was played early in May before her Majesty and the Prince
Consort, and a large audience.   Later in the season, there were
several representations of the comedy (with a farce, "Mr. Night-
ingale's Diary," written by Charles Dickens for himself and Mr.
Mark Lemon) in the Hanover Square Rooms.

But in the interval between the Macready banquet and the play at Devonshire House, Charles Dickens underwent great family trouble and sorrow. His father, whose health had been declining for some time, became seriously ill, and Charles Dickens was summoned from Malvern to attend upon him. Mr. John Dickens died on the Thirty-first March. On the Fourteenth April, Charles Dickens had gone from Malvern to preside at the annual dinner of the General Theatrical Fund, and found his children all well at Devonshire Terrace. He was playing with his baby, Dora, before he went to the dinner ; soon after he left the house the child died suddenly in her nurse's arms. The sad news was communicated to the father after his duties at the dinner were over. The next day, Mr. Forster went to Malvern to break the news to Mrs. Dickens, and she and her sister returned with him to London, and the Malvern lodgings were given up. But Mrs. Dickens being still out of health, and London being more than usually full (this being the year of the Great Exhibition), Charles Dickens decided to let the town house again for a few months, and engaged the Fort House, Broadstairs, from the beginning of May until November. This, which was his longest sojourn at Broadstairs, was also the last, as the following summer he changed his seaside resort, and never returned to that pretty little watering-place, although he always retained an affectionate interest in it.

The lease of the Devonshire Terrace house was to expire this year. It was now too small for his family, so he could not renew it, although he left it with regret. From the beginning of the year, he had been in negotiation for a house in Tavistock Square, in which his friend Mr. Frank Stone had lived for some years. Many letters which follow are on the subject of this house and the improvements Charles Dickens made in it. His brother-in-law, Henry Austin— himself an architect—superintended the "works" at Tavistock House, as he did afterwards those at Gad's Hill—and there are many characteristic letters to Mr. Austin while these works were in progress. In the autumn, as a letter written in August to Mr. Stone will show, an exchange of houses was made—Mr. Stone removing with his family to Devonshire Terrace until his own new house was ready—while the alterations in Tavistock House went on, and Charles Dickens removed into it from Broadstairs, in November.

His eldest son was now an Eton boy. He had been one of the party and had played a small part in the play at Rockingham Castle, in the Christmas holidays, and his father's letters to Mrs. Watson at the beginning of this year have reference to this play.

This year Charles Dickens wrote and published "The Haunted

Man," which he had found himself unable to finish for the previous Christmas. It was the last of the Christmas *books*. He abandoned them in favour of a Christmas number of "Household Words," which he continued annually for many years in "Household Words" and "All the Year Round," and in which he had the collaboration of other writers. "The Haunted Man" was dramatised and produced at the Adelphi Theatre, under the management of Mr. Benjamin Webster. Charles Dickens read the book himself, at Tavistock House, to a party of actors and actresses.

At the end of the year he wrote the first number of "Bleak House," although it was not published until March of the following year. With the close attention and the hard work he gave, from the time of its starting, to his weekly periodical, he found it to be most desirable, now, in beginning a new monthly serial, that he should be ready with some numbers in advance before the appearance of the first number.

A provincial tour for the "Guild" took place at the end of the year. A letter to his wife, from Clifton, in November, gives a notion of the general success and enthusiasm with which the plays were attended. The "new Hardman," to whom he alludes as taking that part in Sir E. B. Lytton's comedy in the place of Mr. Forster, was Mr. John Tenniel, who was a new addition, and a very valuable and pleasant one, to the company. Mr. Topham, the delightful water-colour painter, Mr. Dudley Costello, and Mr. Wilkie Collins were also new recruits to the company of "splendid strollers" about this time. A letter to Mr. Wills, asking him to take a part in the comedy, is given here. He never did *act* with the company, but he complied with Charles Dickens' desire that he should be "in the scheme" by giving it all sorts of assistance, and almost invariably being one of the party in the provincial tours.

We give in this year the first letter to Mr. Layard (now Sir Austen H. Layard), the great Nineveh traveller, for whom Charles Dickens, as his letters show, conceived at once the affectionate friendship which went on increasing from this time for the rest of his life.

DEVONSHIRE TERRACE,
Sunday Night, Fifth January, 1851.

Sir Edward
Bulwer
Lytton.

MY DEAR BULWER,

I am so sorry to have missed you! I had gone down to Forster, comedy in hand.

I think it *most admirable*.* Full of character, strong in

* "Not So Bad as We Seem; or, Many Sides to a Character."

interest, rich in capital situations, and *certain to go nobly.* You
know how highly I thought of "Money," but I sincerely think these
three acts finer.   I did not think of the slight suggestions you
make, but I said, *en passant,* that perhaps the drunken scene
might do better on the stage a little concentrated.   I don't believe
it would require even that, with the leading-up which you propose.
I cannot say too much of the comedy to express what I think and
feel concerning it ; and I look at it, too, remember, with the yellow
eye of an actor !   I should have taken to it (need I say so !) *con
amore* in any case, but I should have been jealous of your
reputation, exactly as I appreciate your generosity.   If I had a
misgiving of ten lines I should have scrupulously mentioned it.

Stone will take the Duke capitally ; and I will answer for his
being got into doing it *very well.*   Looking down the perspective
of a few winter evenings here, I am confident about him.   Forster
will be thoroughly sound and real.   Lemon is so surprisingly
sensible and trustworthy on the stage, that I don't think any
actor could touch his part as he will ; and I hope you will have
opportunities of testing the accuracy of this prediction.   Egg ought
to do the Author to absolute perfection.   As to Jerrold—there he
stands in the play !   I would propose Leech (well made up) for
Easy.   He is a good name, and I see nothing else for him.

This brings me to my own part.   If we had anyone, or could
get anyone, for Wilmot, I could do (I think) something so near
your meaning in Sir Gilbert, that I let him go with a pang.
Assumption has charms for me—I hardly know for how many
wild reasons—so delightful, that I feel a loss of, oh ! I can't say
what exquisite foolery, when I lose a chance of being someone in
voice, etc. not at all like myself.   But—I speak quite freely,
knowing you will not mistake me—I know from experience that
we could find nobody to hold the play together in Wilmot if I
didn't do it.   I think I could touch the gallant, generous, careless
pretence, with the real man at the bottom of it, so as to take the
audience with him from the first scene.   I am quite sure I understand your meaning ; and I am absolutely certain that as Jerrold,
Forster, and Stone came in, I could, as a mere little bit of
mechanics, present them better by doing that part, and paying as
much attention to their points as my own, than another amateur
actor could.   Therefore I throw up my cap for Wilmot, and hereby
devote myself to him, heart and head !

I ought to tell you that in a play we once rehearsed and never
played (but rehearsed several times, and very carefully), I saw
Lemon do a piece of reality with a rugged pathos in it, which I
felt, as I stood on the stage with him, to be extraordinarily good.

In the serious part of Sir Gilbert he will surprise you. And he has an intuitive discrimination in such things which will just keep the suspicious part from being too droll at the outset—which will just show a glimpse of something in the depths of it.

The moment I come back to town (within a fortnight, please God!) I will ascertain from Forster where you are. Then I will propose to you that we call our company together, agree upon one general plan of action, and that you and I immediately begin to see and book our Vice-Presidents, etc. Further, I think we ought to see about the Queen. I would suggest our playing first about three weeks before the opening of the Exhibition, in order that it may be the town talk before the country people and foreigners come. Macready thinks with me that a very large sum of money may be got in London.

I propose (for cheapness and many other considerations) to make a theatre expressly for the purpose, which we can put up and take down—say in the Hanover Square Rooms—and move into the country. As Watson wanted something of a theatre made for his forthcoming Little Go, I have made it a sort of model of what I mean, and shall be able to test its working powers before I see you. Many things that, for portability, were to be avoided in Mr. Hewitt's theatre, I have replaced with less expensive and weighty contrivances.

Now, my dear Bulwer, I have come to the small hours, and am writing alone here, as if *I* were writing something to do what your comedy will. At such a time the temptation is strong upon me to say a great deal more, but I will only say this—in mercy to you—that I do devoutly believe that this plan carried, will entirely change the status of the literary man in England, and make a revolution in his position, which no Government, no power on earth but his own, could ever effect. I have implicit confidence in the scheme—so splendidly begun—if we carry it out with a stedfast energy. I have a strong conviction that we hold in our hands the peace and honour of men of letters for centuries to come, and that you are destined to be their best and most enduring benefactor.

Oh! what a procession of New Years might walk out of all this, after we are very dusty!

Ever yours faithfully.

P.S.—I have forgotten something. I suggest this title: " Knowing the World ; or, Not So Bad as We Seem."

The Hon.
Mrs.
Watson.

DEVONSHIRE TERRACE, *Twenty-fourth January*, 1851.

MY DEAR MRS. WATSON,

Kate will have told you, I daresay, that my despondency on coming to town was relieved by a talk with Lady John Russell, of which you were the subject, and in which she spoke of you with an earnestness of old affection and regard that did me good. I date my recovery (which has been slow) from that hour. I am still feeble, and liable to sudden outbursts of causeless rage and demoniacal gloom, but I shall be better presently. What a thing it is, that we can't be always innocently merry and happy with those we like best without looking out at the back windows of life! Well, one day perhaps—after a long night—the blinds on that side of the house will be down for ever, and nothing left but the bright prospect in front.

Concerning supper-toast (of which I feel bound to make some mention), you did, as you always do, right, and exactly what was most agreeable to me.

My love to your excellent husband (I wonder whether he and the dining-room have got to rights yet!), and to the jolly little boys and the calm little girl. Somehow, I shall always think of Lord Spencer as eternally walking up and down the platform at Rugby, in a high chill wind, with no apparent hope of a train—as I left him; and somehow I always think of Rockingham, after coming away, as if I belonged to it and had left a bit of my heart behind, which it is so very odd to find wanting twenty times a day.

Ever, dear Mrs. Watson, faithfully yours, and his.

The same.

DEVONSHIRE TERRACE, *Tuesday Night,*
Twenty-eighth January, 1851.

MY DEAR, DEAR MRS. WATSON,

I presume you mean Mr. Stafford and Mr. Stopford to pay Wilson (as I have instructed him) a guinea each? Am I right? In that just case I still owe you a guinea for *my* part. I was going to send you a post-office order for that amount, when a faint sense of absurdity mantled my ingenuous visage with a blush, and I thought it better to owe you the money until we meet. I hope it may be soon!

I believe I may lay claim to the mysterious inkstand, also to a volume lettered on the back, "Shipwrecks and Disasters at Sea, II.," which I left when I came down at Christmas. Will you take care of them as hostages until we effect an exchange?

Charley went back in great spirits, threatening to write to George. It was a very wet night, and John took him to the railway. He said, on his return : "Mas'r Charles went off very gay, sir. He found some young gen'lmen as was his friends in the train, sir." "Come," said I, "I am glad of that. How many were there? Two or three?" "Oh dear, sir, there was a matter of forty, sir! All with their heads out o' the coach windows, sir, a-hallooing 'Dickens!' all over the station!"

Her ladyship* and the ward of the FIZ-ZISH-UN. send their best loves, in which I heartily join. If you and your dear husband come to town before we bring out Bulwer's comedy, I think we must have a snug reading of it.

Ever, dear Mrs. Watson, faithfully yours.

DEVONSHIRE TERRACE,   Mr. Mark
Friday, Thirty-first January, 1851.   Lemon.

MY DEAR LEMON,

We are deeply sorry to receive the mournful intelligence of your calamity. But we know that you will both have found comfort in that blessed belief, from which the sacred figure with the child upon His knee is, in all stages of our lives, inseparable, for of such is the kingdom of God!

We join in affectionate loves to you and your dear wife. She well deserves your praise, I am sure.

Ever affectionately yours.

DEVONSHIRE TERRACE,   Mr. W. H.
Monday, Tenth February, 1851.   Wills.

MY DEAR WILLS,

There is a small part in Bulwer's comedy, but very good what there is—not much—my servant, who opens the play, which I should be very glad if you would like to do.

Pray understand that there is no end of men who would do it, and that if you have the least objection to the trouble, I don't make this the expression of a wish even. Otherwise, I would like you to be in the scheme, which is a very great and important one, and which cannot have too many men who are steadily—not flightily, like some of our friends—in earnest, and who are not to be lightly discouraged.

If you do the part, I would like to have a talk with you about the secretarial duties. They must be performed by someone I clearly see, and will require good business direction. I should like to put some young fellow, to whom such work and its remuneration would be an object, under your eye, if we could find one entire and perfect chrysolite anywhere. Let me know whether I am to

---

* Lady Clutterbuck—a part in "Used Up," played by Mrs. Dickens at the Rockingham Theatricals.

rate you on the ship's books or not.   If yes, consider yourself "called" to the reading (by Macready) at Forster's rooms, on Wednesday, the nineteenth, at three.

Ever yours.

HÔTEL WAGRAM, PARIS,
Thursday, Twelfth February, 1851.

Mrs. Charles
Dickens.

MY DEAREST KATE,

I received your letter this morning (on returning from an expedition to a market thirteen miles away, which involved the necessity of getting up at five), and am delighted to have such good accounts of all at home.

We had D'Orsay to dinner yesterday, and I am hurried to dress now, in order to pay a promised visit to his *atelier*.   He was very happy with us, and is much improved both in spirits and looks.   Lord and Lady Castlereagh live downstairs here, and we went to them in the evening, and afterwards brought him upstairs to smoke.   To-night we are going to see Lemaître in the renowned "Belphégor" piece.   To-morrow at noon we leave Paris for Calais (the Boulogne boat does not serve our turn), and unless the weather for crossing should be absurd, I shall be at home, please God, early on the evening of Saturday.   It continues to be delightful weather here—gusty, but very clear and fine.   Leech and I had a charming country walk before breakfast this morning at Poissy, and enjoyed it very much.   The rime was on the grass and trees, and the country most delicious.

Spencer Lyttelton is a capital companion on a trip, and a great addition to the party.   We have got on famously and been very facetious.

Ever most affectionately.

DEVONSHIRE TERRACE, *Friday Night, late,*
Twenty-first February, 1851.

Miss Mary
Boyle.

MY DEAR MISS BOYLE,

I have devoted a couple of hours this evening to going very carefully over your paper (which I had read before) and to endeavouring to bring it closer, and to lighten it, and to give it that sort of compactness which a habit of composition, and of disciplining one's thoughts like a regiment, and of studying the art of putting each soldier into his right place, may have gradually taught me to think necessary.   I hope, when you see it in print, you will not be alarmed by my use of the pruning-knife.   I have tried to exercise it with the utmost delicacy and discretion, and to suggest to you, especially towards the end, how this sort of writing (regard being had to the size of the journal in which it appears) requires to be compressed, and is made pleasanter by compression. This all reads very solemnly, but only because I want you to read it (I mean the article) with as loving an eye as I have truly tried to touch it with a loving and gentle hand. I propose to call it "My Mahogany Friend." The other name is too long, and I think not attractive. Until I go to the office to-morrow and see what is actually in hand, I am not certain of the number in which it will appear, but Georgy shall write on Monday and tell you. We are always a fortnight in advance of the public, or the mechanical work could not be done. I think there are many things in it that are *very pretty*. The Katie part is particularly well done. If I don't say more, it is because I have a heavy sense, in all cases, of the responsibility of encouraging anyone to enter on that thorny track, where the prizes are so few and the blanks so many ; where——

But I won't write you a sermon. With the fire going out, and the first shadows of a new story hovering in a ghostly way about me (as they usually begin to do, when I have finished an old one), I am in danger of doing the heavy business, and becoming a heavy guardian, or something of that sort, instead of the light and airy Joe.

So good-night, and believe that you may always trust me, and never find a grim expression (towards you) in any that I wear.

Ever yours.

Twenty-first February, 1851.   Mr. David Roberts, R.A.

Oh my dear Roberts, if you knew the trouble we have had and the money we pay for Drury Lane for one night for the benefit, you would never dream of it for the dinner. *There isn't possibility of getting a theatre.*

I will do all I can for your charming little daughter, and hope to squeeze in half-a-dozen ladies at the last ; but we must not breathe the idea or we shall not dare to execute it, there will be such an outcry.

Faithfully yours.

DEVONSHIRE TERRACE, *Twenty-seventh February*, 1851.   Mr. W. C. Macready.

MY DEAR MACREADY,

Forster told me to-day that you wish Tennyson's sonnet to be read after your health is given on Saturday. I am perfectly certain that it would not do at that time. I am quite convinced that the audience would not receive it, under those exciting circumstances, as it ought to be received. If I had to read it, I would on no account undertake to do so at that period, in a great room crowded with a dense company. I have an instinctive assurance that it would fail. Being with Bulwer this morning, I communicated your wish to him, and he immediately felt as I do. I could enter into many reasons which induce me to form this opinion. But I believe that you have that confidence in me that I may spare you the statement of them.

I want to know one thing from you. As I shall be obliged to be at the London Tavern in the afternoon of to-morrow, Friday (I write, observe, on Thursday night), I shall be much helped in the arrangements if you will send me your answer by a messenger (addressed here) on the receipt of this. Which would you prefer —that "Auld Lang Syne" should be sung after your health is given and before you return thanks, or after you have spoken?

I cannot forbear a word about last night. I think I have told you sometimes, my much-loved friend, how, when I was a mere boy, I was one of your faithful and devoted adherents in the pit; I believe as true a member of that true host of followers as it has ever boasted. As I improved myself and was improved by favouring circumstances in mind and fortune, I only became the more earnest (if it were possible) in my study of you. No light portion of my life arose before me when the quiet vision to which I am beholden, in I don't know how great a degree, or for how much—who does?—faded so nobly from my bodily eyes last night. And if I were to try to tell you what I felt—of regret for its being past for ever, and of joy in the thought that you could have taken your leave of *me* but in God's own time—I should only blot this paper with some drops that would certainly not be of ink, and give very faint expression to very strong emotions.

What is all this in writing? It is only some sort of relief to my full heart, and shows very little of it to you; but that's something, so I let it go.

Ever, my dearest Macready,
Your most affectionate Friend.

Sir Edward
Bulwer
Lytton.

DEVONSHIRE TERRACE,
Tuesday Night, Fourth March, 1851.

MY DEAR BULWER,
I know you will be glad to hear what I have to tell you.
I wrote to the Duke of Devonshire this morning, enclosing him the rough proof of the scheme, and plainly telling him what we wanted—*i.e.* to play for the first time at his house, to the Queen and Court. Within a couple of hours he wrote me as follows:

"DEAR SIR,

"I have read with very great interest the prospectus of the new endowment which you have confided to my perusal.

"Your manner of doing so is a proof that I am honoured by your goodwill and approbation.

"I'm truly happy to offer you my earnest and sincere co-operation. My services, my house, and my subscription will be at your orders. And I beg you to let me see you before long, not merely to converse upon this subject, but because I have long had the greatest wish to improve our acquaintance, which has, as yet, been only one of crowded rooms."

This is quite princely, I think, and will push us along as brilliantly as heart could desire. Don't you think so too?

Yesterday Lemon and I saw the Secretary of the National Provident Institution (the best Office for the purpose, I am inclined to think) and stated all our requirements. We appointed to meet the chairman and directors next Tuesday; so on the day of our reading and dining I hope we shall have that matter in good train.

The theatre is also under consultation; and directly after the reading we shall go briskly to work in all departments.

I hear nothing but praises of your Macready speech—of its eloquence, delicacy, and perfect taste, all of which it is good to hear, though I know it all before-hand as well as most men can tell it me.

Ever cordially.

KNUTSFORD LODGE, GREAT MALVERN,
Twentieth March, 1851.

Mr. David
Roberts,
R.A.

MY DEAR ROBERTS,

Mrs. Dickens has been unwell, and I am here with her. I want you to give a quarter of an hour to the perusal of the enclosed prospectus; to consider the immense value of the design, if it be successful, to artists young and old; and then to bestow your favourable consideration on the assistance I am going to ask of you for the sake and in the name of the cause.

For the representation of the new comedy Bulwer has written for us, to start this scheme, I am having an ingenious theatre made by Webster's people, for erection on certain nights in the Hanover Square Rooms. But it will first be put up in the Duke of Devonshire's house, where the first representation will take place before a brilliant company, including (I believe) the Queen.

Now, will you paint us a scene—the scene of which I enclose Bulwer's description from the prompter's book? It will be a cloth

, with a set-piece. It should be sent to your studio or put up in a theatre painting-room, as you would prefer. I have asked Stanny to do another scene, Edwin Landseer, and Louis Haghe. The Devonshire House performance will probably be on Monday, the Twenty-eighth of April. I should want to have the scenery complete by the twentieth, as it would require to be elaborately worked and rehearsed. *You* could do it in no time after sending in your pictures, and will you?

What the value of such aid would be I need not say. I say no more of the reasons that induce me to ask it, because if they are not in the prospectus they are nowhere.

On Monday and Tuesday nights I shall be in town for rehearsal, but until then I shall be here. Will you let me have a line from you in reply?

My dear Roberts, ever faithfully yours.

Description of the Scene proposed:

STREETS OF LONDON IN THE TIME OF GEORGE I.

In perspective, an alley inscribed DEADMAN'S LANE; a large, old-fashioned, gloomy, mysterious house in the corner, marked No. 1. (*This No. 1, Deadman's Lane, has been constantly referred to in the play as the abode of a mysterious female figure, who enters masked, and passes into this house on the scene being disclosed.*) It is night, and there are moonlight mediums.

Sir Edward
Bulwer
Lytton.

DEVONSHIRE TERRACE,
Tuesday Morning, Twenty-fifth March, 1851.

MY DEAR BULWER,

Coming home at midnight last night after our first rehearsal, I find your letter. I write to entreat you, if you make any change in the first three acts, to let it be only of the slightest kind. Because we are now fairly under way, everybody is already drilled into his place, and in two or three rehearsals those acts will be in a tolerably presentable state.

It is of vital importance that we should get the last two acts *soon*. The Queen and Prince are coming—Phipps wrote me yesterday the most earnest letter possible—the time is fearfully short, and we *must* have the comedy in such a state as that it will go like a machine. Whatever you do, for Heaven's sake don't be persuaded to endanger that!

Even at the risk of your falling into the pit with despair at beholding anything of the comedy in its present state, if you can by any possibility come down to Covent Garden Theatre to-night, do. I hope you will see in Lemon the germ of a very fine presentation of Sir Geoffrey. I think Topham, too, will do Easy admirably.

We really did wonders last night in the way of arrangements. I see the ground-plan of the first three acts distinctly. The dressing and furnishing and so forth, will be a perfect picture, and I will answer for the men in three weeks' time.

In great haste, my dear Bulwer,
Ever faithfully yours.

H. W. OFFICE, *Monday, Twenty-sixth March*, 1851.   Mrs. Charles Dickens.

MY DEAREST KATE,

I reserve all news of the play until I come down. The Queen appoints the Thirtieth of April. There is no end of trouble.

My father slept well last night, and is as well this morning (they send word) as anyone in such a state, so cut and slashed, can be. I have been waiting at home for Bulwer all the morning (it is now two), and am now waiting for Lemon before I go up there. I will not close this note until I have been.

It is raining here incessantly. The streets are in a most miserable state. A van, containing the goods of some unfortunate family moving, has broken down close outside, and the whole scene is a picture of dreariness.

The children are quite well and very happy. I had Dora down this morning, who was quite charmed to see me. That Miss Ketteridge appointed two to-day for seeing the house, and probably she is at this moment disparaging it.

My father is very weak and low, but not worse, I hope, than might be expected. I am going home to dine with the children. By working here late to-night (coming back after dinner) I can finish what I have to do for the play. Therefore I hope to be with you to-morrow, in good time for dinner.

Ever affectionately.

GREAT MALVERN, *Twenty-ninth March*, 1851.   Mrs. Cowden Clarke.

MY DEAR MRS. COWDEN CLARKE,

Ah, those were days indeed, when we were so fatigued at dinner that we couldn't speak, and so revived at supper that we couldn't go to bed; when wild in inns the noble savage ran; and all the world was a stage, gas-lighted in a double sense—by the Young Gas and the old one! When Emmeline Montague (now Compton, and the mother of two children) came to rehearse in our new comedy * the other night, I nearly fainted. The gush of recollection was so overpowering that I couldn't bear it.

I use the portfolio † for managerial papers still. That's something.

* "Not so Bad as We Seem."
† An embroidered blotting-book given by Mrs. Cowden Clarke.

But all this does not thank you for your book.* I have not got it yet (being here with Mrs. Dickens, who has been very un-well), but I shall be in town early in the week, and shall bring it down to read quietly on these hills, where the wind blows as freshly as if there were no Popes and no Cardinals whatsoever—nothing the matter anywhere. I thank you a thousand times, beforehand, for the pleasure you are going to give me. I am full of faith. Your sister Emma, she is doing work of some sort on the P.S. side of the boxes, in some dark theatre, *I know*, but where, I wonder. W.† has not proposed to her yet, has he? I understood he was going to offer his hand and heart, and lay his leg ‡ at her feet.

Ever faithfully yours.

Mr. W. H.
Wills.

DEVONSHIRE TERRACE
Thursday Morning, Third April, 1851.

MY DEAR WILLS,

I took my threatened walk last night, but it yielded little but generalities.

However, I thought of something for *to-night*, that I think will make a splendid paper. I have an idea that it might be connected with the gas paper (making gas a great agent in an effective police), and made one of the articles. This is it: "A Night in a Station-House." If you would go down to our friend Mr. Yardley, at Scotland Yard, and get a letter or order to the acting chief authority at that station-house in Bow Street, to enable us to hear the charges, observe the internal economy of the station-house all night, go round to the cells with the visiting policeman, etc., I would stay there, say from twelve to-night to four or five in the morning. We might have a "night-cap," a fire, and some tea at the office hard by. If you could conveniently borrow an hour or two from the night we could both go. If not, I would go alone. It would make a wonderful good paper at a most appropriate time, when the back slums of London are going to be invaded by all sorts of strangers.

You needn't exactly say that *I* was going *in propriâ* (unless it were necessary), and, of course, you wouldn't say that I propose to-night, because I am so worn by the sad arrangements in which I am engaged, and by what led to them, that I cannot take my

* One of the series in "The Girlhood of Shakespeare's Heroines," dedicated to Charles Dickens.

† Wilmot, Mr. Macready's prompter, who was engaged to accompany the acting-tours.

‡ A wooden one.

natural rest. But to-morrow night we go to the gas-works. I might not be so disposed for this station-house observation as I shall be to-night for a long time, and I see a most singular and admirable chance for us in the descriptive way, not to be lost.

Therefore, if you will arrange the thing before I come down at four this afternoon, any of the Scotland Yard people will do it, I should think; if our friend by any accident should not be there, I will go into it.

If they should recommend any other station-house as better for the purpose, or would think it better for us to go to more than one under the guidance of some trustworthy man, of course we will pay any man and do as they recommend. But I think one topping station-house would be best.

Faithfully ever.

DEVONSHIRE TERRACE, *Nineteenth April*, 1851.   Mr. Thomas
MY DEAR MITTON,   Mitton.

I have been in trouble, or I should have written to you sooner. My wife has been, and is, far from well. My poor father's death caused me much distress. I came to London last Monday to preside at a public dinner—played with little Dora, my youngest child, before I went, and was told when I left the chair that she had died in a moment. I am quite happy again, but I have undergone a good deal.

I am not going back to Malvern, but have let this house until September, and taken the "Fort," at Broadstairs.

Faithfully yours.

DEVONSHIRE TERRACE,   Sir Edward
Monday, Twenty-eighth April, 1851.   Bulwer
MY DEAR BULWER,   Lytton.

The Duke has read the play. He asked for it a week ago, and had it. He has been at Brighton since. He called here before eleven on Saturday morning, but I was out on the play business, so I went to him at Devonshire House yesterday. He almost knows the play by heart. He is supremely delighted with it, and critically understands it. In proof of the latter part of this sentence I may mention that he had made two or three memoranda of trivial doubtful points, *every one of which had attracted our attention in rehearsal*, as I found when he showed them to me. He thoroughly understands and appreciates the comedy of the Duke—threw himself back in his chair and laughed, as I say of Walpole, "till I thought he'd have choked," about his first Duchess, who was a Percy. He suggested that he shouldn't say :

"You know how to speak to the heart of a Noble," because it was not likely that he would call himself a Noble. He thought we might close up the Porter and Softhead a little more (already done), and was so charmed and delighted to recall the comedy that he was more pleased than any boy you ever saw when I repeated two or three of the speeches in my part for him. He is coming to the rehearsal to-day (we rehearse now at Devonshire House, three days a-week, all day long), and, since he read the play, has conceived a most magnificent and noble improvement in the Devonshire House plan, by which, I daresay, we shall get another thousand or fifteen hundred pounds. There is not a grain of distrust or doubt in him. I am perfectly certain that he would confide to me, and does confide to me, his whole mind on the subject.

More than this, the Duke comes out the best man in the play. I am happy to report to you that Stone does the honourable manly side of that pride inexpressibly better than I should have supposed possible in him. The scene where he makes that reparation to the slandered woman is *certain* to be an effect. He is *not* a jest upon the order of Dukes, but a great tribute to them. I have sat looking at the play (as you may suppose) pretty often, and carefully weighing every syllable of it. I see, in the Duke, the most estimable character in the piece. I am as sure that I represent the audience in this as I am that I hear the words when they are spoken before me. The first time that scene with Hardman was seriously done, it made an effect on the company that quite surprised and delighted me; and whenever and wherever it is done (but most of all at Devonshire House) the result will be the same.

Everyone is greatly improved. I wrote an earnest note to Forster a few days ago on the subject of his being too loud and violent. He has since subdued himself with the most admirable pains, and improved the part a thousand per cent. All the points are gradually being worked and smoothed out with the utmost neatness all through the play. They are all most heartily anxious and earnest, and, upon the least hitch, will do the same thing twenty times over. The scenery, furniture, etc. are rapidly advancing towards completion, and will be beautiful. The dresses are a perfect blaze of colour, and there is not a pocket-flap or a scrap of lace that has not been made according to Egg's drawings to the quarter of an inch. Every wig has been made from an old print or picture. From the Duke's snuff-box to Will's Coffee-house, you will find everything in perfect truth and keeping. I have resolved that whenever we come to a weak place in the acting, it must, somehow or other, be made a strong one. The places that I used to be most afraid of are among the best points now.

Will you come to the dress rehearsal on the Tuesday evening before the Queen's night? There will be no one present but the Duke.

I write in the greatest haste, for the rehearsal time is close at hand, and I have the master carpenter and gasman to see before we begin.

Miss Coutts is one of the most sensible of women, and if I had not seen the Duke yesterday, I would have shown her the play directly. But there can't be any room for anxiety on the head that has troubled you so much. You may clear it from your mind as completely as the Gunpowder Plot.

In great haste, ever cordially.

Saturday, Twenty-fourth May, 1851. Mr. W. C.
Macready.

MY DEAR MACREADY,

We are getting in a good heap of money for the Guild. The comedy has been very much improved, in many respects, since you read it. The scene to which you refer is certainly one of the most telling in the play. And there *is* a farce to be produced on Tuesday next, wherein a distinguished amateur will sustain a variety of assumption-parts, and in particular, Samuel Weller and Mrs. Gamp, of which I say no more. I am pining for Broadstairs, where the children are at present. I lurk from the sun, during the best part of the day, in a villainous compound of darkness, canvas, sawdust, general dust, stale gas (involving a vague smell of pepper), and disenchanted properties. But I hope to get down on Wednesday or Thursday.

Ah! you country gentlemen, who live at home at ease, how little do you think of us among the London fleas! But they tell me you are coming in for Dorsetshire. You must be very careful, when you come to town to attend to your parliamentary duties, never to ask your way of people in the streets. They will misdirect you for what the vulgar call "a lark," meaning, in this connection, a jest at your expense. Always go into some respectable shop or apply to a policeman. You will know him by his being dressed in blue, with very dull silver buttons, and by the top of his hat being made of sticking-plaster. You may perhaps see in some odd place an intelligent-looking man, with a curious little wooden table before him and three thimbles on it. He will want you to bet, but don't do it. He really desires to cheat you. And don't buy at auctions where the best plated goods are being knocked down for next to nothing. These, too, are delusions. If you wish to go to the play to see real good acting (though a little more subdued than perfect tragedy should be), I would recommend you to see —— at the Theatre Royal, Drury Lane. Anybody will show it to you. It is near the Strand, and you may know it by seeing no company whatever at any of the doors. Cab fares are eighteen pence a mile. A mile London measure is half a Dorsetshire mile, recollect. Porter is twopence per pint; what is called stout is fourpence. The Zoological Gardens are in the Regent's Park, and the price of admission is one shilling. Of the streets, I would recommend you to see Regent Street and the Quadrant, Bond Street, Piccadilly, Oxford Street, and Cheapside. I think these will please you after a time, though the tumult and bustle will at first bewilder you. If I can serve you in any way, pray command me. And with my best regards to your happy family, so remote from this Babel,

Believe me, my dear Friend,
Ever affectionately yours.

P.S.—I forgot to mention just now that the black equestrian figure you will see at Charing Cross, as you go down to the House, is a statue of *King Charles the First*.

The Earl of
Carlisle.   BROADSTAIRS, *Eighth July*, 1851.

MY DEAR LORD CARLISLE,

We shall be delighted to see you, if you will come down on Saturday. Mr. Lemon may perhaps be here, with his wife, but no one else. And we can give you a bed that may be surpassed, with a welcome that certainly cannot be.

The general character of Broadstairs as to size and accommodation was happily expressed by Miss Eden, when she wrote to the Duke of Devonshire (as he told me), saying how grateful she felt to a certain sailor, who asked leave to see her garden, for not plucking it bodily up, and sticking it in his button-hole.

As we think of putting mignonette-boxes outside the windows, for the younger children to sleep in by-and-by, I am afraid we should give your servant the cramp if we hardily undertook to lodge him. But in case you should decide to bring one, he is easily disposable hard by.

Don't come by the boat. It is rather tedious, and both departs and arrives at inconvenient hours. There is a railway train from the Dover terminus to Ramsgate, at half-past twelve in the day, which will bring you in three hours. Another at half-past four in the afternoon. If you will tell me by which you come (I hope the former), I will await you at the terminus with my little brougham.

You will have for a night-light in the room we shall give you, the North Foreland lighthouse. That and the sea and air are our only lions. It is a very rough little place, but a very pleasant one, and you will make it pleasanter than ever to me.

> Faithfully yours always.

BROADSTAIRS, KENT, *Eleventh July*, 1851.

MY DEAR MRS. WATSON,

I am so desperately indignant with you for writing me that short apology for a note, and pretending to suppose that under any circumstances I could fail to read with interest anything *you* wrote to me, that I have more than half a mind to inflict a regular letter upon you. If I were not the gentlest of men I should do it!

Poor dear Haldimand, I have thought of him so often. That kind of decay is so inexpressibly affecting and piteous to me, that I have no words to express my compassion and sorrow. When I was at Abbotsford, I saw in a vile glass case the last clothes Scott wore. Among them an old white hat, which seemed to be tumbled and bent and broken by the uneasy, purposeless wandering, hither and thither, of his heavy head. It so embodied Lockhart's pathetic description of him when he tried to write, and laid down his pen and cried, that it associated itself in my mind with broken powers and mental weakness from that hour. I fancy Haldimand in such another, going listlessly about that beautiful place, and remembering the happy hours we have passed with him, and his goodness and truth, I think what a dream we live in, until it seems for the moment the saddest dream that ever was dreamed. Pray tell us if you hear more of him. We really loved him.

To go to the opposite side of life, let me tell you that a week or so ago I took Charley and three of his schoolfellows down the river gipsying. I secured the services of Charley's godfather (an old friend of mine,* and a noble fellow with boys), and went down to Slough, accompanied by two immense hampers from Fortnum and Mason, on (I believe) the wettest morning ever seen out of the tropics.

It cleared before we got to Slough ; but the boys, who had got up at four (we being due at eleven), had horrible misgivings that we might not come, in consequence of which we saw them looking into the carriages before us, all face. They seemed to have no bodies whatever, but to be all face ; their countenances lengthened to that surprising extent. When they saw us, the faces shut up as if they were upon strong springs, and their waistcoats developed themselves in the usual places. When the first hamper came out

* Mr. Thomas Beard.

of the luggage-van, I was conscious of their dancing behind the guard; when the second came out with bottles in it, they all stood wildly on one leg. We then got a couple of flys to drive to the boat-house. I put them in the first, but they couldn't sit still a moment, and were perpetually flying up and down like the toy figures in the sham snuff-boxes. In this order we went on to "Tom Brown's, the tailor's," where they all dressed in aquatic costume, and then to the boat-house, where they all cried in shrill chorus for "Mahogany"—a gentleman so called by reason of his sunburnt complexion, a waterman by profession. (He was likewise called during the day "Hog" and "Hogany," and seemed to be unconscious of any proper name whatsoever.) We embarked, the sun shining now, in a galley with a striped awning, which I had ordered for the purpose, and all rowing hard, went down the river. We dined in a field; what I suffered for fear those boys should get drunk, the struggles I underwent in a contest of feeling between hospitality and prudence, must ever remain untold. I feel, even now, old with the anxiety of that tremendous hour. They were very good, however. The speech of one became thick, and his eyes too like lobsters' to be comfortable, but only temporarily. He recovered, and I suppose outlived the salad he took. I have heard nothing to the contrary, and I imagine I should have been implicated on the inquest if there had been one. We had tea and rashers of bacon at a public-house, and came home, the last five or six miles in a prodigious thunderstorm. This was the great success of the day, which they certainly enjoyed more than anything else. The dinner had been great, and Mahogany had informed them, after a bottle of light champagne, that he never would come up the river "with ginger company" any more. But the getting so completely wet through was the culminating part of the entertainment. You never in your life saw such objects as they were; and their perfect unconsciousness that it was at all advisable to go home and change, or that there was anything to prevent their standing at the station two mortal hours to see me off, was wonderful. As to getting them to their dames with any sort of sense that they were damp, I abandoned the idea. I thought it a success when they went down the street as civilly as if they were just up and newly dressed, though they really looked as if you could have rubbed them to rags with a touch, like saturated curl-paper.

I am sorry you have not been able to see our play, which I suppose you won't now, for I take it you are not going on Monday, the twenty-first, our last night in town? It is worth seeing, not for the getting up (which modesty forbids me to approve), but for the little bijou it is, in the scenery, dresses, and appointments. They are such as never can be got together again, because such men as Stanfield, Roberts, Grieve, Haghe, Egg, and others, never can be again combined in such a work. Everything has been done at its best from all sorts of authorities, and it is really very beautiful to look at.

I find I am "used up" by the Exhibition. I don't say "there is nothing in it"—there's too much. I have only been twice; so many things bewildered me. I have a natural horror of sights, and the fusion of so many sights in one has not decreased it. I am not sure that I have seen anything but the fountain and perhaps the Amazon. It is a dreadful thing to be obliged to be false, but when anyone says, "Have you seen —— !" I say, "Yes," because if I don't, I know he'll explain it, and I can't bear that. —— took all the school one day. The school was composed of a hundred "infants," who got among the horses' legs in crossing to the main entrance from the Kensington Gate, and came reeling out from between the wheels of coaches undisturbed in mind. They were clinging to horses, I am told, all over the park.

When they were collected and added up by the frantic monitors, they were all right. They were then regaled with cake, etc., and went tottering and staring all over the place; the greater part wetting their forefingers and drawing a wavy pattern on every accessible object. One infant strayed. He was not missed. Ninety and nine were taken home, supposed to be the whole collection, but this particular infant went to Hammersmith. He was found by the police at night, going round and round the turnpike, which he still supposed to be a part of the Exhibition. He had the same opinion of the police, also of Hammersmith workhouse, where he passed the night. When his mother came for him in the morning, he asked when it would be over? It was a great Exhibition, he said, but he thought it long.

As I begin to have a foreboding that you will think the same of this act of vengeance of mine, this present letter, I shall make an end of it, with my heartiest and most loving remembrances to Watson. I should have liked him of all things to have been in the Eton expedition, tell him, and to have heard a song (by-the-bye, I have forgotten that) sung in the thunderstorm, solos by Charley, chorus by the friends, describing the career of a booby who was plucked at college, every verse ending :

> I don't care a fig what the people may think,
> But what WILL the governor say !

which was shouted with a deferential jollity towards myself, as a governor who had that day done a creditable action, and proved himself worthy of all confidence.

> Ever, dear Mrs. Watson,
>> Most sincerely yours.

Mr. Frank Stone.

"HOUSEHOLD WORDS," *Sunday, Twentieth July*, 1851.

MY DEAR STONE,

I have been considering the great house question since you kindly called yesterday evening, and come to the conclusion that I had better not let it go. I am convinced it is the prudent thing for me to do, and that I am very unlikely to find the same comforts for the rising generation elsewhere, for the same money. Therefore, as Robins no doubt understands that you would come to me yesterday—passing his life as he does amidst every possible phase of such negotiations—I think it hardly worth while to wait for the receipt of his coming letter. If you will take the trouble to call on him in the morning, and offer the £1450, I shall be very much obliged to you. If you will receive from me full power to conclude the purchase (subject of course to my solicitor's approval of the lease), pray do. I give you *carte blanche* to £1500, but I think the £1450 ought to win the day.

I don't make any apologies for thrusting this honour upon you, knowing what a thorough-going old pump you are. Lemon and his wife are coming here, after rehearsal, to a gipsy sort of cold dinner. Time, half-past three. Viands, pickled salmon and cold pigeon-pie. Occupation afterwards, lying on the carpet as a preparation for histrionic strength. Will you come with us from the Hanover Square Rooms?

> Ever affectionately.

Mr. Charles Knight.

> BROADSTAIRS, KENT,
> *Sunday, Twenty-seventh July*, 1851.

MY DEAR KNIGHT,

A most excellent Shadow!* I have sent it up to the printer, and Wills is to send you a proof. Will you look carefully at all the earlier part, where the use of the past tense instead of the present a little hurts the picturesque effect? I understand each phase of the thing to be *always a thing present before the mind's eye*—a shadow passing before it. Whatever is done, must be *doing*. Is it not so? For example, if I did the Shadow of Robinson Crusoe, I should not say he *was* a boy at Hull when his father lectured him about going to sea, and so forth; but he *is* a boy at Hull. There he is, in that particular Shadow, eternally

---

* Mr. Charles Knight was writing a series of papers in "Household Words" called "Shadows."

a boy at Hull; his life to me is a series of shadows, but there is no "was" in the case. If I choose to go to his manhood, I can. These shadows don't change as realities do. No phase of his existence passes away, if I choose to bring it to this unsubstantial and delightful life, the only death of which, to me, is *my* death, and thus he is immortal to unnumbered thousands. If I am right, will you look at the proof through the first third or half of the papers, and see whether the Factor comes before us in that way? If not, it is merely the alteration of the verb here and there that is requisite.

I cannot say that I derive a comfortable impression of —— from his note, or that I think him easy to be hopefully assisted; but I am almost ashamed of building up any opinion on such slight premises. He writes about his books rather as if he saw his future biography in his mind's eye, with this letter in it. Is it so? or am I a Beast whom Begging-Letter Writers have made out of a Beautiful Prince?

You say you are coming down to look for a place next week. Now, Jerrold says he is coming on Thursday, by the cheap express at half-past twelve, to return with me for the play early on Monday morning. Can't you make that a holiday too? I have promised him our only spare bed, but we'll find you a bed hard by, and shall be delighted "to eat and drink you," as an American once wrote to me. We will make expeditions to Herne Bay, Canterbury, where not? and drink deep draughts of fresh air. Come! They are beginning to cut the corn. You will never see the country so pretty. If you stay in town these days, you'll do nothing. Say you'll come!

Ever affectionately.

BROADSTAIRS, KENT,
Saturday, Twenty-third August, 1851.

Mr. Frank Stone.

MY DEAR STONE,

A "dim vision" occurs to me, arising out of your note; also presents itself to the brains of my other half.

Supposing you should find, on looking onward, a possibility of your being houseless at Michaelmas, what do you say to using Devonshire Terrace as a temporary encampment? It will not be in its usual order, but we would take care that there should be as much useful furniture of all sorts there, as to render it unnecessary for you to move a stick. If you should think this a convenience, then I should propose to you to pile your furniture in the middle of the rooms at Tavistock House, and go out to Devonshire Terrace two or three weeks *before* Michaelmas, to enable my workmen to commence their operations. This might be to our mutual convenience, and therefore I suggest it. Certainly the sooner I can begin on Tavistock House the better. And possibly your going into Devonshire Terrace might relieve you from a difficulty that would otherwise be perplexing.

I make this suggestion (I need not say to *you*) solely on the chance of its being useful to both of us. If it were merely convenient to me, you know I shouldn't dream of it. Such an arrangement, while it would cost you nothing, would perhaps enable you to get your new house into order comfortably, and do exactly the same thing for me.

Ever affectionately.

Mr. Henry Austin.

BROADSTAIRS, *Sunday, Seventh September*, 1851.

MY DEAR HENRY,

I am in that state of mind which you may (once) have seen described in the newspapers as "bordering on distraction;" the house given up to me, the fine weather going on (soon to break, I daresay), the painting season oozing away, my new book waiting to be born, and

NO WORKMEN ON THE PREMISES,

along of my not hearing from you!! I have torn all my hair off, and constantly beat my unoffending family. Wild notions have occurred to me of sending in my own plumber to do the drains. Then I remember that you have probably written to prepare *your* man, and restrain my audacious hand. Then Stone presents himself, with a most exasperatingly mysterious visage, and says that a rat has appeared in the kitchen, and it's his opinion (Stone's, not the rat's) that the drains want "compo-ing;" for the use of which explicit language I could fell him without remorse. In my horrible desire to "compo" everything, the very postman becomes my enemy because he brings no letter from you; and, in short, I don't see what's to become of me unless I hear from you to-morrow which I have not the least expectation of doing.

Going over the house again, I have materially altered the plans —abandoned conservatory and front balcony—decided to make Stone's painting-room the drawing-room (it is nearly six inches higher than the room below), to carry the entrance passage right through the house to a back door leading to the garden, and to reduce the once intended drawing-room—now school-room—to a manageable size, making a door of communication between the new drawing-room and the study. Curtains and carpets, on a scale of awful splendour and magnitude, are already in preparation, and still—still—

NO WORKMEN ON THE PREMISES.

To pursue this theme is madness. Where are you? When are you coming home? Where is THE.man who is to do the work? Does he know that an army of artificers must be turned in at once, and the whole thing finished out of hand? O rescue me from my present condition. Come up to the scratch, I entreat and implore you!

I send this to Lætitia to forward,

> Being, as you well know why,
> Completely floored by N. W., I
> *Sleep.*

I hope you may be able to read this. My state of mind does not admit of coherence.

Ever affectionately.

P.S.—No WORKMEN ON THE PREMISES!
Ha! ha! ha! (I am laughing demoniacally.)

EXTRACT FROM LETTER TO MR. STONE.

Eighth September, 1851.   Mr. Frank Stone.

You never saw such a sight as the sands between this and Margate presented yesterday. This day fortnight a steamer laden with cattle going from Rotterdam to the London market, was wrecked on the Goodwin—on which occasion, by-the-bye, the coming in at night of our Salvage Luggers laden with dead cattle, which were hoisted up upon the pier, where they lay in heaps, was a most picturesque and striking sight. The sea since Wednesday has been very rough, blowing in straight upon the land. Yesterday, the shore was strewn with hundreds of oxen, sheep, and pigs (and with bushels upon bushels of apples,) in every state and stage of decay—burst open, rent asunder, lying with their stiff hoofs in the air, or with their great ribs yawning like the wrecks of ships—tumbled and beaten out of shape, and yet with a horrible sort of humanity about them. Hovering among these carcases was every kind of water-side plunderer, pulling the horns out, getting the hides off, chopping the hoofs with poleaxes, etc. etc., attended by no end of donkey carts, and spectral horses with scraggy necks, galloping wildly up and down as if there were something maddening in the stench. I never beheld such a demoniacal business!

Very faithfully yours.

Mr. Henry
Austin.

BROADSTAIRS, *Monday, Eighth September*, 1851.

MY DEAR HENRY,

Your letter, received this morning, has considerably allayed
the anguish of my soul. Our letters crossed, of course, as letters
under such circumstances always do.

I am perpetually wandering (in fancy) up and down the house *
and tumbling over the workmen; when I feel that they are gone
to dinner I become low, when I look forward to their total abstinence on Sundays, I am wretched. The gravy at dinner has a taste
of glue in it. I smell paint in the sea. Phantom lime attends
me all the day long. I dream that I am a carpenter and can't partition off the hall. I frequently dance (with a distinguished company)
in the drawing-room, and fall in the kitchen for want of a pillar.

A great to-do here. A steamer lost on the Goodwins yesterday,
and our men bringing in no end of dead cattle and sheep. I stood
a supper for them last night, to the unbounded gratification of
Broadstairs. They came in from the wreck very wet and tired,
and very much disconcerted by the nature of their prize—which,
I suppose, after all, will have to be recommitted to the sea, when
the hides and tallow are secured. One lean-faced boatman mur-
mured, when they were all ruminative over the bodies as they lay
on the pier: " Couldn't sassages be made on it ?" but retired in
confusion shortly afterwards, overwhelmed by the execrations of
the bystanders.   Ever affectionately.

P.S.—Sometimes I think ——'s bill will be too long to be
added up until Babbage's calculating-machine shall be improved
and finished. Sometimes that there is not paper enough ready
made, to carry it over and bring it forward upon.

I dream, also, of the workmen every night. They make faces
at me, and won't do anything.

The same.

BROADSTAIRS, *Sunday, Twenty-first September*, 1851.

MY DEAR HENRY,

It is quite clear we could do nothing else with the drains
than what you have done. Will it be at all a heavy item in the
estimate ?

If there be the *least* chance of a necessity for the pillar, let us
have it. Let us dance in peace, whatever we do, and only go into
the kitchen by the staircase. Have they cut the door between
the drawing-room, and the study yet? The foreman will let
Shoolbred know when the feat is accomplished.

* Tavistock House.

Oh! and did you tell him of another brass ventilator in the dining-room, opening into the dining-room flue?

I am getting a complete set of a certain distinguished author's works prepared for a certain distinguished architect, which I hope he will accept, as a slight, though very inadequate, etc. etc.; affectionate, etc.; so heartily and kindly taking so much interest, etc. etc.

Ever affectionately.

BROADSTAIRS, *Sunday, Twenty-eighth September*, 1851.   The Hon. Miss Eden.*

MY DEAR MISS EDEN,

Many thanks for the grapes; which must have come from the identical vine a man ought to sit under. They were a prodigy of excellence.

I have been concerned to hear of your indisposition, but thought the best thing I could do, was to make no formal calls when you were really ill. I have been suffering myself from another kind of malady—a severe, spasmodic, house-buying-and-repairing attack—which has left me extremely weak and all but exhausted. The seat of the disorder has been the pocket.

I had the kindest of notes from the kindest of men this morning, and am going to see him on Wednesday. Of course I mean the Duke of Devonshire. Can I take anything to Chatsworth for you?

Very faithfully yours.

BROADSTAIRS, KENT, *Seventh October*, 1851.   Mr. Henry Austin.

MY DEAR HENRY,

O! O! O! D—— the Pantechnicon. O!

I will be at Tavistock House at twelve on Saturday, and then will wait for you until I see you. If we return together—as I hope we shall—our express will start at half-past four, and we ought to dine (somewhere about Temple Bar) at three.

The infamous —— says the stoves shall be fixed to-morrow.

Oh! if this were to last long; the distraction of the new book, the whirling of the story through one's mind, escorted by workmen, the imbecility, the wild necessity of beginning to write, the not being able to do so, the, O! I should go—— O!

Ever affectionately.

BROADSTAIRS, KENT, *Tenth October*, 1851.   Miss Mary Boyle.

ON THE DEATH OF HER MOTHER.

MY DEAR MISS BOYLE,

Your remembrance at such a time—not thrown away upon me, trust me—is a sufficient assurance that you know how truly

---

* Miss Eden had a cottage at Broadstairs, and was residing there at this time.

I feel towards you, and with what an earnest sympathy I must think of you now.

God be with you! There is indeed nothing terrible in such a death, nothing that we would undo, nothing that we may remember otherwise than with deeply thankful, though with softened hearts.

Kate sends you her affectionate love. I enclose a note from Georgina. Pray give my kindest remembrances to your brother Cavendish, and believe me now and ever,

Faithfully your Friend.

Mr. Eeles.

" HOUSEHOLD WORDS " OFFICE,
Wednesday Evening, Twenty-second October, 1851.

MY DEAR MR. EELES,

I send you the list I have made for the book-backs. I should like the " History of a Short Chancery Suit " to come at the bottom of one recess, and the " Catalogue of Statues of the Duke of Wellington " at the bottom of the other. If you should want more titles, and will let me know how many, I will send them to you. Faithfully yours.

LIST OF IMITATION BOOK-BACKS.

Tavistock House, 1851.

Five Minutes in China. 3 vols.

Forty Winks at the Pyramids. 2 vols.

Abernethy on the Constitution. 2 vols.

Mr. Green's Overland Mail. 2 vols.

Captain Cook's Life of Savage. 2 vols.

A Carpenter's Bench of Bishops. 2 vols.

Toots' Universal Letter - Writer. 2 vols.

Orson's Art of Etiquette.

Downeaster's Complete Calculator.

History of the Middling Ages. 6 vols.

Jonah's Account of the Whale.

Captain Parry's Virtues of Cold Tar.

Kant's Ancient Humbugs. 10 vols.

Bowwowdom. A Poem.

The Quarrelly Review. 4 vols.

The Gunpowder Magazine. 4 vols.

Steele. By the Author of "Ion."

The Art of Cutting the Teeth.

Matthew's Nursery Songs. 2 vols.

Paxton's Bloomers. 5 vols.

On the Use of Mercury by the Ancient Poets.

Drowsy's Recollections of Nothing. 3 vols.

Heavyside's Conversations with Nobody. 3 vols.

Commonplace Book of the Oldest Inhabitant. 2 vols.

Growler's Gruffiology, with Appendix. 4 vols.

The Books of Moses and Sons. 2 vols.

Burke (of Edinburgh) on the Sublime and Beautiful. 2 vols.

Teazer's Commentaries.

King Henry the Eighth's Evidences of Christianity. 5 vols.

Miss Biffin on Deportment.

Morrison's Pills Progress. 2 vols.

Lady Godiva on the Horse.

Munchausen's Modern Miracles. 4 vols.

Richardson's Show of Dramatic Literature. 12 vols.

Hansard's Guide to Refreshing Sleep. As many volumes as possible.

OFFICE OF "HOUSEHOLD WORDS,"
Saturday, Twenty-fifth October, 1851.

Mr. Henry
Austin.

MY DEAR HENRY,

On the day of our departure, I thought we were going—backward—at a most triumphant pace; but yesterday we rather recovered. The painters still mislaid their brushes every five minutes, and chiefly whistled in the intervals; and the carpenters (especially the Pantechnicon) continued to look sideways with one eye down pieces of wood, as if they were absorbed in the contemplation of the perspective of the Thames Tunnel, and had entirely relinquished the vanities of this transitory world; but still there was an improvement, and it is confirmed to-day. White lime is to be seen in kitchens, the bath-room is gradually resolving itself from an abstract idea into a fact—youthful, extremely youthful, but a fact. The drawing-room encourages no hope whatever, nor the study. Staircase painted. Irish labourers howling in the school-room, but I don't know why. I see nothing. Gardener vigorously lopping the trees, and really letting in the light and air. Foreman sweet-tempered but uneasy. Inimitable hovering gloomily through the premises all day, with an idea that a little more work is done when he flits, bat-like, through the rooms, than when there is no one looking on. Catherine all over paint. Mister McCann, encountering Inimitable in doorways, fades obsequiously into areas, and there encounters him again, and swoons with confusion. Several reams of blank paper constantly spread on the drawing-room walls, and sliced off again, which looks like insanity. Two men still clinking at the new stair-rails. I think they must be learning a tune; I cannot make out any other object in their proceedings.

Since writing the above, I have been up there again, and found the young paper-hanger putting on his slippers, and looking hard at the walls of the servant's room at the top of the house, as if he meant to paper it one of these days. May Heaven prosper his intentions!

Ever affectionately.

CLIFTON, *Thirteenth November*, 1851.

Mrs. Charles
Dickens.

MY DEAREST KATE,

I have just received your second letter, and am quite delighted to find that all is going on so vigorously, and that you are in such a methodical, business-like, and energetic state. I shall come home by the express on Saturday morning, and shall hope to be at home between eleven and twelve.

We had a noble night last night. The room (which is the largest but one in England) was crammed in every part. The effect of from thirteen to fourteen hundred people, all well dressed, and all seated in one unbroken chamber, except that the floor rose high towards the end of the hall, was most splendid, and we never played to a better audience. The enthusiasm was prodigious; the place delightful for speaking in; no end of gas; another hall for a dressing-room; an immense stage; and every possible convenience. We were all thoroughly pleased, I think, with the whole thing, and it was a very great and striking success. To-morrow-night, having the new Hardman, I am going to try the play with all kinds of cuts, taking out, among other things, some half-dozen printed pages of "Will's Coffee House."

We are very pleasant and cheerful. They are all going to Matthew Davenport Hill's to lunch this morning, and to see some woods about six or seven miles off. I prefer being quiet, and shall go out at my leisure and call on Elliott. We are very well lodged and boarded, and living high up on the Downs, are quite out of the filth of Bristol.

I saw old Landor at Bath, who has bronchitis. When he was last in town, "Kenyon drove him about, by God, half the morning, under a most damnable pretence of taking him to where Walter was at school, and they never found the confounded house!" He had in his pocket on that occasion a souvenir for Walter in the form of a Union shirt-pin, which is now in my possession, and shall be duly brought home.

I am tired enough, and shall be glad when to-morrow night is over. We expect a very good house. Forster came up to town after the performance last night, and promised to report to you that all was well. Jerrold is in extraordinary force. I don't think I ever knew him so humorous. And this is all my news, which is quite enough. I am continually thinking of the house in the midst of all the bustle, but I trust it with such confidence to you that I am quite at my ease about it.

Ever, my dearest Kate,
Most affectionately yours.

P.S.—I forgot to say that Topham has suddenly come out as a juggler, and swallows candles, and does wonderful things with the poker very well indeed, but with a bashfulness and embarrassment extraordinarily ludicrous.

TAVISTOCK HOUSE, TAVISTOCK SQUARE,   Mr. Eeles.
Seventeenth November, 1851.

DEAR MR. EELES,

I must thank you for the admirable manner in which you have done the book-backs in my room. I feel personally obliged to you, I assure you, for the interest you have taken in my whim, and the promptitude with which you have completely carried it out.

Faithfully yours.

TAVISTOCK HOUSE, *Thursday Afternoon*,   Mrs.
Fifth December, 1851.   Gaskell.

MY DEAR MRS. GASKELL,

I write in great haste to tell you that Mr. Wills, in the utmost consternation, has brought me your letter, just received (four o'clock), and that it is *too late* to recall your tale. I was so delighted with it that I put it first in the number (not hearing of any objection to my proposed alteration by return of post), and the number is now made up in the printer's hands. I cannot possibly take the tale out—it has departed from me.

I am truly concerned for this, but I hope you will not blame me for what I have done in perfect good faith. Any recollection of me from your pen cannot (as I think you know) be otherwise than truly gratifying to me ; but with my name on every page of "Household Words," there would be—or at least I should feel— an impropriety in so mentioning myself. I was particular, in changing the author, to make it "Hood's *Poems*" in the most important place—I mean where the captain is killed—and I hope and trust that the substitution will not be any serious drawback to the paper in any eyes but yours. I would do anything rather than cause you a minute's vexation arising out of what has given me so much pleasure, and I sincerely beseech you to think better of it, and not to fancy that any shade has been thrown on your charming writing, by

The unfortunate but innocent.

TAVISTOCK HOUSE, TAVISTOCK SQUARE,   Mr. Austen
Sixteenth December, 1851.   Henry
   Layard.

MY DEAR LAYARD,

I want to renew your recollection of "the last time we parted"—not at Wapping Old Stairs, but at Miss Coutts'—when we vowed to be more intimate after all nations should have departed from Hyde Park, and I should be able to emerge from my cave on the seashore.

Can you, and will you, be in town on Wednesday, the last day of the present old year?   If yes, will you dine with us at a quarter after six, and see the New Year in with such extemporaneous follies of an exploded sort (in genteel society) as may occur to us?   Both Mrs. Dickens and I would be really delighted if this should find you free to give us the pleasure of your society.

Believe me always, very faithfully yours.

Mrs.
Gaskell.

TAVISTOCK HOUSE, *Sunday,*
Twenty-first December, 1851.

MY DEAR MRS. GASKELL,

If you were not the most suspicious of women, always looking for soft sawder in the purest metal of praise, I should call your paper delightful, and touched in the tenderest and most delicate manner.   Being what you are, I confine myself to the observation that I have called it " A Love Affair at Cranford," and sent it off to the printer. Faithfully yours ever.

Mr. Peter
Cunning-
ham.

TAVISTOCK HOUSE, *Twenty-sixth December*, 1851.

MY DEAR CUNNINGHAM,

About the three papers.

1st.   With Mr. Plowman of Oxford, Wills will communicate.

2nd.   (Now returned.)   I have seen, in nearly the same form, before.   The list of names is overwhelming.

3rd.   I am not at all earnest in the Savage matter; firstly, because I think so tremendous a vagabond never could have obtained an honest living in any station of existence or at any period of time; and secondly, because I think it of the highest importance that such an association as our Guild should not appear to resent upon society the faults of individuals who were flagrantly impracticable.

At its best, it is liable to that suspicion, as all such efforts have been on the part of many jealous persons, to whom it *must* look for aid.   And any step that in the least encourages it is one of a fatal kind.

I do *not* think myself, but this is merely an individual opinion, that Savage *was* a man of genius, or that anything of his writing would have attracted much notice but for the bastard's reference to his mother.   For these reasons combined, I should not be inclined to add my subscription of two guineas to yours, unless the inscription were altered as I have altered it in pencil.   But in that case I should be very glad to respond to your suggestion, and to snuff out all my smaller disinclination.

Faithfully yours ever.

1852.

NARRATIVE.

IN the summer of this year, Charles Dickens hired a house at Dover for three months, whither he went with his family. At the end of this time he sent his children and servants back to Tavistock House, and crossed over to Boulogne, with his wife and sister-in-law, to inspect that town and its neighbourhood, with a view of making it his summer quarters in the following year. Many amateur performances were given in the provinces in aid of the fund for the Guild of Literature and Art; Charles Dickens, as usual, taking the whole management on his own shoulders.

In March, the first number of "Bleak House" appeared, and he was at work on this book all through the year, as well as being constantly occupied with his editorship of "Household Words."

We have, in the letters for this year, Charles Dickens' first to Lord John Russell (afterwards the Earl Russell); a friend whom he held in the highest estimation, and to whom he was always grateful for many personal kindnesses. We have also his first letter to Mr. Wilkie Collins, with whom he became most intimately associated in literary work. The affectionate friendship he had for him, the high value in which he held him as a brother-artist, are constantly expressed in Charles Dickens' own letters to Mr. Collins, and in his letters to other friends.

"Those gallant men" (in the letter to Mr. J. Crofton Croker) had reference to an antiquarian club, called the Noviomagians, who were about to give a dinner in honour of Sir Edward Belcher and Captain Kellett, the officers in command of the Arctic Exploring Expedition, to which Charles Dickens was also invited. Mr. Crofton Croker was the president of this club, and to denote his office it was customary to put on a cocked hat after dinner.

The "lost character" he writes of in a letter to Mrs. Watson, refers to two different decipherings of his handwriting; this sort of study being in fashion then, and he and his friends at Rockingham Castle deriving much amusement from it.

The letter, dated Twenty-sixth March, to Mr. (afterwards Dr.) James Bower Harrison (a cousin of Mr. Harrison Ainsworth, and the writer of many scientific works), was on the subject of an article, written by that gentleman for "Household Words," on the injurious effects of the manufacture of lucifer matches on the employed.

The letter dated Ninth July was in answer to an anonymous correspondent, who wrote to him as follows: " I venture to trespass on your attention with one serious query, touching a sentence in the last number of 'Bleak House.' Do the supporters of Christian missions to the heathen really deserve the attack that is conveyed in the sentence about Jo' seated in his anguish on the doorstep of the Society for the Propagation of the Gospel in Foreign Parts? The allusion is severe, but is it just? Are such boys as Jo' neglected? What are ragged schools, town missions, and many of those societies I regret to see sneered at in the last number of 'Household Words'?"

Our last letter in this year, to Mr. G. Linnæus Banks, was in acknowledgment of one from him on the subject of a proposed public dinner to Charles Dickens, to be given by the people of Birmingham, when they were also to present him with a salver and a diamond ring. The dinner was given in the following year, and the ring and salver (the latter an artistic specimen of Birmingham ware) were duly presented by Mr. Banks, who acted as honorary secretary, in the names of the subscribers, at the rooms of the Birmingham Fine Arts Association. Mr. Banks, and the artist, Mr. J. C. Walker, were the originators of this demonstration.

Mr. W. C.
Macready.

TAVISTOCK HOUSE, *Thirty-first January*, 1852.

MY DEAR MACREADY,

If the "taxes on knowledge" mean the stamp duty, the paper duty, and the advertisement duty, they seem to me to be unnecessarily confounded, and unfairly too.

I have already declined to sign a petition for the removal of the stamp duty on newspapers. I think the reduced duty is some protection to the public against the rash and hasty launching of blackguard newspapers. I think the newspapers are made extremely accessible to the poor man at present, and that he would not derive the least benefit from the abolition of the stamp. It is not at all clear to me, supposing he wants *The Times* a penny cheaper, that he would get it a penny cheaper if the tax were taken off. If he supposes he would get in competition two or three new journals as good to choose from, he is mistaken; not knowing the immense resources and the gradually perfective machinery necessary to the production of such a journal. It appears to me to be a fair tax enough, very little in the way of individuals, not embarrassing to the public in its mode of being levied, and requiring some small consideration and pauses from the American kind of newspaper projectors. Further, a committee has reported in favour of the repeal, and the subject may be held to need no present launching.

The repeal of the paper duty would benefit the producers of periodicals immensely. It would make a very large difference to me, in the case of such a journal as "Household Words." But the gain to the public would be very small. It would not make the difference of enabling me, for example, to reduce the price of "Household Words," by its fractional effect upon a copy, or to increase the quantity of matter. I might, in putting the difference into my pocket, improve the quality of the paper a little, but not one man in a thousand would notice it. It *might* (though I am not sure even of this) remove the difficulties in the way of a deserving periodical with a small sale. Charles Knight holds that it would. But the case, on the whole, appeared to me so slight, when I went to Downing Street with a deputation on the subject, that I said (in addressing the Chancellor of the Exchequer) I could not honestly maintain it for a moment as against the soap duty, or any other pressing on the mass of the poor.

The advertisement duty has this preposterous anomaly, that a footman in want of a place pays as much in the way of tax for the expression of his want, as Professor Holloway pays for the whole list of his miraculous cures.

But I think, at this time especially, there is so much to be considered in the necessity the country will be under of having money, and the necessity of justice it is always under, to consider the physical and moral wants of the poor man's home, as to justify a man in saying : "I must wait a little, all taxes are more or less objectionable, and so no doubt are these, but we must have some ; and I have not made up my mind that all these things that are mixed up together *are* taxes on knowledge in reality."

We are always with you in spirit, and always talking about you. I am obliged to conclude very hastily, being beset to-day with business engagements. Saw the lecture and was delighted ; thought the idea admirable. Again, loves upon loves to dear Mrs. Macready and to Miss Macready also, and Kate and all the house. I saw —— play (O Heaven !) "Macbeth," the other night, in three hours and fifty minutes, which is quick, I think.

Ever and always affectionately.

TAVISTOCK HOUSE,
Sunday Night, Fifteenth February, 1852.

Sir Edward
Bulwer
Lytton.

MY DEAR BULWER,

I left Liverpool at four o'clock this morning, and am so blinded by excitement, gas, and waving hats and handkerchiefs, that I can hardly see to write, but I cannot go to bed without telling you what a triumph we have had. Allowing for the necessarily heavy expenses of all kinds, I believe we can hardly fund less than a Thousand Pounds out of this trip alone. And, more than that, the extraordinary interest taken in the idea of the Guild by "this grand people of England" down in these vast hives, and the enthusiastic welcome they give it, assure me that we may do what we will if we will only be true and faithful to our design. There is a social recognition of it which I cannot give you the least idea of. I sincerely believe that we have the ball at our feet, and may throw it up to the very Heaven of Heavens. And I don't speak for myself alone, but for all our people, and not least of all for Forster, who has been absolutely stunned by the tremendous earnestness of these great places.

To tell you (especially after your affectionate letter) what I would have given to have had you there would be idle. But I can most seriously say that all the sights of the earth turned pale in my eyes, before the sight of three thousand people with one heart among them, and no capacity in them, in spite of all their efforts, of sufficiently testifying to you how they believe you to be right, and feel that they cannot do enough to cheer you on. They understood the play (*far better acted by this time than ever you have seen it*) as well as you do. They allowed nothing to escape them. They rose up, when it was over, with a perfect fury of delight, and the Manchester people sent a requisition after us to Liverpool to say that if we will go back there in May, when we act at Birmingham (as of course we shall) they will joyfully undertake to fill the Free Trade Hall again. Among the Tories of Liverpool the reception was equally enthusiastic. We played, two nights running, to a hall crowded to the roof—more like the opera at Genoa or Milan than anything else I can compare it to. We dined at the Town Hall magnificently, and it made no difference in the response. I said what we were quietly determined to do (when the Guild was given as the toast of the night), and really they were so noble and generous in their encouragement that I should have been more ashamed of myself than I hope I ever shall be, if I could have felt conscious of having ever for a moment faltered in the work.

I will answer for Birmingham—for any great working town to which we chose to go. We have won a position for the idea which years upon years of labour could not have given it. I believe its worldly fortunes have been advanced in this last week fifty years at least. I feebly express to you what Forster (who couldn't be at Liverpool, and has not those shouts ringing in his ears) has felt from the moment he set foot in Manchester. Believe me we may carry a perfect fiery cross through the North of England, and over the Border, in this cause, if need be—not only to the enrichment of the cause, but to the lasting enlistment of the people's sympathy.

I have been so happy in all this that I could have cried on the shortest notice any time since Tuesday. And I do believe that our whole body would have gone to the North Pole with me if I had shown them good reason for it.

I hope I am not so tired but that you may be able to read this. I have been at it almost incessantly, day and night for a week, and I am afraid my handwriting suffers. But in all other respects I am only a giant refreshed.

We meet next Saturday you recollect? Until then, and ever afterwards, Believe me, heartily yours.

TAVISTOCK HOUSE, *Third March,* 1852.　Mrs. Cowden Clarke.

MY DEAR MRS. CLARKE,
　　　It is almost an impertinence to tell you how delightful your flowers were to me ; for you who thought of that beautiful and delicately-timed token of sympathy and remembrance, must know it very well already.

I do assure you that I have hardly ever received anything with so much pleasure in all my life. They are not faded yet—are on my table here—but never can fade out of my remembrance.

I should be less than a Young Gas, and more than an old Manager—that commemorative portfolio is here too—if I could relieve my heart of half that it could say to you. All my house are my witnesses that you have quite filled it, and this note is my witness that I can *not* empty it.

　　　Ever faithfully and gratefully your Friend.

TAVISTOCK HOUSE, *Sixth March,* 1852.　Mr. J. Crofton Croker.

MY DEAR SIR,
　　　I have the greatest interest in those gallant men, and should have been delighted to dine in their company. I feel truly obliged to you for your kind remembrance on such an occasion.

But I am engaged to Lord Lansdowne on Wednesday, and can only drink to them in spirit, which I have often done when they have been farther off.

I hope you will find occasion to put on your cocked hat, that they may see how terrific and imposing " a fore-and-after " can be made on shore.　　　　　　　　Faithfully yours always.

LONDON, TAVISTOCK HOUSE, *Twenty-sixth March,* 1852.　Mr. James Bower Harrison.

DEAR SIR,
　　　I beg to thank you for your interesting pamphlet, and to add that I shall be very happy to accept an article from you on

the subject for "Household Words." I should already have suggested to you that I should have great pleasure in receiving contributions from one so well and peculiarly qualified to treat of many interesting subjects, but that I felt a delicacy in encroaching on your other occupations. Will you excuse my remarking that to make an article on this particular subject useful, it is essential to address the employed as well as the employers? In the case of the Sheffield grinders the difficulty was, for many years, not with the masters, but the men. Painters who use white lead are with the greatest difficulty persuaded to be particular in washing their hands, and I daresay that I need not remind you that one could not generally induce domestic servants to attend to the commonest sanitary principles in their work without absolutely forcing them to experience their comfort and convenience.

Dear Sir, very faithfully yours.

TAVISTOCK HOUSE, Sixth April, 1852.

The Hon.
Mrs.
Watson.

MY DEAR MRS. WATSON,

My "lost character" was one of those awful documents occasionally to be met with, which WILL be everywhere. It glared upon me from every drawer I had, fell out of books, lurked under keys, hid in empty inkstands, got into portfolios, frightened me by inscrutably passing into locked despatch-boxes, and was not one character, but a thousand. This was when I didn't want it. I look for it this morning, and it is nowhere! Probably will never be beheld again.

But it was very unlike this one; and there is no doubt that when these ventures come out good, it is only by lucky chance and coincidence. She never mentioned my love of order before, and it is so remarkable (being almost a *dis*order), that she ought to have fainted with surprise when my handwriting was first revealed to her.

I was very sorry to leave Rockingham the other day, and came away in quite a melancholy state. The Birmingham people were very active; and the Shrewsbury gentry quite transcendent. I hope we shall have a very successful and dazzling trip. It is delightful to me to think of your coming to Birmingham; and, by-the-bye, if you will tell me in the previous week what hotel accommodation you want, Mr. Wills will look to it with the greatest pleasure.

Your bookseller ought to be cashiered. I suppose "he" (as Rogers calls everybody's husband) went out hunting with the idea of diverting his mind from dwelling on its loss. Abortive effort!

Ever, dear Mrs. Watson, most faithfully yours.

TAVISTOCK HOUSE, *Twenty-ninth June*, 1852. Mr. Charles
MY DEAR KNIGHT, Knight.

A thousand thanks for the Shadow, which is charming.
May you often go (out of town) and do likewise!

I dined with Charles Kemble, yesterday, to meet Emil Devrient,
the German actor. He said (Devrient is my antecedent) that
Ophelia *spoke* the snatches of ballads in their German version
of " Hamlet," because they didn't know the airs. Tom Taylor
said that you had published the airs in your " Shakespeare." I
said that if it were so, I knew you would be happy to place them
at the German's service. If you have got them and will send
them to me, I will write to Devrient (who knows no English) a
French explanation and reminder of the circumstance, and will tell
him that you responded like a man and a—I was going to say
publisher, but you are nothing of the sort, except as Tonson.*
Then indeed you are every inch a pub. !

Ever affectionately.

TAVISTOCK HOUSE, *Wednesday, Thirtieth June*, 1852. The
MY DEAR LORD, Lord John
Russell.

I am most truly obliged to you for your kind note, and for
your so generously thinking of me in the midst of your many
occupations. I do assure you that your ever ready consideration
had already attached me to you in the warmest manner, and made
me very much your debtor. I thank you unaffectedly and very
earnestly, and am proud to be held in your remembrance.

Believe me always, yours faithfully and obliged.

TAVISTOCK HOUSE, TAVISTOCK SQUARE, Anonymous
Ninth July, 1852. Corre-
spondent.
SIR,

I have received your letter of yesterday's date, and shall
content myself with a brief reply.

There was a long time during which benevolent societies were
spending immense sums on missions abroad, when there was no
such thing as a ragged school in England, or any kind of associated
endeavour to penetrate to those horrible domestic depths in which
such schools are now to be found, and where they were, to my
most certain knowledge, neither placed nor discovered by the
Society for the Propagation of the Gospel in Foreign Parts.

If you think the balance between the home mission and the
foreign mission justly held in the present time, I do not. I

* Mr. Charles Knight played the part of Jacob Tonson in " Not So Bad
as We Seem."

abstain from drawing the strange comparison that might be drawn
between the sums even now expended in endeavours to remove
the darkest ignorance and degradation from our very doors,
because I have some respect for mistakes that may be founded
in a sincere wish to do good. But I present a general suggestion
of the still-existing anomaly (in such a paragraph as that which
offends you), in the hope of inducing some people to reflect on this
matter, and to adjust the balance more correctly. I am decidedly
of opinion that the two works, the home and the foreign, are *not*
conducted with an equal hand, and that the home claim is by far
the stronger and the more pressing of the two.

Indeed, I have very grave doubts whether a great commercial
country, holding communication with all parts of the world, can
better Christianise the benighted portions of it than by the
bestowal of its wealth and energy on the making of good Christians at home, and on the utter removal of neglected and untaught
childhood from its streets, before it wanders elsewhere. For, if it
steadily persists in this work, working downward to the lowest,
the travellers of all grades whom it sends abroad will be good,
exemplary, practical missionaries, instead of undoers of what the
best professed missionaries can do.

These are my opinions, founded, I believe, on some knowledge
of facts and some observation. If I could be scared out of them,
let me add in all good humour, by such easily-impressed words as
"antichristian" or "irreligious," I should think that I deserved
them in their real signification.

I have referred in vain to page 312 of "Household Words" for
the sneer to which you call my attention. Nor have I, I assure
you, the least idea where else it is to be found.

I am, Sir, your faithful Servant.

10, CAMDEN CRESCENT, DOVER,
Twenty-second July, 1852.

Miss Mary
Boyle.

MY DEAR MARY,

This is indeed a noble letter. The description of the family
is quite amazing. I *must* return it myself to say that I HAVE
appreciated it.

I am going to do "Used Up" at Manchester on the Second of
September. O, think of that! With another Mary!!! How
can I ever say, "*Dear* Joe, if you like!" The voice may fully
frame the falsehood, but the heart—the heart, Mr. Wurzel—will
have no part in it.

My dear Mary, you do scant justice to Dover. It is not quite a place to my taste, being too bandy (I mean musical, no reference to its legs), and infinitely too genteel.   But the sea is very fine, and the walks are quite remarkable.   There are two ways of going to Folkestone, both lovely and striking in the highest degree ; and there are heights, and downs, and country roads, and I don't know what, everywhere.

To let you into a secret, I am not quite sure that I ever did like, or ever shall like, anything quite so well as "Copperfield." But I foresee, I think, some very good things in "Bleak House." I shouldn't wonder if they were the identical things that D'Israeli sees looming in the distance.   I behold them in the months ahead and weep.

Watson seemed, when I saw him last, to be holding on as by a sheet-anchor to theatricals at Christmas.   Then, O rapture ! but be still, my fluttering heart.

This is one of what I call my wandering days before I fall to work.   I seem to be always looking at such times for something I have not found in life, but may possibly come to a few thousands of years hence, in some other part of some other system.   God knows.   At all events I won't put your pastoral little pipe out of tune by talking about it.   I'll go and look for it on the Canterbury road among the hop-gardens and orchards.

Ever faithfully your Friend,

JOE.

10, CAMDEN CRESCENT, DOVER,   Mr. Charles
Sunday, First August, 1852.   Knight.

MY DEAR KNIGHT,

I don't see why you should go to the Ship, and I won't stand it.   The state apartment will be occupied by the Duke of Middlesex * (whom I think you know), but we can easily get a bed for you hard by.   Therefore, you will please to drive here next Saturday evening.   Our regular dinner hour is half-past five. If you are later, you will find something ready for you.

If you go on in that way about your part, I shall think you want to play Mr. Gabblewig.   Your rôle, though a small one on the stage, is a large one off it ; and no man is more important to the Guild, both on and off.

My dear friend Watson !   Dead after an illness of four days. He dined with us this day three weeks.   I loved him as my heart, and cannot think of him without tears.

Ever affectionately.

* The character played by Mr. Frank Stone in Sir E. B. Lytton's comedy.

Mr. Mark
Lemon.

DOVER, *Fifth August*, 1852.

MY DEAR MARK,

Poor dear Watson was dead when the paragraph in the paper appeared. He was buried in his own church yesterday. Last Sunday three weeks (the day before he went abroad) he dined with us, and was quite well and happy. She has come home, is at Rockingham with the children, and does not weakly desert his grave, but sets up her rest by it from the first. He had been wandering in his mind a little before his death, but recovered consciousness, and fell asleep (she says) quite gently and peacefully in her arms.

I loved him very much, and God knows he deserved it.

Ever affectionately.

The Earl of
Carlisle.

10, CAMDEN CRESCENT, DOVER,
Thursday, Fifth August, 1852.

MY DEAR LORD CARLISLE,

'Peared to me (as Uncle Tom would say) until within these last few days, that I should be able to write to you, joyfully accepting your Saturday's invitation after Newcastle, in behalf of all whom it concerned. But the Sunderland people rushed into the field to propose our acting there on that Saturday, the only possible night. And as it is the concluding Guild expedition, and the Guild has a paramount claim on us, I have been obliged to knock my own inclinations on the head, cut the throat of my own wishes, and bind the Company hand and foot to the Sunderland lieges. I don't mean to tell them now of your invitation until we shall have got out of that country. There might be rebellion. We are staying here for the autumn.

Is there any hope of your repeating your visit to these coasts?

Ever faithfully yours.

The Hon.
Mrs.
Watson.

10, CAMDEN CRESCENT, DOVER,
Fifth August, 1852.

ON THE DEATH OF MR. WATSON.

MY DEAR, DEAR MRS. WATSON,

I cannot bear to be silent longer, though I know full well —no one better, I think—how your love for him, and your trust in God, and your love for your children will have come to the help of such a nature as yours, and whispered better things than any friendship can, however faithful and affectionate.

We held him so close in our hearts—all of us here—and have been so happy with him, and so used to say how good he was, and what a gentle, generous, noble spirit he had, and how he shone out among commoner men as something so real and genuine, and full of every kind of worthiness, that it has often brought the tears into my eyes to talk of him; we have been so accustomed to do this when we looked forward to years of unchanged intercourse, that now, when everything but truth goes down into the dust, those recollections which make the sword so sharp pour balm into the wound.   And if it be a consolation to us to know the virtues of his character, and the reasons that we had for loving him, O how much greater is your comfort who were so devoted to him, and were the happiness of his life!

We have thought of you every day and every hour; we think of you now in the dear old house, and know how right it is, for his dear children's sake, that you should have bravely set up your rest in the place consecrated by their father's memory, and within the same summer shadows that fall upon his grave.   We try to look on, through a few years, and to see the children brightening it, and George a comfort and a pride and an honour to you; and although it is hard to think of what we have lost, we know how something of it will be restored by your example and endeavours, and the blessing that will descend upon them.   We know how the time will come when some reflection of that cordial, unaffected, most affectionate presence, which we can never forget, and never would forget if we could—such is God's great mercy—will shine out of your boy's eyes upon you, his best friend and his last consoler, and fill the void there is now.

May God, who has received into His rest through this affliction as good a man as ever I can know and love and mourn for on this earth, be good to you, dear friends, through these coming years! May all those compassionate and hopeful lessons of the great Teacher who shed divine tears for the dead bring their full comfort to you!   I have no fear of that, my confidence is certainty.

I cannot write what I wish; I had so many things to say, I seem to have said none.   It is so with the remembrances we send. I cannot put them into words.

If you should ever set up a record in the little church, I would try to word it myself, and God knows out of the fulness of my heart, if you should think it well.

My dear Friend,

Yours, with the truest affection and sympathy.

T

HÔTEL DES BAINS, BOULOGNE,
Tuesday Night, Fifth October, 1852.

ON THE DEATH OF MRS. MACREADY.

MY DEAREST MACREADY,

I received your melancholy letter while we were staying at Dover, a few days after it was written; but I thought it best not to write to you until you were at home again, among your dear children.

Its tidings were not unexpected to us, had been anticipated in many conversations, often thought of under many circumstances; but the shock was scarcely lessened by this preparation. The many happy days we have passed together came crowding back; all the old cheerful times arose before us; and the remembrance of what we had loved so dearly and seen under so many aspects— all natural and delightful and affectionate and ever to be cherished —was, how pathetic and touching you know best!

But my dear, dear Macready, this is not the first time you have felt that the recollection of great love and happiness associated with the dead soothes while it wounds. And while I can imagine that the blank beside you may grow wider every day for many days to come, I *know*—I think—that from its depths such comfort will arise as only comes to great hearts like yours, when they can think upon their trials with a steady trust in God.

My dear friend, I have known her so well, have been so happy in her regard, have been so light-hearted with her, have interchanged so many tender remembrances of you with her when you were far away, and have seen her ever so simply and truly anxious to be worthy of you, that I cannot write as I would and as I know I ought. As I would press your hand in your distress, I let this note go from me. I understand your grief, I deeply feel the reason that there is for it, yet in that very feeling find a softening consolation that must spring up a hundred-thousandfold for you. May Heaven prosper it in your breast, and the spirits that have gone before, from the regions of mercy to which they have been called, smooth the path you have to tread alone! Children are left to you. Your good sister (God bless her!) is by your side. You have devoted friends, and more reasons than most men to be self-reliant and steadfast. Something is gone that never in this world can be replaced, but much is left, and it is a part of her life, her death, her immortality.

Catherine and Georgina, who are with me here, send you their overflowing love and sympathy. We hope that in a little while, and for a little while at least, you will come among us, who have known the happiness of being in this bond with you, and will not exclude us from participation in your past and future.

Ever, my dearest Macready, with unchangeable affection,

Yours in all love and truth.

Mr. W. H. Wills.

HÔTEL DES BAINS, BOULOGNE,
Tuesday, Twelfth October, 1852.

MY DEAR WILLS,

H. W.

I have thought of the Christmas number, but not very successfully, because I have been (and still am) constantly occupied with "Bleak House." I purpose returning home either on Sunday or Monday, as my work permits, and we will, immediately thereafter, dine at the office and talk it over, so that you may get all the men to their work.

The fault of ——'s poem, besides its intrinsic meanness as a composition, is that it goes too glibly with the comfortable ideas (of which we have had a great deal too much in England since the Continental commotions) that a man is to sit down and make himself domestic and meek, no matter what is done to him. It wants a stronger appeal to rulers in general to let men do this, fairly, by governing them well. As it stands, it is at about the tract-mark ("Dairyman's Daughter," etc.) of political morality, and don't think that it is necessary to write *down* to any part of our audience. I always hold that to be as great a mistake as can be made.

I wish you would mention to Thomas,[*] that I think the paper on hops *extremely well done.* He has caught quite the idea we want, and caught it in the best way. In pursuing the bridge subject, I think it would be advisable to look up the *Thames police.* I have a misty notion of some capital papers coming out of it. Will you see to this branch of the tree among the other branches?

MYSELF.

To Chapman I will write. My impression is that I shall not subscribe to the Hood monument, as I am not at all favourable to such posthumous honours.

Ever faithfully.

---

[*] Mr. Moy Thomas, who was at this time one of the regular contributors to " Household Words,"

Mr. W. H.
Wills.

HÔTEL DES BAINS, BOULOGNE,
Wednesday Night, Thirteenth October, 1852.

MY DEAR WILLS,

I am grievously depressed by the number; it is so exceedingly bad. If you have anything else to put first, don't put ——'s paper first. (There is nothing better for a beginning in the number as it stands, but this is very bad.) It is a mistake to think of it as a first article. The article itself is in the main a mistake. Firstly, the subject requires the greatest discretion and nicety of touch. And secondly, it is all wrong and self-contradictory. Nobody can for a moment suppose that " sporting " amusements are the sports of the PEOPLE; the whole gist of the best part of the description is to show that they are the amusements of a peculiar and limited class. The greater part of them are at a miserable discount (horse-racing excepted, which has been already sufficiently done in H. W.), and there is no reason for running amuck at them at all.º I have endeavoured to remove much of my objection (and I think have done so), but both in purpose and in any general address, it is as wide of a first article as anything can well be. It would do best in the opening of the number.

About Sunday in Paris there is no kind of doubt. Take it out. Such a thing as that crucifixion, unless it were done in a masterly manner, we have no business to stagger families with. Besides, the name is a comprehensive one, and should include a quantity of fine matter. Lord bless me, what I could write under that head !

Strengthen the number, pray, by anything good you may have. It is a very dreary business as it stands.

Ever faithfully.

P.S.—I want a name for Miss Martineau's paper.

TRIUMPHANT CARRIAGES (OR TRIUMPHAL).
DUBLIN STOUTHEARTEDNESS.
PATIENCE AND PREJUDICE.

Take which you like best.

Mr. John
Watkins.

MONDAY, *Eighteenth October,* 1852.

SIR,

On my return to town I find the letter awaiting me which you did me the favour to address to me, I believe—for it has no date—some days ago.

I have the greatest tenderness for the memory of Hood, as I had for himself. But I am not very favourable to posthumous memorials in the monument way, and I should exceedingly regret to see any such appeal as you contemplate made public, remembering another public appeal that was made and responded to after Hood's death. I think that I best discharge my duty to my deceased friend, and best consult the respect and love with which I remember him, by declining to join in any such public endeavours as that which you (in all generosity and singleness of purpose, I am sure) advance. I shall have a melancholy gratification in privately assisting to place a simple and plain record over the remains of a great writer that should be as modest as he was himself, but I regard any other monument in connection with his mortal resting-place as a mistake.

I am, Sir, your faithful Servant.

OFFICE OF "HOUSEHOLD WORDS,"   Rev. James
Tuesday, Nineteenth October, 1852.   White.

MY DEAR WHITE,

We are now getting our Christmas extra number together, and I think you are the boy to do, if you will, one of the stories.

I propose to give the number some fireside name, and to make it consist entirely of short stories supposed to be told by a family sitting round the fire. *I don't care about their referring to Christmas at all;* nor do I design to connect them together otherwise than by their names, as : ·

THE GRANDFATHER'S STORY.
THE FATHER'S STORY.
THE DAUGHTER'S STORY.
THE SCHOOLBOY'S STORY.
THE CHILD'S STORY.
THE GUEST'S STORY.
THE OLD NURSE'S STORY.

The grandfather might very well be old enough to have lived in the days of the highwaymen. Do you feel disposed, from fact, fancy, or both, to do a good winter-hearth story of a highwayman? If you do, I embrace you (per post), and throw up a cap I have purchased for the purpose into mid-air.

Think of it and write me a line in reply. We are all well and blooming.

Are you never coming to town any more? Never going to drink port again, metropolitaneously, but *always* with Fielden*?

Ever faithfully, my dear White.

ATHENÆUM, *Monday, Twenty-second November*, 1852.   The Hon.
Mrs.
Watson.

MY DEAR MRS. WATSON,

Having just now finished my work for the time being, I turn in here in the course of a rainy walk, to have the gratification

---

* The Rev. R. Fielden, a clergyman resident at Bonchurch.

of writing a few lines to you. If my occupations with this same right hand were less numerous, you would soon be tired of me, I should write to you so often.

You ask Catherine a question about " Bleak House." Its circulation is half as large again as "Copperfield" ! I have just now come to the point I have been patiently working up to in the writing, and I hope it will suggest to you a pretty and affecting thing. In the matter of " Uncle Tom's Cabin," I partly though not entirely agree with Mr. James. No doubt a much lower art will serve for the handling of such a subject in fiction, than for a launch on the sea of imagination without such a powerful bark ; but there are many points in the book very admirably done. There is a certain St. Clair, a New Orleans gentleman, who seems to me to be conceived with great power and originality. If he had not "a Grecian outline of face," which I began to be a little tired of in my earliest infancy, I should think him unexceptionable. He has a sister too, a maiden lady from New England, in whose person the besetting weaknesses and prejudices of the Abolitionists themselves, on the subject of the blacks, are set forth in the liveliest and truest colours, and with the greatest boldness.

I have written for " Household Words " of this next publication-day an article on the State funeral,* showing why I consider it altogether a mistake, to be temperately but firmly objected to ; which I daresay will make a good many of the admirers of such things highly indignant. It may have right and reason on its side, however, none the less.

Charley and I had a great talk at Dover about his going into the army, when I thought it right to set before him fairly and faithfully the objections to that career, no less than its advantages. The result was that he asked in a very manly way for time to consider. So I appointed to go down to Eton on a certain day at the beginning of this month, and resume the subject. We resumed it accordingly at the White Hart, at Windsor, and he came to the conclusion that he would rather be a merchant, and try to establish some good house of business, where he might find a path perhaps for his younger brothers, and stay at home, and make himself the head of that long, small procession. I was very much pleased with him indeed ; he showed a fine sense and a fine feeling in the whole matter. We have arranged, therefore, that he shall leave Eton at Christmas, and go to Germany after the holidays, to become well acquainted with that language, now most essential in such a walk of life as he will probably tread.

And I think this is the whole of my news. We are always

* The great Duke of Wellington's funeral.

talking of you at home. Mary Boyle dined with us a little while ago. You look out, I imagine, on a waste of water. When I came from Windsor, I thought I must have made a mistake and got into a boat (in the dark) instead of a railway-carriage. I am ever, with the best and truest wishes of my heart, my dear Mrs. Watson,

Your most affectionate Friend.

OFFICE OF "HOUSEHOLD WORDS,"
Monday, Twenty-second November, 1852.
Rev. James White.

MY DEAR WHITE,

First and foremost, there is no doubt whatever of your story suiting "Household Words." It is a very good story indeed, and would be serviceable at any time. I am not quite so clear of its suiting the Christmas number, for this reason. You know what the spirit of the Christmas number is. When I suggested the stories being about a highwayman, I got hold of that idea as being an adventurous one, including various kinds of wrong, expressing a state of society no longer existing among us, and pleasant to hear (therefore) from an old man. Now, your highwayman not being a real highwayman after all, the kind of suitable Christmas interest I meant to awaken in the story is not in it. Do you understand ? For an ordinary number it is quite unobjectionable. If you should think of any other idea, narratable by an old man, which you think would strike the chord of the season ; and if you should find time to work it out during the short remainder of this month, I should be greatly pleased to have it. In any case this story goes straightway into type.

I think you will find some good going in the next "Bleak House." I write shortly, having been working my head off.

Ever affectionately yours.

OFFICE OF "HOUSEHOLD WORDS,"
Wednesday, First December, 1852.
Mrs. Gaskell.

MY DEAR MRS. GASKELL,

I send you the proof of "The Old Nurse's Story," with my proposed alteration. I shall be glad to know whether you approve of it. To assist you in your decision, I send you, also enclosed, the original ending. And I have made a line with ink across the last slip but one, where the alteration begins. Of course if you wish to enlarge, explain, or re-alter, you will do it. Do not keep the proof longer than you can help, as I want to get to press with all despatch.

Ever faithfully yours.

Mr. W. H.
Wills.

TAVISTOCK HOUSE,
Thursday, Ninth December, 1852.

MY DEAR WILLS,

I am driven mad by dogs, who have taken it into their accursed heads to assemble every morning in the piece of ground opposite, and who have barked this morning *for five hours without intermission* ; positively rendering it impossible for me to work, and so making what is really ridiculous quite serious to me. I wish, between this and dinner, you would send John to see if he can hire a gun, with a few caps, some powder, and a few charges of small shot. If you duly commission him with a card, he can easily do it. And if I get those implements up here to-night, I'll be the death of some of them to-morrow morning.

Ever faithfully.

Rev. James
White.

TAVISTOCK HOUSE,
·*Thursday Evening, Ninth December*, 1852.

MY DEAR WHITE,

I hear you are not going to poor Macready's. Now, don't you think it would do you good to come here instead? *I* say it would, and I ought to know! We can give you everything but a bed (all ours are occupied in consequence of the boys being at home), and shall all be delighted to see you. Leave the bed to us, and we'll find one hard by. I say nothing of the last day of the old year, and the dancing out of that good old worthy that will take place here (for you might like to hear the bells at home) ; but after the twentieth, I shall be comparatively at leisure, and good for anything or nothing. Don't you consider it your duty to your family to come? *I* do, and again I say that I ought to know.

Our best love to Mrs. White and Lotty—happily so much better, we rejoice to hear—and all.

So no more at present from

THE INIMITABLE B.

Mrs.
Gaskell.

TAVISTOCK HOUSE,
Friday, Seventeenth December, 1852.

MY DEAR MRS. GASKELL,

I received your kind note yesterday morning with the truest gratification, for I *am* the writer of "The Child's Story" as well as of "The Poor Relation's." I assure you, you have given me the liveliest and heartiest pleasure by what you say of it.

I don't claim for my ending of "The Nurse's Story" that it would have made it a bit better. All I can urge in its behalf is, that it is what I should have done myself. But there is no doubt of the story being admirable as it stands, and there *is* some doubt

(I think) whether Forster would have found anything wrong in it, if he had not known of my hammering over the proofs in making up the number, with all the three endings before me.

Ever faithfully yours.

TAVISTOCK HOUSE,
Monday, Twentieth December, 1852.

Mr. W.
Wilkie
Collins.

MY DEAR COLLINS,

If I did not know that you are likely to have a forbearing remembrance of my occupation, I should be full of remorse for not having sooner thanked you for " Basil."

Not to play the sage or the critic (neither of which parts, I hope, is at all in my line), but to say what is the friendly truth, I may assure you that I have read the book with very great interest, and with a very thorough conviction that you have a call to this same art of fiction. I think the probabilities here and there require a little more respect than you are disposed to show them, and I have no doubt that the prefatory letter would have been better away, on the ground that a book (of all things) should speak for and explain itself. But the story contains admirable writing, and many clear evidences of a very delicate discrimination of character. It is delightful to find throughout that you have taken great pains with it besides, and have "gone at it" with a perfect knowledge of the jolter-headedness of the conceited idiots who suppose that volumes are to be tossed off like pancakes, and that any writing can be done without the utmost application, the greatest patience, and the steadiest energy of which the writer is capable.

For all these reasons I have made " Basil's " acquaintance with great gratification, and entertain a high respect for him. And I hope that I shall become intimate with many worthy descendants of his, who are yet in the limbo of creatures waiting to be born.

Always faithfully yours.

P.S.—I am open to any proposal to go anywhere any day or days this week. Fresh air and change in any amount I am ready for. If I could only find an idle man (this is a general observation), he would find the warmest recognition in this direction.

TAVISTOCK HOUSE,
Monday Evening, Twentieth December, 1852.

Mr. Frank
Stone,
A.R.A.

MY DEAR STONE,

Every appearance of brightness ! Shall I expect you to-morrow morning ? If so, at what hour ?

I think of taking train afterwards, and going down for a walk on Chatham lines. If you can spare the day for fresh air and an impromptu bit of fish and chop, I can recommend you one of the most delightful of men for a companion. O, he is indeed refreshing ! ! !   Ever affectionately yours.

Mr. W. H.   OFFICE OF "HOUSEHOLD WORDS,"

Mr. W. H. Wills.

OFFICE OF "HOUSEHOLD WORDS,"
Christmas Eve, 1852.

MY DEAR WILLS,

I have gone carefully through the number—an awful one for the amount of correction required—and have made everything right. If my mind could have been materialised, and drawn along the tops of all the spikes on the outside of the Queen's Bench prison, it could not ·have been more agonised than by the ——, which, for imbecility, carelessness, slovenly composition, relatives without antecedents, universal chaos, and one absorbing whirlpool of jolter-headedness, beats anything in print and paper I have ever "gone at" in my life.

· I shall come and see how you are to-morrow. Meantime everything is in perfect trim in these parts, and I have sent down to Stacey to come here and top up with a final interview before I go.

Just after I had sent the messenger off to you, yesterday, concerning the toll-taker memoranda, the other idea came into my head, and in the most obliging manner came out of it.

Ever faithfully yours.

Mr G. Linnæus Banks.

TAVISTOCK HOUSE,
Sunday, Twenty-sixth December, 1852.

MY DEAR SIR,

I will not attempt to tell you how affected and gratified I am by the intelligence your kind letter conveys to me. Nothing would be more welcome to me than such a mark of confidence and approval from such a source, nothing more precious, or that I could set a higher worth upon.

I hasten to return the gauges, of which I have marked· one as the size of the finger, from which this token will never more be absent as long as I live.

With feelings of the liveliest gratitude and cordiality towards the many friends who so honour me, and with many thanks to you for the genial earnestness with which you represent them,

I am, my dear Sir, very faithfully yours.

1853.

NARRATIVE.

IN this year, Charles Dickens was still writing "Bleak House," and went to Brighton for a short time in the spring. In May he had an attack of illness, a return of an old trouble of an inflammatory pain in the side, which was short but very severe while it lasted. Immediately on his recovery, early in June, a departure from London for the summer was resolved upon. He had decided upon trying Boulogne this year for his holiday sojourn, and as soon as he was strong enough to travel, he, his wife, and sister-in-law went there in advance of the family, taking up their quarters at the Hôtel des Bains, to find a house, which was speedily done. The pretty little Villa des Moulineaux, and its excellent landlord, at once took his fancy, and in that house, and in another on the same ground, also belonging to M. Beaucourt, he passed three very happy summers. And he became as much attached to "Our French Watering Place" as to "Our English" one. Having written a sketch of Broadstairs under that name in "Household Words," he did the same of Boulogne under the former title.

During the summer, besides his other work, he was employed in dictating "The Child's History of England," which he published in "Household Words," and which was the only book he ever wrote by dictation. But, as at Broadstairs and other seaside homes, he had always plenty of relaxation and enjoyment in the visits of his friends. In September he finished "Bleak House," and in October he started with Mr. Wilkie Collins and Mr. Egg from Boulogne, on an excursion through parts of Switzerland and Italy; his wife and family going home at the same time, and himself returning to Tavistock House early in December. His eldest son, Charles, had left Eton some time before this, and had gone for the completion of his education to Leipsic. He was to leave Germany at the end of the year, therefore it was arranged that he should meet the travellers in Paris on their homeward journey, and they all returned together.

Just before Christmas Charles Dickens went to Birmingham in fulfilment of an offer which he had made at the dinner given to him at Birmingham on the Sixth of January (of which he writes to Mr. Macready in the first letter that follows here), to give two readings from his own books for the benefit of the New Midland Institute. They were his first public readings. He read "The Christmas Carol" on one evening, and "The Cricket on the

Hearth " on the next, before enormous audiences. The success was so great, and the sum of money realised for the institute so large, that he consented to give a second reading of " The Christmas Carol," remaining another night in Birmingham for the purpose, on the condition that seats were reserved, at prices within their means, for the working men. And to his great satisfaction they formed a large proportion, and were among the most enthusiastic and appreciative of his audience. He was accompanied by his wife and sister-in-law, and on this occasion a breakfast was given to him after his last reading, at which a silver flower-basket, duly inscribed, was very gracefully presented to *Mrs.* Charles Dickens.

The letters in this year require little explanation. Those to his wife and sister-in-law and Mr. Wills give a little history of his Italian journey. At Naples he found his excellent friend Sir James Emerson Tennent, with his wife and daughter, with whom he joined company in the ascent of Vesuvius.

The two letters to M. Regnier, the distinguished actor of the Théâtre Français—with whom Charles Dickens had formed a sincere friendship during his first residence in Paris—on the subject of a projected benefit to Miss Kelly, need no explanation.

Mr. John Delane, editor of *The Times,* and always a highly-esteemed friend of Charles Dickens, had given him an introduction to a school at Boulogne, kept by two English gentlemen, one a clergyman and the other a former Eton master, the Rev. W. Bewsher and Mr. Gibson. He had at various times four boys at this school, and very frequently afterwards he expressed his gratitude to Mr. Delane for having given him the introduction, which turned out so satisfactory in every respect.

The letter of grateful acknowledgment from Mr. Poole and Charles Dickens to Lord Russell was for the pension for which the old dramatic author was indebted to that nobleman, and which enabled him to live comfortably until the end of his life.

A note to Mr. Marcus Stone was sent with a copy of "The Child's History of England." The sketch referred to was one of "Jo'," in "Bleak House," which showed great feeling and artistic promise, since fully fulfilled by the young painter, but very remarkable in a boy so young as he was at that time. The letter to Mr. Stanfield, in seafaring language, is a specimen of the playful way in which he frequently addressed that dear friend.

*" A curiosity from *him*. No date. No signature."*—W. H. W.

MY DEAR WILLS,

I have not a shadow of doubt about Miss Martineau's story. It is certain to tell. I think it very effectively, admirably done; a fine plain purpose in it; quite a singular novelty. For the last story in the Christmas number it will be great. I couldn't wish for a better.

Mrs. Gaskell's ghost story I have got this morning; have not yet read. It is long.

H.M.S. Tavistock, Second January, 1853.

Yoho, old salt! Neptun' ahoy! You don't forget, messmet, as you was to meet Dick Sparkler and Mark Porpuss on the fok'sle of the good ship *Owssel Words*, Wednesday next, half-past four? Not you; for when did Stanfell ever pass his word to go anywheers and not come? Well. Belay, my heart of oak, belay! Come alongside the *Tavistock* same day and hour, 'stead of *Owssel Words*. Hail your shipmets, and they'll drop over the side and join you, like two new shillings a-droppin' into the purser's pocket. Damn all lubberly boys and swabs, and give *me* the lad with the tarry trousers, which shines to me like di'mings bright!

TAVISTOCK HOUSE, Friday Night,
Fourteenth January, 1853.

MY DEAREST MACREADY,

I have been much affected by the receipt of your kindest and best of letters; for I know out of the midst of what anxieties it comes to me, and I appreciate such remembrance from my heart. You and yours are always with us, however. It is no new thing for you to have a part in any scene of my life. It very rarely happens that a day passes without our thoughts and conversation travelling to Sherborne. We are so much there that I cannot tell you how plainly I see you as I write.

I know you would have been full of sympathy and approval if you had been present at Birmingham, and that you would have concurred in the tone I tried to take about the eternal duties of the arts to the people. I took the liberty of putting the court and that kind of thing out of the question, and recognising nothing *but* the arts and the people. The more we see of life and its brevity, and the world and its varieties, the more we know that no exercise of our abilities in any art, but the addressing of it to the great ocean of humanity in which we are drops, and not to bye-ponds (very stagnant) here and there, ever can or ever will lay the foundations of an endurable retrospect. Is it not so? *You* should have as much practical information on this subject, now, my dear friend, as any man.

My dearest Macready, I cannot forbear this closing word. I still look forward to our meeting as we used to do in the happy times we have known together, so far as your old hopefulness and energy are concerned. And I think I never in my life have been more glad to receive a sign, than I have been to hail that which I find in your handwriting.

Some of your old friends at Birmingham are full of interest and enquiry. I am ever, and no matter where I am—am quite as much in a crowd as alone—my dearest Macready,

Your affectionate and most attached Friend.

Mr. W. H.
Wills.

1, JUNCTION PARADE, BRIGHTON,
Thursday Night, Fourth March, 1853.

MY DEAR WILLS,

.I am sorry, but Brutus sacrifices unborn children of his own as well as those of other people. "The Sorrows of Childhood," long in type, and long a mere mysterious name, must come out. The paper really is, like the celebrated ambassadorial appointment, "too bad."

"A Doctor of Morals," *impossible of insertion as it stands.* A mere puff, with all the difficult facts of the question blinked, and many statements utterly at variance with what I am known to have written. It is exactly because the great bulk of offences in a great number of places are committed by professed thieves, that it will not do to have pet prisoning advocated without grave remonstrance and great care. That class of prisoner is not to be reformed. We must begin at the beginning and prevent, by stringent correction and supervision of wicked parents, that class of prisoner from being regularly supplied as if he were a human necessity.

Do they teach trades in workhouses and try to fit *their* people (the worst part of them) for society? Come with me to Tothill Fields Bridewell, and I will show you what a workhouse-girl is. Or look to my "Walk in a Workhouse" (in "H. W.") and to the glance at the youths I saw in one place positively kept like wolves.

Mr. —— thinks prisons could be made nearly self-supporting. Have you any idea of the difficulty that is found in disposing of Prison-work, or does he think that the Tread-mills didn't grind the air because the State or the Magistracy objected to the competition of prison-labour with free-labour, but because the work *could not be got?*

I never can have any kind of prison-discipline disquisition in

"H. W." that does not start with the first great principle I have laid down, and that does not protest against Prisons being considered *per se*. Whatever chance is given to a man in a prison must be given to a man in a refuge for distress.

The article in itself is very good, but it must have these points in it, otherwise I am not only compromising opinions I am known to hold, but the journal itself is blowing hot and cold, and playing fast and loose in a ridiculous way.

"Starting a Paper in India" is very droll to us. But it is full of references that the public don't understand, and don't in the least care for. Bourgeois, brevier, minion, and nonpareil, long primer, turn-ups, dunning advertisements, and reprints, back forme, imposing-stone, and locking-up, are all quite out of their way, and a sort of slang that they have no interest in.

Let me see a revise when you have got it together, and if you can strengthen it—do. I mention all the objections that occur to me as I go on, not because you can obviate them (except in the case of the prison-paper), but because if I make a point of doing so always you will feel and judge the more readily both for yourself and me too when I take an Italian flight.

YOU:
How are the eyes getting on?

ME:
I have been at work all day.

Ever faithfully.

TAVISTOCK HOUSE, *Third May*, 1853. Mrs. Gaskell.
MY DEAR MRS. GASKELL,

The subject is certainly NOT too serious, so sensibly treated. I have no doubt that you may do a great deal of good by pursuing it in "Household Words." I thoroughly agree in all you say in your note, have similar reasons for giving it some anxious consideration, and shall be greatly interested in it. Pray decide to do it. Send the papers, as you write them, to me. Meanwhile I will think of a name for them, and bring it to bear upon yours, if I think yours improvable. I am sure you may rely on being widely understood and sympathised with.

Forget that I called those two women my dear friends! Why, if I told you a fiftieth part of what I have thought about them, you would write me the most suspicious of notes, refusing to receive the fiftieth part of that. So I don't write, particularly as you laid your injunctions on me concerning Ruth. In revenge, I will now mention one word that I wish you would take out when-

ever you reprint that book. She would never—I am ready to
make affidavit before any authority in the land—have called her
seducer "Sir," when they were living at that hotel in Wales. A
girl pretending to be what she really was would have done it, but
she—never!
                                            Ever most faithfully yours.

Monsieur
Regnier.   TAVISTOCK HOUSE, *Monday, Ninth May*, 1853.

MY DEAR REGNIER,

I meant to have spoken to you last night about a matter
in which I hope you can assist me, but I forgot it. I think I
must have been quite *bouleversé* by your supposing (as you pretended to do, when you went away) that it was not a great pleasure
and delight to me to see you act!

There is a certain Miss Kelly,[*] now sixty-two years old, who
was once one of the very best of English actresses, in the greater
and better days of the English theatre. She has much need of a
benefit, and I am exerting myself to arrange one for her, on or
about the Ninth of June, if possible, at the St. James's Theatre.
The first piece will be an entertainment of her own, and she will
act in the last. Between these two (and at the best time of the
night), it would be a great attraction to the public, and a great
proof of friendship to me, if you would act. If we could manage,
through your influence and with your assistance, to present a little
French vaudeville, such as "*Le bon Homme jadis*," it would make
the night a grand success.

Mitchell's permission, I suppose, would be required. That I
will undertake to apply for, if you tell me that you are willing to
help us, and that you could answer for the other necessary actors
in the little French piece, whatever the piece might be, that you
would choose for the purpose. Pray write me a short note in
answer, on this point.

I ought to tell you that the benefit will be "under distinguished
patronage." The Duke of Devonshire, the Duke of Leinster, the
Duke of Beaufort, etc. etc., are members of the committee with
me, and I have no doubt that the audience will be of the *élite*.

I have asked Mr. Chapman to come to me to-morrow, to
arrange for the hiring of the theatre. Mr. Harley (a favourite
English comedian whom you may know) is our secretary. And if
I could assure the committee to-morrow afternoon of your co-operation, I am sure they would be overjoyed.
                                            Votre tout dévoué.

[*] Still living [1882], and in sadly necessitous circumstances. She has
just been made the subject of a memorial to the Prime Minister, praying for
a pension on the Civil List. Miss Kelly is *now* dead [1892].

TAVISTOCK HOUSE, *Twentieth May*, 1853.   Monsieur Regnier.

MY DEAR REGNIER,

I am heartily obliged to you for your kind letter respecting Miss Kelly's benefit. It is to take place *on Thursday, the Sixteenth June*; Thursday the Ninth (the day originally proposed) being the day of Ascot Races, and therefore a bad one for the purpose.

Mitchell, like a brave *garçon* as he is, most willingly consents to your acting for us. Will you think what little French piece it will be best to do, in order that I may have it ready for the bills?

Ever faithfully yours, my dear Regnier.

BOULOGNE, *Monday, Thirteenth June*, 1853.   Mr. W. H. Wills.

MY DEAR WILLS,

You will be glad, I know, to hear that we had a delightful passage yesterday, and that I made a perfect phenomenon of a dinner. It is raining hard to-day, and my back feels the draught; but I am otherwise still mending.

I have signed, sealed, and delivered a contract for a house (once occupied for two years by a man I knew in Switzerland), which is not a large one, but stands in the middle of a great garden, with what the landlord calls a "forest" at the back, and is now surrounded by flowers, vegetables, and all manner of growth. A queer, odd, French place, but extremely well supplied with all table and other conveniences, and strongly recommended.

The address is :

> Château des Moulineaux,
> Rue Beaurepaire, Boulogne.

There is a coach-house, stabling for half-a-dozen horses, and I don't know what.

We take possession this afternoon, and I am now laying in a good stock of creature comforts. So no more at present from

Yours ever faithfully.

CHÂTEAU DES MOULINEAUX, BOULOGNE,   The same.
Saturday Night, Eighteenth June, 1853.

MY DEAR WILLS,

"BLEAK HOUSE."

Thank God I have done half the number with great care, and hope to finish on Thursday or Friday next. O how thankful I feel to be able to have done it, and what a relief to get the number out !

GENERAL MOVEMENTS OF INIMITABLE.

I don't think (I am not sure) I shall come to London until after the completion of "Bleak House," No. 18—the number after this now in hand—for it strikes me that I am better here at present. I have picked up in the most extraordinary manner, and I believe you would never suppose to look at me that I had had that week or barely an hour of it. If there should be any occasion for our meeting in the meantime, a run over here would do you no harm, and we should be delighted to see you at any time. If you suppose this place to be in a street, you are much mistaken. It is in the country, though not more than ten minutes' walk from the post-office, and is the best doll's-house of many rooms, in the prettiest French grounds, in the most charming situation I have ever seen; the best place I have ever lived in abroad, except at Genoa. You can scarcely imagine the beauty of the air in this richly-wooded hill-side. As to comforts in the house, there are all sorts of things, beginning with no end of the coldest water and running through the most beautiful flowers down to English foot-baths and a Parisian liqueur-stand.

I think that's all at present.

Ever, my dear Wills, faithfully yours.

Mr. Frank
Stone,
A.R.A.

CHÂTEAU DES MOULINEAUX, RUE BEAUREPAIRE,
BOULOGNE, *Thursday, Twenty-third June*, 1853.

MY DEAR PUMPION,

I take the earliest opportunity, after finishing my number—ahem!—*to write you a line, and to report myself (thank God!) brown, well, robust, vigorous, open to fight any man in England of my weight, and growing a moustache. Any person of undoubted pluck, in want of a customer, may hear of me at the bar of Bleak House, where my money is down.

I think there is an abundance of places here that would suit you well enough; and Georgina is ready to launch on voyages of discovery and observation with you. But it is necessary that you should consider for how long a time you want it, as the folks here let much more advantageously for the tenant when they know the term—don't like to let without. It seems to me that the best thing you can do is to get a paper of the South Eastern tidal trains, fix your day for coming over here in five hours, let me know the day, and come and see how you like the place. *I* like it better than ever. We can give you a bed (two to spare, at a pinch three), and show you a garden and a view or so. The town is not so cheap as places farther off, but you get a great deal for your money, and by far the best wine at tenpence a bottle that I have ever drank anywhere. I really desire no better.

I may mention for your guidance (for I count upon your coming to overhaul the general aspect of things), that you have nothing on earth to do with your luggage when it is once in the boat, *until after you have walked ashore.* That you will be filtered with the rest of the passengers through a hideous, whitewashed, quarantine-looking custom-house, where a stern man of military aspect will demand your passport. That you will have nothing of the sort, but will produce your card with this addition: "Restant à Boulogne, chez M. Charles Dickens, Château des Moulineaux." That you will then be passed out at a little door, like one of the ill-starred prisoners on the bloody September night, into a yelling and shrieking crowd, cleaving the air with the names of the different hotels, exactly seven thousand six hundred and fifty-four in number. And that your heart will be on the point of sinking with dread, then you will find yourself in the arms of the Sparkler of Albion.

Ever affectionately.

Mr. W. H. Wills.

BOULOGNE, *Wednesday, Twenty-seventh July,* 1853.

MY DEAR WILLS,

I have thought of another article to be called "Frauds upon the Fairies," *à propos* of George Cruikshank's editing. Half playfully and half seriously, I mean to protest most strongly against alteration, for any purpose, of the beautiful little stories which are so tenderly and humanly useful to us in these times, when the world is too much with us early and late; and then to re-write "Cinderella" according to Total Abstinence, Peace Society, and Bloomer principles, and expressly for their propagation.

I shall want his book of "Hop o' my Thumb" (Forster noticed it in the last *Examiner*), and the most simple and popular version of "Cinderella" you can get me. I shall not be able to do it until after finishing "Bleak House," but I shall do it the more easily for having the books by me. So send them, if convenient, in your next parcel.

Ever faithfully.

The same.

BOULOGNE, *Sunday, Seventh August,* 1853.

MY DEAR WILLS,

Can't possibly write autographs until I have written "Bleak House." My work has been very hard since I have been here; and when I throw down my pen of a day, I throw down myself, and can take up neither article.

The " C. P."* is very well done, but I cannot make up my mind to lend my blow to the great Forge-bellows of puffery at work. I so heartily desired to have nothing to do with it, that I wish you would cancel this article altogether, and substitute something else. As to the guide-books, I think they are a sufficiently flatulent botheration in themselves, without being discussed. A lurking desire is always upon me to put Mr. ——'s speech on Accidents to the public, as chairman of the Brighton Railway, against his pretensions as a chairman of public instructors and guardians. And I don't know but that I may come to it at some odd time. This strengthens me in my wish to avoid the bellows.

How two men can have gone, one after the other, to the Camp, and have written nothing about it, passes my comprehension. I have been in great doubt about the end of ——. I wish you would suggest to him from me, when you see him, how wrong it is. Surely he cannot be insensible to the fact that military preparations in England at this time mean Defence. Woman, says ——, means Home, love, children, Mother. Does he not find any protection for these things in a wise and moderate means of Defence; and is not the union between these things and those means one of the most natural, significant, and plain in the world?

I wish you would send friend Barnard here a set of " Household Words," in a paid parcel (on the other side is an inscription to be neatly pasted into vol. i. before sending), with a post-letter beforehand from yourself, saying that I had begged you to forward the books, feeling so much obliged to him for his uniform attention and politeness. Also that you will not fail to continue his set, as successive volumes appear.

ASPECTS OF NATURE.

We have had a tremendous sea here. Steam-packet in the harbour frantic, and dashing her brains out against the stone walls.

Ever faithfully.

Mr. W. C.
Macready.

CHÂTEAU DES MOULINEAUX, BOULOGNE,
Sunday, Twenty-fourth August, 1853.

MY DEAREST MACREADY,

Some unaccountable delay in the transmission here of the parcel which contained your letter, caused me to come into the receipt of it a whole week after its date. I immediately wrote to Miss Coutts, who has written to you, and I hope some good may come of it. I know it will not be her fault if none does. I was very much concerned to read your account of poor Mrs. Warner,†

* Crystal Palace.
† A very celebrated actress at this time, who was dying of cancer.

and to read her own plain and unaffected account of herself. Pray assure her of my cordial sympathy and remembrance, and of my earnest desire to do anything in my power to help to put her mind at ease.

We are living in a beautiful little country place here, where I have been hard at work ever since I came, and am now (after an interval of a week's rest) going to work again to finish "Bleak House." Kate and Georgina look forward, I assure you, to their Sherborne visit, when I—a mere forlorn wanderer—shall be roaming over the Alps into Italy. I saw "The Midsummer Night's Dream" of the Opéra Comique, done here (very well) last night. The way in which a poet named Willyim Shay Kes Peer gets drunk in company with Sir John Foll Stayffe, fights with a noble knight, Lor Latimeer (who is in love with a maid of honour you may have read of in history, called Mees Oleevia), and promises not to do so any more on observing symptoms of love for him in the Queen of England, is very remarkable. Queen Elizabeth, too, in the profound and impenetrable disguise of a black velvet mask, two inches deep by three broad, following him into taverns and worse places, and enquiring of persons of doubtful reputation for "the sublime Williams," was inexpressibly ridiculous. And yet the nonsense was done with a sense quite admirable.

I have been very much struck by the book you sent me. It is one of the wisest, the manliest, and most serviceable I ever read. I am reading it again with the greatest pleasure and admiration.

Ever most affectionately yours,

My dear Macready.

VILLA DES MOULINEAUX, BOULOGNE,   The Hon.
Saturday, Twenty-seventh August, 1853.   Mrs. Watson.

MY DEAR MRS. WATSON,

I received your letter—most welcome and full of interest to me—when I was hard at work finishing "Bleak House." We are always talking of you; and I had said but the day before, that one of the first things I would do on my release would be to write to you. To finish the topic of "Bleak House" at once, I will only add that I like the conclusion very much and think it *very pretty indeed.* The story has taken extraordinarily, especially during the last five or six months, when its purpose has been gradually working itself out. It has retained its immense circulation from the first, beating dear old "Copperfield" by a round ten thousand or more. I have never had so many readers. We had a little reading of the final double number here the night before last, and it made a great impression I assure you.

We are all extremely well, and like Boulogne very much indeed. I laid down the rule before we came, that we would know nobody here, and we *do* know nobody here. We evaded callers as politely as we could, and gradually came to be understood and left to ourselves. It is a fine bracing air, a beautiful open country, and an admirable mixture of town and country. Things are tolerably cheap, and exceedingly good ; the people very cheerful, good-looking, and obliging ; the houses very clean ; the distance to London short, and easily traversed. I think if you came to know the place (which I never did myself until last October, often as I have been through it), you could be but in one mind about it.

Charley is still at Leipzig. I shall take him up somewhere on the Rhine, to bring him home for Christmas, as I come back on my own little tour. He has been in the Hartz Mountains on a walking tour, and has written a journal thereof, which he has sent home in portions. It has cost about as much in postage as would have bought a pair of ponies.

I contemplate starting from here on Monday, the Tenth of October ; Catherine, Georgina, and the rest of them will then go home. I shall go first by Paris and Geneva to Lausanne, for it has a separate place in my memory. If the autumn should be very fine (just possible after such a summer), I shall then go by Chamounix and Martigny, over the Simplon to Milan, thence to Genoa, Leghorn, Pisa, and Naples, thence, I hope, to Sicily. Back by Bologna, Florence, Rome, Verona, Mantua, etc., to Venice and home by Germany, arriving in good time for Christmas Day. Three nights in Christmas week, I have promised to read in the Town Hall at Birmingham, for the benefit of a new and admirable institution for working men projected there. The Friday will be the last night, and I shall read the "Carol" to two thousand working people, stipulating that they shall have that night entirely to themselves.

It just occurs to me that I mean to engage, for the two months odd, a travelling servant. I have not yet got one. If you should happen to be interested in any good foreigner, well acquainted with the countries and the languages, who would like such a master, how delighted I should be to like *him !*

Ever since I have been here, I have been very hard at work, often getting up at daybreak to write through many hours. I have never had the least return of illness, thank God, though I was so altered (in a week) when I came here, that I doubt if you would have known me. I am redder and browner than ever at the present writing, with the addition of a rather formidable and fierce moustache. Lowestoft I know, by walking over there from

Yarmouth, when I went down on an exploring expedition, previous to "Copperfield." It is a fine place. I saw the name "Blunderstone" on a direction-post between it and Yarmouth, and took it from the said direction-post for the book. In some of the descriptions of Chesney Wold, I have taken many bits, chiefly about trees and shadows, from observations made at Rockingham. I wonder whether you have ever thought so! I shall hope to hear from you again soon, and shall not fail to write again before I go away. There seems to be nothing but "I" in this letter; but "I" know, my dear friend, that you will be more interested in that letter in the present connection, than in any other I could take from the alphabet.

If I were to give you a hint of what we feel at the sight of your handwriting, and at the receipt of a word from yourself about yourself, and the dear boys, and the precious little girls, I should begin to be sorrowful, which is rather the tendency of my mind at the close of another long book.

Ever, my dear Mrs. Watson,

Yours, with true affection and regard.

Château des Moulineaux,
Rue Beaurepaire, Boulogne.

Mr. Peter Cunningham.

My dear Cunningham,

A note—Cerberus-like—of three heads.

First. I know you will be glad to hear that the manager is himself again. Vigorous, brown, energetic, muscular; the pride of Albion and the admiration of Gaul.

Secondly. I told Wills when I left home, that I was quite pained to see the end of your excellent "Bowl of Punch" altered. I was unaffectedly touched and gratified by the heartiness of the original; and saw no earthly, celestial, or subterranean objection to its remaining, as it did not so unmistakably apply to me as to necessitate the observance of my usual precaution in the case of such references, by any means.

Thirdly. If you ever have a holiday that you don't know what to do with, *do* come and pass a little time here. Excellent light wines on the premises, French cookery, millions of roses, two cows (for milk punch), vegetables cut for the pot, and handed in at the kitchen window; five summer-houses, fifteen fountains (with no water in 'em), and thirty-seven clocks (keeping, as I conceive, Australian time; having no reference whatever to the hours on this side of the globe).

I know, my dear Cunningham, that the British nation can ill afford to lose you; and that when the Audit Office mice are away, the cats of that great public establishment will play. But pray consider that the bow may be sometimes bent too long, and that over-arduous application, even in patriotic service, is to be avoided. No one can more highly estimate your devotion to the best interests of Britain than I. But I wish to see it tempered with a wise consideration for your own amusement, recreation, and pastime. All work and no play may make Peter a dull boy as well as Jack. And (if I may claim the privilege of friendship to remonstrate) I would say that you do not take enough time for your meals. Dinner, for instance, you habitually neglect. Believe me, this rustic repose will do you good. Winkles also are to be obtained in these parts, and it is well remarked by Poor Richard, that a bird in the handbook is worth two in the bush.

Ever cordially yours.

Mr. Walter
Savage
Landor.

TAVISTOCK HOUSE, LONDON,
Eighth September, 1853.

MY DEAR LANDOR,

I am in town for a day or two, and Forster tells me I may now write to thank you for the happiness you have given me by honouring my name with such generous mention, on such a noble place, in your great book. I believe he has told you already that I wrote to him from Boulogne, not knowing what to do, as I had not received the precious volume, and feared you might have some plan of sending it to me, with which my premature writing would interfere.

You know how heartily and inexpressibly I prize what you have written to me, or you never would have selected me for such a distinction. I could never thank you enough, my dear Landor, and I will not thank you in words any more. Believe me, I receive the dedication like a great dignity, the worth of which I hope I thoroughly know. The Queen could give me none in exchange that I wouldn't laughingly snap my fingers at.

Walter is a very good boy, and comes home from school with honourable commendation. He passed last Sunday in solitary confinement (in a bath-room) on bread and water, for terminating a dispute with the nurse by throwing a chair in her direction. It is the very first occasion of his ever having got into trouble, for he is a great favourite with the whole house, and one of the most amiable boys in the boy-world. (He comes out on birthdays in a blaze of shirt-pin.)

If I go and look at your house, as I shall if I go to Florence, I shall bring you back another leaf from the same tree as I plucked the last from.

Ever, my dear Landor,

Heartily and affectionately yours.

VILLA DES MOULINEAUX, BOULOGNE,
Monday, Twelfth September, 1853.

Mr. John
Delane.

MY DEAR DELANE,

I am very much obliged to you, I assure you, for your frank and full reply to my note. Nothing could be more satisfactory, and I have to-day seen Mr. Gibson and placed my two small representatives under his charge. His manner is exactly what you describe him. I was greatly pleased with his genuineness altogether.

We remain here until the tenth of next month, when I am going to desert my wife and family and run about Italy until Christmas. If I can execute any little commission for you or Mrs. Delane—in the Genoa street of silversmiths, or anywhere else—I shall be delighted to do so. I have been in the receipt of several letters from Macready lately, and rejoice to find him quite himself again, though I have great misgivings that he will lose his eldest boy before he can be got to India.

I never saw anything so ridiculous as this place at present. They expected the Emperor ten or twelve days ago, and put up all manner of triumphal arches made of evergreens, which look like tea-leaves now, and will take a withered and weird appearance hardly to be foreseen, long before the twenty-fifth, when the visit is vaguely expected to come off. In addition to these faded garlands all over the leading streets, there are painted eagles hoisted over gateways and sprawling across a hundred ways, which have been washed out by the rain and are now being blistered by the sun, until they look horribly ludicrous. And a number of our benighted compatriots who came over to see a perfect blaze of *fêtes*, go wandering among these shrivelled preparations and staring at ten thousand flag-poles without any flags upon them, with a kind of indignant curiosity and personal injury quite irresistible. With many thanks,

Very faithfully yours.

BOULOGNE, *Sunday, Eighteenth September,* 1853.

Mr. W. H.
Wills.

MY DEAR WILLS,

COURIER.

Edward Kaub will bring this. He turned up yesterday, accounting for his delay by waiting for a written recommendation, and having at the last moment (as a foreigner, not being an Englishman) a passport to get. I quite agree with you as to his appearance and manner, and have engaged him. It strikes me that it would be an excellent beginning if you would deliver him a neat and appropriate address, telling him what in your conscience you can find to tell of me favourably as a master, and particularly impressing upon him *readiness and punctuality* on his part as the great things to be observed. I think it would have a much better effect than anything I could say in this stage, if said from yourself. But I shall be much obliged to you if you will act upon this hint forthwith.

Ever faithfully.

The
Lord John
Russell.

VILLA DES MOULINEAUX, BOULOGNE,
Wednesday, Twenty-first September, 1853.

MY DEAR LORD,

Your note having been forwarded to me here, I cannot forbear thanking you with all my heart for your great kindness. Mr. Forster had previously sent me a copy of your letter to him, together with the expression of the high and lasting gratification he had in your handsome response. I know he feels it most sincerely.

I became the prey of a perfect spasm of sensitive twinges, when I found that the close of "Bleak House" had not penetrated to "the wilds of the North" when your letter left those parts. I was so very much interested in it myself when I wrote it here last month, that I have a fond sort of faith in its interesting its readers. But for the hope that you may have got it by this time, I should refuse comfort. That supports me.

I fear there is not much chance of my being able to execute any little commission for Lady John anywhere in Italy. But I am going across the Alps, returning home to London for Christmas Day, and should indeed be happy if I could do her any dwarf service.

You will be interested, I think, to hear that Poole lives happily on his pension, and lives within it. He is quite incapable of any mental exertion, and what he would have done without it I cannot imagine. I send it to him at Paris every quarter. It is something, even amid the estimation in which you are held, which is but a foreshadowing of what shall be by-and-by as the people advance, to be so gratefully remembered, as he, with the best reason, remembers you. Forgive my saying this. But the manner of that transaction, no less than the matter, is always fresh in my memory in association with your name, and I cannot help it.

My dear Lord,
Yours very faithfully and obliged.

BOULOGNE, *Wednesday,*
Twenty-first September, 1853.

MY DEAR MRS. WATSON,

The courier was unfortunately engaged. He offered to recommend another, but I had several applicants, and begged Mr. Wills to hold a grand review at the "Household Words" office, and select the man who is to bring me down as his victim. I am extremely sorry the man you recommend was not to be had. I should have been so delighted to take him.

I am finishing "The Child's History," and clearing the way through "Household Words," in general, before I go on my trip. I forget whether I told you that Mr. Egg the painter and Mr. Collins are going with me. The other day I was in town. In case you should not have heard of the condition of that deserted village, I think it worth mentioning. All the streets of any note were unpaved, mountains high, and all the omnibuses were sliding down alleys, and looking into the upper windows of small houses. At eleven o'clock one morning I was positively *alone* in Bond Street. I went to one of my tailors, and he was at Brighton. A smutty-faced woman among some gorgeous regimentals, half finished, had not the least idea when he would be back. I went to another of my tailors, and he was in an upper room, with open windows and surrounded by mignonette-boxes, playing the piano in the bosom of his family. I went to my hosier's, and two of the least presentable of "the young men" of that elegant establishment were playing at draughts in the back shop. (Likewise I beheld a porter-pot hastily concealed under a Turkish dressing-gown of a golden pattern.) I then went wandering about to look for some ingenious portmanteau, and near the corner of St. James's Street saw a solitary being sitting in a trunk-shop, absorbed in a book which, on a close inspection, I found to be "Bleak House." I thought this looked well, and went in. And he really was more interested in seeing me, when he knew who I was, than any face I had seen in any house, every house I knew being occupied by painters, including my own. I went to the Athenæum that same night, to get my dinner, and it was shut up for repairs. I went home late, and had forgotten the key and was locked out.

Preparations were made here, about six weeks ago, to receive the Emperor, who is not come yet. Meanwhile our countrymen (deluded in the first excitement) go about staring at these arrangements, and *will* persist in speaking an unknown tongue to the French people, who *will* speak English to them.

We are all quite well. Going to drop two small boys here, at school with a former Eton tutor highly recommended to me.

Charley was heard of a day or two ago. He says his professor "is very short-sighted, always in green spectacles, always drinking weak beer, always smoking a pipe, and always at work." The last qualification seems to appear to Charley the most astonishing one.

Ever, my dear Mrs. Watson,
Most affectionately yours.

Rev. James White.

BOULOGNE, Thirtieth September, 1853.

MY DEAR WHITE,

As you wickedly failed in your truth to the writer of books you adore, I write something that I hoped to have said, and meant to have said, in the confidence of the Pavilion among the trees.

Will you write another story for the Christmas No. ? It will be exactly (I mean the Xmas No.) on the same plan as the last.

Loves from all to all, and my particular love to Mrs. White.

Ever cordially yours.

Mrs. Charles Dickens.

HÔTEL DE LONDRES, CHAMOUNIX,
Thursday Night, Twentieth October, 1853.

MY DEAREST KATE,

We came here last night after a very long journey over very bad roads, from Geneva, and leave here (for Martigny, by the Tête Noire) at six to-morrow morning. Next morning early we mean to try the Simplon.

After breakfast to-day we ascended to the Mer de Glace—wonderfully different at this time of the year from when we saw it—a great portion of the ascent being covered with snow, and the climbing very difficult. Regardless of my mule, I walked up and walked down again, to the great admiration of the guides, who pronounced me "an Intrepid." The little house at the top being closed for the winter, and Edward having forgotten to carry any brandy, we had nothing to drink at the top—which was a considerable disappointment to the Inimitable, who was streaming with perspiration from head to foot. But we made a fire in the snow with some sticks, and after a not too comfortable rest came down again. It took a long time—from ten to three.

The appearance of Chamounix at this time of the year is very remarkable. The travellers are over for the season, the inns are generally shut up, all the people who can afford it are moving off to Geneva, the snow is low on the mountains, and the general desolation and grandeur extraordinarily fine. I wanted to pass by the Col de Balme, but the snow lies too deep upon it.

You would have been quite delighted if you could have seen the warmth of our old Lausanne friends, and the heartiness with which they crowded down on a fearfully bad morning to see us off. We passed the night at the Ecu de Genève, in the rooms once our old rooms—at that time (the day before yesterday) occupied by the Queen of the French (ex- I mean) and Prince Joinville and his family.

Tell Sydney that all the way here from Geneva, and up to the Sea of Ice this morning, I wore his knitting, which was very comfortable indeed. I mean to wear it on the long mule journey to Martigny to-morrow.

We get on extremely well. Edward continues as before. He had never been here, and I took him up to the Mer de Glace this morning, and had a mule for him.

I shall leave this open, as usual, to add a word or two on our arrival at Martigny. We have had an amusingly absurd incident this afternoon. When we came here, I saw added to the hotel— our old hotel, and I am now writing in the room where we once dined at the table d'hôte—some baths, cold and hot, down on the margin of the torrent below. This induced us to order three hot baths. Thereupon the keys of the bath-rooms were found with immense difficulty, women ran backwards and forwards across the bridge, men bore in great quantities of wood, a horrible furnace was lighted, and a smoke was raised which filled the whole valley. This began at half-past three, and we congratulated each other on the distinction we should probably acquire by being the cause of the conflagration of the whole village. We sat by the fire until half-past five (dinner-time), and still no baths. Then Edward came up to say that the water was as yet only "tippit," which we suppose to be tepid, but that by half-past eight it would be in a noble state. Ever since the smoke has poured forth in enormous volume, and the furnace has blazed, and the women have gone and come over the bridge, and piles of wood have been carried in ; but we observed a general avoidance of us by the establishment which still looks like a failure. We have had a capital dinner, the dessert whereof is now on the table. When we arrived, at nearly seven last night, all the linen in the house, newly washed, was piled in the sitting-room, all the curtains were taken down, and all the chairs piled bottom upwards. They cleared away as much as they could directly, and had even got the curtains up at breakfast this morning.

I am looking forward to letters at Genoa, though I doubt if we shall get there (supposing all things right at the Simplon) before Monday night or Tuesday morning. I found there last night what F—— would call "Mr. Smith's" story of Mont Blanc, and took it to bed to read. It is extremely well and unaffectedly done. You would be interested in it.

MARTIGNY, *Friday Afternoon, Twenty-first October.*

Safely arrived here after a most delightful day, without a cloud. I walked the whole way. The scenery most beautifully presented. We are in the hotel where our old St. Bernard party assembled.

I should like to see you all very much indeed.

Ever affectionately.

Mrs. Charles Dickens.

HÔTEL DE LA VILLE, MILAN,
Twenty-fifth October, 1853.

MY DEAREST CATHERINE,

The road from Chamounix here takes so much more time than I supposed (for I travelled it day and night, and my companions don't at all understand the idea of never going to bed) that we only reached Milan last night, though we had been travelling twelve and fifteen hours a day. We crossed the Simplon on Sunday, when there was not (as there is not now) a particle of cloud in the whole sky, and when the pass was as nobly grand and beautiful as it possibly can be. There was a good deal of snow upon the top, but not across the road, which had been cleared. We crossed the Austrian frontier yesterday, and, both there and at the gate of Milan, received all possible consideration and politeness.

I have not seen Bairr yet. He has removed from the old hotel to a larger one at a few hours' distance. The head-waiter remembered me very well last night after I had talked to him a little while, and was greatly interested in hearing about all the family, and about poor Roche. The boy we used to have at Lausanne is now seventeen-and-a-half—very tall, he says. The elder girl, fifteen, very like her mother, but taller and more beautiful. He described poor Mrs. Bairr's death (I am speaking of the head-waiter before mentioned) in most vivacious Italian. It was all over in ten minutes, he said. She put her hands to her head one day, down in the courtyard, and cried out that she heard little bells ringing violently in her ears. They sent off for Bairr, who was close by. When she saw him, she stretched out her arms, said in English, "Adieu, my dear!" and fell dead. He has not married again, and he never will. She was a good woman (my friend went on), excellent woman, full of charity, loved the poor, but *un poco furiosa*—that was nothing!

The new hotel is just like the old one, admirably kept, excellently furnished, and a model of comfort. I hope to be at Genoa on Thursday morning, and to find your letter there. We have agreed to drop Sicily, and to return home by way of Marseilles. Our projected time for reaching London is the tenth of December.

As this house is full, I daresay we shall meet some one we know at the table d'hôte to-day. It is extraordinary that the only travellers we have encountered, since we left Paris, have been one horribly vapid Englishman and wife whom we dropped at Basle, one boring Englishman whom we found (and, thank God, left) at Geneva, and two English maiden ladies, whom we found sitting on a rock (with parasols) the day before yesterday, in the most magnificent part of the Gorge of Gondo, the most awful portion of the Simplon—there awaiting their travelling chariot, in which, with their money, their parasols, and a perfect shop of baskets, they were carefully *locked up* by an English servant in sky blue and silver buttons. We have been in the most extra-ordinary vehicles—like swings, like boats, like Noah's arks, like barges and enormous bedsteads. After dark last night, a land-lord, where we changed horses, discovered that the luggage would certainly be stolen from *questo porco d'uno carro*—this pig of a cart—his complimentary description of our carriage, unless cords were attached to each of the trunks, which cords were to hang down so that we might hold them in our hands all the way, and feel any tug that might be made at our treasures. You will imagine the absurdity of our jolting along some twenty miles in this way, exactly as if we were in three shower-baths and were afraid to pull the string.

We are going to the Scala to-night, having got the old box belonging to the hotel, the old key of which is lying beside me on the table. There seem to be no singers of note here now, and it appears for the time to have fallen off considerably. I shall now bring this to a close, hoping that I may have more interesting jottings to send you about the old scenes and people, from Genoa, where we shall stay two days. You are now, I take it, at Mac-ready's. I shall be greatly interested by your account of your visit there. We often talk of you all.

Edward's Italian is (I fear) very weak. When we began to get really into the language, he reminded me of poor Roche in Germany. But he seems to have picked up a little this morning. He has been unfortunate with the unlucky Egg, leaving a pair of his shoes (his favourite shoes) behind in Paris, and his flannel dressing-gown yesterday morning at Domo d'Ossola. In all other respects he is just as he was.

Egg and Collins have gone out to kill the lions here, and I take advantage of their absence to write to you, Georgy, and Miss Coutts. Wills will have told you, I daresay, that Cerjat accom-panied us on a miserably wet morning, in a heavy rain, down the lake. By-the-bye, the wife of one of his cousins, born in France of

German parents, living in the next house to Haldimand's, is one of the most charming, natural, open-faced, and delightful women I ever saw. Madame de —— is set up as the great attraction of Lausanne ; but this capital creature shuts her up altogether. We have called her (her—the real belle), ever since, the early closing movement.

I am impatient for letters from home ; confused ideas are upon me that you are going to White's, but I have no notion when.

Take care of yourself, and God bless you.

Ever most affectionately.

Miss
Hogarth.

HÔTEL DE LA VILLA, MILAN,
Tuesday, Twenty-fifth October, 1853.

MY DEAR GEORGY,

I have walked to that extent in Switzerland (walked over the Simplon on Sunday, as an addition to the other feats) that one pair of the new strong shoes has gone to be mended this morning, and the other is in but a poor way ; the snow having played the mischief with them.

On the Swiss side of the Simplon, we slept at the beastliest little town, in the wildest kind of house, where some fifty cats tumbled into the corridor outside our bedrooms all at once in the middle of the night—whether through the roof or not I don't know ; for it was dark when we got up—and made such a horrible and terrific noise that we started out of our beds in a panic. I strongly objected to opening the door lest they should get into the room and tear at us ; but Edward opened his, and laid about him until he dispersed them. At Domo d'Ossola we had three immense bedrooms (Egg's bed twelve feet wide !), and a sala of imperceptible extent in the dim light of two candles and a wood fire ; but were very well and very cheaply entertained. Here we are, as you know, housed in the greatest comfort.

We continue to get on very well together. We really do admirably. I lose no opportunity of inculcating the lesson that it is of no use to be out of temper in travelling, and it is very seldom wanted for any of us. Egg is an excellent fellow, and full of good qualities ; I am sure a generous and staunch man at heart, and a good and honourable nature.

I shall hope to hear from you and shall be very glad indeed to do so. No more at present.

Ever most affectionately.

CROCE DI MALTA, GENOA,
Friday Night, Twenty-ninth October, 1853.

MY DEAREST CATHERINE,

As we arrived here later than I had expected (in consequence of the journey from Milan being most horribly slow) I received your welcome letter only this morning. I write this before going to bed, that I may be sure of not being taken by any engagement off the post time to-morrow.

We came in last night between seven and eight. The railroad to Turin is finished and opened to within twenty miles of Genoa. Its effect upon the whole town, and especially upon that part of it lying down beyond the lighthouse and away by San Pietro d'Arena, is quite wonderful. I only knew the place by the lighthouse, so numerous were the new buildings, so wide the streets, so busy the people, and so thriving and busy the many signs of commerce. To-day I have seen ——, the ——, the ——, and the ——, the latter of whom live at Nervi, fourteen or fifteen miles off, towards Porto Fino. First, of the ——. They are just the same, except that Mrs. ——'s face is larger and fuller, and her hair rather gray. As I rang at their bell she came out walking, and stared at me. "What! you don't know me?" said I; upon which she recognised me very warmly, and then said in her old quiet way: "I expected to find a ruin. We heard you had been so ill; and I find you younger and better-looking than ever. But it's so strange to see you without a bright waistcoat. Why haven't you got a bright waistcoat on?" I apologised for my black one, and was sent upstairs, when B—— presently appeared in a hideous and demoniacal night-dress, having turned out of bed to greet his distinguished countryman. After a long talk, in the course of which I arranged to dine there on Sunday early, before starting by the steamer for Naples, and in which they told me every possible and impossible particular about their minutest affairs, and especially about S——'s marriage, I set off for G——'s. I had found letters from him here, and he had been here over and over again, and had driven out no end of times to the Gate to leave messages for me, and really is (in his strange uncouth way) crying glad to see me. I found him and his wife in a little comfortable country house, overlooking the sea, sitting in a small summer-house on wheels, exactly like a bathing-machine. I found her rather pretty, extraordinarily cold and composed, a mere piece of furniture, *talking broken English*. Through eight months in the year they live in this country place. She never reads, never works, never talks, never gives an order or directs anything, has only a taste for going to the theatre (where she never speaks either) and buying clothes.

X

They sit in the garden all day, dine at four, *smoke their cigars,* go in at eight, sit about till ten, and then go to bed.   The greater part of this I had from G—— himself in a particularly unintelligible confidence in the garden, the only portion of which that I could clearly understand were the words "and one thing and another," repeated one hundred thousand times.   He described himself as being perfectly happy, and seemed very fond of his wife. "But that," said his father-in-law to me this morning, looking like the figure-head of a ship, with a nutmeg-grater for a face, "that he ought to be, and must be, and is bound to be—he couldn't help it."

Then I went on to the T——'s, and found them living in a beautiful situation in a ruinous Albaro-like palace.   Coming upon them unawares, I found T——, with a pointed beard, smoking a great German pipe, in a pair of slippers; the two little girls very pale and faint from the climate, in a singularly untidy state—one (heaven knows why!) without stockings, and both with their little short hair cropped in a manner never before beheld, and a little bright bow stuck on the top of it.   C—— said she had invented this headgear as a picturesque thing, adding that perhaps it was— and perhaps it was not.   She was greatly flushed and agitated, but looked very well, and seems to be greatly liked here.   We had disturbed her at her painting in oils, and I have rather received an impression that, what with that, and what with music, the household affairs went a little to the wall.   T—— was teaching the two little girls the multiplication table in a disorderly old billiard-room, with all manner of maps in it.

Having obtained a gracious permission from the lady of the school, I am going to show my companions the Sala of the Peschiere this morning.   It is raining intensely hard in the regular Genoa manner, so that I can hardly hope for Genoa's making as fine an impression as I could desire.   Our boat for Naples is a large French mail-boat, and we hope to get there on Tuesday or Wednesday.   If the day after you receive this you write to the Poste Restante, Rome, it will be the safest course.   Friday's letter write Poste Restante, Florence.   You refer to a letter you suppose me to have received from Forster—to whom my love. No letter from him has come to hand.

I will resume my report of this place in my next.   In the meantime I will not fail to drink dear Katey's health to-day. Edward has just come in with mention of an English boat on Tuesday morning, superior to French boat to-morrow, and faster. I shall enquire at the Consulate and take the best.   When I next write I will give you our route in detail.

I am pleased to hear of Mr. Robson's success in a serious part,* as I hope he will now be a fine actor. I hope you will enjoy yourself at Macready's, though I fear it must be sometimes but a melancholy visit.

Good-bye, my dear, and believe me ever most affectionately.

Sunday, Thirtieth October.

We leave for Naples to-morrow morning by the Peninsular and Oriental Company's steamer the *Valletta*. I send a sketch of our movements that I have at last been able to make.

Mrs. G—— quite came out yesterday. So did Mrs. B—— (in a different manner), by violently attacking Mrs. T—— for painting ill in oils when she might be playing well on the piano. It rained hard all yesterday, but is finer this morning. We went over the Peschiere in the wet afternoon. The garden is sorely neglected now, and the rooms are all full of boarding-school beds, and most of the fireplaces are closed up, but the old beauty and grandeur of the place were in it still.

I will think of Charley (from whom I have heard here) and soon write to him definitely. At present I think he had better join me at Boulogne. I shall not bring the little boys over, as, if we keep our time, it would be too long before Christmas Day.

Ever most affectionately yours.

Miss
Hogarth

CROCE DI MALTA, GENOA,
Saturday, Twenty-ninth October, 1853.

MY DEAREST GEORGY,

We had thirty-one hours consecutively on the road between this and Milan, and arrived here in a rather damaged condition. We live at the top of this immense house, overlooking the port and sea, pleasantly and airily enough, though it is no joke to get so high, and though the apartment is rather vast and faded.

The old walks are pretty much the same as ever, except that they have built behind the Peschiere on the San Bartolomeo hill, and changed the whole town towards San Pietro d'Arena, where we seldom went. The Bisagno looks just the same, strong just now, and with very little water in it. "Vicoli" stink exactly as they used to, and are fragrant with the same old flavour of very rotten cheese kept in very hot blankets. The Mezzaro pervades them as before. The old Jesuit college in the Strada Nuova is under the present government the Hôtel de Ville; and a very splendid caffé with a terrace garden has arisen between it and

* "Desmarets" in Mr. Tom Taylor's play, "Plot and Passion."

Palavicini's old palace. Another new and handsome caffé has been built in the Piazza Carlo Felice, between the old caffé and the Strada Carlo Felice. The old beastly gate and guard-house on the Albaro road are still in their dear old beastly state, and the whole of the road is just as it was. The man without legs is still in the Strada Nuova; but the beggars in general are all cleared off, and our old one-armed Belisario made a sudden evaporation a year or two ago. I am going to the Peschiere to-day. The puppets are here, and the opera is open, but only with a buffo company, and without a buffet. We went to the Scala, where they did an opera of Verdi's, called "Il Trovatore," and a poor enough ballet. The whole performance miserable indeed. I wish you were here to take some of the old walks. It is quite strange to walk about alone. Good-bye, my dear Georgy. Pray tell me how Kate is. I rather fancy from her letter, though I scarcely know why, that she is not quite as well as she was at Boulogne. I was charmed with your account of the Plornishghenter and everything and everybody else.

Ever most affectionately yours.

Miss
Hogarth.

HÔTEL DES ÉTRANGERS, NAPLES,
Friday Night, Fourth November, 1853.

MY DEAREST GEORGY,

Instead of embarking on Monday at Genoa, we were delayed (in consequence of the boat's being a day later when there are thirty-one days in the month) until Tuesday. Going aboard that morning at half-past nine, we found the steamer more than full of passengers from Marseilles, and in a state of confusion not to be described. We could get no places at the table, got our dinners how we could on deck, had no berths or sleeping accommodation of any kind, and had paid heavy first-class fares! To add to this, we got to Leghorn too late to steam away again that night, getting the ship's papers examined first—as the authorities said so, not being favourable to the new express English ship, English officered—and we lay off the lighthouse all night long. The scene on board beggars description. Ladies on the tables, gentlemen under the tables, and ladies and gentlemen lying indiscriminately on the open deck, arrayed like spoons on a sideboard. No mattresses, no blankets, nothing. Towards midnight, attempts were made by means of an awning and flags to make this latter scene remotely approach an Australian encampment; and we three lay together on the bare planks covered with overcoats. We were all gradually dozing off when a perfectly tropical rain fell, and in a moment drowned the whole ship. The rest of the night was passed upon the stairs, with an immense jumble of men and women. When anybody came up for any purpose we all fell down; and when anybody came down we all fell up again. Still, the good-humour in the English part of the passengers was quite extraordinary. There were excellent officers aboard, and the first mate lent me his cabin to wash in in the morning, which I afterwards lent to Egg and Collins. Then we and the Emerson Tennents (who were aboard) and the captain, the doctor, and the second officer went off on a jaunt together to Pisa, as the ship was to lie at Leghorn all day.

The captain was a capital fellow, but I led him, facetiously, such a life all day, that I got almost everything altered at night. Emerson Tennent, with the greatest kindness, turned his son out of his state room (who, indeed, volunteered to go in the most amiable manner), and I got a good bed there. The store-room down by the hold was opened for Egg and Collins, and they slept with the moist sugar, the cheese in cut, the spices, the cruets, the apples and pears—in a perfect chandler's shop; in company with what the ——'s would call a "hold gent"—who had been so horribly wet through overnight that his condition frightened the authorities—a cat, and the steward—who dozed in an armchair, and all night long fell headforemost, once in every five minutes, on Egg, who slept on the counter or dresser. Last night I had the steward's own cabin, opening on deck, all to myself. It had been previously occupied by some desolate lady, who went ashore at Civita Vecchia. There was little or no sea, thank Heaven, all the trip; but the rain was heavier than any I have ever seen, and the lightning very constant and vivid. We were, with the crew, some two hundred people; with boats, at the utmost stretch, for one hundred perhaps. I could not help thinking what would happen if we met with any accident; the crew being chiefly Maltese, and evidently fellows who would cut off alone in the largest boat on the least alarm. The speed (it being the crack express ship for the India mail) very high; also the running through all the narrow rocky channels. Thank God, however, here we are; though the more sensible and experienced part of the passengers agreed with me this morning that it was not a thing to try often. We had an excellent table after the first day, the best wines and so forth, and the captain and I swore eternal friendship. Ditto the first officer and the majority of the passengers. We got into the bay about seven this morning, but could not land until noon. We towed from Civita Vecchia the entire Greek navy, I believe, consisting of a little brig-of-war, with great guns, fitted as a steamer, but disabled by having burst the bottom of her boiler in her first run. She was just big enough to carry the captain and a crew of six or so, but the captain was so covered with buttons and gold that there never would have been room for him on board to put these valuables away if he hadn't worn them, which he consequently did, all night.

Whenever anything was wanted to be done, as slackening the tow-rope or anything of that sort, our officers roared at this miserable potentate, in violent English, through a speaking-trumpet, of which he couldn't have understood a word under the most favourable circumstances, so he did all the wrong things first, and the right things always last. The absence of any knowledge of anything not English on the part of the officers and stewards was most ridiculous. I met an Italian gentleman on the cabin steps, yesterday morning, vainly endeavouring to explain that he wanted a cup of tea for his sick wife. And when we were coming out of the harbour at Genoa, and it was necessary to order away that boat of music you remember, the chief officer (called aft for the purpose, as "knowing something of Italian,") delivered himself in this explicit and clear manner to the principal performer: "Now, signora, if you don't sheer off, you'll be run down; so you had better trice up that guitar of yours, and put about."

We get on as well as possible, and it is extremely pleasant and interesting, and I feel that the change is doing me great and real service, after a long continuous strain upon the mind; but I am pleased to think that we are at our farthest point, and I look forward with joy to coming home again, to my old room, and the old walks, and all the old pleasant things.

I wish I had arranged, or could have done so—for it would not have been easy—to find some letters here. It is a blank to stay for five days in a place without any.

I am afraid this is a dull letter, for I am very tired. You must take the will for the deed, my dear, and good-night.

Ever most affectionately.

Mrs. Charles
Dickens.

HÔTEL DES ÉTRANGERS, NAPLES,
Friday Night, Fourth November, 1853.

MY DEAREST CATHERINE,

We arrived here at midday—two days after our intended time, under circumstances which I reserve for Georgina's letter, by way of variety—in what Forster used to call good health and sp—p—pirits. We have a charming apartment opposite the sea, a little lower down than the Victoria—in the direction of the San Carlo Theatre—and the windows are now wide open as on an English summer night. The first persons we found on board at

Genoa, were Emerson Tennent, Lady Tennent, their son and daughter. They are all here too, in an apartment over ours, and we have all been constantly together in a very friendly way, ever since our meeting. We dine at the table d'hôte—made a league together on board—and have been mutually agreeable. They have no servant with them, and have profited by Edward. He goes on perfectly well, is always cheerful and ready, has been sleeping on board (upside down, I believe), in a corner, with his head in the wet and his heels against the side of the paddle-box— but has been perpetually gay and fresh.

As soon as we got our luggage from the custom-house, we packed complete changes in a bag, set off in a carriage for some warm baths, and had a most refreshing cleansing after our long journey. There was an odd Neapolitan attendant—a steady old man—who, bringing the linen into my bath, proposed to "soap me." Upon which I called out to the other two that I intended to have everything done to me that could be done, and gave him directions accordingly. I was frothed all over with Naples soap, rubbed all down, scrubbed with a brush, had my nails cut, and all manner of extraordinary operations performed. He was as much disappointed (apparently) as surprised not to find me dirty, and kept on ejaculating under his breath, "Oh, Heaven! how clean this Englishman is!" He also remarked that the Englishman is as fair as a beautiful woman. Some relations of Lord John Russell's, going to Malta, were aboardship, and we were very pleasant. Likewise there was a Mr. Young aboard—an agreeable fellow, not very unlike Forster in person—who introduced himself as the brother of the Miss Youngs whom we knew at Boulogne. He was musical and had much good-fellowship in him, and we were very agreeable together also. On the whole I became decidedly popular, and was embraced on all hands when I came over the side this morning. We are going up Vesuvius, of course, and to Herculaneum and Pompeii, and the usual places. The Tennents will be our companions in most of our excursions, but we shall leave them here behind us. Naples looks just the same as when we left it, except that the weather is much better and brighter.

On the day before we left Genoa, we had another dinner with G—— at his country place. He was the soul of hospitality, and really seems to love me. You would have been quite touched if you could have seen the honest warmth of his affection. On the occasion of this second banquet, Egg made a brilliant mistake that perfectly convulsed us all. I had introduced all the games with great success, and we were playing at the "What advice would you

have given that person ?" game.   The advice was " Not to bully
his fellow-creatures."   Upon which, Egg triumphantly and with the
greatest glee, screamed, "Mr. B——!" utterly forgetting S——'s
relationship, which I had elaborately impressed upon him.   The
effect was perfectly irresistible and uncontrollable ; and the little
woman's way of humouring the joke was in the best taste and the
best sense.   While I am upon Genoa I may add, that when we
left the Croce the landlord, in hoping that I was satisfied, told me
that as I was an old inhabitant, he had charged the prices " as to
a Genoese."   They certainly were very reasonable.

Mr. and Mrs.* Sartoris have lately been staying in this house,
but are just gone.   It is kept by an English waiting-maid who
married an Italian courier, and is extremely comfortable and clean.
I am getting impatient to hear from you with all home news, and
shall be heartily glad to get to Rome, and find my best welcome
and interest at the post-office there.

That ridiculous —— and her mother were at the hotel at
Leghorn the day before yesterday, where the mother (poor old lady !)
was so ill'from the fright and anxiety consequent on her daughter's
efforts at martyrdom, that it is even doubtful whether she will
recover.   I learnt from a lady friend of ——, that all this nonsense
originated at Nice, where she was stirred up by Free Kirk parsons
—itinerant—any one of whom I take her to be ready to make a
semi-celestial marriage with.   The dear being who told me all
about her was a noble specimen—single, forty, in a clinging flounced
black silk dress, which wouldn't drape, or bustle, or fall, or do anything of that sort—and with a leghorn hat on her head, at least (I
am serious) *six feet round.*   The consequence of its immense size,
was, that whereas it had an insinuating blue decoration in the
form of a bow in front, it was so out of her knowledge behind, that
it was all battered and bent in that direction—and, viewed from
that quarter, she looked drunk.

My best love to Mamey and Katey, and Sydney the king of the
nursery, and Harry and the dear little Plornishghenter.   I kiss
almost all the children I encounter in remembrance of their sweet
faces, and talk to all the mothers who carry them.   I hope to hear
nothing but good news from you, and to find nothing but good
spirits in your expected letter when I come to Rome.   I already
begin to look homeward, being now 'at the remotest part of the
journey, and to anticipate the pleasure of return.

Ever most affectionately.

* Miss Adelaide Kemble.

Rome, *Sunday Night,*
Thirteenth November, 1853.

Miss
Hogarth.

MY DEAREST GEORGY,

We arrived here yesterday afternoon, at between three and four. On sending to the post-office this morning, I received your pleasant little letter, and one from Miss Coutts, who is still at Paris. But to my amazement there was none from Catherine! You mention her writing, and I cannot but suppose that your two letters must have been posted together. However, I received none from her, and I have all manner of doubts respecting the plainness of its direction. They will not produce the letters here as at Genoa, but persist in looking them out at the post-office for you. I shall send again to-morrow, and every day until Friday, when we leave here.

One night, at Naples, Edward came in, open-mouthed, to the table d'hôte where we were dining with the Tennents, to announce "The Marchese Garofalo." I at first thought it must be the little parrot-marquess who was once your escort from Genoa; but I found him to be a man (married to an Englishwoman) whom we used to meet at Ridgway's. He was very glad to see me, and I afterwards met him at dinner at Mr. Lowther's, our chargé d'affaires. Mr. Lowther was at the Rockingham play, and is a very agreeable fellow. We had an exceedingly pleasant dinner of eight, preparatory to which I was near having the ridiculous adventure of not being able to find the house and coming back dinnerless. I went in an open carriage from the hotel in all state, and the coachman, to my surprise, pulled up at the end of the Chiaja. "Behold the house," says he, "of Il Signor Larthoor!"—at the same time pointing with his whip into the seventh heaven, where the early stars were shining. "But the Signor Larthoor," returns the Inimitable darling, "lives at Pausilippo." "It is true," says the coachman (still pointing to the evening star), "but he lives high up the Salita Sant' Antonio, where no carriage ever yet ascended, and that is the house" (evening star as aforesaid), "and one must go on foot. Behold the Salita Sant' Antonio!" I went up it, a mile and a half I should think. I got into the strangest places, among the wildest Neapolitans—kitchens, washing-places, archways, stables, vineyards—was baited by dogs, answered in profoundly unintelligible Neapolitan, from behind lonely locked doors, in cracked female voices, quaking with fear; could hear of no such Englishman or any Englishman. By-and-by I came upon a Polenta-shop in the clouds, where an old Frenchman, with an umbrella like a faded tropical leaf (it had not rained for six weeks) was staring at nothing at all, with a snuff-box in his hand. To him I appealed concerning the Signor Larthoor. "Sir," said he, with the sweetest politeness, "can you speak French?" "Sir," said I, "a little." "Sir," said he, "I presume the Signor Lootheere"—you will observe that he changed the name according to the custom of his country—"is an Englishman." I admitted that he was the victim of circumstances and had that misfortune. "Sir," said he, "one word more. *Has* he a servant with a wooden leg?" "Great Heaven, sir," said I, "how do I know? I should think not, but it is possible." "It is always," said the Frenchman, "possible. Almost all the things of the world are always possible." "Sir," said I—you may imagine my condition and dismal sense of my own absurdity, by this time—"that is true." He then took an immense pinch of snuff, wiped the dust off his umbrella, led me to an arch commanding a wonderful view of the bay of Naples, and pointed deep into the earth from which I had mounted. "Below there, near the lamp, one finds an Englishman, with a servant with a wooden leg. It is always possible that he is the Signor Lootheere." I had been asked at six, and it was now getting on for seven. I went down again in a state of perspiration and misery not to be described, and without the faintest hope of finding the place. But as I was going down to the lamp, I saw the strangest staircase up a dark corner, with a man in a white-waistcoat (evidently hired) standing on the top of it fuming. I dashed in at a venture, found it was the place, made the most of the whole story, and was indescribably popular. The best of it was, that as nobody ever did find the place, he had put a servant at the bottom of the Salita, to "wait for an English gentleman." The servant (as he presently pleaded), deceived by the moustache, had allowed the English gentleman to pass unchallenged.

The night before we left Naples we were at the San Carlo, where, with the Verdi rage of our old Genoa time, they were again doing the "Trovatore." It seemed rubbish on the whole to me, but was very fairly done. I think "La Tenco," the prima donna, will soon be a great hit in London. She is a very remarkable singer and a fine actress, to the best of my judgment on such premises. There seems to be no opera here at present. There was a Festa in St. Peter's to-day, and the Pope passed to the Cathedral in state. We were all there.

We leave here, please God, on Friday morning, and post to Florence in three days and a half. We came here by Vetturino. Upon the whole, the roadside inns are greatly improved since our time. Half-past three and half-past four have been, however, our usual times of rising on the road.

I was in my old place at the Coliseum this morning, and it

was as grand as ever. With that exception the ruined part of Rome—the real original Rome—looks smaller than my remembrance made it. It is the only place on which I have yet found that effect. We are in the old hotel.

You are going to Bonchurch I suppose? will be there, perhaps, when this letter reaches you? I shall be pleased to think of you as at home again, and making the commodious family mansion look natural and home-like. I don't like to think of my room without anybody to peep into it now and then. Here is a world of travelling arrangements for me to settle, and here are Collins and Egg looking sideways at me with an occasional imploring glance as beseeching me to settle it. So I leave off. Good-night.

Ever, my dearest Georgy,

Most affectionately yours.

HÔTEL DES ILES BRITANNIQUES, PIAZZA DEL POPOLO, ROME, *Monday, Fourteenth November*, 1853.

Sir James Emerson Tennent.

MY DEAR TENNENT,

As I never made a good bargain in my life—except once, when, on going abroad, I let my house on excellent terms to an admirable tenant, who never paid anything—I sent Edward into the Casa Dies yesterday morning, while I invested the premises from the outside, and carefully surveyed them. It is a very clean, large, bright-looking house at the corner of Via Gregoriana; not exactly in a part of Rome I should pick out for living in, and on what I should be disposed to call the wrong side of the street. However, this is not to the purpose. Signor Dies has no idea of letting an apartment for a short time—scouted the idea of a month —signified that he could not be brought to the contemplation of two months—was by no means clear that he could come down to the consideration of three. This of course settled the business speedily.

This hotel is no longer kept by the Melloni I spoke of, but is even better kept than in his time, and is a very admirable house. I have engaged a small apartment for you to be ready on Thursday afternoon. If you would like to change to ours, which is a very good one, on Friday morning, you can of course do so. As our dining-room is large, and there is no table d'hôte here, I will order dinner in it for our united parties at six on Thursday. You will be able to decide how to arrange for the remainder of your stay, after being here and looking about you—two really necessary considerations in Rome.

Pray make my kind regards to Lady Tennent, and Miss Tennent, and your good son, who became homeless for my sake. Mr. Egg and Mr. Collins desire to be also remembered.

It has been beautiful weather since we left Naples, until to-day, when it rains in a very dogged, sullen, downcast, and determined manner. We have been speculating at breakfast on the possibility of its raining in a similar manner at Naples, and of your wandering about the hotel, refusing consolation.

I grieve to report the Orvieto considerably damaged by the general vine failure, but still far from despicable. Montefiascone (the Est wine you know) is to be had here; and we have had one bottle in the very finest condition, and one in a second-rate state.

Believe me always, very faithfully yours.

ROME, Monday, Fourteenth November, 1853.

Mrs. Charles Dickens.

MY DEAREST CATHERINE,

As I have mentioned in my letter to Georgy (written last night but posted with this), I received her letter without yours, to my unbounded astonishment. This morning, on sending again to the post-office, I at last got yours, and most welcome it is with all its contents.

I found Layard at Naples, who went up Vesuvius with us, and was very merry and agreeable. He is travelling with Lord and Lady Somers, and Lord Somers being laid up with an attack of malaria fever, Layard had a day to spare. Craven, who was Lord Normanby's Secretary of Legation in Paris, now lives at Naples, and is married to a French lady. He is very hospitable and hearty, and seemed to have vague ideas that something might be done in a pretty little private theatre he has in his house. He told me of Fanny Kemble and the Sartoris's being here. I have also heard of Thackeray's being here—I don't know how truly. Lockhart* is here, and, I fear, very ill. I mean to go and see him.

We are living in the old hotel. I don't know whether you recollect an apartment at the top of the house, to which we once ran up with poor Roche to see the horses start in the race at the Carnival time? That is ours, in which I at present write. We have a large back dining-room, a handsome front drawing-room, looking into the Piazza del Popolo, and three front bedrooms, all on a floor. The whole costs us about four shillings a day each. The hotel is better kept than ever. There is a little kitchen to each apartment where the dinner is kept hot. There is no house comparable to it in Paris, and it is better than Mivart's. We start for Florence, post, on Friday morning, and I am bargaining for a carriage to take us on to Venice.

Edward is an excellent servant, and always cheerful and ready for his work. I am perfectly pleased with him, and would rather

<hr>

* The son-in-law and biographer of Sir Walter Scott.

have him than an older hand. Poor dear Roche comes back to my mind, though, often.

We have had delightful weather, with one day's exception, until to-day, when it rained very heavily and suddenly. Egg and Collins have gone to the Vatican, and I am "going" to try whether I can hit out anything for the Christmas number.

I have not come across any English whom I know except Layard and the Emerson Tennents, who will be here on Thursday from Civita Vecchia, and are to dine with us. The losses up to this point have been two pairs of shoes (one mine and one Egg's), Collins' snuff-box, and Egg's dressing-gown.

We observe the managerial punctuality in all our arrangements, and have not had any difference whatever.

I introduced myself to Salvatore at Vesuvius, and reminded him of the night when poor Le Gros fell down the mountains. He was full of interest directly, remembered the very hole, put on his gold-banded cap, and went up with us himself. He did not know that Le Gros was dead, and was very sorry to hear it. He asked after the ladies, and hoped they were very happy, to which I answered "Very." The cone is completely changed since our visit, is not at all recognisable as the same place; and there is no fire from the mountain, though there is a great deal of smoke. Its last demonstration was in 1850.

I shall be glad to think of your all being at home again, as I suppose you will be soon after the receipt of this. I shall be very happy to be at home again myself, and to embrace you; for of course I miss you *very much*, though I feel that I could not have done a better thing to clear my mind and freshen it up again, than make this expedition. If I find Charley much ahead of me, I shall start on through a night or so to meet him, and leave the others to catch us up. I look upon the journey as almost closed at Turin. My best love to Mamey, and Katey, and Sydney, and Harry, and the darling Plornishghenter. We often talk about them, and both my companions do so with interest. They always send all sorts of messages to you, which I never deliver. God bless you! Take care of yourself.

Ever most affectionately.

ROME, *Thursday Afternoon,*
Seventeenth November, 1853.
Mr. W. H. Wills.

MY DEAR WILLS,

Just as I wrote the last words of the enclosed little story for the Christmas number just now, Edward brought in your letter. Also one from Forster (tell him) which I have not yet opened. I will write again—and write to him—from Florence. I am delighted to have news of you.

The enclosed little paper for the Christmas number is in a character that nobody else is likely to hit, and which is pretty sure to be considered pleasant. Let Forster have the MS. with the proof, and I know he will correct it to the minutest point. I have a notion of another little story, also for the Christmas number. If I can do it at Venice, I will, and send it straight on. But it is not easy to work under these circumstances. In travelling we generally get up about three; and in resting we are perpetually roaming about in all manner of places. Not to mention my being laid hold of by all manner of people.

KEEP "HOUSEHOLD WORDS" IMAGINATIVE! is the solemn and continual Conductorial Injunction. Delighted to hear of Mrs. Gaskell's contributions.

In making up the Christmas number, don't consider my paper or papers, with any reference saving to where they will fall best. I have no liking, in the case, for any particular place.

All perfectly well. Companion moustaches (particularly Egg's) dismal in the extreme.

Ever faithfully.

FLORENCE, Monday, Twenty-first November, 1853.

Mr. W. H.
Wills.

H. W.

MY DEAR WILLS,

I sent you by post from Rome, on Wednesday last, a little story for the Christmas number, called "The Schoolboy's Story." I have an idea of another short one to be called "Nobody's Story," which I hope to be able to do at Venice, and to send you straight home before this month is out. I trust you have received the first safely.

Edward continues to do extremely well. He is always, early and late, what you have seen him. He is a very steady fellow, a little too bashful for a courier even; settles prices of everything now, as soon as we come into an hotel; and improves fast. His knowledge of Italian is painfully defective, and, in the midst of a howling crowd at a post-house or railway station, this deficiency perfectly stuns him. I was obliged last night to get out of the carriage, and pluck him from a crowd of porters who were putting our baggage into wrong conveyances—by cursing and ordering about in all directions. I should think about ten substantives, the names of ten common objects, form his whole Italian stock. It matters very little at the hotels, where a great deal of French is spoken now ; but, on the road, if none of his party knew Italian, it would be a very serious inconvenience indeed.

Will you write to Ryland if you have not heard from him, and ask him what the Birmingham reading-nights are really to be? For it is ridiculous enough that I positively don't know. Can't a Saturday Night in a Truck District, or a Sunday Morning among the Ironworkers (a fine subject) be knocked out in the course of the same visit?

If you should see any managing man you know in the Oriental and Peninsular Company, I wish you would very gravely mention to him from me that if they are not careful what they are about with their steamship *Valletta*, between Marseilles and Naples, they will suddenly find that they will receive a blow one fine day in *The Times*, which it will be a very hard matter for them ever to recover. When I sailed in her from Genoa, there had been taken on board, *with no caution in most cases from the agent, or hint of discomfort*, at least forty people of both sexes for whom there was no room whatever. I am a pretty old traveller as you know, but I never saw anything like the manner in which pretty women were compelled to lie among the men in the great cabin and on the bare decks. The good humour was beyond all praise, but the natural indignation very great ; and I was repeatedly urged to stand up for the public in "Household Words," and to write a plain description of the facts to *The Times*. If I had done either, and merely mentioned that all these people paid heavy first-class fares, I will answer for it that they would have been beaten off the station in a couple of months. I did neither, because I was the best of friends with the captain and all the officers, and never saw such a fine set of men ; so admirable in the discharge of their duty, and so zealous to do their best by everybody. It is impossible to praise them too highly. But there is a strong desire at all the ports along the coast to throw impediments in the way of the English service, and to favour the French and Italian boats. In these boats (which I know very well) great care is taken of the passengers, and the accommodation is very good. If the Peninsular and Oriental add to all this the risk of such an exposure as they are *certain* to get (if they go on so) in *The Times*, they are dead sure to get a blow from the public which will make them stagger again. I say nothing of the number of the passengers and the room in the ship's boats, though the frightful consideration the contrast presented must have been in more minds than mine. I speak only of the taking people for whom there is no sort of accommodation as the most decided swindle, and the coolest, I ever did with my eyes behold.   Ever, my dear Wills, faithfully yours.

VENICE, *Friday, Twenty-fifth November,* 1853.

MY DEAREST GEORGY,

We found an English carriage from Padua at Florence, and
hired it to bring it back again. We travelled post with four horses
all the way (from Padua to this place there is a railroad) and
travelled all night. We left Florence at half-past six in the
morning, and got to Padua at eleven next day—yesterday. The
cold at night was most intense. I don't think I have ever felt it
colder. But our carriage was very comfortable, and we had some
wine and some rum to keep us warm. We came by Bologna
(where we had tea) and Ferrara. You may imagine the delays in
the night when I tell you that each of our passports, after receiving
six visés at Florence, received in the course of the one night, *nine
more,* every one of which was written and sealed ; somebody being
slowly knocked out of bed to do it every time! It really was excruciating.

Landor had sent me a letter to his son, and on the day before
we left Florence I thought I would go out to Fiesoli and leave it.
So I got a little one-horse open carriage and drove off alone. We
were within half a mile of the Villa Landoro, and were driving
down a very narrow lane like one of those at Albaro, when I saw
an elderly lady coming towards us, very well dressed in silk of the
Queen's blue, and walking freshly and briskly against the wind at
a good round pace. It was a bright, cloudless, very cold day, and
I thought she walked with great spirit, as if she enjoyed it. I
also thought (perhaps that was having him in my mind) that her
ruddy face was shaped like Landor's. All of a sudden the coachman pulls up, and looks enquiringly at me. "What's the matter?"
says I. "Ecco la Signora Landoro?" says he. "For the love of
Heaven, don't stop," says I. "*I* don't know her, I am only going
to the house to leave a letter—go on!" Meanwhile she (still
coming on) looked at me, and I looked at her, and we were both a
good deal confused, and so went our several ways. Altogether, I
think it was as disconcerting a meeting as I ever took part in, and
as odd a one. Under any other circumstances I should have
introduced myself, but the separation made the circumstances so
peculiar that "I didn't like."

The Plornishghenter is evidently the greatest, noblest, finest,
cleverest, brightest, and most brilliant of boys. Your account of
him is most delightful, and I hope to find another letter from you
somewhere on the road, making me informed of his demeanour on
your return. On which occasion, as on every other, I have no
doubt he will have distinguished himself as an irresistibly attracting, captivating May-Roon-Ti-Goon-Ter. Give him a good many

kisses for me. I quite agree with Syd as to his ideas of paying attention to the old gentleman. It's not bad, but deficient in originality. The usual deficiency of an inferior intellect with so great a model before him. I am very curious to see whether the Plorn remembers me on my reappearance.

I meant to have gone to work this morning, and to have tried a second little story for the Christmas number of "Household Words," but my letters have (most pleasantly) put me out, and I defer all such wise efforts until to-morrow. Egg and Collins are out in a gondola with a "servitore di piazza."

You will find this but a stupid letter, but I really have no news. We go to the opera, whenever there is one, see sights, eat and drink, sleep in a natural manner two or three nights, and move on again. Edward was a little crushed at Padua yesterday. He had been extraordinarily cold all night in the rumble, and had got out our clothes to dress, and I think must have been projecting a five or six hours' sleep, when I announced that he was to come on here in an hour and a half to get the rooms and order dinner. He fell into a sudden despondency of the profoundest kind, but was quite restored when we arrived here between eight and nine. We found him waiting at the Custom House with a gondola in his usual brisk condition.

It is extraordinary how few English we see. With the exception of a gentlemanly young fellow (in a consumption I am afraid), married to the tiniest little girl, in a brown straw hat, and travelling with his sister and her sister, and a consumptive single lady, travelling with a maid and a Scotch terrier christened Trotty Veck, we have scarcely seen any, and have certainly spoken to none, since we left Switzerland. These were aboard the *Valletta*, where the captain and I indulged in all manner of insane suppositions concerning the straw hat—the "Little Matron" we called her; by which name she soon became known all over the ship. The day we entered Rome, and the moment we entered it, there was the Little Matron, alone with antiquity—and Murray—on the wall. The very first church I entered, there was the Little Matron. On the last afternoon, when I went alone to St. Peter's, there was the Little Matron and her party. The best of it is, that I was extremely intimate with them, invited them to Tavistock House when they come home in the spring, and have not the faintest idea of their name.

There was no table d'hôte at Rome, or at Florence, but there is one here, and we dine at it to-day, so perhaps we may stumble upon somebody. I have heard from Charley this morning, who appoints (wisely) Paris as our place of meeting. I had a letter

Y

from Coote,* at Florence, informing me that his volume of "House-hold Songs" was ready, and requesting permission to dedicate it to me. Which of course I gave.

I am beginning to think of the Birmingham readings. I suppose you won't object to be taken to hear them? This is the last place at which we shall make a stay of more than one day. We shall stay at Parma one, and at Turin one, and then we shall come hard and fast home. I feel almost there already, and shall be delighted to close the pleasant trip, and get back to my own Piccola Camera—if, being English, you understand what *that* is. I will not wait over to-morrow, tell Kate, for her letter; but will write then, whether or no.

Ever, my dearest Georgy,

Most affectionately yours.

Mr. Marcus Stone.

TAVISTOCK HOUSE, *Nineteenth December*, 1853.

MY DEAR MARCUS,

You made an excellent sketch from a book of mine which I have received (and have preserved) with great pleasure. Will you accept from me, in remembrance of it, *this* little book? I believe it to be true, though it may be sometimes not as genteel as history has a habit of being.

Faithfully yours.

1854.

NARRATIVE.

THE summer of this year was also spent at Boulogne, M. Beaucourt being again the landlord; but the house, though still on the same "property," stood on the top of the hill, above the Moulineaux, and was called the Villa du Camp de Droite.

In the early part of the year Charles Dickens paid several visits to the English provinces, giving readings from his books at many of the large manufacturing towns, and always for some good and charitable purpose.

He was still at work upon "Hard Times," which was finished during the summer, and was constantly occupied with "Household Words." Many of the letters for this year are to the contributors to this journal. The last is an unusually interesting one. He had for some time past been much charmed with the writings of a certain Miss Berwick, who he knew to be a contributor under a

---

* Mr. Charles Coote, a gentleman for whom Charles Dickens had a great regard and respect, travelled with the amateur company, as director of the music.

feigned name.   When at last the lady confided her real name, and he discovered in the young poetess the daughter of his dear friends, Mr.* and Mrs. Procter, the "new sensation" caused him intense surprise, and the greatest pleasure and delight.   Miss Adelaide Procter was, from this time, a frequent contributor to "Household Words," more especially to the Christmas numbers.

There are really very few letters in this year requiring any explanation — many explaining themselves, and many having allusion to incidents in the past year, which have been duly noted by us for 1853.

The portrait mentioned in the letter to Mr. Collins, for which Charles Dickens was sitting to Mr. E. M. Ward, R.A., was to be one of a series of oil sketches of the then celebrated literary men of the day, in their studies.   We believe this portrait to be now in the possession of Mrs. Ward.

In explanation of the letter to Mr. John Saunders on the subject of the production of the latter's play, called "Love's Martyrdom," we will give the dramatist's own words :

"Having printed for private circulation a play entitled 'Love's Martyrdom,' and for which I desired to obtain the independent judgment of some of our most eminent literary men, before seeking the ordeal of the stage, I sent a copy to Mr. Dickens, and the letter in question is his acknowledgment.

*   *   *   *

"He immediately took steps for the introduction of the play to the theatre.   At first he arranged with Mr. Phelps, of Sadler's Wells, but subsequently, with that gentleman's consent, removed it to the Haymarket.   There it was played with Miss Helen Faucit in the character of Margaret, Miss Swanborough (who shortly after married and left the stage) as Julia, Mr. Barry Sullivan as Franklyn, and Mr. Howe as Laneham.

"As far as the play itself was concerned, it was received on all sides as a genuine dramatic and poetic success, achieved, however, as an eminent critic came to my box to say, through greater difficulties than he had ever before seen a dramatic work pass through. The time has not come for me to speak freely of these, but I may point to two of them : the first being the inadequate rehearsals, which caused Mr. Dickens to tell me on the stage, four or five days only before the first performance, that the play was not then in as good a state as it would have been in at Paris three weeks earlier. The other was the breakdown of a performer of a most important secondary part ; a collapse so absolute that he was changed by the management before the second representation of the piece."

* The poet "Barry Cornwall."

This ill-luck of the beginning pursued the play to its close.

"The Haymarket Theatre was at the time in the very lowest state of prostration, through the Crimean War; the habitual frequenters were lovers of comedy, and enjoyers of farce and burlesque; and there was neither the money nor the faith to call to the theatre by the usual methods, vigorously and discriminatingly pursued, the multitudes that I believed could have been so called to a better and more romantic class of comedy.

"Even under these and other similarly depressing circumstances, the nightly receipts were about £60, the expenses being £80; and on the last—an author's—night, there was an excellent and enthusiastic house, yielding, to the best of my recollection, about £140, but certainly between £120 and £140. And with that night—the sixth or seventh—the experiment ended."

Mr. Walter
Savage
Landor.

TAVISTOCK HOUSE, *Seventh January*, 1854.

MY DEAR LANDOR,

I heartily assure you that to have your name coupled with anything I have done is an honour and a pleasure to me. I cannot say that I am sorry that you should have thought it necessary to write to me, for it is always delightful to me to see your hand, and to know (though I want no outward and visible sign as an assurance of the fact) that you are ever the same generous, earnest, gallant man.

Catherine and Georgina send their kind loves. So does Walter Landor, who came home from school with high judicial commendation and a prize into the bargain.

Ever, my dear Landor, affectionately yours.

The Hon.
Mrs.
Watson.

TAVISTOCK HOUSE, *Friday, Thirteenth January*, 1854.

MY DEAR MRS. WATSON,

On the very day after I sent the Christmas number to Rockingham, I heard of your being at Brighton. I should have sent another there, but that I had a misgiving I might seem to be making too much of it. For, when I thought of the probability of the Rockingham copy going on to Brighton, and pictured to myself the advent of two of those very large envelopes at once at Junction House at breakfast time, a sort of comic modesty overcame me. I was heartily pleased with the Birmingham audience, which was a very fine one. I never saw, nor do I suppose anybody ever did, such an interesting sight as the working people's night. There were two thousand five hundred of them there, and a more delicately observant audience it is impossible to imagine. They lost nothing, misinterpreted nothing, followed everything closely, laughed and cried with most delightful earnestness, and animated me to that extent that I felt as if we were all bodily going up into the clouds together. It is an enormous place for the purpose; but I had considered all that carefully, and I believe made the most distant person hear as well as if I had been reading in my own room. I was a little doubtful before I began on the first night whether it was quite practicable to conceal the requisite effort; but I soon had the satisfaction of finding that it was, and that we were all going on together, in the first page, as easily, to all appearance, as if we had been sitting round the fire.

Few things that I saw, when I was away, took my fancy so much as the Electric Telegraph, piercing, like a sunbeam, right through the cruel old heart of the Coliseum at Rome. And on the summit of the Alps, among the eternal ice and snow, there it was still, with its posts sustained against the sweeping mountain winds by clusters of great beams—to say nothing of its being at the bottom of the sea as we crossed the Channel.

Ever, my dear Mrs. Watson,
Most faithfully yours.

TAVISTOCK HOUSE, LONDON, *Thirteenth January*, 1854.   Mr. Frederick Grew.*

MY DEAR SIR,

I beg, through you, to assure the artisans' committee in aid of the Birmingham and Midland Institute, that I have received the resolution they have done me the honour to agree upon for themselves and their fellow-workmen, with the highest gratification. I awakened no pleasure or interest among them at Birmingham which they did not repay to me with abundant interest. I have their welfare and happiness sincerely at heart, and shall ever be their faithful friend.

Your obedient Servant.

TAVISTOCK HOUSE, *Monday,*   Miss Mary Boyle.
Sixteenth January, 1854.

MY DEAR MARY,

It is all very well to pretend to love me as you do. Ah! If you loved as *I* love, Mary! But, when my breast is tortured by the perusal of such a letter as yours, Falkland, Falkland, madam, becomes my part in "The Rivals," and I play it with desperate earnestness.

As thus :

FALKLAND (*to Acres*). Then you see her, sir, sometimes?
ACRES.   See her! Odds beams and sparkles, yes. See her acting! Night after night.

---

* Secretary to the Artisans' Committee in aid of the Birmingham and Midland Institute.

FALKLAND (*aside and furious*).   Death and the devil!   Acting, and I
not there!   Pray, sir (*with constrained calmness*), what
does she act?

ACRES.   Odds, monthly nurses and babbies!   Sairey Gamp and Betsy
Prig, "which, wotever it is, my dear (*mimicking*), I likes
it brought reg'lar and draw'd mild!"   *That's* very like
her.

FALKLAND.   Confusion!   Laceration!   Perhaps, sir, perhaps she sometimes acts—ha! ha! perhaps she sometimes acts, I say—
eh! sir?—a—ha, ha, ha! a fairy? (*With great bitterness.*)

ACRES.   Odds, gauzy pinions and spangles, yes!   You should hear
her sing as a fairy.   You should see her dance as a fairy.
Tol de rol lol—la—lol—liddle diddle. (*Sings and
dances.*)   *That's* very like her.

FALKLAND.   Misery!   while I, devoted to her image, can scarcely write a
line now and then, or pensively read aloud to the people
of Birmingham. (*To him.*)   And they applaud her, no
doubt they applaud her, sir.   And she—I see her!
Curtsies and smiles!   And they—curses on them! they
laugh and—ha, ha, ha! and clap their hands—and say it's
very good.   Do they not say it's very good, sir?   Tell
me.   Do they not?

ACRES.   Odds, thunderings and pealings, of course they do! and the
third fiddler, little Tweaks, of the county town, goes into
fits.   Ho, ho, ho, I can't bear it (*mimicking*); take me
out!   Ha, ha, ha!   O what a one she is!   She'll be the
death of me.   Ha, ha, ha, ha!   *That's* very like her!

FALKLAND.   Damnation!   Heartless Mary! (*Rushes out.*)

Scene opens, and discloses coals of fire, heaped up into form of
letters, representing the following inscription:

When the praise thou meetest
To thine ear is sweetest,
O then

REMEMBER JOE!

(*Curtain falls.*)

M. De
Cerjat.

TAVISTOCK HOUSE, *Monday,*
Sixteenth January, 1854.

MY DEAR CERJAT,

Guilty.   The accused pleads guilty, but throws himself
upon the mercy of the court.   He humbly represents that his
usual hour for getting up, in the course of his travels, was three
o'clock in the morning, and his usual hour for going to bed, nine
or ten the next night.   That the places in which he chiefly
deviated from these rules of hardship, were Rome and Venice;
and that at those cities of fame he shut himself up in solitude, and
wrote Christmas papers for the incomparable publication known as
"Household Words."   That his correspondence at all times,
arising out of the business of the said "Household Words" alone,

was very heavy. That his offence, though undoubtedly committed, was unavoidable, and that a nominal punishment will meet the justice of the case.

We had only three bad days out of the whole time. After Naples, which was very hot, we had very cold, clear, bright weather. When we got to Chamounix, we found the greater part of the inns shut up and the people gone. No visitors whatsoever, and plenty of snow. These were the very best circumstances under which to see the place, and we stayed a couple of days at the Hôtel de Londres (hastily re-furbished for our entertainment), and climbed through the snow to the Mer de Glace, and thoroughly enjoyed it. Then we went, in mule procession (I walking), to the old hotel at Martigny, where Collins was ill, and I suppose I bored Egg to death by talking all the evening about the time when you and I were there together. Naples (a place always painful to me, in the intense degradation of the people) seems to have only three classes of inhabitants left in it—priests, soldiers (standing army one hundred thousand strong), and spies. Of macaroni we ate very considerable quantities everywhere; also, for the benefit of Italy, we took our share of every description of wine. At Naples, I found Layard, the Nineveh traveller, who is a friend of mine and an admirable fellow; so we fraternised and went up Vesuvius together, and ate more macaroni and drank more wine. At Rome, the day after our arrival, they were making a saint at St. Peter's; on which occasion I was surprised to find what an immense number of pounds of wax candles it takes to make the regular, genuine article. From Turin to Paris, over the Mont Cenis, we made only one journey. The Rhone, being frozen and foggy, was not to be navigated, so we posted from Lyons to Chalons, and everybody else was doing the like, and there were no horses to be got, and we were stranded at midnight in amazing little cabarets, with nothing worth mentioning to eat in them, except the iron stove, which was rusty, and the billiard-table, which was musty. We left Turin on a Tuesday evening, and arrived in Paris on a Friday evening; where I found my son Charley, hot—or I should rather say cold—from Germany, with his arms and legs so grown out of his coat and trousers, that I was ashamed of him, and was reduced to the necessity of taking him, under cover of night, to a ready-made establishment in the Palais Royal, where they put him into balloon-waisted pantaloons, and increased my confusion. Leaving Calais on the evening of Sunday, the Tenth of December; fact of distinguished author's being aboard, was telegraphed to Dover; thereupon authorities of Dover Railway detained train to London for distinguished author's arrival, rather to the exasperation of British public. D. A. arrived at home between ten and eleven that night, thank God, and found all well and happy.

I think you see *The Times*, and if so, you will have seen a very graceful and good account of the Birmingham readings. It was the most remarkable thing that England could produce, I think, in the way of a vast intelligent assemblage ; and the success was most wonderful and prodigious—perfectly overwhelming and astounding altogether. They wound up by giving my wife a piece of plate, having given me one before ; and when you come to dine here (may it be soon !) it shall be duly displayed in the centre of the table.

Tell Mrs. Cerjat, to whom my love, and all our loves, that I have highly excited them at home here by giving them an account in detail of all your daughters ; further, that the way in which Catherine and Georgina have questioned me and cross-questioned me about you all, notwithstanding, is maddening. Mrs. Watson has been obliged to pass her Christmas at Brighton alone with her younger children, in consequence of her two eldest boys coming home to Rockingham from school with the whooping-cough. The quarantine expires to-day, however ; and she drives here, on her way back into Northamptonshire, to-morrow.

The sad affair of the Preston strike remains unsettled ; and I hear, on strong authority, that if that were settled, the Manchester people are prepared to strike next. Provisions very dear, but the people very temperate and quiet in general. So ends this jumble, which looks like the index to a chapter in a book, I find, when I read it over.

Ever, my dear Cerjat, heartily your Friend.

Mr. Arthur
Ryland.

TAVISTOCK HOUSE, Eighteenth January, 1854.

MY DEAR SIR,

I am quite delighted to find that you are so well satisfied, and that the enterprise has such a light upon it. I think I never was better pleased in my life than I was with my Birmingham friends.

That principle of fair representation of all orders carefully carried out, I believe, will do more good than any of us can yet foresee. Does it not seem a strange thing to consider that I have never yet seen with these eyes of mine, a mechanic in any recognised position on the platform of a Mechanics' Institution ?

Mr. Wills may be expected to sink, shortly, under the ravages of letters from all parts of England, Ireland, and Scotland, proposing readings. He keeps up his spirits, but I don't see how they are to carry him through.

I am, my dear Sir, with much regard, too,

Very faithfully yours.

TAVISTOCK HOUSE, *Thirtieth January*, 1854.   Mr. Charles
Knight.

MY DEAR KNIGHT,

Indeed there is no fear of my thinking you the owner of a cold heart. I am more than three parts disposed, however, to be ferocious with you for ever writing down such a preposterous truism.

My satire is against those who see figures and averages, and nothing else—the representatives of the wickedest and most enormous vice of this time—the men who, through long years to come, will do more to damage the real useful truths of political economy than I could do (if I tried) in my whole life; the addled heads who would take the average of cold in the Crimea during twelve months as a reason for clothing a soldier in nankeens on a night when he would be frozen to death in fur, and who would comfort the labourer in travelling twelve miles a day to and from his work, by telling him that the average distance of one inhabited place from another in the whole area of England, is not more than four miles. Bah! What have you to do with these?

I shall put the book upon a private shelf (after reading it), by "Once upon a Time." I should have buried my pipe of peace and sent you this blast of my war-horn three or four days ago, but that I had been reading to a little audience of three thousand five hundred at Bradford.

Ever affectionately yours.

TAVISTOCK HOUSE, *Eighteenth February*, 1854.   Mrs.
Gaskell.

MY DEAR MRS. GASKELL,

I am sorry to say that I am not one of the Zoologicals, or I should have been delighted to have had a hand in the introduction of a child to the lions and tigers. But Wills shall send up to the gardens this morning, and see if Mr. Mitchell, the secretary, can be found. If he be producible, I have no doubt that I can send you what you want in the course of the day.

Such has been the distraction of *my* mind in *my* story, that I have twice forgotten to tell you how much I liked the Modern Greek Songs. The article is printed and at press for the very next number as ever is.

Don't put yourself out at all as to the division of the story into parts; I think you had better write it in your own way. When we come to get a little of it into type, I have no doubt of being able to make such little suggestions as to breaks of chapters as will carry us over all that easily.

My dear Mrs. Gaskell,
Always faithfully yours.

Rev. James
White.

TAVISTOCK HOUSE,
Tuesday, Seventh March, 1854.

MY DEAR WHITE,

I am tardy in answering your letter; but "Hard Times," and an immense amount of enforced correspondence, are my excuse. To you a sufficient one, I know.

As I should judge from outward and visible appearances, I have exactly as much chance of seeing the Russian fleet reviewed by the Czar as I have of seeing the English fleet reviewed by the Queen.

"Club Law" made me laugh very much when I went over it in the proof yesterday. It is most capitally done, and not (as I feared it might be) too directly. It is in the next number but one.

Mrs. —— has gone stark mad—and stark naked—on the spirit-rapping imposition. She was found t'other day in the street, clothed only in her chastity, a pocket-handkerchief and a visiting card. She had been informed, it appeared, by the spirits, that if she went out in that trim she would be invisible. She is now in a madhouse, and, I fear, hopelessly insane. One of the curious manifestations of her disorder is that she can bear nothing black. There is a terrific business to be done, even when they are obliged to put coals on her fire.

—— has a thing called a Psycho-grapher, which writes at the dictation of spirits. It delivered itself, a few nights ago, of this extraordinarily lucid message :

X. Y. Z. !

upon which it was gravely explained by the true believers that "the spirits were out of temper about something." Said —— had a great party on Sunday, when it was rumoured "a count was going to raise the dead." I stayed till the ghostly hour, but the rumour was unfounded, for neither count nor plebeian came up to the spiritual scratch. It is really inexplicable to me that a man of his calibre can be run away with by such small deer.

À propos of spiritual messages comes in Georgina, and, hearing that I am writing to you, delivers the following enigma to be conveyed to Mrs. White :

"Wyon of the Mint lives *at* the Mint."

Feeling my brain going after this, I only trust it with loves from all to all.

Ever faithfully.

Mr. Charles Knight.

TAVISTOCK HOUSE, *Seventeenth March*, 1854.

MY DEAR KNIGHT,

I have read the article with much interest. It is most conscientiously done, and presents a great mass of curious information condensed into a surprisingly small space.

I have made a slight note or two here and there, with a soft pencil, so that a touch of indiarubber will make all blank again.

And I earnestly entreat your attention to the point (I have been working upon it, weeks past, in "Hard Times") which I have jocosely suggested on the last page but one. The English are, so far as I know, the hardest-worked people on whom the sun shines. Be content if, in their wretched intervals of pleasure, they read for amusement and do no worse. They are born at the oar, and they live and die at it. Good God, what would we have of them!

Affectionately yours always.

Mr. W. H. Wills.

OFFICE OF "HOUSEHOLD WORDS,"
No. 16, WELLINGTON STREET, NORTH STRAND,
Wednesday, Twelfth April, 1854.

*　　　　*　　　　*　　　　*

I know all the walks for many and many miles round about Malvern, and delightful walks they are. I suppose you are already getting very stout, very red, very jovial (in a physical point of view) altogether.

Mark and I walked to Dartford from Greenwich, last Monday, and found Mrs. —— acting "The Stranger" (with a strolling company from the Standard Theatre) in Mr. Munn's schoolroom. The stage was a little wider than your table here, and its surface was composed of loose boards laid on the school forms. Dogs sniffed about it during the performances, and *the* carpenter's high-lows were ostentatiously taken off and displayed in the proscenium.

We stayed until a quarter to ten, when we were obliged to fly to the railroad, but we sent the landlord of the hotel down with the following articles:

> 1 bottle superior old port,
> 1   do.   do.   golden sherry,
> 1   do.   do.   best French Brandy,
> 1   do.   do.   1st quality old Tom gin,
> 1   do.   do.   prime Jamaica rum,
> 1   do.   do.   small still Isla whiskey,
> 1 kettle boiling water, two pounds finest
>   white lump sugar,
>
> Our cards,
> 1 lemon,   and
> Our compliments.

The effect we had previously made upon the theatrical company by being beheld in the first two chairs—there was nearly a pound in the house—was altogether electrical.

My ladies send their kindest regards, and are disappointed at your not saying that you drink two-and-twenty tumblers of the limpid element every day. The children also unite in "loves," and the Plornishghenter, on being asked if he would send his, replies "Yes—man," which we understand to signify cordial acquiescence.

Forster just come back from lecturing at Sherborne. Describes said lecture as "Blaze of Triumph."

H. W. AGAIN.

Miss—I mean Mrs.—Bell's story very nice. I have sent it to the printer, and entitled it "The Green Ring and the Gold Ring."

This apartment looks desolate in your absence; but, O Heavens, how tidy!

Mrs. Wills supposed to have gone into a convent at Somers Town.

My dear Wills,
Ever faithfully yours.

Mr. B. W.
Procter.

TAVISTOCK HOUSE, Saturday Night,
Fifteenth April, 1854.

MY DEAR PROCTER,

I have read "The Fatal Revenge." Don't do what the minor theatrical people call "despi-ser" me, but I think it's very bad. The concluding narrative is by far the most meritorious part of the business. Still, the people are so very convulsive and tumble down so many places, and are always knocking other people's bones about in such a very irrational way, that I object. The way in which earthquakes won't swallow the monsters, and volcanoes in eruption won't boil them, is extremely aggravating. Also their habit of bolting when they are going to explain anything.

You have sent me a very different and a much better book; and for that I am truly grateful. With the dust of "Maturin" in my eyes, I sat down and read "The Death of Friends," and the dust melted away in some of those tears it is good to shed. I remember to have read "The Back-room Window" some years ago, and I have associated it with you ever since. It is a most delightful paper. But the two volumes are all delightful, and I have put them on a shelf where you sit down with Charles Lamb again, with Talfourd's vindication of him hard by.

We never meet. I hope it is not irreligious, but in this strange London I have an inclination to adapt a portion of the Church Service to our common experience. Thus:

"We have left unmet the people whom we ought to have met, and we have met the people whom we ought not to have met, and there seems to be no help in us."

But I am always, my dear Procter,

(At a distance),

Very cordially yours.

TAVISTOCK HOUSE, *Twenty-first April*, 1854.

Mrs. Gaskell.

MY DEAR MRS. GASKELL,

I safely received the paper from Mr. Shaen, welcoming it with three cheers, and instantly despatched it to the printer, who has it in hand now.

I have no intention of striking. The monstrous claims at domination made by a certain class of manufacturers, and the extent to which the way is made easy for working men to slide down into discontent under such hands, are within my scheme; but I am not going to strike, so don't be afraid of me. But I wish you would look at the story yourself, and judge where and how near I seem to be approaching what you have in your mind. The first two months of it will show that. I will "make my will" on the first favourable occasion. We were playing games last night, and were fearfully clever. Always, my dear Mrs. Gaskell,

Faithfully yours.

TAVISTOCK HOUSE,
Friday Evening, Nineteenth May, 1854.

Rev. W. Harness.

MY DEAR HARNESS,

On Thursday, the first of June, we shall be delighted to come. (Might I ask for the mildest whisper of the dinner-hour?) I am more than ever devoted to your niece, if possible, for giving me the choice of two days, as on the second of June I am a fettered mortal.

I heard a manly, Christian sermon last Sunday at the Foundling —with *great satisfaction*. If you should happen to know ·the preacher of it, pray thank him from me.

Ever cordially yours.

TAVISTOCK HOUSE, *Twenty-sixth May*, 1854.

Rev. James White.

MY DEAR WHITE,

Here is Conolly * in a dreadful state of mind because you won't dine with him on the seventh of June next to meet Stratford-

* The well-known Dr. Conolly, of Hanwell.

on-Avon people, writing to me, to ask me to write to you and ask you what you mean by it.

What *do* you mean by it?

It appears to Conolly that your supposing you *can* have anything to do is a clear case of monomania, one of the slight instances of perverted intellect, wherein a visit to him cannot fail to be beneficial. After conference with my learned friend I am of the same opinion.

Ever faithfully yours.

Mr. Frank
Stone,
A.R.A.

TAVISTOCK HOUSE, *Thirtieth May*, 1854.

MY DEAR STONE,

I can*not* stand a total absence of ventilation, and I should have liked (in an amiable and persuasive manner) to have punched T——'s head, and opened the register stoves. I saw the supper tables, sir, in an empty state, and was charmed with them. Likewise I recovered myself from a swoon, occasioned by long contact with an unventilated man of a strong flavour from Copenhagen, by drinking an unknown species of celestial lemonade in that enchanted apartment.

I am grieved to say that on Saturday I stand engaged to dine, at three weeks' notice, with one B——, a man who has read every book that ever was written, and is a perfect gulf of information. Before exploding a mine of knowledge he has a habit of closing one eye and wrinkling up his nose, so that he seems perpetually to be taking aim at you and knocking you over with a terrific charge. Then he looks again, and takes another aim. So you are always on your back, with your legs in the air.

How can a man be conversed with, or walked with, in the county of Middlesex, when he is reviewing the Kentish Militia on the shores of Dover, or sailing, every day for three weeks, between Dover and Calais? Ever affectionately.

P.S.—"Humphry Clinker" is certainly Smollett's best. I am rather divided between "Peregrine Pickle" and "Roderick Random," both extraordinarily good in their way, which is a way without tenderness; but you will have to read them both, and I send the first volume of "Peregrine" as the richer of the two.

Mr. Peter
Cunning-
ham.

TAVISTOCK HOUSE, *Seventh June*, 1854.

MY DEAR CUNNINGHAM,

I cannot become one of the committee for Wilson's statue, after entertaining so strong an opinion against the expediency of such a memorial in poor dear Talfourd's case. But I will subscribe my three guineas, and will pay that sum to the account at Coutts' when I go there next week, before leaving town.

"The Goldsmiths" admirably done throughout. It is a book I have long desired to see done, and never expected to see half so well done. Many thanks to you for it.

Ever faithfully yours.

VILLA DU CAMP DE DROITE,
Thursday, Twenty-second June, 1854.

Mr. W. H. Wills.

MY DEAR WILLS,

I have nothing to say, but having heard from you this morning, think I may as well report all well.

We have a most charming place here. It beats the former residence all to nothing. We have a beautiful garden, with all its fruits and flowers, and a field of our own, and a road of our own away to the Column, and everything that is airy and fresh. The great Beaucourt hovers about us like a guardian genius, and I imagine that no English person in a carriage could by any possibility find the place.

Of the wonderful inventions and contrivances with which a certain inimitable creature has made the most of it, I will say nothing, until you have an opportunity of inspecting the same. At present I will only observe that I have written exactly seventy-two words of "Hard Times," since I have been here.

The children arrived on Tuesday night, by London boat, in every stage and aspect of sea-sickness.

The camp is about a mile off, and huts are now building for (they say) sixty thousand soldiers. I don't imagine it to be near enough to bother us.

If the weather ever should be fine, it might do you good sometimes to come over with the proofs on a Saturday, when the tide serves well, before you and Mrs. W. make your annual visit. Recollect there is always a bed, and no sudden appearance will put us out.

Ever faithfully.

VILLA DU CAMP DE DROITE, BOULOGNE,
Wednesday Night, Twelfth July, 1854.

Mr. W. Wilkie Collins.

MY DEAR COLLINS,

Bobbing up, corkwise, from a sea of "Hard Times," I beg to report this tenement—AMAZING!!! Range of view and air, most free and delightful; hill-side garden, delicious; field, stupendous; speculations in haycocks already effected by the undersigned, with the view to the keeping up of a "home" at rounders.

I hope to finish and get to town by next Wednesday night, the nineteenth; what do you say to coming back with me on the following Tuesday? The interval I propose to pass in a career of amiable dissipation and unbounded license in the metropolis. If you will come and breakfast with me about midnight—anywhere —any day, and go to bed no more until we fly to these pastoral retreats, I shall be delighted to have so vicious an associate.

Will you undertake to let Ward know that if he still wishes me to sit to him, he shall have me as long as he likes, at Tavistock House, on Monday, the 24th, from ten A.M.?

I have made it understood here that we shall want to be taken the greatest care of this summer, and to be fed on nourishing meats. Several new dishes have been rehearsed and have come out very well. I have met with what they call in the City "a parcel" of the celebrated 1846 champagne. It is a very fine wine, and calculated to do us good when weak.

The camp is about a mile off. Voluptuous English authors reposing from their literary fatigues (on their laurels) are expected, when all other things fail, to lie on straw in the midst of it when the days are sunny, and stare at the blue sea until they fall asleep. (About one hundred and fifty soldiers have been at various times billeted on Beaucourt since we have been here, and he has clinked glasses with them every one, and read a MS. book of his father's, on soldiers in general, to them all.)

I shall be glad to hear what you say to these various proposals. I write with the Emperor in the town, and a great expenditure of tricolour floating thereabouts, but no stir makes its way to this inaccessible retreat. It is like being up in a balloon. Lionising Englishmen and Germans start to call, and are found lying imbecile in the road half-way up. Ha! ha! ha!

Ever faithfully.

P.S.—The cobbler has been ill these many months, and unable to work; has had a carbuncle in his back, and has it cut three times a week. The little dog sits at the door so unhappy and anxious to help, that I every day expect to see him beginning a pair of top boots.

Miss Hogarth.

OFFICE OF "HOUSEHOLD WORDS,"
Saturday, Twenty-second July, 1854.

MY DEAR GEORGINA,

Neither you nor Catherine did justice to Collins' book.* I think it far away the cleverest novel I have ever seen written by a new hand. It is in some respects masterly. " Valentine

* "Hide and Seek."

Blyth" is as original and as well done as anything can be. The scene where he shows his pictures is full of an admirable humour. Old Mat is admirably done. In short, I call it a very remarkable book, and I have been very much surprised by its great merit.

Tell Kate, with my love, that she will receive to-morrow, in a little parcel, the complete proofs of "Hard Times."

They will not be corrected, but she will find them pretty plain. I am just now going to put them up for her. I saw Grisi the night before last in "Lucrezia Borgia"—finer than ever. Last night I was drinking gin-slings till daylight, with Buckstone of all people, who saw me looking at the Spanish dancers, and insisted on being convivial. I have been in a blaze of dissipation altogether, and have succeeded (I think) in knocking the remembrance of my work out.

London is far hotter than Naples.

Ever affectionately.

BOULOGNE, Wednesday, Second August, 1854. Mr. W. H.
Wills.

MY DEAR WILLS,

I will endeavour to come off my back (and the grass) to do an opening paper for the starting number of "North and South." I can't positively answer for such a victory over the idleness into which I have delightfully sunk, as the achievement of this feat; but let us hope.

During a fête on Monday night the meteor flag of England (forgotten to be struck at sunset) was *stolen ! ! !*

Manage the proofs of "H. W." so that I may not have to correct them on a Sunday. I am not going over to the Sabbatarians, but like the haystack (particularly) on a Sunday morning.

I should like John to call on M. Henri, Townshend's servant, 21, Norfolk Street, Park Lane, and ask him if, when he comes here with his master, he can take charge of a trap bat and ball. If yea, then I should like John to proceed to Mr. Darke, Lord's Cricket Ground, and purchase said trap bat and ball of the best quality. Townshend is coming here on the fifteenth, probably will leave town a day or two before.

Pray be in a condition to drink a glass of 1846 champagne when *you* come.

I think I have no more to say at present. I cannot sufficiently admire my prodigious energy in coming out of a stupor to write this letter.

Ever faithfully.

z

VILLA DU CAMP DE DROITE, BOULOGNE,
Thursday, Seventeenth August, 1854.

MY DEAR MRS. GASKELL,

I sent your MS. off to Wills yesterday, with instructions to forward it to you without delay. I hope you will have received it before this notification comes to hand.

The usual festivity of this place at present—which is the blessing of soldiers by the ten thousand—has just now been varied by the baptising of some new bells, lately hung up (to my sorrow and lunacy) in a neighbouring church. An English lady was god-mother; and there was a procession afterwards, wherein an English gentleman carried "the relics" in a highly suspicious box, like a barrel organ; and innumerable English ladies in white gowns and bridal wreaths walked two and two, as if they had all gone to school again.

At a review, on the same day, I was particularly struck by the commencement of the proceedings, and its singular contrast to the usual military operations in Hyde Park. Nothing would induce the general commanding-in-chief to begin, until chairs were brought for all the lady-spectators. And a detachment of about a hundred men deployed into all manner of farmhouses to find the chairs. Nobody seemed to lose any dignity by the transaction either.

Faithfully yours always.

VILLA DU CAMP DE DROITE, BOULOGNE,
Saturday, Nineteenth August, 1854.

MY DEAR HARNESS,

Yes. The book came from me. I could not put a memo-randum to that effect on the title-page, in consequence of my being here.

I am heartily glad you like it. I know the piece you mention, but am far from being convinced by it. A great misgiving is upon me, that in many things (this thing among the rest) too many are martyrs to *our* complacency and satisfaction, and that we must give up something thereof for their poor sakes.

My kindest regards to your sister, and my love (if I may send it) to another of your relations.

Always, very faithfully yours.

VILLA DU CAMP DE DROITE, BOULOGNE,
Wednesday, Sixth September, 1854.

*   *   *   *

Any Saturday on which the tide serves your purpose (next Saturday excepted) will suit me for the flying visit you hint at; and we shall be delighted to see you. If you could come here in dry weather you would find it as pretty, airy, and pleasant a situation as you ever saw. We illuminated the whole front of the house last night *—eighteen windows—and an immense palace of light was seen sparkling on this hill-top for miles and miles away. I rushed to a distance to look at it, and never saw anything of the same kind half so pretty.

The town looks like one immense flag, it is so decked out with streamers ; and as the royal yacht approached yesterday—the whole range of the cliff tops lined with troops, and the artillery matches in hand, all ready to fire the great guns the moment she made the harbour ; the sailors standing up in the prow of the yacht, the Prince in a blazing uniform, left alone on the deck for everybody to see—a stupendous silence, and then such an infernal blazing and banging as never was heard. It was almost as fine a sight as one could see under a deep-blue sky. 'In our own proper illumination I laid on all the servants, all the children now at home, all the visitors (it is the annual "Household Words" time), one to every window, with everything ready to light up on the ringing of a big dinner-bell by your humble correspondent. St. Peter's on Easter Monday was the result.

Ever affectionately.

Boulogne, *Tuesday,*
Twenty-Sixth September, 1854.

Mr. W.
Wilkie
Collins.

MY DEAR COLLINS,

First, I have to report that I received your letter with much pleasure.

Secondly, that the weather has entirely changed. It is so cool that we have not only a fire in the drawing-room regularly, but another to dine by. The delicious freshness of the air is charming, and it is generally bright and windy besides.

Thirdly, that V——'s intellectual faculties appear to have developed suddenly. He has taken to borrowing money ; from which I infer (as he had no intention whatever of repaying) that his mental powers are of a high order. Having got a franc from me, he fell upon Mrs. Dickens for five sous. She declining to enter into the transaction, he beleaguered that feeble little couple, Harry and Sydney, into paying two sous each for "tickets" to behold the ravishing spectacle of an utterly-non-existent-and-therefore-impossible-to-be-produced toy theatre. He eats stony apples, and harbours designs upon his fellow-creatures until he has become light-headed. From the couch rendered uneasy by this disorder

* On the occasion of the Prince Consort's visit to the camp at Boulogne.

he has arisen with an excessively protuberant forehead, a dull
slow eye, a complexion of a leaden hue, and a croaky voice. He
has become a horror to me, and I resort to the most cowardly
expedients to avoid meeting him. He, on the other hand, wanting
another franc, dodges me round those trees at the corner, and at
the back door; and I have a presentiment upon me that I shall
fall a sacrifice to his cupidity at last.

On the Sunday night after you left, or rather on the Monday
morning at half-past one, Mary was taken *very ill*. English
cholera. She was sinking so fast, and the sickness was so
exceedingly alarming, that it evidently would not do to wait for
Elliotson.* I caused everything to be done that we had naturally
often thought of, in a lonely house so full of children, and fell back
upon the old remedy; though the difficulty of giving even it was
rendered very great by the frightful sickness. Thank God, she
recovered so favourably that by breakfast time she was fast asleep.
She slept twenty-four hours, and has never had the least uneasiness
since. I heard—of course afterwards—that she had had an attack
of sickness two nights before. I think that long ride and those
late dinners had been too much for her. Without them I am
inclined to doubt whether she would have been ill.

Last Sunday as ever was, the theatre took fire at half-past
eleven in the forenoon. Being close by the English Church, it
showered hot sparks into that temple through the open windows.
Whereupon the congregation shrieked and rose and tumbled out
into the street; —— benignly observing to the only ancient female
who would listen to him, "I fear we must part;" and afterwards
being beheld in the street—in his robes and with a kind of sacred
wildness on him—handing ladies over the kennel into shops and
other structures, where they had no business whatever, or the least
desire to go. I got to the back of the theatre, where I could see
in through some great doors that had been forced open, and whence
the spectacle of the whole interior, burning like a red-hot cavern,
was really very fine, even in the daylight. Meantime the soldiers
were at work, "saving" the scenery by pitching it into the next
street; and the poor little properties (one spinning-wheel, a feeble
imitation of a water-wheel, and a basketful of the dismalest
artificial flowers very conspicuous) were being passed from hand
to hand with the greatest excitement, as if they were rescued
children or lovely women. In four or five hours the whole place
was burnt down, except the outer walls. Never in my days did I
behold such feeble endeavours in the way of extinguishment. On

* Dr. Elliotson happened, most fortunately, to be staying at Boulogne at
this time.

an average I should say it took ten minutes to throw half a gallon of water on the great roaring heap; and every time it was insulted in this way it gave a ferocious burst, and everybody ran off. Beaucourt has been going 'about for two days in a clean collar; which phenomenon evidently means something, but I don't know what. Elliotson reports that the great conjurer lives at his hotel, has extra wine every day, and fares expensively. Is he the devil?

I have heard from the Kernel.* Wa'al, sir, sayin' as he minded to locate himself with us for a week. I expected to have heard from him again this morning, but have not.

The Plornish-Maroon desires his duty. He had a fall yesterday, through overbalancing himself in kicking his nurse.

Ever faithfully.

BOULOGNE, *Friday, Thirteenth October*, 1854.

MY DEAR STONE,

Mr. Frank Stone, A.R.A.

Having some little matters that rather press on my attention to see to in town, I have made up my mind to relinquish the walking project, and come straight home (by way of Folkestone) on Tuesday. I shall be due in town at midnight, and shall hope to see you next day, with the top of your coat-collar mended.

Everything that happens here we suppose to be an announcement of the taking of Sebastopol. When a church-clock strikes, we think it is the joy-bell, and fly out of the house in a burst of nationality—to 'sneak in again. If they practise firing at the camp, we are sure it is the artillery celebrating the fall of the Russian, and we become enthusiastic in a moment. I live in constant readiness to illuminate the whole house. Whatever anybody says I believe; everybody says, every day, that Sebastopol is in flames. Sometimes the Commander-in-Chief has blown himself up, with seventy-five thousand men. Sometimes he has "cut" his way through Lord Raglan, and has fallen back on the advancing body of the Russians, one hundred and forty-two thousand strong, whom he is going to "bring up" (I don't know where from, or how, or when, or why) for the destruction of the Allies. All these things, in the words of the catechism, "I steadfastly believe," until I become a mere driveller, a moonstruck, babbling, staring, credulous, imbecile, greedy, gaping, wooden-headed, addle-brained, wool-gathering, dreary, vacant, obstinate civilian.

Ever, my fellow-countryman, affectionately.

* Mr. Egg.

Mr. John
Saunders.   TAVISTOCK HOUSE, *Twenty-sixth October*, 1854.

DEAR SIR,

I have had much gratification and pleasure in the receipt of your obliging communication. Allow me to thank you for it, in the first place, with great cordiality.

Although I cannot say that I came without any prepossessions to the perusal of your play (for I had favourable inclinings towards it before I began), I *can* say that I read it with the closest attention, and that it inspired me with a strong interest, and a genuine and high admiration. The parts that involve some of the greatest difficulties of your task appear to me those in which you shine most. I would particularly instance the end of Julia as a very striking example of this. The delicacy and beauty of her redemption from her weak rash lover, are very far indeed beyond the range of any ordinary dramatist, and display the true poetical strength.

As your hopes now centre in Mr. Phelps, and in seeing the child of your fancy on his stage, I will venture to point out to you not only what I take to be very dangerous portions of "Love's Martyrdom" as it stands, *for presentation on the stage*, but portions which I believe Mr. Phelps will speedily regard in that light when he sees it before him in the persons of live men and women on the wooden boards. Knowing him, I think he will be then as violently discouraged as he is now generously exalted; and it may be useful to you to be prepared for the consideration of those passages.

I do not regard it as a great stumbling-block that the play of modern times best known to an audience proceeds upon the main idea of this, namely, that there was a hunchback who, because of his deformity, mistrusted himself. But it is certainly a grain in the balance when the balance is going the wrong way, and therefore it should be most carefully trimmed. The incident of the ring is an insignificant one to look at over a row of gaslights, is difficult to convey to an audience, and the least thing will make it ludicrous. If it be so well done by Mr. Phelps himself as to be otherwise than ludicrous, it will be disagreeable. If it be either, it will be perilous, and doubly so, because you revert to it. The quarrel scene between the two brothers in the third act is now so long that the justification of blind passion and impetuosity—which can alone bear out Franklyn, before the bodily eyes of a great concourse of spectators, in plunging at the life of his own brother —is lost. That the two should be parted, and that Franklyn should again drive at him, and strike him, and then wound him, is a state of things to set the sympathy of an audience in the wrong direction, and turn it from the man you make happy to the man you leave unhappy. I would on no account allow the artist to appear, attended by that picture more than once. All the most sudden inconstancy of Clarence I would soften down. Margaret must act much better than any actress I have ever seen, if all her lines fall in pleasant places; therefore, I think she needs compression too.

All this applies solely to the theatre. If you ever revise the sheets for readers, will you note in the margin the broken laughter and the appeals to the Deity? If, on summing them up, you find you want them all, I would leave them as they stand by all means. If not, I would blot accordingly.

It is only in the hope of being slightly useful to you by anticipating what I believe Mr. Phelps will discover—or what, if ever he should pass it, I have a strong conviction the audience will find out—that I have ventured on these few hints. Your concurrence with them generally, on reconsideration, or your preference for the poem as it stands, can not in the least affect my interest in your success. On the other hand, I have a perfect confidence in your not taking my misgivings ill; they arise out of my sincere desire for the triumph of your work.

With renewed thanks for the pleasure you have afforded me,

I am, dear Sir, faithfully yours.

TAVISTOCK HOUSE, *First November*, 1854.   Mr. W. C.
(And a constitutionally foggy day.)   Macready.

MY DEAREST MACREADY,

I thought it better not to encumber the address to working men with details. Firstly, because they would detract from whatever fiery effect the words may have in them; secondly, because writing and petitioning and pressing a subject upon members and candidates are now so clearly understood; and thirdly, because the paper was meant as an opening to a persistent pressure of the whole question on the public, which would yield other opportunities of touching on such points.

In the number *for next week*—not this—is one of those following-up articles called "A Home Question." It is not written by me, but is generally of my suggesting, and is exceedingly well done by a thorough and experienced hand. I think you will find in it, generally, what you want. I have told the printers to send you a proof by post as soon as it is corrected—that is to say, as soon as some insertions I made in it last night are in type and in their places.

My dear old Parr, I don't believe a word you write about

King John! That is to say, I don't believe you take into account the enormous difference between the energy summonable-up in your study at Sherborne and the energy that will fire up in you (without so much as saying "With your leave" or "By your leave") in the Town Hall at Birmingham. I know you, you ancient codger, I know you! Therefore I will trouble you to be so good as to do an act of honesty after you have been to Birmingham, and to write to me, "Ingenuous boy, you were correct. I find I could have read 'em 'King John' with the greatest ease."

In that vast hall in the busy town of Sherborne, in which our illustrious English novelist is expected to read next month—though he is strongly of opinion that he is deficient in power, and too old—I wonder what accommodation there is for reading! because our illustrious countryman likes to stand at a desk breast-high, with plenty of room about him, a sloping top, and a ledge to keep his book from tumbling off. If such a thing should not be there, however, on his arrival, I suppose even a Sherborne carpenter could knock it up out of a deal board. *Is* there a deal board in Sherborne though? I should like to hear Katey's * opinion on that point.

In this week's "Household Words" there is an exact portrait of our Boulogne landlord, which I hope you will like. I think of opening the next long book I write with a man of juvenile figure and strong face, who is always persuading himself that he is infirm. What do you think of the idea? I should like to have your opinion about it. I would make him an impetuous passionate sort of fellow, devilish grim upon occasion, and of an iron purpose. Droll, I fancy?

—— is getting a little too fat, but appears to be troubled by the great responsibility of directing the whole war. He doesn't seem to be quite clear that he has got the ships into the exact order he intended, on the sea point of attack at Sebastopol. We went to the play last Saturday night with Stanfield, whose "high lights" (as Maclise calls those knobs of brightness on the top of his cheeks) were more radiant than ever. We talked of you, and I told Stanny how they are imitating his "Acis and Galatea" sea in "Pericles," at Phelps'. He didn't half like it; but I added, in nautical language, that it was merely a piratical effort achieved by a handful of porpoise-faced swabs, and that brought him up with a round turn, as we say at sea.

We are looking forward to the twentieth of next month with great pleasure. Ever, my dearest Macready,

Most affectionately yours.

* Mr. Macready's daughter.

TAVISTOCK HOUSE, *Wednesday,*
First November, 1854.

MY DEAR MRS. WATSON,

The "Walk" is not my writing. It is very well done by a close imitator. Why I found myself so "used up" after "Hard Times" I scarcely know, perhaps because I intended to do nothing in that way for a year, when the idea laid hold of me by the throat in a very violent manner, and because the compression and close condensation necessary for that disjointed form of publication gave me perpetual trouble. But I really was tired, which is a result so very incomprehensible that I can't forget it. I have passed an idle autumn in a beautiful situation, and am dreadfully brown and big.

If you carry out that bright Croydon idea, rely on our glad co-operation, only let me know all about it a few days beforehand; and if you feel equal to the contemplation of the moustache (which has been cut lately) it will give us the heartiest pleasure to come and meet you. This in spite of the terrific duffery of the Crystal Palace. It is a very remarkable thing in itself; but to have so very large a building continually crammed down one's throat, and to find it a new page in "The Whole Duty of Man" to go there, is a little more than even I (and you know how amiable I am) can endure.

You always like to know what I am going to do, so I beg to announce that on the nineteenth of December I am going to read the "Carol" at Reading, where I undertook the presidency of the Literary Institution on the death of poor dear Talfourd. Then I am going on to Sherborne, in Dorsetshire, to do the like for another institution, which is one of the few remaining pleasures of Macready's life. Then I am coming home for Christmas Day. Then I believe I must go to Bradford, in Yorkshire, to read once more to a little fireside party of four thousand. Then I am coming home again to get up a new little version of "The Children in the Wood" (yet to be written, by-the-bye), for the children to act on Charley's birthday.

I am full of mixed feeling about the war—admiration of our valiant men, burning desires to cut the Emperor of Russia's throat, and something like despair to see how the old cannon-smoke and blood-mists obscure the wrongs and sufferings of the people at home. When I consider the Patriotic Fund on the one hand, and on the other the poverty and wretchedness engendered by cholera, of which in London alone, an infinitely larger number of English people than are likely to be slain in the whole Russian war have miserably and needlessly died—I feel as if the world had been pushed back five hundred years. If you are reading new books just now I think you will be interested with a controversy between Whewell and Brewster, on the question of the shining orbs about us being inhabited or no. Whewell's book is called, "On the Plurality of Worlds;" Brewster's, "More Worlds than One." I shouldn't wonder if you know all about them. They bring together a vast number of points of great interest in natural philosophy, and some very curious reasoning on both sides, and leave the matter pretty much where it was.

We had a fine absurdity in connection with our luggage, when we left Boulogne. The barometer had within a few hours fallen about a foot, in honour of the occasion, and it was a tremendous night, blowing a gale of wind and raining a little deluge. The luggage (pretty heavy as you may suppose), in a cart drawn by two horses, stuck fast in a rut in our field, and couldn't be moved. Our man, made a lunatic by the extremity of the occasion, ran down to the town to get two more horses to help it out, when he returned with those horses and carter B, the most beaming of men ; carter A, who had been soaking all the time by the disabled vehicle, descried in carter B the acknowledged enemy of his existence, took his own two horses out, and walked off with them ! After which, the whole set-out remained in the field all night, and we came to town, thirteen individuals, with one comb and a pocket-handkerchief. I was upside-down during the greater part of the passage.

Dr. Rae's account of Franklin's unfortunate party is deeply interesting ; but I think hasty in its acceptance of the details, particularly in the statement that they had eaten the dead bodies of their companions, which I don't believe. Franklin, on a former occasion, was almost starved to death, had gone through all the pains of that sad end, and lain down to die, and no such thought had presented itself to any of them. In famous cases of shipwreck, it is very rare indeed that any person of any humanising education or refinement resorts to this dreadful means of prolonging life. In open boats, the coarsest and commonest men of the shipwrecked party have done such things ; but I don't remember more than one instance in which an officer had overcome the loathing that the idea had inspired. Dr. Rae talks about their *cooking* these remains too. I should like to know where the fuel came from.

Ever, my dear Mrs. Watson, affectionately yours.

TAVISTOCK HOUSE,
Friday Night, Third November, 1854.

Mr.
Clarkson
Stanfield,
R.A.

MY DEAR STANNY,

This is not to remind you that we meet at the Athenæum next Monday at five, because none but a mouldy swab as never broke biscuit or lay out on the for'sel-yardarm in a gale of wind ever forgot an appointment with a messmate.

But what I want you to think of at your leisure is this: when our dear old Macready was in town last, I saw it would give him so much interest and pleasure if I promised to go down and read my "Christmas Carol" to the little Sherborne Institution, which is now one of the few active objects he has in the life about him, that I came out with that promise in a bold—I may say a swaggering way. Consequently, on Wednesday, the twentieth of December, I am going down to see him, with Kate and Georgina, returning to town in good time for Christmas, on Saturday, the twenty-third. Do you think you could manage to go and return with us? I really believe there is scarcely anything in the world that would give him such extraordinary pleasure as such a visit; and if you would empower me to send him an intimation that he may expect it, he will have a daily joy in looking forward to the time (I am seriously sure) which we—whose light has not gone out, and who are among our old dear pursuits and associations—can scarcely estimate.

I don't like to broach the idea in a careless way, and so I propose it thus, and ask you to think of it.

Ever most affectionately yours.

TAVISTOCK HOUSE,
Sunday, Seventeenth December, 1854.

Miss
Procter.

MY DEAR MISS PROCTER,

You have given me a new sensation. I did suppose that nothing in this singular world could surprise me, but you have done it.

You will believe my congratulations on the delicacy and talent of your writing to be sincere. From the first, I have always had an especial interest in that Miss Berwick, and have over and over again questioned Wills about her. I suppose he has gone on gradually building up an imaginary structure of life and adventure for her, but he has given me the strangest information! Only yesterday week, when we were "making up" "The Poor Travellers," as I sat meditatively poking the office fire, I said to him, "Wills, have you got that Miss Berwick's proof back, of the little sailor's song?" "No," he said. "Well, but why not?"

I asked him. "Why, you know," he answered, "as I have often told you before, she don't live at the place to which her letters are addressed, and so there's always difficulty and delay in communicating with her." "Do you know what age she is?" I said. Here he looked unfathomably profound, and returned, "Rather advanced in life." "You said she was a governess, didn't you?" said I; to which he replied in the most emphatic and positive manner, "A governess."

He then came and stood in the corner of the hearth, with his back to the fire, and delivered himself like an oracle concerning you. He told me that early in life (conveying to me the impression of about a quarter of a century ago) you had had your feelings desperately wounded by some cause, real or imaginary—"It does not matter which," said I, with the greatest sagacity—and that you had then taken to writing verses. That you were of an unhappy temperament, but keenly sensitive to encouragement. That you wrote after the educational duties of the day were discharged. That you sometimes thought of never writing any more. That you had been away for some time "with your pupils." That your letters were of a mild and melancholy character, and that you did not seem to care as much as might be expected about money. All this time I sat poking the fire, with a wisdom upon me absolutely crushing; and finally I begged him to assure the lady that she might trust me with her real address, and that it would be better to have it now, as I hoped our further communications, etc. etc. etc. You must have felt enormously wicked last Tuesday, when I, such a babe in the wood, was unconsciously prattling to you. But you have given me so much pleasure, and have made me shed so many tears, that I can only think of you now in association with the sentiment and grace of your verses.

So pray accept the blessing and forgiveness of Richard Watts, though I am afraid you come under both his conditions of exclusion.*

Very faithfully yours.

---

* The inscription on the house in Rochester known as "Watts' Charity" is to the effect that it furnishes a night's lodging for six poor travellers—"not being ROGUES or PROCTORS."

1855.

NARRATIVE.

In the beginning of this year, Charles Dickens gave public readings at Reading, Sherborne, and Bradford in Yorkshire, to which reference is made in the first following letters. Besides this, he was fully occupied in getting up a play for his children, which was acted on the Sixth January. Mr. Planché's fairy extravaganza of "Fortunio and his Seven Gifted Servants" was the play selected, the parts being filled by all his own children and some of their young friends, and Charles Dickens, Mr. Mark Lemon, and Mr. Wilkie Collins playing with them, the only grown-up members of the company. In February, Charles Dickens made a short trip to Paris with Mr. Wilkie Collins, with an intention of going on to Bordeaux, which was abandoned on account of bad weather. Out of the success of the children's play at Tavistock House rose a scheme for a serious play at the same place. Mr. Collins undertaking to write a melodrama for the purpose, and Mr. Stanfield to paint scenery and drop-scene, Charles Dickens turned one of the rooms of the house into a very perfect little theatre, and in June "The Lighthouse" was acted for three nights, with "Mr. Nightingale's Diary" and "Animal Magnetism" as farces; the actors being himself and several members of the original amateur company,—the actresses, his two daughters and his sister-in-law. Mr. Stanfield, after entering most heartily into the enterprise, and giving constant time and attention to the painting of his beautiful scenes, was unfortunately ill and unable to attend the first performance. We give a letter to him, reporting its great success.

In the summer Charles Dickens made a speech at a great meeting at Drury Lane Theatre on the subject of "Administrative Reform," of which he wrote to Mr. Macready. On this subject of "Administrative Reform," too, we give two letters to Mr. Layard, who also spoke at the Drury Lane meeting.

Charles Dickens had made a promise to give another reading at Birmingham for the funds of the institute which still needed help; and in a letter to Mr. Arthur Ryland, asking him to fix a time for it, he gives the first idea of a selection from "David Copperfield," which was afterwards one of the most popular of his readings.

He was at all times fond of making excursions for a day—or two or three days—to Rochester and its neighbourhood; and after one of these, this year, he wrote to Mr. Wills that he had seen a "small freehold" to be sold, *opposite* the house on which he had

fixed his childish affections (and which he calls in *this* letter the
"Hermitage," its real name being "Gad's Hill Place"). The
latter house was not, at that time, to be had, and he made some
approach to negotiations as to the other "little freehold," which,
however, did not come to anything. Soon after, Mr. Wills, by an
accident, discovered that Gad's Hill Place, the property of Miss
Lynn, the well-known authoress, and a constant contributor to
"Household Words," was itself for sale; and a negotiation for its
purchase commenced, which was not, however, completed until the
following spring.

Later in the year the performance of "The Lighthouse" was
repeated, for a charitable purpose, at the Campden House theatre.

This autumn was passed at Folkestone. Charles Dickens had
decided upon spending the following winter in Paris, and the
family proceeded there from Folkestone in October, making a halt
at Boulogne; from whence his sister-in-law preceded the party to
Paris, to secure lodgings, with the help of Lady Olliffe.* He
followed, to make his choice of the apartments that had been
found, and he wrote to his wife and to Mr. Wills, giving a description of the Paris house. Here he began "Little Dorrit." In a
letter to Mrs. Watson, from Folkestone, he gives her the name
which he had first proposed for this story—"Nobody's Fault."

Mr. and Mrs. Hogarth occupied Tavistock House during the
absence of Charles Dickens from England, and his eldest son,
being now engaged in business, remained with them, coming to
Paris only for Christmas. Three of his boys were at school at
Boulogne at this time, and one, Walter Landor, at Wimbledon,
studying for an Indian army appointment.

We are sorry to have only two short notes addressed to the late
Mr. W. M. Thackeray. The first comes in this year, the second in
the year 1858. We give them both, as we are glad to have the
two names associated together in this work.

Mrs. Winter, to whom are addressed two letters in this year,
was a very dear friend and companion of Charles Dickens in his
youth.

Miss Emily Jolly was a contributor to "Household Words," and
is also the authoress of "Mr. Arle," and many other clever novels.

Captain Morgan was a captain in the American merchant service.
He was an intimate friend of Mr. Leslie, R.A., by whom he was
made known to Charles Dickens. It may interest our readers to
know that the character of Captain Jorgan, in the Christmas
Number for 1860, was suggested by this pleasant sailor, for whom
Charles Dickens had a hearty liking.

* Wife of Sir Joseph Olliffe, then physician to the British Embassy.

PROLOGUE TO "THE LIGHTHOUSE."

(Spoken by CHARLES DICKENS.)

Slow music all the time, unseen speaker, curtain down.

A story of these rocks where doomed ships come
To cast their wrecks upon the steps of home,
Where solitary men, the long year through—
The wind their music and the brine their view—
Warn mariners to shun the beacon-light ;
A story of those rocks is here to-night.
Eddystone Lighthouse

　　　　　　　　　　　　[Exterior view discovered.

　　　　　　　　In its ancient form ;
Ere he who built it wish'd * for the great storm
That shiver'd it to nothing ; once again
Behold outgleaming on the angry main !
Within it are three men ; to these repair
In our frail bark of Fancy, swift as air !
They are but shadows, as the rower grim
Took none but shadows in his boat with him.
So be *ye* shades, and, for a little space,
The real world a dream without a trace.
Return is easy.　It will have ye back
Too soon to the old beaten dusty track ;
For but one hour forget it.　Billows rise,
Blow winds, fall rain, be black, ye midnight skies ;
And you who watch the light, arise ! arise !

　　　　　　　[Exterior view rises and discovers the scene.

THE SONG OF THE WRECK.

I.

The wind blew high, the waters raved
　　A ship drove on the land,
A hundred human creatures saved,
　　Kneeled down upon the sand.
Threescore were drowned, threescore were thrown
　　Upon the black rocks wild,
And thus among them, left alone,
　　They found one helpless child.

II.

A seaman rough, to shipwreck bred,
　　Stood out from all the rest,
And gently laid the lonely head
　　Upon his honest breast.
And travelling o'er the desert wide,
　　It was a solemn joy,
To see them, ever side by side,
　　The sailor and the boy.

---

* Henry Winstanley, the builder of the first Eddystone Lighthouse in 1696, considered it so strong that he expressed a wish that he might be in it during the greatest storm that ever blew.　He had his wish, and was in his Lighthouse when it was blown away in a terrific storm in 1703.

III.

In famine, sickness, hunger, thirst,
  These two were still but one,
Until the stroug man drooped the first,
  And felt his labours done.
Then to a trusty friend he spake,
  " Across the desert wide,
O take the poor boy for my sake ! "
      And kissed the child and died.

IV.

Toiling along in weary plight,
  Through heavy jungle mire,
These two came later every night
  To warm them at the fire.
Until the captain said one day,
  " O seaman good and kind,
To save thyself now come away,
  And leave the boy behind ! "

V.

The child was slumb'ring near the blaze,
  " O captain, let him rest
Until it sinks, when God's own ways
  Shall teach us what is best ! "
They watched the whitened ashy heap,
  They touched the child in vain ;
They did not leave him there asleep,
  He never woke again.

This song was sung to the music of "Little Nell," a ballad composed by the late Mr. George Linley, to the words of Miss Charlotte Young, and dedicated to Charles Dickens. He was very fond of it, and his eldest daughter had been in the habit of singing it to him constantly since she was quite a child.

M. De
Cerjat.

TAVISTOCK HOUSE, Third January, 1855.

MY DEAR CERJAT,

    When your Christmas letter did not arrive according to custom, I felt as if a bit of Christmas had fallen out and there was no supplying the piece. However, it was soon supplied by yourself, and the bowl became round and sound again.

The Christmas number of " Household Words," I suppose, will reach Lausanne about midsummer. The first ten pages or so—all under the head of " The First Poor Traveller "—are writte . by me, and I hope you will find, in the story of the soldier which they contain, something that may move you a little. It moved me *not* a little in the writing, and I believe has touched a va t number of people. We have sold eighty thousand of it.

I am but newly come home from reading :t Reading, and at

Sherborne, in Dorsetshire, and at Bradford, in Yorkshire. Wonderful audiences! and the number at the last place three thousand seven hundred. And yet but for the noise of their laughing and cheering, they "went" like one man.

The absorption of the English mind in the war is, to me, a melancholy thing. Every other subject of popular solicitude and sympathy goes down before it. I fear I clearly see that for years to come domestic reforms are shaken to the root; every miserable red-tapist flourishes war over the head of every protester against his humbug; and everything connected with it is pushed to such an unreasonable extent, that, however kind and necessary it may be in itself, it becomes ridiculous. For all this it is an indubitable fact, I conceive, that Russia MUST BE stopped, and that the future peace of the world renders the war imperative upon us. The Duke of Newcastle lately addressed a private letter to the newspapers, entreating them to exercise a larger discretion in respect of the letters of "Our Own Correspondents," against which Lord Raglan protests as giving the Emperor of Russia information for nothing which would cost him (if indeed he could get it at all) fifty or a hundred thousand pounds a year. The communication has not been attended with much effect, so far as I can see. In the meantime I do suppose we have the wretchedest Ministry that ever was —in whom nobody not in office of some sort believes—yet whom there is nobody to displace. The strangest result, perhaps, of years of Reformed Parliaments that ever the general sagacity did *not* forsake.

Let me recommend you, as a brother-reader of high distinction, two comedies, both Goldsmith's—"She Stoops to Conquer" and "The Good-natured Man." Both are so admirable and so delightfully written that they read wonderfully. A friend of mine, Forster, who wrote "The Life of Goldsmith," was very ill a year or so ago, and begged me to read to him one night as he lay in bed, "something of Goldsmith's." I fell upon "She Stoops to Conquer," and we enjoyed it with that wonderful intensity, that I believe he began to get better in the first scene, and was all right again in the fifth act.

I am charmed by your account of Haldimand, to whom my love. Tell him Sydney Smith's daughter has privately printed a life of her father with selections from his letters, which has great merit, and often presents him exactly as he used to be. I have strongly urged her to publish it, and I think she will do so, about March.

My eldest boy has come home from Germany to learn a business Birmingham (I think), first of all. The whole nine are well ny. Ditto, Mrs. Dickens. Ditto, Georgina. My two girls are full of interest in yours; and one of mine (as I think I told you when I was at the Elysée) is curiously like one of yours in the face. They are all agog now about a great fairy play, which is to come off here next Monday. The house is full of spangles, gas, Jew theatrical tailors, and pantomime carpenters. We all unite in kindest and best loves to dear Mrs. Cerjat and all the blooming daughters. And I am, with frequent thoughts of you and cordial affection, ever, my dear Cerjat,

Your faithful Friend.

TAVISTOCK HOUSE, Third January, 1855.

MY DEAR MARY,

This is a word of heartfelt greeting, in exchange for yours, which came to me most pleasantly, and was received with a cordial welcome. If I had leisure to write a letter, I should write you, at this point, perhaps the very best letter that ever was read; but, being in the agonies of getting up a gorgeous fairy play for the children, on Charley's birthday (besides having the work of half-a-dozen to do as a regular thing), I leave the merits of the wonderful epistle to your lively fancy.

Enclosing a kiss, if you will have the kindness to return it when done with.

I have just been reading my "Christmas Carol" in Yorkshire. I should have lost my heart to the beautiful young landlady of my hotel (age twenty-nine, dress, black frock and jacket, exquisitely braided) if it had not been safe in your possession.

Many, many happy years to you! My regards to that obstinate old Wurzell and his dame, when you have them under lock and key again.*

Ever affectionately yours.

TAVISTOCK HOUSE,
Twenty-seventh January, 18!

MY DEAR MRS. GASKELL,

Let me congratulate you on the conclusion of your ̃
not because it is the end of a task to which you had conce
dislike (for I imagine you to have got the better of that d
by this time), but because it is the vigorous and powerful
plishment of an anxious labour. It seems to me that y
felt the ground thoroughly firm under your feet, and hav
on with a force and purpose that MUST now give you plea

You will not, I hope, allow that non-lucid interval of
faction with yourself (and me?), which beset you for a

---

* Captain Cavendish Boyle was governor of the military prison ̃

Sorry:
The defect on the previous page was that way in the original book we reproduced.

two once upon a time, to linger in the shape of any disagreeable association with "Household Words." I shall still look forward to the large sides of paper, and shall soon feel disappointed if they don't begin to reappear.

I thought it best that Wills should write the business letter on the conclusion of the story, as that part of our communications had always previously rested with him. I trust you found it satisfactory? I refer to it, not as a matter of mere form, but because I sincerely wish everything between us to be beyond the possibility of misunderstanding or reservation.

Dear Mrs. Gaskell, very faithfully yours.

TAVISTOCK HOUSE,
Monday, Twenty-ninth January, 1855.

Mr. Arthur Ryland.

MY DEAR MR. RYLAND,

I have been in the greatest difficulty—which I am not yet out of—to know what to read at Birmingham. I fear the idea of next month is now impracticable. Which of two other months do you think would be preferable for your Birmingham objects? Next May, or next December?

Having already read two Christmas books at Birmingham, I should like to get out of that restriction, and have a swim in the broader waters of one of my long books. I have been poring over "Copperfield" (which is my favourite), with the idea of getting a reading out of it, to be called by some such name as "Young Housekeeping and Little Emily." But there is still the huge difficulty that I constructed the whole with immense pains, and have so woven it up and blended it together, that I cannot yet so separate the parts as to tell the story of David's married life with Dora, and the story of Mr. Peggotty's search for his niece, within the time. This is my object. If I could possibly bring it to bear, it would make a very attractive reading, with a strong interest in it, and a certain completeness.

This is exactly the state of the case. I don't mind confiding to you, that I never can approach the book with perfect composure (it had such perfect possession of me when I wrote it), and that I no sooner begin to try to get it into this form, than I begin to read it all, and to feel that I cannot disturb it. I have not been unmindful of the agreement we made at parting, and I have sat staring at the backs of my books for an inspiration. This project is the only one that I have constantly reverted to, and yet I have made no progress in it!

Faithfully yours always.

Monsieur
Regnier.

TAVISTOCK HOUSE, LONDON,
Saturday Evening, Third February, 1855.

MY DEAR REGNIER,

I am coming to Paris for a week, with my friend Collins—son of the English painter who painted our green lanes and our cottage children so beautifully. Do not tell this to Le Vieux. Unless I have the ill fortune to stumble against him in the street I shall not make my arrival known to him.

I purpose leaving here on Sunday, the eleventh, but I shall stay that night at Boulogne to see two of my little boys who are at school there. We shall come to Paris on Monday, the twelfth, arriving there in the evening.

Now, *mon cher*, do you think you can, without inconvenience, engage me for a week an apartment—cheerful, light, and wholesome—containing a comfortable *salon et deux chambres à coucher*. I do not care whether it is an hotel or not, but the reason why I do not write for an apartment to the Hôtel Brighton is, that there they expect one to dine at home (I mean in the apartment) generally; whereas, as we are coming to Paris expressly to be always looking about us, we want to dine wherever we like every day. Consequently, what we want to find is a good apartment, where we can have our breakfast but where we shall never dine.

Can you engage such accommodation for me? If you can, I shall feel very much obliged to you. If the apartment should happen to contain a little bed for a servant I might perhaps bring one, but I do not care about that at all. I want it to be pleasant and gay, and to throw myself *en garçon* on the festive *diableries de Paris*.

All the children send their loves to the two brave boys and the Normandy *bonnes*.

I shall hope for a short answer from you one day next week. My dear Regnier,

Always faithfully yours.

Mr. W. H.
Wills.

OFFICE OF "HOUSEHOLD WORDS,"
Friday, Ninth February, 1855.

MY DEAR WILLS,

I want to alter the arrangements for to-morrow, and put you to some inconvenience.

When I was at Gravesend t'other day, I saw, at Gad's Hill—just opposite to the Hermitage, where Miss Lynn used to live—a little freehold to be sold. The spot and the very house are literally "a dream of my childhood," and I should like to look at it before I go to Paris. With that purpose I must go to Strood by the

North Kent, at a quarter-past ten to-morrow morning, and I want you, strongly booted, to go with me! (I know the particulars from the agent.)

Can you? Let me know. If you can, can you manage so that we can take the proofs with us? If you can't, will you bring them to Tavistock House at dinner time to-morrow, half-past five? Forster will dine with us, but no one else.

Ever faithfully.

TAVISTOCK HOUSE, Miss King.
Friday Evening, Ninth February, 1855.

MY DEAR MISS KING,

I wish to get over the disagreeable part of my letter in the beginning. I have great doubts of the possibility of publishing your story in portions.

But I think it possesses *very great merit.* My doubts arise partly from the nature of the interest which I fear requires presentation as a whole, and partly on your manner of relating the tale. The people do not sufficiently work out their own purposes in dialogue and dramatic action. You are too much their exponent; what you do for them, they ought to do for themselves. With reference to publication in detached portions (or, indeed, with a reference to the force of the story in any form), that long stoppage and going back to possess the reader with the antecedents of the clergyman's biography, are rather crippling. I may mention that I think the boy (the child of the second marriage) a little too "slangy." I know the kind of boyish slang which belongs to such a character in these times; but, considering his part in the story, I regard it as the author's function to elevate such a characteristic, and soften it into something more expressive of the ardour and flush of youth, and its romance. It seems to me, too, that the dialogues between the lady and the Italian maid are conventional but not natural. This observation I regard as particularly applying to the maid, and to the scene preceding the murder. Supposing the main objection surmountable, I would venture then to suggest to you the means of improvement in this respect.

The paper is so full of good touches of character, passion, and natural emotion, that I very much wish for a little time to reconsider it, and to try whether condensation here and there would enable us to get it say into four parts. I am not sanguine of this, for I observed the difficulties as I read it the night before last; but I am very unwilling, I assure you, to decline what has so much merit.

I am going to Paris on Sunday morning for ten days or so. I purpose being back again within a fortnight. If you will let me think of this matter in the meanwhile, I shall at least have done all I can to satisfy my own appreciation of your work.

But if, in the meantime, you should desire to have it back with any prospect of publishing it through other means, a letter—the shortest in the world—from you to Mr. Wills at the " Household Words " office will immediately produce it. I repeat with perfect sincerity that I am much impressed by its merits, and that if I had read it as the production of an entire stranger, I think it would have made exactly this effect upon me.

My dear Miss King,

Very faithfully yours.

Miss
Hogarth.

HÔTEL MEURICE, PARIS,
Friday, Sixteenth February, 1855

MY DEAR GEORGY,

I heard from home last night; but the posts are so delayed and put out by the snow, that they come in at all sorts of times except the right times, and utterly defy all calculation. Will you tell Catherine with my love, that I will write to her again to-morrow afternoon; I hope she may then receive my letter by Monday morning, and in it I purpose telling her when I may be expected home. The weather is so severe and the roads are so bad, that the journey to and from Bordeaux seems out of the question. We have made up our minds to abandon it for the present, and to return about Tuesday night or Wednesday. Collins continues in a queer state, but is perfectly cheerful under the stoppage of his wine and other afflictions.

We have a beautiful apartment, very elegantly furnished, very thickly carpeted, and as warm as any apartment in Paris *can* be in such weather. We are very well waited on and looked after. We breakfast at ten, read and write till two, and then I go out walking all over Paris, while the invalid sits by the fire or is deposited in a café. We dine at five, in a different restaurant every day, and at seven or so go to the theatre—sometimes to two theatres, sometimes to three. We get home about twelve, light the fire, and drink lemonade, to which *I* add rum. We go to bed between one and two. I live in peace, like an elderly gentleman, and regard myself as in a negative state of virtue and respectability.

The theatres are not particularly good, but I have seen Lemaître act in the most wonderful and astounding manner. I am afraid we must go to the Opéra Comique on Sunday. To-morrow we dine with Regnier, and to-day with the Olliffes.

"La Joie fait Peur," at the Français, delighted me. Exquisitely played and beautifully imagined altogether. Last night we went to the Porte St. Martin to see a piece (English subject) called "Jane Osborne," which the characters pronounce "Ja Nosbornune." The seducer was Lord Nottingham. The comic Englishwoman's name (she kept lodgings and was a very bad character) was Missees Christmas. She had begun to get into great difficulties with a gentleman of the name of Meestair Cornhill, when we were obliged to leave, at the end of the first act, by the intolerable stench of the place. The whole theatre must be standing over some vast cess-pool. It was so alarming that I instantly rushed into a café and had brandy.

My ear has gradually become so accustomed to French, that I understand the people at the theatres (for the first time) with perfect ease and satisfaction. I walked about with Regnier for an hour and a half yesterday, and received many compliments on my angelic manner of speaking the celestial language. There is a winter Franconi's now, high up on the Boulevards, just like the round theatre on the Champs Elysées, and as bright and beautiful. A clown from Astley's is all in high favour there at present. He talks slang English (being evidently an idiot), as if he felt a perfect confidence that everybody understands him. His name is Boswell, and the whole cirque rang last night with cries for Boz Zwilllll! Boz Zweellll! Boz Zwuallll! etc. etc. etc. etc.

I must begin to look out for the box of bon-bons for the noble and fascinating Plornish-Maroon. Give him my love and a thousand kisses.

The following stab to Anne—she forgot to pack me any shaving soap.

Ever, my dear Georgy, most affectionately yours.

HÔTEL MEURICE, PARIS, Mr. W. H.
Friday, Sixteenth February, 1855. Wills.

MY DEAR WILLS,

I received your letter yesterday evening. I am living like Gil Blas and doing nothing. I am very much obliged to you, indeed, for the trouble you have kindly taken about the little freehold. It is clear to me that its merits resolve themselves into the view and the spot. If I had more money these considerations might, with me, overtop all others. But, as it is, I consider the matter quite disposed of, finally settled in the negative, and to be thought no more about. I shall not go down and look at it, as I could add nothing to your report.

Paris is finer than ever, and I go wandering about it all day. I suppose, as an old farmer said of Scott, I am "makin' mysel'" all the time; but I seem to be rather a free-and-easy sort of superior vagabond.

I live in continual terror of P——, and am strongly fortified within doors, with a means of retreat into my bedroom always ready. Up to the present blessed moment, his staggering form has not appeared.

As to yesterday's post from England, I have not, at the present moment, the slightest idea where it may be. It is under the snow somewhere, I suppose; but nobody expects it, and *Galignani* reprints every morning leaders from *The Times* of about a fortnight or three weeks old.

Collins, who is not very well, sends his "penitent regards," and says he is enjoying himself as much as a man with the weight of a broken promise on his conscience can.

Ever, my dear Wills, faithfully yours.

Miss King.   TAVISTOCK HOUSE, *Twenty-fourth February*, 1855.

MY DEAR MISS KING,

I have gone carefully over your story again, and quite agree with you that the episode of the clergyman could be told in a very few lines. Startling as I know it will appear to you, I am bound to say that I think the purpose of the whole tale would be immensely strengthened by great compression. I doubt if it could not be told more forcibly in half the space.

It is certainly too long for "Household Words," and I fear my idea of it is too short for you. I am, if possible, more unwilling than I was at first to decline it; but the more I have considered it, the longer it has seemed to grow. Nor can I ask you to try to present it free from that objection, because I already perceive the difficulty, and pain, of such an effort.

To the best of my knowledge, you are wrong about the Lady at last, and to the best of my observation, you do not express what you explain yourself to mean in the case of the Italian attendant. I have met with such talk in the romances of Maturin's time—certainly never in Italian life.

These, however, are slight points easily to be compromised in an hour. The great obstacle I must leave wholly to your own judgment, in looking over the tale again.

Believe me always, very faithfully yours.

TAVISTOCK HOUSE, LONDON,
Sunday, Twenty-fifth February, 1855.

MY DEAR OLLIFFE,

As soon as I came home I communicated with ——— on the subject we spoke of. The best report I can make is to send you his written account of the questions. How is it? The thaw here (which began yesterday morning) is of a very earnest description. Everything is weeping. All the buildings have severe colds in their heads, all the window-sills are in the first stage of measles, all the water-pipes are bursting, all the streets are great black heaps of mud.

Five hundred thousand pairs of pattens are now going to church, and the bells are making such an intolerable uproar that I can't hear myself think.

I don't know what is to be done to Lady Olliffe if she ever comes to London again without writing word of her arrival.

Believe me always,
Very faithfully yours.

TAVISTOCK HOUSE, *Twenty-sixth February, 1855.*

MY DEAR MR. RYLAND,

Charley came home, I assure you, perfectly delighted with his visit to you, and rapturous in his accounts of your great kindness to him.

It appears to me that the first question in reference to my reading (I have not advanced an inch in my "Copperfield" trials by-the-bye) is, whether you think you could devise any plan in connection with the room at Dee's, which would certainly bring my help in money up to five hundred pounds. That is what I want. If it could be done by a subscription for two nights, for instance, I would not be chary of my time and trouble. But if you cannot see your way clearly to that result in that connection, then I think it would be better to wait until we can have the Town Hall at Christmas. I have promised to read, about Christmas time, at Sheffield and at Peterboro'. I *could* add Birmingham to the list, then, if need were. But what I want is, to give the institution in all five hundred pounds. That is my object, and nothing less will satisfy me.

Will you think it over, taking counsel with whomsoever you please, and let me know what conclusion you arrive at? Only think of me as subservient to the institution.

My dear Mr. Ryland, always very faithfully yours.

Mr. David
Roberts,
R.A.

TAVISTOCK HOUSE,
Twenty-eighth February, 1855.

MY DEAR DAVID ROBERTS,

I hope to make it quite plain to you, in a few words, why I think it right to stay away from the Lord Mayor's dinner to the club. If I did not feel a kind of rectitude involved in my non-acceptance of his invitation, your note would immediately induce me to change my mind.

Entertaining a strong opinion on the subject of the City Corporation as it stands, and the absurdity of its pretensions in an age perfectly different, in all conceivable respects, from that to which it properly belonged as a reality, I have expressed that opinion on more than one occasion, within a year or so, in "Household Words." I do not think it consistent with my respect for myself, or for the art I profess, to blow hot and cold in the same breath; and to laugh at the institution in print, and accept the hospitality of its representative while the ink is staring us all in the face. There is a great deal too much of this among us, and it does not elevate the earnestness or delicacy of literature.

This is my sole consideration. Personally I have always met the present Lord Mayor on the most agreeable terms, and I think him an excellent one. As between you, and me, and him, I cannot have the slightest objection to your telling him the truth. On a more private occasion, when he was not keeping his state, I should be delighted to interchange any courtesy with that honourable and amiable gentleman, Mr. Moon.

Believe me always cordially yours.

Mr. W. M.
Thackeray.

TAVISTOCK HOUSE,
Friday Evening, Twenty-third March, 1855.

MY DEAR THACKERAY,

I have read in *The Times* to-day an account of your last night's lecture, and cannot refrain from assuring you in all truth and earnestness that I am profoundly touched by your generous reference to me. I do not know how to tell you what a glow it spread over my heart. Out of its fulness I do entreat you to believe that I shall never forget your words of commendation. If you could wholly know at once how you have moved me, and how you have animated me, you would be the happier I am very certain.

Faithfully yours ever.

TAVISTOCK HOUSE,
Friday, Twenty-ninth March, 1855.

MY DEAR FORSTER,

I have hope of Mr. Morley,* whom one cannot see without knowing to be a straightforward, earnest man. I also think Higgins † will materially help them.‡ Generally, I quite agree with you that they hardly know what to be at; but it is an immensely difficult subject to start, and they must have every allowance. At any rate, it is not by leaving them alone and giving them no help, that they can be urged on to success. (Travers, too, I think, a man of the Anti-Corn-Law-League order.)

Higgins told me, after the meeting on Monday night, that on the previous evening he had been closeted with ——, whose letter in that day's paper he had put right for *The Times.* He had never spoken to —— before, he said, and found him a rather muddle-headed Scotchman as to his powers of conveying his ideas. He (Higgins) had gone over his documents judicially, and with the greatest attention; and not only was —— wrong in every particular (except one very unimportant circumstance), but, in reading documents to the House, had stopped short in sentences where no stop was, and by so doing had utterly perverted their meaning.

This is to come out, of course, when said —— gets the matter on. I thought the case so changed, before I knew this, by his letter and that of the other shipowners, that I told Morley, when I went down to the theatre, that I felt myself called upon to relieve him from the condition I had imposed.

For the rest, I am quite calmly confident that I only do justice to the strength of my opinions, and use the power which circumstances have given me, conscientiously and moderately, with a right object, and towards the prevention of nameless miseries. I should be now reproaching myself if I had not gone to the meeting, and, having been, I am very glad.

A good illustration of a Government office. T—— very kindly wrote to me to suggest that "Houses of Parliament" illustration. After I had dined on Wednesday, and was going to jog slowly down to Drury Lane, it suddenly came into my head that perhaps his details were wrong. I had just time to turn to the "Annual Register," and *not one of them was correct!*

This is, of course, in close confidence.

Ever affectionately.

* Chairman of the "Administrative Reform League" Meeting at Drury Lane Theatre.

† Mr. Higgins, best known as a writer in *The Times,* under the name of "Jacob Omnium."

‡ The Members of the Administrative Reform League.

Mr. Austen
Henry
Layard.

TAVISTOCK HOUSE,
Tuesday Evening, Third April, 1855.

DEAR LAYARD,

Since I had the pleasure of seeing you again at Miss Coutts' (really a greater pleasure to me than I could easily tell you), I have thought a good deal of the duty we all owe you of helping you as much as we can. Being on very intimate terms with Lemon, the editor of " Punch " (a most affectionate and true-hearted fellow), I mentioned to him in confidence what I had at heart. You will find yourself the subject of their next large cut, and of some lines in an earnest spirit. He again suggested the point to Mr. Shirley Brookes, one of their regular corps, who will do what is right in *The Illustrated London News* and *The Weekly Chronicle*, papers that go into the hands of large numbers of people. I have also communicated with Jerrold, whom I trust, and have begged him not to be diverted from the straight path of help to the most useful man in England on all possible occasions. Forster I will speak to carefully, and I have no doubt it will quicken him a little ; not that we have anything to complain of in his direction. If you ever see any new loophole, cranny, or needle's-eye, through which I can present your case to " Household Words," I most earnestly entreat you, as your staunch friend and admirer—you *can* have no truer—to indicate it to me at any time or season, and to count upon my being Damascus steel to the core.

All this is nothing ; because all these men, and thousands of others, dote upon you. But I know it would be a comfort to me, in your hard-fighting place, to be assured of such sympathy, and therefore only I write.

You have other recreations for your Sundays in the session, I daresay, than to come here. But it is generally a day on which I do not go out, and when we dine at half-past five in the easiest way in the world, and smoke in the peacefulest manner. Perhaps one of these Sundays after Easter you might not be indisposed to begin to dig us out ?

And I should like, on a Saturday of your appointing, to get a few of the serviceable men I know—such as I have mentioned—about you here. Will you think of this, too, and suggest a Saturday for our dining together ?

I am really ashamed and moved that you should do your part so manfully and be left alone in the conflict. I felt you to be all you are the first moment I saw you. I know you will accept my regard and fidelity for what they are worth.

Dear Layard, very heartily yours.

MY DEAR MARIA,

A necessity is upon me now—as at most times—of wandering about in my old wild way, to think. I could no more resist this on Sunday or yesterday than a man can dispense with food, or a horse can help himself from being driven. I hold my inventive capacity on the stern condition that it must master my whole life, often have complete possession of me, make its own demands upon me, and sometimes, for months together, put everything else away from me. If I had not known long ago that my place could never be held, unless I were at any moment ready to devote myself to it entirely, I should have dropped out of it very soon. All this I can hardly expect you to understand—or the restlessness and waywardness of an author's mind. You have never seen it before you, or lived with it, or had occasion to think or care about it, and you cannot have the necessary consideration for it. "It is only half-an-hour,"—"It is only an afternoon,"—"It is only an evening," people say to me over and over again; but they don't know that it is impossible to command one's self sometimes to any stipulated and set disposal of five minutes,—or that the mere consciousness of an engagement will sometimes worry a whole day. These are the penalties paid for writing books. Whoever is devoted to an art must be content to deliver himself wholly up to it, and to find his recompense in it. I am grieved if you suspect me of not wanting to see you, but I can't help it; I must go my way whether or no.

I thought you would understand that in sending the card for the box I sent an assurance that there was nothing amiss. I am pleased to find that you were all so interested with the play. My ladies say that the first part is too painful and wants relief. I have been going to see it a dozen times, but have never seen it yet, and never may. Madame Céleste is injured thereby (you see how unreasonable people are!), and says in the green-room, "M. Dickens est artiste! Mais il n'a jamais vu 'Janet Pride!'"

It is like a breath of fresh spring air to know that that unfortunate baby of yours is out of her one close room, and has about half-a-pint of very doubtful air per day. I could only become her Godfather on the condition that she had five hundred gallons of open air at any rate every day of her life; and you would soon see a rose or two in the face of my other little friend, Ella, if you opened all your doors and windows throughout the whole of all fine weather, from morning to night.

I am going off; I don't know where or how far, to ponder about

I. don't know what.　Sometimes I am half in the mood to set off for France, sometimes I think I will go and walk about on the seashore for three or four months, sometimes I look towards the Pyrenees, sometimes Switzerland.　I made a compact with a great Spanish authority last week, and vowed I would go to Spain. Two days afterwards Layard and I agreed to go to Constantinople when Parliament rises.　To-morrow I shall probably discuss with somebody else the idea of going to Greenland or the North Pole. The end of all this, most likely, will be, that I shall shut myself up in some out-of-the-way place I have not yet thought of, and go desperately to work there.

Once upon a time I didn't do such things you say.　No.　But I have done them through a good many years now, and they have become myself and my life.

Ever affectionately.

Mr. Austen
Henry
Layard.

TAVISTOCK HOUSE, *Tuesday, Tenth April*, 1855.

DEAR LAYARD,　·

I shall of course observe the strictest silence, at present, in reference to your resolutions.　It will be a most acceptable occupation to me to go over them with you, and I have not a doubt of their producing a strong effect out of doors.

There is nothing in the present time at once so galling and so alarming to me as the alienation of the people from their own public affairs.　I have no difficulty in understanding it.　They have had so little to do with the game through all these years of Parliamentary Reform, that they have sullenly laid down their cards, and taken to looking on.　The players who are left at the table do not see beyond it, conceive that gain and loss and all the interest of the play are in their hands, and will never be wiser until they and the table and the lights and the money are all overturned together.　And I believe the discontent to be so much the worse for smouldering, instead of blazing openly, that it is extremely like the general mind of France before the breaking out of the first Revolution, and is in danger of being turned by any one of a thousand accidents—a bad harvest—the last strain too much of aristocratic insolence or incapacity—a defeat abroad—a mere chance at home—into such a devil of a conflagration as never has been beheld since.

Meanwhile, all our English tuft-hunting, toad-eating, and other manifestations of accursed gentility—to say nothing of the Lord knows who's defiances of the proven truth before six hundred and fifty men—ARE expressing themselves every day.　So, every day, the disgusted millions with this unnatural gloom are confirmed and hardened in the very worst of moods. Finally, round all this is an atmosphere of poverty, hunger, and ignorant desperation, of the mere existence of which perhaps not one man in a thousand of those not actually enveloped in it, through the whole extent of this country, has the least idea.

It seems to me an absolute impossibility to direct the spirit of the people at this pass until it shows itself. If they began to bestir themselves in the vigorous national manner; if they would appear in political reunion, array themselves peacefully but in vast numbers against a system that they know to be rotten altogether, make themselves heard like the sea all round this island, I for one should be in such a movement heart and soul, and should think it a duty of the plainest kind to go along with it, and try to guide it by all possible means. But you can no more help a people who do not help themselves than you can help a man who does not help himself. And until the people can be got up from the lethargy, which is an awful symptom of the advanced state of their disease, I know of nothing that can be done beyond keeping their wrongs continually before them.

I shall hope to see you soon after you come back. Your speeches at Aberdeen are most admirable, manful, and earnest. I would have such speeches at every market-cross, and in every town-hall, and among all sorts and conditions of men; up in the very balloons, and down in the very diving-bells.

Ever, cordially yours.

TAVISTOCK HOUSE,
Saturday, Fourteenth April, 1855.

Mr. John
Forster.

MY DEAR FORSTER,

I cannot express to you how very much delighted I am with the "Steele." I think it incomparably the best of the series. The pleasanter humanity of the subject may commend it more to one's liking, but that again requires delicate handling, which you have given to it in a most charming manner. It is surely not possible to approach a man with a finer sympathy, and the assertion of the claims of literature throughout is of the noblest and most gallant kind.

I don't agree with you about the serious papers in *The Spectator*, which I think (whether they be Steele's or Addison's) are generally as indifferent as the humour of *The Spectator* is delightful. And I have always had a notion that Prue understood her husband very well, and held him in consequence, when a fonder woman with less show of caprice must have let him go. But these are points of opinion. The paper is masterly, and all I have got to say is, that if —— had a grain of the honest sentiment with which it over-flows, he never would or could have made so great a mistake.

Ever affectionately.

Mr. Mark
Lemon.

Tavistock House,
Thursday, Twenty-sixth April, 1855.

ON THE DEATH OF AN INFANT.

My dear Mark,

I will call for you at two, and go with you to Highgate, by all means.

Leech and I called on Tuesday evening and left our loves. I have not written to you since, because I thought it best to leave you quiet for a day. I have no need to tell you, my dear fellow, that my thoughts have been constantly with you, and that I have not forgotten (and never shall forget) who sat up with me one night when a little place in my house was left empty.

It is hard to lose any child, but there are many blessed sources of consolation in the loss of a baby.

Ever affectionately yours.

P.S.—Our kindest loves to Mrs. Lemon.

Mr. Clarkson
Stanfield,
R.A.

Tavistock House,
Sunday, Twentieth May, 1855.

My dear Stanny,

I have a little lark in contemplation, if you will help it to fly.

Collins has done a melodrama (a regular old-style melodrama), in which there is a very good notion. I am going to act it, as an experiment, in the children's theatre here—I, Mark, Collins, Egg, and my daughter Mary, the whole dram. pers.; our families and yours the whole audience; for I want to make the stage large and shouldn't have room for above five-and-twenty spectators. Now, there is only one scene in the piece, and that, my tarry lad, is the inside of a lighthouse. Will you come and paint it for us one night, and we'll all turn to and help? It is a mere wall, of course, but Mark and I have sworn that you must do it. If you will say yes, I should like to have the tiny flats made, after you have looked at the place, and not before. On Wednesday in this week I am good for a steak and the play, if you will make your own appointment here; or any day next week except Thursday. Write me a line in reply. We mean to burst on an astonished world with the melodrama, without any note of preparation. So don't say a syllable to Forster if you should happen to see him.

Ever affectionately yours.

TAVISTOCK HOUSE, *Tuesday Afternoon, Six o'clock,*   Mr.
Twenty-second May, 1855.   Clarkson
Stanfield,
MY DEAR STANNY,   R.A.

Your note came while I was out walking. Even if I had been at home I could not have managed to dine together to-day, being under a beastly engagement to dine out. Unless I hear from you to the contrary, I shall expect you here some time to-morrow, and will remain at home. I only wait your instructions to get the little canvases made. O, what a pity it is not the outside of the light'us, with the sea a-rowling agin it! Never mind, we'll get an effect out of the inside, and there's a storm and shipwreck "off;" and the great ambition of my life will be achieved at last, in the wearing of a pair of very coarse petticoat trousers. So hoorar for the salt sea, mate, and bouse up!

Ever affectionately,
DICKY.

TAVISTOCK HOUSE, *Twenty-third May,* 1855.   Mr. Mark
Lemon.
MY DEAR MARK,

Stanny says he is only sorry it is not the outside of the lighthouse with a raging sea and a transparent light. He enters into the project with the greatest delight, and I think we shall make a capital thing of it.

It now occurs to me that we may as well do a farce too. I should like to get in a little part for Katey, and also for Charley, if it were practicable. What do you think of "Animal Mag."? You and I in our old parts; Collins, Jeffrey; Charley, the Markis; Katey and Mary (or Georgina), the two ladies? Can you think of anything merry that is better? It ought to be broad, as a relief to the melodrama, unless we could find something funny with a story in it too. I rather incline myself to "Animal Mag." Will you come round and deliver your sentiments?

Ever affectionately.

TAVISTOCK HOUSE,   Mr. Frank
Thursday, Twenty-fourth May, 1855.   Stone,
A.R.A.
MY DEAR STONE,

Great projects are afoot here for a grown-up play in about three weeks' time. Former schoolroom arrangements to be reversed —large stage and small audience. Stanfield bent on desperate effects, and all day long with his coat off, up to his eyes in distemper colours.

Will you appear in your celebrated character of Mr. Nightingale? I want to wind up with that popular farce, we all playing our old parts. Ever affectionately.

2 B

Mr. Frank
Stone,
A.R.A.

TAVISTOCK HOUSE, *Twenty-fourth May*, 1855.

MY DEAR STONE,

That's right! You will find the words come back very quickly. Why, *of course* your people are to come, and if Stanfield don't astonish 'em, I'm a Dutchman. O Heaven, if you could hear the ideas he proposes to me, making even *my* hair stand on end!

Will you get Marcus or some similar bright creature to copy out old Nightingale's part for you, and then return the book? This is the prompt-book, the only one I have; and Katey and Georgina (being also in wild excitement) want to write their parts out with all despatch.

Ever affectionately.

Mr. W.
Wilkie
Collins.

TAVISTOCK HOUSE,
Thursday, Twenty-fourth May, 1855.

MY DEAR COLLINS,

I shall expect you to-morrow evening at "Household Words." I have written a little ballad for Mary—"The Story of the Ship's Carpenter and the Little Boy, in the Shipwreck."

Let us close up with "Mr. Nightingale's Diary." Will you look whether you have a book of it, or your part?

Ever faithfully.

Mrs.
Trollope.

TAVISTOCK HOUSE,
Tuesday Morning, Nineteenth June, 1855.

MY DEAR MRS. TROLLOPE,

I was out of town on Sunday, or I should have answered your note immediately on its arrival. I cannot have the pleasure of seeing the famous "medium" to-night, for I have some theatricals at home. But I fear I shall not in any case be a good subject for the purpose, as I altogether want faith in the thing.

I have not the least belief in the awful unseen world being available for evening parties at so much per night; and, although I should be ready to receive enlightenment from any source, I must say I have very little hope of it from the spirits who express themselves through mediums, as I have never yet observed them to talk anything but nonsense, of which (as Carlyle would say) there is probably enough in these days of ours, and in all days, among mere mortality.

Very faithfully yours,

TAVISTOCK HOUSE,
Wednesday, Twentieth June, 1855.

Mr. Clarkson Stanfield, R.A.

MY DEAR STANNY,

I write a hasty note to let you know that last night was perfectly wonderful ! ! !

Such an audience ! Such a brilliant success from first to last ! The Queen had taken it into her head in the morning to go to Chatham, and had carried Phipps with her. He wrote to me asking if it were possible to give him a quarter of an hour. I got through that time before the overture, and he came without any dinner, so influenced by eager curiosity. Lemon and I did every conceivable absurdity, I think, in the farce ; and they never left off laughing. At supper I proposed your health, which was drunk with nine times nine, and three cheers over. We then turned to at Scotch reels (having had no exercise), and danced in the maddest way until five this morning.

It is as much as I can do to guide the pen.

Ever most affectionately yours.

TAVISTOCK HOUSE,
Saturday, Thirtieth June, 1855.

Mr. W. C. Macready.

MY VERY DEAR MACREADY,

I write shortly, after a day's work at my desk, rather than lose a post in answering your enthusiastic, earnest, and young— how young, in all the best side of youth—letter.

To tell you the truth, I confidently expected to hear from you. I knew that if there were a man in the world who would be interested in, and who would approve of, my giving utterance to whatever was in me at this time, it would be you. I was as sure of you as of the sun this morning.

The subject is surrounded by difficulties ; the Association is sorely in want of able men ; and the resistance of all the phalanx, who have an interest in corruption and mismanagement, is the resistance of a struggle against death. But the great, first, strong necessity is to rouse the people up, to keep them stirring and vigilant, to carry the war dead into the tent of such creatures as ——, and ring into their souls (or what stands for them) that the time for dandy insolence is gone for ever. It may be necessary to come to that law of primogeniture (I have no love for it), or to come to even greater things ; but this is the first service to be done, and unless it is done, there is not a chance. For this, and to encourage timid people to come in, I went to Drury Lane the other night ; and I wish you had been there and had seen and heard the people.

The Association will be proud to have your name and gift. When we sat down on the stage the other night, and were waiting a minute or two to begin, I said to Morley, the chairman (a thoroughly fine earnest fellow), "this reminds me so of one of my dearest friends, with a melancholy so curious, that I don't know whether the place feels familiar to me or strange." He was full of interest directly, and we went on talking of you until the moment of his getting up to open the business.

They are going to print my speech in a tract form, and send it all over the country. I corrected it for the purpose last night. We are all well. Charley in the City; all the boys at home for the holidays; three prizes brought home triumphantly (one from the Boulogne waters and one from Wimbledon); I taking dives into a new book, and runs at leap-frog over "Household Words;" and Anne going to be married—which is the only bad news.

Ever, my dearest Macready, with unalterable affection and attachment,   Your faithful Friend.

Mrs. Winter.   TAVISTOCK HOUSE,
                                    Saturday, Thirtieth June, 1855.

MY DEAR MRS. WINTER,
        I am truly grieved to hear of your affliction in the loss of your darling baby. But if you be not, even already, so reconciled to the parting from that innocent child for a little while, as to bear it gently and with a softened sorrow, I know that that not unhappy state of mind must soon arise. The death of infants is a release from so much chance and change—from so many casualties and distresses—and is a thing so beautiful in its serenity and peace—that it should not be a bitterness, even in a mother's heart. The simplest and most affecting passage in all the noble history of our Great Master, is His consideration for little children; and in reference to yours, as many millions of bereaved mothers poor and rich will do in reference to theirs until the end of time, you may take the comfort of the generous words, "And He took a child and set it in the midst of them."

In a book, by one of the greatest English writers, called "A Journey from this World to the Next," a parent comes to the distant country beyond the grave, and finds the little girl he had lost so long ago, engaged in building a bower to receive him in, when his aged steps should bring him there at last. He is filled with joy to see her, so young—so bright—so full of promise—and is enraptured to think that she never was old, wan, tearful, withered. This is always one of the sources of consolation in the deaths of children. With no effort of the fancy, with nothing to undo, you will always be able to think of the pretty creature you have lost, *as a child* in heaven.

A poor little baby of mine lies in Highgate cemetery—and I laid her just as you think of laying yours, in the catacombs there, until I made a resting-place for all of us in the free air.

It is better that I should not come to see you. I feel quite sure of that, and will think of you instead.

God bless and comfort you! Mrs. Dickens and her sister send their kindest condolences to yourself and Mr. Winter. I add mine with all my heart. Affectionately your Friend.

TAVISTOCK HOUSE, *Sunday, Eighth July,* 1855. Mr. W. Wilkie Collins.

MY DEAR COLLINS,

I don't know whether you may have heard from Webster,* or whether the impression I derived from Mark's manner on Friday may be altogether correct. But it strongly occurred to me that Webster was going to decline the play, and that he really has worried himself into a fear of playing Aaron.

Now, when I got this into my head—which was during the rehearsal—I considered two things :—firstly, how we could best put about the success of the piece more widely and extensively even than it has yet reached ; and secondly, how you could be best assisted against a bad production of it hereafter, or no production of it. I thought I saw immediately, that the point would be to have this representation noticed in the newspapers. So I waited until the rehearsal was over and we had profoundly astonished the family, and then asked Colonel Waugh what he thought of sending some cards for Tuesday to the papers. He highly approved, and I yesterday morning directed Mitchell to send to all the morning papers, and to some of the weekly ones—a dozen in the whole.

I dined at Lord John's yesterday (where Meyerbeer was, and said to me after dinner: "Ah, mon ami illustre! que c'est noble de vous entendre parler d'haute voix morale, à la table d'un ministre!" for I gave them a little bit of truth about Sunday that was like bringing a Sebastopol battery among the polite company), I say, after this long parenthesis, I dined at Lord John's, and found great interest and talk about the play, and about what everybody who had been here had said of it. And I was confirmed in my decision that the thing for you was the invitation to the papers. Hence I write to tell you what I have done. Ever faithfully.

NOTE (by Mr. Wilkie Collins).—This characteristically kind endeavour to induce managers of theatres to produce "The Lighthouse," after the amateur

* Mr. Benjamin Webster, then Manager of the Adelphi Theatre.

performances of the play, was not attended with any immediate success. The work remained in the author's desk until Messrs. Robson and Emden undertook the management of the Olympic Theatre. They opened their first season with "The Lighthouse;" the part of Aaron Gurnock being performed by Mr. F. Robson.—W. C.

Miss Emily
Jolly.

3, ALBION VILLAS, FOLKESTONE, KENT,
Tuesday, Seventeenth July, 1855.

DEAR MADAM,

Your manuscript, entitled a "Wife's Story," has come under my own perusal within these last three or four days. I recognise in it such great merit and unusual promise, and I think it displays so much power and knowledge of the human heart, that I feel a strong interest in you as its writer.

I have begged the gentleman, who is in my confidence as to the transaction of the business of "Household Words," to return the MS. to you by the post, which (as I hope) will convey this note to you. My object is this: I particularly entreat you to consider the catastrophe. You write to be read, of course. The close of the story is unnecessarily painful—will throw off numbers of persons who would otherwise read it, and who (as it stands) will be deterred by hearsay from so doing, and is so tremendous a piece of severity, that it will defeat your purpose. All my knowledge and experience, such as they are, lead me straight to the recommendation that you will do well to spare the life of the husband, and of one of the children. Let her suppose the former dead, from seeing him brought in wounded and insensible—lose nothing of the progress of her mental suffering afterwards when that doctor is in attendance upon her—but bring her round at last to the blessed surprise that her husband is still living, and that a repentance which can be worked out, *in the way of atonement for the misery she has occasioned to the man whom she so ill repaid for his love, and made so miserable,* lies before her. So will you soften the reader whom you now as it were harden, and so you will bring tears from many eyes, which can only have their spring in affectionately and *gently* touched hearts. I am perfectly certain that with this change, all the previous part of your tale will tell for twenty times as much as it can in its present condition. And it is because I believe you have a great fame before you if you do justice to the remarkable ability you possess, that I venture to offer you this advice in what I suppose to be the beginning of your career.

I observe some parts of the story which would be strengthened, even in their psychological interest, by condensation here and there. If you will leave that to me, I will perform the task as conscientiously and carefully as if it were my own. But the suggestion I offer for your acceptance, no one but yourself can act upon.

Let me conclude this hasty note with the plain assurance that I have never been so much surprised and struck by any manuscript I have read, as I have been by yours.

Your faithful Servant.

3, ALBION VILLAS, FOLKESTONE,
Tuesday, Seventeenth July, 1855.

Mr. W.
Wilkie
Collins.

MY DEAR COLLINS,

Walter goes back to school on the First of August. Will you come out of school to this breezy vacation on the same day, or rather *this day fortnight, July Thirty-first?* for that is the day on which he leaves us, and we begin (here's a parent!) to be able to be comfortable. Why a boy of that age should seem to have on at all times a hundred and fifty pair of double-soled boots, and to be always jumping a bottom stair with the whole hundred and fifty, I don't know. But the woeful fact is within my daily experience.

We have a very pleasant little house, overlooking the sea, and I think you will like the place. It rained, in honour of our arrival, with the greatest vigour yesterday. I went out after dinner to buy some nails (you know the arrangements that would be then in progress), and I stopped in the rain, about halfway down a steep, crooked street, like a crippled ladder, to look at a little coachmaker's, where there had just been a sale. Speculating on the insolvent coachmaker's business, and what kind of coaches he could possibly have expected to get orders for in Folkestone, I thought, "What would bring together fifty people now, in this little street, at this little rainy minute?" On the instant, a brewer's van, with two mad horses in it, and the harness dangling about them—like the trappings of those horses you are acquainted with, who bolted through the starry courts of heaven—dashed by me, and in that instant, such a crowd as would have accumulated in Fleet Street sprang up magically. Men fell out of windows, dived out of doors, plunged down courts, precipitated themselves down steps, came down waterspouts, instead of rain, I think, and I never saw so wonderful an instance of the gregarious effect of an excitement.

A man, a woman, and a child had been thrown out on the horses taking fright and the reins breaking. The child is dead, and the woman very ill, but will probably recover, and the man has a hand broken and other mischief done to him.

Let me know what Wigan * says. If he does not take the play, and readily too, I would recommend you not to offer it elsewhere. You have gained great reputation by it, have done your position a deal of good, and (as I think) stand so well with it, that it is a pity to engender the notion that you care to stand better.   Ever faithfully.

Miss Emily
Jolly.

3, ALBION VILLAS, FOLKESTONE,
Twenty-first July, 1855.

DEAR MADAM,

I did not enter, in detail, on the spirit of the alteration I propose in your story; because I thought it right that you should think out that for yourself if you applied yourself to the change. I can now assure you that you describe it exactly as I had conceived it; and if I had wanted anything to confirm me in my conviction of its being right, our both seeing it so precisely from the same point of view, would be ample assurance to me.

I would leave her new and altered life to be inferred. It does not appear to me either necessary or practicable (within such limits) to do more than that. Do not be uneasy if you find the alteration demanding time. I shall quite understand that, and my interest will keep. *When* you finish the story, send it to Mr. Wills. Besides being in daily communication with him, I am at the office once a week; and I will go over it in print, before the proof is sent to you.   Very faithfully yours.

Mr. W. H.
Wills.

FOLKESTONE, *Sixteenth September*, 1855.

MY DEAR WILLS,

Scrooge is delighted to find that Bob Cratchit is enjoying his holiday in such a delightful situation; and he says (with that warmth of nature which has distinguished him since his conversion), "Make the most of it, Bob; make the most of it."

[I am just getting to work on No. 3 of the new book, and am in the hideous state of mind belonging to that condition.]

I have not a word of news. I am steeped in my story, and rise and fall by turns into enthusiasm and depression.

                                                 Ever faithfully.

The Hon.
Mrs.
Watson.

FOLKESTONE, *Sunday, Sixteenth September*, 1855.

MY DEAR MRS. WATSON,

This will be a short letter, but I hope not unwelcome. If you knew how often I write to you—in intention—I don't know where you would find room for the correspondence.

* Mr. Alfred Wigan was, at this time, Manager of the Olympic Theatre.

Catherine tells me that you want to know the name of my new book. I cannot bear that you should know it from anyone but me. It will not be made public until the end of October; the title is:

"NOBODY'S FAULT."

Keep it as the apple of your eye—an expressive form of speech, though I have not the least idea of what it means.

Next, I wish to tell you that I have appointed to read at Peterboro' on Tuesday, the Eighteenth of December. I have told the Dean that I cannot accept his hospitality, and that I am going with Mr. Wills to the inn, therefore I shall be absolutely at your disposal, and shall be more than disappointed if you don't stay with us. As the time approaches will you let me know your arrangements, and whether Mr. Wills can bespeak any rooms for you in arranging for me? Georgy will give you our address in Paris as soon as we shall have settled there. We shall leave here, I think, in rather less than a month from this time.

You know my state of mind as well as I do; indeed, if you don't know it much better, it is not the state of mind I take it to be. How I work, how I walk, how I shut myself up, how I roll down hills and climb up cliffs; how the new story is everywhere—heaving in the sea, flying with the clouds, blowing in the wind; how I settle to nothing, and wonder (in the old way) at my own incomprehensibility. I am getting on pretty well, have done the first two numbers, and am just now beginning the third; which egotistical announcements I make to you because I know you will be interested in them.

I think of inserting an advertisement in *The Times*, offering to submit the Plornishghenter to public competition, and to receive fifty thousand pounds if such another boy cannot be found, and to pay five pounds (my fortune) if he can.

Ever, my dear Mrs. Watson, affectionately yours.

FOLKESTONE, *Sunday, Thirtieth September*, 1855.

Mr. W. Wilkie Collins.

MY DEAR COLLINS,

Welcome from the bosom of the deep! If a hornpipe will be acceptable to you at any time (as a reminder of what the three brothers were always doing), I shall be, as the chairman says at Mr. Evans', "happy to oblige."

I have almost finished No. 3, in which I have relieved my indignant soul with a scarifier. Sticking at it day after day, I am the *in*completest letter-writer imaginable—seem to have no idea of holding a pen for any other purpose but that book. My fair Laura has not yet reported concerning Paris, but I should

think will have done so before I see you.   And now to that point.
I purpose being in town on *Monday, the eighth,* when I promised
to dine with Forster.   Of course the H. W. stories are at your
disposition.   At the office I will tell you the idea of the Christmas
number, which will put you in train, I hope, for a story.   I have
postponed the shipwreck idea for a year, as it seemed to require
more force from me than I could well give it with the weight of a
new start upon me.

We missed you very much, and the Plorn was quite inconsolable.
We slide down Cæsar occasionally.

They launched the boat, the rapid building of which you
remember, the other day.   All the fishermen in the place, all the
nondescripts, and all the boys, pulled at it with ropes from six A.M.
to four P.M.   Every now and then the ropes broke, and they all
fell down in the shingle.   The obstinate way in which the beastly
thing wouldn't move was so exasperating that I wondered they
didn't shoot it, or burn it.   Whenever it moved an inch they all
cheered ; whenever it wouldn't move they all swore.   Finally,
when it was quite given over, someone tumbled against it accidentally (as it appeared to me, looking out of my window here),
and it instantly shot about a mile into the sea, and they all stood
looking at it helplessly.

Kind regards to Pigott,* in which all unite.

                                               Ever faithfully.

Mr. W. C.   FOLKESTONE, *Thursday, Fourth October,* 1855.
Macready.
MY DEAREST MACREADY,

I have been hammering away in that strenuous manner at
my book, that I have had leisure for scarcely any letters but such
as I have been obliged to write ; having a horrible temptation
when I lay down my book-pen to run out on the breezy downs
here, tear up the hills, slide down the same, and conduct myself
in a frenzied manner, for the relief that only exercise gives me.

Your letter to Miss Coutts in behalf of little Miss Warner I
despatched straightway.   She is at present among the Pyrenees,
and a letter from her crossed that one of mine in which I enclosed
yours, last week.

Pray stick to that dim notion you have of coming to Paris !
How delightful it would be to see your aged countenance and
perfectly bald head in that capital !   It will renew your youth to
visit a theatre (previously dining at the Trois Frères) in company
with the jocund boy who now addresses you.   Do, do stick to it.

---

* Mr. Edward F. S. Pigott, now in the Lord Chamberlain's Office as
Examiner of Plays.

You will be pleased to hear, I know, that Charley has gone into Baring's house under very auspicious circumstances. Mr. Bates, of that firm, had done me the kindness to place him at the brokers' where he was. And when said Bates wrote to me a fortnight ago to say that an excellent opening had presented itself at Baring's, he added that the brokers gave Charley "so high a character for ability and zeal" that it would be unfair to receive him as a volunteer, and he must begin at a fifty-pound salary, to which I graciously consented.

As to the suffrage, I have lost hope even in the ballot. We appear to me to have proved the failure of representative institutions without an educated and advanced people to support them. What with teaching people to "keep in their stations," what with bringing up the soul and body of the land to be a good child, or to go to the beershop, to go a-poaching and go to the devil; what with having no such thing as a middle class (for though we are perpetually bragging of it as our safety, it is nothing but a poor fringe on the mantle of the upper); what with flunkyism, toadyism, letting the most contemptible lords come in for all manner of places, reading *The Court Circular* for the New Testament, I do reluctantly believe that the English people are habitually consenting parties to the miserable imbecility into which we have fallen, *and never will help themselves out of it.* Who is to do it, if anybody is, God knows. But at present we are on the down-hill road to being conquered, and the people WILL be content to bear it, sing "Rule Britannia," and WILL NOT be saved.

In No. 3 of my new book I have been blowing off a little of indignant steam which would otherwise blow me up, and with God's leave I shall walk in the same all the days of my life; but I have no present political faith or hope—not a grain.

I am going to read the "Carol" here to-morrow in a long carpenter's shop, which looks far more alarming as a place to hear — in than the Town Hall at Birmingham.

It is blowing a gale here from the south-west and raining like mad. Ever most affectionately.

2, RUE ST. FLORENTIN,   Mrs. Charles
Tuesday, Sixteenth October, 1855.   Dickens.

MY DEAREST CATHERINE,
We have had the most awful job to find a place that would in the least suit us, for Paris is perfectly full, and there is nothing to be got at any sane price. However, we have found two apartments—an *entresol* and a first floor, with a kitchen and

servants' room at the top of the house, at No. 49, Avenue des Champs Elysées.

You must be prepared for a regular Continental abode. There is only one window in each room, but the front apartments all look upon the main street of the Champs Elysées, and the view is delightfully cheerful. There are also plenty of rooms. They are not over and above well furnished, but by changing furniture from rooms we don't care for to rooms we *do* care for, we shall be able to make them home-like and presentable. I think the situation itself almost the finest in Paris; and the children will have a window from which to look on the busy life outside.

We could have got a beautiful apartment in the Rue Faubourg St. Honoré for a very little more, most elegantly furnished; but the greater part of it was on a courtyard, and it would never have done for the children. What you have to expect is a regular French residence, which a little habitation will make pretty and comfortable, with nothing showy in it, but with plenty of rooms, and with that wonderful street in which the Barrière de l'Etoile stands outside. The amount of rooms is the great thing, and I believe it to be the place best suited for us, at a not unreasonable price in Paris.

Georgina and Lady Olliffe send their loves.

Ever affectionately.

49, Avenue des Champs Elysées, Paris,
Sunday Night, Twenty-first October, 1855.

Mr. W. H.
Wills.

My dear Wills,

I will try my hand at that paper for H. W. to-morrow, if I can get a yard of flooring to sit upon; but we have really been in that state of topsy-turvyhood that even that has been an unattainable luxury, and may yet be for eight-and-forty hours or so, for anything I see to the contrary.

I have two floors here—*entresol* and first—in a doll's house, but really pretty within, and the view without, astounding, as you will say when you come. The house is on the Exposition side, about half a quarter of a mile above Franconi's, of course on the other side of the way, and close to the Jardin d'Hiver. We have no fewer than six rooms (besides the back ones) looking on the Champs Elysées, with the wonderful life perpetually flowing up and down. We have no spare-room, but excellent stowage for the whole family, including a capital dressing-room for me, and a really slap-up kitchen near the stairs.

But, sir—but—when Georgina, the servants, and I were here for the first night (Catherine and the rest being at Boulogne), I heard Georgy restless—turned out—asked : " What's the matter ? " " Oh, it's dreadfully dirty. I can't sleep for the smell of my room "—imagine all my stage-managerial energies multiplied at daybreak by a thousand. Imagine the porter, the porter's wife, the porter's wife's sister, a feeble upholsterer of enormous age from round the corner, and all his workmen (four boys), summoned. Imagine the partners in the proprietorship of the apartment, the martial little man with François-Prussian beard, also summoned. Imagine your inimitable chief briefly explaining that dirt is not in his way, and that he is driven to madness, and that he devotes himself to no coat and a dirty face, until the apartment is thoroughly purified. Imagine co-proprietors at first astounded, then urging that "it's not the custom," then wavering, then affected, then confiding their utmost private sorrows to the Inimitable, offering new carpets (accepted), embraces (not accepted), and really responding like French bricks. Sallow, unbrushed, unshorn, awful, stalks the Inimitable through the apartment until last night. Then all the improvements were concluded, and you must picture it as the smallest place you ever saw, but as exquisitely cheerful and vivacious, clean as anything human can be, and with a moving panorama always outside, which is Paris in itself.

I thought we were to give £1700 for the house at Gad's Hill. Are we bound to £1800 ? Considering the improvements to be made, it is a little too much, isn't it ? I have a strong impression that at the utmost we were only to divide the difference, and not to pass £1750. You will set me right if I am wrong. But I don't think I am.

Ever, my dear Wills, faithfully.

Avenue des Champs Elysées,
Wednesday, Twenty-fourth October, 1855.

Mr. W. H Wills.

MY DEAR WILLS,

In the Gad's Hill matter, I too would like to try the effect of "not budging." *So do not go beyond the* £1700. Considering what I should have to expend on the one hand, and the low price of stock on the other, I do not feel disposed to go beyond that mark. They won't let a purchaser escape for the sake of the £100, I think. And Austin was strongly of opinion, when I saw him last, that £1700 was enough.

You cannot think how pleasant it is to me to find myself generally known and liked here. If I go into a shop to buy anything, and give my card, the officiating priest or priestess brightens up, and says : " *Ah ! c'est l'écrivain célèbre ! Monsieur porte un nom très-distingué. Mais ! je suis honoré et intéressé de voir Monsieur Dick-in.   Je lis un des livres de monsieur tous les jours*" (in the *Moniteur*).   And a man who brought some little vases home last night, said : "*On connaît bien en France que Monsieur Dick-in prend sa position sur la dignité de la littérature. Ah ! c'est grande chose !   Et ses caractères*" (this was to Georgina, while he unpacked) "*sont si spirituellement tournées !   Cette Madame Tojare*" (Todgers), "*ah ! qu'elle est drôle et précisément comme une dame que je connais à Calais.*"

Ever faithfully.

Monsieur Regnier.

Wednesday, Twenty-first November, 1855.

MY DEAR REGNIER,

In thanking you for the box you kindly sent me the day before yesterday, let me thank you a thousand times for the delight we derived from the representation of your beautiful and admirable piece.*   I have hardly ever been so affected and interested in any theatre.   Its construction is in the highest degree excellent, the interest absorbing, and the whole conducted by a masterly hand to a touching and natural conclusion.

Through the whole story from beginning to end, I recognise the true spirit and feeling of an artist, and I most heartily offer you and your fellow-labourer my felicitations on the success you have achieved.   That it will prove a very great and lasting one, I cannot for a moment doubt.

O my friend !   If I could see an English actress with but one hundredth part of the nature and art of Madame Plessy, I should believe our English theatre to be in a fair way towards its regeneration.   But I have no hope of ever beholding such a phenomenon.   I may as well expect ever to see upon an English stage an accomplished artist, able to write and to embody what he writes, like you. Faithfully yours ever.

Madame Viardot.

49, AVENUE DES CHAMPS ELYSÉES, *Monday, Third December, 1855.*

DEAR MADAME VIARDOT,

Mrs. Dickens tells me that you have only borrowed the first number of "Little Dorrit," and are going to send it back. Pray do nothing of the sort, and allow me to have the great pleasure of sending you the succeeding numbers as they reach me. I have had such delight in your great genius, and have so high an interest in it and admiration of it, that I am proud of the honour of giving you a moment's intellectual pleasure.

Believe me, very faithfully yours.

* "La Joconda."

DEAR FRIEND,

I am always delighted to hear from you. Your genial earnestness does me good to think of. And every day of my life I feel more and more that to be thoroughly in earnest is everything, and to be anything short of it is nothing. You see what we have been doing to our valiant soldiers.† You see what miserable humbugs we are. And because we have got involved in meshes of aristocratic red tape to our unspeakable confusion, loss, and sorrow, the gentlemen who have been so kind as to ruin us are going to give us a day of humiliation and fasting the day after to-morrow. I am sick and sour to think of such things at this age of the world. . . . I am in the first stage of a new book, which consists in going round and round the idea, as you see a bird in his cage go about and about his sugar before he touches it.

Always most cordially yours.

1856.

NARRATIVE.

CHARLES DICKENS having taken an apartment in Paris for the winter months, 49, Avenue des Champs Elysées, was there with his family until the middle of May. He much enjoyed this winter sojourn, meeting many old friends, making new friends, and interchanging hospitalities with the French artistic world. He had also many friends from England to visit him. Mr. Wilkie Collins had an *appartement de garçon* hard by, and the two companions were constantly together. The Rev. James White and his family also spent their winter in Paris, having taken an apartment at 49, Avenue des Champs Elysées, and the girls of the two families had the same masters, and took their lessons together. After the Whites' departure, Mr. Macready paid Charles Dickens a visit, occupying the vacant apartment.

During this winter Charles Dickens was, however, constantly backwards and forwards between Paris and London on "Household Words" business, and was also at work on his "Little Dorrit."

While in Paris he sat for his portrait to the great Ary Scheffer. It was exhibited at the Royal Academy Exhibition of this year, and is now in the National Portrait Gallery.

The summer was again spent at Boulogne, and once more at the

---

* This and another Letter to Captain Morgan, which appears under date of 1860, were published in *Scribner's Monthly*, October, 1877.

† This letter was written during the Crimean war.

Villa des Moulineaux, where Charles Dickens received constant visits from his English friends, Mr. Wilkie Collins taking up his quarters for many weeks in a little cottage in the garden; and there the idea of another play, to be acted at Tavistock House, was first started. Many of the letters for this year have reference to this play, and will show the interest which Charles Dickens took in it, and the immense amount of care and pains given by him to the careful carrying out of this favourite amusement.

The Christmas number of "Household Words," written by Charles Dickens and Mr. Collins, called "The Wreck of the *Golden Mary*," was planned by the two friends during this summer holidays.

It was in this year that one of the great wishes of his life was to be realised, the much-coveted house—Gad's Hill Place—having been purchased by him, and the cheque written on the 14th of March —on a "Friday," as he writes to his sister-in-law in a letter of this date. He frequently remarked that all the important, and so far fortunate, events of his life had happened to him on a Friday. So that, contrary to the usual superstition, that day had come to be looked upon by his family as his "lucky" day.

The allusion to the "plainness" of Miss Boyle's handwriting is good-humouredly ironical; that lady's writing being by no means famous for its legibility.

The "Anne" mentioned in the letter to his sister-in-law, which follows the one to Miss Boyle, was the faithful servant who had lived with the family so long; and who, having left to be married the previous year, had found it a very difficult matter to recover from her sorrow at this parting. And the "godfather's present" was for a son of Mr. Edmund Yates.

The explanation of the remark to Mr. Wills (6th April), that he had paid the money to Mr. Poole, is that Charles Dickens was the trustee through whom the dramatist received his pension.

The letter to the Duke of Devonshire has reference to the peace illuminations after the Crimean war.

The M. Forgues for whom, at Mr. Collins' request, he wrote á short biography of himself, was the editor of the *Revue des Deux Mondes.*

The speech at the London Tavern was on behalf of the Artists' Benevolent Fund.

Miss Kate Macready had sent some clever poems to "Household Words," with which Charles Dickens had been much pleased. He makes allusion to these in the two remaining letters to Mr. Macready.

"I did write it for you" (letter to Mrs. Watson, 17th October), refers to that part of "Little Dorrit" which treats of the visit of the Dorrit family to the Great St. Bernard. An expedition which it will be remembered he made himself, in company with Mr. and Mrs. Watson and other friends.

The letter to Mrs. Horne refers to a joke about the name of a friend of this lady's, who had once been brought by her to Tavistock House. The letter to Mr. Mitton concerns the lighting of the little theatre at Tavistock House.

The last letter for this year is in answer to one from Mr. Kent, asking Charles Dickens to sit to Mr. John Watkins for his photograph. We should add, however, that he did subsequently give this gentleman some sittings.

49, CHAMPS ELYSÉES, *Sunday, Sixth January*, 1856.   Mr. W. H.
Wills.

MY DEAR WILLS,

I should like Morley to do a Strike article, and to work into it the greater part of what is here. But I cannot represent myself as holding the opinion that all strikes among this unhappy class of society, who find it so difficult to get a peaceful hearing, are always necessarily wrong, because I don't think so. To open a discussion of the question by saying that the men are "*of course* entirely and painfully in the wrong," surely would be monstrous in anyone. Show them to be in the wrong here, but in the name of the eternal heavens show why, upon the merits of this question. Nor can I possibly adopt the representation that these men are wrong because by throwing themselves out of work they throw other people, possibly without their consent. If such a principle had anything in it, there could have been no civil war, no raising by Hampden of a troop of horse, to the detriment of Buckinghamshire agriculture, no self-sacrifice in the political world. And O, good God, when —— treats of the suffering of wife and children, can he suppose that these mistaken men don't feel it in the depths of their hearts, and don't honestly and honourably, most devoutly and faithfully believe that for those very children, when they shall have children, they are bearing all these miseries now !   Ever faithfully.

49, CHAMPS ELYSÉES, PARIS,   Mr. Mark
Monday, Seventh January, 1856.   Lemon.

MY DEAR MARK,

In a piece at the Ambigu, called the "Rentrée à Paris," a mere scene in honour of the return of the troops from the Crimea the other day, there is a novelty which I think it worth letting you know of, as it is easily available, either for a serious or a comic interest—the introduction of a supposed electric telegraph. The

2 c

scene is the railway terminus at Paris, with the electric telegraph office on the prompt side, and the clerks *with their backs to the audience*—much more real than if they were, as they infallibly would be, staring about the house—working the needles; and the little bell perpetually ringing. There are assembled to greet the soldiers, all the easily and naturally imagined elements of interest —old veteran fathers, young children, agonised mothers, sisters and brothers, girl lovers—each impatient to know of his or her own object of solicitude. Enter to these a certain marquis, full of sympathy for all, who says : "My friends, I am one of you. My brother has no commission yet. He is a common soldier. I wait for him as well as all brothers and sisters here wait for *their* brothers. Tell me whom you are expecting." Then they all tell him. Then he goes into the telegraph-office, and sends a message down the line to know how long the troops will be. Bell rings. Answer handed out on slip of paper. "Delay on the line. Troops will not arrive for a quarter of an hour." General disappointment. "But we have this brave electric telegraph, my friends," says the marquis. "Give me your little messages, and I'll send them off." General rush round the marquis. Exclamations : "How's Henri ?" "My love to Georges ;" "Has Guillaume forgotten Elise ?" "Is my son wounded ?" "Is my brother promoted ?" etc. etc. Marquis composes tumult. Sends message—such a regiment, such a company—"Elise's love to Georges." Little bell rings, slip of paper handed out—"Georges in ten minutes will embrace his Elise. Sends her a thousand kisses." Marquis sends message— such a regiment, such a company—"Is my son wounded ?" Little bell rings. · Slip of paper handed out—"No. He has not yet upon him those marks of bravery in the glorious service of his country which his dear old father bears " (father being lamed and invalided). Last of all the widowed mother. Marquis sends message—such a regiment, such a company—"Is my only son safe ?" Little bell rings. Slip of paper handed out—"He was first upon the heights of Alma." General cheer. Bell rings again, another slip of paper handed out. "He was made a sergeant at Inkermann." Another cheer. Bell rings again, another slip of paper handed out. "He was made colour-sergeant at Sebastopol." Another cheer. Bell rings again, another slip of paper handed out. "He was the first man who leaped with the French banner on the Malakhoff tower." Tremendous cheer. Bell rings again, another slip of paper handed out. "But he was struck down there by a musket-ball, and—— Troops have proceeded. Will arrive in half a minute after this." Mother abandons all hope ; general commiseration ; troops rush in, down a platform ; son only wounded, and embraces her.

As I have said, and as you will see, this is available for any purpose. But done with equal distinction and rapidity, it is a tremendous effect, and got by the simplest means in the world. There is nothing in the piece, but it was impossible not to be moved and excited by the telegraph part of it.

I have written to Beaucourt about taking that breezy house—a little improved—for the summer, and I hope you and yours will come there often and stay there long. My present idea, if nothing should arise to uproot me sooner, is to stay here until the middle of May, then plant the family at Boulogne, and come with Catherine and Georgy home for two or three weeks.

We are up to our knees in mud here. Literally in vehement despair, I walked down the avenue outside the Barrière de l'Etoile here yesterday, and went straight on among the trees. I came back with top-boots of mud on. Nothing will cleanse the streets. Numbers of men and woman are for ever scooping and sweeping in them, and they are always one lake of yellow mud. All my trousers go to the tailor's every day, and are ravelled out at the heels every night. Washing is awful.

Tell Mrs. Lemon, with my love, that I have bought her some Eau d'Or, in grateful remembrance of her knowing what it is, and crushing the tyrant of her existence by resolutely refusing to be put down when that monster would have silenced her. You may imagine the loves and messages that are now being poured in upon me by all of them, so I will give none of them; though I am pretending to be very scrupulous about it, and am looking (I have no doubt) as if I were writing them down with the greatest care.

Ever affectionately.

49, CHAMPS ELYSÉES,
Saturday, Nineteenth January, 1856.

Mr. W.
Wilkie
Collins.

MY DEAR COLLINS,

I had no idea you were so far on with your book, and heartily congratulate you on being within sight of land.

It is excessively pleasant to me to get your letter, as it opens a perspective of theatrical and other lounging evenings, and also of articles in "Household Words." It will not be the first time that we shall have got on well in Paris, and I hope it will not be by many a time the last.

I purpose coming over, early in February, and therefore we can return in a jovial manner together. As soon as I know my day of coming over, I will write to you again, and (as the merchants —say Charley—would add) "communicate same" to you.

I have been sitting to Scheffer to-day—conceive this, if you please, with No. 5 upon my soul—four hours !! I am so addle-headed and bored, that if you were here, I should propose an instantaneous rush to the Trois Frères. Under existing circumstances I have no consolation.

I think THE portrait * is the most astounding thing ever beheld upon this globe. It has been shrieked over by the united family as "Oh! the very image!" I went down to the *entresol* the moment I opened it, and submitted it to the Plorn—then engaged, with a half-franc musket, in capturing a Malakhoff of chairs. He looked at it very hard, and gave it as his opinion that it was Misser Hegg. We suppose him to have confounded the Colonel with Jollins. I met Madame Georges Sand the other day at a dinner got up by Madame Viardot for that great purpose. The human mind cannot conceive any one more astonishingly opposed to all my preconceptions. If I had been shown her in a state of repose, and asked what I thought her to be, I should have said: "The Queen's monthly nurse." *Au reste*, she has nothing of the *bas bleu* about her, and is very quiet and agreeable.

The way in which mysterious Frenchmen call and want to embrace me, suggests to any one who knows me intimately, such infamous lurking, slinking, getting behind doors, evading, lying—so much mean resort to craven flights, dastard subterfuges, and miserable poltroonery—on my part, that I merely suggest the arrival of cards like this:

* Of Mr. Wilkie Collins.

—and I then write letters of terrific *empressement*, with assurances of all sorts of profound considerations, and never by any chance become visible to the naked eye.

At the Porte St. Martin they are doing the " Orestes," put into French verse by Alexandre Dumas. Really one of the absurdest things I ever saw. The scene of the tomb, with all manner of classical females, in black, grouping themselves on the lid, and on the steps, and on each other, and in every conceivable aspect of obtrusive impossibility, is just like the window of one of those artists in hair, who address the friends of deceased persons. To-morrow week a fête is coming off at the Jardin d'Hiver, next door but one here, which I must certainly go to—the fête of the company of the Folies Nouvelles! The ladies of the company are to keep stalls, and are to sell to Messieurs the Amateurs orange-water and lemonade. Paul le Grand is to promenade among the company, dressed as Pierrot. Kalm, the big-faced comic singer, is to do the like, dressed as a Russian Cossack. The entertainments are to conclude with " La Polka des Bêtes féroces, par la Troupe entière des Folies Nouvelles." I wish, without invasion of the rights of British subjects, or risk of war, —— could be seized by French troops, brought over, and made to assist.

The *appartement* has not grown any bigger since you last had the joy of beholding me, and upon my honour and word I live in terror of asking —— to dinner, lest she should not be able to get in at the dining-room door. I *think* (am not sure) the dining-room would hold her, if she could be once passed in, but I don't see my way to that. Nevertheless, we manage our own family dinners very snugly there, and have good ones, as I think you will say, every day at half-past five.

I have a notion that we may knock out a *series* of descriptions for H. W. without much trouble. It is very difficult to get into the Catacombs, but my name is so well known here that I may succeed. I find that the guillotine can be got set up in private, like Punch's show. What do you think of *that* for an article? I find myself underlining words constantly. It is not my nature. It is mere imbecility after the four hours' sitting.

Ever cordially.

49, CHAMPS ELYSÉES, PARIS,
Twenty-eighth January, 1856.

Miss Mary Boyle.

MY DEAR MARY,

I am afraid you will think me an abandoned ruffian for not having acknowledged your more than handsome warm-hearted letter before now. But, as usual, I have been so occupied, and so glad to get up from my desk and wallow in the mud (at present about six feet deep here), that pleasure correspondence is just the last thing in the world I have had leisure to take to. Business correspondence with all sorts and conditions of men and women, O my Mary! is one of the dragons I am perpetually fighting; and the more I throw it, the more it stands upon its hind legs, rampant, and throws me.

Yes, on that bright cold morning when I left Peterboro', I felt that the best thing I could do was to say that word that I would do anything in an honest way to avoid saying, at one blow, and make off. I was so sorry to leave you all! You can scarcely imagine what a chill and blank I felt on that Monday evening at Rockingham. It was so sad to me, and engendered a constraint so melancholy and peculiar, that I doubt if I were ever much more out of sorts in my life. Next morning, when it was light and sparkling out of doors, I felt more at home again. But when I came in from seeing poor dear Watson's grave, Mrs. Watson asked me to go up in the gallery, which I had last seen in the days of our merry play. We went up, and walked into the very part he had made and was so fond of, and she looked out of one window and I looked out of another, and for the life of me I could not decide in my own heart whether I should console or distress her by going and taking her hand, and saying something of what was naturally in my mind. So I said nothing, and we came out again; on the whole perhaps it was best; for I have no doubt we understood each other very well without speaking a word.

Sheffield was a tremendous success and an admirable audience. They made me a present of table-cutlery after the reading was over; and I came away by the mail-train within three-quarters of an hour, changing my dress and getting on my wrappers partly in the fly, partly at the inn, partly on the platform. When we got among the Lincolnshire fens it began to snow. That changed to sleet, that changed to rain; the frost was all gone as we neared London, and the mud has all come. At two or three o'clock in the morning I stopped at Peterboro' again, and thought of you all disconsolately. The lady in the refreshment-room was very hard upon me, harder even than those fair enslavers usually are. She gave me a cup of tea, as if I were a hyena and she my cruel keeper with a strong dislike to me. I mingled my tears with it, and had a petrified bun of enormous antiquity in miserable meekness.

It is clear to me that climates are gradually assimilating over a great part of the world, and that in the most miserable part of our year there is very little to choose between London and Paris, except that London is not so muddy. I have never seen dirtier or worse weather than we have had here since I returned. In desperation I went out to the Barrières last Sunday on a headlong walk, and came back with my very eyebrows smeared with mud. Georgina is usually invisible during the walking time of the day. A turned-up nose may be seen in the midst of splashes, but nothing more.

I am settling to work again, and my horrible restlessness immediately assails me. It belongs to such times. As I was writing the preceding page, it suddenly came into my head that I would get up and go to Calais. I don't know why; the moment I got there I should want to go somewhere else. But, as my friend the Boots says (see Christmas number "Household Words"): "When you come to think what a game you've been up to ever since you was in your own cradle, and what a poor sort of chap you are, and how it's always yesterday with you, or else to-morrow, and never to-day, that's where it is."

My dear Mary, would you favour me with the name and address of the professor that taught you writing, for I want to improve myself? Many a hand have I seen with many characteristics of beauty in it—some loopy, some dashy, some large, some small, some sloping to the right, some sloping to the left, some not sloping at all; but what I like in *your* hand, Mary, is its plainness, it is like print. Them as runs may read just as well as if they stood still. I should have thought it was copper-plate if I hadn't known you. They send all sorts of messages from here, and so do I, with my best regards to Bedgy and pardner and the blessed babbies. When shall we meet again, I wonder, and go somewhere! Ah!—

Believe me ever, my dear Mary,
Yours truly and affectionately,
JOE.

(That doesn't look plain.)

JOE.

"HOUSEHOLD WORDS," Miss
Friday, Eighth February, 1856. Hogarth.

MY DEAR GEORGY,

I must write this at railroad speed, for I have been at it all day, and have numbers of letters to cram into the next half-hour. I began the morning in the City, for the Theatrical Fund; went on to Shepherd's Bush; came back to leave cards for Mr. Baring and Mr. Bates; ran across Piccadilly to Stratton Street, stayed there an hour, and shot off here. Am going to dine with Mark and Webster at half-past four, and finish the evening at the Adelphi.

The dinner was very successful. Charley was in great force, and floored Peter Cunningham and the Audit Office on a question about some bill transactions with Barings'. The other guests were Bradbury and Evans, Shirley Brooks, Forster, and that's all. The dinner admirable. I never had a better. All the wine I sent down from Tavistock House. Anne waited, and looked well and happy, very much brighter altogether. It gave me great pleasure to see her so improved. Just before dinner I got all the letters from home. They could not have arrived more opportunely.

The godfather's present looks charming now it is engraved, and John is just now going off to take it to Mrs. Yates. To-morrow Wills and I are going to Gad's Hill. It will occupy the whole day, and will just leave me time to get home to dress for dinner.

And that's all that I have to say, except that I am grieved to hear about the Plorn's black eye, and fear that I shall find it in the green and purple state on my return.

Ever affectionately.

<table>
<tr><td>Mr. Douglas
Jerrold.</td><td style="text-align:right">" HOUSEHOLD WORDS " OFFICE,
Sixth March, 1856.</td></tr>
</table>

MY DEAR JERROLD,

Buckstone has been with me to-day in a state of demi-semi-distraction, by reason of Macready's dreading his asthma so much as to excuse himself (of necessity, I know) from taking the chair for the fund on the occasion of their next dinner. I have promised to back Buckstone's entreaty to you to take it; and although I know that you have an objection which you once communicated to me, I still hold (as I did then) that it is a reason *for*, and not against. Pray reconsider the point. Your position in connection with dramatic literature has always suggested to me that there would be a great fitness and grace in your appearing in this post. I am convinced that the public would regard it in that light, and I particularly ask you to reflect that we never can do battle with the Lords, if we will not bestow ourselves to go into places which they have long monopolised. Now pray discuss this matter with yourself once more. If you can come to a favourable conclusion I shall be really delighted, and will of course come from Paris to be by you; if you cannot come to a favourable conclusion I shall be really sorry, though I of course most readily defer to your right to regard such a matter from your own point of view.

Ever faithfully yours.

"HOUSEHOLD WORDS,
Friday, Fourteenth March, 1856.

MY DEAR GEORGY,

I am amazed to hear of the snow (I don't know why, but it excited John this morning beyond measure); though we have had the same east wind here, and *the* cold and *my* cold have both been intense.

Yesterday evening Webster, Mark, Stanny, and I went to the Olympic, where the Wigans ranged us in a row in a gorgeous and immense private box, and where we saw "Still Waters Run Deep." I laughed (in a conspicuous manner) to that extent at Emery, when he received the dinner-company, that the people were more amused by me than by the piece. I don't think I ever saw anything meant to be funny that struck me as so extraordinarily droll. I couldn't get over it at all. After the piece we went round, by Wigan's invitation, to drink with him. It being positively impossible to get Stanny off the stage, we stood in the wings during the burlesque. Mrs. Wigan seemed really glad to see her old manager, and the company overwhelmed him with embraces. They had nearly all been at the meeting in the morning.

This day I have paid the purchase-money for Gad's Hill Place. After drawing the cheque, I turned round to give it to Wills (£1790), and said: "Now isn't it an extraordinary thing—look at the day—Friday! I have been nearly drawing it half-a-dozen times, when the lawyers have not been ready, and here it comes round upon a Friday, as a matter of course."

Kiss the noble Plorn a dozen times for me, and tell him I drank his health yesterday, and wished him many happy returns of the day; also that I hope he will not have broken all his toys before I come back.

Ever affectionately.

49, CHAMPS ELYSÉES, PARIS,
Saturday, Twenty-second March, 1856.

MY DEAR MACREADY,

I want you—you being quite well again, as I trust you are, and resolute to come to Paris—so to arrange your order of march as to let me know beforehand when you will come and how long you will stay. We owe Scribe and his wife a dinner, and I should like to pay the debt when you are with us. Ary Scheffer too would be delighted to see you again. If I could arrange for a certain day I would secure them. We cannot afford (you and I, I mean) to keep much company, because we shall have to look in at a theatre or so, I daresay!

It would suit my work best, if I could keep myself clear until Monday, the Seventh of April. But in case that day should be too late for the beginning of your brief visit with a deference to any other engagements you have in contemplation, then fix an earlier one, and I will make "Little Dorrit" curtsy to it. My recent visit to London and my having only just now come back have thrown me a little behindhand : but I hope to come up with a wet sail in a few days.

You should have seen the ruins of Covent Garden Theatre ! I went in the moment I got to London—four days after the fire. Although the audience part and the stage were so tremendously burnt out that there was not a piece of wood half the size of a lucifer-match for the eye to rest on, though nothing whatever remained but bricks and smelted iron lying on a great black desert, the theatre still looked so wonderfully like its old self grown gigantic that I never saw so strange a sight. The wall dividing the front from the stage still remained, and the iron pass-doors stood ajar in an impossible and inaccessible frame. The arches that supported the stage were there, and the arches that supported the pit; and in the centre of the latter lay something like a Titanic grape-vine that a hurricane had pulled up by the roots, twisted, and flung down there; this was the great chandelier. Gye had kept the men's wardrobe at the top of the house over the great entrance staircase ; when the roof fell in it came down bodily, and all that part of the ruins was like an old Babylonic pavement, bright rays tesselating the black ground, sometimes in pieces so large that I could make out the clothes in the "Trovatore."

I should run on for a couple of hours if I had to describe the spectacle as I saw it, wherefore I will immediately muzzle myself. All Parisian novelties you shall see and hear for yourself.

Ever, my dearest Macready,

Your affectionate Friend.

P.S.—Mr. F.'s aunt sends her defiant respects.

Mr. W. C. Macready.

49, AVENUE DES CHAMPS ELYSÉES, PARIS, *Thursday Night, Twenty-seventh March,* 1856. (*After post time.*)

MY DEAREST MACREADY,

If I had had any idea of your coming (see how naturally I use the word when I am three hundred miles off !) to London so soon, I would never have written one word about the jump over next week. I am vexed that I did so, but as I did I will not now propose a change in the arrangements, as I know how methodical you tremendously old fellows are. That's your secret I suspect.

That's the way in which the blood of the Mirabels mounts in your aged veins, even at your time of life.

How charmed I shall be to see you, and we all shall be, I will not attempt to say. On that expected Sunday you will lunch at Amiens but not dine, because we shall wait dinner for you, and you will merely have to tell that driver in the glazed hat to come straight here. When the Whites left I added their little apartment to this little apartment, consequently you shall have a snug bedroom (is it not waiting expressly for you?) overlooking the Champs Élysées. As to the arm-chair in my heart, no man on earth——but, good God! you know all about it.

You will find us in the queerest of little rooms all alone, except that the son of Collins the painter (who writes a good deal in "Household Words") dines with us every day. Scheffer and Scribe shall be admitted for one evening, because they know how to appreciate you. The Emperor we will not ask unless you expressly wish it; it makes a fuss.

If you have no appointed hotel at Boulogne, go to the Hôtel des Bains, there demand "Marguerite," and tell her that I commended you to her special care. It is the best house within my experience in France; Marguerite the best housekeeper in the world.

I shall charge at "Little Dorrit" to-morrow with new spirits. The sight of you is good for my boyish eyes, and the thought of you for my dawning mind. Give the enclosed lines a welcome, then send them on to Sherborne.

Ever yours, most affectionately and truly.

49, CHAMPS ELYSÉES, PARIS,
Sunday, Sixth April, 1856.

MY DEAR WILLS,

CHRISTMAS.

Collins and I have a mighty original notion (mine in the beginning) for another play at Tavistock House. I propose opening on Twelfth Night the theatrical season of that great establishment. But now a tremendous question. Is

MRS. WILLS!

game to do a Scotch housekeeper, in a supposed country-house, with Mary, Katey, Georgina, etc.? If she can screw her courage up to saying "Yes," that country-house opens the piece in a singular way, and that Scotch housekeeper's part shall flow from the present pen. If she says "No" (but she won't), no Scotch housekeeper can be. The Tavistock House season of four nights pauses for a reply. Scotch song (new and original) of Scotch housekeeper would pervade the piece.

You

, had better pause for breath.

Ever faithfully.

Mrs. Charles
Dickens.

TAVISTOCK HOUSE, *Monday, Fifth May*, 1856.

MY DEAR CATHERINE,

I did nothing at Dover (except for "Household Words"), and have not begun "Little Dorrit," No. 8, yet. But I took twenty-mile walks in the fresh air, and perhaps in the long run did better than if I had been at work. The report concerning Scheffer's portrait I had from Ward. It is in the best place in the largest room, but I find the *general* impression of the artists exactly mine. They almost all say that it wants something; that nobody could mistake whom it was meant for, but that it has something disappointing in it, etc. etc. Stanfield likes it better than any one of the other painters, I think. His own picture is magnificent. And Frith, in a "Little Child's Birthday Party," is quite delightful. There are many interesting pictures. When you see Scheffer, tell him from me that Eastlake, in his speech at the dinner, referred to the portrait as "a contribution from a distinguished man of genius in France, worthy of himself and of his subject." The school-room and dining-room I have brought into habitable condition and comfortable appearance. Charley and I breakfast at half-past eight, and meet again at dinner when he does not dine in the City, or has no engagement. He looks very well.

The audiences at Gye's are described to me as absolute marvels of coldness. No signs of emotion can be hammered out of them. Panizzi sat next me at the Academy dinner, and took it very ill that I disparaged ———. The amateurs here are getting up another pantomime, but quarrel so violently among themselves that I doubt its ever getting on the stage. Webster expounded his scheme for rebuilding the Adelphi to Stanfield and myself last night, and I felt bound to tell him that I thought it wrong from beginning to end. This is all the theatrical news I know.

Ever affectionately.

Miss
Hogarth.

TAVISTOCK HOUSE, *Monday, Fifth May*, 1856.

MY DEAR GEORGY,

You will not be much surprised to hear that I have done nothing yet (except for H. W.), and have only just settled down into a corner of the schoolroom. The extent to which John and I wallowed in dust for four hours yesterday morning, getting things neat and comfortable about us, you may faintly imagine. At four in the afternoon came Stanfield, to whom I no sooner described the notion of the new play, than he immediately upset all my new arrangements by making a proscenium of the chairs, and planning the scenery with walking-sticks. One of the least things he did was getting on the top of the long table, and hanging over the bar in the middle window where that top sash opens, as if he had got a hinge in the middle of his body. He is immensely excited on the subject. Mark has a farce ready for the managerial perusal, but it won't do.

I went to Dover theatre on Friday night, which was a miserable spectacle. The pit is boarded over, and it is a drinking and smoking place. It was "for the benefit of Mrs. ——," and the town had been very extensively placarded with "Don't forget Friday." I made out four and ninepence (I am serious) in the house, when I went in. We may have warmed up in the course of the evening to twelve shillings. A Jew played the grand piano; Mrs. —— sang no end of songs (with not a bad voice, poor creature); Mr. —— sang comic songs fearfully, and danced clog hornpipes capitally; and a miserable woman, shivering in a shawl and bonnet, sat in the side-boxes all the evening, nursing Master ——, aged seven months. It was a most forlorn business, and I should have contributed a sovereign to the treasury if I had known how.

I walked to Deal and back that day, and on the previous day walked over the downs towards Canterbury in a gale of wind. It was better than still weather after all, being wonderfully fresh and free.

If the Plorn were sitting at this schoolroom window in the corner, he would see more cats in an hour than he ever saw in his life. I never saw so many, I think, as I have seen since yesterday morning.

There is a painful picture of a great deal of merit (Egg has bought it) in the exhibition, painted by the man who did those little interiors of Forster's. It is called "The Death of Chatterton." The dead figure is a good deal like Arthur Stone; and I was touched on Saturday to see that tender old file standing before it, crying under his spectacles at the idea of seeing his son dead. It was a very tender manifestation of his gentle old heart.

This sums up my news, which is no news at all. Kiss the Plorn for me, and expound to him that I am always looking forward to meeting him again, among the birds and flowers in the garden on the side of the hill at Boulogne.

Ever affectionately.

Mr. T. Ross.
Mr. J.
Kenny.

GENTLEMEN,

I have received a letter signed by you (which I assume to be written mainly on behalf of what are called Working-Men and their families) inviting me to attend a meeting in our Parish Vestry Hall this evening on the subject of the stoppage of the Sunday bands in the Parks.

I thoroughly agree with you that those bands have afforded an innocent and healthful enjoyment on the Sunday afternoon, to which the people have a right. But I think it essential that the working people should, of themselves and by themselves, assert that right. They have been informed, on the high authority of their first Minister (lately rather in want of House of Commons votes, I am told), that they are almost indifferent to it. The correction of that mistake, if official omniscience can be mistaken, lies with themselves. In case it should be considered by the meeting, which I prefer for this reason not to attend, expedient to unite with other Metropolitan parishes in forming a fund for the payment of such expenses as may be incurred in peaceably and numerously representing to the governing powers that the harmless recreation they have taken away is very much wanted, I beg you to put down my name as a subscriber of ten pounds.

And I am, your faithful Servant.

The Duke of
Devonshire.

MY DEAR DUKE OF DEVONSHIRE,

Allow me to thank you with all my heart for your kind remembrance of me on Thursday night. My house was already engaged to Miss Coutts', and I to—the top of St. Paul's, where the sight was most wonderful! But seeing that your cards gave me leave to present some person not named, I conferred them on my excellent friend Dr. Elliotson, whom I found with some fire-workless little boys in a desolate condition, and raised to the seventh heaven of happiness. You are so fond of making people happy, that I am sure you approve.

Always your faithful and much obliged.

Mr. W.
Wilkie
Collins.

MY DEAR COLLINS,

I have never seen anything about myself in print which has much correctness in it—any biographical account of myself I mean. I do not supply such particulars when I am asked for them by editors and compilers, simply because I am asked for them every day. If you want to prime Forgues, you may tell him without fear of anything wrong, that I was born at Portsmouth on the Seventh of February, 1812; that my father was in the Navy Pay Office; that I was taken by him to Chatham when I was very young, and lived and was educated there till I was twelve or thirteen, I suppose; that I was then put to a school near London, where (as at other places) I distinguished myself like a brick; that I was put in the office of a solicitor, a friend of my father's, and didn't much like it: and after a couple of years (as well as I can remember) applied myself with a celestial or diabolical energy to the study of such things as would qualify me to be a first-rate parliamentary reporter—at that time a calling pursued by many clever men who were young at the Bar; that I made my début in the gallery (at about eighteen, I suppose), engaged on a voluminous publication no longer in existence, called *The Mirror of Parliament*; that when *The Morning Chronicle* was purchased by Sir John Easthope, and acquired a large circulation, I was engaged there, and that I remained there until I had begun to publish "Pickwick," when I found myself in a condition to relinquish that part of my labours; that I left the reputation behind me of being the best and most rapid reporter ever known, and that I could do anything in that way under any sort of circumstances, and often did. (I daresay I am at this present writing the best shorthand writer in the world.)

That I began, without any interest or introduction of any kind, to write fugitive pieces for the old "Monthly Magazine," when I was in the gallery for *The Mirror of Parliament*; that my faculty for descriptive writing was seized upon the moment I joined *The Morning Chronicle*, and that I was liberally paid there and handsomely acknowledged, and wrote the greater part of the short descriptive "Sketches by Boz" in that paper; that I had been a writer when I was a mere baby, and always an actor from the same age; that I married the daughter of a writer to the signet in Edinburgh, who was the great friend and assistant of Scott, and who first made Lockhart known to him.

And that here I am.

Finally, if you want any dates of publication of books, tell Wills and he'll get them for you.

This is the first time I ever set down even these particulars, and, glancing them over, I feel like a wild beast in a caravan describing himself in the keeper's absence.

                                                      Ever faithfully.

P.S.—I made a speech last night at the London Tavern, at the end of which all the company sat holding their napkins to their eyes with one hand, and putting the other into their pockets. A hundred people or so contributed nine hundred pounds then and there.

Mr. Mark
Lemon.

VILLA DES MOULINEAUX, BOULOGNE,
Sunday, Fifteenth June, 1856.

MY DEAR OLD BOY,

This place is beautiful—a burst of roses. Your friend Beaucourt (who *will not* put on his hat) has thinned the trees and greatly improved the garden. Upon my life, I believe there are at least twenty distinct smoking-spots expressly made in it.

And as soon as you can see your day in next month for coming over with Stanny and Webster, will you let them both know?

There is a fête here to-night in honour of the Imperial baptism, and there will be another to-morrow. The Plorn has put on two bits of ribbon (one pink and one blue), which he calls "companys," to celebrate the occasion. The fact that the receipts of the fêtes are to be given to the sufferers by the late floods reminds me that you will find at the passport office a tin-box, condescendingly and considerately labelled in English:

FOR THE OVERFLOWINGS,

which the chief officer clearly believes to mean, for the sufferers from the inundations.

I observe more "Mingles" in the laundresses' shops, and one inscription, which looks like the name of a duet or chorus in a playbill, "Here they mingle."

And that is all my present intelligence.

Ever affectionately.

The same.

H. W. OFFICE, *Second July,* 1856.

MY DEAR MARK,

I am concerned to hear that you are ill, that you sit down before fires and shiver, and that you have stated times for doing so, like the demons in the melodramas, and that you mean to take a week to get well in.

Make haste about it, like a dear fellow, and keep up your spirits, because I have made a bargain with Stanny and Webster that they shall come to Boulogne to-morrow week, Thursday the Tenth, and stay a week. And you know how much pleasure we shall all miss if you are not among us—at least for some part of the time.

If you find any unusually light appearance in the air at Brighton, it is a distant refraction (I have no doubt) of the gorgeous and shining surface of Tavistock House, now transcendently painted. The theatre partition is put up, and is a work of such terrific solidity, that I suppose it will be dug up, ages hence, from the ruins of London, by that Australian of Macaulay's who is to be impressed by its ashes. I have wandered through the spectral halls of the Tavistock mansion two nights, with feelings of the profoundest depression. I have breakfasted there, like a criminal in Pentonville (only not so well). It is more like Westminster Abbey by midnight than the lowest-spirited man—say you at present for example—can well imagine.

There has been a wonderful robbery at Folkestone, by the new manager of the Pavilion, who succeeded Giovannini. He had in keeping £16,000 of a foreigner's, and bolted with it, as he supposed, but in reality with only £1400 of it. The Frenchman had previously bolted with the whole, which was the property of his mother. With him to England the Frenchman brought a "lady," who was, all the time and at the same time, endeavouring to steal all the money from him and bolt with it herself. The details are amazing, and all the money (a few pounds excepted) has been got back.

Ever, my dear Boy, your affectionate Friend.

TAVISTOCK HOUSE,* *London, Fifth July,* 1856.   Mr. Washington Irving.

MY DEAR IRVING,

If you knew how often I write to you individually and personally in my books, you would be no more surprised in seeing this note than you were in seeing me do my duty by that flowery julep (in what I dreamily apprehend to have been a former state of existence) at Baltimore.

Will you let me present to you a cousin of mine, Mr. B———, who is associated with a merchant's house in New York? Of course he wants to see you, and know you. How can *I* wonder at that? How can anybody?

I had a long talk with Leslie at the last Academy dinner (having previously been with him in Paris), and he told me that you were flourishing. I suppose you know that he wears a moustache—so do I for the matter of that, and a beard too—and that he looks like a portrait of Don Quixote.

Holland House has four-and-twenty youthful pages in it now— twelve for my lord, and twelve for my lady; and no clergyman coils his leg up under his chair all dinner-time, and begins to uncurve it when the hostess goes. No wheeled chair runs smoothly in with that beaming face in it; and ———'s little cotton pocket-handkerchief helped to make (I believe) this very sheet of

* Written at Boulogne, on paper with London address printed on it.

paper. A half-sad, half-ludicrous story of Rogers is all I will sully it with. You know, I daresay, that for a year or so before his death he wandered, and lost himself like one of the Children in the Wood, grown up there and grown down again. He had Mrs. Procter and Mrs. Carlyle to breakfast with him one morning—only those two. Both excessively talkative, very quick and clever, and bent on entertaining him. When Mrs. Carlyle had flashed and shone before him for about three-quarters of an hour on one subject, he turned his poor old eyes on Mrs. Procter, and pointing to the brilliant discourser with his poor old finger, said (indignantly), "Who is *she?*" Upon this, Mrs. Procter, cutting in, delivered (it is her own story) a neat oration on the life and writings of Carlyle, and enlightened him in her happiest and airiest manner; all of which he heard, staring in the dreariest silence, and then said (indignantly, as before), "And who are *you?*"   Ever, my dear Irving,

          Most affectionately and truly yours.

Mr. Walter
Savage
Landor.

          VILLA DES MOULINEAUX, BOULOGNE,
                    Saturday Evening, Fifth July 1856.

MY DEAR LANDOR,

          I write to you so often in my books, and my writing of letters is usually so confined to the numbers that I *must* write, and in which I have no kind of satisfaction, that I am afraid to think how long it is since we exchanged a direct letter. But talking to your namesake this very day at dinner, it suddenly entered my head that I would come into my room here as soon as dinner should be over, and write, "My dear Landor, how are you?" for the pleasure of having the answer under your own hand. That you *do* write, and that pretty often, I know beforehand. Else why do I read *The Examiner?*

We were in Paris from October to May (I perpetually flying between that city and London), and there we found out, by a blessed accident, that your godson was horribly deaf. I immediately consulted the principal physician of the Deaf and Dumb Institution there (one of the best aurists in Europe), and he kept the boy for three months, and took unheard-of pains with him. He is now quite recovered, has done extremely well at school, has brought home a prize in triumph, and will be eligible to "go up" for his India examination soon after next Easter. Having a direct appointment, he will probably be sent out soon after he has passed, and so will fall into that strange life "up the country," before he well knows he is alive, which indeed seems to be rather an advanced stage of knowledge.

And there in Paris, at the same time, I found Marguerite Power and little Nelly, living with their mother and a pretty sister, in a very small, neat apartment, and working (as Marguerite told me) hard for a living. All that I saw of them filled me with respect, and revived the tenderest remembrances of Gore House. They are coming to pass two or three weeks here for a country rest, next month. We had many long talks concerning Gore House, and all its bright associations; and I can honestly report that they hold no one in more gentle and affectionate remembrance than you. Marguerite is still handsome, though she had the small-pox two or three years ago, and bears the traces of it here and there, by daylight. Poor little Nelly (the quicker and more observant of the two) shows some little tokens of a broken-off marriage in a face too careworn for her years, but is a very winning and sensible creature.

We are expecting Mary Boyle too, shortly.

I have just been propounding to Forster if it is not a wonderful testimony to the homely force of truth, that one of the most popular books on earth has nothing in it to make anyone laugh or cry? Yet I think, with some confidence, that you never did either over any passage in "Robinson Crusoe." In particular, I took Friday's death as one of the least tender and (in the true sense) least sentimental things ever written. It is a book I read very much; and the wonder of its prodigious effect on me and everyone, and the admiration thereof, grows on me the more I observe this curious fact.

Kate and Georgina send you their kindest loves, and smile approvingly on me from the next room, as I bend over my desk. My dear Landor, you see many I daresay, and hear from many I have no doubt, who love you heartily; but we silent people in the distance never forget you. Do not forget us, and let us exchange affection at least. Ever your Admirer and Friend.

VILLA DES MOULINEAUX, NEAR BOULOGNE,   The Duke of
Saturday Night, Fifth July, 1856.   Devonshire.

MY DEAR DUKE OF DEVONSHIRE,

From this place where I am writing my way through the summer, in the midst of rosy gardens and sea airs, I cannot forbear writing to tell you with what uncommon pleasure I received your interesting letter, and how sensible I always am of your kindness and generosity. You were always in the mind of my household during your illness; and to have so beautiful, and fresh, and manly an assurance of your recovery from it, under your own hand, is a privilege and delight that I will say no more of.

I am so glad you like Flora. It came into my head one day that we have all had our Floras, and that it was a half-serious, half-ridiculous truth which had never been told. It is a wonderful gratification to me to find that everybody knows her. Indeed, some people seem to think I have done them a personal injury, and that their individual Floras (God knows where they are, or who !) are each and all Little Dorrit's !

We were all grievously disappointed that you were ill when we played Mr. Collins' "Lighthouse" at my house. If you had been well, I should have waited upon you with my humble petition that you would come and see it ; and if you had come I think you would have cried, which would have charmed me. I hope to produce another play at home next Christmas, and if I can only persuade you to see it from a special arm-chair, and can only make you wretched, my satisfaction will be intense. May I tell you, to beguile a moment, of a little "Tag," or end of a piece, I saw in Paris this last winter, which struck me as the prettiest I had ever met with ? The piece was not a new one, but a revival at the Vaudeville—"Les Mémoires du Diable." Admirably constructed, very interesting, and extremely well played. The plot is, that a certain M. Robin has come into possession of the papers of a deceased lawyer, and finds some relating to the wrongful withholding of an estate from a certain baroness, and to certain other frauds (involving even the denial of the marriage to the deceased baron, and the tarnishing of his good name) which are so very wicked that he binds them up in a book and labels them "Mémoires du Diable." Armed with this knowledge he goes down to the desolate old château in the country—part of the wrested-away estate—from which the baroness and her daughter are going to be ejected. He informs the mother that he can right her and restore the property, but must have, as his reward, her daughter's hand in marriage. She replies : "I cannot promise my daughter to a·man of whom I know nothing. The gain would be an unspeakable happiness, but I resolutely decline the bargain." The daughter, however, has observed all, and she comes forward and says : "Do what you have promised my mother you can do, and I am yours." Then the piece goes on to its development, in an admirable way, through the unmasking of all the hypocrites. Now, M. Robin, partly through his knowledge of the secret ways of the old château (derived from the lawyer's papers), and partly through his going to a masquerade as the devil—the better to explode what he knows on the hypocrites—is supposed by the servants at the château really to be the devil. At the opening of the last act he suddenly appears there before the young lady, and she screams, but, recovering and laughing, says : "You are not really the —— ? " "Oh dear no ! " he replies, "have no connection with him. But these people down here are so frightened and absurd ! See this little toy on the table ; I open it ; here's a little bell. They have a notion that whenever this bell rings I shall appear. Very ignorant, is it not ? " "Very, indeed," says she. "Well," says M. Robin, "if you should want me very much to appear, try the bell, if only for a jest. Will you promise ? " Yes, she promises, and the play goes on. At last he has righted the baroness completely, and has only to hand her the last document, which proves her marriage and restores her good name. Then he says : "Madame, in the progress of these endeavours I have learnt the happiness of doing good for its own sake. I made a necessary bargain with you : I release you from it. I have done what I undertook to do. I wish you and your amiable daughter all happiness. Adieu ! I take my leave." Bows himself out. People on the stage astonished. Audience astonished—incensed. The daughter is going to cry, when she looks at the box on the table, remembers the bell, runs to it and rings it, and he rushes back and takes her to his heart ; upon which we all cry with pleasure, and then laugh heartily.

This looks dreadfully long, and perhaps you know it already. If so, I will endeavour to make amends with Flora in future numbers.

I saw Paxton* now and then when you were ill, and always received from him most encouraging accounts. I don't know how heavy he is going to be (I mean in the scale), but I begin to think Daniel Lambert must have been in his family.

Ever your Grace's faithful and obliged.

Mr. W. C.
Macready.

VILLA DES MOULINEAUX, BOULOGNE,
Tuesday, Eighth July, 1856.

MY DEAREST MACREADY,

I perfectly agree with you in your appreciation of Katie's poem, and shall be truly delighted to publish it in "Household Words." It shall go into the very next number we make up. We are a little in advance (to enable Wills to get a holiday), but as I remember, the next number made up will be published in three weeks.

We are pained indeed to read your reference to my poor boy. God keep him and his father. I trust he is not conscious of much suffering himself. If that be so, it is, in the midst of the distress, a great comfort.

* Sir Joseph Paxton.

"Little Dorrit" keeps me pretty busy as you may suppose. The beginning of No. 10—the first line—now lies upon my desk. It would not be easy to increase upon the pains I take with her anyhow.

We are expecting Stanfield on Thursday, and Peter Cunningham and his wife on Monday. I would we were expecting you! This is as pretty and odd a little French country house as could be found anywhere; and the gardens are most beautiful.

In "Household Words," next week, pray read "The Diary of Anne Rodway" (in two not long parts). It is by Collins, and I think possesses great merit and real pathos.

Being in town the other day, I saw Gye by accident, and told him, when he praised —— to me, that she was a very bad actress. "Well!" said he, "you may say anything, but if anybody else had told me that I should have stared." Nevertheless, I derived an impression from his manner that she had not been a profitable speculation in respect of money. That very same day Stanfield and I dined alone together at the Garrick, and drank your health. We had had a ride by the river before dinner (of course he would go and look at boats), and had been talking of you.

I know of nothing of public interest that is new in France, except that I am changing my moustache into a beard.

Ever, my dearest Macready,

Most affectionately yours.

Mr. Frank
Stone,
A.R.A.

VILLA DES MOULINEAUX, BOULOGNE,
Wednesday, Ninth July, 1856.

MY DEAR STONE,

I have got a capital part for you in the farce,* not a difficult one to learn, as you never say anything but "Yes" and "No." You are called in the *dramatis personæ* an able-bodied British seaman, and you are never seen by mortal eye to do anything (except inopportunely producing a mop) but stand about the deck of the boat in everybody's way, with your hair immensely touzled, one brace on, your hands in your pockets, and the bottoms of your trousers tucked up. Yet you are inextricably connected with the plot, and are the man whom everybody is enquiring after. I think it is a very whimsical idea and extremely droll. It made me laugh heartily when I jotted it all down yesterday.

Ever affectionately.

* The farce alluded to, however, was never written.

VILLA DES MOULINEAUX, BOULOGNE,
Sunday, Thirteenth July, 1856.

Mr. W.
Wilkie
Collins.

MY DEAR COLLINS,

We are all sorry that you are not coming until the middle of next month, but we hope that you will then be able to remain, so that we may all come back together about the Tenth of October. I think (recreation allowed, etc.) that the play will take that time to write. The ladies of the *dram. pers.* are frightfully anxious to get it under way, and to see you locked up in the pavilion ; apropos of which noble edifice I have omitted to mention that it is made a more secluded retreat than it used to be, and is greatly improved by the position of the door being changed. It is as snug and as pleasant as possible ; and the Genius of Order has made a few little improvements about the house (at the rate of about tenpence apiece), which the Genius of Disorder will, it is hoped, appreciate.

I cannot tell you what a high opinion I have of Anne Rodway. I took " Extracts " out of the title because it conveyed to the many-headed an idea of incompleteness—of something unfinished—and is likely to stall some readers off. I read the first part at the office with strong admiration, and read the second on the railway coming back here, being in town just after you had started on your cruise. My behaviour before my fellow-passengers was weak in the extreme, for I cried as much as you could possibly desire. Apart from the genuine force and beauty of the little narrative, and the admirable personation of the girl's identity and point of view, it is done with an amount of honest pains and devotion to the work which few men have better reason to appreciate than I, and which no man can have a more profound respect for. I think it excellent, feel a personal pride and pleasure in it which is a delightful sensation, and know no one else who could have done it.

Of myself I have only to report that I have been hard at it with " Little Dorrit." This last week I sketched out the notion, characters, and progress of the farce, and sent it off to Mark, who has been ill of an ague. It ought to be very funny. The cat business is too ludicrous to be treated of in so small a sheet of paper, so I must describe it *vivâ voce* when I come to town. French has been so insufferably conceited since he shot tigerish cat No. 1 (intent on the noble Dick, with green eyes three inches in advance of her head), that I am afraid I shall have to part with him. All the boys likewise (in new clothes and ready for church) are at this instant prone on their stomachs behind bushes, whoosh-ing and crying (after tigerish cat No. 2) : " French ! " " Here she comes ! " " There she goes ! " etc. I dare not put my head out of window for fear of being shot (it is as like a *coup d'état* as

possible), and tradesmen coming up the avenue cry plaintively:
"*Ne tirez pas, Monsieur Fleench; c'est moi—boulanger. Ne tirez
pas, mon ami.*"

Likewise I shall have to recount to you the secret history of a
robbery at the Pavilion at Folkestone, which you will have to
write.

Tell Piggot, when you see him, that we shall all be much
pleased if he will come down at his own convenience while you are
here, and stay a few days with us.

I shall have more than one notion of future work to suggest to
you while we are beguiling the dreariness of an arctic winter in
these parts. May they prosper!

Kind regards from all to the dramatic poet of the establishment,
and to the D. P.'s mother and brother.

Ever yours.

P.S.—If "The Flying Dutchman" should be done again, pray
do go and see it. Webster expressed his opinion to me that it was
"a neat piece." I implore you to go and see a neat piece.

Mr. W. H.
Wills.

Boulogne, *Thursday, Seventh August,* 1856.

My dear Wills,

I do not feel disposed to record those two Chancery cases;
firstly, because I would rather have no part in engendering in the
mind of any human creature, a hopeful confidence in that den of
iniquity.

And secondly, because it seems to me that the real philosophy
of the facts is altogether missed in the narrative. The wrong
which chanced to be set right in these two cases was done, as all
such wrong is, mainly because these wicked courts of equity, with
all their means of evasion and postponement, give scoundrels confidence in cheating. If justice were cheap, sure, and speedy, few such
things could be. It is because it has become (through the vile
dealing of those courts and the vermin they have called into
existence) a positive precept of experience that a man had better
endure a great wrong than go, or suffer himself to be taken, into
Chancery, with the dream of setting it right. It is because of this
that such nefarious speculations are made.

Therefore I see nothing at all to the credit of Chancery in these
cases, but everything to its discredit. And as to owing it to
Chancery to bear testimony to its having rendered justice in two
such plain matters, I have no debt of the kind upon my conscience.

In haste, ever faithfully.

BOULOGNE, *Friday, Eighth August,* 1856.

MY DEAREST MACREADY,

I like the second little poem very much indeed, and think (as you do) that it is a great advance upon the first. Please to note that I make it a rule to pay for everything that is inserted in "Household Words," holding it to be a part of my trust to make my fellow-proprietors understand that they have no right to unrequited labour. Therefore, when Wills (who has been ill and is gone for a holiday) does his invariable spiriting gently, don't make Katey's case different from Adelaide Procter's.

I am afraid there is no possibility of my reading Dorsetshirewards. I have made many conditional promises thus: "I am very much occupied; but if I read at all, I will read for your institution in such an order on my list." Edinburgh, which is No. 1, I have been obliged to put as far off as next Christmas twelvemonth. Bristol stands next. The working men at Preston come next. And so, if I were to go out of the record and read for your people, I should bring such a house about my ears as would shake "Little Dorrit" out of my head.

Being in town last Saturday, I went to see Robson in a burlesque of "Medea." It is an odd but perfectly true testimony to the extraordinary power of his performance (which is of a very remarkable kind indeed), that it points the badness of ——'s acting in a most singular manner, by bringing out what she might do and does not. The scene with Jason is perfectly terrific; and the manner in which the comic rage and jealousy does not pitch itself over the floor at the stalls is in striking contrast to the manner in which the tragic rage and jealousy does. He has a frantic song and dagger dance, about ten minutes long altogether, which has more passion in it than —— could express in fifty years.

Ever, my dear Macready, affectionately yours.

TAVISTOCK HOUSE, *Sunday Morning,* *Twenty-eighth September,* 1856.

MY DEAR WILLS,

I suddenly remember this morning that in Mr. Curtis' article, "Health and Education," I left a line which must come out. It is in effect that the want of healthy training leaves girls in a fit state to be the subjects of mesmerism. I would not on any condition hurt Elliotson's feelings (as I should deeply) by leaving that depreciatory kind of reference in any page of H. W. He has suffered quite enough without a stab from a friend. So pray, whatever the inconvenience may be in what Bradbury calls "the Friars," take that passage out. By some extraordinary accident, after observing it, I forgot to do it.

Ever faithfully.

TAVISTOCK HOUSE, *Saturday, Fourth October*, 1856.

MY DEAR MAMEY,

The preparations for the play are already beginning, and it is christened (this is a great dramatic secret, which I suppose you know already) "The Frozen Deep."

Tell Katey, with my best love, that if she fail to come back six times as red, hungry, and strong as she was when she went away, I shall give her part to somebody else.

We shall all be very glad to see you both back again. When I say "we" I include the birds (who send their respectful duty) and the Plorn.

Ever, my dear Mamey, your affectionate Father.

TAVISTOCK HOUSE, *Tuesday, Seventh October*, 1856.

MY DEAR MRS. WATSON,

I *did* write it for you; and I hoped, in writing it, that you would think so. All those remembrances are fresh in my mind, as they often are, and gave me an extraordinary interest in recalling the past. I should have been grievously disappointed if you had not been pleased, for I took aim at you with a most determined intention.

Let me congratulate you most heartily on your handsome Eddy having passed his examination with such credit. I am sure there is a spirit shining out of his eyes, which will do well in that manly and generous pursuit. You will naturally feel his departure very much, and so will he; but I have always observed within my experience, that the men who have left home young have, many long years afterwards, had the tenderest love for it, and for all associated with it. That's a pleasant thing to think of, as one of the wise and benevolent adjustments in these lives of ours.

I have been so hard at work (and shall be for the next eight or nine months), that sometimes I fancy I have a digestion, or a head, or nerves, or some odd encumbrance of that kind, to which I am altogether unaccustomed, and am obliged to rush at some other object for relief; at present the house is in a state of tremendous excitement, on account of Mr. Collins having nearly finished the new play we are to act at Christmas, which is very interesting and extremely clever. I hope this time you will come and see it. We purpose producing it on Charley's birthday, Twelfth Night; but we shall probably play four nights altogether—"The Lighthouse " on the last occasion—so that if you could come for the two last nights, you would see both the pieces. I am going to try and do better than ever, and already the schoolroom is in the hands of carpenters; men from underground habitations in theatres, who look as if they lived entirely upon smoke and gas, meet me at unheard-of hours. Mr. Stanfield is perpetually measuring the boards with a chalked piece of string and an umbrella, and all the elder children are wildly punctual and businesslike to attract managerial commendation. If you don't come, I shall do something antagonistic—try to unwrite No 11, I think. I should particularly like you to see a new and serious piece so done. Because I don't think you know, without seeing, how good it is!!!

None of the children suffered, thank God, from the Boulogne risk. The three little boys have gone back to school there, and are all well. Katey came away ill, but it turned out that she had the whooping-cough for the second time. She has been to Brighton, and comes home to-day. I hear great accounts of her, and I hope to find her quite well when she arrives presently. I am afraid Mary Boyle has been praising the Boulogne life too highly. Not that I deny, however, our having passed some very pleasant days together, and our having had great pleasure in her visit.

You will object to me dreadfully, I know, with a beard (though not a great one); but if you come and see the play, you will find it necessary there, and will perhaps be more tolerant of the fearful object afterwards. I need not tell you how delighted we should be to see George, if you would come together. Pray tell him so, with my kind regards. I like the notion of Wentworth and his philosophy of all things. I remember a philosophical gravity upon him, a state of suspended opinion as to myself, it struck me, when we last met, in which I thought there was a great deal of oddity and character.

Charley is doing very well at Baring's, and attracting praise and reward to himself. Within this fortnight there turned up from the West Indies, where he is now a chief justice, an old friend of mine, of my own age, who lived with me in lodgings in the Adelphi, when I was just Charley's age. He had a great affection for me at that time, and always supposed I was to do some sort of wonders. It was a very pleasant meeting indeed, and he seemed to think it so odd that I shouldn't be Charley!

This is every atom of no-news that will come out of my head, and I firmly believe it is all I have in it—except that a cobbler at Boulogne, who had the nicest of little dogs, that always sat in his sunny window watching him at work, asked me if I would bring the dog home, as he couldn't afford to pay the tax for him. The cobbler and the dog being both my particular friends, I complied. The cobbler parted with the dog heart-broken. When the dog got home here, my man, like an idiot as he is, tied him up and then untied him. The moment the gate was open, the dog (on the very day after his arrival) ran out. Next day, Georgy and I saw him lying, all covered with mud, dead, outside the neighbouring church. How am I ever to tell the cobbler? He is too poor to come to England, so I feel that I must lie to him for life, and say that the dog is fat and happy. Mr. Plornish, much affected by this tragedy, said: "I s'pose, pa, I shall meet the cobbler's dog" (in heaven).

Pray write to me again some day, and I can't be too busy to be happy in the sight of your familiar hand, associated in my mind with so much that I love and honour.

Ever, my dear Mrs. Watson, most faithfully yours.

Mrs. Horne.   TAVISTOCK HOUSE, TAVISTOCK SQUARE,
                                    October Twentieth, 1856.

MY DEAR MRS. HORNE,

I answer your note by return of post, in order that you may know that the Stereoscopic Nottage has not written to me yet. Of course I will not lose a moment in replying to him when he does address me.

We shall be greatly pleased to see you again. You have been very, very often in our thoughts and on our lips, during this long interval.

And "she" is near you, is she? O I remember her well! And I am still of my old opinion! Passionately devoted to her sex as I am (they are the weakness of my existence), I still consider her a failure.. She had some extraordinary christian-name, which I forget. Lashed into verse by my feelings, I am inclined to write:

> My heart disowns
> Ophelia Jones;

only I think it was a more sounding name.

> Are these the tones—
> Volumnia Jones?

No. Again it seems doubtful.

> God bless her bones,
> Petronia Jones.

I think not.

> Carve I on stones
> Olympia Jones.

Can *that* be the name? Fond memory favours it more than any other. My love to her.

Ever, my dear Mrs. Horne, very faithfully yours.

TAVISTOCK HOUSE, *First December*, 1856. The Duke of Devonshire.

MY DEAR DUKE OF DEVONSHIRE,

The moment the first bill is printed for the first night of the new play I told you of, I send it to you, in the hope that you will grace it with your presence. There is not one of the old actors whom you will fail to inspire as no one else can; and I hope you will see a little result of the friendly union of the arts, that you may think worth seeing, and that you can see nowhere else.

We propose repeating it on Thursday, the Eighth; Monday, the Twelfth; and Wednesday, the Fourteenth of January. I do not encumber this note with so many bills, and merely mention those nights in case any one of them should be more convenient to you than the first.

But I shall hope for the first, unless you dash me (N.B.—I put Flora into the current number on purpose that this might catch you softened towards me, and at a disadvantage). If there is hope of your coming, I will have the play clearly copied, and will send it to you to read beforehand. With the most grateful remembrances, and the sincerest good wishes for your health and happiness,

I am ever, my dear Duke of Devonshire,

Your faithful and obliged.

TAVISTOCK HOUSE, Mr. Thomas
Wednesday, Third December, 1856. Mitton.

MY DEAR MITTON,

The inspector from the fire office—surveyor, by-the-bye, they called him—duly came. Wills described him as not very pleasant in his manners. I derived the impression that he was so exceedingly dry, that if *he* ever takes fire, he must burn out, and can never otherwise be extinguished.

Next day I received a letter from the secretary, to say that the said surveyor had reported great additional risk from fire, and that the directors, at their meeting next Tuesday, would settle the extra amount of premium to be paid.

Thereupon I thought the matter was becoming complicated, and wrote a common-sense note to the secretary (which I begged might be read to the directors), saying that I was quite prepared to pay any extra premium, but setting forth the plain state of the case. (I did not say that the Lord Chief Justice, the Chief Baron, and half the Bench were coming; though I felt a temptation to make a joke about burning them all.)

Finally, this morning comes up the secretary to me (yesterday having been the great Tuesday), and says that he is requested by the directors to present their compliments, and to say that they could not think of charging for any additional risk at all; feeling convinced that I would place the gas (which they considered to be the only danger) under the charge of one competent man. I then explained to him how carefully and systematically that was all arranged, and we parted with drums beating and colours flying on both sides.

Ever faithfully.

TAVISTOCK HOUSE,
Saturday Evening, Thirteenth December, 1856.

Mr. W. C.
Macready.

MY DEAREST MACREADY,

We shall be charmed to squeeze Willie's friend in, and it shall be done by some undiscovered power of compression on the second night, Thursday, the fourteenth. Will you make our compliments to his honour, the Deputy Fiscal, present him with the enclosed bill, and tell him we shall be cordially glad to see him? I hope to entrust him with a special shake of the hand, to be forwarded to our dear boy (if a hoary sage like myself may venture on that expression) by the next mail.

I would have proposed the first night, but that is too full. You may faintly imagine, my venerable friend, the occupation of these also gray hairs, between "Golden Marys," "Little Dorrits," 'Household Wordses," four stage-carpenters entirely boarding on the premises, a carpenter's shop erected in the back garden, size always boiling over on all the lower fires, Stanfield perpetually elevated on planks and splashing himself from head to foot, Telbin requiring impossibilities of smart gasmen, and a legion of prowling nondescripts for ever shrinking in and out. Calm amidst the wreck, your aged friend glides away on the "Dorrit" stream, forgetting the uproar for a stretch of hours, refreshing himself with a ten or twelve miles' walk, pitches headforemost into foaming rehearsals, placidly emerges for editorial purposes, smokes over buckets of distemper with Mr. Stanfield aforesaid, again calmly floats upon the "Dorrit" waters.

Ever, my dear Macready, most affectionately yours.

TAVISTOCK HOUSE, *Fifteenth December*, 1856. Miss Power.

MY DEAR MARGUERITE,

I am not *quite* clear about the story; not because it is otherwise than exceedingly pretty, but because I· am rather in a difficult position as to stories just now. Besides beginning a long one by Collins with the new year (which will last five or six months), I have, as I always have at this time, a considerable .residua of stories written for the Christmas number, not suitable to it, and yet available for the general purposes of "Household Words." This limits my choice for the moment to stories that have some decided specialities (or a great deal of story) in them.

But I will look over the accumulation before you come, and I hope you will never see your little friend again but in print.

You will find us expecting you on the night of the twenty-fourth, and heartily glad to welcome you. The most terrific preparations are in hand for the play on Twelfth Night. There has been a painter's shop in the school-room; a gasfitter's shop all over the basement; a dressmaker's shop at the top of the house; a tailor's shop in my dressing-room. Stanfield has been incessantly on scaffoldings for two months; and your friend has been writing "Little Dorrit," etc. etc., in corners, like the sultan's groom, who was turned upside-down by the genie.

Kindest love, from all, and from me.   Ever affectionately.

TAVISTOCK HOUSE, *Christmas Eve*, 1856. Mr. William
Charles
Kent.

MY DEAR SIR,

I cannot leave your letter unanswered, because I am really anxious that you should understand why I cannot comply with your request.

Scarcely a week passes without my receiving requests from various quarters to sit for likenesses, to be taken by all the processes ever invented. Apart from my having an invincible objection to the multiplication of my countenance in the shop-windows, I have not, between my avocations and my needful recreation, the time to comply with these proposals. At this moment there are three cases out of a vast number, in which I have said: "If I sit at all, it shall be to you first, to you second, and to you third." But I assure you, I consider myself almost as unlikely to go through these three conditional achievements as I am to go to China. Judge when I am likely to get to Mr. Watkins!

. I highly esteem and thank you for your sympathy with my writings. I doubt if I have a more genial reader in the world.

Very faithfully yours.

1857.

NARRATIVE.

THIS was a very full year in many ways. In February, Charles Dickens obtained possession of Gad's Hill, and was able to turn workmen into it. In April he stayed, with his wife and sister-in-law, for a week or two at Wate's Hotel, Gravesend, to be at hand to superintend the beginning of his alterations of the house, and from thence we give a letter to Lord Carlisle. He removed his family to Gad's Hill, for a summer residence, in June; and he finished "Little Dorrit" there early in the summer. One of his first visitors at Gad's Hill was the famous writer, Hans Christian Andersen. In January "The Frozen Deep" had been played at the Tavistock House theatre with such success, that it was necessary to repeat it several times and the theatre was finally demolished at the end of that month. In June Charles Dickens heard, with great grief, of the death of his dear friend Douglas Jerrold; and as a testimony of admiration for his genius and affectionate regard for himself, it was decided to organise, under the management of Charles Dickens, a series of entertainments, "in memory of the late Douglas Jerrold," the fund produced by them (a considerable sum) to be presented to Mr. Jerrold's family. The amateur company, including many of Mr. Jerrold's colleagues on "Punch," gave subscription performances of "The Frozen Deep;" the Gallery of Illustration, in Regent Street, being engaged for the purpose. Charles Dickens gave two readings at St. Martin's Hall of "The Christmas Carol" (to such immense audiences and with such success, that the idea of giving public readings for his *own* benefit first occurred to him). The professional actors, among them the famous veteran actor, Mr. T. P. Cooke, gave a performance of Mr. Jerrold's plays of "The Rent Day" and "Black-eyed Susan," in which Mr. T. P. Cooke sustained the character which he had originally "made" when the latter play was first produced. A lecture was given by Mr. Thackeray, and another by Mr. W. H. Russell. Finally, the Queen having expressed a desire to see "The Frozen Deep," which had been much talked of during that season, there was another performance before her Majesty and the Prince Consort at the Gallery of Illustration in July, and at the end of that month Charles Dickens read his "Carol" in the Free Trade Hall, at Manchester. And to wind up the "Memorial Fund" entertainments, "The Frozen Deep" was played again at Manchester, also in the great Free Trade Hall, at the end of August. For the business of these entertainments he secured the assistance of Mr. Arthur Smith, of whom he writes to Mr. Forster, at this time: "I have got hold of Arthur Smith, as the best man of business I know, and go to work with him to-morrow morning." And when he began his own public readings, both in town and country, he felt himself most fortunate in having the co-operation of this invaluable man of business, and also of his zealous friendship and pleasant companionship.

In July, his second son, Walter Landor, went to India as a cadet in the "Company's service," from which he was afterwards transferred to the 42nd Royal Highlanders. His father and his elder brother went to Southampton to see him off. From this place Charles Dickens wrote to Mr. Edmund Yates, a young man in whom he had been interested from his boyhood, both for the sake of Mr. Yates' parents and for his own sake, and for whom he had always an affectionate regard.

In September Charles Dickens made a short tour in the North of England, with Mr. Wilkie Collins, out of which arose "The Lazy Tour of Two Idle Apprentices," written by them jointly, and published in "Household Words." Some letters to Miss Hogarth during this expedition are given here, parts of which (as is the case with many letters to his eldest daughter and his sister-in-law) have been published in Mr. Forster's book.

The letters which follow are almost all on the various subjects mentioned in our Narrative, and need little explanation.

His letter to Mr. Procter makes allusion to a legacy lately left to that friend.

The letters to Mr. Dilke, the original and much-respected proprietor of *The Athenæum*, and to Mr. Forster, on the subject of the "Literary Fund," refer, as the letters indicate, to a battle which they were carrying on together with that institution.

A letter to Mr. Frank Stone is an instance of his kind, patient, and judicious criticism of a young writer, and the letter which follows it shows how thoroughly it was understood and how perfectly appreciated by the authoress of the "Notes" referred to. Another instance of the same kind criticism is given in a second letter this year to Mr. Edmund Yates.

At the end of this Narrative we give a prologue to the play of "The Frozen Deep." It was spoken at Tavistock House by Mr. John Forster; and at the public performances of the play, by Charles Dickens.

2 E

PROLOGUE.

Curtain rises.   Mists and darkness.   Soft music throughout.

One savage footprint on the lonely shore,
Where one man listen'd to the surge's roar ;
Not all the winds that stir the mighty sea
Can ever ruffle in the memory.
If such its interest and thrall, O then
Pause on the footprints of heroic men,
Making a garden of the desert wide
Where PARRY conquer'd death and FRANKLIN died.

To that white region where the Lost lie low,
Wrapp'd in their mantles of eternal snow ;
Unvisited by change, nothing to mock
Those statues sculptured in the icy rock,
We pray your company ; that hearts as true
(Though nothings of the air) may live for you ;
Nor only yet that on our little glass
A faint reflection of those wilds may pass.

But, that the secrets of the vast Profound
Within us, an exploring hand may sound,
Testing the region of the ice-bound soul,
Seeking the passage at its northern pole,
Soft'ning the horrors of its wintry sleep,
Melting the surface of that "Frozen Deep."

Vanish ye mists !   But ere this gloom departs,
And to the union of three sister arts
We give a winter evening, good to know
That in the charms of such another show,
That in the fiction of a friendly play,
The Arctic sailors, too, put gloom away,
Forgot their long night, saw no starry dome,
Hail'd the warm sun, and were again at Home.

Vanish ye mists !   Not yet do we repair
To the still country of the piercing air ;
But seek, before we cross the troubled seas,
An English hearth and Devon's waving trees.

Mr. B. W. Procter.

TAVISTOCK HOUSE, *Second January,* 1857.

MY DEAR PROCTER,

I have to thank you for a delightful book which has given me unusual pleasure.   My delight in it has been a little dashed by certain farewell verses, but I have made up my mind (and you have no idea of the obstinacy of my character) not to believe them.

Perhaps it is not taking a liberty—perhaps it is—to congratulate you on Kenyon's remembrance.   Either way I can't help doing it with all my heart, for I know no man in the world (myself excepted) to whom I would rather the money went.

Affectionately yours ever.

TAVISTOCK HOUSE, *Ninth January,* 1857.

MY DEAR TENNENT,

I must thank you for your earnest and affectionate letter. It has given me the greatest pleasure, mixing the play in my mind confusedly and delightfully with Pisa, the Valetta, Naples, Herculanæum—God knows what not.

As to the play itself; when it is made as good as my care can make it, I derive a strange feeling out of it, like writing a book in company; a satisfaction of a most singular kind, which has no exact parallel in my life; a something that I suppose to belong to a labourer in art alone, and which has to me a conviction of its being actual truth without its pain that I never could adequately state if I were to try never so hard.

You touch so kindly and feelingly on the pleasure such little pains give, that I feel quite sorry you have never seen this drama in progress during the last ten weeks here. Every Monday and Friday evening during that time we have been at work upon it. I assure you it has been a remarkable lesson to my young people in patience, perseverance, punctuality, and order; and, best of all, in that kind of humility which is got from the earnest knowledge that whatever the right hand finds to do must be done with the heart in it, and in a desperate earnest.

When I changed my dress last night (though I did it very quickly), I was vexed to find you gone. I wanted to have secured you for our green-room supper, which was very pleasant. If by any accident you should be free next Wednesday night (our last), pray come to that green-room supper. It would give me cordial pleasure to have you there.

Ever, my dear Tennent, very heartily yours.

TAVISTOCK HOUSE,
Monday Night, Seventeenth January, 1857.

MY DEAR CERJAT,

So wonderfully do good (epistolary) intentions become confounded with bad execution, that I assure you I laboured under a perfect and most comfortable conviction that I had answered your Christmas Eve letter of 1855. More than that, in spite of your assertions to the contrary, I still strenuously believe that I did so! I have more than half a mind ("Little Dorrit" and my other occupations notwithstanding) to charge you with having forgotten my reply!! I have even a wild idea that Townshend reproached me, when the last old year was new, with writing to you instead of to him!!! We will argue it out, as well as we can argue anything without poor dear Haldimand, when I come back to Elysée.

In any case, however, don't discontinue your annual letter, because it has become an expected and a delightful part of the season to me.

With one of the prettiest houses in London, and every conceivable (and inconceivable) luxury in it, Townshend is voluntarily undergoing his own sentence of transportation in Nervi, a beastly little place near Genoa, where you would as soon find a herd of wild elephants in any villa as comfort. He has a notion that he *must* be out of England in the winter, but I believe him to be altogether wrong (as I have just told him in a letter), unless he could just take his society with him.

Workmen are now battering and smashing down my theatre here, where we have just been acting a new play of great merit, done in what I may call (modestly speaking of the getting-up, and not of the acting) an unprecedented way. I believe that anything so complete has never been seen. We had an act at the North Pole, where the slightest and greatest thing the eye beheld were equally taken from the books of the Polar voyagers. Out of thirty people, there were certainly not two who might not have gone straight to the North Pole itself, completely furnished for the winter! And now it is a mere chaos of scaffolding, ladders, beams, canvases, paint-pots, sawdust, artificial snow, gas-pipes, and ghastliness. I have taken such pains with it for these ten weeks in all my leisure hours, that I feel now shipwrecked—as if I had never been without a play on my hands before. A third topic comes up as this ceases.

Down at Gad's Hill, near Rochester, in Kent—Shakespeare's Gad's Hill, where Falstaff engaged in the robbery—is a quaint little country-house of Queen Anne's time. I happened to be walking past, a year and a half or so ago, with my sub-editor of "Household Words," when I said to him: "You see that house? It has always a curious interest for me, because when I was a small boy down in these parts I thought it the most beautiful house (I suppose because of its famous old cedar-trees) ever seen. And my poor father used to bring me to look at it, and used to say that if I ever grew up to be a clever man perhaps I might own that house, or such another house. In remembrance of which, I have always in passing looked to see if it was to be sold or let, and it has never been to me like any other house, and it has never changed at all." We came back to town, and my friend went out to dinner. Next morning he came to me in great excitement, and said: "It is written that you were to have that house at Gad's Hill. The lady I had allotted to me to take down to dinner yesterday began to speak of that neighbourhood. 'You know it?'

I said; 'I have been there to-day.' 'O yes,' said she, 'I know it very well. I was a child there, in the house they call Gad's Hill Place. My father was the rector, and lived there many years. He has just died, has left it to me, and I want to sell it.' 'So,' says the sub-editor, 'you must buy it. Now or never!'." I did, and hope to pass next summer there, though I may, perhaps, let it afterwards, furnished, from time to time.

All about myself I find, and the little sheet nearly full! But I know, my dear Cerjat, the subject will have its interest for you, so I give it its swing. Mrs. Watson was to have been at the play, but most unfortunately had three children sick of gastric fever, and could not leave them. She was here some three weeks before, looking extremely well in the face, but rather thin. I hope you detected a remembrance of our happy visit to the Great St. Bernard in a certain number of "Little Dorrit"? Tell Mrs. Cerjat, with my love, that the opinions I have expressed to her on the subject of cows have become matured in my mind by experience and venerable age; and that I denounce the race as humbugs, who have been getting into poetry and all sorts of places without the smallest reason. Haldimand's housekeeper is an awful woman to consider. Pray give him our kindest regards and remembrances, if you ever find him in a mood to take it. We often, often talk of our old days at Lausanne.

Adieu, my dear fellow; ever cordially yours.

TAVISTOCK HOUSE, *Twenty-eighth January*, 1857.   Mr. W. C. Macready.

MY DEAREST MACREADY,

Your friend and servant is as calm as Pecksniff, saving for his knitted brows now turning into cordage over "Little Dorrit." The theatre has disappeared, the house is restored to its usual conditions of order, the family are tranquil and domestic, dove-eyed peace is enthroned in this study, fire-eyed radicalism in its master's breast.

I am glad to hear that our poetess is at work again, and shall be very much pleased to have some more contributions from her.

We dined yesterday at Frederick Pollock's. I begged an amazing photograph of you, and brought it away. It strikes me as one of the most ludicrous things I ever saw in my life. I think of taking a public-house, and having it copied larger, for the size. You may remember it? Very square and big—the Saracen's Head with its hair cut, and in modern gear? Staring very hard? As your particular friend, I would not part with it on any consideration. I will never get such a wooden head again.

Ever affectionately.

Sir Edward
Bulwer
Lytton.

TAVISTOCK HOUSE,
Wednesday, Twenty-eighth January, 1857.

MY DEAR BULWER,

I thought Wills had told you as to the Guild (for I begged
him to) that he can do absolutely nothing until our charter is
seven years old.   It is the stringent and express prohibition of the
Act of Parliament—for which things you members, thank God,
are responsible and not I.   When I observed this clause (which was
just as we were going to grant a pension, if we could agree on a
good subject), I caused our Counsel's opinion to be taken on it,
and there is not a doubt about it.   I immediately recommended
that there should be no expenses—that the interest on the capital
should be all invested as it accrued—that the chambers should be
given up and the clerk discharged—and that the Guild should
have the use of the "Household Words" office rent free, and the
services of Wills on the same terms.   All of which was done.

A letter is now copying, to be sent round to all the members,
explaining, with the New Year, the whole state of the thing.
You will receive this.   It appears to me that it looks wholesome
enough.   But if a strong idiot comes and binds your hands, or
mine, or both, for seven years, what is to be done against him?

As to greater matters than this, however—as to all matters on
this teeming Earth—it appears to me that the House of Commons
and Parliament altogether, is just the dreariest failure and
nuisance that has bothered this much-bothered world.

Ever yours.

Miss Mary
Boyle.

TAVISTOCK HOUSE, *Seventh February,* 1857.

MY DEAR MARY,

Half-a-dozen words on this, my birthday, to thank you for
your kind and welcome remembrance, and to assure you that your
Joseph is proud of it.

For about ten minutes after his death, on each occasion of that
event occurring, Richard Wardour was in a floored condition.
And one night, to the great terror of Devonshire, the Arctic
Regions, and Newfoundland (all of which localities were afraid to
speak to him, as his ghost sat by the kitchen fire in its rags), he
very nearly did what he never did—went and fainted off, dead,
again.   But he always plucked up, on the turn of ten minutes,
and became facetious.

Likewise he chipped great pieces out of all his limbs (solely,
as I imagine, from moral earnestness and concussion of passion,
for I never knew him to hit himself in any way) and terrified

Aldersley* to that degree, by lunging at him to carry him into the cave, that the said Aldersley always shook like a mould of jelly, and muttered, "This is an awful thing!"

Ever affectionately.

TAVISTOCK HOUSE, *Sunday, Eighth February,* 1857.   Rev. James White.

MY DEAR WHITE,

Your note about the *Golden Mary* gave me great pleasure; though I don't believe in one part of it; for I honestly believe that your story, as really belonging to the rest of the narrative, had been generally separated from the other stories, and greatly liked. I had not that particular shipwreck that you mention in my mind (indeed I doubt if I know it), and John Steadiman merely came into my head as a staunch sort of name that suited the character. The number has done "Household Words" great service, and has decidedly told upon its circulation.

You should have come to the play. I much doubt if anything so complete will ever be seen again; the result was most remarkable even to me.

When are you going to send something more to H. W.? Are you lazy?? Low-spirited??? Pining for Paris????

Ever affectionately.

OFFICE OF "HOUSEHOLD WORDS,"   Mr. W. C. Dilke.
Thursday, Nineteenth March, 1857.

MY DEAR MR. DILKE,

Forster has another notion about the Literary Fund. Will you name a day next week—that day being neither Thursday nor Saturday—when we shall hold solemn council there at half-past four?

For myself, I beg to report that I have my war-paint on, that I have buried the pipe of peace, and am whooping for committee scalps.

Ever faithfully yours.

GRAVESEND, KENT, *Tenth April,* 1857.   Miss Emily Jolly.

DEAR MADAM,

As I am away from London for a few days, your letter has been forwarded to me.

I can honestly encourage and assure you that I believe the depression and want of confidence under which you describe yourself as labouring to have no sufficient foundation.

* The part played in "The Frozen Deep" by its author, Mr. Wilkie Collins.

First as to "Mr. Arle." I have constantly heard it spoken of with great approval, and I think it a book of considerable merit. If I were to tell you that I see no evidence of inexperience in it, that would not be true. I think a little more stir and action to be desired also; but I am surprised at your being despondent about it, for I assure you that I had supposed it (always remembering that it is your first novel) to have met with a very good reception.

I can bring to my memory—here, with no means of reference at hand—only two papers of yours that have been unsuccessful at "Household Words." I think the first was called "The Brook." It appeared to me to break down upon a confusion that pervaded it, between a Coroner's Inquest and a Trial. I have a general recollection of the mingling of the two, as to facts and forms that should have been kept apart, in some inextricable manner that was beyond my powers of disentanglement. The second was about a wife's writing a Novel and keeping the secret from her husband until it was done. I did not think the incident of sufficient force to justify the length of the narrative. But there is nothing fatal in either of these mischances.

Mr. Wills told me, when I spoke to him of the latter paper, that you had it in contemplation to offer a longer story to "Household Words." If you should do so, I assure you I shall be happy to read it myself, and that I shall have a sincere desire to accept it, if possible.

I can give you no better counsel than to look into the life about you, and to strive for what is noblest and true. As to further encouragement, I do not, I can most strongly add, believe that you have any reason to be downhearted.

Very faithfully yours.

The Earl of
Carlisle.

GRAVESEND, KENT,
Wednesday, Fifteenth April, 1857.

MY DEAR LORD CARLISLE,

I am writing by the river-side for a few days, and at the end of last week —— appeared here with your note of introduction. I was not in the way; but as —— had come express from London with it, Mrs. Dickens opened it, and gave her (in the limited sense which was of no use to her) an audience. She did not quite seem to know what she wanted of me. But she said she had understood at Stafford House that I had a theatre in which she could read; with a good deal of modesty and diffidence she at last got so far. Now, my little theatre turns my house out of window, costs fifty pounds to put up, and is only two months taken down ; therefore, is quite out of the question. This Mrs. Dickens explained, and also my profound inability to do anything for ——'s readings which they could not do for themselves. She appeared fully to understand the explanation, and indeed to have anticipated for herself how powerless I must be in such a case.

She described herself as being consumptive, and as being subject to an effusion of blood from the lungs ; about the last condition, one would think, poor woman, for the exercise of public elocution as an art.

Between ourselves, I think the whole idea a mistake, and have thought so from its first announcement. It has a fatal appearance of trading upon Uncle Tom, and am I not a man and a brother? which you may be by all means, and still not have the smallest claim to my attention as a public reader. The town is over-read from all the white squares on the draught-board ; it has been considerably harried from all the black squares—now with the aid of old banjoes, and now with the aid of Exeter Hall ; and I have a very strong impression that it is by no means to be laid hold of from this point of address. I myself, for example, am the meekest of men, and in abhorrence of slavery yield to no human creature, and yet I don't admit the sequence that I want Uncle Tom (or Aunt Tomasina) to expound "King Lear" to me. And I believe my case to be the case of thousands.

I trouble you with this much about it, because I am naturally desirous you should understand that if I could possibly have been of any service, or have suggested anything to this poor lady, I would not have lost the opportunity. But I cannot help her, and I assure you that I cannot honestly encourage her to hope. I fear her enterprise has no hope in it.

In your absence I have always followed you through the papers, and felt a personal interest and pleasure in the public affection in which you are held over there.* At the same time I must confess that I should prefer to have you here, where good public men seem to me to be dismally wanted. I have no sympathy with demagogues, but am a grievous Radical, and think the political signs of the times to be just about as bad as the spirit of the people will admit of their being. In all other respects I am as healthy, sound, and happy as your kindness can wish. So you will set down my political despondency as my only disease.

I am, dear Lord Carlisle,
Yours very faithfully and obliged.

* The Earl of Carlisle was at this time Viceroy of Ireland.

Mr. John
Forster.
TAVISTOCK HOUSE, *Thirteenth May*, 1857.

MY DEAR FORSTER,

I have gone over Dilke's memoranda, and I think it quite right and necessary that those points should be stated. Nor do I see the least difficulty in the way of their introduction into the pamphlet. But I do not deem it possible to get the pamphlet written and published before the dinner. I have so many matters pressing on my attention, that I cannot turn to it immediately on my release from my book just finished. It shall be done and distributed early next month.

As to anything being lost by its not being in the hands of the people who dine (as you seem to think), I have not the least misgiving on that score. They would say, if it were issued, just what they will say without it.

Lord Granville is committed to taking the chair, and will make the best speech he can in it. The pious B——— will cram him with as many distortions of the truth as his stomach may be strong enough to receive. R. B———, with Bardolphian eloquence, will cool his nose in the modest merits of the institution. T——— will make a neat and appropriate speech on both sides, round the corner and over the way. And all this would be done exactly to the same purpose and in just the same strain, if twenty thousand copies of the pamphlet had been circulated.

Ever affectionately.

Rev. James
White.
TAVISTOCK HOUSE,
Friday, Twenty-second May, 1857.

MY DEAR WHITE,

My emancipation having been effected on Saturday, the ninth of this month, I take some shame to myself for not having sooner answered your note. But the host of things to be done as soon as I was free, and the tremendous number of ingenuities to be wrought out at Gad's Hill, have kept me in a whirl of their own ever since.

We purpose going to Gad's Hill for the summer on the First of June; as, apart from the master's eye being a necessary ornament to the spot, I clearly see that the workmen yet lingering in the yard must be squeezed out by bodily pressure, or they will never go. How will this suit you and yours? If you will come down, we can take you all in, on your way north; that is to say, we shall have that ample verge and room enough, until about the eighth; when Hans Christian Andersen (who has been "coming" for about three years) will come for a fortnight's stay in England.

I shall like you to see the little old-fashioned place. It strikes me as being comfortable.

Believe me, ever affectionately yours.

TAVISTOCK HOUSE,
Saturday Morning, Thirtieth May, 1857.

Miss Emily
Jolly.

DEAR MADAM,

I read your story, with all possible attention, last night. I cannot tell you with what reluctance I write to you respecting it, for my opinion of it is not favourable, although I perceive your heart in it, and great strength.

Pray understand that I claim no infallibility. I merely express my honest opinion, formed against my earnest desire. I do not lay it down as law for others, though, of course, I believe that many others would come to the same conclusion. It appears to me that the story is one that cannot possibly be told within the compass to which you have limited yourself. The three principal people are, every one of them, in the wrong with the reader, and you cannot put any of them right, without making the story extend over a longer space of time, and without anatomising the souls of the actors more slowly and carefully. Nothing would justify the departure of Alice, but her having some strong reason to believe that in taking that step, *she saved her lover.* In your intentions as to that lover's transfer of his affections to Eleanor, I descry a striking truth; but I think it confusedly wrought out, and all but certain to fail in expressing itself. Eleanor, I regard as forced and overstrained. The natural result is, that she carries a train of anti-climax after her. I particularly notice this at the point when she thinks she is going to be drowned.

The whole idea of the story is sufficiently difficult to require the most exact truth and the greatest knowledge and skill in the colouring throughout. In this respect I have no doubt of its being extremely defective. The people do not talk as such people would; and the little subtle touches of description which, by making the country house and the general scene real, would give an air of reality to the people (much to be desired) are altogether wanting. The more you set yourself to the illustration of your heroine's passionate nature, the more indispensable this attendant atmosphere of truth becomes. It would, in a manner, oblige the reader to believe in her. Whereas, for ever exploding like a great firework without any background, she glares and wheels and hisses, and goes out, and has lighted nothing.

Lastly, I fear she is too convulsive from beginning to end. Pray reconsider, from this point of view, her brow, and her eyes, and her drawing herself up to her full height, and her being a perfumed presence, and her floating into rooms, also her asking people how they dare, and the like, on small provocation. When she hears her music being played, I think she is particularly objectionable.

I have a strong belief that if you keep this story by you three or four years, you will form an opinion of it not greatly differing from mine. There is so much good in it, so much reflection, so much passion and earnestness, that, if my judgment be right, I feel sure you will come over to it. On the other hand, I do not think that its publication, as it stands, would do you service, or be agreeable to you hereafter.

I have no means of knowing whether you are patient in the pursuit of this art; but I am inclined to think that you are not, and that you do not discipline yourself enough. When one is impelled to write this or that, one has still to consider: "How much of this will tell for what I mean? How much of it is my own wild emotion and superfluous energy—how much remains that is truly belonging to this ideal character and these ideal circumstances?" It is in the laborious struggle to make this distinction, and in the determination to try for it, that the road to the correction of faults lies. [Perhaps I may remark, in support of the sincerity with which I write this, that I am an impatient and impulsive person myself, but that it has been for many years the constant effort of my life to practise at my desk what I preach to you.]

I should not have written so much, or so plainly, but for your last letter to me. It seems to demand that I should be strictly true with you, and I am so in this letter, without any reservation either way.　　　　　　　　　　　　　Very faithfully yours.

Mr. Frank Stone, A.R.A.

OFFICE OF "HOUSEHOLD WORDS,"
Monday, First June, 1857.

MY DEAR STONE,

I know that what I am going to say will not be agreeable; but I rely on the authoress's good sense; and say it, knowing it to be the truth.

These "Notes" are destroyed by too much smartness. It gives the appearance of perpetual effort, stabs to the heart the nature that is in them, and wearies by the manner and not by the matter. It is the commonest fault in the world (as I have constant occasion to observe here), but it is a very great one. Just as you couldn't bear to have an épergne or a candlestick on your table, supported by a light figure always on tiptoe and evidently in an impossible attitude for the sustainment of its weight, so all readers would be more or less oppressed and worried by this presentation of everything in one smart point of view; when they know it must have other, and weightier, and more solid properties.   Airiness and good spirits are always delightful, and are inseparable from notes of a cheerful trip; but they should sympathise with many things as well as see them in a lively way.   It is but a word or a touch that expresses this humanity, but without that little embellishment of good nature there is no such thing as humour.   In this little MS. everything is too much patronised and condescended to, whereas the slightest touch of feeling for the rustic who is of the earth earthy, or of sisterhood with the homely servant who has made her face shine in her desire to please, would make a difference that the writer can scarcely imagine without trying it.   The only relief in the twenty-one slips is the little bit about the chimes.   It *is* a relief, simply because it is an indication of some kind of sentiment.   You don't want any sentiment laboriously made out in such a thing.   You don't want any maudlin show of it.   But you do want a pervading suggestion that it is there.   It makes all the difference between being playful and being cruel.   Again I must say, above all things—especially to young people writing: For the love of God don't condescend! Don't assume the attitude of saying, "See how clever I am, and what fun everybody else is!"   Take any shape but that.

I observe an excellent quality of observation throughout, and think the boy at the shop, and all about him, particularly good.   I have no doubt whatever that the rest of the journal will be much better if the writer chooses to make it so.   If she considers for a moment within herself, she will know that she derived pleasure from everything she saw, because she saw it with innumerable lights and shades upon it, and bound to humanity by innumerable fine links; she cannot possibly communicate anything of that pleasure to another by showing it from one little limited point only, and that point, observe, the one from which it is impossible to detach the exponent as the patroness of a whole universe of inferior souls. This is what everybody would mean in objecting to these notes (supposing them to be published), that they are too smart and too flippant.

As I understand this matter to be altogether between us three, and as I think your confidence, and hers, imposes a duty of friendship on me, I discharge it to the best of my ability.   Perhaps I make more of it than you may have meant or expected; if so, it is because I am interested and wish to express it.   If there had been anything in my objection not perfectly easy of removal, I might, after all, have hesitated to state it; but that is not the case.

A very little indeed would make all this gaiety as sound and wholesome and good-natured in the reader's mind as it is in the writer's.
                                                    · Affectionately always.

GAD'S HILL PLACE, HIGHAM,
Thursday, Fourth June, 1857.

MY DEAR ——,

Coming home here last night, from a day's business in
London, I found your most excellent note awaiting me, in which I
have had a pleasure to be derived from none but good and natural
things.   I can now honestly assure you that I believe you will write
well, and that I have a lively hope that I may be the means of
showing you yourself in print one day.   Your powers of graceful
and light-hearted observation need nothing but the little touches on
which we are both agreed.   And I am perfectly sure that they will
be as pleasant to you as to anyone, for nobody can see so well as
you do, without feeling kindly too.

To confess the truth to you, I was half sorry, yesterday, that I
had been so unreserved ; but not half as sorry, yesterday, as I am
glad to-day.   You must not mind my adding that there is a noble
candour and modesty in your note, which I shall never be able to
separate from you henceforth.   Affectionately yours always.

GAD'S HILL, *Saturday, Sixth June*, 1857.

MY DEAR HENRY,

Here is a very serious business on the great estate respecting
the water supply.   Last night they had pumped the well dry merely
in raising the family supply for the day ; and this morning (very
little water having been got into the cisterns) it is dry again !   It
is pretty clear to me that we must look the thing in the face, and
at once bore deeper, dig, or do some beastly thing or other, to secure
this necessary in abundance.   Meanwhile I am in a most plaintive
and forlorn condition without your presence and counsel.   I raise
my voice in the wilderness and implore the same ! ! !

Wild legends are in circulation among the servants how that
Captain Goldsmith on the knoll above—the skipper in that crow's-
nest of a house—has millions of gallons of water always flowing for
him. Can he have damaged my well ? Can we imitate him, and have
our millions of gallons ? Goldsmith or I must fall, so I conceive.

If you get this, send me a telegraph message informing me
when I may expect comfort.   I am held by four of the family
while I write this, in case I should do myself a mischief—it
certainly won't be taking to drinking water.

Ever affectionately (most despairingly).

TAVISTOCK HOUSE, *Monday, Thirteenth July*, 1857.

Mr. W. C.
Macready.

MY DEAREST MACREADY,

Many thanks for your Indian information. I shall act upon it in the most exact manner. Walter sails next Monday. Charley and I go down with him to Southampton next Sunday. We are all delighted with the prospect of seeing you at Gad's Hill. These are my Jerrold engagements : On Friday, the twenty-fourth, I have to repeat my reading at St. Martin's Hall ; on Saturday, the twenty-fifth, to repeat "The Frozen Deep" at the Gallery of Illustration for the last time. On Thursday, the thirtieth, or Friday, the thirty-first, I shall probably read at Manchester. Deane, the general manager of the Exhibition, is going down to-night, and will arrange all the preliminaries for me. If you and I went down to Manchester together, and were there on a Sunday, he would give us the whole Exhibition to ourselves. It is probable, I think (as he estimates the receipts of a night at about seven hundred pounds), that we may, in about a fortnight or so after the reading, play "The Frozen Deep" at Manchester. But of this contingent engagement I at present know no more than you do.

Now, will you, upon this exposition of affairs, choose your own time for coming to us, and, when you have made your choice, write to me at Gad's Hill? I am going down this afternoon for rest (which means violent cricket with the boys) after last Saturday night ; which was a teaser, but triumphant. The St. Martin's Hall audience was, I must confess, a very extraordinary thing. The two thousand and odd people were like one, and their enthusiasm was something awful.

Yet I have seen that before, too. Your young remembrance cannot recall the man ; but he flourished in my day—a great actor, sir—a noble actor—thorough artist ! I have seen him do wonders in that way. He retired from the stage early in life (having a monomaniacal delusion that he was old), and is said to be still living in your county.

Ever, my dearest Macready,
Most affectionately yours.

TAVISTOCK HOUSE, *Sunday, Nineteenth July*, 1857.

Mr.
Edmund
Yates.

MY DEAR YATES,

Although I date this ashore, I really write it from Southampton. I have come here on an errand which will grow familiar to you before you know that Time has flapped his wings over your head. Like me, you will find those babies grow to be young men before you are quite sure they are born. Like me, you will have great teeth drawn with a wrench, and will only then know that you ever cut them. I am here to send Walter away over what they call, in Green Bush melodramas, "the Big Drink," and I don't at all know this day how he comes to be mine, or I his.

I don't write to say this—or to say how, seeing Charley and he going aboard the ship before me just now, I suddenly came into possession of a photograph of my own back at sixteen and twenty, and also into a suspicion that I had doubled the last age. I merely write to mention that Telbin and his wife are going down to Gad's Hill with us, about mid-day next Sunday, and that if you and Mrs. Yates will come too, we shall be delighted to have you. We can give you a bed, and you can be in town (if you have such a savage necessity) by twenty minutes before ten on Monday morning.

I was very much pleased (as I had reason to be) with your account of the reading in *The Daily News*. I thank you heartily.

IN REMEMBRANCE OF THE LATE MR. DOUGLAS JERROLD.

Mr. T. P.
Cooke.

COMMITTEE'S OFFICE, GALLERY OF ILLUSTRATION,
REGENT STREET, *Thursday, Thirtieth July*, 1857.

MY DEAR MR. COOKE,

I cannot rest satisfied this morning without writing to congratulate you on your admirable performance of last night. It was so fresh and vigorous, so manly and gallant, that I felt as if it splashed against my theatre-heated face, along with the spray of the breezy sea. What I felt everybody felt; I should feel it quite an impertinence to take myself out of the crowd, therefore, if I could by any means help doing so. But I can't; so I hope you will feel that you bring me on yourself, and have only yourself to blame.

Always faithfully yours.

Mrs.
Compton.

GAD'S HILL PLACE, HIGHAM BY ROCHESTER,
Sunday Night, Second August, 1857.

MY DEAR MRS. COMPTON,

We are going to play "The Frozen Deep" (pursuant to requisition from town magnates, etc.) at Manchester, at the New Free Trade Hall, on the nights of Friday and Saturday, the Twenty-first and Twenty-second August.

The place is out of the question for my girls. Their action could not be seen, and their voices could not be heard. You and I have played, there and elsewhere, so sociably and happily, that I am emboldened to ask you whether you would play my sister-in-law Georgina's part (Compton and babies permitting).

We shall go down in the old pleasant way, and shall have the Art Treasures Exhibition to ourselves on the Sunday ; when even "he" (as Rogers always called every pretty woman's husband) might come and join us.

What do you say ? What does he say ? and what does baby say ? When I use the term "baby," I use it in two tenses— present and future.

Answer me at this address, like the Juliet I saw at Drury Lane —when was it?—yesterday. And whatever your answer is, if you will say that you and Compton will meet us at the North Kent Station, London Bridge, next Sunday at a quarter before one, and will come down here for a breath of sweet air and stay all night, you will give your old friends great pleasure. Not least among them,

Yours faithfully.

GAD's HILL PLACE, HIGHAM BY ROCHESTER,   Mr. W. C.
Monday, Third August, 1857.   Macready.

MY DEAREST MACREADY,

I read at Manchester last Friday. As many thousand people were there as you like to name. The collection of pictures in the Exhibition is wonderful. And the power with which the modern English school asserts itself is a very gratifying and delightful thing to behold. The care for the common people, in the provision made for their comfort and refreshment, is also admirable and worthy of all commendation. But they want more amusement, and particularly (as it strikes me) *something in motion,* though it were only a twisting fountain. The thing is too still after their lives of machinery, and art flies over their heads in consequence.

I hope you have seen my tussle with the "Edinburgh." I saw the chance last Friday week, as I was going down to read the "Carol" in St. Martin's Hall. Instantly turned to, then and there, and wrote half the article. Flew out of bed early next morning, and finished it by noon. Went down to the Gallery of Illustration (we acted that night), did the day's business, corrected the proofs in Polar costume in dressing-room, broke up two numbers of "Household Words" to get it out directly, played in "Frozen Deep" and "Uncle John," presided at supper of company, made no end of speeches, went home and gave in completely for four hours, then got sound asleep, and next day was as fresh as you used to be in the far-off days of your lusty youth.

Ever and ever affectionately.

2 F

Mr. Frank
Stone,
A.R.A.

TAVISTOCK HOUSE,
Sunday Afternoon, Ninth August, 1857.

MY DEAR STONE,

Now here, without any preface, is a good, confounding, stunning question for you—would you like to play "Uncle John" on the two nights at Manchester?

It is not a long part. You could have a full rehearsal on the Friday, and I could sit in the wing at night and pull you through all the business. Perhaps you might not object to being in the thing in your own native place, and the relief to me would be enormous.

It's a capital part, and you are a capital old man. You know the play as we play it, and the Manchester people don't. Say the word, and I'll send you my own book by return of post.

The agitation and exertion of Richard Wardour are so great to me, that I cannot rally my spirits in the short space of time I get. The strain is so great to make a show of doing it, that I want to be helped out of "Uncle John" if I can. Think of yourself far more than me; but if you half think you are up to the joke, and half doubt your being so, then give me the benefit of the doubt and play the part.

Ever affectionately.

Mr. Henry
Austin.

GAD'S HILL PLACE,
Saturday, Fifteenth August, 1857.

MY DEAR HENRY,

At last, I am happy to inform you, we have got at a famous spring!! It rushed in this morning, ten foot deep. And our friends talk of its supplying "a ton a minute for yourself and your family, sir, for nevermore."

They ask leave to bore ten feet lower, to prevent the possibility of what they call "a choking with sullage." Likewise, they are going to insert "a rose-headed pipe;" at the mention of which implement, I am (secretly) well-nigh distracted, having no idea of what it means. But I have said "Yes," besides instantly standing a bottle of gin. Can you come back, and can you get down on Monday morning, to advise and endeavour to decide on the mechanical force we shall use for raising the water?

Ever affectionately.

Mr. Frank
Stone,
A.R.A.

GAD'S HILL PLACE,
Monday, Seventeenth August, 1857.

MY DEAR STONE,

I received your kind note this morning, and write this reply here to take to London with me and post in town, being bound for that village and three days' drill of the professional ladies who are to succeed the Tavistock girls.

My book I enclose. You will not find the situations or business difficult, with me on the spot to put you right.

Now, as to the dress. You will want a pair of pumps and a pair of white silk socks ; these you can get at Manchester. The extravagantly and anciently-frilled shirts that I have had got up for the part, I will bring you down ; large white waistcoat, I will bring you down ; large white hat, I will bring you down ; dressing-gown, I will bring you down ; white gloves and ditto choker you can get at Manchester. There then remain only a pair of common nankeen tights, to button below the calf, and blue wedding-coat. The nankeen tights you had best get made at once ; my "Uncle John" coat I will send you down in a parcel by to-morrow's train, to have altered in Manchester to your shape and figure. You will then be quite independent of Christian chance and Jewish Nathan, which latter potentate is now at Canterbury with the cricket amateurs, and might fail.

As I have already suggested, with a careful rehearsal on Friday morning, and with me at the wing at night to put you right, you will find yourself sliding through it easily. There is nothing in the least complicated in the business. As to the dance, you have only to knock yourself up for a twelvemonth and it will go nobly.

After all, too, if you *should*, through any unlucky breakdown, come to be afraid of it, I am no worse off than I was before, if I have to do it at last. Keep your pecker up with that.

I am heartily obliged to you, my dear old boy, for your affectionate and considerate note, and I wouldn't have you do it, really and sincerely—immense as the relief will be to me—unless you are quite comfortable in it, and able to enjoy it.

Ever affectionately.

OFFICE OF "HOUSEHOLD WORDS,"
Tuesday, Eighteenth August, 1857.

Mr. Frank Stone, A.R.A.

MY DEAR STONE,

I sent you a telegraph message last night, in total contradiction of the letter you received from me this morning.

The reason was simply this : Arthur Smith and the other business men, both in Manchester and here, urged upon me, in the strongest manner, that they were afraid of the change ; that it was well known in Manchester that I had done the part in London ; that there was a danger of its being considered disrespectful in me to give it up ; also that there was a danger that it might be thought that I did so at the last minute, after an immense let, whereas I might have done it at first, etc. etc. etc. Having no desire but for the success of our object, and a becoming recognition on my part of the kind Manchester public's cordiality, I gave way, and thought it best to go on.

I do so against the grain, and against every inclination, and against the strongest feeling of gratitude to you. My people at home will be miserable too when they hear I am going to do it. If I could have heard from you sooner, and got the bill out sooner, I should have been firmer in considering my own necessity of relief. As it is, I sneak under; and I hope you will feel the reasons, and approve.

Ever affectionately.

Mr. Henry Austin.

GAD'S HILL PLACE, Wednesday,
Second September, 1857.

MY DEAR HENRY,

The second conspirator has been here this morning to ask whether you wish the windlass to be left in the yard, and whether you will want him and his mate any more, and, if so, when? Of course he says (rolling something in the form of a fillet in at one broken tooth all the while, and rolling it out at another) that they could wish fur to have the windlass if it warn't any ways a hill conwenience fur to fetch her away. I have told him that if he will come back on Friday he shall have your reply. Will you, therefore, send it me by return of post? He says he'll "look up" (as if he was an astronomer) "a Friday arterdinner."

On Monday I am going away with Collins for ten days or a fortnight, on a "tour in search of an article" for "Household Words." We have not the least idea where we are going; but <i>he</i> says, "Let's look at the Norfolk coast," and <i>I</i> say, "Let's look at the back of the Atlantic." I don't quite know what I mean by that; but have a general impression that I mean something knowing.

I am horribly used up after the Jerrold business. Low spirits, low pulse, low voice, intense reaction. If I were not like Mr. Micawber, "falling back for a spring" on Monday, I think I should slink into a corner and cry.

Ever affectionately.

Miss Hogarth.

ALLONDY, CUMBERLAND,
Wednesday Night, Ninth September, 1857.

MY DEAR GEORGY,

*   *   *   *   *

Think of Collins' usual luck with me! We went up a Cumberland mountain yesterday—a huge black hill, fifteen hundred feet high. We took for a guide a capital innkeeper hard by. It rained in torrents—as it only does rain in a hill country—the whole time. At the top, there were black mists and the darkness of night. It then came out that the innkeeper had not been up for twenty years, and he lost his head and himself altogether; and we couldn't get down again! What wonders the Inimitable performed with his compass until it broke with the heat and wet of his pocket, no matter; it did break, and then we wandered about, until it was clear to the Inimitable that the night must be passed there, and the enterprising travellers probably die of cold. We took our own way about coming down, struck, and declared that the guide might wander where he would, but we would follow a watercourse we lighted upon, and which must come at last to the river. This necessitated amazing gymnastics; in the course of which performances, Collins fell into the said watercourse with his ankle sprained, and the great ligament of the foot and leg swollen I don't know how big.

How I enacted Wardour over again in carrying him down, and what a business it was to get him down; I may say in Gibbs' words: "Vi lascio a giudicare!" But he was got down somehow, and we got off the mountain somehow; and now I carry him to bed, and into and out of carriages, exactly like Wardour in private life. I don't believe he will stand for a month to come. He has had a doctor, and can wear neither shoe nor stocking, and has his foot wrapped up in a flannel waistcoat, and has a breakfast saucer of liniment, and a horrible dabbling of lotion incessantly in progress. We laugh at it all, but I doubt very much whether he can go on to Doncaster. It will be a miserable blow to our H. W. scheme, and I say nothing about it as yet; but he is really so crippled that I doubt the getting him there. We have resolved to fall to work to-morrow morning and begin our writing; and there, for the present, that point rests.

This is a little place with fifty houses, five bathing-machines, five girls in straw hats, five men in straw hats, and no other company. The little houses are all in half-mourning—yellow stone on white stone, and black; and it reminds me of what Broadstairs might have been if it had not inherited a cliff, and had been an Irishman. But this is a capital little homely inn, looking out upon the sea; and we are really very comfortably lodged. We have a very obliging and comfortable landlady; and it is a clean nice place in a rough wild country. We came here haphazard, but could not have done better.

We lay last night at a place called Wigton—also in half-mourning—with the wonderful peculiarity that it had no population, no business, no streets to speak of; but five linendrapers within range of our small windows, one linendraper's next door, and five more linendrapers round the corner.* I ordered a night-light in my bedroom. A queer little old woman brought me one of the common Child's night-lights, and seeming to think that I looked at it with interest, said: "It's joost a vara keeyourious thing, sir, and joost new coom oop. It'll burn awt hoors a' end, an no gootther, nor no waste, nor ony sike a thing, if you can creedit what I say, seein' the airticle."   Ever affectionately.

Miss
Hogarth.

LANCASTER, *Saturday Night, Twelfth September*, 1857.

MY DEAR GEORGY,

I received your letter at Allonby yesterday, and was de-lighted to get it. We came back to Carlisle last night (to a capital inn, kept by Breach's brother), and came on here to-day. We are on our way to Doncaster; but, although it is not a hundred miles from here, we shall have, as well as I can make out the complicated list of trains, to sleep at Leeds to-morrow night.

Accustomed as you are to the homage which men delight to render to the Inimitable, you would be scarcely prepared for the proportions it assumes in this northern country. Station-masters assist him to alight from carriages, deputations await him in hotel entries, innkeepers bow down before him and put him into regal rooms, the town goes down to the platform to see him off, and Collins' ankle goes into the newspapers ! ! !

It is a great deal better than it was, and he can get into new hotels and up the stairs with two thick sticks, like an admiral in a farce. His spirits have improved in a corresponding degree, and he contemplates cheerfully the keeping house at Doncaster. I thought (as I told you) he would never have gone there, but he seems quite up to the mark now. Of course he can never walk out, or see anything of any place.

The landlady of the little inn at Allonby lived at Greta Bridge, in Yorkshire, when I went down there before "Nickleby," and was smuggled into the room to see me, when I was secretly found out. She is an immensely fat woman now. "But I could tuck my arm round her waist then, Mr. Dickens," the landlord said when she told me the story as I was going to bed the night before last. "And can't you do it now," I said, "you insensible dog? Look at me! Here's a picture!" Accordingly, I got round as much of her as I could; and this gallant action was the most successful I have ever performed, on the whole. I think it was the dullest little place I ever entered; and what with the monotony of an idle sea, and what with the monotony of another sea in the room (occasioned by Collins' perpetually holding his ankle over a pail of salt water, and laving it with a milk jug), I struck yesterday, and came away.

We are in a very remarkable old house here, with genuine old rooms and an uncommonly quaint staircase. I have a state bedroom, with two enormous red four-posters in it, each as big as Charley's room at Gad's Hill. Bellew is to preach here to-morrow. "And we know he is a friend of yours, sir," said the landlord, when he presided over the serving of the dinner (two little salmon trout; a sirloin steak; a brace of partridges; seven dishes of sweets; five dishes of dessert, led off by a bowl of peaches; and in the centre an enormous bride-cake—"We always have it here, sir," said the landlord, "custom of the house.") Collins turned pale, and estimated the dinner at half a guinea each.

This is the stupidest of letters, but all description is gone or going, into "The Lazy Tour of Two Idle Apprentices."

Ever affectionately, my dearest Georgy.

ANGEL HOTEL, DONCASTER,   Miss
Tuesday, Fifteenth September, 1857.   Hogarth.

MY DEAR GEORGY,

I found your letter here on my arrival yesterday. I had hoped that the wall would have been almost finished by this time, and the additions to the house almost finished too—but patience, patience !

We have very good, clean, and quiet apartments here, on the second floor, looking down into the main street, which is full of horse jockeys, bettors, drunkards, and other blackguards, from morning to night—and all night. The races begin to-day and last till Friday, which is the Cup Day. I am not going to the course this morning, but have engaged a carriage (open, and pair) for to-morrow and Friday.

"The Frozen Deep's" author gets on as well as could be expected. He can hobble up and down stairs when absolutely necessary, and limps to his bedroom on the same floor. He talks of going to the theatre to-night in a cab, which will be the first occasion of his going out, except to travel, since the accident. He sends his kind regards and thanks for enquiries and condolence. I am perpetually tidying the rooms after him, and carrying all sorts of untidy things which belong to him into his bedroom, which is a picture of disorder. You will please to imagine mine, airy and clean, little dressing-room attached, eight water-jugs (I never saw such a supply), capital sponge-bath, perfect arrangement, and exquisite neatness. We breakfast at half-past eight, and fall to work for H. W. afterwards. Then I go out, and—hem ! look for subjects.   Ever affectionately.

Mr. Arthur
Ryland.

GAD'S HILL PLACE,
Saturday Evening, Third October, 1857.

MY DEAR SIR,

I have had the honour and pleasure of receiving your letter of the twenty-eighth of last month, informing me of the distinction that has been conferred upon me by the council of the Birmingham and Midland Institute.

Allow me to assure you with much sincerity, that I am highly gratified by having been elected one of the first honorary members of that establishment. Nothing could have enhanced my interest in so important an undertaking; but the compliment is all the more welcome to me on that account.

I accept it with a due sense of its worth, with many acknowledgments and with all good wishes.

I am ever, my dear Sir, very faithfully yours.

Mr. Edmund
Yates.

TAVISTOCK HOUSE,
Monday Night, Sixteenth November, 1857.

MY DEAR YATES,

I retain the story with pleasure; and I need not tell you that you are not mistaken in the last lines of your note.

Excuse me, on that ground, if I say a word or two as to what I think (I mention it with a view to the future) might be better in the paper. The opening is excellent. But it passes too completely into the Irishman's narrative, does not light it up with the life about it, or the circumstances under which it is delivered, and does not carry through it, as I think it should with a certain indefinable subtleness, the thread with which you begin your weaving. I will tell Wills to send me the proof, and will try to show you what I mean when I shall have gone over it carefully.

Faithfully yours always.

Mr. Frank
Stone,
A.R.A.

TAVISTOCK HOUSE,
Wednesday, Thirteenth December, 1857.

MY DEAR STONE,

I find on enquiry that the "General Theatrical Fund" has relieved non-members in one or two instances; but that it is exceedingly unwilling to do so, and would certainly not do so again, saving on some very strong and exceptional case. As its trustee, I could not represent to it that I think it ought to sail into those open waters, for I very much doubt the justice of such cruising, with a reference to the interests of the patient people who support it out of their small earnings.

Affectionately ever.

BOOK III.

1858 TO 1870.

1858.

ALL through this year, Charles Dickens was constantly moving about from place to place. After much and careful consideration, he had come to the determination for the future of giving readings for his own benefit. And although in the spring he gave one reading of his "Christmas Carol" for a charity, all the other readings, beginning from the Twenty-ninth of April, and ever after, were for himself. In the autumn he made reading tours in England, Scotland, and Ireland, always accompanied by his friend and secretary, Mr. Arthur Smith. At Newcastle, Charles Dickens was joined by his daughters, who accompanied him in his Scotch tour. The letters to his sister-in-law, and to his eldest daughter, are given here, and will be given in future reading tours, as they form a complete diary of his life and movements at these times. To avoid the constant repetition of the two names, the beginning of the letters will be dispensed with in all cases where they follow each other in unbroken succession.

We give the short note to Mr. Langford—well known for many years to all literary people in London—on account of the interest of its subject. Mr. Langford published the note in *The Daily News* almost immediately after the lamented death of George Eliot.

The Mr. Frederick Lehmann mentioned in the letter written from Sheffield, had married a daughter of Mr. Robert Chambers, and niece of Mrs. Wills. Coming to settle in London a short time after this date, Mr. and Mrs. Lehmann became intimately known to Charles Dickens and his family—more especially to his eldest daughter, to whom they have been, and are, the kindest and truest of friends. The "pretty little boy" mentioned as being under Mrs. Wills' care, is their eldest son.

The "little speech" alluded to in this first letter to Mr. Macready was one made by Charles Dickens at a public dinner, which was given in aid of the Hospital for Sick Children, in Great Ormond Street. He afterwards (early in April) gave a reading from his "Christmas Carol" for the same charity.

The Christmas number of "Household Words," mentioned in a

letter to Mr. Wilkie Collins, was called "A House to Let," and contained stories written by Charles Dickens, Mr. Wilkie Collins, and other contributors to "Household Words."

At the end of this year we give a letter addressed to Mr. Blanchard Jerrold, who, when he was writing the life of his father, requested Charles Dickens to write a few personal reminiscences of Mr. Douglas Jerrold, for the purpose of publication in his book.

Mr. W.
Wilkie
Collins.

TAVISTOCK HOUSE, *Sunday, Seventeenth January,* 1858.

MY DEAR WILKIE,

I am very sorry to receive so bad an account of the foot; but I hope it is all in the past tense now.

I met with an incident the other day, which I think is a good deal in your way, for introduction either into a long or short story. Dr. Sutherland and Dr. Monro went over St. Luke's with me (only last Friday), to show me some distinctly and remarkably-developed types of insanity. Among other patients, we passed a deaf and dumb man, now afflicted with incurable madness too, of whom they said that it was only when his madness began to develop itself in strongly-marked mad actions, that it began to be suspected, "though it had been there, no doubt, some time." This led me to consider, suspiciously, what employment he had been in, and so to ask the question. "Aye," says Dr. Sutherland, "that is the most remarkable thing of all, Mr. Dickens. He was employed in the transmission of electric-telegraph messages; and it is impossible to conceive what delirious despatches that man may have been sending about all over the world!"

Rejoiced to hear such good report of the play.

Ever faithfully.

Mr. Joseph
Langford.

TAVISTOCK HOUSE, W.C., *Eighteenth January,* 1858.

MY DEAR LANGFORD,

Will you—by such roundabout ways and methods as may present themselves—convey the note of thanks (enclosed) to the author of "Scenes of Clerical Life," whose two first stories I can never say enough of, I think them so truly admirable. But if those two volumes, or a part of them, were not written by a woman, then should I begin to believe that I am a woman myself.

Faithfully yours always.

Mr.
Edmund
Yates.

TAVISTOCK HOUSE, *Tuesday, Second February,* 1858.

MY DEAR YATES,

Your quotation is, as I supposed, all wrong. The text is *not* "which his 'owls was organs." When Mr. Harris went into an empty dog-kennel, to spare his sensitive nature the anguish of overhearing Mrs. Harris' exclamations on the occasion of the birth of her first child (the Princess Royal of the Harris family), "he never took his hands away from his ears, or came out once, till he was showed the baby." On encountering that spectacle, he was (being of a weakly constitution) "took with fits." For this distressing complaint he was medically treated; the doctor "collared him, and laid him on his back upon the airy stones"—please to observe what follows—"and she was told, to ease her mind, his 'owls was organs."

That is to say, Mrs. Harris, lying exhausted on her bed, in the first sweet relief of freedom from pain, merely covered with the counterpane, and not yet "put comfortable," hears a noise apparently proceeding from the back-yard, and says, in a flushed and hysterical manner: "What 'owls are those? Who is a-'owling? Not my ugebond?" Upon which the doctor, looking round one of the bottom posts of the bed, and taking Mrs. Harris' pulse in a reassuring manner, says, with much admirable presence of mind: "Howls, my dear madam?—no, no, no! What are we thinking of? Howls, my dear Mrs. Harris? Ha, ha, ha! Organs, ma'am, organs. Organs in the streets, Mrs. Harris; no howls."

Yours faithfully.

TAVISTOCK HOUSE,
Tuesday, Second February, 1858.

Mr. W. M. Thackeray.

MY DEAR THACKERAY,

The wisdom of Parliament, in that expensive act of its greatness which constitutes the Guild, prohibits that corporation *from doing anything* until it shall have existed in a perfectly useless condition for seven years. This clause (introduced by some private-bill magnate of official might) seemed so ridiculous, that nobody could believe it to have this meaning; but as I felt clear about it when we were on the very verge of granting an excellent literary annuity, I referred the point to counsel, and my construction was confirmed without a doubt.

It is therefore needless to enquire whether an association in the nature of a provident society could address itself to such a case as you confide to me. The prohibition has still two or three years of life in it.

But, assuming the gentleman's title to be considered as an "author" as established, there is no question that it comes within the scope of the Literary Fund. They would habitually "lend" money if they did what I consider to be their duty; as it is they only give money, but they give it in such instances.

I have forwarded the envelope to the Society of Arts, with a request that they will present it to Prince Albert, approaching H.R.H. in the Siamese manner.

Ever faithfully.

Mr. John Forster.

TAVISTOCK HOUSE,
Wednesday Night, Third February, 1858.

MY DEAR FORSTER,

I beg to report two phenomena:

1. An excellent little play in one act, by Marston, at the Lyceum; title, "A Hard Struggle;" as good as "La Joie fait Peur," though not at all like it.

2. Capital acting in the same play, by Mr. Dillon. Real good acting, in imitation of nobody, and honestly made out by himself!!

I went (at Marston's request) last night, and cried till I sobbed again. I have not seen a word about it from Oxenford.* But it is as wholesome and manly a thing altogether as I have seen for many a day. (I would have given a hundred pounds to have played Mr. Dillon's part.)

Ever affectionately.

Dr. Westland Marston.

TAVISTOCK HOUSE,
Wednesday, Third February, 1858.

MY DEAR MARSTON,

I most heartily and honestly congratulate you on your charming little piece. It moved me more than I could easily tell you, if I were to try. Except "La Joie fait Peur," I have seen nothing nearly so good, and there is a subtlety in the comfortable presentation of the child who is to become a devoted woman for Reuben's sake, which goes a long way beyond Madame de Girardin. I am at a loss to let you know how much I admired it last night, or how heartily I cried over it. A touching idea, most delicately conceived and wrought out by a true artist and poet, in a spirit of noble, manly generosity, that no one should be able to study without great emotion.

It is extremely well acted by all concerned; but Mr. Dillon's performance is really admirable, and deserving of the highest commendation. It is good in these days to see an actor taking such pains, and expressing such natural and vigorous sentiment. There is only one thing I should have liked him to change. I am much mistaken if any man—least of all any such man—would crush a

---

* Mr. John Oxenford, at this time the dramatic critic of *The Times.*

letter written by the hand of the woman he loved. Hold it to his heart unconsciously and look about for it the while, he might; or he might do anything with it that expressed a habit of tenderness and affection in association with the idea of her; but he would never crush it under any circumstances. He would as soon crush her heart.

You will see how closely I went with him by my minding so slight an incident in so fine a performance. There is no one who could approach him in it; and I am bound to add that he surprised me as much as he pleased me.

I think it might be worth while to try the people at the Français with the piece. They are very good in one-act plays; such plays take well there, and this seems to me well suited to them. If you would like Samson or Regnier to read the play (in English) I know them well, and would be very glad indeed to tell them that I sent it with your sanction because I had been so much struck by it.

Faithfully yours always.

TAVISTOCK HOUSE, LONDON, W.C.,   Monsieur
Thursday, Eleventh February, 1858.   Regnier.

MY DEAR REGNIER,

I want you to read the enclosed little play. You will see that it is in one act—about the length of "La Joie fait Peur." It is now acting at the Lyceum Theatre here, with very great success. The author is Mr. Westland Marston, a dramatic writer of reputation, who wrote a very well-known tragedy called "The Patrician's Daughter," in which Macready and Miss Faucit acted (under Macready's management at Drury Lane) some years ago.

This little piece is so very powerful on the stage, its interest is so simple and natural, and the part of Reuben is such a very fine one, that I cannot help thinking you might make one grand *coup* with it, if with your skilful hand you arranged it for the Français. I have communicated this idea of mine to the author, "*et là-dessus je vous écris*." I am anxious to know your opinion, and shall expect with much interest to receive a little letter from you at your convenience.

Ever, my dear Regnier, faithfully your Friend.

TAVISTOCK HOUSE, *Saturday*,   The same.
Twentieth February, 1858.

MY DEAR REGNIER,

Let me thank you with all my heart for your most patient

and kind letter. I made its contents known to Mr. Marston, and I enclose you his reply. You will see that he cheerfully leaves the matter in your hands, and abides by your opinion and discretion.

You need not return his letter, my friend. There is great excitement here this morning, in consequence of the failure of the Ministry last night to carry the bill they brought in to please your Emperor and his troops. I, for one, am extremely glad of their defeat.

"Le vieux P——," I have no doubt, will go staggering down the Rue de la Paix to-day, with his stick in his hand and his hat on one side, predicting the downfall of everything, in consequence of this event. His handwriting shakes more and more every quarter, and I think he mixes a great deal of cognac with his ink. He always gives me some astonishing piece of news (which is never true), or some suspicious public prophecy (which is never verified), and he always tells me he is dying (which he never is).

Adieu, my dear Regnier; accept a thousand thanks from me, and believe me, now and always,

Your affectionate and faithful Friend.

Mr. W. C. Macready.

TAVISTOCK HOUSE, Fifteenth March, 1858.

MY DEAREST MACREADY,

I have safely received your cheque this morning, and will hand it over forthwith to the honorary secretary of the hospital. I hope you have read the little speech in the hospital's publication of it. They had it taken by their own shorthand-writer, and it is done verbatim.

You may be sure that it is a good and kind charity. It is amazing to me that it is not at this day ten times as large and rich as it is. But I hope and trust that I have happily been able to give it a good thrust onward into a great course. I am devising all sorts of things in my mind, and am in a state of energetic restlessness incomprehensible to the calm philosophers of Dorsetshire. What a dream it is, this work and strife, and how little we do in the dream after all! Only last night, in my sleep, I was bent upon getting over a perspective of barriers, with my hands and feet bound. Pretty much what we are all about, waking, I think?

But, Lord! (as I said before) you smile pityingly, not bitterly, at this hubbub, and moralise upon it, in the calm evenings when there is no school at Sherborne.

Ever affectionately and truly.

TAVISTOCK HOUSE, TAVISTOCK SQUARE, LONDON, W.C.,   Mrs.
Wednesday, Fourteenth April, 1858.   Hogge.*

MY DEAR MRS. HOGGE,

After the profoundest cogitation, I come reluctantly to the conclusion that I do not know that orphan. If you were the lady in want of him, I should certainly offer *myself.* But as you are not, I will not hear of the situation.

It is wonderful to think how many charming little people there must be, to whom this proposal would be like a revelation from Heaven. Why don't I know one, and come to Kensington, boy in hand, as if I had walked (I wish to God I had) out of a fairy tale! But no, I do *not* know that orphan. He is crying somewhere, by himself, at this moment. I can't dry his eyes. He is being neglected by some ogress of a nurse. I can't rescue him.

I will make a point of going to the Athenæum on Monday night; and if I had five hundred votes to give, Mr. Macdonald should have them all, for your sake.

I grieve to hear that you have been ill, but I hope that the spring, *when* it comes, will find you blooming with the rest of the flowers.

Very faithfully yours.

TAVISTOCK HOUSE, TAVISTOCK SQUARE, LONDON, W.C.,   Mr.
Wednesday, Twenty-eighth April, 1858.   Edmund Yates.

MY DEAR YATES,

For a good many years I have suffered a great deal from charities, but never anything like what I suffer now. The amount of correspondence they inflict upon me is really incredible. But this is nothing. Benevolent men get behind the piers of the gates, lying in wait for my going out; and when I peep shrinkingly from my study-windows, I see their pot-bellied shadows projected on the gravel. Benevolent bullies drive up in hansom cabs (with engraved portraits of their benevolent institutions hanging over the aprons, like banners on their outward walls), and stay long at the door. Benevolent area-sneaks get lost in the kitchens and are found to impede the circulation of the knife-cleaning machine. My man has been heard to say (at The Burton Arms) "that if it was a wicious place, well and good—*that* an't door work; but that wen all the Christian wirtues is always a-shoulderin' and a-helberin' on you in the 'all, a-tryin' to git past you and cut upstairs into master's room, why no wages as you couldn't name wouldn't make it up to you."

Persecuted ever.

* Niece to the Rev. W. Harness.

Mrs. Yates.

TAVISTOCK HOUSE, TAVISTOCK SQUARE, W.C.,
Saturday Evening, Fifteenth May, 1858.

MY DEAR MRS. YATES,*

Pray believe that I was sorry with all my heart to miss
you last Thursday, and to learn the occasion of your absence;
also that, whenever you can come, your presence will give me a
new interest in that evening. No one alive can have more delightful associations with the lightest sound of your voice than I
have; and to give you a minute's interest and pleasure in acknowledgment of the uncountable hours of happiness you gave me
when you were a mysterious angel to me, would honestly gratify
my heart.

Very faithfully and gratefully yours.

M. De
Cerjat.

GAD'S HILL, *Wednesday, Seventh July*, 1858.

MY DEAR CERJAT,

I should vainly try to tell you—so I *won't* try—how
affected I have been by your warm-hearted letter, or how
thoroughly well convinced I always am of the truth and earnestness of your friendship. I thank you, my dear, dear fellow, with
my whole soul. I fervently return that friendship and I highly
cherish it.

You want to know all about me? I am still reading in London
every Thursday, and the audiences are very great, and the success
immense. On the Second of August I am going away on a tour
of some four months in England, Ireland, and Scotland. I shall
read, during that time, not fewer than four or five times a week.
It will be sharp work; but probably a certain musical clinking will
come of it, which will mitigate the hardship.

At this present moment I am on my little Kentish freehold
(*not* in top-boots, and not particularly prejudiced that I know of),
looking on as pretty a view out of my study window as you will
find in a long day's English ride. My little place is a grave red
brick house, which I have added to and stuck bits upon in all
manner of ways, so that it is as pleasantly irregular, and as
violently opposed to all architectural ideas, as the most hopeful
man could possibly desire. The robbery was committed before
the door, on the man with the treasure, and Falstaff ran away
from the identical spot of ground now covered by the room in
which I write. A little rustic alehouse, called The Sir John
Falstaff, is over the way—has been over the way, ever since, in
honour of the event. Cobham Woods and Park are behind the
house; the distant Thames in front; the Medway, with Rochester,

* The charming actress, the mother of Mr. Edmund Yates.

and its old castle and cathedral, on one side. The whole stupendous property is on the old Dover Road.

The blessed woods and fields have done me a world of good, and I am quite myself again. The children are all as happy as children can be. My eldest daughter, Mary, keeps house, with a state and gravity becoming that high position; wherein she is assisted by her sister Katie, and by her aunt Georgina, who is, and always has been, like another sister. Two big dogs, a bloodhound and a St. Bernard, direct from a convent of that name, where I think you once were, are their principal attendants in the green lanes. These latter instantly untie the neckerchiefs of all tramps and prowlers who approach their presence, so that they wander about without any escort, and drive big horses in basketphaetons through murderous bye-ways, and never come to grief. They are very curious about your daughters, and send all kinds of loves to them and to Mrs. Cerjat, in which I heartily join.

You will have read in the papers that the Thames in London is most horrible. I have to cross Waterloo or London Bridge to get to the railroad when I come down here, and I can certify that the offensive smells, even in that short whiff, have been of a most head-and-stomach-distending nature. Nobody knows what is to be done; at least everybody knows a plan, and everybody else knows it won't do; in the meantime cartloads of chloride of lime are shot into the filthy stream, and do something I hope. You will know, before you get this, that the American telegraph line has parted again, at which most men are sorry, but very few surprised. This is all the news, except that there is an Italian Opera at Drury Lane, price eighteenpence to the pit, where Viardot, by far the greatest artist of them all, sings, and which is full when the dear opera can't let a box; and except that the weather has been exceptionally hot, but is now quite cool. On the top of this hill it has been cold, actually cold at night, for more than a week past.

My dear Cerjat, I have written lightly enough, because I want you to know that I am becoming cheerful and hearty. God bless you! I love you, and I know that you love me.

Ever your attached and affectionate.

WEST HOE, PLYMOUTH,   Miss
Thursday, Fifth August, 1858.   Hogarth.

MY DEAREST GEORGY,

I received your letter this morning with the greatest pleasure, and read it with the utmost interest in all its domestic details.

We had a most wonderful night at Exeter. It is to be regretted that we cannot take the place again on our way back. It was a prodigious cram, and we turned away no end of people. But not only that, I think they were the finest audience I have ever read to. I don't think I ever read, in some respects, so well; and I never beheld anything like the personal affection which they poured out upon me at the end. It was really a remarkable sight, and I shall always look back upon it with pleasure.

Last night here was not so bright. There are quarrels of the strangest kind between the Plymouth people and the Stonehouse people. The room is at Stonehouse (Tracy says the wrong room; there being a Plymouth room in this hotel, and he being a Plymouthite). We had a fair house, but not at all a great one. All the notabilities come this morning to "Little Dombey." For "Mrs. Gamp and the Boots," to-night, we have also a very promising let. But the races are on, and there are two public balls to-night, and the yacht squadron are all at Cherbourg to boot.

The room is a very handsome one, but it is on the top of a windy and muddy hill, leading (literally) to nowhere; and it looks (except that it is new and *mortary*) as if the subsidence of the waters after the Deluge might have left it where it is. I have to go right through the company to get to the platform. Big doors slam and resound when anybody comes in; and all the company seem afraid of one another. Nevertheless they were a sensible audience last night, and much impressed and pleased.

Tracy is in the room (wandering about, and never finishing a sentence), and sends all manner of sea-loves to you and the dear girls. I send all manner of land-loves to you from myself, out of my heart of hearts, and also to my dear Plorn and the boys.

Arthur sends his kindest love. He knows only two characters. He is either always corresponding, like a Secretary of State, or he is transformed into a rout-furniture dealer of Rathbone Place, and drags forms about with the greatest violence, without his coat.

Ever, dearest Georgy, your most affectionate.

Miss
Dickens.

LONDON, *Saturday, Seventh August,* 1858.

MY DEAREST MAMEY,

The closing night at Plymouth was a very great scene, and the morning there was exceedingly good too. You will be glad to hear that at Clifton last night, a torrent of five hundred shillings bore Arthur away, pounded him against the wall, flowed on to the seats over his body, scratched him, and damaged his best dress suit. All to his unspeakable joy.

This is a very short letter, but I am going to the Burlington

Arcade, desperately resolved to have all those wonderful instruments put into operation on my head, with a view to refreshing it.

Ever your affectionate.

SHREWSBURY, *Thursday, Twelfth August*, 1858.

A wonderful audience last night at Wolverhampton. If such a thing can be, they were even quicker and more intelligent than the audience I had in Edinburgh. They were so wonderfully good and were so much on the alert this morning by nine o'clock for another reading, that we are going back there at about our Bradford time. I never saw such people. And the local agent would take no money, and charge no expenses of his own.

This place looks what Plorn would call "ortily" dull. Local agent predicts, however, "great satisfaction to Mr. Dickens, and excellent attendance." I have just been to look at the hall, where everything was wrong, and where I have left Arthur making a platform for me out of dining-tables.

I have not felt the fatigue to any extent worth mentioning; though I get, every night, into the most violent heats. We are going to dine at three o'clock (it wants a quarter now) and have not been here two hours, so I have seen nothing of Clement.

Tell Georgy with my love, that I read in the same room in which we acted, but at the end opposite to that where our stage was. We are not at the inn where the amateur company put up, but at The Lion, where the fair Miss Mitchell was lodged alone. We have the strangest little rooms (sitting-room and two bedrooms altogether), the ceilings of which I can touch with my hand. The windows bulge out over the street, as if they were little stern-windows in a ship. And a door opens out of the sitting-room on to a little open gallery with plants in it, where one leans over a queer old rail, and looks all downhill and slantwise at the crookedest black and yellow old houses, all manner of shapes except straight shapes. To get into this room we come through a china closet; and the man in laying the cloth has actually knocked down, in that repository, two geraniums and Napoleon Bonaparte.

I think that's all I have to say, except that at the Wolverhampton theatre they played "Oliver Twist" last night (Mr. Toole the Artful Dodger), "in consequence of the illustrious author honouring the town with his presence."

John's spirits have been equable and good since we rejoined him. Berry has always got something the matter with his digestion—seems to me the male gender of Maria Jolly, and ought to take nothing but Revalenta Arabica.

Ever your affectionate Father.

ADELPHI HOTEL, LIVERPOOL,
Friday Night, Twentieth August, 1858.

I write to report that my cold is decidedly better, thank God (though still bad), and that I hope to be able to stagger through to-night. After dinner yesterday I began to recover my voice, and I think I sang half the Irish Melodies to myself, as I walked about to test it. I got home at half-past ten, and mustard-poulticed and barley-watered myself tremendously.

I have been very hard to sleep, and last night I was all but sleepless. This morning I was very dull and seedy; but I got a good walk, and picked up again. It has been blowing all day, and I fear we shall have a sick passage over to Dublin to-morrow night.

Tell Mamie (with my dear love to her and Katie) that I will write to her from Dublin—probably on Sunday. Tell her too that the stories she told me in her letter were not only capital stories in themselves, but *excellently told* too.

What Arthur's state has been to-night—he, John, Berry, and Boylett, all taking money and going mad together—you *cannot* imagine. They turned away hundreds, sold all the books, rolled on the ground of my room knee-deep in checks, and made a perfect pantomime of the whole thing. He has kept quite well, I am happy to say, and sends a hundred loves.

Ever affectionately.

MORRISON'S HOTEL, DUBLIN,
Monday, Twenty-third August, 1858.

We had a nasty crossing here. We left Holyhead at one in the morning, and got here at six. Arthur was incessantly sick the whole way. I was not sick at all, but was in as healthy a condition otherwise as humanity need be. We are in a beautiful hotel. Our sitting-room is exactly like the drawing-room at the Peschiere in all its dimensions. I never saw two rooms so exactly resembling one another in their proportions. Our bedrooms too are excellent, and there are baths and all sorts of comforts.

The Lord Lieutenant is away, and the place looks to me as if its professional life were away too. Nevertheless, there are numbers of people in the streets. Somehow, I hardly seem to think we are going to do enormously here; but I have scarcely any reason for supposing so (except that a good many houses are shut up); and I *know* nothing about it, for Arthur is now gone to the agent and to the room. The men came by boat direct from Liverpool. They had a rough passage, were all ill, and did not get here till noon yesterday. Donnybrook Fair, or what remains of it, is going on, within two or three miles of Dublin. They went out there yesterday in a jaunting-car, and John described it to us at dinner-time (with his eyebrows lifted up, and his legs well asunder), as "Johnny Brooks' Fair;" at which Arthur, who was drinking bitter ale, nearly laughed himself to death. Berry is always unfortunate, and when I asked what had happened to Berry on board the steamboat, it appeared that "an Irish gentleman which was drunk, and fancied himself the captain, wanted to knock Berry down."

I am surprised by finding this place very much larger than I had supposed it to be. Its bye-parts are bad enough, but cleaner, too, than I had supposed them to be, and certainly very much cleaner than the old town of Edinburgh. The man who drove our jaunting-car yesterday hadn't a piece in his coat as big as a penny roll, and had had his hat on (apparently without brushing it) ever since he was grown up. But he was remarkably intelligent and agreeable, with something to say about everything. For instance, when I asked him what a certain building was, he didn't say "courts of law" and nothing else, but: "Av you plase, sir, it's the foor coorts o' looyers, where Misther O'Connell stood his trial wunst, ye'll remimber, sir, afore I tell ye of it." When we got into the Phœnix Park, he looked round him as if it were his own, and said: "THAT's a park, sir, av yer plase." I complimented it, and he said: "Gintlemen tills me as they'r bin, sir, over Europe, and never see a park aqualling ov it. 'Tis eight mile roond, sir, ten mile and a half long, and in the month of May the hawthorn trees are as beautiful as brides with their white jewels on. Yonder's the vice-regal lodge, sir; in them two corners lives the two sicretirries, wishing I was them, sir. There's air here, sir, av yer plase! There's scenery here, sir! There's mountains—thim, sir! Yer coonsider it a park, sir? It is that, sir!"

You should have heard John in my bedroom this morning endeavouring to imitate a bath-man, who had resented his interference, and had said as to the shower-bath: "Yer'll not be touching *that*, young man. Divil a touch yer'll touch o' that insthrument, young man!" It was more ridiculously unlike the reality than I can express to you, yet he was so delighted with his powers that he went off in the absurdest little gingerbeery giggle, backing into my portmanteau all the time.

I shall write to Katie next, and then to Aunty. My cold, I am happy to report, is very much better. I lay in the wet all night on deck, on board the boat, but am not as yet any the worse for it. Arthur was quite insensible when we got to Dublin, and stared at our luggage without in the least offering to claim it. He left his kindest love for all before he went out.

Ever, my dearest Mamie,

Your most affectionate Father.

Miss
Hogarth.

MORRISON'S HOTEL, DUBLIN,
Wednesday, Twenty-fifth August, 1858.

I begin my letter to you to-day, though I don't know when I may send it off. We had a very good house last night. For "Little Dombey," this morning, we have an immense stall let—already more than two hundred—and people are now fighting in the agent's shop to take more.

They were a highly excitable audience last night, but they certainly did not comprehend—internally and intellectually comprehend—"The Chimes" as a London audience do. I am quite sure of it. I very much doubt the Irish capacity of receiving the pathetic; but of their quickness as to the humorous there can be no doubt. I shall see how they go along with Little Paul, in his death, presently.

We meant, as I said in a letter to Katie, to go to Queenstown yesterday and bask on the seashore. But there is always so much to do that we couldn't manage it after all. We expect a tremendous house to-morrow night as well as to-day. I have become a wonderful Irishman—must play an Irish part some day—and Arthur's only relaxation is when I enact "John and the Boots," which I consequently do enact all day long. The papers are full of remarks upon my white tie, and describe it as being of enormous size, which is a wonderful delusion, because, as you very well know, it is a small tie. Generally, I am happy to report, the Emerald press is in favour of my appearance, and likes my eyes. But one gentleman comes out with a letter at Cork, wherein he says that although only forty-six I look like an old man. *He* is a rum customer, I think.

John has given it up altogether as to rivalry with the Boots, and did not come into my room this morning at all. Boots appeared triumphant and alone. He was waiting for me at the hotel-door last night. "Whaa't sart of a hoose, sur?" he asked me. "Capital." "The Lard be praised fur the 'onor o' Dooblin!"

Arthur buys bad apples in the streets and brings them home and doesn't eat them, and then I am obliged to put them in the balcony because they make the room smell faint. Also he meets countrymen with honeycomb on their heads, and leads them (by the buttonhole when they have one) to this gorgeous establishment and requests the bar to buy honeycomb for his breakfast ; then it stands upon the sideboard uncovered and the flies fall into it. He buys owls, too, and castles, and other horrible objects, made in bog-oak ; and he is perpetually snipping pieces out of newspapers and sending them all over the world. While I am reading he conducts the correspondence, and his great delight is to show me seventeen or eighteen letters when I come, exhausted, into the retiring-place. Berry has not got into any particular trouble for forty-eight hours, except that he is all over boils. I have prescribed the yeast, but ineffectually. It is indeed a sight to see him and John sitting in pay-boxes, and surveying Ireland out of pigeon-holes.

Same Evening before Bed-time.

Everybody was at "Little Dombey" to-day, and although I had some little difficulty to work them up in consequence of the excessive crowding of the place, and the difficulty of shaking the people into their seats, the effect was unmistakable and profound. The crying was universal, and they were extraordinarily affected. There is no doubt we could stay here a week with that one reading, and fill the place every night. Hundreds of people have been there to-night, under the impression that it would come off again. It was a most decided and complete success.

Here follows a dialogue (but it requires imitation), which I had yesterday morning with a little boy of the house—landlord's son, I suppose—about Plorn's age. I am sitting on the sofa writing, and find him sitting beside me.

INIMITABLE. Holloa, old chap.

YOUNG IRELAND. Hal-loo !

INIMITABLE (*in his delightful way*). What a nice old fellow you are. I am very fond of little boys.

YOUNG IRELAND. Air yer ! Ye'r right.

INIMITABLE. What do you learn, old fellow !

YOUNG IRELAND (*very intent on Inimitable, and always childish, except in his brogue*). I lairn wureds of three sillibils, and wureds of two sillibils, and wureds of one sillibil.

INIMITABLE (*gaily*). Get out, you humbug ! You learn only words of one syllable.

YOUNG IRELAND (*laughs heartily*). You may say that it is mostly wureds of one sillibil.

INIMITABLE. Can you write !

YOUNG IRELAND. Not yet. Things comes by deegrays.

INIMITABLE. Can you cipher !

YOUNG IRELAND (*very quickly*). Wha'at's that !

INIMITABLE. Can you make figures !

YOUNG IRELAND. I can make a nought, which is not easy, being roond.

INIMITABLE. I say, old boy, wasn't it you I saw on Sunday morning in the hall, in a soldier's cap? You know—in a soldier's cap?

YOUNG IRELAND (*cogitating deeply*). Was it a very good cap?

INIMITABLE. Yes.

YOUNG IRELAND. Did it fit unkommon?

INIMITABLE. Yes.

YOUNG IRELAND. Dat was me!

There are two stupid old louts at the room, to show people into their places, whom John calls "them two old Paddies," and of whom he says, that he "never see nothing like them (snigger) hold idiots" (snigger). They bow and walk backwards before the grandees, and our men hustle them while they are doing it.

We walked out last night, with the intention of going to the theatre; but the Piccolomini establishment (they were doing the "Lucia") looked so horribly like a very bad jail, and the Queen's looked so blackguardly, that we came back again, and went to bed. I seem to be always either in a railway carriage, or reading, or going to bed. I get so knocked up, whenever I have a minute to remember it, that then I go to bed as a matter of course.

I am looking forward to the last Irish reading on Thursday, with great impatience. But when we shall have turned this week, once knocked off Belfast, I shall see land, and shall (like poor Timber in the days of old) "keep up a good heart."

Ever, my dearest Georgy, most affectionately.

Miss Dickens.

BELFAST, *Saturday, Twenty-eighth August,* 1858.

When I went down to the Rotunda at Dublin on Thursday night, I said to Arthur, who came rushing at me: "You needn't tell me. I know all about it." The moment I had come out of the door of the hotel (a mile off), I had come against the stream of people turned away. I had struggled against it to the room. There, the crowd in all the lobbies and passages was so great, that I had a difficulty in getting in. They had broken all the glass in the pay-boxes. Our men were flattened against walls and squeezed against beams. Ladies stood all night with their chins against my platform. Other ladies sat all night upon my steps. You never saw such a sight. And the reading went tremendously! It is much to be regretted that we troubled ourselves to go anywhere else in Ireland.

We arrived here yesterday at two. The same scene was repeated with the additional feature, that the people are much rougher here than in Dublin, and that there was a very great uproar at the opening of the doors, which, the police in attendance being quite inefficient and only looking on, it was impossible to check. Arthur was in the deepest misery because shillings got into stalls, and halfcrowns got into shillings, and stalls got nowhere, and there was immense confusion. It ceased, however, the moment I showed myself; and all went most brilliantly, in spite of a great piece of the cornice of the ceiling falling with a great crash within four or five inches of the head of a young lady on my platform (I was obliged to have people there), and in spite of my gas suddenly going out at the time of the game of forfeits at Scrooge's nephew's, through some Belfastian gentleman accidentally treading on the flexible pipe, and needing to be relighted.

We shall not get to Cork before mid-day on Monday; it being difficult to get from here on Sunday. We hope to be able to start away to-morrow morning to see the Giant's Causeway (some sixteen miles off), and in that case we shall sleep at Dublin to-morrow night, leaving here by the train at half-past three in the afternoon. Dublin, you must understand, is on the way to Cork. This is a fine place, surrounded by lofty hills. The streets are very wide, and the place is very prosperous. The whole ride from Dublin here is through a very picturesque and various country; and the amazing thing is, that it is all particularly neat and orderly, and that the houses (outside at all events) are all brightly whitewashed and remarkably clean. I want to climb one of the neighbouring hills before this morning's "Dombey."

Our men are deeply interested in the success, and are as zealous and ardent as possible.

Ever, my dearest Mamie,
Your most affectionate Father.

MORRISON'S HOTEL, DUBLIN,
Sunday Night, Twenty-ninth August, 1858.

Miss
Hogarth.

I am so delighted to find your letter here to-night (eleven o'clock), and so afraid that, in the wear and tear of this strange life, I have written to Gad's Hill in the wrong order, and have not written to you, as I should, that I resolve to write this before going to bed. You will find it a wretchedly stupid letter; but you may imagine, my dearest girl, that I am tired.

The success at Belfast has been equal to the success here. Enormous! I think them a better audience, on the whole, than Dublin; and the personal affection there was something overwhelming. I wish you and the dear girls could have seen the people look at me in the street; or heard them ask me, as I hurried to the hotel after reading last night, to " do me the honour to shake hands, Misther Dickens, and God bless you, sir ; not ounly for the light you've been to me this night, but for the light you've been in mee house, sir (and God love your face !) this many a year." Every night, by-the-bye, since I have been in Ireland, the ladies have beguiled John out of the bouquet from my coat. And yesterday morning, as I had showered the leaves from my geranium in reading " Little Dombey," they mounted the platform, after I was gone, and picked them all up as keepsakes !

I have never seen *men* go in to cry so undisguisedly as they did at that reading yesterday afternoon. They made no attempt whatever to hide it, and certainly cried more than the women. As to the " Boots " at night, and " Mrs. Gamp " too, it was just one roar with me and them, for they made me laugh so that sometimes I *could not* compose my face to go on.

You must not let the new idea of poor dear Landor efface the former image of the fine old man. I wouldn't blot him out, in his tender gallantry, as he sat upon that bed at Forster's that night, for a million of wild mistakes at eighty years of age.

Tell the girls that Arthur and I have each ordered at Belfast a trim, sparkling, slap-up *Irish jaunting-car ! ! !* I flatter myself we shall astonish the Kentish people. It is the oddest carriage in the world, and you are always falling off. But it is gay and bright in the highest degree. Wonderfully Neapolitan.

What with a sixteen-mile ride before we left Belfast, and a sea-beach walk, and a two-o'clock dinner, and a seven-hours' railway ride since, I am—as we say here—" a thrifle weary." But I really am in wonderful force, considering the work. For which I am, as I ought to be, very thankful.

Arthur was exceedingly unwell last night—could not cheer up at all. He was so very unwell that he left the hall (!) and became invisible after my five minutes' rest. I found him at the hotel in a jacket and slippers, and with a hot bath just ready. He was in the last stage of prostration. The local agent was with me, and proposed that he (the wretched Arthur) should go to his office and balance the accounts then and there. He went, in the jacket and slippers, and came back in twenty minutes, *perfectly well*, in consequence of the admirable balance. He is now sitting opposite to me ON THE BAG OF SILVER (it must be dreadfully hard), writing to Boulogne.

Best love to Mamie and Katie, and dear Plorn, and all the boys left when this comes to Gad's Hill ; also to my dear good Anne, and her little woman.

                                        Ever affectionately.

GAD'S HILL PLACE, HIGHAM BY ROCHESTER, KENT,
Monday, Sixth September, 1858.

MY DEAR WILKIE,

First, let me report myself here for something less than eight-and-forty hours. I come last (and direct—a pretty hard journey) from Limerick.

The work is very hard, sometimes overpowering; but I am none the worse for it, and arrived here quite fresh.

Secondly, will you let me recommend the enclosed letter from Wigan, as the groundwork of a capital article, in your way, for H. W.? There is not the least objection to a plain reference to him, or to Phelps, to whom the same thing happened a year or two ago, near Islington, in the case of a clever and capital little daughter of his. I think it a capital opportunity for a discourse on gentility, with a glance at those other schools which advertise that the "sons of gentlemen only" are admitted, and a just recognition of the greater liberality of our public schools. There are tradesmen's sons at Eton, and Charles Kean was at Eton, and Macready (also an actor's son) was at Rugby. Some such title as "Scholastic Flunkeydom," or anything infinitely contemptuous, would help out the meaning. Surely such a schoolmaster must swallow all the silver forks that the pupils are expected to take when they come, and are not expected to take away with them when they go. And of course he could not exist, unless he had flunkey customers by the dozen.

Secondly—no, this is thirdly now—about the Christmas number. I have arranged so to stop my readings, as to be available for it on *Fifteenth of November*, which will leave me time to write a good article, if I clear my way to one. Do you see your way to our making a Christmas number of this idea that I am going very briefly to hint? Some disappointed person, man or woman, prematurely disgusted with the world, for some reason or no reason (the person should be young, I think) retires to an old lonely house, or an old lonely mill, or anything you like, with one attendant, resolved to shut out the world, and hold no communion with it. The one attendant sees the absurdity of the idea, pretends to humour it, but really tries to slaughter it. Everything that happens, everybody that comes near, every breath of human interest that floats into the old place from the village, or the heath, or the four cross-roads near which it stands, and from which belated travellers stray into it, shows beyond mistake that you can't shut out the world; that you are in it, to be of it; that you get into a false position the moment you try to sever yourself from it; and that you must mingle with it, and make the best of it, and make the best of yourself into the bargain.

If we could plot out a way of doing this together, I would not be afraid to take my part. If we could not, could we plot out a way of doing it, and taking in stories by other hands? If we could not do either (but I think we could), shall we fall back upon a round of stories again? That I would rather not do, if possible. Will you think about it?

Ever, my dear Wilkie, affectionately yours.

STATION HOTEL, YORK,
Friday, Tenth September, 1858.

Miss Mary
Boyle.

DEAREST MEERY, .

First let me tell you that all the magicians and spirits in your employ have fulfilled the instructions of their wondrous mistress to admiration. Flowers have fallen in my path wherever I have trod; and when they rained upon me at Cork I was more amazed than you ever saw me.

Secondly, receive my hearty and loving thanks for that same. (Excuse a little Irish in the turn of that sentence, but I can't help it.)

I really cannot tell you how truly and tenderly I feel your letter, and how gratified I am by its contents. Your truth and attachment are always so precious to me that I can*not* get my heart out on my sleeve to show it you. It is like a child, and at the sound of some familiar voices, "goes and hides."

You know what an affection I have for Mrs. Watson, and how happy it made me to see her again—younger, much, than when I first knew her in Switzerland.

God bless you always!   Ever affectionately yours.

ROYAL HOTEL, SCARBOROUGH,
Sunday, Twelfth September, 1858.

Miss
Hogarth.

MY DEAREST GEORGY,

We had a very fine house indeed at York. At Harrogate yesterday; the queerest place, with the strangest people in it, leading the oddest lives of dancing, newspaper reading, and tables d'hôte. The piety of York obliging us to leave that place for this at six this morning, and there being no night train from Harrogate, we had to engage a special engine. We got to bed at one, and were up again before five; which, after yesterday's fatigues, leaves me a little worn out at this present.

We have a charming room, overlooking the sea. Leech is here (living within a few doors), with the partner of his bosom, and his young family. I write at ten in the morning, having been here two hours; and you will readily suppose that I have not seen him.

Of news, I have not the faintest breath. I seem to have been doing nothing all my life but riding in railway-carriages and reading. The railway of the morning brought us through Castle Howard, and under the woods of Easthorpe, and then just below Malton Abbey. It was a most lovely morning, and, tired as I was, I couldn't sleep for looking out of window.

Yesterday, at Harrogate, two circumstances occurred which gave Arthur great delight. Firstly, he chafed his legs sore with his black bag of silver. Secondly, the landlord asked him as a favour, " If he could oblige him with a little silver." He obliged him directly with some forty pounds' worth; and I suspect the landlord to have repented of having approached the subject. After the reading last night we walked over the moor to the railway, three miles, leaving our men to follow with the luggage in a light cart. They passed us just short of the railway, and John was making the night hideous and terrifying the sleeping country, by *playing the horn* in prodigiously horrible and unmusical blasts.

My dearest love, of course, to the dear girls, and to the noble Plorn. Apropos of children, there was one gentleman at the " Little Dombey " yesterday morning, who exhibited, or rather concealed, the profoundest grief. After crying a good deal without hiding it, he covered his face with both his hands, and laid it down on the back of the seat before him, and really shook with emotion. He was not in mourning, but I supposed him to have lost some child in old time. There was a remarkably good fellow of thirty or so, too, who found something so very ludicrous in " Toots," that he *could not* compose himself at all, but laughed until he sat wiping his eyes with his handkerchief. And whenever he felt " Toots " coming again he began to laugh and wipe his eyes afresh, and when he came he gave a kind of cry, as if it were too much for him. It was uncommonly droll, and made me laugh heartily.

Ever, dear Georgy, your most affectionate.

SCARBOROUGH ARMS, LEEDS,
Wednesday, Fifteenth September, 1858.

Miss Dickens.

MY DEAREST MAMIE,

I have added a pound to the cheque. I would recommend your seeing the poor railway man again and giving him ten shillings, and telling him to let you see him again in about a week. If he be then still unable to lift weights and handle heavy things, I would then give him another ten shillings, and so on.

Since I wrote to Georgy from Scarborough, we have had, thank God, nothing but success. The Hull people (not generally considered excitable, even on their own showing) were so enthusiastic, that we were obliged to promise to go back there for two readings.

Arthur told you, I suppose, that he had his shirt-front and waistcoat torn off last night? He was perfectly enraptured in consequence. Our men got so knocked about that he gave them five shillings apiece on the spot. John passed several minutes upside down against a wall, with his head amongst the people's boots. He came out of the difficulty in an exceedingly touzled condition, and with his face much flushed. For all this, and their being packed as you may conceive they would be packed, they settled down the instant I went in, and never wavered in the closest attention for an instant. It was a very high room, and required a great effort.

These streets look like a great circus with the season just finished. All sorts of garish triumphal arches were put up for the Queen, and they have got smoky, and have been looked out of countenance by the sun, and are blistered and patchy, and half up and half down, and are hideous to behold. Spiritless men (evidently drunk for some time in the royal honour) are slowly removing them, and on the whole it is more like the clearing away of "The Frozen Deep" at Tavistock House than anything within your knowledge—with the exception that we are not in the least sorry, as we were then. Vague ideas are in Arthur's head that when we come back to Hull, we are to come here, and are to have the Town Hall (a beautiful building), and read to the million. I can't say yet. That depends. I remember that when I was here before (I came from Rockingham to make a speech), I thought them a dull and slow audience. I hope I may have been mistaken. I never saw better audiences than the Yorkshire audiences generally.

I am so perpetually at work or asleep, that I have not a scrap of news.

Tell the servants that I remember them, and hope they will live with us many years.

Ever, my dearest Mamie,
Your most affectionate Father.

Miss
Hogarth.

KING'S HEAD, SHEFFIELD,
Friday, Seventeenth September, 1858.

I write you a few lines to Tavistock House, thinking you may not be sorry to find a note from me there on your arrival from Gad's Hill.

Halifax was too small for us. I never saw such an audience though. They were really worth reading to for nothing, though I didn't do exactly that.   It is as horrible a place as I ever saw, I think.

The trains are so strange and unintelligible in this part of the country that we were obliged to leave Halifax at eight this morning, and breakfast on the road—at Huddersfield again, where we had an hour's wait.   Wills was in attendance on the platform, and took me (here at Sheffield, I mean) out to Frederick Lehmann's house to see Mrs. Wills.   She looked pretty much the same as ever, I thought, and was taking care of a very pretty little boy.   The house and grounds are as nice as anything *can* be in this smoke.   A heavy thunderstorm is passing over the town, and it is raining hard too.

This is a stupid letter, my dearest Georgy, but I write in a hurry, and in the thunder and lightning, and with the crowd of to-night before me.

Ever most affectionately.

STATION HOTEL, NEWCASTLE-ON-TYNE,   Miss
Sunday, Twenty-sixth September, 1858.   Hogarth.

EXTRACT.

The girls (as I have no doubt they have already told you for themselves) arrived here in good time yesterday, and in very fresh condition.   They persisted in going to the room last night, though I had arranged for their remaining quiet.

We have done a vast deal here.   I suppose you know that we are going to Berwick, and that we mean to sleep there and go on to Edinburgh on Monday morning, arriving there before noon? If it be as fine to-morrow as it is to-day, the girls will see the coast piece of railway between Berwick and Edinburgh to great advantage.   I was anxious that they should, because that kind of pleasure is really almost the only one they are likely to have in their present trip.

Stanfield and Roberts are in Edinburgh, and the Scottish Royal Academy gave them a dinner on Wednesday, to which I was very pressingly invited.   But, of course, my going was impossible.   I read twice that day.

I read at Sunderland in a beautiful new theatre, and (I thought to myself) quite wonderfully.   Such an audience I never beheld for rapidity and enthusiasm.   The room in which we acted (converted into a theatre afterwards) was burnt to the ground a year or two ago.   We found the hotel, so bad in our time, really good. I walked from Durham to Sunderland, and from Sunderland to Newcastle.

My best love to the noble Plornish.   If he is quite reconciled to

2 H

the postponement of his trousers, I should like to behold his first appearance in them.   But, if not, as he is such a good fellow, I think it would be a pity to disappoint and try him.

And now, my dearest Georgy, I think I have said all I have to say before I go out for a little air.   I had a very hard day yesterday, and am tired.

Ever your most affectionate.

Mr. John
Forster.

TAVISTOCK HOUSE, TAVISTOCK SQUARE, LONDON,
Sunday, Tenth October, 1858.

MY DEAR FORSTER,

As to the truth of the readings, I cannot tell you what the demonstrations of personal regard and respect are.   How the densest and most uncomfortably-packed crowd will be hushed in an instant when I show my face.   How the youth of colleges, and the old men of business in the town, seem equally unable to get near enough to me when they cheer me away at night.   How common people and gentlefolks will stop me in the streets and say: "Mr. Dickens, will you let me touch the hand that has filled my home with so many friends?"   And if you saw the mothers, and fathers, and sisters, and brothers in mourning, who invariably come to "Little Dombey," and if you studied the wonderful expression of comfort and reliance with which they hang about me, as if I had been with them, all kindness and delicacy, at their own little death-bed, you would think it one of the strangest things in the world.

As to the mere effect, of course I don't go on doing the thing so often without carefully observing myself and the people too in every little thing, and without (in consequence) greatly improving in it.

At Aberdeen, we were crammed to the street twice in one day. At Perth (where I thought when I arrived there literally could be nobody to come), the nobility came posting in from thirty miles round, and the whole town came and filled an immense hall.   As to the effect, if you had seen them after Lilian died, in "The Chimes," or when Scrooge woke and talked to the boy outside the window, I doubt if you would ever have forgotten it.   And at the end of "Dombey" yesterday afternoon, in the cold light of day, they all got up, after a short pause, gentle and simple, and thundered and waved their hats with that astonishing heartiness and fondness for me, that for the first time in all my public career they took me completely off my legs, and I saw the whole eighteen hundred of them reel on one side as if a shock from without had shaken the hall.

The dear girls have enjoyed themselves immensely, and their

trip has been a great success. I hope I told you (but I forget whether I did or no) how splendidly Newcastle* came out. I am reminded of Newcastle at the moment because they joined me there.

I am anxious to get to the end of my readings, and to be at home again, and able to sit down and think in my own study. But the fatigue, though sometimes very great indeed, hardly tells upon me at all. And although all our people, from Smith downwards, have given in, more or less, at times, I have never been in the least unequal to the work, though sometimes sufficiently disinclined for it. My kindest and best love to Mrs. Forster.

Ever affectionately.

ROYAL HOTEL, DERBY,
Friday, Twenty-second October, 1858.

Miss Dickens.

MY DEAREST MAMIE,

I am writing in a very poor condition; I have a bad cold all over me, pains in my back and limbs, and a very sensitive and uncomfortable throat. There was a great draught up some stone steps near me last night, and I daresay that caused it.

The weather on my first two nights at Birmingham was so intolerably bad—it blew hard, and never left off raining for one single moment—that the houses were not what they otherwise would have been. On the last night the weather cleared, and we had a grand house.

Last night at Nottingham was almost, if not quite, the most amazing we have had. It is not a very large place, and the room is by no means a very large one. Here, it is a pretty room, but not large.

Arthur and I have considered Plornish's joke in all the immense number of aspects in which it presents itself to reflective minds. We have come to the conclusion that it is the best joke ever made. Give the dear boy my love, and the same to Georgy, and the same to Katey, and take the same yourself. Arthur (excessively low and inarticulate) mutters that he "unites."

[We knocked up Boylett, Berry, and John so frightfully yesterday, by tearing the room to pieces and altogether reversing it, as late as four o'clock, that we gave them a supper last night. They shine all over to-day, as if it had been entirely composed of grease.]

Ever, my dearest Mamie,
Your most affectionate Father.

* The birthplace of Mr. Forster.

Miss
Hogarth.

WOLVERHAMPTON,
Wednesday, Third November, 1854.

Little Leamington is represented as the dullest and worst of audiences. I found it very good indeed, even in the morning.

The evening being fine, and blue being to be seen in the sky beyond the smoke, we expect to have a very full hall. Tell Mamey and Katey that if they had been with us on the railway to-day between Leamington and this place, they would have seen (though it is only an hour and ten minutes by the express) fires and smoke indeed. We came through a part of the Black Country that you know, and it looked at its blackest. All the furnaces seemed in full blast, and all the coal-pits to be working.

It is market-day here, and the ironmasters are standing out in the street (where they always hold high change), making such an iron hum and buzz, that they confuse me horribly. In addition there is a bellman announcing something—not the readings, I beg to say—and there is an excavation being made in the centre of the open place, for a statue, or a pump, or a lamp-post, or something or other, round which all the Wolverhampton boys are yelling and struggling.

My best love to the dear girls, and to Plorn, and to you, Marguerite and Ellen Stone not forgotten. All yesterday and to-day I have been doing everything to the tune of:

And the day is dark and dreary.

Ever, dearest Georgy,
Your most affectionate and faithful.

P.S.—I hope the brazier is intolerably hot, and half stifles all the family. Then, and not otherwise, I shall think it in satisfactory work.

Rev. James
White.

TAVISTOCK HOUSE, TAVISTOCK SQUARE, LONDON, W.C.,
Friday, Fifth November, 1858.

MY DEAR WHITE,

May I entreat you to thank Mr. Carter very earnestly and kindly in my name, for his proffered hospitality; and, further, to explain to him that since my readings began, I have known them to be incompatible with all social enjoyments, and have neither set foot in a friend's house nor sat down to a friend's table in any one of all the many places I have been to, but have rigidly kept myself to my hotels. To this resolution I must hold until the last. There is not the least virtue in it. It is a matter of stern necessity, and I submit with the worst grace possible.

Will you let me know, either at Southampton or Portsmouth,

whether any of you, and how many of you, if any, are coming over, so that Arthur Smith may reserve good seats? Tell Lotty I hope she does not contemplate coming to the morning reading; I always hate it so myself.

Ever, my dear White, affectionately yours.

* TAVISTOCK HOUSE, *Twenty-sixth November*, 1858.   Mr.
Blanchard
Jerrold.

      *   *   *   *   *

It has been a gloomy task, and has made my heart heavy. It is not likely that I can furnish you with any new particulars of interest concerning your lamented father. Such details of his life and struggles as I have often heard from himself are better known to you than to me; and my praises of him can make no new sound in your ears.

But as you wish me to note down for you my last remembrance and experience of him, I proceed to do so. It is natural that my thoughts should first rush back (as they instantly do) to the days when he began to be known to me, and to the many happy hours I afterwards passed in his society.

Few of his friends, I think, can have had more favourable opportunities of knowing him, in his gentlest and most affectionate aspect, than I have had. He was one of the gentlest and most affectionate of men. I remember very well that when I first saw him, in or about the year 1835—when I went into his sick room in St. Michael's Grove, Brompton, and found him propped up in a great chair, bright-eyed, and eager and quick in spirit, but very lame in body—he gave me an impression of tenderness. It never became dissociated from him. There was nothing cynical or sour in his heart as I knew it. In the company of children and young people he was particularly happy, and showed to extraordinary advantage. He never was so gay, so sweet-tempered, so pleasing, and so pleased as then. Among my own children I had observed this many and many a time. When they and I came home from Italy in 1845, your father went to Brussels to meet us in company with our friends, Mr. Forster and Mr. Maclise. We all travelled together about Belgium for a little while, and all came home together. He was the delight of the children all the time, and they were his delight. He was in his most brilliant spirits, and I doubt if he were ever more humorous in his life. But the most enduring impression that he left upon us who were grown up—and we have all often spoken of it since—was that Jerrold, in his amiable capacity of being easily pleased, in his freshness, in his good-nature, in his cordiality, and in the unrestrained openness of his heart, had quite captivated us.

* Printed in "The Life of Douglas Jerrold," by Blanchard Jerrold.

Of his generosity I had a proof, within these two or three years, which it saddens me to think of now. There had been an estrangement between us—not on any personal subject, and not involving an angry word—and a good many months had passed without my once seeing him in the street, when it fell out that we dined, each with his own separate party, in the strangers' room of a club. Our chairs were almost back to back, and I took mine after he was seated at dinner. I said not a word (I am sorry to remember) and did not look that way. Before we had sat so, long, he openly wheeled his chair round, stretched out both his hands in a most engaging manner, and said aloud, with a bright and loving face that I can see as I write to you: "For God's sake, let us be friends again! Life's not long enough for this!"

On Sunday, May 31st, 1857, I had an appointment to meet him at the Gallery of Illustration, in Regent Street. We had been advising our friend, Mr. Russell, in the condensation of his lectures on the war in the Crimea, and we had engaged with him to go over the last of the series there at one o'clock that day. Arriving some minutes before the time, I found your father sitting alone in the hall. "There must be some mistake," he said: no one else was there; the place was locked up; he had tried all the doors; and he had been waiting there a quarter of an hour by himself. I sat down by him in a niche in the staircase, and he told me that he had been very unwell for three or four days. A window in his study had been newly painted, and the smell of the paint (he thought it must be that) had filled him with nausea and turned him sick, and he felt quite weak and giddy through not having been able to retain any food. He was a little subdued at first and out of spirits; but we sat there half an hour talking, and when we came out together he was quite himself.

In the shadow I had not observed him closely; but when we got into the sunshine of the streets, I saw that he looked ill. We were both engaged to dine with Mr. Russell at Greenwich, and I thought him so ill then that I advised him not to go, but to let me take him or send him home in a cab. He complained, however, of having turned so weak—we had now strolled as far as Leicester Square—that he was fearful he might faint in the cab, unless I could get him some restorative, and unless he could "keep it down." I deliberated for a moment whether to turn back to the Athenæum, where I could have got a little brandy for him, or to take him on into Covent Garden for the purpose; meanwhile, he stood leaning against the rails of the enclosure, looking for the moment very ill indeed. Finally, we walked on to Covent Garden, and before we had gone fifty yards he was very much better. On our way Mr.

Russell joined us. He was then better still, and walked between us unassisted. I got him a hard biscuit and a little weak cold brandy and water, and begged him by all means to try to eat. He broke up and ate the greater part of the biscuit, and then was much refreshed and comforted by the brandy; he said that he felt the sickness was overcome at last, and that he was quite a new man; it would do him good to have a few quiet hours in the air, and he would go with us to Greenwich. I still tried to dissuade him, but he was by this time bent upon it, and his natural colour had returned, and he was very hopeful and confident.

We strolled through the Temple on our way to a boat, and I have a lively recollection of him stamping about Elm Tree Court, with his hat in one hand and the other pushing his hair back, laughing in his heartiest manner at a ridiculous remembrance we had in common, which I had presented in some exaggerated light to divert him. We found our boat and went down the river, and looked at the *Leviathan*,* which was building, and talked all the way. It was a bright day, and as soon as we reached Greenwich we got an open carriage and went out for a drive about Shooter's Hill. In the carriage Mr. Russell read us his lecture, and we discussed it with great interest; we planned out the ground of Inkermann on the heath, and your father was very earnest indeed. The subject held us so that we were graver than usual; but he broke out at intervals in the same hilarious way as in the Temple, and he over and over again said to me, with great satisfaction, how happy he was that he had "quite got over that paint!"

The dinner-party was a large one, and I did not sit near him at table. But he and I arranged before we went in to dinner that he was only to eat of some simple dish that we agreed upon, and was only to drink sherry-and-water. We broke up very early, and before I went away with Mr. Leech, who was to take me to London, I went round to Jerrold, for whom someone else had a seat in a carriage, and put my hand upon his shoulder, asking him how he was. He turned round to show me a glass beside him with a little wine-and-water in it. "I have kept to the prescription; it has answered as well as this morning's, my dear old boy; I have quite got over the paint, and I am perfectly well." He was really elated by the relief of having recovered, and was as quietly happy as I ever saw him. We exchanged "God bless you!" and shook hands.

I went down to Gad's Hill next morning, where he was to write to me after a little while, appointing his own time for coming to see me there. A week afterwards another passenger in the

* Afterwards called the *Great Eastern.*

railway carriage in which I was on my way to London Bridge opened his morning paper and said, " Douglas Jerrold is dead ! "

*   *   *   *   *

Mr. Albert Smith.

TAVISTOCK HOUSE, TAVISTOCK SQUARE, LONDON, W.C.,
Wednesday Night, First December, 1858.

MY DEAR ALBERT,

I cannot tell you how grieved I am for poor dear Arthur (even you can hardly love him better than I do), or with what anxiety I shall wait for further news of him.

Pray let me know how he is to-morrow. Tell them at home that Olliffe is the kindest and gentlest of men—a man of rare experience and opportunity—perfect master of his profession, and to be confidently and implicitly relied upon. There is no man alive, in whose hands I would more thankfully trust myself.

I will write a cheery word to the dear fellow in the morning.

Ever faithfully.

Mr. Arthur Smith.

TAVISTOCK HOUSE, TAVISTOCK SQUARE, LONDON, W.C.,
Thursday, Second December, 1858.

MY DEAR ARTHUR,

I cannot tell you how surprised and grieved I was last night to hear from Albert of your severe illness. It is not my present intention to give you the trouble of reading anything like a letter, but I MUST send you my loving word, and tell you how we all think of you.

And here am I going off to-morrow to that meeting at Manchester without *you !* the wildest and most impossible of moves as it seems to me. And to think of my coming back by Coventry, on Saturday, to receive the chronometer—also without you !

If you don't get perfectly well soon, my dear old fellow, I shall come over to Paris to look after you, and to tell Olliffe (give him my love, and the same for Lady Olliffe) what a Blessing he is. With kindest regards to Mrs. Arthur and her sister,

Ever heartily and affectionately yours.

Mr. Frank Stone, A.R.A.

TAVISTOCK HOUSE, TAVISTOCK SQUARE, LONDON, W.C.,
Monday, Thirteenth December, 1858.

MY DEAR STONE,

Many thanks for these discourses. They are very good, I think, as expressing what many men have felt and thought; otherwise not specially remarkable. They have one fatal mistake, which is a canker at the root of their ever being widely useful. Half the misery and hypocrisy of the Christian world arises (as I take it) from a stubborn determination to refuse the New Testament as a sufficient guide in itself, and to force the Old Testament into alliance with it—whereof comes all manner of camel-swallowing and of gnat-straining. But so to resent this miserable error, or to (by any implication) depreciate the divine goodness and beauty of the New Testament, is to commit even a worse error. And to class Jesus Christ with Mahomet is simply audacity and folly. I might as well hoist myself on to a high platform, to inform my disciples that the lives of King George the Fourth and of King Alfred the Great belonged to one and the same category.

Ever affectionately.

Sunday, Nineteenth December, 1858.   Mr. B. W.
TAVISTOCK HOUSE,   Procter.

MY DEAR PROCTER,

A thousand thanks for the little song. I am charmed with it, and shall be delighted to brighten "Household Words" with such a wise and genial light. I no more believe that your poetical faculty has gone by, than I believe that you have yourself passed to the better land. You and it will travel thither in company, rely upon it. So I still hope to hear more of the trade-songs, and to learn that the blacksmith has hammered out no end of iron into good fashion of verse, like a cunning workman, as I know him of old to be.

Very faithfully yours, my dear Procter.

1859.

NARRATIVE.

DURING the winter, Charles Dickens was living at Tavistock House, removing to Gad's Hill for the summer early in June, and returning to London in November. At this time a change was made in his weekly journal. "Household Words" became absolutely his own property—Mr. Wills being his partner and editor, as before—and was "incorporated with 'All the Year Round,'" under which title it was known thenceforth. The office was still in Wellington Street, but in a different house. The first number with the new name appeared on the Thirtieth April, and it contained the opening of "A Tale of Two Cities."

The first letter which follows shows that a proposal for a series of readings in America had already been made to Charles Dickens. It was carefully considered and abandoned for the time. But the proposal was constantly renewed, and the idea never wholly relinquished for many years before he actually decided on making so distant a "reading tour."

Mr. Procter contributed to the early numbers of "All the Year Round" some very spirited "Songs of the Trades." We give notes from Charles Dickens to the veteran poet, both in the last year, and in this year, expressing his strong approval of them.

The letter and note to Mr. (afterwards Sir Antonio) Panizzi, for which we are indebted to Mr. Louis Fagan, one of Sir A. Panizzi's executors, show the warm sympathy and interest which he always felt for the cause of Italian liberty, and for the sufferings of the State prisoners who at this time took refuge in England.

We give a little note to the dear friend and companion of Charles Dickens' daughters, "Lotty" White, because it is a pretty specimen of his writing, and because the young girl, who is playfully "commanded" to get well and strong, died early in July of this year. She was, at the time this note was written, first attacked with the illness which was fatal to all her sisters. Mamie and Katie Dickens went from Gad's Hill to Bonchurch to pay a last visit to their friend, and he wrote to his eldest daughter there. Also we give notes of loving sympathy and condolence to the bereaved father and mother.

In the course of this summer Charles Dickens was not well, and went for a week to his old favourite, Broadstairs—where Mr. Wilkie Collins and his brother, Mr. Charles Allston Collins, were staying—for sea-air and change, preparatory to another reading tour, in England only. His letter from Peterborough to Mr. Frank Stone, giving him an account of a reading at Manchester (Mr. Stone's native town), was one of the last ever addressed to that affectionate friend, who died very suddenly, in November, to the great grief of Charles Dickens. The letter to Mr. Thomas Longman, which closes this year, was one of introduction to that gentleman of young Marcus Stone, then just beginning his career as an artist, and to whom the premature death of his father made it doubly desirable that he should have powerful helping hands.

Charles Dickens refers, in a letter to Mrs. Watson, to his portrait by Mr. Frith, which was finished at the end of 1858. It was painted for Mr. Forster, and is now in the "Forster Collection" at the South Kensington Museum.

The Christmas number of this year, again written by several hands, was "The Haunted House." In November, his story of "A Tale of Two Cities" was finished in "All the Year Round," and in December was published, complete, with dedication to Lord John Russell.

GAD'S HILL PLACE, HIGHAM BY ROCHESTER,   Mr. W. P.
Wednesday, Twelfth January, 1859.   Frith, R.A.

MY DEAR FRITH,

At eleven on Monday morning next, the gifted individual whom you will transmit to posterity, will be at Watkins'. Table also shall be there, and chair. Velvet coat likewise if the tailor should have sent it home. But the garment is more to be doubted than the man whose signature here follows.

Faithfully yours always.

TAVISTOCK HOUSE, TAVISTOCK SQUARE, LONDON, W.C.,   Mr. Arthur
Wednesday, Twenty-sixth January, 1859.   Smith.

MY DEAR ARTHUR,

Will you first read the enclosed letters, having previously welcomed, with all possible cordiality, the bearer, Mr. Thomas C. Evans, from New York?

You having read them, let me explain that Mr. Fields is a highly respectable and influential man, one of the heads of the most classical and most respected publishing house in America; that Mr. Richard Grant White is a man of high reputation; and that Felton is the Greek Professor in their Cambridge University, perhaps the most distinguished scholar in the States.

The address to myself, referred to in one of the letters, being on its way, it is quite clear that I must give some decided and definite answer to the American proposal. Now, will you carefully discuss it with Mr. Evans before I enter on it at all? Then, will you dine here with him on Sunday—which I will propose to him—and arrange to meet at half-past four for an hour's discussion?

The points are these:

First. I have a very grave question within myself whether I could go to America at all.

Secondly. If I did go, I could not possibly go before the autumn.

Thirdly. If I did go, how long must I stay?

Fourthly. If the stay were a short one, could *you* go?

Fifthly. What is his project? What could I make? What occurs to you upon his proposal?

I have told him that the business arrangements of the readings have been from the first so entirely in your hands, that I enter upon nothing connected with them without previous reference to you.

Ever faithfully.

TAVISTOCK HOUSE, *Tuesday, First February*, 1859.

MY DEAR CERJAT,

I received your always welcome annual with even more interest than usual this year, being (in common with my two girls and their aunt) much excited and pleased by your account of your daughter's engagement. Apart from the high sense I have of the affectionate confidence with which you tell me what lies so tenderly on your own heart, I have followed the little history with a lively sympathy and regard for her. I hope, with you, that it is full of promise, and that you will all be happy in it. The separation, even in the present condition of travel (and no man can say how much the discovery of a day may advance it), is nothing. And so God bless her and all of you, and may the rosy summer bring her all the fulness of joy that we all wish her.

To pass from the altar to Townshend (which is a long way), let me report him severely treated by Bully, who rules him with a paw of iron; and complaining, moreover, of indigestion. He drives here every Sunday, but at all other times is mostly shut up in his beautiful house, where I occasionally go and dine with him *tête-à-tête*, and where we always talk of you and drink to you. That is a rule with us from which we never depart. He is "seeing a volume of poems through the press;" rather an expensive amusement. He has not been out at night (except to this house) save last Friday, when he went to hear me read "The Poor Traveller," "Mrs. Gamp," and "The Trial" from "Pickwick." He came into my room at St. Martin's Hall, and I fortified him with weak brandy-and-water. You will be glad to hear that the said readings are a greater *furore* than they ever have been, and that every night on which they now take place—once a week— hundreds go away, unable to get in, though the hall holds thirteen hundred people. I dine with —— to-day, by-the-bye, along with his agent; concerning whom I observe him to be always divided between an unbounded confidence and a little latent suspicion. He always tells me that he is a gem of the first water; oh yes, the best of business men! and then says that he did not quite like his conduct respecting that farm-tenant and those hay-ricks.

There is a general impression here, among the best informed, that war in Italy, to begin with, is inevitable, and will break out before April. I know a gentleman at Genoa (Swiss by birth),[*] deeply in with the authorities at Turin, who is already sending children home.

In England we are quiet enough. There is a world of talk, as

---

[*] M. De la Rue and his wife (an English lady) were the dearest friends, in Genoa, of Charles Dickens.

you know, about Reform bills; but I don't believe there is any general strong feeling on the subject. According to my perceptions, it is undeniable that the public has fallen into a state of indifference about public affairs, mainly referable, as I think, to the people who administer them—and there I mean the people of all parties—which is a very bad sign of the times. The general mind seems weary of debates and honourable members, and to have taken *laissez-aller* for its motto.

My affairs domestic (which I know are not without interest for you) flow peacefully. My eldest daughter is a capital housekeeper, heads the .table gracefully, delegates certain appropriate duties to her sister and her aunt, and they are all three devotedly attached. Charley, my eldest boy, remains in Barings' house. Your present correspondent is more popular than he ever has been. I rather think that the readings in the country have opened up a new public who were outside before; but however that may be, his books have a wider range than they ever had, and his public welcomes are prodigious. Said correspondent is at present overwhelmed with proposals to go and read in America. Will never go, unless a small fortune be first paid down in money on this side of the Atlantic. Stated the figure of such payment, between ourselves, only yesterday. Expects to hear no more of it, and assuredly will never go for less. You don't say, my dear Cerjat, when you are coming to England! Somehow I feel that this marriage ought to bring you over, though I don't know why. You shall have a bed here and a bed at Gad's Hill, and we will go and see strange sights together. When I was in Ireland, I ordered the brightest jaunting-car that ever was seen. It has just this minute arrived per steamer from Belfast. Say you are coming, and you shall be the first man turned over by it; somebody must be (for my daughter Mary drives anything that can be harnessed, and I know of no English horse that would understand a jaunting-car coming down a Kentish hill), and you shall be that somebody if you will. They turned the basket-phaeton over, last summer, in a bye-road, Mary and the other two—and had to get it up again; which they did, and came home as if nothing had happened.

Ever your attached and affectionate Friend.

TAVISTOCK HOUSE,
Monday Night, Fourteenth March, 1859.

Mr. Antonio
Panizzi.

MY DEAR PANIZZI,

If you should feel no delicacy in mentioning, or should see no objection to mentioning, to Signor Poerio, or any of the wronged

Neapolitan gentlemen to whom it is your happiness and honour to be a friend on their arrival in this country, an idea that has occurred to me, I should regard it as a great kindness in you if you would be my exponent. I think you will have no difficulty in believing that I would not, on any consideration, obtrude my name or projects upon any one of those noble souls, if there were any reason of the slightest kind against it. And if you see any such reason, I pray you instantly to banish my letter from your thoughts.

It seems to me probable that some narrative of their ten years' suffering will, somehow or other, sooner or later, be by some of them laid before the English people. The just interest and indignation alive here, will (I suppose) elicit it. False narratives and garbled stories will, in any case, of a certainty get about. If the true history of the matter is to be told, I have that sympathy with them and respect for them which would, all other considerations apart, render it unspeakably gratifying to me to be the means of its diffusion. What I desire to lay before them is simply this. If for my new successor to "Household Words" a narrative of their ten years' trial could be written, I would take any conceivable pains to have it rendered into English, and presented in the sincerest and best way to a very large and comprehensive audience. It should be published exactly as you might think best for them, and remunerated in any way that you might think generous and right. They want no mouthpiece and no introducer, but perhaps they might have no objection to be associated with an English writer, who is possibly not unknown to them by some general reputation, and who certainly would be animated by a strong public and private respect for their honour, spirit, and unmerited misfortunes. This is the whole matter; assuming that such a thing is to be done, I long for the privilege of helping to do it. These gentlemen might consider it an independent means of making money, and I should be delighted to pay the money.

In my absence from town, my friend and sub-editor, Mr. Wills (to whom I had expressed my feeling on the subject), has seen, I think, three of the gentlemen together. But as I hear, returning home to-night, that they are in your good hands, and as nobody can be a better judge than you of anything that concerns them, I at once decide to write to you and take no other step whatever. Forgive me for the trouble I have occasioned you in the reading of this letter, and never think of it again if you think that by pursuing it you would cause them an instant's uneasiness.

Believe me, very faithfully yours.

TAVISTOCK HOUSE,
Saturday, Nineteenth March, 1859.

Mr. B. W.
Procter.

MY DEAR PROCTER,

I think the songs are simply ADMIRABLE! and I have no doubt of this being a popular feature in "All the Year Round." I would not omit the sexton, and I would not omit the spinners and weavers; and I would omit the hack-writers, and (I think) the alderman; but I am not so clear about the chorister. The pastoral I a little doubt finding audience for; but I am not at all sure yet that my doubt is well founded.

Had I not better send them all to the printer, and let you have proofs kept by you for publishing? I shall not have to make up the first number of "All the Year Round" until early in April. I don't like to send the manuscript back, and I never do like to do so when I get anything that I know to be thoroughly, soundly, and unquestionably good. I am hard at work upon my story, and expect a magnificent start. With hearty thanks,

Ever yours affectionately.

TAVISTOCK HOUSE, TAVISTOCK SQUARE, LONDON, W.C.,
Tuesday, Twenty-ninth March, 1859.

Mr.
Edmund
Yates.

MY DEAR EDMUND,

1. I think that no one seeing the place can well doubt that my house at Gad's Hill is the place for the letter-box.* The wall is accessible by all sorts and conditions of men, on the bold high road, and the house altogether is the great landmark of the whole neighbourhood. Captain Goldsmith's *house* is up a lane considerably off the high road; but he has a garden *wall* abutting on the road itself.

2. "The Pic-Nic Papers" were originally sold to Colburn, for the benefit of the widow of Mr. Macrone, of St. James's Square, publisher, deceased. Two volumes were contributed—of course gratuitously—by writers who had had transactions with Macrone. Mr. Colburn, wanting three volumes in all for trade purposes, added a third, consisting of an American reprint. Of that volume I didn't know, and don't know, anything. The other two I edited, gratuitously as aforesaid, and wrote the Lamplighter's story in. It was all done many years ago. There was a preface originally, delicately setting forth how the book came to be.

3. I suppose —— to be, as Mr. Samuel Weller expresses it somewhere in "Pickwick," "ravin' mad with the consciousness o' willany." Under their advertisement in *The Times* to-day, you

---

* Mr. Edmund Yates, at this time, held a place in the Post Office.

will see, without a word of comment, the shorthand writer's verbatim report of the judgment.

Ever faithfully.

Mr. Antonio
Panizzi.

"ALL THE YEAR ROUND" OFFICE,
Thursday, Seventh April, 1859.

MY DEAR PANIZZI,

If you don't know, I think you should know that a number of letters are passing through the post-office, purporting to be addressed to the charitable by "Italian Exiles in London," asking for aid to raise a fund for a tribute to "London's Lord Mayor," in grateful recognition of the reception of the Neapolitan exiles. I know this to be the case, and have no doubt in my own mind that the whole thing is an imposture and a "do." The letters are signed "Gratitudine Italiana."

Ever faithfully yours.

Miss White.

TAVISTOCK HOUSE, TAVISTOCK SQUARE, LONDON, W.C.,
Monday, Eighteenth April, 1859.

MY DEAR LOTTY,

This is merely a notice to you that I must positively insist on your getting well, strong, and into good spirits, with the least possible delay. Also, that I look forward to seeing you at Gad's Hill sometime in the summer, staying with the girls, and heartlessly putting down the Plorn. You know that there is no appeal from the Plorn's inimitable father. What _he_ says must be done. Therefore I send you my love (which please take care of), and my commands (which please obey).   Ever your affectionate.

The Hon.
Mrs.
Watson.

TAVISTOCK HOUSE, TAVISTOCK SQUARE, LONDON, W.C.,
Tuesday, Thirty-first May, 1859.

MY DEAR MRS. WATSON,

You surprise me by supposing that there is ever latent a defiant and roused expression in the undersigned lamb ! Apart from this singular delusion of yours, and wholly unaccountable departure from your usual accuracy in all things, your satisfaction with the portrait is a great pleasure to me. It has received every conceivable pains at Frith's hands, and ought on his account to be good. It is a little too much (to my thinking) as if my next-door neighbour were my deadly foe, uninsured, and I had just received tidings of his house being afire ; otherwise very good.

I cannot tell you how delighted we shall be if you would come to Gad's Hill. You should see some charming woods and a rare old castle, and you should have a snug room looking over a

Kentish prospect, with every facility in it for pondering on the beauties of its master's beard! *Do* come, but you positively *must not* come and go on the same day.

My small boy is perfectly happy at Southsea, and likes the school very much. I had the finest letter two or three days ago, from another of my boys—Frank Jeffrey—at Hamburg. In this wonderful epistle he says: "Dear papa, I write to tell you that I have given up all thoughts of being a doctor. My conviction that I shall never get over my stammering is the cause; all professions are barred against me. The only thing I should like to be is a gentleman-farmer, either at the Cape, in Canada, or Australia. With my passage paid, fifteen pounds, a horse, and a rifle, I could go two or three hundred miles up country, sow grain, buy cattle, and in time be very comfortable."

Considering the consequences of executing the little commission by the next steamer, I perceived that the first consequence of the fifteen pounds would be that he would be robbed of it—of the horse, that it would throw him—and of the rifle, that it would blow his head off; which probabilities I took the liberty of mentioning, as being against the scheme.

Ever believe me, my dear Mrs. Watson,
Your faithful and affectionate.

TAVISTOCK HOUSE, *Sunday, Fifth June,* 1859.　Mrs. White.

MY DEAR MRS. WHITE,

I do not write to you this morning because I have anything to say—I well know where your consolation is set, and to what beneficent figure your thoughts are raised—but simply because you are so much in my mind that it is a relief to send you and dear White my love. You are always in our hearts and on our lips. May the great God comfort you! You know that Mary and Katie are coming on Thursday. They will bring dear Lotty what she little needs with you by her side—love; and I hope their company will interest and please her. There is nothing that they, or any of us, would not do for her. She is a part of us all, and has belonged to us, as well as to you, these many years.

Ever your affectionate and faithful.

GAD'S HILL, HIGHAM BY ROCHESTER, KENT,　Miss
Monday, Thirteenth June, 1859.　Dickens.

MY DEAREST MAMIE,

On Saturday night I found, very much to my surprise and pleasure, the photograph on my table at Tavistock House. It is not a very pleasant or cheerful presentation of my daughters; but

2 I

it is wonderfully like for all that, and in some details remarkably good.   When I came home here yesterday I tried it in the large Townshend stereoscope, in which it shows to great advantage.   It is in the little stereoscope at present on the drawing-room table. One of the balustrades of the destroyed old Rochester Bridge has been (very nicely) presented to me by the contractor for the works, and has been duly stonemasoned and set up on the lawn behind the house.   I have ordered a sun-dial for the top of it, and it will be a very good object indeed.   The Plorn is highly excited to-day by reason of an institution which he tells me (after questioning George) is called the "Cobb, or Bodderin," holding a festival at The Falstaff.   He is possessed of some vague information that they go to Higham Church, in pursuance of some old usage, and attend service there, and afterwards march round the village.   It so far looks probable that they certainly started off at eleven very spare in numbers, and came back considerably recruited, which looks to me like the difference between going to church and coming to dinner.   They bore no end of bright banners and broad sashes, and had a band with a terrific drum, and are now (at half-past two) dining at The Falstaff, partly in the side room on the ground-floor, and partly in a tent improvised this morning.   The drum is hung up to a tree in The Falstaff garden, and looks like a tropical sort of gourd.   I have presented the band with five shillings, which munificence has been highly appreciated.   Ices don't seem to be provided for the ladies in the gallery—I mean the garden ; they are prowling about there, endeavouring to peep in at the beef and mutton through the holes in the tent, on the whole, in a debased and degraded manner.

Turk somehow cut his foot in Cobham Lanes yesterday, and Linda hers.   They are both lame, and looking at each other.   Fancy Mr. Townshend not intending to go for another three weeks, and designing to come down here for a few days—with Henri and Bully —on Wednesday !   I wish you could have seen him alone with me on Saturday ; he was so extraordinarily earnest and affectionate on my belongings and affairs in general, and not least of all on you and Katie, that he cried in a most pathetic manner, and was so affected that I was obliged to leave him among the flower-pots in the long passage at the end of the dining-room.   It was a very good piece of truthfulness and sincerity, especially in one of his years, able to take life so easily.

Mr. and Mrs. Wills are here now (but I daresay you know it from your aunt), and return to town with me to-morrow morning. We are now going on to the castle.   Mrs. Wills was very droll last night, and told me some good stories.   My dear, I wish particularly to impress upon you and dear Katie (to whom I send my other best love) that I hope your stay will not be very long. I don't think it very good for either of you, though of course I know that Lotty will be, and must be, and should be the first consideration with you both. I am very anxious to know how you found her and how you are yourself.

Best love to dear Lotty and Mrs. White. We are always talking about you all.

Ever, dearest Mamie, your affectionate Father.

GAD'S HILL PLACE, HIGHAM BY ROCHESTER, KENT,   Rev. James
Thursday, Seventh July, 1859.   White.

MY DEAR WHITE,

I send my heartiest and most affectionate love to Mrs. White and you, and to Clara. You know all that I could add; you have felt it all; let it be unspoken and unwritten—it is expressed within us.

Do you not think that you could all three come here, and stay with us? You and Mrs. White should have your own large room and your own ways, and should be among us when you felt disposed, and never otherwise. I do hope you would find peace here. Can it not be done?

.We have talked very much about it among ourselves, and the girls are strong upon it. Think of it—do.

Ever your affectionate.

GAD'S HILL PLACE, HIGHAM BY ROCHESTER, KENT,   Mrs.
Twenty-first August, 1859.   Cowden
    Clarke.

MY DEAR MRS. COWDEN CLARKE,

I cannot tell you how much pleasure I have derived from the receipt of your earnest letter. Do not suppose it possible that such praise can be "less than nothing" to your old manager. It is more than all else.

Here in my little country house on the summit of the hill where Falstaff did the robbery, your words have come to me in the most appropriate and delightful manner. When the story can be read all at once, and my meaning can be better seen, I will send it to you (sending it to Dean Street, if you tell me of no better way), and it will be a hearty gratification to think that you and your good husband are reading it together. For you must both take notice, please, that I have a reminder of you always before me. On my desk, here, stand two green leaves* which I every morning

* A porcelain paper-weight with two green leaves enamelled on it, between which were placed the initials C. D. A present from Mrs. C. Clarke.

station in their ever-green place at my elbow. The leaves on the oak-trees outside the window are less constant than these, for they are with me through the four seasons.

Lord! to think of the bygone day when you were stricken mute (was it not at Glasgow?) and, being mounted on a tall ladder at a practicable window, stared at Forster, and with a noble constancy refused to utter word! Like the Monk among the pictures with Wilkie, I begin to think *that* the real world, and this the sham that goes out with the lights.

God bless you both.

Ever faithfully yours.

Mr. John
Forster.

GAD'S HILL,
Thursday Night, Twenty-fifth August, 1859.

MY DEAR FORSTER,

Heartily glad to get your letter this morning.

I cannot easily tell you how much interested I am by what you tell me of our brave and excellent friend the Chief Baron,* in connection with that ruffian. I followed the case with so much interest, and have followed the miserable knaves and asses who have perverted it since, with so much indignation, that I have often had more than half a mind to write and thank the upright judge who tried him. I declare to God that I believe such a service one of the greatest that a man of intellect and courage can render to society. Of course I saw the beast of a prisoner (with my mind's eye) delivering his cut-and-dried speech, and read in every word of it that no one but the murderer could have delivered or conceived it. Of course I have been driving the girls out of their wits here, by incessantly proclaiming that there needed no medical evidence either way, and that the case was plain without it. Lastly, of course (though a merciful man—because a merciful man I mean), I would hang any Home Secretary (Whig, Tory, Radical, or otherwise) who should step in between that black scoundrel and the gallows. I can*not* believe—and my belief in all wrong as to public matters is enormous—that such a thing will be done.

I am reminded of Tennyson, by thinking that King Arthur would have made short work of the amiable ——, whom the newspapers strangely delight to make a sort of gentleman of. How fine the "Idylls" are! Lord! what a blessed thing it is to read a man who can write! I thought nothing could be grander than the first poem till I came to the third; but when I had read the last, it seemed to be absolutely unapproached and unapproachable.

* Sir Frederick Pollock.

To come to myself. I have written and begged the "All the Year Round" publisher to send you directly four weeks' proofs beyond the current number, that are in type. I hope you will like them. Nothing but the interest of the subject, and the pleasure of striving with the difficulty of the forms of treatment, nothing in the mere way of money, I mean, could also repay the time and trouble of the incessant condensation. But I set myself the little task of making a *picturesque* story, rising in every chapter with characters true to nature, but whom the story itself should express, more than they should express themselves, by dialogue. I mean, in other words, that I fancied a story of incident might be written, in place of the bestiality that *is* written under that pretence, pounding the characters out in its own mortar, and beating their own interests out of them. If you could have read the story all at once, I hope you wouldn't have stopped halfway.

As to coming to your retreat, my dear Forster, think how helpless I am. I am not well yet. I have an instinctive feeling that nothing but the sea will restore me, and I am planning to go and work at Ballard's, at Broadstairs, from next Wednesday to Monday. I generally go to town on Monday afternoon. All Tuesday I am at the office, on Wednesday I come back here, and go to work again. I don't leave off till Monday comes round once more. I am fighting to get my story done by the first week in October. On the Tenth of October I am going away to read for a fortnight at Ipswich, Norwich, Oxford, Cambridge, and a few other places. Judge what my spare time is just now!

I am very much surprised and very sorry to find from the enclosed that Elliotson has been ill. I never heard a word of it.

It is raining, intensely hot, and stormy. Eighteen creatures, like little tortoises, have dashed in at the window and fallen on the paper since I began this paragraph ● (that was one!). I am a wretched sort of creature in my way, but it is a way that gets on somehow. And all ways have the same finger-post at the head of them, and at every turning in them.

Ever affectionately.

ALBION, BROADSTAIRS,
Friday, Second September, 1859.

MY DEAREST MAMIE AND KATIE,

I have been "moved" here, and am now (Ballard having added to the hotel a house we lived in three years) in our old dining-room and sitting-room, and our old drawing-room as a bedroom. My cold is so bad, both in my throat and in my chest, that I can't bathe in the sea; Tom Collin dissuaded me—thought

Miss Dickens and Miss Katie Dickens.

it "bad"—but I get a heavy shower-bath at Mrs. Crampton's every morning. The baths are still hers and her husband's, but they have retired and live in "Nuckells"—are going to give a stained-glass window, value three hundred pounds, to St. Peter's Church. Tom Collin is of opinion that the Miss Dickenses has growed two fine young women—leastwise, asking pardon, ladies. An evangelical family of most disagreeable girls prowl about here and trip people up with tracts, which they put in the path with stones upon them to keep them from blowing away. Charles Collins and I having seen a bill yesterday—about a mesmeric young lady who did feats, one of which was set forth in the bill, in a line by itself, as

THE RIGID LEGS,

—were overpowered with curiosity, and resolved to go. It came off in the Assembly Room, now more exquisitely desolate than words can describe. Eighteen shillings was the "take." Behind a screen among the company, we heard mysterious gurglings of water before the entertainment began, and then a slippery sound which occasioned me to whisper C. C. (who laughed in the most ridiculous manner), "Soap." It proved to be the young lady washing herself. She must have been wonderfully dirty, for she took a world of trouble, and didn't come out clean after all—in a wretched dirty muslin frock, with blue ribbons. She was the alleged mesmeriser, and a boy who distributed bills the alleged mesmerised. It was a most preposterous imposition, but more ludicrous than any poor sight I ever saw. The boy is clearly out of a pantomime, and when he pretended to be in a mesmeric state, made the company back by going in among them head over heels, backwards, half-a-dozen times, in a most insupportable way. The pianist had struck; and the manner in which the lecturer implored "some lady" to play a "polker," and the manner in which no lady would; and in which the few ladies who were there sat with their hats on, and the elastic under their chins, as if it were going to blow, is never to be forgotten. I have been writing all the morning, and am going for a walk to Ramsgate. This is a beast of a letter, but I am not well, and have been addling my head.

Ever, dear Girls, your affectionate Father.

Mr. W. Wilkie Collins.

GAD'S HILL PLACE, HIGHAM BY ROCHESTER, KENT, *Friday Night, Sixteenth September,* 1859.

MY DEAR WILKIE,

Just a word to say that I have received yours, and that I look forward to the reunion on Thursday, when I hope to have the satisfaction of recounting to you the plot of a play that has been laid before me for commending advice.

Ditto to what you say respecting the *Great Eastern*. I went right up to London Bridge by the boat that day, on purpose that I might pass her. I thought her the ugliest and most unshiplike thing these eyes ever beheld. I wouldn't go to sea in her, shiver my ould timbers and rouse me up with a monkey's tail (man-of-war metaphor), not to chuck a biscuit into Davy Jones' weather eye, and see double with my own old toplights.

Turk has been so good as to produce from his mouth, for the wholesome consternation of the family, eighteen feet of worm. When he had brought it up, he seemed to think it might be turned to account in the housekeeping and was proud. Pony has kicked a shaft off the cart, and is to be sold. Why don't you buy her? she'd never kick with you.

Barber's opinion is, that them fruit-trees, one and all, is touchwood, and not fit for burning at any gentleman's fire; also that the stocking of this here garden is worth less than nothing, because you wouldn't have to grub up nothing, and something takes a man to do it at three-and-sixpence a day. Was "left desponding" by your reporter.

I have had immense difficulty to find a man for the stable-yard here. Barber having at last engaged one this morning, I enquired if he had a decent hat for driving in, to which Barber returned this answer:

"Why, sir, not to deceive you, that man flatly say that he never have wore that article since man he was!"

I am consequently fortified into my room, and am afraid to go out to look at him.

Ever affectionately.

GAD'S HILL PLACE, HIGHAM BY ROCHESTER, KENT, *Saturday, Fifteenth October*, 1859.

Monsieur Regnier.

MY DEAR REGNIER,

You will receive by railway parcel the proof-sheets of a story of mine, that has been for some time in progress in my weekly journal, and that will be published in a complete volume about the middle of November. Nobody but Forster has yet seen the latter portions of it, or will see them until they are published. I want you to read it for two reasons. Firstly, because I hope it is the best story I have written. Secondly, because it treats of a very remarkable time in France; and I should very much like to know what you think of its being dramatised for a French theatre. If you should think it likely to be done, I should be glad to take some steps towards having it well done. The story is an extraordinary success here, and I think the end of it is certain to make a still greater sensation.

Don't trouble yourself to write to me, *mon ami*, until you shall have had time to read the proofs. Remember, they are *proofs*, and *private*; the latter chapters will not be before the public for five or six weeks to come. Believe me, ever faithfully yours.

P.S.—The story (I daresay you have not seen any of it yet) is called "A Tale of Two Cities."

Mr. Frank
Stone,
A.R.A.

PETERBOROUGH,
Wednesday Evening, Nineteenth October, 1859.

MY DEAR STONE,

We had a splendid rush last night. They were a far finer audience than on the previous night; I think the finest I have ever read to. They took every word of the "Dombey" in quite an amazing manner, and after the child's death, paused a little, and then set up a shout that it did one good to hear. Mrs. Gamp then set in with a roar, which lasted till I had done. I think everybody for the time forgot everything but the matter in hand. It was as fine an instance of thorough absorption in a fiction as any of us are likely to see ever again.

—— (in an exquisite red mantle), accompanied by her sister (in another exquisite red mantle) and by the deaf lady (who leaned a black head-dress, exactly like an old-fashioned tea-urn without a top, against the wall), was charming. HE* couldn't get at her on account of the pressure. HE tried to peep at her from the side door, but she (ha, ha, ha!) was unconscious of his presence. I read to her, and goaded him to madness. He is just sane enough to send his kindest regards.

This is a place which—except the cathedral, with the loveliest front I ever saw—is like the back door to some other place. It is, I should hope, the deadest and most utterly inert little town in the British dominions. The magnates have taken places, and the bookseller is of opinion that "such is the determination to do honour to Mr. Dickens that the doors *must* be opened half an hour before the appointed time." You will picture to yourself Arthur's quiet indignation at this, and the manner in which he remarked to me at dinner, "that he turned away twice Peterborough last night."

A very pretty room—though a Corn Exchange—and a room

---

* Mr. Arthur Smith.

we should have been glad of at Cambridge, as it is large, bright, and cheerful, and wonderfully well lighted.

No more at present from,   Yours affectionately.

TAVISTOCK HOUSE, TAVISTOCK SQUARE, LONDON W.C., *Wednesday, Sixteenth November,* 1859.

MY DEAR REGNIER,

I send you ten thousand thanks for your kind and explicit letter. What I particularly wished to ascertain from you was, whether it is likely the Censor would allow such a piece to be played in Paris. In the case of its being likely, then I wished to have the piece as well done as possible, and would even have proposed to come to Paris to see it rehearsed. But I very much doubted whether the general subject would not be objectionable to the Government, and what you write with so much sagacity and with such care convinces me at once that its representation would be prohibited. Therefore I altogether abandon and relinquish the idea. But I am just as heartily and cordially obliged to you for your interest and friendship, as if the book had been turned into a play five hundred times. I again thank you ten thousand times, and am quite sure that you are right. I only hope you will forgive my causing you so much trouble, after your hard work.

Macready, we are all happy to hear from himself, is going to leave the dreary tomb in which he lives, at Sherborne, and to remove to Cheltenham, a large and handsome place, about four or five hours' railway journey from London, where his poor girls will at least see and hear some life. Madame Céleste was with me yesterday, wishing to dramatise "A Tale of Two Cities" for the Lyceum, after bringing out the Christmas pantomime. I gave her my permission and the book; but I fear that her company (troupe) is a very poor one.

This is all the news I have, except (which is no news at all) that I feel as if I had not seen you for fifty years, and that

I am ever your attached and faithful Friend.

TAVISTOCK HOUSE, *Monday, Twenty-eighth November,* 1859.

MY DEAR LONGMAN,

I am very anxious to present to you, with the earnest hope that you will hold him in your remembrance, young Mr. Marcus Stone, son of poor Frank Stone, who died suddenly but a little week ago. You know, I daresay, what a start this young man made in the last exhibition, and what a favourable notice his picture attracted. He wishes to make an additional opening for himself in the illustration of books. He is an admirable draughts-man, has a most dexterous hand, a charming sense of grace and beauty, and a capital power of observation. These qualities in him I know well of my own knowledge. He is in all things modest, punctual, and right; and I would answer for him, if it were needful, with my head.

If you will put anything in his way, you will do it a second time, I am certain.

Faithfully yours always.

1860.

NARRATIVE.

THIS winter was the last spent at Tavistock House. Charles Dickens had for some time been inclining to the idea of making his home altogether at Gad's Hill, giving up his London house, and taking a furnished house for the sake of his daughters for a few months of the London season. And, as his daughter Kate was to be married this summer to Mr. Charles Collins, this intention was confirmed and carried out. He made arrangements for the sale of Tavistock House to Mr. Davis, a Jewish gentleman, and he gave up possession of it in September. Up to this time Gad's Hill had been furnished merely as a temporary summer residence—pictures, library, and all best furniture being left in the London house. He now set about beautifying and making Gad's Hill thoroughly comfortable and homelike. And there was not a year afterwards, up to the time of his death, that he did not make some addition or improvement to it. He also furnished, as a private residence, a sitting-room and some bedrooms at his offices in Wellington Street, to be used, when there was no house in London, as town quarters by himself, his daughter, and his sister-in-law.

He began in this summer his occasional papers for "All the Year Round," which he called "The Uncommercial Traveller," and which were continued at intervals in his journal until 1869.

In the autumn of this year he began another story, to be published weekly in "All the Year Round." The letter to Mr. Forster, which we give, tells him of this beginning and gives him the name of the book. The first number of "Great Expectations" appeared on the first December. The Christmas number, this time, was written jointly by Charles Dickens and Mr. Wilkie Collins. The scene was laid at Clovelly, and they made a journey together into Devonshire and Cornwall, for the purpose of this story, in November.

We give a letter to Mr. Forster on one of his books on the Commonwealth, the "Impeachment of the Five Members;" which, as with other letters on the subject of Mr. Forster's own works, was not used by himself for obvious reasons. Mr. H. F. Chorley was the well-known musical critic, and a very dear and intimate friend of Charles Dickens and his family.

A letter to his daughter Mamie (who, after her sister's marriage, paid a visit with her dear friends the White family to Scotland, where she had a serious illness) introduces a recent addition to the family, who became an important member of it, and one to whom Charles Dickens was very tenderly attached—her little white Pomeranian dog "Mrs. Bouncer" (so called after the celebrated lady of that name in "Box and Cox"). It is quite necessary to make this formal introduction of the little pet animal (who lived to be a very old dog and died in 1874), because future letters to his daughter contain constant references and messages to "Mrs. Bouncer," which would be quite unintelligible without this explanation. "Boy," also referred to in this letter, was his daughter's horse. The little dog and the horse were gifts to Mamie Dickens from her friends Mr. and Mrs. Arthur Smith, and the sister of the latter, Miss Craufurd.

TAVISTOCK HOUSE, *Monday, Second January,* 1860. Mr. W. C. Macready.

MY DEAREST MACREADY,

A happy New Year to you, and many happy years! I cannot tell you how delighted I was to receive your Christmas letter, or with what pleasure I have received Forster's emphatic accounts of your health and spirits. But when was I ever wrong! And when did I not tell you that you were an impostor in pretending to grow older as the rest of us do, and that you had a secret of your own for reversing the usual process! It happened that I read at Cheltenham a couple of months ago, and that I have rarely seen a place that so attracted my fancy. I had never seen it before. Also I believe the character of its people to have greatly changed for the better. All sorts of long-visaged prophets had told me that they were dull, stolid, slow, and I don't know what more that is disagreeable. I found them exactly the reverse in all respects; and I saw an amount of beauty there—well—that is not to be more specifically mentioned to you young fellows.

Katie dined with us yesterday, looking wonderfully well, and singing "Excelsior" with a certain dramatic fire in her, whereof I seem to remember having seen sparks afore now. Etc. etc. etc.

Ever, my dear Macready, your most affectionate.

Mr. W.
Wilkie
Collins.

TAVISTOCK HOUSE, TAVISTOCK SQUARE, LONDON, W.C.,
Saturday Night, Seventh January, 1860.

MY DEAR WILKIE,

I have read this book * with great care and attention. There cannot be a doubt that it is a very great advance on all your former writing, and most especially in respect of tenderness. In character it is excellent. Mr. Fairlie as good as the lawyer, and the lawyer as good as he. Mr. Vesey and Miss Halcombe, in their different ways, equally meritorious. Sir Percival, also, is most skilfully shown, though I doubt (you see what small points I come to) whether any man ever showed uneasiness by hand or foot without being forced by nature to show it in his face too. The story is very interesting, and the writing of it admirable.

I seem to have noticed, here and there, that the great pains you take express themselves a trifle too much, and you know that I always contest your disposition to give an audience credit for nothing, which necessarily involves the forcing of points on their attention, and which I have always observed them to resent when they find it out—as they always will and do. But on turning to the book again, I find it difficult to take out an instance of this. It rather belongs to your habit of thought and manner of going about the work. Perhaps I express my meaning best when I say that the three people who write the narratives in these proofs have a DISSECTIVE property in common, which is essentially not theirs but yours; and that my own effort would be to strike more of what is got *that way* out of them by collision with one another, and by the working of the story.

You know what an interest I have felt in your powers from the beginning of our friendship, and how very high I rate them? *I* know that this is an admirable book, and that it grips the difficulties of the weekly portion and throws them in a masterly style. No one else could do it half so well. I have stopped in every chapter to notice some instance of ingenuity, or some happy turn of writing; and I am absolutely certain that you never did half so well yourself.

So go on and prosper, and let me see some more, when you have enough (for your own satisfaction) to show me. I think of coming in to back you up if I can get an idea for my series of gossiping papers. One of these days, please God, we may do a story together; I have very odd half-formed notions, in a mist, of something that might be done that way.

Ever affectionately.

* "The Woman in White."

* TAVISTOCK HOUSE, TAVISTOCK SQUARE, W.C.,
Friday Night, Third February, 1860.

MY DEAR CHORLEY,

I can most honestly assure you I think "Roccabella" a very remarkable book indeed. Apart—quite apart—from my interest in you, I am certain that if I had taken it up under any ordinarily favourable circumstances as a book of which I knew nothing whatever, I should not—could not—have relinquished it until I had read it through. I had turned but a few pages, and come to the shadow on the bright sofa at the foot of the bed, when I knew myself to be in the hands of an artist. That rare and delightful recognition I never lost for a moment until I closed the second volume at the end. I am "a good audience" when I have reason to be, and my girls would testify to you, if there were need, that I cried over it heartily. Your story seems to me remarkably ingenious. I had not the least idea of the purport of the sealed paper until you chose to enlighten me; and then I felt it to be quite natural, quite easy, thoroughly in keeping with the character and presentation of the Liverpool man. The position of the Bell family in the story has a special air of nature and truth; is quite new to me, and is so dexterously and delicately done that I find the deaf daughter no less real and distinct than the clergyman's wife. The turn of the story round that damnable Princess I pursued with a pleasure with which I could pursue nothing but a true interest; and I declare to you that if I were put upon finding anything better than the scene of Roccabella's death, I should stare round my bookshelves very much at a loss for a long time. Similarly, your characters have really surprised me. From the lawyer to the Princess, I swear to them as true; and in your fathoming of Rosamond altogether, there is a profound wise knowledge that I admire and respect with a heartiness not easily overstated in words.

I am not quite with you as to the Italians. Your knowledge of the Italian character seems to me surprisingly subtle and penetrating; but I think we owe it to those most unhappy men and their political wretchedness to ask ourselves mercifully, whether their faults are not essentially the faults of a people long oppressed and priest-ridden;—whether their tendency to slink and conspire is not a tendency that spies in every dress, from the triple crown to a lousy head, have engendered in their ancestors through generations? Again, like you, I shudder at the distresses that come of these unavailing risings; my blood runs hotter, as yours does, at the

* This and all other Letters addressed to Mr. H. F. Chorley were printed in " Autobiography, Memoir, and Letters of Henry Fothergill Chorley," compiled by Mr. H. G. Hewlett.

thought of the leaders safe, and the instruments perishing by hundreds; yet what is to be done? Their wrongs are so great that they *will* rise from time to time somehow. It would be to doubt the eternal providence of God to doubt that they will rise successfully at last. Unavailing struggles against a dominant tyranny precede all successful turning against it. And is it not a little hard in us Englishmen, whose forefathers have risen so often and striven against so much, to look on, in our own security, through microscopes, and detect the motes in the brains of men driven mad? Think, if you and I were Italians, and had grown from boyhood to our present time, menaced in every day through all these years by that infernal confessional, dungeons, and soldiers, could we be better than these men? Should we be so good? I should not, I am afraid, if I know myself. Such things would make of me a moody, bloodthirsty, implacable man, who would do anything for revenge; and if I compromised the truth—put it at the worst, habitually—where should I ever have had it before me? In the old Jesuits' college at Genoa, or the Chiaja at Naples, in the churches of Rome, at the University of Padua, on the Piazzo San Marco, at Venice, where? And the Government is in all these places, and in all Italian places. I have seen something of these men. I have known Mazzini and Gallenga; Manin was tutor to my daughters in Paris; I have had long talks about scores of them with poor Ary Scheffer, who was their best friend. I have gone back to Italy after ten years, and found the best men I had known there exiled or in jail. I believe they have the faults you ascribe to them (nationally, not individually), but I could not find it in my heart, remembering their miseries, to exhibit those faults without referring them back to their causes. You will forgive my writing this, because I write it exactly as I write my cordial little tribute to the high merits of your book. If it were not a living reality to me, I should care nothing about this point of disagreement; but you are far too earnest a man, and far too able a man, to be left unremonstrated with by an admiring reader. You cannot write so well without influencing many people. If you could tell me that your book had but twenty readers, I would reply, that so good a book will influence more people's opinions, through those twenty, than a worthless book would through twenty thousand; and I express this with the perfect confidence of one in whose mind the book has taken, for good and all, a separate and distinct place.

Accept my thanks for the pleasure you have given me. The poor acknowledgment of testifying to that pleasure wherever I go will be my pleasure in return. And so, my dear Chorley, good night, and God bless you.　　　　Ever faithfully yours.

11, WELLINGTON STREET NORTH, STRAND, LONDON, W.C.,
Wednesday, Second May, 1860.

MY DEAR FORSTER,

It did not occur to me in reading your most excellent, interesting, and remarkable book,* that it could with any reason be called one-sided. If Clarendon had never written his "History of the Rebellion," then I can understand that it might be. But just as it would be impossible to answer an advocate who had misstated the merits of a case for his own purpose, without, in the interests of truth, and not of the other side merely, re-stating the merits and showing them in their real form, so I cannot see the practicability of telling what you had to tell without in some sort championing the misrepresented side, and I think that you don't do that as an advocate, but as a judge.

The evidence has been suppressed and coloured, and the judge goes through it and puts it straight. It is not *his* fault if it all goes one way and tends to one plain conclusion. Nor is it his fault that it goes the further when it is laid out straight, or seems to do so, because it was so knotted and twisted up before.

I can understand any man's, and particularly Carlyle's, having a lingering respect that does not like to be disturbed for those (in the best sense of the word) loyal gentlemen of the country who went with the king and were so true to him. But I don't think Carlyle sufficiently considers that the great mass of those gentlemen *didn't know the truth*, that it was a part of their loyalty to believe what they were told on the king's behalf, and that it is reasonable to suppose that the king was too artful to make known to *them* (especially after failure) what were very acceptable designs to the desperate soldiers of fortune about Whitehall. And it was to me a curious point of adventitious interest arising out of your book, to reflect on the probability of their having been as ignorant of the real scheme in Charles' head, as their descendants and followers down to this time, and to think with pity and admiration that they believed the cause to be so much better than it was. This is a notion I was anxious to have expressed in our account of the book in these pages. For I don't suppose Clarendon, or any other such man, to sit down and tell posterity something that he has not "tried on" in his own time. Do you?

In the whole narrative I saw nothing anywhere to which I demurred. I admired it all, went with it all, and was proud of my friend's having written it all. I felt it to be all square and sound and right, and to be of enormous importance in these times. Firstly, to the people who (like myself) are so sick of the short-

* "The Arrest of the Five Members."

comings of representative government as to have no interest in it. Secondly, to the humbugs at Westminster who have come down— a long, long way—from those men, as you know. When the Great Remonstrance came out, I was in the thick of my story, and was always busy with it; but I am very glad I didn't read it then, as I shall read it now to much better purpose. All the time I was at work on the "Two Cities," I read no books but such as had the air of the time in them.

To return for a final word to the Five Members. I thought the marginal references overdone. Here and there, they had a comical look to me for that reason, and reminded me of shows and plays where everything is in the bill.

Lastly, I should have written to you—as I had a strong inclina- tion to do, and ought to have done, immediately after reading the book—but for a weak reason; of all things in the world I have lost heart in one—I hope no other—I cannot, times out of calcula- tion, make up my mind to write a letter.

Ever, my dear Forster, affectionately yours.

M. De Cerjat.

TAVISTOCK HOUSE, *Thursday, Third May,* 1860.

MY DEAR CERJAT,

The date of this letter would make me horribly ashamed of myself, if I didn't know that *you* know how difficult letter-writing is to one whose trade it is to write.

You asked me on Christmas Eve about my children. My second daughter is going to be married in the course of the summer to Charles Collins, the brother of Wilkie Collins, the novelist. The father was one of the most famous painters of English green lanes and coast pieces. He was bred an artist; is a writer, too, and does "The Eye Witness," in "All the Year Round." He is a gentleman, accomplished, and amiable. My eldest daughter has not yet started any conveyance on the road to matrimony (that I know of); but it is likely enough that she will, as she is very agree- able and intelligent. They are both very pretty. My eldest boy, Charley, has been in Barings' house for three or four years, and is now going to Hong Kong, strongly backed up by Barings, to buy tea on his own account, as a means of forming a connection and seeing more of the practical part of a merchant's calling, before starting in London for himself. His brother Frank (Jeffrey's god- son) I have just recalled from France and Germany, to come and learn business, and qualify himself to join his brother on his return from the Celestial Empire. The next boy, Sydney Smith, is designed for the navy, and is in training at Portsmouth, awaiting his nomination. He is about three foot high, with the biggest eyes ever seen, and is known in the Portsmouth parts as "Young Dickens, who can do everything."

Another boy is at school in France; the youngest of all has a private tutor at home. I have forgotten the second in order, who is in India. He went out as ensign of a non-existent native regiment, got attached to the Forty-second Highlanders, one of the finest regiments in the Queen's service; has remained with them ever since, and got made a lieutenant by the chances of the rebellious campaign, before he was eighteen. Miss Hogarth, always Miss Hogarth, is the guide, philosopher, and friend of all the party, and a very close affection exists between her and the girls. I doubt if she will ever marry. I don't know whether to be glad of it or sorry for it.

I have laid down my pen and taken a long breath after writing this family history. I have also considered whether there are any more children, and I don't think there are. If I should remember two or three others presently, I will mention them in a postscript.

We think Townshend looking a little the worse for the winter, and we perceive Bully to be decidedly old upon his legs, and of a most diabolical turn of mind. When they first arrived the weather was very dark and cold, and kept them indoors. It has since turned very warm and bright, but with a dusty and sharp east wind. They are still kept indoors by this change, and I begin to wonder what change will let them out.

Public matters here are thought to be rather improving; the deep mistrust of the gentleman in Paris being counteracted by the vigorous state of preparation into which the nation is getting. You will have observed, of course, that we establish a new defaulter in respect of some great trust, about once a quarter. The last one, the cashier of a City bank, is considered to have distinguished himself greatly, a quarter of a million of money being high game.

No, my friend, I have not shouldered my rifle yet, but I should do so on more pressing occasion. Every other man in the row of men I know—if they were all put in a row—is a volunteer, though. There is a tendency rather to overdo the wearing of the uniform; but that is natural enough in the case of the youngest men. The turn-out is generally very creditable indeed. At the ball they had (in a perfectly unventilated building), their new leather belts and pouches smelt so fearfully that it was, as my eldest daughter said, like shoemaking in a great prison. She, consequently, distinguished herself by fainting away in the most inaccessible place in the whole structure, and being brought out (horizontally) by a file of volunteers, like some slain daughter of Albion whom they were carrying into the street to rouse the indignant valour of the populace.

Lord, my dear Cerjat, when I turn to that page of your letter where you write like an ancient sage in whom the fire has paled into a meek-eyed state of coolness and virtue, I half laugh and half cry! *You* old! *You* a sort of hermit? Boh! Get out.

When shall you and I meet, and where? Must I come to see Townshend? I begin to think so.

Ever, my dear Cerjat, your affectionate and faithful.

GAD'S HILL, *Tuesday, Fifth June*, 1860.

Sir Edward
Bulwer
Lytton.

MY DEAR BULWER LYTTON,

I am very much interested and gratified by your letter concerning "A Tale of Two Cities." I do not quite agree with you on two points, but that is no deduction from my pleasure.

In the first place, although the surrender of the feudal privileges (on a motion seconded by a nobleman of great rank) was the occasion of a sentimental scene, I see no reason to doubt, but on the contrary, many reasons to believe, that some of these privileges had been used to the frightful oppression of the peasant, quite as near to the time of the Revolution as the doctor's narrative, which, you will remember, dates long before the Terror. And surely when the new philosophy was the talk of the salons and the slang of the hour, it is not unreasonable or unallowable to suppose a nobleman wedded to the old cruel ideas, and representing the time going out, as his nephew represents the time coming in; as to the condition of the peasant in France generally at that day, I take it that if anything be certain on earth it is certain that it was intolerable. No *ex post facto* enquiries and provings by figures will hold water, surely, against the tremendous testimony of men living at the time.

There is a curious book printed at Amsterdam, written to make out no case whatever, and tiresome enough in its literal dictionary-like minuteness, scattered up and down the pages of which is full authority for my marquis. This is "Mercier's Tableau de Paris." Rousseau is the authority for the peasant's shutting up his house when he had a bit of meat. The tax-taker was the authority for the wretched creature's impoverishment.

I am not clear, and I never have been clear, respecting that canon of fiction which forbids the interposition of accident in such a case as Madame Defarge's death. Where the accident is inseparable from the passion and emotion of the character, where it is strictly consistent with the whole design, and arises out of some culminating proceeding on the part of the character which the whole story has led up to, it seems to me to become, as it were, an act of divine justice. And when I use Miss Pross (though this is quite another question) to bring about that catastrophe, I have the positive intention of making that half-comic intervention a part of the desperate woman's failure, and of opposing that mean death—instead of a desperate one in the streets, which she wouldn't have minded—to the dignity of Carton's wrong or right; this *was* the design, and seemed to be in the fitness of things.

Now, as to the reading. I am sorry to say that it is out of the question this season. I have had an attack of rheumatism—quite a stranger to me—which remains hovering about my left side, after having doubled me up in the back, and which would disable me from standing for two hours. I have given up all dinners and town engagements, and come to my little Falstaff House here, sensible of the necessity of country training all through the summer. Smith would have proposed any appointment to see you on the subject, but he has been dreadfully ill with tic. Whenever I read in London, I will gladly put a night aside for your purpose, and we will plot to connect your name with it, and give it some speciality. But this could not be before Christmas time, as I should not be able to read sooner, for in the hot weather it would be useless. Let me hear from you about this when you have considered it. It would greatly diminish the expenses, remember.

Ever affectionately and faithfully.

The
Lord John
Russell.

GAD'S HILL PLACE, HIGHAM BY ROCHESTER, KENT,
Sunday, Seventeenth June, 1860.

MY DEAR LORD JOHN RUSSELL,

I cannot thank you enough for your kind note and its most welcome enclosure. My sailor-boy comes home from Portsmouth to-morrow, and will be overjoyed. His masters have been as anxious for getting his nomination as though it were some distinction for themselves.

Ever your faithful and obliged.

The Earl of
Carlisle.

GAD'S HILL PLACE, HIGHAM BY ROCHESTER, KENT,
Wednesday, Eighth August, 1860.

MY DEAR LORD CARLISLE,

Coming back here after an absence of three days in town, I find your kind and cordial letter lying on my table. I heartily thank you for it, and highly esteem it. I understand that the article on the spirits to which you refer was written by R. B—— (he played an Irish porter in one scene of Bulwer's comedy at Devonshire House). Between ourselves, I think it must be taken with a few grains of salt, imperial measure. The experiences referred to " came off" at ——, where the spirit of —— (among an extensive and miscellaneous bodiless circle) *dines* sometimes ! Mr. ——, the high priest of the mysteries, I have some considerable reason—derived from two honourable men—for mistrusting. And that some of the disciples are very easy of belief I know.

All goes well with me, thank God ! I should be thoroughly delighted to see you again, and to show you where the Falstaff robbery was done. My eldest daughter keeps my house, and it is one I was extraordinarily fond of when a child.

My dear Lord Carlisle, ever affectionately yours.

P.S.—I am prowling about, meditating a new book.

Mr. W. H. Wills.

OFFICE OF " ALL THE YEAR ROUND," *Tuesday, Fourth September,* 1860.

MY DEAR WILLS,

Your description of your sea-castle makes your room here look uncommonly dusty. Likewise the costermongers in the street outside, and the one customer (drunk, with his head on the table) in the Crown Coffee House over the way, in York Street, have an earthy, and, as I may say, a land-lubberly aspect. Cape Horn, to the best of *my* belief, is a tremendous way off, and there are more bricks and cabbage-leaves between this office and that dismal point of land than *you* can possibly imagine.

Coming here from the station this morning, I met, coming from the execution of the Wentworth murderer, such a tide of ruffians as never could have flowed from any point but the gallows. Without any figure of speech it turned one white and sick to behold them.

Tavistock House is cleared to-day, and possession delivered up. I must say that in all things the purchaser has behaved thoroughly well, and that I cannot call to mind any occasion when I have had money dealings with a Christian that have been so satisfactory, considerate, and trusting.

I am ornamented at present with one of my most intensely preposterous and utterly indescribable colds. If you were to make a voyage from Cape Horn to Wellington Street, you would scarcely recognise in the bowed form, weeping eyes, rasped nose, and snivelling wretch whom you would encounter here, the once gay and sparkling, etc. etc.

Everything else here is as quiet as possible. Wilkie looked in to-day, going to Gloucestershire for a week. The office is full of discarded curtains and coverings from Tavistock House, which

Georgina is coming up this evening to select from and banish. Mary is in raptures with the beauties of Dunkeld, but is not very well in health. The Admiral (Sydney) goes up for his examination to-morrow. If he fails to pass with credit, I will never believe in anybody again, so in that case look out for your own reputation with me.

I beg to send my kind regard to Mrs. Wills, and to enquire how she likes wearing a hat, which of course she does. I also want to know from her in confidence whether *Criollm festidiniog llymthll y wodd?*

Yesterday I burnt, in the field at Gad's Hill, the accumulated letters and papers of twenty years. They sent up a smoke like the genie when he got out of the casket on the seashore; and as it was an exquisite day when I began, and rained very heavily when I finished, I suspect my correspondence of having overcast the face of the heavens.

Ever faithfully.

P.S.—Kind regards to Mr. and Mrs. Novelli.*

Hullah's daughter (an artist) tells me that certain female students have addressed the Royal Academy, entreating them to find a place for their education. I think it a capital move, for which I can do something popular and telling in *The Register.* Adelaide Procter is active in the business, and has a copy of their letter. Will you write to her for that, and anything else she may have about it, telling her that I strongly approve, and want to help them myself?

GAD'S HILL PLACE, HIGHAM BY ROCHESTER, KENT,
Friday Night, Fourteenth September, 1860.

The Hon.
Mrs.
Watson.

MY DEAR MRS. WATSON,

I lose no time in answering your letter; and first as to business, the school in the High Town at Boulogne was excellent. The boys all English, the two proprietors an old Eton master and one of the Protestant clergymen of the town. The teaching unusually sound and good. The manner and conduct developed in the boys quite admirable. But I have never seen a gentleman so perfectly acquainted with boy-nature as the Eton master. There was a perfect understanding between him and his charges; nothing pedantic on his part, nothing slavish on their parts. The result was, that either with him or away from him, the boys combined an ease and frankness with a modesty and sense of responsibility that was really above all praise. Alfred went from there to

---

* With whom Mr. and Mrs. Wills were staying at Aberystwith.

a great school at Wimbledon, where they train for India and the artillery and engineers. Sydney went from there to Mr. Barrow, at Southsea. In both instances the new masters wrote to me of their own accord, bearing quite unsolicited testimony to the merits of the old, and expressing their high recognition of what they had done. These things speak for themselves.

Sydney has just passed his examination as a naval cadet and come home, all eyes and gold buttons. He has twelve days' leave before going on board the training-ship. Katie and her husband are in France, and seem likely to remain there for an indefinite period. Mary is on a month's visit in Scotland; Georgina, Frank, and Plorn are at home here; and we all want Mary and her little dog back again. I have sold Tavistock House, am making this rather complete in its way, and am on the restless eve of beginning a new big book; but mean to have a furnished house in town (in some accessible quarter) from February or so to June. May we meet there.

Your handwriting is always so full of pleasant memories to me, that when I took it out of the post-office at Rochester this afternoon it quite stirred my heart. But we must not think of old times as sad times, or regard them as anything but the fathers and mothers of the present. We must all climb steadily up the mountain after the talking bird, the singing tree, and the yellow water, and must all bear in mind that the previous climbers who were scared into looking back got turned into black stone.

Mary Boyle was here a little while ago, as affectionate at heart as ever, as young, and as pleasant. Of course we talked often of you. So let me know when you are established in Halfmoon Street, and I shall be truly delighted to come and see you.

For my attachments are strong attachments and never weaken. In right of bygones, I feel as if "all Northamptonshire" belonged to me, as all Northumberland did to Lord Bateman in the ballad. In memory of your warming your feet at the fire in that waste of a waiting-room when I read at Brighton, I have ever since taken that watering-place to my bosom as I never did before. And you and Switzerland are always one to me, and always inseparable.

Charley was heard of yesterday, from Shanghai, going to Japan, intending to meet his brother Walter at Calcutta, and having an idea of beguiling the time between whiles by asking to be taken as an amateur with the English Chinese forces. Everybody caressed him and asked him everywhere, and he seemed to go.

Ever affectionately yours.

GAD'S HILL PLACE, HIGHAM BY ROCHESTER, KENT,
Sunday, Twenty-third September, 1860.

Mr.
Edmund
Yates.

MY DEAR E. Y.,*

I did not write to you in your bereavement, because I knew
that the girls had written to you, and because I instinctively shrunk
from making a form of what was so real. *You* knew what a loving
and faithful remembrance I always had of your mother as a part
of my youth—no more capable of restoration than my youth itself.
All the womanly goodness, grace, and beauty of my drama went
out with her. To the last I never could hear her voice without
emotion. I think of her as of a beautiful part of my own youth,
and this dream that we are all dreaming seems to darken.

But it is not to say this that I write now. It comes to the
point of my pen in spite of me.

"Holding up the Mirror" is in next week's number. I have
taken out all the personal part of it. Not because I disliked it
(for, indeed, I thought it the best part of the paper), but because
it rather grated on me, going over the proof at that time, as a
remembrance that would be better reserved a little while. Also
because it made rather a mixture of yourself as an individual, with
something that does not belong or attach to you as an individual.
You can have the MS.; and as a part of a paper describing your
own juvenile remembrances of a theatre, there it is, needing no
change or adaptation. Ever faithfully.

GAD'S HILL PLACE, HIGHAM BY ROCHESTER, KENT,
Sunday, Twenty-third September, 1860.

Miss
Dickens.

MY DEAREST MAMIE,

If you had been away from us and ill with anybody in the
world but our dear Mrs. White, I should have been in a state of
the greatest anxiety and uneasiness about you. But as I know it
to be impossible that you could be in kinder or better hands, I was
not in the least restless about you, otherwise than as it grieved me
to hear of my poor dear girl's suffering such pain. I hope it is
over now for many a long day, and that you will come back to us
a thousand times better in health than you left us.

Don't come back too soon. Take time and get well restored.
There is no hurry, the house is not near to-rights yet, and though
we all want you, and though Boy wants you, we all (including
Boy) deprecate a fatiguing journey being taken too soon.

As to the carpenters, they are absolutely maddening. They are
always at work, yet never seem to do anything. Lillie was down

* On the death of his mother.

on Friday, and said (his eye fixed on Maidstone, and rubbing his hand to conciliate his moody employer) that "he didn't think there would be very much left to do after Saturday, the Twenty-ninth."

I didn't throw him out of the window. Your aunt tells you all the news, and leaves me no chance of distinguishing myself, I know. You have been told all about my brackets in the drawing-room, all about the glass rescued from the famous stage-wreck at Tavistock House, all about everything here and at the office. The office is really a success. As comfortable, cheerful, and private as anything of the kind can possibly be.

I took the Admiral (but this you know too, no doubt) to Dollond's, the mathematical instrument maker's, last Monday, to buy that part of his outfit. His sextant (which is about the size and shape of a cocked hat), on being applied to his eye, entirely concealed him. Not the faintest vestige of the distinguished officer behind it was perceptible to the human vision. All through the City, people turned round and stared at him with the sort of pleasure people take in a little model. We went on to Chatham this day week, in search of some big man-of-war's-man who should be under obligation to salute him—unfortunately found none. But this no doubt you know too, and all my news falls flat.

I am driven out of my room by paint, and am writing in the best spare room. The whole prospect is excessively wet; it does not rain now, but yesterday it did tremendously, and it rained very heavily in the night. We are even muddy; and that is saying a great deal in this dry country of chalk and sand. Everywhere the corn is lying out and saturated with wet. The hops (nearly every-where) look as if they had been burnt.

In my mind's eye I behold Mrs. Bouncer, still with some traces of her late anxiety on her faithful countenance, balancing herself a little unequally on her bow fore-legs, pricking up her ears, with her head on one side, and slightly opening her intellectual nostrils. I send my loving and respectful duty to her.

To dear Mrs. White say anything from me that is loving and grateful.

My dearest Mamie,
Ever and ever your most affectionate Father.

Miss
Hogarth.

OFFICE OF "ALL THE YEAR ROUND,"
Monday Night, Twenty-fourth September, 1860.

MY DEAREST GEORGY,

At the Waterloo station we were saluted with "Hallo ! here's Dickens !" from divers naval cadets, and Sir Richard Bromley introduced himself to me, who had his cadet son with him, a friend of Sydney's. We went down together, and the boys were in the closest alliance. Bromley being Accountant-General of the Navy, and having influence on board, got their hammocks changed so that they would swing side by side, at which they were greatly pleased. The moment we stepped on board, the "Hul-lo! here's Dickens!" was repeated on all sides, and the Admiral (evidently highly popular) shook hands with about fifty of his messmates. Taking Bromley for my model (with whom I fraternised in the most pathetic manner), I gave Sydney a sovereign before stepping over the side. He was as little overcome as it was possible for a boy to be, and stood waving the gold-banded cap as we came ashore in a boat.

There is no denying that he looks very small aboard a great ship, and that a boy must have a strong and decided speciality for the sea to take to such a life. Captain Harris was not on board, but the other chief officers were, and were highly obliging. We went over the ship. I should say that there can be little or no individuality of address to any particular boy, but that they all tumble through their education in a crowded way. The Admiral's servant (I mean our Admiral's) had an idiotic appearance, but perhaps it did him injustice (a mahogany-faced marine by station). The Admiral's washing apparatus is about the size of a muffin-plate, and he could easily live in his chest. The meeting with Bromley was a piece of great good fortune, and the dear old chap could not have been left more happily.

Ever, my dearest Georgy, your most affectionate.

OFFICE OF "ALL THE YEAR ROUND,"   Miss Power.
Tuesday, Twenty-fifth September, 1860.

MY DEAR MARGUERITE,

I like the article exceedingly, and think the translation *admirable*—spirited, fresh, bold, and evidently faithful. I will get the paper into the next number I make up, No. 78. I will send a proof to you for your correction, either next Monday, or this day week. Or would you like to come here next Monday and dine with us at five, and go over to Madame Céleste's opening? Then you could correct your paper on the premises, as they drink their beer at the beer-shops.

Some of the introductory remarks on French literature I propose to strike out, as a little too essayical for this purpose, and likely to throw out a large portion of the large audience at starting, as suggesting some very different kind of article. My daring pen shall have imbued its murderous heart with ink before you see the proof.   Ever affectionately.

Mr. John
Forster.

GAD'S HILL PLACE, HIGHAM BY ROCHESTER, KENT,
Thursday, Fourth October, 1860.

MY DEAR FORSTER,

It would be a great pleasure to me to come to you, an immense pleasure, and to sniff the sea I love (from the shore); but I fear I must come down one morning and come back at night. I will tell you why.

Last week, I got to work on a new story. I called a council of war at the office on Tuesday. It was perfectly clear that the one thing to be done was, for me to strike in. I have therefore decided to begin a story, the length of the "Tale of Two Cities," on the First of December—begin publishing, that is. I must make the most I can out of the book. When I come down, I will bring you the first two or three weekly parts. The name is, "GREAT EXPECTATIONS." I think a good name?

Now the preparations to get ahead, combined with the absolute necessity of my giving a good deal of time to the Christmas number, will tie me to the grindstone pretty tightly. It will be just as much as I can hope to do. Therefore, what I hoped would be a few days at Eastbourne diminish to a few hours.

I took the Admiral down to Portsmouth. Every maritime person in the town knew him. He seemed to know every boy on board the *Britannia*, and was a tremendous favourite evidently. It was very characteristic of him that they good-naturedly helped him, he being so very small, into his hammock at night. But he couldn't rest in it on these terms, and got out again to learn the right way of getting in independently. Official report stated that "after a few spills, he succeeded perfectly, and went to sleep." He is perfectly happy on board, takes tea with the captain, leads choruses on Saturday nights, and has an immense marine for a servant.

I saw Edmund Yates at the office, and he told me that during all his mother's wanderings of mind, which were almost incessant at last, she never once went back to the old Adelphi days until she was just dying, when he heard her say, in great perplexity: "I can *not* get the words."

Ever, my dear Forster, affectionately.

Mr. W.
Wilkie
Collins.

OFFICE OF "ALL THE YEAR ROUND,"
Wednesday, Twenty-fourth October, 1860.

MY DEAR WILKIE,

I have been down to Brighton to see Forster, and found your letter there on arriving by express this morning. I also found a letter from Georgina, describing that Mary's horse went down suddenly on a stone, and how Mary was thrown, and had her riding-habit torn to pieces, and has a deep cut just above the knee —fortunately not in the knee itself, which is doing exceedingly well, but which will probably incapacitate her from walking for days and days to come. It is well it was no worse. The accident occurred at Milton, near Gravesend, and they found Mary in a public-house there, wonderfully taken care of and looked after.

Your account of your passage goes to my heart through my stomach. What a pity I was not there on board to present that green-visaged, but sweet-tempered and uncomplaining spectacle of imbecility, at which I am so expert under stormy circumstances, in the poet's phrase :

As I sweep
Through the deep,
When the stormy winds do blow.

What a pity I am not there, at Meurice's, to sleep the sleep of infancy through the long plays where the gentlemen stand with their backs to the mantelpieces. What a pity I am not with you to make a third at the Trois Frères, and drink no end of bottles of Bordeaux, without ever getting a touch of redness in my (poet's phrase again) "innocent nose." But I must go down to Gad's to-night, and get to work again. Four weekly numbers have been ground off the wheel, and at least another must be turned before we meet. They shall be yours in the slumberous railway-carriage, when we start on the First of November.

I don't think Forster is at all in good health. He was tremendously hospitable and hearty. I walked six hours and a half on the downs yesterday, and never stopped or sat. Early in the morning, before breakfast, I went to the nearest baths to get a shower-bath. They kept me waiting longer than I thought reasonable, and seeing a man in a cap in the passage, I went to him and said : "I really must request that you'll be good enough to see about this shower-bath ;" and it was Hullah ! waiting for another bath.

Rumours were brought into the house on Saturday night, that there was a "ghost" up at Larkins' monument. Plorn was frightened to death, and I was apprehensive of the ghost's spreading and coming here, and causing "warning" and desertion among the servants. Frank was at home, and Andrew Gordon was with us. Time, nine o'clock. Village talk and credulity, amazing. I armed the two boys with a short stick apiece, and shouldered my double-barrelled gun, well loaded with shot. "Now observe," says I to the domestics, "if anybody is playing tricks and has got a head, I'll blow it off." Immense impression. New groom evidently convinced that he has entered the service of a blood-thirsty demon. We ascend to the monument. Stop at the gate. Moon is rising. Heavy shadows. "Now, look out!" (from the bloodthirsty demon, in a loud, distinct voice). "If the ghost is here and I see him, so help me God I'll fire at him!" Suddenly, as we enter the field, a most extraordinary noise responds—terrific noise—human noise—and yet superhuman noise. B. T. D. brings piece to shoulder. "Did you hear that, pa?" says Frank. "I did," says I. Noise repeated—portentous, derisive, dull, dismal, damnable. We advance towards the sound. Something white comes lumbering through the darkness. An asthmatic sheep! Dead, as I judge, by this time. Leaving Frank to guard him, I took Andrew with me, and went all round the monument, and down into the ditch, and examined the field well, thinking it likely that somebody might be taking advantage of the sheep to frighten the village. Drama ends with discovery of no one, and triumphant return to rum-and-water.

Ever affectionately.

Sir John
Bowring.

GAD'S HILL, Wednesday, Thirty-first October, 1860.

MY DEAR SIR JOHN,*

First let me congratulate you on your marriage and wish you all happiness and prosperity.

Secondly, I must tell you that I was greatly vexed with the Chatham people for not giving me early notice of your lecture. In that case I should (of course) have presided, as President of the Institution, and I should have asked you to honour my Falstaff house here. But when they made your kind intention known to me, I had made some important business engagements at the "All the Year Round" office for that evening, which I could not possibly forego. I charged them to tell you so, and was going to write to you when I found your kind letter.

We heard of your accident here, and of your "making nothing of it." I said that you didn't make much of disasters, and that you took poison (from natives) as quite a matter of course in the way of business.

Faithfully yours.

Miss
Hogarth.

BIDEFORD, NORTH DEVON,
Thursday Night, First November, 1860.

MY DEAREST GEORGY,

I write (with the most impracticable iron pen on earth) to report our safe arrival here, in a beastly hotel. We start to-morrow

* Sir John Bowring, formerly Her Majesty's Plenipotentiary in China and Governor of Hong Kong.

morning at nine on a two days' posting between this and Liskeard in Cornwall. We are due in Liskeard (but nobody seems to know anything about the roads) on Saturday afternoon, and we purpose making an excursion in that neighbourhood on Sunday, and coming up from Liskeard on Monday by Great Western fast train, which will get us to London, please God, in good time on Monday evening. There I shall hear from you, and know whether dear Mamie will move to London too.

We had a pleasant journey down here, and a beautiful day. No adventures whatever. Nothing has happened to Wilkie, and he sends love.

We had stinking fish for dinner, and have been able to drink nothing, though we have ordered wine, beer, and brandy-and-water. There is nothing in the house but two tarts and a pair of snuffers. The landlady is playing cribbage with the landlord in the next room (behind a thin partition), and they seem quite comfortable.

Ever, my dearest Georgy, your most affectionate.

GAD'S HILL PLACE, HIGHAM BY ROCHESTER, KENT,
Tuesday, Fourth December, 1860.

Mr. Austen
Henry
Layard.

MY DEAR LAYARD,

I know you will readily believe that I would come if I could, and that I am heartily sorry I cannot.

A new story of my writing, nine months long, is just begun in "All the Year Round." A certain allotment of my time when I have that story-demand upon me, has, all through my author life, been an essential condition of my health and success. I have just returned here to work so many hours every day for so many days. It is really impossible for me to break my bond.

There is not a man in England who is more earnestly your friend and admirer than I am. The conviction that you know it, helps me out through this note. You are a man of so much mark to me, that I even regret your going into the House of Commons—for which assembly I have but a scant respect. But I would not mention it to the Southwark electors if I could come to-morrow; though I should venture to tell them (and even that your friends would consider very impolitic) that I think them very much honoured for having such a candidate for their suffrages.

My daughter and sister-in-law want to know what you have done with your "pledge" to come down here again. If they had votes for Southwark they would threaten to oppose you—but would never do it. I was solemnly sworn at breakfast to let you know that we should be delighted to see you. Bear witness that I kept my oath.

Ever, my dear Layard,
Faithfully yours.

Miss Mary
Boyle.

OFFICE OF "ALL THE YEAR ROUND,"
Friday, Twenty-eighth December, 1860.

MY DEAR MARY,

I cannot tell you how much I thank you for the beautiful cigar-case, and how seasonable, and friendly, and good, and warm-hearted it looked when I opened it at Gad's Hill. Besides which, it is a cigar-case, and will hold cigars; two crowning merits that I never yet knew to be possessed by any article claiming the same name. For all of these reasons, but more than all because it comes from you, I love it, and send you eighteen hundred and sixty kisses, with one in for the new year.

I have no news, except that I am not quite well, and am being doctored. Pray read "Great Expectations." I think it is very droll. It is a very great success, and seems universally liked. I suppose because it opens funnily, and with an interest too.

I pass my time here (I am staying here alone) in working, taking physic, and taking a stall at a theatre every night. On Boxing Night I was at Covent Garden. A dull pantomime was "worked" (as we say) better than I ever saw a heavy piece worked on a first night, until suddenly and without a moment's warning, every scene on that immense stage fell over on its face, and disclosed chaos by gaslight behind! There never was such a business; about sixty people who were on the stage being extinguished in the most remarkable manner. Not a soul was hurt. In the uproar, some moon-calf rescued a porter pot, six feet high (out of which the clown had been drinking when the accident happened), and stood it on the cushion of the lowest proscenium box, P.S., beside a lady and gentleman, who were dreadfully ashamed of it. The moment the house knew that nobody was injured, they directed their whole attention to this gigantic porter pot in its genteel position (the lady and gentleman trying to hide behind it), and roared with laughter. When a modest footman came from behind the curtain to clear it, and took it up in his arms like a Brobdingnagian baby, we all laughed more than ever we had laughed in our lives. I don't know why.

We have had a fire here, but our people put it out before the parish-engine arrived, like a drivelling perambulator, with *the beadle in it*, like an imbecile baby. Popular opinion, disappointed in the fire having been put out, snowballed the beadle. God bless it!

Over the way at the Lyceum, there is a very fair Christmas piece, with one or two uncommonly well-done nigger songs—one remarkably gay and mad, done in the finale to a scene. Also a very nice transformation, though I don't know what it means.

The poor actors waylay me in Bow Street to represent their necessities; and I often see one cut down a court when he beholds me coming, cut round Drury Lane to face me, and come up towards me near this door in the freshest and most accidental way, as if I was the last person he expected to see on the surface of this globe. The other day there thus appeared before me (simultaneously with a scent of rum in the air) one aged and greasy man, with a pair of pumps under his arm. He said he thought if he could get down to somewhere (I think it was Newcastle), he would get "taken on" as Pantaloon, the existing Pantaloon being "a stick, sir—a mere muff." I observed that I was sorry times were so bad with him. "Mr. Dickens, you know our profession, sir—no one knows it better, sir—there is no right feeling in it. I was Harlequin on your own circuit, sir, for five-and-thirty years, and was displaced by a boy, sir!—a boy!"

So no more at present, from, my dear Mary,

Your ever affectionate

JOE.

P.S.—DON'T I pine neither?

DEAR FRIEND,

Captain Morgan.

I am heartily obliged to you for your seasonable and welcome remembrance. It came to the office (while I was there) in the pleasantest manner, brought by two seafaring men as if they had swum across with it. I have already told —— what I am very well assured of concerning you, but you are such a noble fellow that I must not pursue that subject. But you will at least take my cordial and affectionate thanks. . . . We have a touch of most beautiful weather here now, and this country is most beautiful too. I wish I could carry you off to a favourite spot of mine between this and Maidstone, where I often smoke your cigars and think of you. We often take our lunch on a hillside there in the summer, and then I lie down on the grass—a splendid example of laziness —and say, "Now for my Morgan!"

My daughter and her aunt declare that they know the true scent of the true article (which I don't in the least believe), and sometimes they exclaim, "That's not a Morgan," and the worst of it is they were once right by accident. . . . I hope you will have seen the Christmas number of "All the Year Round."* Here

* "A Message from the Sea."

and there in the description of the sea-going hero, I have given a touch or two of remembrance of Somebody you know; very heartily desiring that thousands of people may have some faint reflection of the pleasure I have for many years derived from the contemplation of a most amiable nature and most remarkable man.

Ever affectionately yours.

1861.

NARRATIVE.

THIS, as far as his movements were concerned, was again a very unsettled year with Charles Dickens. He hired a furnished house in the Regent's Park, which he, with his household, occupied for some months. During the season he gave several readings at St. James's Hall. After a short summer holiday at Gad's Hill, he started, in the autumn, on a reading tour in the English provinces. Mr. Arthur Smith, being seriously ill, could not accompany him in this tour; and Mr. Headland, who was formerly in office at St. Martin's Hall, was engaged as business-manager of these readings. Mr. Arthur Smith died in October, and Charles Dickens' distress at the loss of this loved friend and companion is touchingly expressed in many of his letters of this year.

There are also sorrowful allusions to the death of his brother-in-law, Mr. Henry Austin, which sad event likewise happened in October. And the letter to Mrs. Austin ("Letitia") has reference to her affliction.

In June of this year he paid a short visit to Sir E. B. Lytton at Knebworth, accompanied by his daughter and sister-in-law, who also joined him in Edinburgh during his autumn tour. But this course of readings was brought rather suddenly to an end on account of the death of the Prince Consort.

Besides being constantly occupied with the business of these readings, Charles Dickens was still at work on his story of "Great Expectations," which was appearing weekly in "All the Year Round." The story closed on the Third of August, when it was published as a whole in three volumes, and inscribed to Mr. Chauncey Hare Townshend. The Christmas number of "All the Year Round" was called "Tom Tiddler's Ground," to which Charles Dickens contributed three stories.

The first letter in this year is given more as a specimen of the claims which were constantly being made upon Charles Dickens' time and patience, than because we consider the letter itself to contain much public interest; excepting, indeed, as showing his always considerate and courteous replies to such constant applications.

"The fire" mentioned in the letter to Mr. Forster was the great fire in Tooley Street. Young Mr. Morgan, the son of Captain Morgan, was, during the years he passed in England, a constant visitor at Gad's Hill. The "Elwin" mentioned in the letter written from Bury St. Edmunds, was the Rev. Whitwell Elwin, a Norfolk clergyman well known in the literary world, and who was for many years editor of "The Quarterly Review."

The explanation of the letter to Mr. John Agate, of Dover, we give in that gentleman's own words:

"There are few public men with the strain upon their time and energies which he had particularly (and which I know better now that I have read his life), who would have spared the time to have written such a long courteous letter.

"I wrote to him rather in anger, and left the letter myself at The Lord Warden, as I and my family were very much disappointed, after having purchased our tickets so long before, to find we could not get into the room, as money was being received, but his kind letter explained all."

OFFICE OF "ALL THE YEAR ROUND," *   Anonymous.
26, WELLINGTON STREET, W.C.,
Tuesday Evening, Eighth January, 1861.

DEAR SIR,

I feel it quite hopeless to endeavour to present my position before you, in reference to such a letter as yours, in its plain and true light. When you suppose it would have cost Mr. Thackeray "but a word" to use his influence to obtain you some curatorship or the like, you fill me with the sense of impossibility of leading you to a more charitable judgment of Mr. Dickens.

Nevertheless, I will put the truth before you. Scarcely a day of my life passes, or has passed for many years, without bringing me some letters similar to yours. Often they will come by dozens—scores—hundreds. My time and attention would be pretty well occupied without them, and the claims upon me (some very near home), for all the influence and means of help that I do and do not possess, are not commonly heavy. I have no power to aid you towards the attainment of your object. It is the simple exact truth, and nothing can alter it. So great is the disquietude I con-

* The same house, but the numbering of Wellington Street had been altered since 1860.

stantly undergo from having to write to some new correspondent in this strain, that, God knows, I would resort to another relief if I could.

Your studies from nature appear to me to express an excellent observation of nature, in a loving and healthy spirit. But what then? The dealers and dealers' prices of which you complain will not be influenced by that honest opinion. Nor will it have the least effect upon the President of the Royal Academy, or the Directors of the School of Design. Assuming your supposition to be correct that these authorities are adverse to you, I have no more power than you have to render them favourable. And assuming them to be quite disinterested and dispassionate towards you, I have no voice or weight in any appointment that any of them make.

I write under the pressure of occupation and business, and therefore write briefly.

Faithfully yours.

Sir Edward
Bulwer
Lytton.

OFFICE OF " ALL THE YEAR ROUND,"
Wednesday, Twenty-third January, 1861.

MY DEAR BULWER LYTTON,

I am delighted to receive your letter, and to look forward with confidence to having such a successor in August. I can honestly assure you that I never have been so pleased at heart in all my literary life, as I am in the proud thought of standing side by side with you before this great audience.

In regard of the story,* I have perfect faith in such a master-hand as yours; and I know that what such an artist feels to be terrible and original, is unquestionably so. You whet my interest by what you write of it to the utmost extent.

Believe me ever affectionately yours.

M. De
Cerjat.

OFFICE OF " ALL THE YEAR ROUND,"
Friday, First February, 1861.

MY DEAR CERJAT,

You have read in the papers of our heavy English frost. At Gad's Hill it was so intensely cold, that in our warm dining-room on Christmas Day we could hardly sit at the table. In my study on that morning, long after a great fire of coal and wood had been lighted, the thermometer was I don't know where below freezing. The bath froze, and all the pipes froze, and remained in a stony state for five or six weeks. The water in the bedroom-jugs froze, and blew up the crockery. The snow on the top of the

---

* "A Strange Story."

house froze, and was imperfectly removed with axes.   My beard froze as I walked about, and I couldn't detach my cravat and coat from it until I was thawed at the fire.   My boys and half the officers stationed at Chatham skated away without a check to Gravesend—five miles off—and repeated the performance for three or four weeks.   At last the thaw came, and then everything split, blew up, dripped, poured, perspired, and got spoilt.   Since then we have had a small visitation of the plague of servants; the cook (in a riding-habit) and the groom (in a dress-coat and jewels) having mounted Mary's horse and mine, in our absence, and scoured the neighbouring country at a rattling pace.   And when I went home last Saturday, I innocently wondered how the horses came to be out of condition, and gravely consulted the said groom on the subject, who gave it as his opinion "which they wanted reg'lar work."   We are now coming to town until midsummer.   Having sold my own house, to be more free and independent, I have taken a very pretty furnished house, No. 3, Hanover Terrace, Regent's Park.   This, of course, on my daughter's account.   For I have very good and cheerful bachelor rooms here, with an old servant in charge, who is the cleverest man of his kind in the world, and can do anything, from excellent carpentery to excellent cookery, and has been with me three-and-twenty years.

The American business is the greatest English sensation at present.   I venture to predict that the struggle of violence will be a very short one, and will be soon succeeded by some new compact between the Northern and Southern States.   Meantime the Lancashire mill-owners are getting very uneasy.

The Italian state of things is not regarded as looking very cheerful.   What from one's natural sympathies with a people so oppressed as the Italians, and one's natural antagonism to a pope and a Bourbon (both of which superstitions I do suppose the world to have had more than enough of), I agree with you concerning Victor Emmanuel, and greatly fear that the Southern Italians are much degraded.   Still, an united Italy would be of vast importance to the peace of the world, and would be a rock in Louis Napoleon's way, as he very well knows.   Therefore the idea must be championed, however much against hope.

My eldest boy, just home from China, was descried by Townshend's Henri the moment he landed at Marseilles, and was by him borne in triumph to Townshend's rooms.   The weather was snowy, slushy, beastly; and Marseilles was, as it usually is to my thinking, well-nigh intolerable.   My boy could not stay with Townshend, as he was coming on by express train; but he says: "I sat with him and saw him dine.   He had a leg of lamb, and a tremendous cold." That is the whole description I have been able to extract from him.

This journal is doing gloriously, and "Great Expectations" is a great success. I have taken my third boy, Frank (Jeffrey's godson), into this office. If I am not mistaken, he has a natural literary taste and capacity, and may do very well with a chance so congenial to his mind, and being also entered at the Bar.

Dear me, when I have to show you about London, and we dine *en garçon* at odd places, I shall scarcely know where to begin. Only yesterday I walked out from here in the afternoon, and thought I would go down by the Houses of Parliament. When I got there, the day was so beautifully bright and warm, that I thought I would walk on by Millbank, to see the river. I walked straight on *for three miles* on a splendid broad esplanade overhanging the Thames, with immense factories, railway works, and whatnot erected on it, and with the strangest beginnings and ends of wealthy streets pushing themselves into the very Thames. When I was a rower on that river, it was all broken ground and ditch, with here and there a public-house or two, an old mill, and a tall chimney. I had never seen it in any state of transition, though I suppose myself to know this rather large city as well as anyone in it.

* * * * *

Mr. E. M.
Ward, R.A.

3, HANOVER TERRACE, REGENT'S PARK,
Saturday Night, Ninth March, 1861.

MY DEAR WARD,

I cannot tell you how gratified I have been by your letter, and what a splendid recompense it is for any pleasure I am giving you. Such generous and earnest sympathy from such a brother-artist gives me true delight. I am proud of it, believe me, and moved by it to do all the better.

Ever faithfully yours.

Sir Edward
Bulwer
Lytton.

3, HANOVER TERRACE, REGENT'S PARK,
Sunday, Twenty-eighth April, 1861.

MY DEAR BULWER LYTTON,

My story will finish in the first week in August. Yours ought to begin in the last week of July, or the last week but one. Wilkie Collins will be at work to follow you. The publication has made a very great success with "Great Expectations," and could not present a finer time for you.

The question of length may be easily adjusted.

Of the misgiving you entertain I cannot of course judge until you give me leave to rush to the perusal. I swear that I never thought I had half so much self-denial as I have shown in this case! I think I shall come out at Exeter Hall as a choice vessel on the strength of it. In the meanwhile I have quickened the printer and told him to get on fast.

You cannot think how happy you make me by what you write of "Great Expectations." There is nothing like the pride of making such an effect on such a writer as you.

Ever faithfully.

3, HANOVER TERRACE, REGENT'S PARK,
Wednesday, Eighth May, 1861.

Sir Edward Bulwer Lytton.

MY DEAR BULWER LYTTON,

I am anxious to let you know that Mr. Frederic Lehmann, who is coming down to Knebworth to see you (with his sister Mrs. Benzon) is a particular friend of mine, for whom I have a very high and warm regard. Although he will sufficiently enlist your sympathy on his own behalf, I am sure that you will not be the less interested in him because I am.

Ever faithfully yours.

3, HANOVER TERRACE,
Sunday, Twelfth May, 1861.

The same.

MY DEAR BULWER LYTTON,

I received your revised proofs only yesterday, and I sat down to read them last night. And before I say anything further I may tell you that I COULD NOT lay them aside, but was obliged to go on with them in my bedroom until I got into a very ghostly state indeed. This morning I have taken them again and have gone through them with the utmost attention.

Of the beauty and power of the writing I say not a word, or of its originality and boldness, or of its quite extraordinary constructive skill. I confine myself solely to your misgiving, and to the question whether there is any sufficient foundation for it.

On the last head I say, without the faintest hesitation, most decidedly there is NOT sufficient foundation for it. I do not share it in the least. I believe that the readers who have never given their minds (or perhaps had any to give) to those strange psychological mysteries in ourselves, of which we are all more or less conscious, will accept your wonders as curious weapons in the armoury of fiction, and will submit themselves to the Art with which said weapons are used. Even to that class of intelligence the marvellous addresses itself from a very strong position; and that class of intelligence is not accustomed to find the marvellous

in such very powerful hands as yours. On more imaginative
readers the tale will fall (or I am greatly mistaken) like a spell.
By readers who combine some imagination, some scepticism, and
some knowledge and learning, I hope it will be regarded as full of
strange fancy and curious study, startling reflections of their own
thoughts and speculations at odd times, and wonder which a
master has a right to evoke.   In the last point lies, to my thinking,
the whole case.   If you were the Magician's servant instead of the
Magician, these potent spirits would get the better of you; but
you *are* the Magician, and they don't, and you make them serve
your purpose.

Occasionally in the dialogue I see an expression here and there
which might—always solely with a reference to your misgivings—
be better away; and I think the vision, to use the word for want
of a better—in the museum, should be made a little less abstruse.
I should not say that, if the sale of the journal was below the sale
of *The Times* newspaper; but as it is probably several thousands
higher, I do.   I would also suggest that after the title we put the
two words—A ROMANCE.   It is an absurdly easy device for getting
over your misgiving with the blockheads, but I think it would be
an effective one.   I don't, on looking at it, like the title.   Here
are a few that have occurred to me.

"The Steel Casket."

"The Lost Manuscript."

"Derval Court."

"Perpetual Youth."

"Maggie."

"Dr. Fenwick."

"Life and Death."

The four last I think the best.   There is an objection to "Dr.
Fenwick" because there has been "Dr. Antonio," and there is a
book of Dumas' which repeats the objection.   I don't think
"Fenwick" startling enough.   It appears to me that a more
startling title would take the (John) Bull by the horns, and would
be a serviceable concession to your misgiving, as suggesting a story
off the stones of the gas-lighted Brentford Road.

The title is the first thing to be settled, and cannot be settled
too soon.

For the purposes of the weekly publication the divisions of the
story will often have to be greatly changed, though afterwards, in
the complete book, you can, of course, divide it into chapters, free
from that reference.   For example: I would end the first chapter
on the third slip at "and through the ghostly streets, under the
ghostly moon, went back to my solitary room."   The rest of what

is now your first chapter might be made Chapter II., and would end the first weekly part.

I think I have become, by dint of necessity and practice, rather cunning in this regard; and perhaps you would not mind my looking closely to such points from week to week. It so happens that if you had written the opening of this story expressly for the occasion its striking incidents could not possibly have followed one another better. One other merely mechanical change I suggest now. I would not have an initial letter for the town, but would state in the beginning that I gave the town a fictitious name. I suppose a blank or a dash rather fends a good many people off—because it always has the effect upon me.

Be sure that I am perfectly frank and open in all I have said in this note, and that I have not a grain of reservation in my mind. I think the story a very fine one, one that no other man could write, and that there is no strength in your misgiving for the two reasons: firstly, that the work is professedly a work of Fancy and Fiction, in which the reader is not required to take anything for Fact; secondly, that it is written by the man who can write it. The Magician's servant does not know what to do with the ghost, and has, consequently, no business with him. The Magician does know what to do with him, and has all the business with him that he can transact.

I am quite at ease on the points that you have expressed yourself as not at ease upon. Quite. I cannot too often say that if they were carried on weak shoulders they would break the bearer down. But in your mastering of them lies the mastery over the reader.

This will reach you at Knebworth, I hope, to-morrow afternoon. Pray give your doubts to the winds of that high spot, and believe that if I had them I would swarm up the flag-staff as nimbly as Margrave and nail the Fenwick colours to the top.

Ever affectionately yours.

3, HANOVER TERRACE, REGENT'S PARK,   Sir Edward
Monday, Twentieth May, 1861.   Bulwer
Lytton.

MY DEAR BULWER LYTTON,

I did not read from Australia till the end, because I was obliged to be hard at work that day, and thought it best that the MS. should come back to you rather than that I should detain it. Of course, I *can* read it, whenever it suits you. As to Isabel's dying and Fenwick's growing old, I would say that, beyond question, whatever the meaning of the story tends to, is the proper end.

All the alterations you mention in your last, are excellent.

As to title, "Margrave, a Tale of Mystery," would be sufficiently striking. I prefer "Wonder" to "Mystery," because I think it suggests something higher and more apart from ordinary complications of plot, or the like, which "Mystery" might seem to mean. Will you kindly remark that the title PRESSES, and that it will be a great relief to have it as soon as possible? The last two months of my story are our best time for announcement and preparation. Of course, it is most desirable that your story should have the full benefit of them.

Ever faithfully.

Lady Olliffe.

LORD WARDEN HOTEL, DOVER,
Sunday, Twenty-sixth May, 1861.

MY DEAR LADY OLLIFFE,

I have run away to this sea-beach to get rid of my neuralgic face.

Touching the kind invitations received from you this morning, I feel that the only course I can take—without being a Humbug—is to decline them. After the middle of June I shall be mostly at Gad's Hill—I know that I cannot do better than keep out of the way of hot rooms and late dinners, and what would you think of me, or call me, if I were to accept and not come!

No, no, no. Be still my soul. Be virtuous, eminent author. Do *not* accept, my Dickens. She is to come to Gad's Hill with her spouse. Await her *there*, my child. (Thus the voice of wisdom.)   My dear Lady Olliffe,

Ever affectionately yours.

Mr. W. C.
Macready.

"ALL THE YEAR ROUND" OFFICE,
Tuesday, Eleventh June, 1861.

MY DEAREST MACREADY,

There is little doubt, I think, of my reading at Cheltenham somewhere about November. I submit myself so entirely to Arthur Smith's arrangements for me, that I express my sentiments on this head with modesty. But I think there is scarcely a doubt of my seeing you then.

I have just finished my book of "Great Expectations," and am the worse for wear. Neuralgic pains in the face have troubled me a good deal, and the work has been pretty close. But I hope that the book is a good book, and I have no doubt of very soon throwing off the little damage it has done me.

What with Blondin at the Crystal Palace and Leotard at

Leicester Square, we seem to be going back to barbaric excitements. I have not seen, and don't intend to see, the Hero of Niagara (as the posters call him), but I have been beguiled into seeing Leotard, and it is at once the most fearful and most graceful thing I have ever seen done.

I am sore afraid that *The Times*, by playing fast and loose with the American question, has very seriously compromised this country. The Americans northward are perfectly furious on the subject; and Motley the historian (a very sensible man, strongly English in his sympathies) assured me the other day that he thought the harm done very serious indeed, and the dangerous nature of the daily widening breach scarcely calculable.

Ever most affectionately, my dearest Macready.

GAD'S HILL, *Monday, First July,* 1861.　Mr. John Forster.

MY DEAR FORSTER,

*　　　*　　　*　　　*　　　*

You will be surprised to hear that I have changed the end of "Great Expectations" from and after Pip's return to Joe's, and finding his little likeness there.

Bulwer (who has been, as I think I told you, extraordinarily taken by the book) so strongly urged it upon me, after reading the proofs, and supported his views with such good reasons, that I resolved to make the change. You shall have it when you come back to town. I have put in a very pretty piece of writing, and I have no doubt the story will be more acceptable through the alteration.

I have not seen Bulwer's changed story. I brought back the first month with me, and I know the nature of his changes throughout; but I have not yet had the revised proofs. He was in a better state at Knebworth than I have ever seen him all these years, a little weird occasionally regarding magic and spirits, but perfectly fair and frank under opposition. He was talkative, anecdotal, and droll; looked young and well, laughed heartily, and enjoyed some games we played with great zest. In his artist character and talk he was full of interest and matter, but that he always is. Socially he seemed to me almost a new man.

The fire I did not see until the Monday morning, but it was blazing fiercely then, and was blazing hardly less furiously when I came down here again last Friday. I was here on the night of its breaking out. If I had been in London I should have been on the scene, pretty surely.

You will be perhaps surprised to hear that it is Morgan's conviction (his son was here yesterday), that the North will put down the South, and that speedily. In his management of his large business, he is proceeding steadily on that conviction. He says that the South has no money and no credit, and that it is impossible for it to make a successful stand. He may be all wrong, but he is certainly a very shrewd man, and he has never been, as to the United States, an enthusiast of any class.

Poor Lord Campbell's seems to me as easy and good a death as one could desire. There must be a sweep of these men very soon, and one feels as if it must fall out like the breaking of an arch—one stone goes from a prominent place, and then the rest begin to drop. So one looks towards Brougham, and Lyndhurst, and Pollock.

I will add no more to this, or I shall not send it; for I am in the first desperate laziness of having done my book, and think of offering myself to the village school as a live example of that vice for the edification of youth.

Ever, my dear Forster, affectionately.

The Hon.
Mrs.
Watson.

GAD'S HILL PLACE, HIGHAM BY ROCHESTER, KENT,
Monday, Eighth July, 1861.

MY DEAR MRS. WATSON,

I have owed you a letter for so long a time that I fear you may sometimes have misconstrued my silence. But I hope that the sight of the handwriting of your old friend will undeceive you if you have, and will put that right.

During the progress of my last story, I have been working so hard that very, very little correspondence—except enforced correspondence on business—has passed this pen. And now that I am free again, I devote a few of my first leisure moments to this note.

You seemed in your last to think that I had forgotten you in respect of the Christmas number. Not so at all. I discussed with them here where you were, how you were to be addressed, and the like; finally left the number in a blank envelope, and did not add the address to it until it would have been absurd to send you such stale bread. This was my fault, but this was all. And I should be so pained at heart if you supposed me capable of failing in my truth and cordiality, or in the warm remembrance of the time we have passed together, that perhaps I make more of it than you meant to do.

My sailor-boy is at home—I was going to write, for the holidays, but I suppose I must substitute "on leave." Under the new regulations, he must not pass out of the *Britannia* before December. The younger boys are all at school, and coming home this week for the holidays. Mary keeps house, of course, and

Katie and her husband surprised us yesterday, and are here now. Charley is holiday-making at Guernsey and Jersey. He has been for some time seeking a partnership in business, and has not yet found one. The matter is in the hands of Mr. Bates, the managing partner in Barings' house, and seems as slow a matter to adjust itself as ever I looked on at. Georgina is, as usual, the general friend and confidante and factotum of the whole party.

Your present correspondent read at St. James's Hall in the beginning of the season, to perfectly astounding audiences; but finding that fatigue and excitement very difficult to manage in conjunction with a story, deemed it prudent to leave off reading in high tide and mid-career, the rather by reason of something like neuralgia in the face. At the end of October I begin again; and if you are at Brighton in November, I shall try to see you there.

This is all about me and mine, and next I want to know why you never come to Gad's Hill, and whether you are never coming. The stress I lay on these questions you will infer from the size of the following note of interrogation ?

I am in the constant receipt of news from Laùsanne. Of Mary Boyle, I daresay you have seen and heard more than I have lately. Rumours occasionally reach me of her acting in every English shire incessantly, and getting in a harvest of laurels all the year round. Cavendish I have not seen for a long time, but when I did see him last, it was at Tavistock House, and we dined together jovially. Mention of that locality reminds me that when you DO come here, you will see the pictures looking wonderfully better, and more precious than they ever did in town. Brought together in country light and air, they really are quite a baby collection and very pretty.

I direct this to Rockingham, supposing you to be there in the summer time. If you are as leafy in Northamptonshire as we are in Kent, you are greener than you have been for some years. I hope you may have seen a large-headed photograph with little legs, representing the undersigned, pen in hand, tapping his forehead to knock an idea out. It has just sprung up so abundantly in all the shops, that I am ashamed to go about town looking in at the picture-windows, which is my delight. It seems to me extra-ordinarily ludicrous, and much more like than the grave portrait done in earnest. It made me laugh when I first came upon it, until I shook again, in open sunlighted Piccadilly.

Pray be a good Christian to me, and don't be retributive in measuring out the time that shall pass before you write to me. And believe me ever,

Your affectionate and faithful.

Mrs. Milner
Gibson.

GAD'S HILL, *Monday, Eighth July,* 1861.

MY DEAR MRS. GIBSON,

I want very affectionately and earnestly to congratulate you on your eldest daughter's approaching marriage. Up to the moment when Mary told me of it, I had foolishly thought of her always as the pretty little girl with the frank loving face whom I saw last on the sands at Broadstairs. I rubbed my eyes and woke at the words "going to be married," and found I had been walking in my sleep some years.

I want to thank you also for thinking of me on the occasion, but I feel that I am better away from it. I should really have a misgiving that I was a sort of shadow on a young marriage, and you will understand me when I say so, and no more.

But I shall be with you in the best part of myself, in the warmth of sympathy and friendship—and I send my love to the dear girl, and devoutly hope and believe that she will be happy. The face that I remember with perfect accuracy, and could draw here, if I could draw at all, was made to be happy and to make a husband so.

I wonder whether you ever travel by railroad in these times! I wish Mary could tempt you to come by any road to this little place.

With kind regard to Milner Gibson, believe me ever,

Affectionately and faithfully yours.

Mr. W.
Wilkie
Collins.

OFFICE OF "ALL THE YEAR ROUND,"
Wednesday, Twenty-eighth August, 1861.

MY DEAR WILKIE,

I have got the "Copperfield" reading ready for delivery, and am now going to blaze away at "Nickleby," which I don't like half as well. Every morning I "go in" at these marks for two or three hours, and then collapse and do nothing whatever (counting as nothing much cricket and rounders).

In my time that curious railroad by the Whitby Moor was so much the more curious, that you were balanced against a counterweight of water, and that you did it like Blondin. But in these remote days the one inn of Whitby was up a back-yard, and oystershell grottoes were the only view from the best private room. Likewise, sir, I have posted to Whitby. "Pity the sorrows of a poor old man."

The sun is glaring in at these windows with an amount of ferocity insupportable by one of the landed interest, who lies upon his back with an imbecile hold on grass, from lunch to dinner. Feebleness of mind and head are the result.

Ever affectionately.

P.S.—The boys have multiplied themselves by fifty daily, and have seemed to appear in hosts (especially in the hottest days) round all the corners at Gad's Hill. I call them the prowlers, and each has a distinguishing name attached, derived from his style of prowling.

GAD'S HILL PLACE, HIGHAM BY ROCHESTER, KENT,   Mr. Arthur
Tuesday, Third September, 1861.   Smith.

MY DEAR ARTHUR,

I cannot tell you how sorry I am to receive your bad account of your health, or how anxious I shall be to receive a better one as soon as you can possibly give it.

If you go away, don't you think in the main you would be better here than anywhere? You know how well you would be nursed, what care we should take of you, and how perfectly quiet and at home you would be, until you become strong enough to take to the Medway. Moreover, I think you would be less anxious about the tour, here, than away from such association. I would come to Worthing to fetch you, I needn't say, and would take the most careful charge of you. I will write no more about this, because I wish to avoid giving you more to read than can be helped; but I do sincerely believe it would be at once your wisest and least anxious course. As to a long journey into Wales, or any long journey, it would never do. Nice is not to be thought of. Its dust, and its sharp winds (I know it well), towards October are very bad indeed.

Ever faithfully.

GAD'S HILL PLACE, HIGHAM BY ROCHESTER, KENT,   Sir Edward
Tuesday, Seventeenth September, 1861.   Bulwer
Lytton.

MY DEAR BULWER LYTTON,

I am delighted with your letter of yesterday—delighted with the addition to the length of the story—delighted with your account of it, and your interest in it—and even more than delighted by what you say of our working in company.

Not one dissentient voice has reached me respecting it. Through the dullest time of the year we held our circulation most gallantly. And it could not have taken a better hold. I saw Forster on Friday (newly returned from thousands of provincial lunatics), and he really was more impressed than I can tell you by what he had seen of it. Just what you say you think it will turn out to be, *he* was saying, almost in the same words.

I am burning to get at the whole story;—and you inflame me in the maddest manner by your references to what I don't know. The exquisite art with which you have changed it, and have overcome the difficulties of the mode of publication, has fairly staggered me. I know pretty well what the difficulties are; and there is no other man who could have done it, I ween.

Ever affectionately.

Mr. John
Watkins.

GAD'S HILL PLACE, HIGHAM BY ROCHESTER, KENT,
Saturday Night, Twenty-eighth September, 1861.

DEAR MR. WATKINS,

In reply to your kind letter I must explain that I have not yet brought down any of your large photographs of myself, and therefore cannot report upon their effect here. I think the "cartes" are all liked.

A general howl of horror greeted the appearance of No. 18, and a riotous attempt was made to throw it out of window. I calmed the popular fury by promising that it should never again be beheld within these walls. I think I mentioned to you when you showed it to me, that I felt persuaded it would not be liked. It has a grim and wasted aspect, and perhaps might be made useful as a portrait of the Ancient Mariner.

I feel that I owe you an apology for being (innocently) a difficult subject. When I once excused myself to Ary Scheffer while sitting to him, he received the apology as strictly his due, and said with a vexed air: "At this moment, *mon cher* Dickens, you look more like an energetic Dutch admiral than anything else;" for which I apologised again.

In the hope that the pains you have bestowed upon me will not be thrown away, but that your success will prove of some use to you, believe me,

Faithfully yours.

Mr. Edmund
Yates.

GAD'S HILL PLACE, HIGHAM BY ROCHESTER, KENT,
Sunday, Sixth October, 1861.

MY DEAR EDMUND,

Coming back here to-day, I find your letter.*

I was so very much distressed last night in thinking of it all, and I find it so very difficult to preserve my composure when I dwell in my mind on the many times fast approaching when I

* On the occasion of the death of Mr. Arthur Smith.

shall sorely miss the familiar face, that I am hardly steady enough yet to refer to the readings like a man. But your kind reference to them makes me desirous to tell you that I took Headland (formerly of St. Martin's Hall, who has always been with us in London) to conduct the business, when I knew that our poor dear fellow could never do it, even if he had recovered strength to go; and that I consulted with himself about it when I saw him for the last time on earth, and that it seemed to please him, and he said: "We couldn't do better." Ever faithfully.

GAD'S HILL PLACE, HIGHAM BY ROCHESTER, KENT, *Sunday, Sixth October*, 1861.

Mr. H. G. Adams.

MY DEAR MR. ADAMS,

My readings are a sad subject to me just now, for I am going away on the twenty-eighth to read fifty times, and I have lost Mr. Arthur Smith—a friend whom I can never replace—who always went with me, and transacted, as no other man ever can, all the business connected with them, and without whom, I fear, they will be dreary and weary to me. But this is not to the purpose of your letter.

I desire to be useful to the Institution of the place with which my childhood is inseparably associated, and I will serve it this next Christmas if I can. Will you tell me when I could do you most good by reading for you? Faithfully yours.

OFFICE OF "ALL THE YEAR ROUND," *Thursday, Tenth October*, 1861.

Miss Dickens.

MY DEAREST MAMIE,

I received your affectionate little letter here this morning, and was very glad to get it. Poor dear Arthur is a sad loss to me, and indeed I was very fond of him. But the readings must be fought out, like all the rest of life.

Ever your affectionate.

GAD'S HILL PLACE, HIGHAM BY ROCHESTER, KENT, *Sunday, Thirteenth October*, 1861.

Mr. W. C. Macready.

MY DEAREST MACREADY,

This is a short note. But the moment I know for certain what is designed for me at Cheltenham, I write to you in order that you may know it from me and not by chance from anyone else.

I am to read there on the evening of Friday, the Third of January, and on the morning of Saturday, the Fourth; as I have nothing to do on Thursday, the Second, but come from Leamington, I shall come to you, please God, for a quiet dinner that day.

The death of Arthur Smith has caused me great distress and anxiety. I had a great regard for him, and he made the reading part of my life as light and pleasant as it *could* be made. I had hoped to bring him to see you, and had pictured to myself how amused and interested you would have been with his wonderful tact and consummate mastery of arrangement. But it's all over.

I begin at Norwich on the twenty-eighth, and am going north in the middle of November. I am going to do "Copperfield," and shall be curious to test its effect on the Edinburgh people. It has been quite a job so to piece portions of the long book together as to make something continuous out of it; but I hope I have got something varied and dramatic. I am also (not to slight *your* book) going to do "Nickleby at Mr. Squeers'." It is clear that both must be trotted out at Cheltenham.

Ever, my dearest Macready, your most affectionate.

Miss
Hogarth.

ROYAL HOTEL, NORWICH,
Tuesday, Twenty-ninth October, 1861.

MY DEAREST GEORGY,

I cannot say that we began well last night. We had not a good hall, and they were a very lumpish audience indeed. This did not tend to cheer the strangeness I felt in being without Arthur, and I was not at all myself. I could have done perfectly if the audience had been bright, but they were an intent and staring audience. They laughed though very well, and the storm made them shake themselves again. But they were not magnetic, and the great big place was out of sorts somehow.

A wet day here, with glimpses of blue. I shall not forget Katey's health at dinner. A pleasant journey down.

Plorn's admission that he likes the school very much indeed, is the great social triumph of modern times.

I am looking forward to Sunday's rest at Gad's, and shall be down by the ten o'clock train from town. I miss poor Arthur dreadfully. It is scarcely possible to imagine how much. It is not only that his loss to me socially is quite irreparable, but that the sense I used to have of compactness and comfort about me while I was reading is quite gone. And when I come out for the ten minutes, when I used to find him always ready for me with something cheerful to say, it is forlorn. I cannot but fancy, too, that the audience must miss the old speciality of a pervading gentleman.

Love to Mamie, if she has come home, and to Bouncer, if *she* has come; also to Marguerite, who I hope is by this time much better.

Ever, my dear Georgy, your most affectionate.

GAD's HILL, *Sunday, Third November*, 1861.   Mrs. Henry Austin.

EXTRACT.

I am heartily glad to hear that you have been out in the air, and I hope you will go again very soon and make a point of continuing to go. There is a soothing influence in the sight of the earth and sky, which God put into them for our relief when He made the world in which we are all to suffer, and strive, and die.

I will not fail to write to you from many points of my tour, and if you ever want to write to me you may be sure of a quick response, and may be certain that I am sympathetic and true.

Ever affectionately.

FOUNTAIN HOTEL, CANTERBURY,   Miss Dickens.
Windy Night, Fourth November, 1861.

MY DEAREST MAMIE,

A word of report before I go to bed. An excellent house to-night, and an audience positively perfect. The greatest part of it stalls, and an intelligent and delightful response in them, like the touch of a beautiful instrument. "Copperfield" wound up in a real burst of feeling and delight.

Ever affectionately.

LORD WARDEN HOTEL, DOVER,   Mr. John Agate.
Wednesday, Sixth November, 1861.

SIR,

I am exceedingly sorry to find, from the letter you have addressed to me, that you had just cause of complaint in being excluded from my reading here last night. It will now and then unfortunately happen when the place of reading is small (as in this case), that some confusion and inconvenience arise from the local agents over-estimating, in perfect good faith and sincerity, the capacity of the room. Such a mistake, I am assured, was made last night; and thus all the available space was filled before the people in charge were at all prepared for that circumstance.

You may readily suppose that I can have no personal knowledge of the proceedings of the people in my employment at such a time. But I wish to assure you very earnestly, that they are all old servants, well acquainted with my principles and wishes, and that they are under the strongest injunction to avoid any approach to

2 M

mercenary dealing; and *to* behave to all comers equally with as much consideration and politeness as they know I should myself display. The recent death of a much-regretted friend of mine, who managed this business for me, and on whom these men were accustomed to rely in any little difficulty, caused them (I have no doubt) to feel rather at a loss in your case. Do me the favour to understand that under any other circumstances you would, as a matter of course, have been provided with any places whatever that could be found, without the smallest reference to what you had originally paid. This is scanty satisfaction to you, but it is so strictly the truth, that yours is the first complaint of the kind I have ever received.

I hope to read in Dover again, but it is quite impossible that I can make any present arrangement for that purpose. Whenever I may return here, you may be sure I shall not fail to remember that I owe you a recompense for a disappointment. In the meanwhile I very sincerely regret it.

Faithfully yours.

Miss
Hogarth.

BEDFORD HOTEL, BRIGHTON,
Thursday, Seventh November, 1861.

MY DEAR GEORGY,

* * * * *

The Duchess of Cambridge comes to-night to "Copperfield." The bad weather has not in the least touched us.

The storm was most magnificent at Dover. All the great side of The Lord Warden next the sea had to be emptied, the break of the sea was so prodigious, and the noise was so utterly confounding. The sea came in like a great sky of immense clouds, for ever breaking suddenly into furious rain. All kinds of wreck were washed in. Miss Birmingham and I saw, among other things, a very pretty brass-bound chest being thrown about like a feather. On Tuesday night, the unhappy Ostend packet could not get in, neither could she go back, and she beat about the Channel until noon yesterday. I saw her come in then, *with five men at the wheel*; such a picture of misery, as to the crew (of passengers there were no signs), as you can scarcely imagine.

The effect at Hastings and at Dover really seems to have outdone the best usual impression, and at Dover they wouldn't go, but sat applauding like mad. The most delicate audience I have seen in any provincial place is Canterbury. The audience with the greatest sense of humour certainly is Dover. The people in the stalls set the example of laughing, in the most curiously unreserved way; and they really laughed when Squeers read the boys' letters, with such cordial enjoyment, that the contagion extended to me, for one couldn't hear them without laughing too.

So, thank God, all goes well, and the recompense for the trouble is in every way great.

Ever affectionately.

GAD'S HILL PLACE, HIGHAM BY ROCHESTER, KENT, *Fifteenth November*, 1861.

The Earl of Carlisle.

MY DEAR LORD CARLISLE,

You knew poor Austin, and what his work was, and how he did it. If you have no private objection to signing the enclosed memorial (which will receive the right signatures before being presented), I think you will have no public objection. I shall be heartily glad if you can put your name to it, and shall esteem your doing so as a very kind service. Will you return the memorial under cover to Mr. Tom Taylor, at the Local Government Act Office, Whitehall? He is generously exerting himself in furtherance of it, and so delay will be avoided.

My dear Lord Carlisle, faithfully yours always.

GAD'S HILL PLACE, HIGHAM BY ROCHESTER, KENT, *Sunday, Seventeenth November*, 1861.

Miss Mary Boyle.

MY DEAR MARY,

I am perfectly enraptured with the quilt. It is one of the most tasteful, lively, elegant things I have ever seen; and I need not tell you that while it is valuable to me for its own ornamental sake, it is precious to me as a rainbow-hint of your friendship and affectionate remembrance.

Please God you shall see it next summer occupying its allotted place of state in my brand-new bedroom here. You shall behold it then, with all cheerful surroundings, the envy of mankind.

My readings have been doing absolute wonders. Your Duchess and Princess came to hear the first "Nickleby" and the "Pickwick Trial," then "Copperfield," at Brighton. I think they were pleased with me, and I am sure I was with them; for they are the very best audience one could possibly desire. I shall always have a pleasant remembrance of them.

Yes, Mary dear, I must say that I like my Carton, and I have a faint idea sometimes that if I had acted him, I could have done something with his life and death.

Believe me, ever your affectionate and faithful

JOE.

Sir Edward
Bulwer
Lytton.

QUEEN'S HEAD HOTEL, NEWCASTLE-ON-TYNE,
Wednesday Night, Twentieth November, 1861.

MY DEAR BULWER LYTTON,

I have read here, this evening, very attentively, Nos. 19 and 20. I have not the least doubt of the introduced matter; whether considered for its policy, its beauty, or its wise bearing on the story, it is decidedly a great improvement. It is at once very suggestive and very new to have these various points of view presented to the reader's mind.

That the audience is good enough for anything that is well presented to it, I am quite sure.

When you can avoid *notes*, however, and get their substance into the text, it is highly desirable in the case of so large an audience, simply because, as so large an audience necessarily reads the story in small portions, it is of the greater importance that they should retain as much of its argument as possible. Whereas the difficulty of getting numbers of people to read notes (which they invariably regard as interruptions of the text, not as strengtheners or elucidators of it) is wonderful.

Ever affectionately.

Miss
Dickens.

QUEEN'S HEAD, NEWCASTLE-ON-TYNE,
Saturday, Twenty-third November, 1861.

MY DEAREST MAMIE,

A most tremendous hall here last night; something almost terrible in the cram. A fearful thing might have happened. Suddenly, when they were all very still over Smike, my gas batten came down, and it looked as if the room was falling. There were three great galleries crammed to the roof, and a high steep flight of stairs, and a panic must have destroyed numbers of people. A lady in the front row of stalls screamed, and ran out wildly towards me, and for one instant there was a terrible wave in the crowd. I addressed that lady laughing (for I knew she was in sight of everybody there), and called out as if it happened every night, "There's nothing the matter, I assure you; don't be alarmed; pray sit down;" and she sat down directly, and there was a thunder of applause. It took some few minutes to mend, and I looked on with my hands in my pockets; for I think if I had turned my back for a moment there might still have been a move. My people were dreadfully alarmed, Boylett in particular, who I suppose had some notion that the whole place might have taken fire.

"But there stood the master," he did me the honour to say afterwards, in addressing the rest, "as cool as ever I see him a-lounging at a railway-station."   Ever affectionately.

P.S.—Duty to Mrs. Bouncer.

BERWICK-ON-TWEED,   Miss
Monday, Twenty-fifth November, 1861.   Hogarth.

I write (in a gale of wind, with a high sea running), to let you know that I go on to Edinburgh at half-past eight to-morrow morning.

A most ridiculous room was designed for me in this odd out-of-the-way place. An immense Corn Exchange made of glass and iron, round, dome-topped, lofty, utterly absurd for any such purpose, and full of thundering echoes, with a little lofty crow's-nest of a stone gallery breast high, deep in the wall, into which it was designed to put *me*! I instantly struck, of course, and said I would either read in a room attached to this house (a very snug one, capable of holding five hundred people) or not at all. Terrified local agents glowered, but fell prostrate.

We left Newcastle yesterday morning in the dark, when it was intensely cold and froze very hard. So it did here. But towards night the wind went round to the S.W., and all night it has been blowing very hard indeed. So it is now.

Tell Mamie that I have the same sitting-room as we had when we came here with poor Arthur, and that my bedroom is the room out of it which she and Katie had. Surely it is the oddest town to read in! But it is taken on poor Arthur's principle that a place in the way pays the expenses of a through journey; and the people would seem to be coming up to the scratch gallantly. It was a dull Sunday, though; O it *was* a dull Sunday, without a book! For I had forgotten to buy one at Newcastle, until it was too late.

I shall hope to hear very soon that the workmen have " broken through," and that you have been in the state apartments, and that upholstery measurements have come off.

There has been a horrible accident in Edinburgh. One of the seven-storey old houses in the High Street fell when it was full of people. Berry was at the bill-poster's house, a few doors off, waiting for him to come home, when he heard what seemed like thunder, and then the air was darkened with dust, " as if an immense quantity of steam had been blown off," and then all that dismal quarter set up shrieks, which he says were most dreadful.

WATERLOO HOTEL, EDINBURGH,   Miss
Wednesday, Twenty-seventh November, 1861.   Dickens.

Mrs. Bouncer must decidedly come with you to Carlisle. She shall be received with open arms. Apropos of Carlisle, let me know *when* you purpose coming there. We shall be there, please God, on the Saturday in good time, as I finish at Glasgow on the Friday night.

Gordon * dined with me yesterday. He is, if anything, rather better, I think, than when we last saw him in town. He was immensely pleased to be with me. I went with him (as his office goes anywhere) right into and among the ruins of the fallen building yesterday. They were still at work trying to find two men (brothers), a young girl, and an old woman, known to be all lying there. On the walls two or three common clocks are still hanging; one of them, judging from the time at which it stopped, would seem to have gone for an hour or so after the fall. Great interest had been taken in a poor linnet in a cage, hanging in the wind and rain high up against the broken wall. A fireman got it down alive, and great exultation has been raised over it. One woman, who was dug out unhurt, staggered into the street, stared all round her, instantly ran away, and has never been heard of since. It is a most extraordinary sight, and of course makes a great sensation.

Miss Dickens.

WATERLOO HOTEL, EDINBURGH,
Friday, Twenty-ninth November, 1861.

I think it is my turn to write to you, and I therefore send a brief despatch, like a telegram, to let you know that in a gale of wind and a fierce rain, last night, we turned away a thousand people. There was no getting into the hall, no getting near the hall, no stirring among the people, no getting out, no possibility of getting rid of them. And yet, in spite of all that, and of their being steaming wet, they never flagged for an instant, never made a complaint, and took up the trial upon their very shoulders, to the last word, in a triumphant roar.

I lunch with Blackwood to-day. He was at the reading last night; a capital audience. Young Blackwood † has also called here. A very good young fellow, I think.

Miss Hogarth.

CARRICK'S ROYAL HOTEL, GLASGOW,
Tuesday, Third December, 1861.

I send you by this post another *Scotsman*. From a paragraph in it, a letter, and an advertisement, you may be able to form some dim guess of the scene at Edinburgh last night. Such a pouring of hundreds into a place already full to the throat, such indescribable confusion, such a rending and tearing of dresses, and yet such a scene of good humour on the whole. I never saw the faintest approach to it. While I addressed the crowd in the room, Gordon addressed the crowd in the street. Fifty frantic

* The Sheriff of Midlothian.
† Mr. William Blackwood, now editor of *Blackwood's Magazine*.

men got up in all parts of the hall and addressed me all at once. Other frantic men made speeches to the walls. The whole Blackwood family were borne in on the top of a wave, and landed with their faces against the front of the platform. I read with the platform crammed with people. I got them to lie down upon it, and it was like some impossible tableau or gigantic picnic; one pretty girl in full dress lying on her side all night, holding on to one of the legs of my table. It was the most extraordinary sight. And yet from the moment I began to the moment of my leaving off, they never missed a point, and they ended with a burst of cheers.

The confusion was decidedly owing to the local agents.

The expenditure of lungs and spirits was (as you may suppose) rather great, and to sleep well was out of the question; I am therefore rather fagged to-day. And as the hall in which I read to-night is a large one, I must make my letter a short one.

My people were torn to ribbons last night. They have not a hat among them, and scarcely a coat.

Give my love to Mamie. To her question, " Will there be war with America?" I answer, " Yes;" I fear the North to be utterly mad, and war to be unavoidable.

Victoria Hotel, Preston,   Mr. W. H.
Friday, Thirteenth December, 1861.   Wills.

My dear Wills,

The news of the Christmas number is indeed glorious, and nothing can look brighter or better than the prospects of the illustrious publication.

Both Carlisle and Lancaster have come out admirably, though I doubted both, as you did. But, unlike you, I always doubted this place. I do so still. It is a poor place at the best (you remember?), and the mills are working half time, and trade is very bad.

The young lady who sells the papers at the station is just the same as ever. Has orders for to-night, and is coming " with a person." " The person?" said I. " Never you mind," said she.

I was so charmed with Robert Chambers' " Traditions of Edinburgh" (which I read in Edinburgh), that I was obliged to write to him and say so.

Will you give my small Admiral, on his personal application, one sovereign? I have told him to come to you for that recognition of his meritorious services.

Ever faithfully.

Mr. W. H.
Wills.

ADELPHI HOTEL, LIVERPOOL,
Sunday, Fifteenth December, 1861.

MY DEAR WILLS,

I sent you a telegram to-day, and I write before the answer has come to hand.

I have been very doubtful what to do here. We have a great let for to-morrow night. The Mayor recommends closing to-morrow, and going on on Tuesday and Wednesday, so does the town clerk, so do the agents. But I have a misgiving that they hardly understand what the public general sympathy with the Queen will be. Further, I feel personally that the Queen has always been very considerate and gracious to me, and I would on no account do anything that might seem unfeeling or disrespectful. I shall attach great weight, in this state of indecision, to your telegram.

The scene at Manchester last night was really magnificent. I had had the platform carried forward to our " Frozen Deep " point, and my table and screen built in with a proscenium and room scenery. When I went in (there was a very fine hall), they applauded in the most tremendous manner; and the extent to which they were taken aback and taken by storm by " Copperfield " was really a thing to see.

Kindest regards, ever faithfully.

Sir Edward
Bulwer
Lytton.

" ALL THE YEAR ROUND " OFFICE,
Eighteenth December, 1861.

MY DEAR BULWER LYTTON,

I have not had a moment in which to write to you. Even now I write with the greatest press upon me, meaning to write in detail in a day or two.

But I have *read*, at all events, though not written. And I say, Most masterly and most admirable ! It is impossible to lay the sheets down without finishing them. I showed them to Georgina and Mary, and they read and read and never stirred until they had read all. There cannot be a doubt of the beauty, power, and artistic excellence of the whole.

I counsel you most strongly NOT to append the proposed dialogue between Fenwick and Faber, and NOT to enter upon any explanation beyond the title-page and the motto, unless it be in some very brief preface. Decidedly I would not help the reader, if it were only for the reason that that anticipates his being in need of help, and his feeling objections and difficulties that require solution. Let the book explain itself. It speaks *for* itself with a noble eloquence.

Ever affectionately.

GAD'S HILL, HIGHAM BY ROCHESTER, KENT,
Saturday, Twenty-eighth December, 1861.

MY DEAR MARY,

On Monday (as you know) I am away again, but I am not sorry to see land and a little rest before me; albeit, these are great experiences of the public heart.

The little Admiral has gone to visit America in the *Orlando*, supposed to be one of the foremost ships in the Service, and the best found, best manned, and best officered that ever sailed from England. He went away much gamer than any giant, attended by a chest in which he could easily have stowed himself and a wife and family of his own proportions.

Ever and always, your affectionate

JOE.

1862.

NARRATIVE.

AT the beginning of this year, Charles Dickens resumed the reading tour which he had commenced at the close of the previous year and continued up to Christmas. The first letter which follows, to Mr. Wills, a New Year's greeting, is written from a railway station between one town and another on this journey. Mr. Macready, who had married for the second time not very long before this, was now settled at Cheltenham. Charles Dickens had arranged to give readings there, chiefly for the pleasure of visiting him, and of having him as one of his audience.

This reading tour went on until the beginning of February. One of the last of the series was in his favourite "beautiful room," the St. George's Hall at Liverpool. In February, he made an exchange of houses with his friends Mr. and Mrs. Hogge (now Mr. and Mrs. Archdale), they going to Gad's Hill, and he and his family to Mr. Hogge's house in Hyde Park Gate South. In March he commenced a series of readings at St. James's Hall, which were continued until the middle of June, when he, very gladly, returned to his country home.

A letter beginning "My dear Girls," addressed to some American ladies who happened to be at Colchester, in the same inn with him when he was reading there, was published by one of them under the name of "Our Letter," in the "St. Nicholas Magazine," New York, in 1877. We think it best to explain it in the young lady's own words, which are as follows:

OUR LETTER.

By M. F. Armstrong.

"From among all my treasures—to each one of which some pleasant history is bound—I choose this letter, written on coarse blue paper.

The letter was received in answer to cigars sent from America to Mr. Dickens.

The 'little public affairs at home' refers to the war of Rebellion.

At Colchester, he read 'The Trial' from 'Pickwick,' and selections from 'Nicholas Nickleby.'

The lady, her two sisters, and her brother were Mr. Dickens' guests at the queer old English inn at Colchester.

Through the softly falling snow we came back together to London, and on the railway platform parted, with a hearty hand-shaking, from the man who will for ever be enshrined in our hearts as the kindest and most generous, not to say most brilliant of hosts."

Mr. Walter Thornbury was one of Charles Dickens' most valuable contributors to "All the Year Round." His letters to Mr. Thornbury about the subjects of his articles for that journal are specimens of his minute and careful attention and personal supervision, never neglected or distracted by any other work on which he might be engaged, were it ever so hard or engrossing.

The letters addressed to Mr. Baylis we give chiefly because one of them has, since Mr. Baylis' death, been added to the collection of MSS. in the British Museum. He was a very intimate and confidential friend of the late Lord Lytton, and accompanied him on a visit to Gad's Hill in this year.

We give an extract from another letter from Charles Dickens to his sister, as a beautiful specimen of a letter of condolence and encouragement to one who was striving, very bravely, but by very slow degrees, to recover from the overwhelming grief of her bereavement. Mr. Wilkie Collins was at this time engaged on his novel of "No Name," which appeared in "All the Year Round," and was threatened with a very serious break-down in health. Charles Dickens wrote the letter which we give, to relieve Mr. Collins' mind as to his work. Happily he recovered sufficiently to make an end to his own story without any help; but the true friendship and kindness which suggested the offer were none the less appreciated, and may, very likely, by lessening Mr. Collins' anxiety, have helped to restore his health. At the end of October in this year, Charles Dickens, accompanied by his daughter and sister-in-law, went to reside for a couple of months in Paris, taking an apartment in the Rue du Faubourg St. Honoré. From thence he wrote to M. Charles Fechter. He had been greatly interested in this fine artist from the time of his first appearance in England, and was always one of his warmest friends and supporters during his stay in this country. M. Fechter was, at this time, preparing for the opening of the Lyceum Theatre, under his own management, at the beginning of the following year.

Just before Christmas, Charles Dickens returned to Gad's Hill. The Christmas number for this year was "Somebody's Luggage."

AT THE BIRMINGHAM STATION,　　Mr. W. H.
Thursday, Second January, 1862.　　Wills.

MY DEAR WILLS,

Being stationed here for an hour, on my way from Leamington to Cheltenham, I write to you.

Firstly, to reciprocate all your cordial and affectionate wishes for the New Year, and to express my earnest hope that we may go on through many years to come, as we have gone on through many years that are gone. And I think we can say that we doubt whether any two men can have gone on more happily and smoothly, or with greater trust and confidence in one another.

A little packet will come to you from Hunt and Roskell's, almost at the same time, I think, as this note.

The packet will contain a claret-jug. I hope it is a pretty thing in itself for your table, and I know that you and Mrs. Wills will like it none the worse because it comes from me.

It is not made of a perishable material, and is so far expressive of our friendship. I have had your name and mine set upon it, in token of our many years of mutual reliance and trustfulness. It will never be so full of wine as it is to-day of affectionate regard.

Ever faithfully yours.

TORQUAY, *Wednesday, Eighth January*, 1862.　　Miss
Hogarth.

MY DEAREST GEORGY,

You know, I think, that I was very averse to going to Plymouth, and would not have gone there again but for poor Arthur. But on the last night I read "Copperfield," and positively enthralled the people. It was a most overpowering effect, and poor Andrew * came behind the screen, after the storm, and cried in the best and manliest manner. Also there were two or three lines of his shipmates and other sailors, and they were

* Lieutenant Andrew Gordon, R.N., son of the Sheriff of Midlothian.

extraordinarily affected. But its culminating effect was on Macready at Cheltenham. When I got home after "Copperfield," I found him quite unable to speak, and able to do nothing but square his dear old jaw all on one side, and roll his eyes (half closed), like Jackson's picture of him. And when I said something light about it, he returned : "No—er—Dickens ! I swear to Heaven that, as a piece of passion and playfulness—er—indescribably mixed up together, it does—er—no, really, Dickens !—amaze me as profoundly as it moves me. But as a piece of art—and you know—er—that I—no, Dickens ! By —— ! I have seen the best art in a great time—it is incomprehensible to me. How is it got at—er—how is it done—er—how one man can—well ? It lays me on my—er—back, and it is of no use talking about it !" With which he put his hand upon my breast and pulled out his pocket-handkerchief, and I felt as if I were doing somebody to his Werner. Katie, by-the-bye, is a wonderful audience, and has a great fund of wild feeling in her. Johnny not at all unlike Plorn.

I have not yet seen the room here, but imagine it to be very small. Exeter I know, and that is small also. I am very much used up, on the whole, for I cannot bear this moist warm climate. It would kill me very soon. And I have now got to the point of -taking so much out of myself with "Copperfield," that I might as well do Richard Wardour.

You have now, my dearest Georgy, the fullest extent of my tidings. This is a very pretty place—a compound of Hastings, Tunbridge Wells, and little bits of the hills about Naples ; but I met four respirators as I came up from the station, and three pale curates without them, who seemed in a bad way.

Ever your affectionate.

Sir Edward
Bulwer
Lytton.

GAD'S HILL PLACE, HIGHAM BY ROCHESTER, KENT,
Friday, Twenty-fourth January, 1862.

MY DEAR BULWER LYTTON,

I have considered your questions, and here follow my replies.

1. I think you undoubtedly *have* the right to forbid the turning of your play into an opera.

2. I do *not* think the production of such an opera in the slightest degree likely to injure the play or to render it a less valuable property than it is now. If it could have any effect on so standard and popular a work as "The Lady of Lyons," the effect would, in my judgment, be beneficial. But I believe the play to be high above any such influence.

3. Assuming you do consent to the adaptation, in a desire to

oblige Oxenford, I would not recommend your asking any pecuniary compensation. This for two reasons: firstly, because the compensation could only be small at the best; secondly, because your taking it would associate you (unreasonably, but not the less assuredly) with the opera.

The only objection I descry is purely one of feeling. Pauline trotting about in front of the float, invoking the orchestra with a limp pocket-handkerchief, is a notion that makes goose-flesh of my back. Also a yelping tenor going away to the wars in a scena half-an-hour long is painful to contemplate. Damas, too, as a bass, with a grizzled bald head, blatantly bellowing about

> Years long ago,
>   When the sound of the drum
> First made his blood glow
>   With a rum ti tum tum—

rather sticks in my throat; but there really seems to me to be no other objection, if you can get over this.

Ever affectionately.

ADELPHI HOTEL, LIVERPOOL,   Miss
Tuesday, Twenty-eighth January, 1862.   Hogarth.

MY DEAREST GEORGY,

The beautiful room was crammed to excess last night, and numbers were turned away. Its beauty and completeness when it is lighted up are most brilliant to behold, and for a reading it is simply perfect. You remember that a Liverpool audience is usually dull, but they put me on my mettle last night, for I never saw such an audience—no, not even in Edinburgh!

I slept horribly last night, and have been over to Birkenhead for a little change of air to-day. My head is dazed and worn by gas and heat, and I fear that "Copperfield" and "Bob" together to-night won't mend it.

I am going to bring the boys some toffee.

Ever affectionately.

GAD'S HILL PLACE, HIGHAM BY ROCHESTER, KENT,   Mr. Baylis.
Saturday, First February, 1862.

MY DEAR MR. BAYLIS,

I have just come home. Finding your note, I write to you at once, or you might do me the wrong of supposing me unmindful of it and you.

I agree with you about Smith himself, and I don't think it necessary to pursue the painful subject. Such things are at an end, I think, for the time being;—fell to the ground with the poor man at Cremorne. If they should be resumed, then they must be attacked; but I hope the fashion (far too much encouraged in its Blondin-beginning by those who should know much better) is over.

It always appears to me that the common people have an excuse in their patronage of such exhibitions which people above them in condition have not. Their lives are full of physical difficulties, and they like to see such difficulties overcome. They go to see them overcome. If I am in danger of falling off a scaffold or a ladder any day, the man who claims that he can't fall from anything is a very wonderful and agreeable person to me.

Faithfully yours always.

The Misses Armstrong.

GAD'S HILL PLACE, HIGHAM BY ROCHESTER, KENT,
Monday, Tenth February, 1862.

MY DEAR GIRLS,

For if I were to write "young friends," it would look like a schoolmaster; and if I were to write "young ladies," it would look like a schoolmistress; and worse than that, neither form of words would look familiar and natural, or in character with our snowy ride that tooth-chattering morning.

I cannot tell you both how gratified I was by your remembrance, or how often I think of you as I smoke the admirable cigars. But I almost think you must have had some magnetic consciousness across the Atlantic, of my whiffing my love towards you from the garden here.

My daughter says that when you have settled those little public affairs at home, she hopes you will come back to England (possibly in united states) and give a minute or two to this part of Kent. Her words are, "a day or two;" but I remember your Italian flights, and correct the message.

I have only just now finished my country readings, and have had nobody to make breakfast for me since the remote ages of Colchester !

Ever faithfully yours.

Mr. Henry F. Chorley.

16, HYDE PARK GATE, SOUTH KENSINGTON GORE, W.,
Saturday, First March, 1862.

MY DEAR CHORLEY,

I was at your lecture * this afternoon, and I hope I may venture to tell you that I was extremely pleased and interested. Both the matter of the materials and the manner of their arrangement were quite admirable, and a modesty and complete absence of any kind of affectation pervaded the whole discourse, which was

* The first of the series on "National Music."

quite an example to the many whom it concerns. If you could be a very little louder, and would never let a sentence go for the thousandth part of an instant until the last word is out, you would find the audience more responsive.

A spoken sentence will never run alone in all its life, and is never to be trusted to itself in its most insignificant member. See it *well out*—with the voice—and the part of the audience is made surprisingly easier. In that excellent description of the Spanish mendicant and his guitar, as well as the very happy touches about the dance and the castanets, the people were really desirous to express very hearty appreciation; but by giving them rather too much to do in watching and listening for latter words, you stopped them. I take the liberty of making the remark, as one who has fought with wild beasts (oratorically) in divers arenas. For the rest nothing could be better. Knowledge, ingenuity, neatness, condensation, good sense, and good taste in delightful combination.

Affectionately always.

16, Hyde Park Gate, South Kensington Gore,
Sunday, Sixteenth March, 1862.

M. De Cerjat.

My dear Cerjat,

My daughter naturally liking to be in town at this time of year, I have changed houses with a friend for three months.

My eldest boy is in business as an Eastern merchant in the City, and will do well if he can find continuous energy; otherwise not. My second boy is with the 42nd Highlanders in India. My third boy, a good steady fellow, is educating expressly for engineers or artillery. My fourth (this sounds like a charade), a born little sailor, is a midshipman in H.M.S. *Orlando*, now at Bermuda, and will make his way anywhere. Remaining two at school, elder of said remaining two very bright and clever. Georgina and Mary keeping house for me; and Francis Jeffrey (I ought to have counted him as the third boy, so we'll take him in here as number two and a half) in my office at present. Now you have the family bill of fare.

You ask me about Fechter and his Hamlet. It was a performance of extraordinary merit; by far the most coherent, consistent, and intelligible Hamlet I ever saw. Some of the delicacies with which he rendered his conception clear were extremely subtle; and in particular he avoided that brutality towards Ophelia which, with a greater or less amount of coarseness, I have seen in all other Hamlets. As a mere *tour de force*, it would have been very remarkable in its disclosure of a perfectly wonderful knowledge of the force of the English language; but its merit was far beyond and above this.   Foreign accent, of course, but not at all a disagreeable one.   And he was so obviously safe and at ease, that you were never in pain for him as a foreigner.   Add to this a perfectly picturesque and romantic "make up," and a remorseless destruction of all conventionalities, and you have the leading virtues of the impersonation.· In Othello he did not succeed.   In Iago he is very good.   He is an admirable artist, and far beyond anyone on our stage.   A real artist and a gentleman.

Last Thursday I began reading again in London—a condensation of "Copperfield," and "Mr. Bob Sawyer's Party," from "Pickwick," to finish merrily.   The success of "Copperfield" is astounding.   It made an impression that *I* must not describe.   I may only remark that I was half dead when I had done; and that although I had looked forward, all through the summer, when I was carefully getting it up, to its being a London sensation; and that although Macready, hearing it at Cheltenham, told me to be prepared for a great effect, it even went beyond my hopes.   I read again next Thursday, and the rush for places is quite furious. Tell Townshend this with my love, if you see him before I have time to write to him; and tell him that I thought the people would never let me go away, they became so excited, and showed it so very warmly.   I am trying to plan out a new book, but have not got beyond trying.

Yours affectionately.

<table>
<tr><td>Mr. Walter
Thornbury.</td><td style="text-align:right">OFFICE OF "ALL THE YEAR ROUND,"
Friday, Eighteenth April, 1862.</td></tr>
</table>

MY DEAR THORNBURY,

The Bow-Street runners ceased out of the land soon after the introduction of the new police.   I remember them very well as standing about the door of the office in Bow Street.   They had no other uniform than a blue dress-coat, brass buttons (I am not even now sure that that was necessary), and a bright red cloth waistcoat.   The waistcoat was indispensable, and the slang name for them was "red-breasts," in consequence.

They kept company with thieves and the like, much more than the detective police do.   I don't know what their pay was, but I have no doubt their principal complements were got under the rose.   It was a very slack institution, and its head-quarters were The Brown Bear, in Bow Street, a public-house of more than doubtful reputation, opposite the police-office; and either the house which is now the theatrical costume maker's, or the next door to it.

Field, who advertises the Secret Enquiry Office, was a Bow-

Street runner, and can tell you all about it; Goddard, who also advertises an enquiry office, was another of the fraternity. They are the only two I know of as yet existing in a "questionable shape."

Faithfully yours always.

GAD'S HILL, ETC., *Wednesday, Second July,* 1862.   Mr. Baylis.

MY DEAR MR. BAYLIS,

I have been in France, and in London, and in other parts of Kent than this, and everywhere but here, for weeks and weeks. Pray excuse my not having (for this reason specially) answered your kind note sooner.

After carefully cross-examining my daughter, I do NOT believe her to be worthy of the fernery. Last autumn we transplanted into the shrubbery a quantity of evergreens previously clustered close to the front of the house, and trained more ivy about the wall and the like. When I ask her where she would have the fernery and what she would do with it, the witness falters, turns pale, becomes confused, and says: "Perhaps it would be better not to have it at all." I am quite confident that the constancy of the young person is not to be trusted, and that she had better attach her fernery to one of her châteaux in Spain, or one of her English castles in the air. None the less do I thank you for your more than kind proposal.

We have been in great anxiety respecting Miss Hogarth, the sudden decline of whose health and spirits has greatly distressed us. Although she is better than she was, and the doctors are, on the whole, cheerful, she requires great care, and fills us with apprehension. The necessity of providing change for her will probably take us across the water very early in the autumn; and this again unsettles home schemes here, and withers many kinds of fern. If they knew (by "they" I mean my daughter and Miss Hogarth) that I was writing to you, they would charge me with many messages of regard. But as I am shut up in my room in a ferocious and unapproachable condition, owing to the great accumulation of letters I have to answer, I will tell them at lunch that I have anticipated their wish. As I know they have bills for me to pay, and are at present shy of producing them, I wish to preserve a gloomy and repellent reputation.

My dear Mr. Baylis, faithfully yours always.

GAD'S HILL, *Tuesday, Seventh October,* 1862.   Mrs. Henry Austin.

*   *   · *   *

I do not preach consolation because I am unwilling to preach at any time, and know my own weakness too well. But in this

2 N

world there is no stay but the hope of a better, and no reliance but on the mercy and goodness of God. Through those two harbours of a shipwrecked heart, I fully believe that you will, in time, find a peaceful resting-place even on this careworn earth. Heaven speed the time, and do you try hard to help it on! It is impossible to say but that our prolonged grief for the beloved dead may grieve them in their unknown abiding-place, and give them trouble. The one influencing consideration in all you do as to your disposition of yourself (coupled, of course, with a real earnest strenuous endeavour to recover the lost tone of spirit) is, that you think and feel you *can* do. I do not in the least regard your change of course in going to Havre as any evidence of instability. But I rather hope it is likely that through such restlessness you will come to a far quieter frame of mind. The disturbed mind and affections, like the tossed sea, seldom calm without an intervening time of confusion and trouble.

But nothing is to be attained without striving. In a determined effort to settle the thoughts, to parcel out the day, to find occupation regularly or to make it, to be up and doing something, are chiefly to be found the mere mechanical means which must come to the aid of the best mental efforts.

It is a wilderness of a day, here, in the way of blowing and raining, and as darkly dismal, at four o'clock, as need be. My head is but just now raised from a day's writing, but I will not lose the post without sending you a word.

Katie was here yesterday, just come back from Clara White's (that was), in Scotland. In the midst of her brilliant fortune, it is too clear to me that she is already beckoned away to follow her dead sisters. Macready was here from Saturday evening to yesterday morning, older but looking wonderfully well, and (what is very rare in these times) with the old thick sweep of hair upon his head. Georgina being left alone here the other day, was done no good to by a great consternation among the servants. On going downstairs, she found Marsh (the stableman) seated with great dignity and anguish in an arm-chair, and incessantly crying out: "I am dead." To which the women servants said, with great pathos (and with some appearance of reason): "No, you ain't, Marsh!" And to which he persisted in replying: "Yes, I am; I am dead!" Some neighbouring vagabond was impressed to drive a cart over to Rochester and fetch the doctor, who said (the patient and his consolers being all very anxious that the heart should be the scene of affliction): "Stomach."

*　　　　*　　　　*　　　　*　　　　*

GAD'S HILL PLACE, HIGHAM BY ROCHESTER, KENT,   Mr. W.
Tuesday Night, Fourteenth October, 1862.   Wilkie
Collins.

MY DEAR WILKIE,

Frank Beard has been here this evening, of course since I posted my this day's letter to you, and has told me that you are not at all well, and how he has given you something which he hopes and believes will bring you round. It is not to convey this insignificant piece of intelligence, or to tell you how anxious I am that you should come up with a wet sheet and a flowing sail (as we say at sea when we are not sick), that I write. It is simply to say what follows, which I hope may save you some mental uneasiness. For I was stricken ill when I was doing "Bleak House," and I shall not easily forget what I suffered under the fear of not being able to come up to time.

Dismiss that fear (if you have it) altogether from your mind. Write to me at Paris at any moment, and say you are unequal to your work, and want me, and I will come to London straight and do your work. I am quite confident that, with your notes and a few words of explanation, I could take it up at any time and do it. Absurdly unnecessary to say that it would be a makeshift! But I could do it at a pinch, so like you as that no one should find out the difference. Don't make much of this offer in your mind; it is nothing, except to ease it. If you should want help, I am as safe as the bank. The trouble would be nothing to me, and the triumph of overcoming a difficulty great. Think it a Christmas number, an "Idle Apprentice," a "Lighthouse," a "Frozen Deep." I am as ready as in any of these cases to strike in and hammer the hot iron out.

You won't want me. You will be well (and thankless!) in no time. But there I am; and I hope that the knowledge may be a comfort to you. Call me, and I come.

As Beard always has a sense of medical responsibility, and says anything important about a patient in confidence, I have merely remarked here that "Wilkie" is out of sorts. Charley (who is here with Katie) has no other cue from me.

Ever affectionately.

PARIS, RUE DU FAUBOURG ST. HONORÉ, 27,   M. Charles
Tuesday, Fourth November, 1862.   Fechter.

MY DEAR FECHTER,

You know, I believe, how our letters crossed, and that I am here until Christmas. Also, you know with what pleasure and readiness I should have responded to your invitation if I had been in London.

Pray tell Paul Féval that I shall be charmed to know him, and that I shall feel the strongest interest in making his acquaintance. It almost puts me out of humour with Paris (and it takes a great deal to do that !) to think that I was not at home to prevail upon him to come with you, and be welcomed to Gad's Hill; but either there or here, I hope to become his friend before this present old year is out. Pray tell him so.

You say nothing in your note of your Lyceum preparations. I trust they are all going on well. There is a fine opening for you, I am sure, with a good beginning; but the importance of a good beginning is very great. If you ever have time and inclination to tell me in a short note what you are about, you can scarcely interest me more, as my wishes and strongest sympathies are for and with your success—*mais cela va sans dire.*

I went to the Châtelet (a beautiful theatre !) the other night to see "Rothomago," but was so mortally *gêné* with the poor nature of the piece and of the acting, that I came out again when there was a week or two (I mean an hour or two, but the hours seemed weeks) yet to get through.

My dear Fechter, very faithfully yours always.

Mrs. Henry
Austin.

PARIS, RUE DU FAUBOURG ST. HONORÉ, 27,
Friday, Seventh November, 1862.

MY DEAR LETITIA,

Your improved account of yourself is very cheering and hopeful. Through determined occupation and action, lies the way. Be sure of it.

I came over to France before Georgina and Mary, and went to Boulogne to meet them coming in by the steamer on the great Sunday—the day of the storm. I stood (holding on with both hands) on the pier at Boulogne, five hours. The Sub-Marine Telegraph had telegraphed their boat as having come out of Folkestone—though the companion boat from Boulogne didn't try it—and at nine o'clock at night, she being due at six, there were no signs of her. My principal dread was, that she would try to get into Boulogne; which she could not possibly have done without carrying away everything on deck. The tide at nine o'clock being too low for any such desperate attempt, I thought it likely that they had run for the Downs and would knock about there all night. So I went to the Inn to dry my pea-jacket and get some dinner anxiously enough, when, at about ten, came a telegram from them at Calais to say they had run in there. To Calais I went, post, next morning, expecting to find them half-dead (of course, they had arrived half-drowned), but I found them elaborately got up to come to Paris by the next train, and the most wonderful thing of all was, that they hardly seemed to have been frightened! Of course, they had discovered at the end of the voyage, that a young bride and her husband, the only other passengers on deck, and with whom they had been talking all the time, were an officer from Chatham whom they knew very well (when dry), just married and going to India! So they all set up housekeeping together at Dessin's at Calais (where I am well known), and looked as if they had been passing a mild summer there.

We have a pretty apartment here, but house-rent is awful to mention. Mrs. Bouncer (muzzled by the Parisian police) is also here, and is a wonderful spectacle to behold in the streets, restrained like a raging Lion.

I learn from our embassy here, that the Emperor has just made an earnest proposal to our Government to unite with France (and Russia, if Russia will) in an appeal to America to stop the brutal war. Our Government's answer is not yet received, but I think I clearly perceive that the proposal will be declined, on the ground "that the time has not yet come."

Ever affectionately.

PARIS, RUE DU FAUBOURG ST. HONORÉ, 27,
Friday, Fifth December, 1862.

Mr. Clarkson Stanfield, R.A.

MY DEAR STANNY,

We have been here for two months, and I shall probably come back here after Christmas (we go home for Christmas week) and stay on into February. But I shall write and propose a theatre before Christmas is out, so this is to warn you to get yourself into working pantomime order!

I hope Wills has duly sent you our new Christmas number. As you may like to know what I myself wrote of it, understand the Dick contributions to be, *his leaving it till called for*, and *his wonderful end, his boots*, and *his brown-paper parcel*.

Since you were at Gad's Hill I have been travelling a good deal, and looking up many odd things for use. I want to know how you are in health and spirits, and it would be the greatest of pleasures to me to have a line under your hand.

God bless you and yours with all the blessings of the time of year, and of all times!

Ever your affectionate and faithful
DICK.

M. Charles
Fechter.

PARIS, *Saturday, Sixth December,* 1862.

MY DEAR FECHTER,

I have read "The White Rose" attentively, and think it an extremely good play. It is vigorously written with a great knowledge of the stage, and presents many striking situations. I think the close particularly fine, impressive, bold, and new.

But I greatly doubt the expediency of your doing *any* historical play early in your management. By the words "historical play," I mean a play founded on any incident in English history. Our public are accustomed to associate historical plays with Shakespeare. In any other hands, I believe they care very little for crowns and dukedoms. What you want is something with an interest of a more domestic and general nature—an interest as romantic as you please, but having a more general and wider response than a disputed succession to the throne can have for Englishmen at this time of day. Such interest culminated in the last Stuart, and has worn itself out. It would be uphill work to evoke an interest in Perkin Warbeck.

I do not doubt the play's being well received, but my fear is that these people would be looked upon as mere abstractions, and would have but a cold welcome in consequence, and would not lay hold of your audience. Now, when you *have* laid hold of your audience and have accustomed them to your theatre, you may produce "The White Rose," with far greater justice to the author, and to the manager also. Wait. Feel your way. Perkin Warbeck is too far removed from analogy with the sympathies and lives of the people for a beginning.

My dear Fechter, ever faithfully yours.

Miss Mary
Boyle.

GAD'S HILL PLACE, HIGHAM BY ROCHESTER, KENT,
Saturday, Twenty-seventh December, 1862.

MY DEAR MARY,

I must send you my Christmas greeting and happy New Year wishes in return for yours; most heartily and fervently reciprocating your interest and affection. You are among the few whom I most care for and best love.

Being in London two evenings in the opening week, I tried to persuade my legs (for whose judgment I have the highest respect) to go to an evening party. But I *could not* induce them to pass Leicester Square. The faltering presentiment under which they laboured so impressed me, that at that point I yielded to their terrors. They immediately ran away to the east, and I accompanied them to the Olympic, where I saw a very good play,

"Camilla's Husband," very well played. Real merit in Mr. Neville and Miss Saville.

We came across directly after the gale, with the Channel all bestrewn with floating wreck, and with a hundred and fifty sick schoolboys from Calais on board. I am going back on the morning after Fechter's opening night, and have promised to read "Copperfield" at the Embassy, for a British charity.

Georgy continues wonderfully well, and she and Mary send you their best love. The house is pervaded by boys; and every boy has (as usual) an unaccountable and awful power of producing himself in every part of the house at every moment, apparently in fourteen pairs of creaking boots.

My dear Mary, ever affectionately your

JOE.

1863.

NARRATIVE.

AT the beginning of this year, Charles Dickens was in Paris for the purpose of giving a reading at the English Embassy.

He remained in Paris until the beginning of February, staying with his servant "John" at the Hôtel du Helder. There was a series of readings in London this season at the Hanover Square Rooms. The Christmas number of "All the Year Round" was entitled "Mrs. Lirriper's Lodgings," to which Charles Dickens contributed the first and last chapters.

The Lyceum Theatre, under the management of M. Fechter, was opened in January with "The Duke's Motto," and the letter given here has reference to this first night.

We regret very much having no letters to Lady Molesworth, who was an old and dear friend of Charles Dickens. But this lady explains to us that she has long ceased to preserve any letters addressed to her.

The "Mr. and Mrs. Humphery" (afterwards Sir William and Lady Humphery), mentioned in the first letter for this year, were dear and intimate friends of his eldest daughter, and were frequent guests in her father's house. Lady Humphery and her sister Lady Olliffe are daughters of the late Mr. William Cubitt, M.P.

The Rev. W. Brookfield, to whom we give two letters in this year, was a clever and remarkably cultivated man. Both he and Mrs. Brookfield were held in high estimation by Charles Dickens.

We have in this year the first letter of Charles Dickens to Mr. Percy Fitzgerald. This gentleman had been a valuable contributor

to his journal before he became personally known to Charles
Dickens. The acquaintance once made soon ripened into friendship, and for the future Mr. Fitzgerald was a constant and always
a welcome visitor to Gad's Hill.

The letter to Mr. Charles Reade alludes to his story, "Hard
Cash," which was then appearing in "All the Year Round." As
a writer, and as a friend, he was held by Charles Dickens in the
highest regard.

Charles Dickens' correspondence with his solicitor and excellent
friend, Mr. Frederic Ouvry (a vice-president of the Society of
Antiquaries), was almost entirely of a business character; but we
are glad to give one or two notes to that gentleman, although of
little public interest, in order to have the name of one of the
kindest of our own friends in this book.

Miss
Dickens.

PARIS, HÔTEL DU HELDER, RUE DU HELDER,
Friday, Sixteenth January, 1863.

MY DEAREST MAMIE,

As I send a line to your aunt to-day and know that you
will not see it, I send another to you to report my safe (and
neuralgic) arrival here. My little rooms are perfectly comfortable,
and I like the hotel better than any I have ever put up at in Paris.
John's amazement at, and appreciation of, Paris are indescribable.
He goes about with his mouth open, staring at everything and
being tumbled over by everybody.

The state dinner at the Embassy, yesterday, coming off in the
room where I am to read, the carpenters did not get in until this
morning. But their platforms were ready—or supposed to be—
and the preparations are in brisk progress. I think it will be a
handsome affair to look at—a very handsome one. There seems
to be great artistic curiosity in Paris, to know what kind of thing
the reading is.

I know a "rela-shon" (with one weak eye), who is in the gun-
making line, very near here. There is a strong family resemblance
—but no muzzle. Lady Molesworth and I have not begun to
"toddle" yet, but have exchanged affectionate greetings. I am
going round to see her presently, and I dine with her on Sunday.
The only remaining news is, that I am beset by mysterious adorers,
and smuggle myself in and out of the house in the meanest and
basest manner.

With kind regard to Mr. and Mrs. Humphery,

Ever, my dearest Mamey, your affectionate Father.

P.S.—*Hommage à Madame B. !*

PARIS, *Sunday, First February*, 1863.   Monsieur
                                                      Regnier.
MY DEAR REGNIER,

I was charmed by the receipt of your cordial and sympathetic letter, and I shall always preserve it carefully as a most noble tribute from a great and real artist.

I wished you had been at the Embassy on Friday evening. The audience was a fine one, and the "Carol" is particularly well adapted to the purpose. It is an uncommon pleasure to me to learn that I am to meet you on Tuesday, for there are not many men whom I meet with greater pleasure than you. Heaven! how the years roll by! We are quite old friends now, in counting by years. If we add sympathies, we have been friends at least a thousand years.

Affectionately yours ever.

HÔTEL DU HELDER, PARIS,   Miss
Sunday, First February, 1863.   Dickens.

MY DEAREST MAMIE,

I cannot give you any idea of the success of the readings here, because no one can imagine the scene of last Friday night at the Embassy. Such audiences and such enthusiasm I have never seen, but the thing culminated on Friday night in a two-hours' storm of excitement and pleasure. They actually recommenced and applauded right away into their carriages and down the street.

You know your parent's horror of being lionised, and will not be surprised to hear that I am half dead of it. I cannot leave here until Thursday (though I am every hour in danger of running away) because I have to dine out, to say nothing of breakfasting— think of me breakfasting!—every intervening day. But my project is to send John home on Thursday, and then to go on a little perfectly quiet tour for about ten days, touching the sea at Boulogne.

I enclose a short note for each of the little boys. Give Harry ten shillings pocket-money, and Plorn six.

The Olliffe girls, very nice. Florence at the readings, prodigiously excited.

PARIS, *Sunday, First February*, 1863.   Miss
                                                      Hogarth

From my hurried note to Mamie, you will get some faint general idea of a new star's having arisen in Paris. But of its brightness you can have no adequate conception.

[John has locked me up and gone out, and the little bell at the door is ringing demoniacally while I write.]

You have never heard me read yet. I have been twice goaded and lifted out of myself into a state that astonished *me* almost as much as the audience. "I have a cold, but no neuralgia, and am as well as can be expected."

I forgot to tell Mamie that I went (with Lady Molesworth) to hear "Faust" last night. It is a splendid work, and perfectly delighted me. But I think it requires too much of the audience to do for a London opera house. The composer must be a very remarkable man indeed. Some management of light throughout the story is also very poetical and fine. We had Carvalho's box. I could hardly bear the thing, it affected me so.

But, as a certain Frenchman said, "No weakness, Danton!" So I leave off.

Ever affectionately.

M. Charles Fechter.

PARIS, *Wednesday, Fourth February,* 1863.

MY DEAR FECHTER,

A thousand congratulations on your great success! Never mind what they say, or do, *pour vous écraser ;* you have the game in your hands. The romantic drama, thoroughly well done (with a touch of Shakespeare now and then), is the speciality of your theatre. Give the public the picturesque, romantic drama, with yourself in it ; and (as I told you in the beginning) you may throw down your gauntlet in defiance of all comers.

It * is a most brilliant success indeed, and it thoroughly rejoices my heart!

Unfortunately I cannot now hope to see "Maquet," because I am packing up and going out to dinner (it is late in the afternoon), and I leave to-morrow morning when all sensible people, except myself, are in bed ; and I do not come back to Paris or near it. I had hoped to see him at breakfast last Monday, but he was not there. Paul Féval was there, and I found him a capital fellow. If I can do anything to help you on with "Maquet" † when I come back, I will most gladly do it.

I shall be heartily pleased to see you again, my dear Fechter, and to share your triumphs with the real earnestness of a real friend. And so go on and prosper, and believe me, as I truly am,

Most cordially yours.

* "The Duke's Motto."
† Alluding to a translation of a play by M. Maquet, which M. Fechter was then preparing for his theatre.

OFFICE OF "ALL THE YEAR ROUND,"
Thursday, Nineteenth February, 1863.

Mr. W. C.
Macready.

MY DEAREST MACREADY,

I have just come back from Paris, where the readings— "Copperfield," "Dombey" and "Trial," and "Carol" and "Trial" —have made a sensation which modesty (my natural modesty) renders it impossible for me to describe. You know what a noble audience the Paris audience is! They were at their very noblest with me.

I was very much concerned by hearing hurriedly from Georgy that you were ill. But when I came home at night, she showed me Katie's letter, and that set me up again. Ah, you have the best of companions and nurses, and can afford to be ill now and then for the happiness of being so brought through it. But don't do it again yet awhile for all that.

Regnier desired to be warmly remembered to you. He looks just as of yore.

Paris generally is about as wicked and extravagant as in the days of the Regency. Madame Viardot in the "Orphée," most splendid. An opera of "Faust," a very sad and noble rendering of that sad and noble story. Stage management remarkable for some admirable, and really poetical, effects of light. In the more striking situations, Mephistopheles surrounded by an infernal red atmosphere of his own. Marguerite by a pale blue mournful light. The two never blending. After Marguerite has taken the jewels placed in her way in the garden, a weird evening draws on, and the bloom fades from the flowers, and the leaves of the trees droop and lose their fresh green, and mournful shadows overhang her chamber window, which was innocently bright and gay at first. I couldn't bear it, and gave in completely.

Fechter doing wonders over the way here, with a picturesque French drama. Miss Kate Terry,[*] in a small part in it, perfectly charming. You may remember her making a noise, years ago, doing a boy at an inn, in "The Courier of Lyons"! She has a tender love-scene in this piece, which is a really beautiful and artistic thing. I saw her do it at about three in the morning of the day when the theatre opened, surrounded by shavings and carpenters, and (of course) with that inevitable hammer going; and I told Fechter: "That is the very best piece of womanly tenderness I have ever seen on the stage, and you'll find that no audience can miss it." It is a comfort to add that it was instantly seized upon, and is much talked of.

Stanfield was very ill for some months, then suddenly picked

[*] Afterwards Mrs. Arthur Lewis.

up, and is really rosy and jovial again. Going to see him when he was very despondent, I told him the story of Fechter's piece (then in rehearsal) with appropriate action ; fighting a duel with the washing-stand, defying the bedstead, and saving the life of the sofa-cushion. This so kindled his old theatrical ardour, that I think he turned the corner on the spot.

With love to Mrs. Macready and Katie, and (be still my heart !) Benvenuta, and the exiled Johnny (not too attentive at school, I hope ?), and the personally-unknown young Parr,

Ever, my dearest Macready, your most affectionate.

Miss Power.

OFFICE OF "ALL THE YEAR ROUND,"
Thursday, Twenty-sixth February, 1863.

MY DEAR MARGUERITE,

I think I have found a first-rate title for your book, with an early and a delightful association in most people's minds, and a strong suggestion of Oriental pictures :

"ARABIAN DAYS AND NIGHTS."

I have sent it to Low's. If they have the wit to see it, do you in your first chapter touch that string, so as to bring a fanciful explanation in aid of the title, and sound it afterwards, now and again, when you come to anything where Haroun al Raschid, and the Grand Vizier, and Mesrour, the chief of the guard, and any of that wonderful *dramatis personæ* are vividly brought to mind.

Ever affectionately.

Mr. Charles Knight.

OFFICE OF "ALL THE YEAR ROUND,"
Wednesday, Fourth March, 1863.

MY DEAR CHARLES KNIGHT,

At a quarter to seven on Monday, the sixteenth, a stately form will be descried breathing birthday cordialities and affectionate amenities, as it descends the broken and gently dipping ground by which the level country of the Clifton Road is attained. A practised eye will be able to discern two humble figures in attendance, which from their flowing crinolines may, without exposing the prophet to the imputation of rashness, be predicted to be women. Though certes their importance, absorbed and as it were swallowed up in the illustrious bearing and determined purpose of the maturer stranger, will not enthrall the gaze that wanders over the forest of San Giovanni as the night gathers in.

Ever affectionately,
G. P. R. JAMES.

EXTRACT.

Mrs. Dallas.*

It is curious to see London gone mad.† Down in the Strand here, the monomaniacal tricks it is playing are grievous to behold, but along Fleet Street and Cheapside it gradually becomes frenzied, dressing itself up in all sorts of odds and ends, and knocking itself about in a most amazing manner. At London Bridge it raves, principally about the Kings of Denmark and their portraits. I have been looking among them for Hamlet's uncle, and have discovered one personage with a high nose, who I think is the man.

Faithfully yours always.

OFFICE OF "ALL THE YEAR ROUND,"
No. 26, WELLINGTON STREET, STRAND, LONDON, W.C.,
Tuesday, Tenth March, 1863.

Mrs. F. Lehmann.

DEAR MRS. LEHMANN,

Two stalls for to-morrow's reading were sent to you by post before I heard from you this morning. Two will always come to you while you remain a Gummidge, and I hope I need not say that if you want more, none could be better bestowed in my sight.

Pray tell Lehmann, when you next write to him, that I find I owe him a mint of money for the delightful Swedish sleigh-bells. They are the wonder, awe, and admiration of the whole country side, and I never go out without them.

Let us make an exchange of child stories. I heard of a little fellow the other day whose mamma had been telling him that a French governess was coming over to him from Paris, and had been expatiating on the blessings and advantages of having foreign tongues. After leaning his plump little cheek against the window glass in a dreary little way for some minutes, he looked round and enquired in a general way, and not as if it had any special application, whether she didn't think "that the Tower of Babel was a great mistake altogether?"

Ever faithfully yours.

OFFICE OF "ALL THE YEAR ROUND," A WEEKLY JOURNAL, ETC. ETC.,
26, WELLINGTON STREET, STRAND,
Thursday, Twelfth March, 1863.

Mrs. Major. ‡

MY DEAR MARY,

I am quite concerned to hear that you and your party (including your brother Willie) paid for seats at my reading last

* Formerly Miss Glyn, the celebrated actress.
† On the occasion of the arrival of the Princess Alexandra in London.
‡ Formerly Miss Talfourd.

night. You must promise me never to do so any more. My old affections and attachments are not so lightly cherished or so easily forgotten as that I can bear the thought of you and yours coming to hear me like so many strangers. It will at all times delight me if you will send a little note to me, or to Georgina, or to Mary, saying when you feel inclined to come, and how many stalls you want. You may always be certain, even on the fullest nights, of room being made for you. And I shall always be interested and pleased by knowing that you are present.

Mind! You are to be exceedingly penitent for last night's offence, and to make me a promise that it shall never be repeated. On which condition accept my noble forgiveness.

Affectionately yours.

Mr. W. C.
Macready.

GAD'S HILL PLACE, HIGHAM BY ROCHESTER, KENT,
Thursday, Thirty-first March, 1863.

MY DEAREST MACREADY,

I mean to go on reading into June. For the sake of the finer effects (in "Copperfield" principally), I have changed from St. James's Hall to the Hanover Square Room. The latter is quite a wonderful room for sound, and so easy that the least inflection will tell anywhere in the place exactly as it leaves your lips; but I miss my dear old shilling galleries—six or eight hundred strong —with a certain roaring sea of response in them, that you have stood upon the beach of many and many a time.

The summer, I hope and trust, will quicken the pace at which you grow stronger again. I am but in dull spirits myself just now, or I should remonstrate with you on your slowness.

Having two little boys sent home from school "to see the illuminations" on the marriage-night, I chartered an enormous van, at a cost of five pounds, and we started in majesty from the office in London, fourteen strong. We crossed Waterloo Bridge with the happy design of beginning the sight at London Bridge, and working our way through the City to Regent Street. In a by-street in the Borough, over against a dead wall and under a railway bridge, we were blocked for four hours. We were obliged to walk home at last, having seen nothing whatever. The wretched van turned up in the course of the next morning; and the best of it was that at Rochester here they illuminated the fine old castle, and really made a very splendid and picturesque thing (so my neighbours tell me).

Ever, my dearest Macready, your most affectionate.

GAD'S HILL PLACE, HIGHAM BY ROCHESTER, KENT,   Mr. W.
Wednesday, Twenty-second April, 1863.   Wilkie
   Collins.

EXTRACT.*

Ah, poor Egg! I knew what you would think and feel about it. When we saw him in Paris on his way out I was struck by his extreme nervousness, and derived from it an uneasy foreboding of his state. What a large piece of a good many years he seems to have taken with him! How often have I thought, since the news of his death came, of his putting his part in the saucepan (with the cover on) when we rehearsed "The Lighthouse;" of his falling out of the hammock when we rehearsed "The Frozen Deep;" of his learning Italian numbers when he ate the garlic in the carriage; of the thousands (I was going to say) of dark mornings when I apostrophised him as "Kernel;" of his losing my invaluable knife in that beastly stage-coach; of his posting up that mysterious book† every night! I hardly know why, but I have always associated that volume most with Venice. In my memory of the dear gentle little fellow, he will be (as since those days he always has been) eternally posting up that book at the large table in the middle of our Venice sitting-room, incidentally asking the name of an hotel three weeks back! And his pretty house is to be laid waste and sold. If there be a sale on the spot I shall try to buy something in loving remembrance of him, good dear little fellow. Think what a great "Frozen Deep" lay close under those boards we acted on! My brother Alfred, Luard, Arthur, Albert, Austin, Egg. Even among the audience Prince Albert and poor Stone! "I heard the"—I forget what it was I used to say—"come up from the great deep;" and it rings in my ears now, like a sort of mad prophecy.

However, this won't do. We must close up the ranks and march on.

    *   *   *   *   *

GAD'S HILL, *Seventeenth May,* 1863.   Rev. W.
   Brookfield.

MY DEAR BROOKFIELD,

It occurs to me that you may perhaps know, or know of, a kind of man that I want to discover.

One of my boys (the youngest) now is at Wimbledon School. He is a docile, amiable boy of fair abilities, but sensitive and shy. And he writes me so very earnestly that he feels the school to be

* On the death of Mr. Egg.
† His travelling journal.

confusingly large for him, and that he is sure he could do better with some gentleman who gave his own personal attention to the education of half-a-dozen or a dozen boys, as to impress me with the belief that I ought to heed his conviction.

Has any such phenomenon as a good and reliable man in this wise ever come in your way? Forgive my troubling you, and believe me,

Cordially yours.

Rev. W.
Brookfield.

GAD's HILL PLACE, HIGHAM BY ROCHESTER, KENT,
Twenty-fourth May, 1863.

MY DEAR BROOKFIELD,

I am most truly obliged to you for your kind and ready help.

When I am in town next week, I will call upon the Bishop of Natal, more to thank him than with the hope of profiting by that gentleman of whom he writes, as the limitation to "little boys" seems to stop the way. I want to find someone with whom this particular boy could remain; if there were a mutual interest and liking, that would be a great point gained.

Why did the kings in the fairy tales want children? I suppose in the weakness of the royal intellect.

Concerning "Nickleby" I am so much of your mind (comparing it with "Copperfield"), that it was a long time before I could take a pleasure in reading it. But I got better, as I found the audience always taking to it. I have been trying, alone by myself, the "Oliver Twist" murder, but have got something so horrible out of it that I am afraid to try it in public.

Ever faithfully yours.

M. De
Cerjat.

GAD's HILL PLACE, HIGHAM BY ROCHESTER, KENT,
Thursday, Twenty-fourth May, 1863.

MY DEAR CERJAT,

I don't wonder at your finding it difficult to reconcile your mind to a French Hamlet; but I assure you that Fechter's is a very remarkable performance, perfectly consistent with itself (whether it be my particular Hamlet, or your particular Hamlet, or no), a coherent and intelligent whole, and done by a true artist. I have never seen, I think, an intelligent and clear view of the whole character so well sustained throughout; and there is a very captivating air of romance and picturesqueness added, which is quite new. Rely upon it, the public were right. The thing could not have been sustained by oddity ; it would have perished upon that, very soon. As to the mere accent, there is far less drawback in that than you would suppose. For this reason, he obviously knows English so thoroughly that you feel he is safe. You are never in pain for him. This sense of ease is gained directly, and then you think very little more about it.

The Colenso and Jowett matter is a more difficult question, but here again I don't go with you. The position of the writers of " Essays and Reviews " is, that certain parts of the Old Testament have done their intended function in the education of the world *as it was* ; but that mankind, like the individual man, is designed by the Almighty to have an infancy and a maturity, and that as it advances, the machinery of its education must advance too. For example : inasmuch as ever since there was a sun and there was vapour, there *must have* been a rainbow under certain conditions, so surely it would be better now to recognise that indisputable fact. Similarly, Joshua might command the sun to stand still, under the impression that it moved round the earth ; but he could not possibly have inverted the relations of the earth and the sun, whatever his impressions were. Again, it is contended that the science of geology is quite as much a revelation to man, as books of an immense age and of (at the best) doubtful origin, and that your consideration of the latter must reasonably be influenced by the former. As I understand the importance of timely suggestions such as these, it is, that the Church should not gradually shock and lose the more thoughtful and logical of human minds ; but should be so gently and considerately yielding as to retain them, and, through them, hundreds of thousands. This seems to me, as I understand the temper and tendency of the time, whether for good or evil, to be a very wise and necessary position. And as I understand the danger, it is not chargeable on those who take this ground, but on those who in reply call names and argue nothing. What these bishops and such-like say about revelation, in assuming it to be finished and done with, I can't in the least understand. Nothing is discovered without God's intention and assistance, and I suppose every new knowledge of His works that is conceded to man to be distinctly a revelation by which men are to guide themselves. Lastly, in the mere matter of religious doctrine and dogmas, these men (Protestants— protestors—successors of the men who protested against human judgment being set aside) talk and write as if they were all settled by the direct act of Heaven ; not as if they had been, as we know they were, a matter of temporary accommodation and adjustment among disputing mortals as fallible as you or I.

Coming nearer home, I hope that Georgina is almost quite well. Mary is neither married nor (that I know of) going to be. She and Katie and a lot of them have been playing croquet outside my window here for the last four days, to a mad and maddening extent. My sailor-boy's ship, the *Orlando*, is fortunately in Chatham Dockyard—so he is pretty constantly at home—while the shipwrights are repairing a leak in her. I am reading in London every Friday just now. Great crams and great enthusiasm. Townshend I suppose to have left Lausanne somewhat about this day. His house in the park is hermetically sealed, ready for him. The Prince and Princess of Wales go about (wisely) very much, and have as fair a chance of popularity as ever prince and princess had. The City ball in their honour is to be a tremendously gorgeous business, and Mary is highly excited by her father's being invited, and she with him. Meantime the unworthy parent is devising all kinds of subterfuges for sending her and getting out of it himself. A very intelligent German friend of mine, just home from America, maintains that the conscription will succeed in the North, and that the war will be indefinitely prolonged. *I* say "No," and that however mad and villainous the North is, the war will finish by reason of its not supplying soldiers. We shall see. The more they brag the more I don't believe in them.

*   *   *   *   *

Mr. Percy Fitzgerald.

GAD'S HILL PLACE,
Saturday Night, Fourth July, 1863.

MY DEAR MR. FITZGERALD,

I have been most heartily gratified by the perusal of your article on my dogs. It has given me an amount and a kind of pleasure very unusual, and for which I thank you earnestly. The owner of the renowned dog Cæsar understands me so sympathetically, that I trust with perfect confidence to his feeling what I really mean in these few words. You interest me very much by your kind promise, the redemption of which I hereby claim, to send me your life of Sterne when it comes out. If you should be in England before this, I should be delighted to see you here. It is a very pretty country, not thirty miles from London; and if you could spare a day or two for its fine walks, I and my two latest dogs, a St. Bernard and a bloodhound, would be charmed with your company as one of ourselves.

Believe me, very faithfully yours.

Friday, Tenth July, 1863. *

DEAR MADAM,

I hope you will excuse this tardy reply to your letter. It is often impossible for me, by any means, to keep pace with my correspondents. I must take leave to say, that if there be any general feeling on the part of the intelligent Jewish people, that I have done them what you describe as "a great wrong," they are a far less sensible, a far less just, and a far less good-tempered people than I have always supposed them to be. Fagin, in "Oliver Twist," is a Jew, because it unfortunately was true of the time to which that story refers, that that class of criminal almost invariably was a Jew. But surely no sensible man or woman of your persuasion can fail to observe—firstly, that all the rest of the wicked *dramatis personæ* are Christians; and secondly, that he is called a "Jew," not because of his religion, but because of his race. If I were to write a story, in which I described a Frenchman or a Spaniard as "the Roman Catholic," I should do a very indecent and unjustifiable thing; but I make mention of Fagin as the Jew, because he is one of the Jewish people, and because it conveys that kind of idea of him which I should give my readers of a Chinaman, by calling him a Chinese.

The enclosed is quite a nominal subscription towards the good object in which you are interested; but I hope it may serve to show you that I have no feeling towards the Jewish people but a friendly one. I always speak well of them, whether in public or in private, and bear my testimony (as I ought to do) to their perfect good faith in such transactions as I have ever had with them; and in my "Child's History of England," I have lost no opportunity of setting forth their cruel persecution in old times.

Dear Madam, faithfully yours.

(In reply to this, the Jewish lady thanked him for his kind letter and its enclosure, still remonstrating and pointing out that though, as he observed, "all the other criminal characters were Christians, they are, at least, contrasted with characters of good Christians; this wretched Fagin stands alone as the Jew."

The reply to *this* letter afterwards was the character of Riah, in "Our Mutual Friend," and some favourable sketches of Jewish character in the lower class, in some articles in "All the Year Round.")

* Answer to letter from Jewish lady, remonstrating with him on injustice to the Jews, shown in the character of Fagin, and asking for a subscription for the benefit of the Jewish poor.

Mr. Ouvry.

GAD'S HILL PLACE, HIGHAM BY ROCHESTER, KENT,
Wednesday Night, Twenty-ninth July, 1863.

MY DEAR OUVRY,

I have had some undefined idea that you were to let me know if you were coming to the archæologs at Rochester. (I myself am keeping out of their way, as having had enough of crowding and speech-making in London.) Will you tell me where you are, whether you are in this neighbourhood or out of it, whether you will come here on Saturday and stay till Monday or till Tuesday morning? If you will come, I *know* I can give you the heartiest welcome in Kent, and I *think* I can give you the best wine in this part of it. Send me a word in reply. I will fetch you from anywhere, at any indicated time.

We have very pretty places in the neighbourhood, and are not uncomfortable people (I believe) to stay with.

Faithfully yours ever.

Mr. John
Bennett.*

† GAD'S HILL PLACE, HIGHAM BY ROCHESTER, KENT,
Monday Night, Fourteenth September, 1863.

MY DEAR SIR,

Since my hall clock was sent to your establishment to be cleaned it has gone (as indeed it always has) perfectly well, but has struck the hours with great reluctance, and after enduring internal agonies of a most distressing nature, it has now ceased striking altogether. Though a happy release for the clock, this is not convenient to the household. If you can send down any confidential person with whom the clock can confer, I think it may have something on its works that it would be glad to make a clean breast of.

Faithfully yours.

Mr. Charles
Reade.

OFFICE OF "ALL THE YEAR ROUND,"
Wednesday, Thirtieth September, 1863.

MY DEAR READE,

I *must* write you one line to say how interested I am in your story, and to congratulate you upon its admirable art and its surprising grace and vigour.

And to hint my hope, at the same time, that you will be able to find leisure for a little dash for the Christmas number. It would be a really great and true pleasure to me if you could.

Faithfully yours always.

* Afterwards Sir John Bennett.
† This letter was published in *The Daily News* after the death of Charles Dickens.

GAD'S HILL PLACE, HIGHAM BY ROCHESTER, KENT,
Wednesday, Seventh October, 1863.

MY DEAREST GEORGY,

You will see by to-day's *Times* that it *was* an earthquake that shook me, and that my watch showed exactly the same time as the man's who writes from Blackheath so near us—twenty minutes past three.

It is a great satisfaction to me to make it out so precisely; I wish you would enquire whether the servants felt it. I thought it was the voice of the cook that answered me, but that was nearly half an hour later. I am strongly inclined to think that there is a peculiar susceptibility in iron—at all events in our part of the country—to the shock, as though there were something magnetic in it. For, whereas my long iron bedstead was so violently shaken I certainly heard nothing rattle in the room.

Ever affectionately.

GAD'S HILL, *Sunday, Twentieth December*, 1863.

MY DEAR WILLS,

I am clear that you took my cold. Why didn't you do the thing completely, and take it away from me? for it hangs by me still.

Will you tell Mrs. Linton that in looking over her admirable account (*most* admirable) of Mrs. Gordon's book, I have taken out the references to Lockhart, not because I in the least doubt their justice, but because I knew him and he liked me; and because one bright day in Rome, I walked about with him for some hours when he was dying fast, and all the old faults had faded out of him, and the now ghost of the handsome man I had first known when Scott's daughter was at the head of his house, had little more to do with this world than she in her grave, or Scott in his, or small Hugh Littlejohn in his. Lockhart had been anxious to see me all the previous day (when I was away on the Campagna), and as we walked about I knew very well that *he* knew very well why. He talked of getting better, but I never saw him again. This makes me stay Mrs. Linton's hand, gentle as it is.

Mrs. Lirriper is indeed a most brilliant old lady. God bless her!

Ever faithfully.

1864.

NARRATIVE.

CHARLES DICKENS was, as usual, at Gad's Hill, with a family and friendly party, at the opening of this year, and had been much shocked and distressed by the news of the sudden death of Mr. Thackeray, brought to him by friends arriving from London on the Christmas Eve of 1863, the day on which it happened. He wrote of this death, in the first letter of the year, to Mr. Wilkie Collins, who was passing the winter in Italy. He tells him, also, of his having got well to work upon a new serial story, the first number of which ("Our Mutual Friend") was published on the First of May.

The year began very sadly for Charles Dickens. On the seventh of February (his own birthday) he received the mournful announcement of the death of his second son, Walter Landor (a lieutenant in the 42nd Royal Highlanders), who had died quite suddenly at Calcutta, on the last night of the year of 1863, at the age of twenty-three. His third son, Francis Jeffrey, had started for India at the end of January.

His annual letter to M. De Cerjat contains an allusion to "another generation beginning to peep above the table"—the children of his son Charles, who had been married three years before, to Miss Bessie Evans.

In the middle of February he removed to a house in London (57, Gloucester Place, Hyde Park), where he made a stay of the usual duration, up to the middle of June, all the time being hard at work upon "Our Mutual Friend" and "All the Year Round." Mr. Marcus Stone was the illustrator of the new monthly work, and we give a specimen of one of many letters which were written to him about his "subjects."

Mr. Charles Knight, with whom for many years Charles Dickens had dined on his birthday, was staying, this spring, in the Isle of Wight. To him he wrote of the death of Walter, and of another melancholy death which happened at this time, and which affected him almost as much. Clara, the last surviving daughter of Mr. and Mrs. White, who had been happily married to Mr. Gordon, of Cluny, not more than two years, had just died at Bonchurch. Her father, as will be seen by the touching allusion to him in this letter, had died a short time after this daughter's marriage.

A letter to Mr. Edmund Ollier has reference to certain additions which Charles Dickens wished him to make to an article (by Mr.

Ollier) on Working Men's Clubs, published in "All the Year Round."

We are glad to have one letter to the Lord Chief Baron, Sir Frederick Pollock, which shows the great friendship and regard Charles Dickens had for him, and his admiration for his qualities in his judicial capacity.

We give a pleasant letter to Mrs. Storrar, for whom, and for her husband, Dr. Storrar, Charles Dickens had affectionate regard. The letter speaks for itself and needs no explanation.

The latter part of the year was uneventful. Hard at work, he passed the summer and autumn at Gad's Hill, taking holidays by receiving visitors at home (among them, this year, Sir J. Emerson Tennent, his wife and daughter, who were kindly urgent for his paying them a return visit in Ireland) and occasional "runs" into France. The last letters we give are his annual one to M. De Cerjat, and a graceful little New Year's note to his dear old friend "Barry Cornwall."

The Christmas number was "Mrs. Lirriper's Legacy," the first and last part written by himself, as in the case of the previous year's "Mrs. Lirriper."

GAD's HILL, *Monday, Twenty-fourth January,* 1864.   Mr. W. Wilkie Collins.

EXTRACT.

MY DEAR WILKIE,

I am horribly behindhand in answering your welcome letter; but I have been so busy, and have had the house so full for Christmas and the New Year, and have had so much to see to in getting Frank out to India, that I have not been able to settle down to a regular long letter, which I mean this to be, but which it may not turn out to be, after all.

First, I will answer your enquiries about the Christmas number and the new book. The Christmas number has been the greatest success of all; has shot ahead of last year; has sold about two hundred and twenty thousand; and has made the name of Mrs. Lirriper so swiftly and domestically famous as never was. I had a very strong belief in her when I wrote about her, finding that she made a great effect upon me; but she certainly has gone beyond my hopes. (Probably you know nothing about her? which is a very unpleasant consideration.) Of the new book, I have done the two first numbers, and am now beginning the third. It is a combination of drollery with romance which requires a great deal of pains and a perfect throwing away of points that might be amplified; but I hope it is *very good.* I confess, in short, that I think it is. Strange to say, I felt at first quite dazed in getting back to the large canvas and the big brushes; and even now, I have a sensation as of acting at the San Carlo after Tavistock House, which I could hardly have supposed would have come upon so old a stager.

You will have read about poor Thackeray's death—sudden, and yet not sudden, for he had long been alarmingly ill. At the solicitation of Mr. Smith and some of his friends, I have done what I would most gladly have excused myself from doing, if I felt I could —written a couple of pages about him in what was his own magazine.

Concerning the Italian experiment, De la Rue is more hopeful than you. He and his bank are closely leagued with the powers at Turin, and he has long been devoted to Cavour; but he gave me the strongest assurances (with illustrations) of the fusion between place and place, and of the blending of small mutually antagonistic characters into one national character, progressing cheeringly and certainly. Of course there must be discouragements and discrepancies in the first struggles of a country previously so degraded and enslaved, and the time, as yet, has been very short.

I should like to have a day with you at the Coliseum, and on the Appian Way, and among the tombs, and with the Orvieto. But Rome and I are wide asunder, physically as well as morally. I wonder whether the dramatic stable, where we saw the marionettes, still receives the Roman public? And Lord! when I think of you in that hotel, how I think of poor dear Egg in the long front drawing-room, giving on to the piazza, posting up that wonderful necromantic volume which we never shall see opened!

*   *   *   *   *

Mr. Marcus
Stone.

57, GLOUCESTER PLACE, HYDE PARK,
Tuesday, Twenty-third February, 1864.

MY DEAR MARCUS,

I think the design for the cover *excellent,* and do not doubt its coming out to perfection. The slight alteration I am going to suggest originates in a business consideration not to be overlooked.

The word "Our" in the title must be out in the open like "Mutual Friend," making the title three distinct large lines— "Our" as big as "Mutual Friend." This would give you too much design at the bottom. I would therefore take out the dustman, and put the Wegg and Boffin composition (which is capital) in its place. I don't want Mr. Inspector or the murder reward bill, because these points are sufficiently indicated in the river at the top. Therefore you can have an indication of the dustman in

Mr. Inspector's place. Note, that the dustman's face should be droll, and not horrible. Twemlow's elbow will still go out of the frame as it does now, and the same with Lizzie's skirts on the opposite side. With these changes, work away!

Mrs. Boffin, as I judge of her from the sketch, "very good, indeed." I want Boffin's oddity, without being at all blinked, to be an oddity of a very honest kind, that people will like.

The doll's dressmaker is immensely better than she was. I think she should now come extremely well. A weird sharpness not without beauty is the thing I want.

Affectionately yours.

57, GLOUCESTER PLACE, W.,   Mr. Charles
Tuesday, First March, 1864.   Knight.

MY DEAR KNIGHT,

We knew of your being in the Isle of Wight, and had said that we should have this year to drink your health in your absence. Rely on my being always ready and happy to renew our old friendship in the flesh. In the spirit it needs no renewal, because it has no break.

Ah poor Mrs. White! A sad, sad story! It is better for poor White that that little churchyard by the sea received his ashes a while ago, than that he should have lived to this time.

My poor boy was on his way home from an up-country station, on sick leave. He had been very ill, but was not so at the time. He was talking to some brother-officers in the Calcutta hospital about his preparations for home, when he suddenly became excited, had a rush of blood from the mouth, and was dead. His brother Frank would arrive out at Calcutta, expecting to see him after six years, and he would have been dead a month.

My "working life" is resolving itself at the present into another book, in twenty green leaves. You work like a Trojan at Ventnor, but you do that everywhere; and that's why you are so young.   Affectionately yours.

P.S.—Serene View! What a placid address!

"ALL THE YEAR ROUND" OFFICE, *March*, 1864.   Mr.
                    Edmund
EXTRACT.   Ollier.

I want the article on "Working Men's Clubs" to refer back to "The Poor Man and his Beer" in No. 1, and to maintain the principle involved in that effort.

Also, emphatically, to show that trustfulness is at the bottom of all social institutions, and that to trust a man, as one of a body of men, is to place him under a wholesome restraint of social opinion, and is a very much better thing than to make a baby of him.

Also, to point out that the rejection of beer in this club, tobacco in that club, dancing or what-not in another club, are instances that such clubs are founded on mere whims, and therefore cannot successfully address human nature in general, and hope to last. Also, again to urge that patronage is the curse and blight of all such endeavours, and to impress upon the working men that they must originate and manage for themselves. And to ask them the question, can they possibly show their detestation of drunkenness better, or better strive to get rid of it from among them, than to make it a hopeless disqualification in all their clubs, and a reason for expulsion.

Also, to encourage them to declare to themselves and their fellow working men that they want social rest and social recreation for themselves and their families; and that these clubs are intended for that laudable and necessary purpose, and do not need educational pretences or flourishes. Do not let them be afraid or ashamed of wanting to be amused and pleased.

*   *   *   *   *

The Lord
Chief Baron.

57, GLOUCESTER PLACE, *Tuesday, Fifteenth March,* 1864.

MY DEAR CHIEF BARON,

Many thanks for your kind letter.

Your answer concerning poor Thackeray I will duly make known to the active spirit in that matter, Mr. Shirley Brooks.

Your kind invitation to me to come and see you and yours, and hear the nightingales, I shall not fail to discuss with Forster, and with an eye to spring. I expect to see him presently; the rather as I found a note from him when I came back yesterday, describing himself somewhat gloomily as not having been well, and as feeling a little out of heart.

It is not out of order, I hope, to remark that you have been much in my thoughts and on my lips lately? For I really have not been able to repress my admiration of the vigorous dignity and sense and spirit, with which one of the best of judges set right one of the dullest of juries in a recent case.

Believe me ever, very faithfully yours.

57, GLOUCESTER PLACE,   Mr. John
Forster.
Tuesday, Twenty-ninth March, 1864.

MY DEAR FORSTER,

Concerning Eliot, I sat down, as I told you, and read the book through with the strangest interest and the highest admiration. I believe it to be as honest, spirited, patient, reliable, and gallant a piece of biography as ever was written, the care and pains of it astonishing, the completeness of it masterly ; and what I particularly feel about it is that the dignity of the man, and the dignity of the book that tells about the man, always go together, and fit each other. This same quality has always impressed me as the great leading speciality of the Goldsmith, and enjoins sympathy with the subject, knowledge of it, and pursuit of it in its own spirit ; but I think it even more remarkable here. I declare that apart from the interest of having been so put into the time, and enabled to understand it, I personally feel quite as much the credit and honour done to literature by such a book. It quite clears out of the remembrance a thousand pitiful things, and sets one up in heart again. I am not surprised in the least by Bulwer's enthusiasm. I was as confident about the effect of the book when I closed the first volume, as I was when I closed the second with a full heart. No man less in earnest than Eliot himself could have done it, and I make bold to add that it never could have been done by a man who was so distinctly born to do the work as Eliot was to do his.

Saturday at Hastings I must give up. I have wavered and considered, and considered and wavered, but if I take that sort of holiday, I must have a day to spare after it, and at this critical time I have not. If I were to lose a page of the five numbers I have purposed to myself to be ready by the publication day, I should feel that I had fallen short. I have grown hard to satisfy, and write very slowly, and I have so much bad fiction, that *will* be thought of when I don't want to think of it, that I am forced to take more care than I ever took.

Ever affectionately.

GAD'S HILL PLACE, HIGHAM BY ROCHESTER, KENT,   Mrs. Storrar.
Sunday Morning, Fifteenth May, 1864.

MY DEAR MRS. STORRAR,

Our family dinner must come off at Gad's Hill, where I have improvements to exhibit, and where I shall be truly pleased to see you and the doctor again. I have deferred answering your note, while I have been scheming and scheming for a day between this time and our departure. But it is all in vain. My engagements have accumulated, and become such a whirl, that no day is left me. Nothing is left me but to get away. I look forward to my release from this dining life with an inexpressible longing after quiet and my own pursuits. What with public speechifying, private eating and drinking, and perpetual simmering in hot rooms, I have made London too hot to hold me and my work together. Mary and Georgina acknowledge the condition of imbecility to which we have become reduced in reference to your kind reminder. They say, when I stare at them in a forlorn way with your note in my hand: "What CAN you do!" To which I can only reply, implicating them: "See what you have brought me to!"

With our united kind regard to yourself and Dr. Storrar, I entreat your pity and compassion for an unfortunate wretch whom a too-confiding disposition has brought to this pass. If I had not allowed my "cheeild" to pledge me to all manner of fellow-creatures, I and my digestion might have been in a state of honourable independence this day.

Faithfully and penitently yours.

Mr. Percy
Fitzgerald.

OFFICE OF "ALL THE YEAR ROUND," ETC. ETC. ETC.,
Wednesday, Twenty-seventh July, 1864.

MY DEAR MR. FITZGERALD,

First, let me assure you that it gave us all real pleasure to see your sister and you at Gad's Hill, and that we all hope you will both come and stay a day or two with us when you are next in England.

Next, let me convey to you the intelligence that I resolve to launch "Miss Manuel," fully confiding in your conviction of the power of the story. On all business points, Wills will communicate with you. I purpose beginning its publication in our first September number, therefore there is no time to be lost.

The only suggestion I have to make as to the MS. in hand and type is, that Captain Fermor wants relief. It is a disagreeable character, as you mean it to be, and I should be afraid to do so much with him, if the case were mine, without taking the taste of him, here and there, out of the reader's mouth. It is remarkable that if you do not administer a disagreeable character carefully, the public have a decided tendency to think that the *story* is disagreeable, and not merely the fictitious person.

What do you think of the title,

NEVER FORGOTTEN ?

It is a good one in itself, would express the eldest sister's pursuit, and glanced at now and then in the text, would hold the reader in suspense. I would propose to add the line,

BY THE AUTHOR OF BELLA DONNA.

Let me know your opinion as to the title.   I need not assure you that the greatest care will be taken of you here, and that we shall make you as thoroughly well and widely known as we possibly can.

Very faithfully yours.

GAD'S HILL PLACE, HIGHAM BY ROCHESTER, KENT,
Friday, Twenty-sixth August, 1861.

Sir James Emerson Tennent.

MY DEAR TENNENT,

Believe me, I fully intended to come to you—did not doubt that I should come—and have greatly disappointed Mary and her aunt, as well as myself, by not coming.   But I do not feel safe in going out for a visit.   The mere knowledge that I had such a thing before me would put me out.   It is not the length of time consumed, or the distance traversed, but it is the departure from a settled habit and a continuous sacrifice of pleasures that comes in question.   This is an old story with me.   I have never divided a book of my writing with anything else, but have always wrought at it to the exclusion of everything else; and it is now too late to change.

After receiving your kind note I resolved to make another trial. But the hot weather and a few other drawbacks did not mend the matter, for I have dropped astern this month instead of going ahead.   So I have seen Forster, and shown him my chains, and am reduced to taking exercise in them, like Baron Trenck.

I am heartily pleased that you set so much store by the dedication.   You may be sure that it does not make me the less anxious to take pains, and to work out well what I have in my mind.

Mary and Georgina unite with me in kindest regards to Lady Tennent and Miss Tennent, and wish me to report that while they are seriously disappointed, they still feel there is no help for it.   I can testify that they had great pleasure in the anticipation of the visit, and that their faces were very long and blank indeed when I began to hint my doubts.   They fought against them valiantly as long as there was a chance, but they see my difficulty as well as anyone not myself can.

Believe me, my dear Tennent, ever faithfully yours.

THE ATHENÆUM,
Wednesday, Twenty-first September, 1864.

Mr. Clarkson Stanfield, R.A.

MY DEAR STANNY,

I met George in the street a few days ago, and he gave me a wonderful account of the effect of your natural element upon you at Ramsgate.   I expect you to come back looking about twenty-nine, and feeling about nineteen.

This morning I have looked in here to put down Fechter as a candidate, on the chance of the committee's electing him some day or other. He is a most devoted worshipper of yours, and would take it as a great honour if you would second him. Supposing you to have not the least objection (of course, if you should have any, I can in a moment provide a substitute), will you write your name in the candidates' book as his seconder when you are next in town and passing this way?

Lastly, if you should be in town on his opening night (a Saturday, and in all probability the Twenty-second of October), will you come and dine at the office and see his new piece?* You have not yet "pronounced" in the matter of that new French stage of his, on which Callcott for the said new piece has built up all manner of villages, camps, Versailles gardens, etc. etc. etc. etc., with no wings, no flies, no looking off in any direction. If you tell me that you are to be in town by that time, I will not fail to refresh your memory as to the precise day.

Believe me, my dear old boy, ever your affectionate

DICK.

Mr. W. H. Wills.

LORD WARDEN HOTEL, DOVER,
Sunday, Sixteenth October, 1864.

MY DEAR WILLS,

I was unspeakably relieved, and most agreeably surprised, to get your letter this morning. I had pictured you as lying there waiting full another week.

I hope you are deriving benefit from the sea, and the shore, and the young ladies on horseback, and the riding-masters, and the schools, and the gallant seamen who never do what England expects of them, in the least.

My expectations of "Mrs. Lirriper's" sale are not so mighty as yours, but I am heartily glad and grateful to be honestly able to believe that she is nothing but a good 'un. It is the condensation of a quantity of subjects and the very greatest pains.

As next week will not be my working-time at "Our Mutual Friend," I shall devote the day of Friday (*not* the evening) to making up news. Therefore I write to say that if you would rather stay where you are than come to London, *don't come.* I shall throw my hat into the ring at eleven, and shall receive all the punishment that can be administered by two Nos. on end like a British Glutton.

Ever.

* "The King's Butterfly."

GAD'S HILL PLACE, HIGHAM BY ROCHESTER,
Tuesday, Twenty-fifth October, 1864.

MY DEAR CERJAT,

Here is a limping brute of a reply to your always-welcome
Christmas letter! But, as usual, when I have done my day's
work, I jump up from my desk and rush into air and exercise, and
find letter-writing the most difficult thing in my daily life.

I hope that your asthmatic tendencies may not be strong just
now; but Townshend's account of the premature winter at
Lausanne is not encouraging, and with us here in England all
such disorders have been aggravated this autumn. However, a
man of your dignity *must* have either asthma or gout, and I hope
you have got the better of the two.

In London there is, as you see by the papers, extraordinarily
little news. At present the apprehension (rather less than it was
thought) of a commercial crisis, and the trial of Müller next
Thursday, are the two chief sensations. I hope that gentleman
will be hanged, and have hardly a doubt of it, though croakers
contrariwise are not wanting. It is difficult to conceive any other
line of defence than that the circumstances proved, taken separately, are slight. But a sound judge will immediately charge the
jury that the strength of the circumstances lies in their being put
together, and will thread them together on a fatal rope.

As to the Church, my friend, I am sick of it. The spectacle
presented by the indecent squabbles of priests of most denomina-
tions, and the exemplary unfairness and rancour with which they
conduct their differences, utterly repel me. And the idea of the
Protestant establishment, in the face of its own history, seeking to
trample out discussion and private judgment, is an enormity so
cool, that I wonder the Right Reverends, Very Reverends, and all
other Reverends, who commit it, can look in one another's faces
without laughing, as the old soothsayers did. Perhaps they can't
and don't. How our sublime and so-different Christian religion is
to be administered in the future I cannot pretend to say, but that
the Church's hand is at its own throat I am fully convinced.
Here, more Popery, there, more Methodism—as many forms of
consignment to eternal damnation as there are articles, and all in
one forever quarrelling body—the Master of the New Testament
put out of sight, and the rage and fury almost always turning on
the letter of obscure parts of the Old Testament, which itself has
been the subject of accommodation, adaptation, varying interpretation without end—these things cannot last. The Church that is
to have its part in the coming time must be a more Christian one,

with less arbitrary pretensions and a stronger hold upon the mantle of our Saviour, as He walked and talked upon this earth.

Of family intelligence I have very little. Charles Collins continuing in a very poor way, and showing no signs of amendment, he and my daughter Katie went to Wiesbaden and thence to Nice, where they are now. I have strong apprehensions that he will never recover, and that she will be left a young widow. All the rest are as they were. Mary neither married nor going to be; Georgina holding them all together and perpetually corresponding with the distant ones; occasional rallyings coming off here, in which another generation begins to peep above the table. I once used to think what a horrible thing it was to be a grandfather. Finding that the calamity falls upon me without my perceiving any other change in myself, I bear it like a man.

Mrs. Watson has bought a house in town, to which she repairs in the season, for the bringing out of her daughter. She is now at Rockingham. Her eldest son is said to be as good an eldest son as ever was, and to make her position there a perfectly independent and happy one. I have not seen him for some years; her I often see; but he ought to be a good fellow, and is very popular in his neighbourhood.

I have altered this place very much since you were here, and have made a pretty (I think an unusually pretty) drawing-room. I wish you would come back and see it. My being on the Dover line, and my being very fond of France, occasion me to cross the Channel perpetually. Whenever I feel that I have worked too much, or am on the eve of overdoing it, and want a change, away I go by the mail-train, and turn up in Paris or anywhere else that suits my humour, next morning. So I come back as fresh as a daisy, and preserve as ruddy a face as though I had never leant over a sheet of paper. When I retire from a literary life I think of setting up as a Channel pilot.

Old days in Switzerland are ever fresh to me, and sometimes I walk with you again, after dark, outside the hotel at Martigny, while Lady Mary Taylour (wasn't it?) sang within very prettily. Lord, how the time goes! How many years ago!

Affectionately yours.

Wednesday, Sixteenth November, 1864.[*]

DEAR MADAM,

I have received your letter with great pleasure, and hope to be (as I have always been at heart) the best of friends with the

[*] In answer to another letter from the "Jewish Lady," in which she gives her reasons for still being dissatisfied with the character of Riah.

Jewish people. The error you point out to me had occurred to me, as most errors do to most people, when it was too late to correct it. But it will do no harm. The peculiarities of dress and manner are fused together for the sake of picturesqueness.

Dear Madam, faithfully yours.

GAD'S HILL, *Wednesday, Thirtieth November*, 1864. Mr. W. H. Wills.

MY DEAR WILLS,

I found the beautiful and perfect Brougham* awaiting me in triumph at the Station when I came down yesterday afternoon. Georgina and Marsh were both highly mortified that it had fallen dark, and the beauties of the carriage were obscured. But of course I had it out in the yard the first thing this morning, and got in and out at both the doors, and let down and pulled up the windows, and checked an imaginary coachman, and leaned back in a state of placid contemplation.

It is the lightest and prettiest and best carriage of the class ever made. But you know that I value it for higher reasons than these. It will always be dear to me—far dearer than anything on wheels could ever be for its own sake—as a proof of your ever generous friendship and appreciation, and a memorial of a happy intercourse and a perfect confidence that have never had a break, and that surely never can have any break now (after all these years) but one.

Ever your faithful.

GAD'S HILL PLACE, HIGHAM BY ROCHESTER, KENT, Mr. B. W. Procter.
Saturday, Thirty-first December, 1864.

MY DEAR PROCTER,

I have reserved my acknowledgment of your delightful note (the youngest note I have had in all this year) until to-day, in order that I might send, most heartily and affectionately, all seasonable good wishes to you and to Mrs. Procter, and to those who are nearest and dearest to you. Take them from an old friend who loves you.

Mamie returns the tender compliments, and Georgina does what the Americans call "endorse them." Mrs. Lirriper is proud to be so remembered, and says over and over again "that it's worth twenty times the trouble she has taken with the narrative, since Barry Cornwall, Esquire, is pleased to like it."

I got rid of a touch of neuralgia in France (as I always do there), but I found no old friends in my voyages of discovery on that side, such as I have left on this.

My dear Procter, ever your affectionate.

* A present from Mr. Wills.

2 P

1865.

NARRATIVE.

FOR this spring a furnished house in Somers Place, Hyde Park, had been taken, which Charles Dickens occupied, with his sister-in-law and daughter, from the beginning of March until June.

During the year he paid two short visits to France.

He was still at work upon "Our Mutual Friend," two numbers of which had been issued in January and February, when the first volume was published, with dedication to Sir James Emerson Tennent. The remaining numbers were issued between March and November, when the complete work was published in two volumes.

The Christmas number, to which Charles Dickens contributed three stories, was called "Doctor Marigold's Prescriptions."

Being out of health, and much overworked, Charles Dickens, at the end of May, took his first short holiday trip into France. And on his way home, and on a day afterwards so fatal to him, the Ninth of June, he was in that most terrible railway accident at Stapleburst. Many of the letters for this year have reference to this awful experience—an experience from the effects of which his nerves never wholly recovered. His letters to Mr. Thomas Mitton and to Mrs. Hulkes (an esteemed friend and neighbour) are graphic descriptions of this disaster. But they do NOT tell of the wonderful presence of mind and energy shown by Charles Dickens when most of the terrified passengers were incapable of thought or action, or of his gentleness and goodness to the dead and dying. The Mr. Dickenson* mentioned in the letter to Mrs. Hulkes soon recovered. He always considers that he owes his life to Charles Dickens, the latter having discovered and extricated him from beneath a carriage before it was too late.

The first letter, to Mr. Kent, is one of congratulation upon his having become the proprietor of *The Sun* newspaper.

The letter to Mrs. Procter is in answer to one from that lady, asking Charles Dickens to write a memoir of her daughter Adelaide, as a preface to a collected edition of her poems.

Mr. William Charles Kent.

GAD'S HILL PLACE, HIGHAM BY ROCHESTER, KENT,
Tuesday, Seventeenth January, 1865.

MY DEAR KENT,

I meant to have written instantly on the appearance of your paper in its beautiful freshness, to congratulate you on its

---

* Now Captain E. Newton Dickenson.

handsome appearance, and to send you my heartiest good wishes for its thriving and prosperous career. Through a mistake of the postman's, that remarkable letter has been tesselated into the Infernal Pavement instead of being delivered in the Strand.

We have been looking and waiting for your being well enough to propose yourself for a mouthful of fresh air. Are you well enough to come on Sunday?

It amuses me to find that you don't see your way with a certain "Mutual Friend" of ours. I have a horrible suspicion that you may begin to be fearfully knowing at somewhere about No. 12 or 13. But you shan't if I can help it.

Your note delighted me because it dwelt upon the places in the number that *I* dwell on. Not that that is anything new in your case, but it is always new to me in the pleasure I derive from it, which is truly inexpressible.

Ever cordially yours.

GAD'S HILL PLACE, HIGHAM BY ROCHESTER, KENT,   Mrs.
Wednesday, Fifteenth February, 1865.   Procter.

MY DEAR MRS. PROCTER,

Of course I will do it, and of course I will do it for the love of you and Procter. You can give me my brief, and we can speak about its details. Once again, of course I will do it, and with all my heart.

I have registered a vow (in which there is not the least merit, for I couldn't help it) that when I am, as I am now, very hard at work upon a book, I never will dine out more than one day in a week. Why didn't you ask me for the Wednesday, before I stood engaged to Lady Molesworth for the Tuesday?

It is so delightful to me to sit by your side anywhere and be brightened up, that I lay a handsome sacrifice upon the altar of "Our Mutual Friend" in writing this note, very much against my will. But for as many years as can be made consistent with my present juvenility, I always have given my work the first place in my life, and what can I do now at 35!—or at least at the two figures, never mind their order.

I send my love to Procter, hoping you may appropriate a little of it by the way.

Affectionately yours.

16, SOMERS PLACE, HYDE PARK,
Saturday Night, Twenty-second April, 1865.

MY DEAREST MACREADY,

A thousand thanks for your kind letter, most heartily welcome.

My frost-bitten foot, after causing me great inconvenience and much pain, has begun to conduct itself amiably. I can now again walk my ten miles in the morning without inconvenience, but am absurdly obliged to sit shoeless all the evening—a very slight penalty, as I detest going out to dinner (which killed the original old Parr by-the-bye).

I am working like a dragon at my book, and am a terror to the household, likewise to all the organs and brass bands in this quarter. Gad's Hill is being gorgeously painted, and we are here until the First of June. I wish I might hope you would be there any time this summer; I really *have* made the place comfortable and pretty by this time.

It is delightful to us to hear such good news of Butty.* She made so deep an impression on Fechter that he always asks me what Ceylon has done for her, and always beams when I tell him how thoroughly well it has made her. As to *you*, you are the youngest man (worth mentioning as a thorough man) that I know. Oh, let me be as young when I am as——did you think I was going to write "old?" No, sir—withdraw from the wear and tear of busy life is my expression.

Poole still holds out at Kentish Town, and says he is dying of solitude. His memory is astoundingly good. I see him about once in two or three months, and in the meantime he makes notes of questions to ask me when I come. Having fallen in arrear of the time, these generally refer to unknown words he has encountered in the newspapers. His three last (he always reads them with tremendous difficulty through an enormous magnifying-glass) were as follows:

1. What's croquet?
2. What's an Albert chain?
3. Let me know the state of mind of the Queen.

When I had delivered a neat exposition on these heads, he turned back to his memoranda, and came to something that the utmost power of the enormous magnifying-glass couldn't render legible. After a quarter of an hour or so, he said: "Oh yes, I know." And then rose and clasped his hands above his head, and said: "Thank God, I am not a dram-drinker."

* Mr. Macready's youngest daughter, Benvenuta.

Do think of coming to Gad's in the summer; and do give my love to Mrs. Macready, and tell her I know she can make you come if she will. Johnny we suppose to be climbing the tree of knowledge somewhere.

My dearest Macready, ever yours most affectionately.

GAD'S HILL, *Monday, Twelfth June*, 1865.   Mr. W. C.
MY DEAREST MACREADY,   Macready.

[*So far in his own writing.*]

Many thanks for your kind words of remembrance.* This is not all in my own hand, because I am too much shaken to write many notes. Not by the beating and dragging of the carriage in which I was—it did not go over, but was caught on the turn, among the ruins of the bridge—but by the work afterwards to get out the dying and dead, which was terrible.

[*The rest in his own writing.*]

Ever your affectionate Friend.

GAD'S HILL PLACE, HIGHAM BY ROCHESTER, KENT,   Mr. Thomas
Tuesday, Thirteenth June, 1865.   Mitton.

MY DEAR MITTON,
I should have written to you yesterday or the day before, if I had been quite up to writing.

I was in the only carriage that did not go over into the stream. It was caught upon the turn by some of the ruin of the bridge, and hung suspended and balanced in an apparently impossible manner. Two ladies were my fellow-passengers, an old one and a young one. This is exactly what passed. You may judge from it the precise length of the suspense: Suddenly we were off the rail, and beating the ground as the car of a half-emptied balloon might. The old lady cried out, "My God!" and the young one screamed. I caught hold of them both (the old lady sat opposite and the young one on my left), and said: "We can't help ourselves, but we can be quiet and composed. Pray don't cry out." The old lady immediately answered: "Thank you. Rely upon me. Upon my soul I will be quiet." We were then all tilted down together in a corner of the carriage, and stopped. I said to them thereupon: "You may be sure nothing worse can happen. Our danger *must* be over. Will you remain here without stirring, while I get out of the window?" They both answered quite collectedly, "Yes,"

* This was a circular note which he sent in answer to innumerable letters of inquiry, after the accident.

and I got out without the least notion what had happened. Fortunately I got out with great caution and stood upon the step. Looking down I saw the bridge gone, and nothing below me but the line of rail. Some people in the two other compartments were madly trying to plunge out of window, and had no idea that there was an open swampy field fifteen feet down below them, and nothing else! The two guards (one with his face cut) were running up and down on the down side of the bridge (which was not torn up) quite wildly. I called out to them: "Look at me. Do stop an instant and look at me, and tell me whether you don't know me." One of them answered: "We know you very well, Mr. Dickens." "Then," I said, "my good fellow, for God's sake give me your key, and send one of those labourers here, and I'll empty this carriage." We did it quite safely, by means of a plank or two, and when it was done I saw all the rest of the train, except the two baggage vans, down in the stream. I got into the carriage again for my brandy flask, took off my travelling hat for a basin, climbed down the brickwork, and filled my hat with water.

Suddenly I came upon a staggering man covered with blood (I think he must have been flung clean out of his carriage), with such a frightful cut across the skull that I couldn't bear to look at him. I poured some water over his face and gave him some drink, then gave him some brandy, and laid him down on the grass, and he said, "I am gone," and died afterwards. Then I stumbled over a lady lying on her back against a little pollard-tree, with the blood streaming over her face (which was lead colour) in a number of distinct little streams from the head. I asked her if she could swallow a little brandy and she just nodded, and I gave her some and left her for somebody else. The next time I passed her she was dead. Then a man, examined at the inquest yesterday (who evidently had not the least remembrance of what really passed) came running up to me and implored me to help him find his wife, who was afterwards found dead. No imagination can conceive the ruin of the carriages, or the extraordinary weights under which the people were lying, or the complications into which they were twisted up among iron and wood, and mud and water.

I don't want to be examined at the inquest and I don't want to write about it. I could do no good either way, and I could only seem to speak about myself, which, of course, I would rather not do. I am keeping very quiet here. I have a—I don't know what to call it—constitutional (I suppose) presence of mind, and was not in the least fluttered at the time. I instantly remembered that I had the MS. of a number with me, and clambered back into the carriage for it. But in writing these scanty words of recollection I feel the shake and am obliged to stop.

Ever faithfully.

GAD'S HILL PLACE, HIGHAM BY ROCHESTER, KENT,
Saturday, Seventeenth June, 1865.*

Mr. Walter Jones.

SIR,

I beg you to assure the Committee of the Newsvendors' Benevolent and Provident Institution, that I have been deeply affected by their special remembrance of me in my late escape from death or mutilation, and that I thank them with my whole heart.

Faithfully yours and theirs.

GAD'S HILL, *Sunday, Eighteenth June,* 1865.

Mrs. Hulkes.

MY DEAR MRS. 'HULKES,

I return *The Examiner* with many thanks. The account is true, except that I *had* brandy. By an extraordinary chance I had a bottle and a half with me. I slung the half-bottle round my neck. But I can understand the describer (whoever he is) making the mistake in perfect good faith, and supposing that I called for brandy, when I really called to the others who were helping: "I have brandy here." The Mr. Dickenson mentioned had changed places with a Frenchman, who did not like the window down, a few minutes before the accident. The Frenchman was killed, and a labourer and I got Mr. Dickenson out of a most extraordinary heap of dark ruins, in which he was jammed upside down. He was bleeding at the eyes, ears, nose, and mouth; but he didn't seem to know that afterwards, and of course I didn't tell him. In the moment of going over the viaduct the whole of his pockets were shaken empty! He had no watch, no chain, no money, no pocket-book, no handkerchief, when we got him out. He had been choking a quarter of an hour when I heard him groaning. If I had not had the brandy to give him at the moment, I think he would have been done for. As it was, I brought him up to London in the carriage with me, and couldn't make him believe he was hurt. He was the first person whom the brandy saved. As I ran back to the carriage for the whole full bottle, I saw the first two people I had helped lying dead. A bit of shade from the hot sun, into which we got the unhurt ladies, soon had as many dead in it as living.

Faithfully yours always.

* This letter was written in reply to the Committee's congratulations to Charles Dickens upon his escape from this accident.

Mr. Arthur
Ryland.

GAD'S HILL PLACE, HIGHAM BY ROCHESTER, KENT,
Wednesday, Twenty-first June, 1865.

MY DEAR MR. RYLAND,

I need not assure you that I regard the unanimous desire of the Town Council Committee as a great honour, and that I feel the strongest interest in the occasion, and the strongest wish to associate myself with it.

But, after careful consideration, I most unwillingly come to the conclusion that I must decline. At the time in question I shall, please God, either have just finished, or be just finishing, my present book. Country rest and reflection will then be invaluable to me, before casting about for Christmas. I am a little shaken in my nervous system by the terrible and affecting incidents of the late railway accident, from which I bodily escaped. I am withdrawing myself from engagements of all kinds, in order that I may pursue my story with the comfortable sense of being perfectly free while it is a-doing, and when it is done. The consciousness of having made this engagement would, if I were to make it, render such sense incomplete, and so open the way to others. This is the real state of the case, and the whole reason for my declining.

Faithfully yours always.

Mrs. F.
Lehmann.

GAD'S HILL PLACE, HIGHAM BY ROCHESTER, KENT,
Tuesday, Twenty-seventh June, 1865.

DEAR MRS. LEHMANN,

Come (with self and partner) on either of the days you name, and you will be heartily welcomed by the humble youth who now addresses you, and will then cast himself at your feet.

I am quite right again, I thank God, and have even got my voice back; I most unaccountably brought somebody else's out of that terrible scene. The directors have sent me a Resolution of Thanks for assistance to the unhappy passengers.

With kind regards to Lehmann, ever yours.

Mr. Percy
Fitzgerald.

OFFICE OF "ALL THE YEAR ROUND,"
Friday, Seventh July, 1865.

MY DEAR FITZGERALD,

I shall be delighted to see you at Gad's Hill on Sunday, and I hope you will bring a bag with you and will not think of returning to London at night.

We are a small party just now, for my daughter Mary has been decoyed to Andover for the election week, in the Conservative interest; think of my feelings as a Radical parent! The wrong-headed member and his wife are the friends with whom she hunts, and she helps to receive (and *deceive*) the voters, which is very awful!

But in the week after next we shall be in great croquet force. I shall hope to persuade you to come back to us then for a few days, and we will try to make you some amends for a dull Sunday. Turn it over in your mind and try to manage it.

Sincerely yours ever.

GAD'S HILL, *Wednesday, Twelfth July*, 1865. Professor Owen, F.R.S.

MY DEAR OWEN,

Studying the gorilla last night for the twentieth time, it suddenly came into my head that I had never thanked you for that admirable treatise. This is to bear witness to my blushes and repentance. If you knew how much interest it has awakened in me, and how often it has set me a-thinking, you would consider me a more thankless beast than any gorilla that ever lived. But happily you do *not* know, and I am not going to tell you.

Believe me, ever faithfully yours.

GAD'S HILL PLACE, HIGHAM BY ROCHESTER, KENT, Sir Edward Bulwer Lytton.
Thursday, Twentieth July, 1865.

MY DEAR BULWER LYTTON,

I am truly sorry to reply to your kind and welcome note that we cannot come to Knebworth on a visit at this time: firstly, because I am tied by the leg to my book. Secondly, because my married daughter and her husband are with us. Thirdly, because my two boys are at home for their holidays.

But if you would come out of that murky electioneering atmosphere and come to us, you don't know how delighted we should be. You should have your own way as completely as though you were at home. You should have a cheery room, and you should have a Swiss châlet all to yourself to write in. *Smoking regarded as a personal favour to the family.* Georgina is so insupportably vain on account of being a favourite of yours, that you might find *her* a drawback; but nothing else would turn out in that way, I hope.

Won't you manage it? *Do* think of it. If, for instance, you would come back with us on that Guild Saturday. I have turned the house upside down and inside out since you were here, and have carved new rooms out of places then non-existent. Pray do think of it, and do manage it. I should be heartily pleased.

I hope you will find the purpose and the plot of my book very plain when you see it as a whole piece. I am looking forward to sending you the proofs complete about the end of next month. It is all sketched out and I am working hard on it, giving it all the pains possible to be bestowed on a labour of love. Your critical opinion two months in advance of the public will be invaluable to me. For you know what store I set by it, and how I think over a hint from you.

I notice the latest piece of poisoning ingenuity in Pritchard's case. When he had made his medical-student boarders sick, by poisoning the family food, he then quietly walked out, took an emetic, and made himself sick. This with a view to ask them, in examination on a possible trial, whether he did not present symptoms at the time like the rest?—A question naturally asked for him and answered in the affirmative. From which I get at the fact.

If your constituency don't bring you in they deserve to lose you, and may the gods continue to confound them! I shudder at the thought of such life as political life. Would there not seem to be something horribly rotten in the system of it, when one stands amazed how any man—not forced into it by position, as you are—can bear to live it?

But the private life here is my point, and again I urge upon you. Do think of it, and Do come.

I want to tell you how I have been impressed by the "Boatman." It haunts me as only a beautiful and profound thing can. The lines are always running in my head, as the river runs with me.

Ever affectionately.

The
Lord John
Russell.

GAD'S HILL PLACE, HIGHAM BY ROCHESTER, KENT,
Wednesday, Sixteenth August, 1865.

MY DEAR LORD RUSSELL,

Mr. Dallas, who is a candidate for the Scotch professional chair left vacant by Aytoun's death, has asked me if I would object to introduce to you the first volume of a book he has in the press with my publishers, on "The Gay Science of Art and Criticism." I have replied I would *not* object, as I have read as many of the sheets as I could get, with extreme pleasure, and as I know you will find it a very winning and brilliant piece of writing. Therefore he will send the proofs of the volume to you as soon as he can get them from the printer (at about the end of this week I take it), and if you read them you will not be hard upon me for bearing the responsibility of his doing so, I feel assured.

I suppose Mr. Dallas to have some impression that his pleasing you with his book might advance his Scottish suit. But all I know is, that he is a gentleman of great attainments and erudition, much distinguished as the writer of the best critical literary pieces in *The Times*, and thoroughly versed in the subjects which Professor Aytoun represented officially.

I beg to send my regard to Lady Russell and all the house, and am ever, my dear Lord Russell,

Your faithful and obliged.

P.S.—I am happy to report that my sailor-boy's captain, relinquishing his ship on sick leave, departs from the mere form of certificate given to all the rest, and adds that his obedience to orders is remarkable, and that he is a highly intelligent and promising young officer.

HÔTEL DU HELDER, PARIS,
Wednesday, Thirteenth September, 1865.

Mr. Marcus Stone.

MY DEAR MARCUS,

I leave here to-morrow, and propose going to the office by tidal train *next Saturday evening*. The sooner I can know about the subjects you take for illustration the better, as I can then fill the list of illustrations to the second volume for the printer, and enable him to make up his last sheet. Necessarily that list is now left blank, as I cannot give him the titles of the subjects, not knowing them myself.

It has been fearfully hot on this side, but is something cooler.

Ever affectionately yours.

P.S.—On glancing over this note, I find it very like the king's love-letter in "Ruy Blas." "Madam, there is a high wind. I have shot six wolves."

I think the frontispiece to the second volume should be the dustyard with the three mounds, and Mr. Boffin digging up the Dutch bottle, and Venus restraining Wegg's ardour to get at him. Or Mr. Boffin might be coming down with the bottle, and Venus might be dragging Wegg out of the way as described.

OFFICE OF "ALL THE YEAR ROUND,"
Saturday, Twenty-third September, 1865.

Mr. Percy Fitzgerald.

MY DEAR FITZGERALD,

I cannot thank you too much for Sultan. He is a noble fellow, has fallen into the ways of the family with a grace and dignity that denote the gentleman, and came down to the railway a day or two since to welcome me home (it was our first meeting), with a profound absence of interest in my individual opinion of him which captivated me completely. I am going home to-day to take him about the country, and improve his acquaintance. You will find a perfect understanding between us, I hope, when you next come to Gad's Hill. (He has only swallowed Bouncer once, and temporarily.)

Your hint that you were getting on with your story and liked it was more than golden intelligence to me in foreign parts. The intensity of the heat, both in Paris and the provinces, was such that I found nothing else so refreshing in the course of my rambles.

With many more thanks for the dog than my sheet of paper would hold,

Believe me, ever very faithfully yours.

Mrs.
Procter.

GAD'S HILL PLACE, HIGHAM BY ROCHESTER, KENT,
Twenty-sixth September, 1865.

MY DEAR MRS. PROCTER,

I have written the little introduction, and have sent it to my printer, in order that you may read it without trouble. But if you would like to keep the few pages of MS., of course they are yours.

It is brief, and I have aimed at perfect simplicity, and an avoidance of all that your beloved Adelaide would have wished avoided. Do not expect too much from it. If there should be anything wrong in fact, or anything that you would like changed for any reason, *of course you will tell me so,* and of course you will not deem it possible that you can trouble me by making any such request most freely.

You will probably receive the proof either on Friday or Saturday. Don't write to me until you have read it.

Ever your affectionate Friend.

Mr. Edmund
Yates.

HÔTEL DU HELDER, PARIS,
Saturday, Thirtieth September, 1865.

MY DEAR EDMUND,

The heat has been excessive on this side of the Channel, and I got a slight sunstroke last Thursday, and was obliged to be doctored and put to bed for a day ; but, thank God, I am all right again. The man who sells the *tisane* on the Boulevards can't keep the flies out of his glasses, and as he wears them on his red velvet bands, the flies work themselves into the ends of the tumblers, trying to get through and tickle the man. If fly life were long enough, I think they would at last. Three paving blouses came to work at the corner of this street last Monday, pulled up a bit of road, sat down to look at it, and fell asleep. On Tuesday one of the blouses spat on his hands and seemed to be going to begin, but didn't. The other two have shown no sign of life whatever.

This morning the industrious one ate a loaf. You may rely upon this as the latest news from the French capital.

Faithfully ever.

GAD'S HILL,
Sunday, Twenty-ninth October, 1865.

Mrs. Procter.

MY DEAR MRS. PROCTER,

The beautiful table-cover was a most cheering surprise to me when I came home last night, and I lost not a moment in finding a table for it, where it stands in a beautiful light and a perfect situation. Accept my heartiest thanks for a present on which I shall set a peculiar and particular value.

Enclosed is the MS. of the introduction. The printers have cut it across and mended it again, because I always expect them to be quick, and so they distribute my "copy" among several hands, and apparently not very clean ones in this instance.

Odd as the poor butcher's feeling appears, I think I can understand it. Much as he would not have liked his boy's grave to be without a tombstone, had he died ashore and had a grave, so he can't bear him to drift to the depths of the ocean unrecorded.

Ever affectionately yours.

GAD'S HILL PLACE, HIGHAM BY ROCHESTER, KENT,
Friday, Third November, 1865.

Mr. W. B. Rye.*

DEAR SIR,

I beg you to accept my cordial thanks for your curious "Visits to Rochester." As I peeped about its old corners with interest and wonder when I was a very little child, few people can find a greater charm in that ancient city than I do.

Believe me, yours faithfully and obliged.

26, WELLINGTON STREET,
Monday, Sixth November, 1865.

Mr. William Charles Kent.

MY DEAR KENT,

No, I *won't* write in this book, because I have sent another to the binder's for you.

I have been unwell with a relaxed throat, or I should have written to you sooner to thank you for your dedication, to assure you that it heartily, most heartily, gratifies me, as the sincere tribute of a true and generous heart, and to tell you that I have been charmed with your book itself.† I am proud of having given a name to anything so picturesque, so sympathetic and spirited.

I hope and believe the "Doctor" is nothing but a good 'un.

---

* Late keeper of printed books at the British Museum, now of Exeter.
† "Footprints on the Road."

He has perfectly astonished Forster, who writes : " Neither good, gooder, nor goodest, but super-excellent ; all through there is such a relish of you at your best, as I could not have believed in, after a long story."

Ever affectionately.

GAD'S HILL PLACE, HIGHAM BY ROCHESTER, KENT,
Thirteenth November, 1865.

MY DEAR CERJAT,

Having achieved my book and my Christmas number, and having shaken myself after two years' work, I send you my annual greeting. How are you ? Asthmatic, I know you will reply ; but as my poor father (who was asthmatic, too, and the jolliest of men) used philosophically to say, " one must have something wrong, I suppose, and I like to know what it is."

In England we are groaning under the brigandage of the butcher, which is being carried to that height that I think I foresee resistance on the part of the middle-class, and some combination in perspective for abolishing the middle-man, whensoever he turns up (which is everywhere) between producer and consumer. The cattle plague is the butcher's stalking-horse, and it is unquestionably worse than it was ; but seeing that the great majority of creatures lost or destroyed have been cows, and likewise that the rise in butchers' meat bears no reasonable proportion to the market prices of the beasts, one comes to the conclusion that the public is done. The commission has ended very weakly and ineffectually, as such things in England rather frequently do ; and everybody writes to *The Times*, and nobody does anything else.

If the Americans don't embroil us in a war before long it will not be their fault. What with their swagger and bombast, what with their claims for indemnification, what with Ireland and Fenianism, and what with Canada, I have strong apprehensions. With a settled animosity towards the French usurper, I believe him to have always been sound in his desire to divide the States against themselves, and that we were unsound and wrong in "letting I dare not wait upon I would." The Jamaica insurrection is another hopeful piece of business. That platform-sympathy with the black—or the native, or the devil—afar off, and that platform indifference to our own countrymen at enormous odds in the midst of bloodshed and savagery, makes me stark wild. Only the other day, here was a meeting of jawbones of asses at Manchester, to censure the Jamaica Governor for his manner of putting down the insurrection ! So we are badgered about New Zealanders and Hottentots, as if they were identical with men in clean shirts at Camberwell, and were to be bound by pen and ink accordingly. So Exeter Hall holds us in mortal submission to missionaries, who (Livingstone always excepted) are perfect nuisances, and leave every place worse than they found it.

Of all the many evidences that are visible of our being ill-governed, no one is so remarkable to me as our ignorance of what is going on under our Government. What will future generations think of that enormous Indian Mutiny being ripened without suspicion, until whole regiments arose and killed their officers? A week ago, red tape, half bouncing and half pooh-poohing what it bounced at, would have scouted the idea of a Dublin jail not being able to hold a political prisoner. But for the blacks in Jamaica being over-impatient and before their time, the whites might have been exterminated, without a previous hint or suspicion that there was anything amiss. *Laissez aller*, and Britons never, never, never !———

Meantime, if your honour were in London, you would see a great embankment rising high and dry out of the Thames on the Middlesex shore, from Westminster Bridge to Blackfriars. A really fine work, and really getting on. Moreover, a great system of drainage. Another really fine work, and likewise really getting on. Lastly, a muddle of railways in all directions possible and impossible, with no general public scheme, no general public super-vision, enormous waste of money, no fixable responsibility, no accountability but under Lord Campbell's Act. I think of that accident in which I was preserved. Before the most furious and notable train in the four-and-twenty hours, the head of a gang of workmen takes up the rails. That train changes its time every day as the tide changes, and that head workman is not provided by the railway company with any clock or watch! Lord Shaftes-bury wrote to me to ask me what I thought of an obligation on railway companies to put strong walls to all bridges and viaducts. I told him, of course, that the force of such a shock would carry away anything that any company could set up, and I added: "Ask the minister what *he* thinks about the votes of the railway interest in the House of Commons, and about his being afraid to lay a finger on it with an eye to his majority."

I seem to be grumbling, but I am in the best of humours. All goes well with me and mine, thank God.

Last night my gardener came upon a man in the garden and fired. The man returned the compliment by kicking him in the groin and causing him great pain. I set off with a great mastiff-bloodhound I have, in pursuit. Couldn't find the evil-doer, but had the greatest difficulty in preventing the dog from tearing two policemen down.   They were coming towards us with professional mystery, and he was in the air on his way to the throat of an eminently respectable constable when I caught him.

It has been blowing here tremendously for a fortnight, but to-day is like a spring day, and plenty of roses are growing over the labourers' cottages.   The *Great Eastern* lies at her moorings beyond the window where I write these words; looks very dull and unpromising.   A dark column of smoke from Chatham Dockyard, where the iron shipbuilding is in progress, has a greater significance in it, I fancy.

*   *   *   *   *

Miss Dickens.

GAD'S HILL PLACE, HIGHAM BY ROCHESTER, KENT,
Tuesday, Fourteenth November, 1865.

MY DEAREST MAMIE,

As you want to know my views of the Sphinx, here they are.   But I have only seen it once; and it is so extraordinarily well done, that it ought to be observed closely several times.

Anyone who attentively notices the flower trick will see that the two little high tables hung with drapery cover each a trap. Each of those tables, during that trick, hides a confederate, who changes the paper cone twice.   When the cone has been changed as often as is required, the trap is closed and the table can be moved.

When the curtain is removed for the performance of the Sphinx trick, there is a covered, that is draped table on the stage, which is never seen before or afterwards.   In front of the middle of it, and between it and the audience, stands one of those little draped tables covering a trap; this is a third trap in the centre of the stage.   The box for the head is then upon IT, and the conjurer takes it off and shows it.   The man whose head is afterwards shown in that box is, I conceive, in the table; that is to say, is lying on his chest in the thickness of the table, in an extremely constrained attitude.   To get him into the table, and to enable him to use the trap in the table through which his head comes into the box, the two hands of a confederate are necessary.   That confederate comes up a trap, and stands in the space afforded by the interval below the stage and the height of the little draped table! his back is towards the audience.   The moment he has assisted the hidden man sufficiently, he closes the trap, and the conjurer then immediately removes the little draped table, and also the drapery of the larger table; when he places the box on the last-named table *with the slide on* for the head to come into it, he stands with his back to the audience and his face to the box, and masks the box considerably to facilitate the insertion of the head.   As soon as he knows the head to be in its place, he undraws the slide. When the verses have been spoken and the trick is done, he loses no time in replacing the slide.. The curtain is then immediately dropped, because the man cannot otherwise be got out of the table, and has no doubt had quite enough of it. With kindest regards to all at Penton,

Ever your most affectionate.

GAD'S HILL,
Thursday, Thirtieth November, 1865.

Mr. Percy
Fitzgerald.

MY DEAR FITZGERALD,

I should have answered your last note long ago but for having been perpetually occupied.

That notice of the ship broker's garden takes my fancy strongly. If I had not been already at work upon the Xmas No. when you suggested it to me, I think I must have tried my hand upon it. As it is, I often revert to it, and go about it and about it, and pat it into new forms, much as the buttermen in the shops (who have something of a literary air at their wooden desks) pat the butter. I have been vexed by not being able to get your story into Dr. Marigold. I tried it again and again, but *could not* adapt its length to the other requirements of the No. Once, I sent it; but I was not easy afterwards, and thought it best to restore the excision, and leave the whole for a regular No. The difficulty of fitting and adjusting this unusual job, is hardly to be imagined without trying it. For the rest, I hope you will like the Doctor—and know him at once—for he speaks for himself in the first paper and the last. Also I recommend to your perusal a certain ghost story, headed "To be taken with a grain of salt." *

Sultan has grown immensely, and is a sight. But he is so accursedly fierce towards other dogs, that I am obliged to take him out muzzled. Also he has an invincible repugnance to soldiers, which, in a military country, is inconvenient. Such is the spirit of the dog that, with his muzzle tight on, he dashed into the heart of a company in heavy marching order (only the other day), and pulled down an objectionable private. Except under such provocations, he is as gentle and docile with me, as a dog can possibly be. Last night, the gardener fired at some man in the garden, upon whom he came suddenly, and who attacked him in a desperate manner. I immediately turned out, unloosed Sultan, and hunted the vagabond. We couldn't get hold of him, but the intelligence of the dog, and the delighted confidence he imparted to me, as he tumbled across country in the dark, were quite enchanting. Two policemen appearing in the distance and making

* This story was written by Mr. Charles Collins.

2 Q

a professional show of stealthiness, had a narrow escape. As he was in the act of flying at them, I was obliged to hold him round the neck with both arms (like the little boy in the snow with the St. Bernard dog, grown up), and call to the Force to vanish in an inglorious manner.

A friend has sent me from America a thoroughbred black Newfoundland dog, since you were here. Sultan (who hates him mortally), he, Linda, I, and three or four small dogs in the nature of canine parasites and toadies, make a show in the lanes and roads which I specially beseech you to come and see. We only want the renowned dog Cæsar to make us matchless.

I hope you are in force and spirits with your new story.

My dear Fitzgerald,

Faithfully yours always.

1866.

NARRATIVE.

THE furnished house hired by Charles Dickens in the spring of this year was in Southwick Place, Hyde Park.

Having entered into negotiations with the Messrs. Chappell for a series of readings to be given in London, in the English provinces, in Scotland and Ireland, Charles Dickens had no leisure for more than his usual editorial work for "All the Year Round." He contributed four parts to the Christmas number, which was entitled "Mugby Junction."

For the future all his English readings were given in connection with the Messrs. Chappell, and never in all his career had he more satisfactory or more pleasant business relations than those connected with these gentlemen. Moreover, out of this connection sprang a sincere friendship on both sides.

Mr. Dolby is so constantly mentioned in future letters, that they themselves will tell of the cordial companionship which existed between Charles Dickens and this able and obliging "manager."

We give in this year the only letter we have been able to procure to Mr. Robert Browning, for the sake of having the name of the poet in our work, and also because he was a dear and valued friend.

The letter to "Lily" was in answer to a child's letter from Miss Lily Benzon, inviting Charles Dickens to a birthday party.

The play alluded to in the letter to M. Fechter was called "A Long Strike," and was performed at the Lyceum Theatre.

Mr. Rusden was at this time Clerk to the House of Parliament, in Melbourne. He was the kindest of friends to the two sons of Charles Dickens, in Australia, from the time that the elder of the two first went out there. And Charles Dickens had the most grateful regard for him, and maintained a frequent correspondence with him, although they never met.

The "Sultan" mentioned in the letters of last year and this year to Mr. Fitzgerald was a noble Irish bloodhound, presented by that gentleman to Charles Dickens. The story of the dog's death is told in a letter to M. De Cerjat, written on New Year's Day 1867.

OFFICE OF "ALL THE YEAR ROUND,"
Saturday, Sixth January, 1866.

Miss Mary Boyle.

MY DEAR MARY,

Feeling pretty certain that I shall never answer your letter unless I answer it at once (I got it this morning), here goes!

I did not dramatise "The Master of Ravenswood," though I did a good deal towards and about the piece, having an earnest desire to put Scott, for once, upon the stage in his own gallant manner. It is *an enormous success,* and increases in attraction nightly. I have never seen the people in all parts of the house so leaning forward, in lines sloping towards the stage, earnestly and intently attentive, as while the story gradually unfolds itself. But the astonishing circumstance of all is, that Miss Leclercq (never thought of for Lucy till all other Lucies had failed) is marvellously good, highly pathetic, and almost unrecognisable in person! What note it touches in her, always dumb until now, I do not pretend to say, but there is no one on the stage who could play the contract scene better, or more simply and naturally, and I find it impossible to see it without crying! Almost everyone plays well, the whole is exceedingly picturesque, and there is scarcely a movement throughout, or a look, that is not indicated by Scott. So you get a life romance with beautiful illustrations, and I do not expect ever again to see a book take up its bed and walk in like manner.

I am charmed to learn that you have had a freeze out of my ghost story. It rather did give me a shiver up the back in the writing. "Dr. Marigold" has just now accomplished his two hundred thousand. My only other news about myself is that I am doubtful whether to read or not in London this season. If I decide to do it at all, I shall probably do it on a large scale.

Many happy years to you, my dear Mary. So prays

Your ever affectionate

Jo.

Mr. William
Charles
Kent.

GAD'S HILL,
Thursday, Eighteenth January, 1866.

MY DEAR KENT,

    I cannot tell you how grieved we all are here to know that you are suffering again. Your patient tone, however, and the hopefulness and forbearing of Fergusson's * course, gives us some reassurance. Apropos of which latter reference I dined with Fergusson at the Lord Mayor's, last Tuesday, and had a grimly-distracted impulse upon me to defy the toast-master and rush into a speech about him and his noble art, when I sat pining under the imbecility of constitutional and corporational idiots. I did seize him for a moment by the hair of his head (in proposing the Lady Mayoress), and derived some faint consolation from the company's response to the reference. O! no man will ever know under what provocation to contradiction and a savage yell of repudiation I suffered at the hands of ———, feebly complacent in the uniform of Madame Tussaud's own military waxers, and almost the worst speaker I ever heard in my life! Mary and Georgina, sitting on either side of me, urged me to "look pleasant." I replied in expressions not to be repeated. Shee (the judge) was just as good and graceful, as he (the member) was bad and gawky.

    Bulwer's "Lost Tales of Miletus" is a most noble book! He is an extraordinary fellow, and fills me with admiration and wonder.

    It is of no use writing to you about yourself, my dear Kent, because you are likely to be tired of that constant companion, and so I have gone scratching (with an exceedingly bad pen) about and about you. But I come back to you to let you know that the reputation of this house as a convalescent hospital stands (like the house itself) very high, and that testimonials can be produced from credible persons who have recovered health and spirits here swiftly. Try us, only try us, and we are content to stake the reputation of the establishment on the result.

                  Ever affectionately yours.

Mr. John
Forster.

OFFICE OF "ALL THE YEAR ROUND,"
Friday, Twenty-sixth January, 1866.

MY DEAR FORSTER,

    I most heartily hope that your doleful apprehensions will prove unfounded. These changes from muggy weather to slight sharp frost, and back again, touch weak places, as I find by my own foot; but the touch goes by. May it prove so with you!

* Sir William Fergusson, the great surgeon.

Yesterday Captain ——, Captain ——, and Captain ——, dined at Gad's. They are, all three, naval officers of the highest reputation. —— is supposed to be the best sailor in our Service. I said I had been remarking at home, *à propos* of the *London*, that I knew of no shipwreck of a large strong ship (not carrying weight of guns) in the open sea, and that I could find none such in the shipwreck books. They all agreed that the unfortunate Captain Martin *must* have been unacquainted with the truth as to what can and what can not be done with a Steamship having rigging and canvas; and that no sailor would dream of turning a ship's stern to such a gale—*unless his vessel could run faster than the sea.* —— said (and the other two confirmed) that the *London* was the better for everything that she lost aloft in such a gale, and that with her head kept to the wind by means of a storm topsail— which is hoisted from the deck and requires no man to be sent aloft, and can be set under the worst circumstances—the disaster could not have occurred. If he had no such sail, he could have improvised it, even of hammocks and the like. They said that under a Board of Enquiry into the wreck, any efficient witness must of necessity state this as the fact, and could not possibly avoid the conclusion that the seamanship was utterly bad; and as to the force of the wind, for which I suggested allowance, they all had been in West Indian hurricanes and in Typhoons, and had put the heads of their ships to the wind under the most adverse circumstances.

I thought you might be interested in this, as you have no doubt been interested in the case. They had a great respect for the unfortunate Captain's character, and for his behaviour when the case was hopeless, but they had not the faintest doubt that he lost the ship and those two hundred and odd lives.

> Ever affectionately.

GAD'S HILL, *Friday, Second February,* 1866.   Mr. Percy Fitzgerald.

MY DEAR FITZGERALD,

I ought to have written to you days and days ago, to thank you for your charming book on Charles Lamb, to tell you with what interest and pleasure I read it as soon as it came here, and to add that I was honestly affected (far more so than your modesty will readily believe) by your intimate knowledge of those touches of mine concerning childhood.

Let me tell you now that I have not in the least cooled, after all, either as to the graceful sympathetic book, or as to the part in it with which I am honoured. It has become a matter of real feeling with me, and I postponed its expression because I couldn't satisfactorily get it out of myself, and at last I came to the conclusion that it must be left in.

My dear Fitzgerald, faithfully yours always.

Miss
Hogarth.

OFFICE OF "ALL THE YEAR ROUND,"
Friday, Ninth February, 1866.

MY DEAREST GEORGY,

*   *   *   *   *

Frank Beard wrote me word that with such a pulse as I described, an examination of the heart was absolutely necessary, and that I had better make an appointment with him alone for the purpose. This I did. I was not at all disconcerted, for I knew well beforehand that the effect could not possibly be without that one cause at the bottom of it. There seems to be degeneration of some functions of the heart. It does not contract as it should. So I have got a prescription of iron, quinine, and digitalis, to set it a-going, and send the blood more quickly through the system. If it should not seem to succeed on a reasonable trial, I will then propose a consultation with someone else. Of course I am not so foolish as to suppose that all my work can have been achieved without *some* penalty, and I have noticed for some time a decided change in my buoyancy and hopefulness—in other words, in my usual " tone."

*   *   *   *   *

Mr. R. M.
Ross.*

GAD'S HILL PLACE, HIGHAM BY ROCHESTER, KENT,
Monday, Nineteenth February, 1866.

DEAR SIR,

I have the honour to acknowledge the receipt of your obliging letter enclosing a copy of the Resolution passed by the members of the St. George Club on my last past birthday. Do me the kindness to assure those friends of mine that I am touched to the heart by their affectionate remembrance, and that I highly esteem it. To have established such relations with readers of my books is a great happiness to me, and one that I hope never to forfeit by being otherwise than manfully and truly in earnest in my vocation.

I am, dear Sir,
Your faithful Servant.

* The honorary secretary of the St. George Club, Manchester.

OFFICE OF "ALL THE YEAR ROUND,"
Tuesday, Twentieth February, 1866.

MY DEAR MRS. BROOKFIELD,

Having gone through your MS. (which I should have done sooner, but that I have not been very well), I write these few following words about it. Firstly, with a limited reference to its unsuitability to these pages. Secondly, with a more enlarged reference to the merits of the story itself.

If you will take any part of it and cut it up (in fancy) into the small portions into which it would have to be divided here for only a month's supply, you will (I think) at once discover the impossibility of publishing it in weekly parts. The scheme of the chapters, the manner of introducing the people, the progress of the interest, the places in which the principal places fall, are all hopelessly against it. It would seem as though the story were never coming, and hardly ever moving. There must be a special design to overcome that specially trying mode of publication, and I cannot better express the difficulty and labour of it than by asking you to turn over any two weekly numbers of "A Tale of Two Cities," or "Great Expectations," or Bulwer's story, or Wilkie Collins', or Reade's, or "At the Bar," and notice how patiently and expressly the thing has to be planned for presentation in these fragments, and yet for afterwards fusing together as an uninterrupted whole.

Of the story itself I honestly say that I think highly. The style is particularly easy and agreeable, infinitely above ordinary writing, and sometimes reminds me of Mrs. Inchbald at her best. The characters are remarkably well observed, and with a rare mixture of delicacy and truthfulness. I observe this particularly in the brother and sister, and in Mrs. Neville. But it strikes me that you constantly hurry your narrative (and yet without getting on) *by telling it, in a sort of impetuous breathless way, in your own person, when the people should tell it and act it for themselves.* My notion always is, that when I have made the people to play out the play, it is, as it were, their business to do it, and not mine. Then, unless you really have led up to a great situation like Basil's death, you are bound in art to make more of it. Such a scene should form a chapter of itself. Impressed upon the reader's memory, it would go far to make the fortune of the book. Suppose yourself telling that affecting incident in a letter to a friend. Wouldn't you describe how you went through the life and stir of the streets and roads to the sick-room? Wouldn't you say what kind of room it was, what time of day it was, whether it was sunlight, starlight, or moonlight? Wouldn't you have a strong impression on your mind of how you were received, when you first met the look of the dying man, what strange contrasts were about you and struck you? I don't want you, in a novel, to present *yourself* to tell such things, but I want the things to be there. You make no more of the situation than the index might, or a descriptive playbill might in giving a summary of the tragedy under representation.

As a mere piece of mechanical workmanship, I think all your chapters should be shorter; that is to say, that they should be subdivided. Also, when you change from narrative to dialogue, or *vice versâ*, you should make the transition more carefully. Also, taking the pains to sit down and recall the principal landmarks in your story, you should then make them far more elaborate and conspicuous than the rest. Even with these changes I do not believe that the story would attract the attention due to it, if it were published even in such monthly portions as the space of "Fraser" would admit of. Even so brightened, it would not, to the best of my judgment, express itself piecemeal. It seems to me to be so constituted as to require to be read "off the reel." As a book in two volumes I think it would have good claims to success, and good chances of obtaining success. But I suppose the polishing I have hinted at (not a meretricious adornment, but positively necessary to good work and good art) to have been first thoroughly administered.

Now, don't hate me, if you can help it. I can afford to be hated by some people, but I am not rich enough to put you in possession of that luxury.

Ever faithfully yours.

Mr. R.
Browning.

6, SOUTHWICK PLACE, HYDE PARK,
Monday, Twelfth March, 1866.

MY DEAR BROWNING,

Will you dine here next Sunday at half-past six punctually, instead of with Forster? I am going to read Thirty times, in London and elsewhere, and as I am coming out with "Doctor Marigold," I had written to ask Forster to come on Sunday and hear me sketch him. Forster says (with his own boldness) that he is sure it would not bore you to have that taste of his quality after dinner. I should be delighted if this should prove true. But I give warning that in that case I shall exact a promise from you to come to St. James's Hall one evening in April or May, and hear "David Copperfield," my own particular favourite.

Ever affectionately yours.

ADELPHI, LIVERPOOL,
Friday, Thirteenth April, 1866.

MY DEAREST GEORGY,

    The reception at Manchester last night was quite a magnificent sight; the whole of the immense audience standing up and cheering. I thought them a little slow with "Marigold," but believe it was only the attention necessary in so vast a place. They gave a splendid burst at the end. And after "Nickleby" (which went to perfection), they set up such a call, that I was obliged to go in again. The unfortunate gasman, a very steady fellow, got a fall off a ladder and sprained his leg. He was put to bed in a public opposite, and was left there, poor man.

    This is the first very fine day we have had. I have taken advantage of it by crossing to Birkenhead and getting some air upon the water. It was fresh and beautiful.

    I send my best love to Mamie, and hope she is better. I am, of course, tired (the pull of "Marigold" upon one's energy, in the Free Trade Hall, was great); but I stick to my tonic, and feel, all things considered, in very good tone. The room here (I mean the hall) being my special favourite and extraordinarily easy, is *almost* a rest!

ADELPHI, LIVERPOOL,
Saturday, Fourteenth April, 1866.

MY DEAREST MAMIE,

    The police reported officially that three thousand people were turned away from the hall last night. I doubt if they were so numerous as that, but they carried in the outer doors and pitched into Dolby with great vigour. I need not add that every corner of the place was crammed. They were a very fine audience, and took enthusiastically every point in "Copperfield" and the "Trial." They made the reading a quarter of an hour longer than usual. One man advertised in the morning paper that he would give thirty shillings (double) for three stalls, but nobody would sell, and he didn't get in.

    Except that I cannot sleep, I really think myself in much better training than I had anticipated. A dozen oysters and a little champagne between the parts every night, constitute the best restorative I have ever yet tried. John appears low, but I don't know why. A letter comes for him daily; the hand is female; whether Smudger's, or a nearer one still and a dearer one, I don't know. So it may or may not be the cause of his gloom.

    "Miss Emily" of Preston is married to a rich cotton lord, rides in open carriages in gorgeous array, and is altogether splendid. With this effective piece of news I close

Miss
Hogarth.

GLASGOW, *Seventeenth April*, 1866.

We arrived here at ten yesterday evening. I don't think the journey shook me at all. Dolby provided a superb cold collation and "the best of drinks," and we dined in the carriage, and I made him laugh all the way.

Every precaution taken to prevent my platform from being captured as it was last time ; but I don't feel at all sure that it will not be stormed at one of the two readings. Wills is to do the genteel to-night at the stalls, and Dolby is to stem the shilling tide *if* he can. The poor gasman cannot come on, and we have got a new one here who is to go to Edinburgh with us. Of Edinburgh we know nothing, but as its first night has always been shady, I suppose it will stick to its antecedents.

I like to hear about Harness and his freshness. The rest has certainly done me good. I slept thoroughly well last night, and feel fresh. What to-night's work, and every night's work this week, may do contrariwise, remains to be seen.

Miss
Dickens.

WATERLOO HOTEL, EDINBURGH,
Wednesday, Eighteenth April, 1866.

We had a tremendous house again last night at Glasgow. Not only that, but they were a most brilliant and delicate audience, and took "Marigold" with a fine sense and quickness not to be surpassed. The shillings pitched into Dolby again, and one man writes a sensible letter in one of the papers this morning, showing to *my* satisfaction (?) that they really had, through the local agent, some cause of complaint. The thundering of applause last night was quite staggering, and my people checked off my reception by the minute-hand of a watch, and stared at one another, thinking I should never begin. I keep quite well, have happily taken to sleeping these last three nights ; and feel, all things considered, very little conscious of fatigue.

I am going to write a line by this post to Katie, from whom I have a note. I hope Harry's leg will now step out in the manner of the famous cork leg in the song.

Miss
Hogarth.

EDINBURGH, *Thursday, Nineteenth April*, 1866.

The house was more than twice better than any first night here previously. They were, as usual here, remarkably intelligent, and the reading went *brilliantly*. I have not sent up any newspapers, as they are generally so poorly written, that you may know beforehand all the commonplaces that they will write. But *The Scotsman* has so pretty an article this morning, and (so far as I know) so true a one, that I will try to post it to you, either from here or Glasgow. It is cold and wet here. Chang is living in this house. John (not knowing it) was rendered perfectly drivelling last night by meeting him on the stairs. The Tartar Dwarf is always twining himself upstairs sideways, and drinks a bottle of whisky per day, and is reported to be a surprising little villain.

WATERLOO HOTEL, EDINBURGH,
Friday, Twentieth April, 1866.

Miss Dickens.

No row at Glasgow last night. Great placards were posted about the town by the anxious Dolby, announcing that no money would be taken at the doors. This kept the crowd off. Two files of policemen and a double staff everywhere did the rest, and nothing could be better-tempered or more orderly. Tremendous enthusiasm with the "Carol" and "Trial." I was dead beat afterwards, but plucked up again, had some supper, slept well, and am quite right to-day. It is a bright day, and the express ride over from Glasgow was very pleasant.

I have a story to answer you and your aunt with. Before I left Southwick Place for Liverpool, I received a letter from Glasgow, saying, "Your little Emily has been woo'd and married and a'! since you last saw her;" and describing her house within a mile or two of the city, and asking me to stay there. I wrote the usual refusal, and supposed Mrs. —— to be some romantic girl whom I had joked with, perhaps at Allison's or where not. On the first night at Glasgow I received a bouquet from ——, and wore one of the flowers. This morning at the Glasgow station, —— appeared, and proved to be the identical Miss Emily, of whose marriage Dolby had told me on our coming through Preston. She was attired in magnificent raiment, and presented the happy ——.

DOWN HOTEL, CLIFTON, *Friday, Eleventh May*, 1866.

Miss Hogarth.

It has been very heavy work getting up at half-past six each morning after a heavy night, and I am not at all well to-day. We had a tremendous hall at Birmingham last night—two thousand one hundred people. I made a most ridiculous mistake. Had "Nickleby" on my list to finish with, instead of "Trial." Read "Nickleby" with great go, and the people remained. Went back again at ten and explained the accident, and said if they liked, I would give them the "Trial." They *did* like, and I had another half-hour of it in that enormous place.

My cold is no better. John fell off a platform about ten feet high yesterday, and fainted. He looks all the colours of the rainbow to-day, but does not seem much hurt beyond being puffed up one hand, arm, and side.

Miss Lily Benzon.*

GAD'S HILL PLACE, HIGHAM BY ROCHESTER, KENT,
Monday, Eighteenth June, 1866.

MY DEAR LILY,

I am sorry that I cannot come to read to you "The Boots at the Holly Tree Inn," as you ask me to do; but the truth is, that I am tired of reading at this present time, and have come into the country to rest and hear the birds sing. There are a good many birds, I daresay, in Kensington Palace Gardens, and upon my word and honour they are much better worth listening to than I am. So let them sing to you as hard as ever they can, while their sweet voices last (they will be silent when the winter comes); and very likely after you and I have eaten our next Christmas pudding and mince-pies, you and I and Uncle Harry may all meet together at St. James's Hall; Uncle Harry to bring you there, to hear the "Boots;" I to receive you there, and read the "Boots;" and you (I hope) to applaud very much, and tell me that you like the "Boots." So, God bless you and me, and Uncle Harry, and the "Boots," and long life and happiness to us all!

Your affectionate Friend.

P.S.—There's a flourish!

Lord Lytton.

GAD'S HILL,
Monday, Sixteenth July, 1866.

MY DEAR LYTTON,

First, let me congratulate you on the honour which Lord Derby has conferred upon the peerage. And next, let me thank you heartily for your kind letter.

I am very sorry to report that we are so encumbered with engagements in the way of visitors coming here that we cannot see our way to getting to Knebworth yet.

Mary and Georgina send you their kind regard, and hope that the delight of coming to see you is only deferred.

Fitzgerald will be so proud of your opinion of his "Mrs. Tillotson," and will (I know) derive such great encouragement from it, that I have faithfully quoted it, word for word, and sent it on to him in Ireland. He is a very clever fellow (you may remember, perhaps, that I brought him to Knebworth on the Guild day), and has charming sisters and an excellent position.

Ever affectionately yours.

* Now Mrs. Stuart Forster.

GAD'S HILL PLACE, HIGHAM BY ROCHESTER, KENT, Mr. B. W.
Monday, Thirteenth August, 1866. Procter.

MY DEAR PROCTER,

I have read your biography of Charles Lamb with inexpressible pleasure and interest. I do not think it possible to tell a pathetic story with a more unaffected and manly tenderness. And as to the force and vigour of the style, if I did not know you I should have made sure that there was a printer's error in the opening of your introduction, and that the word "seventy" occupied the place of "forty."

Let me, my dear friend, most heartily congratulate you on your achievement. It is not an ordinary triumph to do such justice to the memory of such a man. And I venture to add, that the fresh spirit with which you have done it impresses me as being perfectly wonderful.

Ever affectionately yours.

GAD'S HILL, Sir James
Monday, Twentieth August, 1866. Emerson
Tennent.

MY DEAR TENNENT,

I have been very much interested by your extract, and am strongly inclined to believe that the founder of the Refuge for Poor Travellers meant the kind of man to which it refers. Chaucer certainly meant the Pardonere to be a humbug, living on the credulity of the people. After describing the sham reliques he carried, he says :

> But with these relikes whanne that he found
> A poure personne dwelling up on lond
> Upon a day he gat him more moneye
> Than that the personne got in monthes tyme,
> And thus, with fained flattering and japes
> He made the personne, and the people, his apes.

And the worthy Watts (founder of the charity) may have had these very lines in his mind when he excluded such a man.

When I last heard from my boy he was coming to you, and was full of delight and dignity.* My midshipman has just been appointed to the *Bristol*, on the West Coast of Africa, and is on his voyage out to join her. I wish it was another ship and another station. She has been unlucky in losing men.

Faithfully yours ever.

* Henry F. Dickens.

M. Charles
Fechter.

GAD'S HILL,
Tuesday, Fourth September, 1866.

MY DEAR FECHTER,

This morning I received the play to the end of the telegraph scene, and I have since read it twice.

I clearly see the *ground* of Mr. Boucicault's two objections; but I do not see their *force*.

First, as to the writing. If the characters did not speak in a terse and homely way, their idea and language would be inconsistent with their dress and station, and they would lose, as characters, before the audience. The dialogue seems to be exactly what is wanted. Its simplicity (particularly in Mr. Boucicault's part) is often very effective; and throughout there is an honest, straight-to-the-purpose ruggedness in it, like the real life and the real people.

Secondly, as to the absence of the comic element. I really do not see how more of it could be got into the story, and I think Mr. Boucicault underrates the pleasant effect of his own part. The very notion of a sailor, whose life is not among those little courts and streets, and whose business does not lie with the monotonous machinery, but with the four wild winds, is a relief to me in reading the play. I am quite confident of its being an immense relief to the audience when they see the sailor before them, with an entirely different bearing, action, dress, complexion even, from the rest of the men. I would make him the freshest and airiest sailor that ever was seen; and through him I can distinctly see my way out of "the Black Country" into clearer air. (I speak as one of the audience, mind.) I should like something of this contrast to be expressed in the dialogue between the sailor and the Jew, in the second scene of the second act. Again, I feel Widdicomb's part (which is charming, and ought to make the whole house cry) most agreeable and welcome, much better than any amount in such a story, of mere comicality.

It is unnecessary to say that the play is done with a master's hand. Its closeness and movement are quite surprising. Its construction is admirable. I have the strongest belief in its making a great success. But I must add this proviso: I never saw a play so dangerously depending in critical places on strict natural propriety in the manner and perfection in the shaping of the small parts. Those small parts cannot take the play up, but they can let it down. I would not leave a hair on the head of one of them to the chance of the first night, but I would see, to the minutest particular, the make-up of every one of them at a night rehearsal.

Of course you are free to show this note to Mr. Boucicault, and I suppose you will do so ; let me throw out this suggestion to him and you. Might it not ease the way with the Lord Chamberlain's Office, and still more with the audience, when there are Manchester champions in it, if instead of "Manchester" you used a fictitious name ? When I did "Hard Times" I called the scene Coketown. Everybody knew what was meant, but every cotton-spinning town said it was the other cotton-spinning town.

Ever heartily.

Mr. Walter Thornbury.

"ALL THE YEAR ROUND" OFFICE,
Saturday, Fifteenth September, 1866.

MY DEAR THORNBURY,

In reference to your Shakespeare queries, I am not so much enamoured of the first and third subjects as I am of the Ariosto enquiry, which should be highly interesting. But if you have so got the matter in your mind, as that its execution would be incomplete and unsatisfactory to you unless you write all the three papers, then by all means write the three, and I will most gladly take them. For some years I have had so much pleasure in reading you, that I can honestly warrant myself as what actors call "a good audience."

The idea of old stories retold is decidedly a good one. I greatly like the notion of that series. Of course you know De Quincey's paper on the Ratcliffe Highway murderer ? Do you know also the illustration (I have it at Gad's Hill), representing the horrible creature as his dead body lay on a cart, with a piece of wood for a pillow, and a stake lying by, ready to be driven through him ?

I don't *quite* like the title, "The Social History of London." I should better like some title to the effect, "The History of London's Social Changes in so many Years." Such a title would promise more, and better express your intention. What do you think of taking for a first title, "London's Changes" ? You could then add the second title, "Being a History," etc.

I don't at all desire to fix a limit to the series of old stories retold. I would state the general intention at the beginning of the first paper, and go on like Banquo's line.

Don't let your London title remind people, by so much as the place of the word "civilisation," of Buckle. It seems a ridiculous caution, but the indolent part of the public (a large part !) on such points tumble into extraordinary mistakes.

Faithfully yours always.

Mr. Rusden.   *September*, 1866.

MY DEAR SIR,

Again I have to thank you very heartily for your kindness in writing to me about my son. The intelligence you send me concerning him is a great relief and satisfaction to my mind, and I cannot separate those feelings from a truly grateful recognition of the advice and assistance for which he is so much beholden to you, or from his strong desire to deserve your good opinion.

Believe me always, my dear Sir,

Your faithful and truly obliged.

Mr. Percy   GAD'S HILL, *Tuesday, Sixth November,* 1866.
Fitzgerald.   MY DEAR FITZGERALD,

It is always pleasant to me to hear from you, and I hope you will believe that this is not a mere fashion of speech.

Concerning the green covers, I find the leaves to be budding— on questionable newspaper authority; but, upon my soul, I have no other knowledge of their being in embryo! Really, I do not see a chance of my settling myself to such work until after I have accomplished forty-two readings, to which I stand pledged.

I hope to begin this series somewhere about the middle of January, in Dublin. Touching the details of the realisation of this hope, will you tell me in a line as soon as you can—*Is the exhibition room a good room for speaking in?*

Your mention of the late Sultan touches me nearly. He was the finest dog I ever saw, and between him and me there was a perfect understanding. But, to adopt the popular phrase, it was so very confidential that it "went no further." He would fly at anybody else with the greatest enthusiasm for destruction. He has broken loose (muzzled) and come home covered with blood, again and again. And yet he never disobeyed me, unless he had first laid hold of a dog.

You heard of his going to execution, evidently supposing the procession to be a party detached in pursuit of something to kill or eat? It was very affecting. And also of his bolting a blue-eyed kitten, and making me acquainted with the circumstance by his agonies of remorse (or indigestion)?

I cannot find out that there is anyone in Rochester (a sleepy old city) who has anything to tell about Garrick, except what is not true. His brother, the wine merchant, would be more in Rochester way, I think. How on earth do you find time to do all these books?

You make my hair stand on end; an agreeable sensation, for

I am charmed to find that I have any. Why don't you come yourself and look after Garrick? I shall be truly delighted to receive you.

My dear Fitzgerald, always faithfully yours.

GAD'S HILL,
Thursday, Twenty-seventh December, 1866.

DEAR MADAM,

You make an absurd, though common mistake, in supposing that any human creature can help you to be an authoress, if you cannot become one in virtue of your own powers. I know nothing about "impenetrable barriers," "outsiders," and "charmed circles." I know that anyone who can write what is suitable to the requirements of my own journal—for instance—is a person I am heartily glad to discover, and do not very often find. And I believe this to be no rare case in periodical literature. I cannot undertake to advise you in the abstract, as I number my unknown correspondents by the hundred. But if you offer anything to me for insertion in "All the Year Round," you may be sure that it will be honestly read, and that it will be judged by no test but its own merits and adaptability to those pages.

But I am bound to add that I do not regard successful fiction as a thing to be achieved in "leisure moments."

Faithfully yours.

GAD'S HILL PLACE, HIGHAM BY ROCHESTER, KENT,
Friday, Twenty-eighth December, 1866.

MY DEAREST MACREADY,

You will be interested in knowing that, encouraged by the success of summer cricket-matches, I got up a quantity of foot-races and rustic sports in my field here on the twenty-sixth last past: as I have never yet had a case of drunkenness, the landlord of The Falstaff had a drinking-booth on the ground. All the prizes I gave were in money, too. We had two thousand people here. Among the crowd were soldiers, navvies, and labourers of all kinds. Not a stake was pulled up, or a rope slackened, or one farthing's-worth of damage done. To every competitor (only) a printed bill of general rules was given, with the concluding words: "Mr. Dickens puts every man upon his honour to assist in preserving order." There was not a dispute all day, and they went away at sunset rending the air with cheers, and leaving every flag on a six-hundred yards' course as neat as they found it when the gates were opened at ten in the morning. Surely this is a bright sign in the neighbourhood of such a place as Chatham!

2 R

"Mugby Junction" turned, yesterday afternoon, the extraordinary number of two hundred and fifty thousand !

In the middle of next month I begin a new course of readings. If any of them bring me within reach of Cheltenham, with an hour to spare, I shall come on to you, even for that hour. More of this when I am afield and have my list.

I begin to discover in your riper years, that you have been secretly vain of your handwriting all your life. For I swear I see no change in it ! What it always was since I first knew it (a year or two !) it *is*. This I will maintain against all comers.

Ever affectionately, my dearest Macready.

1867.

NARRATIVE.

CHARLES DICKENS took no house in London this spring. He came to his office quarters at intervals, for the series of readings in town ; usually starting off again, on his country tour, the day after a London reading. From some passages in his letters to his daughter and sister-in-law during this country course, it will be seen that (though he made very light of the fact) the great exertion of this work, combined with incessant railway travelling, was beginning to tell upon his health, and he was frequently "heavily beaten" after reading at his best to an enthusiastic audience in a large hall.

During the short intervals between his journeys, he was as constantly and carefully at work upon the business of "All the Year Round" as if he had no other work on hand. A proof of this is given in a letter dated "Fifth February." It is written to a young man (the son of a friend), who wrote a long novel when far too juvenile for such a task, and had submitted it to Charles Dickens for his opinion, with a view to publication. In the midst of his own hard and engrossing occupation he read the book, and the letter which he wrote on the subject needs no remark beyond this, that the young writer received the adverse criticism with the best possible sense, and has since, in his literary profession, profited by the advice so kindly given.

At this time the proposals to Charles Dickens for reading in America, which had been perpetually renewed from the time of his first abandoning the idea, became so urgent and so tempting, that he found at last he must, at all events, give the subject his most serious consideration. He took counsel with his two confidential friends and advisers, Mr. John Forster and Mr. W. H. Wills. They were both, at first, strongly opposed to the undertaking, chiefly on the ground of the trial to his health and strength which it would involve. But they could not deny the counterbalancing advantages. And, after much deliberation it was resolved that Mr. George Dolby should be sent out to take an impression, on the spot, as to the feeling of the United States about the Readings. His report as to the undoubted enthusiasm and urgency on the other side of the Atlantic was impossible to resist. Even the friends of Charles Dickens withdrew their opposition (though still with misgivings as to the effect upon his health, which were but too well founded!), and on the Thirtieth September he telegraphed "Yes" to America.

The "Alfred" alluded to in a letter from Glasgow was Charles Dickens' fourth son, Alfred Tennyson, who had gone to Australia two years previously.

We give, in April, the last letter to one of the friends for whom Charles Dickens had always a most tender love—Mr. Stanfield. He was then in failing health, and in May he died.

In April also we give the first of our few letters to the Hon. Robert Lytton, now the Earl of Lytton, well known (in literature) as "Owen Meredith."

Another death which affected him very deeply happened this summer. Miss Marguerite Power died in July. She had long been very ill, but, until it became impossible for her to travel, she was a frequent and beloved guest at Gad's Hill. The Mrs. Henderson to whom he wrote was Miss Power's youngest sister.

Before Charles Dickens started for America it was proposed to wish him God-speed by a public dinner at the Freemasons' Hall. The proposal was most warmly and fully responded to. His zealous friend, Mr. Charles Kent, willingly undertook the whole work of arrangement of this banquet. It took place on the Second November, and Lord Lytton presided.

On the eighth he left London for Liverpool, accompanied by his daughters, his sister-in-law, his eldest son, Mr. Arthur Chappell, Mr. Charles Collins, Mr. Wilkie Collins, Mr. Kent, and Mr. Wills. The next morning the whole party took a final leave of Charles Dickens on board the *Cuba*, which sailed that day.

We give a letter which he wrote to Mr. J. L. Toole on the morning of the dinner, thanking him for a parting gift and an earnest letter. That excellent comedian was one of his most appreciative admirers, and, in return, he had for Mr. Toole the greatest admiration and respect.

The Christmas number for this year, "No Thoroughfare," was

written by Charles Dickens and Mr. Wilkie Collins. It was dramatised by Mr. Collins chiefly. But, in the midst of all the work of preparation for departure, Charles Dickens gave minute attention to as much of the play as could be completed before he left England. It was produced, after Christmas, at the Adelphi Theatre, where M. Fechter was then acting, under the management of Mr. Benjamin Webster.

M. De
Cerjat.

GAD'S HILL PLACE, HIGHAM BY ROCHESTER, KENT,
New Year's Day, 1867.

MY DEAR CERJAT,

Thoroughly determined to be beforehand with "the middle of next summer," your penitent friend and remorseful correspondent thus addresses you.

The big dog, on a day last autumn, having seized a little girl (sister to one of the servants) whom he knew, and was bound to respect, was flogged by his master, and then sentenced to be shot at seven next morning. He went out very cheerfully with the half-dozen men told off for the purpose, evidently thinking that they were going to be the death of somebody unknown. But observing in the procession an empty wheelbarrow and a double-barrelled gun, he became meditative, and fixed the bearer of the gun with his eyes. A stone deftly thrown across him by the village blackguard (chief mourner) caused him to look round for an instant, and then he fell dead, shot through the heart. Two posthumous children are at this moment rolling on the lawn; one will evidently inherit his ferocity, and will probably inherit the gun. The pheasant was a little ailing towards Christmas Day, and was found dead under some ivy in his cage, with his head under his wing, on the morning of the Twenty-seventh of December, one thousand eight hundred and sixty-six. I, proprietor of the remains of the two deceased, am working hard, getting up "Barbox" and "The Boy at Mugby," with which I begin a new series of readings in London on the fifteenth. Next morning I believe I start into the country. When I read, I *don't* write. I only edit, and have the proof-sheets sent me for the purpose. Here are your questions answered.

As to the Reform question, it should have been, and could have been, perfectly known to any honest man in England that the more intelligent part of the great masses were deeply dissatisfied with the state of representation, but were in a very moderate and patient condition, awaiting the better intellectual cultivation of numbers of their fellows. The old insolent resource of assailing them and making the most audaciously wicked statements that they are politically indifferent, has borne the inevitable fruit. The perpetual taunt, "Where are they?" has called them out with the answer: "Well then, if you *must* know, here we are." The intolerable injustice of vituperating the bribed to an assembly of bribers, has goaded their sense of justice beyond endurance. And now, what they would have taken they won't take, and whatever they are steadily bent upon having they will get. Rely upon it, this is the real state of the case. As to your friend "Punch," you will find him begin to turn at the very selfsame instant when the new game shall manifestly become the losing one. You may notice his shoes pinching him a little already.

My dear fellow, I have no more power to stop that mutilation of my books than you have. It is as certain as that every inventor of anything designed for the public good, and offered to the English Government, becomes *ipso facto* a criminal, to have his heart broken on the circumlocutional wheel. It is as certain as that the whole Crimean story will be retold, whenever this country again goes to war. And to tell the truth, I have such a very small opinion of what the great genteel have done for us, that I am very philosophical indeed concerning what the great vulgar may do, having a decided opinion that they can't do worse.

This is the time of year when the theatres do best, there being still numbers of people who make it a sort of religion to see Christmas pantomimes. Having my annual houseful, I have, as yet, seen nothing. Fechter has neither pantomime nor burlesque, but is doing a new version of the old "Trente Ans de la Vie d'un Joueur." I am afraid he will not find his account in it. On the whole, the theatres, except in the articles of scenery and pictorial effect, are poor enough. But in some of the smaller houses there are actors who, if there were any dramatic head-quarters as a school, might become very good. The most hopeless feature is, that they have the smallest possible idea of an effective and harmonious whole, each "going in" for himself or herself. The music-halls attract an immense public, and don't refine the general taste. But such things as they do are well done of their kind, and always briskly and punctually.

The American yacht race is the last sensation. I hope the general interest felt in it on this side will have a wholesome interest on that. It will be a woeful day when John and Jonathan throw their caps into the ring. The French Emperor is indubitably in a dangerous state. His Parisian popularity wanes, and his army are discontented with him. I hear on high authority that his secret police are always making discoveries that render him desperately uneasy.

You know how we have been swindling in these parts. But perhaps you don't know that Mr. ——, the "eminent" contractor, before he fell into difficulties settled *one million of money* on his wife. Such a good and devoted husband!

My daughter Katie has been very ill of nervous fever. On the Twenty-seventh of December she was in a condition to be brought down here (old high road and post-horses), and has been steadily getting better ever since. Her husband is here too, and is on the whole as well as he ever is or ever will be, I fear.

We played forfeit-games here, last night, and then pool; for a billiard-room has been added to the house since you were here. Come and play a match with me.   Always affectionately.

Miss
Hogarth.

ADELPHI HOTEL, LIVERPOOL,
Monday, Twenty-first January, 1867.

MY DEAREST GEORGY,

First I send you my most affectionate wishes for many, many happy returns of your birthday. That done, from my heart of hearts, I go on to my small report of myself.

The readings have produced such an immense effect here that we are coming back for two more in the middle of February.

It being next to impossible for people to come out at night with horses, we have felt the weather in the stalls, and expect to do so through the week. The enthusiasm has been unbounded. On Friday night I quite astonished myself; but I was taken so faint afterwards that they laid me on a sofa at the hall for half an hour. I attribute it to my distressing inability to sleep at night, and to nothing worse.

Scott does very well indeed. As a dresser he is perfect. In a quarter of an hour after I go into the retiring-room, where all my clothes are airing and everything is set out neatly in its own allotted space, I am ready; and he then goes softly out, and sits outside the door. In the morning he is equally punctual, quiet, and quick. He has his needles and thread, buttons, and so forth, always at hand; and in travelling he is very systematic with the luggage. What with Dolby and what with this skilful valet, everything is made as easy to me as it possibly *can* be.

There is great distress here among the poor (four thousand people relieved last Saturday at one workhouse), and there is great anxiety concerning *seven mail-steamers some days overdue.* Such a circumstance as this last has never been known. It is supposed that some great revolving storm has whirled them all out of their course. One of these missing ships is an American mail, another an Australian mail.

Same Afternoon.

We have been out for four hours in the bitter east wind, and walking on the sea-shore, where there is a broad strip of great blocks of ice.

We have been constantly talking of the terrible Regent's Park accident. I hope and believe that nearly the worst of it is now known.

CHESTER, *Tuesday, Twenty-second January,* 1867. Miss Dickens.

MY DEAREST MAMIE,

We came over here from Liverpool at eleven this forenoon. There was a heavy swell in the Mersey breaking over the boat; the cold was nipping, and all the roads we saw as we came along were wretched. This seems to be a very nice hotel, but it is an extraordinarily cold one. Our reading for to-night is "Marigold" and "Trial."

Barton, the gasman who succeeded the man who sprained his leg, sprained *his* leg yesterday!! And that, not at his work, but in running downstairs at the hotel. However, he has hobbled through it so far, and I hope will hobble on, for he knows his work.

I have seldom seen a place look more hopelessly frozen up than this place does. The hall is like a Methodist chapel in low spirits, and with a cold in its head. A few blue people shiver at the corners of the streets. And this house, which is outside the town, looks like an ornament on an immense twelfth cake baked for 1847.

I am now going to the fire to try to warm myself, but have not the least expectation of succeeding. The sitting-room has two large windows in it, down to the ground and facing due east. The adjoining bedroom (mine) has also two large windows in it, down to the ground and facing due east. The very large doors are opposite the large windows, and I feel as if I were something to eat in a pantry.

HEN AND CHICKENS, BIRMINGHAM, Miss Hogarth.
Thursday, Twenty-fourth January, 1867.

At Chester we read in a snowstorm and a fall of ice. I think it was the worst weather I ever saw. Nevertheless, the people were enthusiastic. At Wolverhampton last night the thaw had thoroughly set in, and it rained heavily. We had not intended to go back there, but have arranged to do so on the day after Ash Wednesday. Last night I was again heavily beaten. We came on here after the reading (it is only a ride of forty minutes), and it was as much as I could do to hold out the journey. But I was not faint, as at Liverpool; I was only exhausted. I am all right this morning; and to-night, as you know, I have a rest. I trust that Charley Collins is better, and that Mamie is strong and well again.   Yesterday I had a note from Katie, which seemed hopeful and encouraging.

Miss
Dickens.

HEN AND CHICKENS, BIRMINGHAM,
Thursday, Twenty-fourth January, 1867.

Since I wrote to your aunt just now, I have received your note addressed to Wolverhampton.

The maimed gasman's foot is much swollen, but he limps about and does his work.   I have doctored him up with arnica.   During the reading last night there was an escape of gas from the side of my top batten, which caught the copper-wire and was within a thread of bringing down the heavy reflector into the stalls.   It was a very ticklish matter, though the audience knew nothing about it.   I saw it, and the gasman and Dolby saw it, and stood at that side of the platform in agonies.   We all three calculated that there would be just time to finish and save it; when the gas was turned out the instant I had done, the thing was at its very last and utmost extremity.   Whom it would have tumbled on, or what might have been set on fire, it is impossible to say.

*   *   *   *   *

Anonymous.

OFFICE OF "ALL THE YEAR ROUND,"
Tuesday, Fifth February, 1867.

DEAR SIR,

I have looked at the larger half of the first volume of your novel, and have pursued the more difficult points of the story through the other two volumes.

You will, of course, receive my opinion as that of an individual writer and student of art, who by no means claims to be infallible.

I think you are too ambitious, and that you have not sufficient knowledge of life or character to venture on so comprehensive an attempt.   Evidences of inexperience in every way, and of your power being far below the situations that you imagine, present themselves to me in almost every page I have read.   It would greatly surprise me if you found a publisher for this story, on trying your fortune in that line, or derived anything from it but weariness and bitterness of spirit.

On the evidence thus put before me, I cannot even entirely satisfy myself that you have the faculty of authorship latent within you.   If you have not, and yet pursue a vocation towards which you have no call, you cannot choose but be a wretched man.   Let me counsel you to have the patience to form yourself carefully, and the courage to renounce the endeavour if you cannot establish your case on a very much smaller scale.   You see around you every day, how many outlets there are for short pieces of fiction in all kinds. Try if you can achieve any success within these modest limits (I have practised in my time what I preach to you), and in the meantime put your three volumes away.

Faithfully yours.

LIVERPOOL, *Friday, Fifteenth February*, 1867. Miss
Hogarth.

MY DEAREST GEORGY,

My short report of myself is that we had an enormous turn-away last night, and do not doubt about having a cram to-night. The day has been very fine, and I have turned it to the whole-somest account by walking on the sands at New Brighton all the morning. I am not quite right, but believe it to be an effect of the railway shaking. There is no doubt of the fact that, after the Staplehurst experience, it tells more and more, instead of (as one might have expected) less and less.

The charming room here greatly lessens the fatigue of this fatiguing week. I read last night with no more exertion than if I had been at Gad's, and yet to eleven hundred people, and with astonishing effect.

GLASGOW, *Sunday, Seventeenth February*, 1867. Miss
Dickens.

MY DEAREST MAMIE,

We arrived here this morning at our time to the moment, five minutes past ten. We turned away great numbers on both nights at Liverpool; and Manchester last night was a splendid spectacle. They cheered to that extent after it was over, that I was obliged to huddle on my clothes (for I was undressing to prepare for the journey), and go back again.

After so heavy a week, it *was* rather stiff to start on this long journey at a quarter to two in the morning; but I got more sleep than I ever got in a railway-carriage before, and it really was not tedious. The travelling was admirable, and a wonderful contrast to my friend the Midland.

I am not by any means knocked up, though I have, as I had in the last series of readings, a curious feeling of soreness all round the body, which I suppose to arise from the great exertion of voice. It is a mercy that we were not both made really ill at Liverpool. On Friday morning I was taken so faint and sick, that I was obliged to leave the table. On the same afternoon the same thing happened to Dolby. We then found that a part of the hotel close to us was dismantled for painting, and that they were at that moment painting a green passage leading to our rooms, with a most horrible mixture of white lead and arsenic. On pursuing the enquiry, I found that the four lady book-keepers in the bar were all suffering from the poison.

BRIDGE OF ALLAN,
Tuesday, Nineteenth February, 1867.

I was very glad to get your letter before leaving Glasgow this morning. This is a poor return for it, but the post goes out early, and we come in late.

Yesterday morning I was so unwell that I wrote to Frank Beard, from whom I shall doubtless hear to-morrow. I mention it, only in case you should come in his way, for I know how perversely such things fall out. I felt it a little more exertion to read afterwards, and I passed a sleepless night after that again; but otherwise I am in good force and spirits to-day. I may say, in the best force.

The quiet of this little place is sure to do me good. The little inn in which we are established seems a capital house of the best country sort.

GLASGOW, *Thursday, Twenty-first February*, 1867.

After two days' rest at the Bridge of Allan I am in renewed force, and have nothing to complain of but inability to sleep. I have been in excellent air all day since Tuesday at noon, and made an interesting walk to Stirling yesterday, and saw its lions, and (strange to relate) was not bored by them. Indeed, they left me so fresh that I knocked at the gate of the prison, presented myself to the governor, and took Dolby over the jail, to his unspeakable interest. We then walked back again to our excellent country inn.

Wonderful as it is to mention, the sun shines here to-day! But to counterbalance that phenomenon I am in close hiding from ——, who has christened his infant son in my name, and, consequently, haunts the building. He and Dolby have already nearly come into collision, in consequence of the latter being always under the dominion of the one idea that he is bound to knock everybody down who asks for me.

*   *   *   *   *   *

[The " Jewish lady," wishing to mark her " appreciation of Mr. Dickens' nobility of character," presented him with a copy of Benisch's Hebrew and English Bible, with this inscription : " Presented to Charles Dickens, in grateful and admiring recognition of his having exercised the noblest quality man can possess—that of atoning for an injury as soon as conscious of having inflicted it."]

The acknowledgment of the gift is the following letter:

BRADFORD, YORKSHIRE,
Friday, First March, 1867.

MY DEAR MRS. ——,

I am working through a series of readings, widely dispersed through England, Scotland, and Ireland, and am so constantly occupied that it is very difficult for me to write letters. I have received your highly-esteemed note (forwarded from my home in Kent), and should have replied to it sooner but that I had a hope of being able to get home and see your present first. As I have not been able to do so, however, and am hardly likely to do so for two months to come, I delay no longer. It is safely awaiting me on my own desk in my own quiet room. I cannot thank you for it too cordially, and cannot too earnestly assure you that I shall always prize it highly. The terms in which you send me that mark of your remembrance are more gratifying to me than I can possibly express to you; for they assure me that there is nothing but goodwill left between you and me and a people for whom I have a real regard, and to whom I would not wilfully have given an offence or done an injustice for any worldly consideration.

Believe me, very faithfully yours.

LEEDS, *Thursday, Seventh March,* 1867.

MY DEAR MRS. FITZGERALD,

Your kind and welcome letter reached me here last night. I cannot tell you how highly I esteem it, or how cordially I reciprocate your friendly regard.

But I must not allow myself to break my rule of always living with my secretary at an hotel on these occasions. My inflexible self-denial in this respect has had much to do with the establishment of a system among the three attendants who travel with us, which otherwise must have become less exact and punctual. Knowing that I am never away, they are always at their posts. In the continual hurry, fatigue, and change of this episodical life, its wear and tear is reduced to the smallest possible amount by its machinery never varying in the least. And I am so fortunate in the zeal and loyalty of my travelling companion, Mr. Dolby, that I should regard myself as a sort of deserter from my colours if I left him to do this anxious work alone. For all these reasons I never promise myself while thus engaged to make a visit; and even in the case of my old friend, Mr. Macready, at Cheltenham, a little while ago, I acted on the Spartan principles which at this present writing are making me very uncomfortable, and with which I have no natural sympathy whatever.

In regard to your son Percy (whom, I hope, by-the-bye, to prevail upon to go with me to Belfast) let me honestly assure you that my editorial existence has had no pleasanter incident in it than its having made me acquainted with his very great abilities, and having made us private friends. It is impossible that he can have a more interested or appreciative reader than he has in me, and no man ever sets foot in my house whom I better like to see there. My daughter and her aunt shall have your messages.

Believe me, with best regards to all your house,

Very faithfully yours.

Miss
Hogarth.

SHELBOURNE HOTEL, DUBLIN,
Friday, Fifteenth March, 1867.

MY DEAREST GEORGY,

We made our journey through an incessant snowstorm on Wednesday night; at last got snowed up among the Welsh mountains in a tremendous storm of wind, came to a stop, and had to dig the engine out. We went to bed at Holyhead at six in the morning of Thursday, and got aboard the packet at two yesterday afternoon. It blew hard, but as the wind was right astern, we only rolled and did not pitch much. As I walked about on the bridge all the four hours, and had cold salt beef and biscuit there and brandy-and-water, you will infer that my Channel training has not worn out.

There is no doubt that great alarm prevails here. This hotel is constantly filling and emptying as families leave the country, and set in a current to the steamers. There is apprehension of some disturbance between to-morrow night and Monday night (both inclusive), and I learn this morning that all the drinking shops are to be closed from to-night until Tuesday. It is rumoured here that the Liverpool people are very uneasy about some apprehended disturbance there at the same time. Very likely you will know more about this than I do, and very likely it may be nothing. There is no doubt whatever that alarm prevails, and the manager of this hotel, an intelligent German, is very gloomy on the subject. On the other hand, there is feasting going on, and I have been asked to dinner-parties by divers civil and military authorities.

Don't *you* be uneasy, I say once again. You may be absolutely certain that there is no cause for it. We are splendidly housed here, and in great comfort.

SHELBOURNE HOTEL, DUBLIN,
Saturday, Sixteenth March, 1867.

Miss
Dickens.

MY DEAREST MAMIE,

I daresay you know already that I held many councils in London about coming to Ireland at all, and was much against it. Everything looked as bad here as need be, but we did very well last night after all.

There is considerable alarm here beyond all question, and great depression in all kinds of trade and commerce. To-morrow being St. Patrick's Day, there are apprehensions of some disturbance, and croakers predict that it will come off between to-night and Monday night. Of course there are preparations on all sides, and large musters of soldiers and police, though they are kept carefully out of sight. One would not suppose, walking about the streets, that any disturbance was impending; and yet there is no doubt that the materials of one lie smouldering up and down the city and all over the country. [I have a letter from Mrs. Bernal Osborne this morning, describing the fortified way in which she is living in her own house in the County Tipperary.]

You may be quite sure that your venerable parent will take good care of himself. If any riot were to break out, I should immediately stop the readings here. At Belfast, we shall have an enormous house. This is all my news, except that I am in perfect force.

SHELBOURNE HOTEL, DUBLIN,
Sunday, Seventeenth March, 1867.

Miss
Hogarth.

Everything remains in appearance perfectly quiet here. The streets are gay all day, now that the weather is improved, and singularly quiet and deserted at night. But the whole place is secretly girt in with a military force. To-morrow night is supposed to be a critical time; but in view of the enormous preparations, I should say that the chances are at least one hundred to one against any disturbance.

The most curious, and for facilities of mere destruction, such as firing houses in different quarters, the most dangerous piece of intelligence imparted to me on authority is, that the Dublin domestic men-servants as a class are all Fenians.

I am perfectly convinced that the worst part of the Fenian business is to come yet.

BELFAST, *Thursday, Twenty-first March*, 1867.

Miss
Dickens.

In spite of public affairs and dismal weather, we are doing wonders in Ireland.

That the conspiracy is a far larger and more important one than would seem from what it has done yet, there is no doubt. I have had a good deal of talk with a certain colonel, whose duty it has been to investigate it, day and night, since last September. That it will give a world of trouble, and cost a world of money, I take to be (after what I have thus learned) beyond all question. One regiment has been found to contain five hundred Fenian soldiers, every man of whom was sworn in the barrack-yard. How information is swiftly and secretly conveyed all over the country, the Government with all its means and money cannot discover; but every hour it is found that instructions, warnings, and other messages are circulated from end to end of Ireland. It is a very serious business indeed.

Miss
Hogarth.

NORWICH, *Friday, Twenty-ninth March,* 1867.

The reception at Cambridge last night was something to be proud of in such a place. The colleges mustered in full force from the biggest guns to the smallest, and went far beyond even Manchester in the roars of welcome and the rounds of cheers. All through the readings, the whole of the assembly, old men as well as young, and women as well as men, took everything with a heartiness of enjoyment not to be described. The place was crammed, and the success the most brilliant I have ever seen.

What we are doing in this sleepy old place I don't know, but I have no doubt it is mild enough.

* * * * *

Mr. Walter
Thornbury.

OFFICE OF "ALL THE YEAR ROUND,"
Monday, First April, 1867.

MY DEAR THORNBURY,

I am very doubtful indeed about "Vaux," and have kept it out of the number in consequence. The mere details of such a rascal's proceedings, whether recorded by himself or set down by the Reverend Ordinary, are not wholesome for a large audience, and are scarcely justifiable (I think) as claiming to be a piece of literature. I can understand Barrington to be a good subject, as involving the representation of a period, a style of manners, an order of dress, certain habits of street life, assembly-room life, and coffee-room life, etc.; but there is a very broad distinction between this and mere Newgate Calendar. The latter would assuredly damage your book, and be protested against to me. I have a conviction of it, founded on constant observation and experience here.

Your kind invitation is extremely welcome and acceptable to me, but I am sorry to add that I must not go a-visiting. For this reason: So incessantly have I been "reading," that I have not once been at home at Gad's Hill since last January, and am little likely to get there before the middle of May. Judge how the master's eye must be kept on the place when it does at length get a look at it after so long an absence! I hope you will descry in this a reason for coming to me again, instead of my coming to you.

The extinct prize-fighters, as a body, I take to be a good subject, for much the same reason as George Barrington. Their patrons were a class of men now extinct too, and the whole ring of those days (not to mention Jackson's rooms in Bond Street) is a piece of social history. Now Vaux is not, nor is he even a phenomenon among thieves.

Faithfully yours always.

GAD'S HILL PLACE, HIGHAM BY ROCHESTER, KENT,
Wednesday, Seventeenth April, 1867.

Hon. Robert Lytton.

MY DEAR ROBERT LYTTON,

It would have been really painful to me, if I had seen you and yours at a Reading of mine in right of any other credentials than my own. Your appreciation has given me higher and purer gratification than your modesty can readily believe. When I first entered on this interpretation of myself (then quite strange in the public ear) I was sustained by the hope that I could drop into some hearts, some new expression of the meaning of my books, that would touch them in a new way. To this hour that purpose is so strong in me, and so real are my fictions to myself, that, after hundreds of nights, I come with a feeling of perfect freshness to that little red table, and laugh and cry with my hearers, as if I had never stood there before. You will know from this what a delight it is to be delicately understood, and why your earnest words cannot fail to move me.

We are delighted to be remembered by your charming wife, and I am entrusted with more messages from this house to her, than you would care to give or withhold, so I suppress them myself and absolve you from the difficulty.

Affectionately yours.

GAD'S HILL PLACE, HIGHAM BY ROCHESTER,
Thursday, Eighteenth April, 1867.

Mr. Clarkson Stanfield, R.A

MY DEAR STANNY,

The time of year reminds me how the months have gone, since I last heard from you through Mrs. Stanfield.

I hope you have not thought me unmindful of you in the meanwhile. I have been almost constantly travelling and reading. England, Ireland, and Scotland have laid hold of me by turns, and I have had no rest. As soon as I had finished this kind of work last year, I had to fall to work upon "All the Year Round" and the Christmas number. I was no sooner quit of that task, and the Christmas season was but run out to its last day, when I was tempted into another course of fifty readings that are not yet over. I am here now for two days, and have not seen the place since Twelfth Night. When a reading in London has been done, I have been brought up for it from some great distance, and have next morning been carried back again. But the fifty will be "paid out" (as we say at sea) by the middle of May, and then I hope to see you.

Reading at Cheltenham the other day, I saw Macready, who sent his love to you. His face was much more massive and as it used to be, than when I saw him previous to his illness. His wife takes admirable care of him, and is on the happiest terms with his daughter Katie. His boy by the second marriage is a jolly little fellow, and leads a far easier life than the children you and I remember, who used to come in at dessert and have each a biscuit and a glass of water, in which last refreshment I was always convinced that they drank, with the gloomiest malignity, "Destruction to the gormandising grown-up company!"

I hope to look up your latest triumphs on the day of the Academy dinner. Of course as yet I have had no opportunity of even hearing of what anyone has done. I have been (in a general way) snowed up for four months. The locomotive with which I was going to Ireland was dug out of the snow at midnight, in Wales. Both passages across were made in a furious snowstorm. The snow lay ankle-deep in Dublin, and froze hard at Belfast. In Scotland it slanted before a perpetual east wind. In Yorkshire, it derived novelty from thunder and lightning. Whirlwinds everywhere I don't mention.

God bless you and yours. If I look like some weather-beaten pilot when we meet, don't be surprised. Any mahogany-faced stranger who holds out his hand to you will probably turn out, on inspection, to be the old original Dick.

Ever, my dear Stanny, your faithful and affectionate.

P.S.—I wish you could have been with me (of course in a snowstorm) one day on the pier at Tynemouth. There was a very heavy sea running, and a perfect fleet of screw merchantmen were plunging in and out on the turn of the tide at high-water. Suddenly there came a golden horizon, and a most glorious rainbow burst out, arching one large ship, as if she were sailing direct for heaven. I was so enchanted by the scene, that I became oblivious of a few thousand tons of water coming on in an enormous roller, and was knocked down and beaten by its spray when it broke, and so completely wetted through and through, that the very pockets in my pocket-book were full of sea.

GAD'S HILL,
Thursday, Eighteenth April, 1867.

Mr. Henry
W. Phillips.

MY DEAR MR. PHILLIPS,*

Although I think the scheme has many good points, I have this doubt: Would boys so maintained at any one of our great public schools stand at a decided disadvantage towards boys not so maintained? Foundation Scholars, in many cases, win their way into public schools and so enforce respect and even assert superiority. In many other cases their patron is a remote and misty person, or Institution, sanctioned by Time and custom. But the proposed position would be a very different one for a student to hold, and boys are too often inconsiderate, proud, and cruel. I should like to know whether this point has received consideration from the projectors of the design?

Faithfully yours always.

OFFICE OF "ALL THE YEAR ROUND,"
Sunday, Nineteenth May, 1867.

Mr. George
Stanfield.†

MY DEAR GEORGE,

When I came up to the house this afternoon and saw what had happened, I had not the courage to ring, though I had thought I was fully prepared by what I heard when I called yesterday. No one of your father's friends can ever have loved him more dearly than I always did, or can have better known the worth of his noble character.

It is idle to suppose that I can do anything for you; and yet I cannot help saying that I am staying here for some days, and that if I could, it would be a much greater relief to me than it could be a service to you.

Your poor mother has been constantly in my thoughts since I saw the quiet bravery with which she preserved her composure. The beauty of her ministration sank into my heart when I saw him for the last time on earth. May God be with her, and with you all, in your great loss.

Affectionately yours always.

---

* Mr. Henry W. Phillips, at this time secretary of the Artists' General Benevolent Society. He was eager to establish some educational system in connection with that institution.

† On the death of his father.

Mr. W. H.
Wills.   *Thursday, Sixth June*, 1867.

MY DEAR WILLS,

I cannot tell you how warmly I feel your letter, or how deeply I appreciate the affection and regard in which it originates. I thank you for it with all my heart.

You will not suppose that I make light of any of your misgivings if I present the other side of the question. Every objection that you make strongly impresses me, and will be revolved in my mind again and again.

When I went to América in '42, I was so much younger, but (I think) very much weaker too. I had had a painful surgical operation performed shortly before going out, and had had the labour from week to week of "Master Humphrey's Clock." My life in the States was a life of continual speech-making (quite as laborious as reading), and I was less patient and more irritable then than I am now. My idea of a course of readings in America is, that it would involve far less travelling than you suppose, that the large first-class rooms would absorb the whole course, and that the receipts would be very much larger than your estimate, unless the demand for the readings is ENORMOUSLY EXAGGERATED ON ALL HANDS. There is considerable reason for this view of the case. And I can hardly think that all the speculators who beset, and all the private correspondents who urge me, are in a conspiracy or under a common delusion.

    *   *   *   *   *

I shall never rest much while my faculties last, and (if I know myself) have a certain something in me that would still be active in rusting and corroding me, if I flattered myself that I was in repose. On the other hand, I think that my habit of easy self-abstraction and withdrawal into fancies has always refreshed and strengthened me in short intervals wonderfully. I always seem to myself to have rested far more than I have worked; and I do really believe that I have some exceptional faculty of accumulating young feelings in short pauses, which obliterates a quantity of wear and tear.

My worldly circumstances (such a large family considered) are very good. I don't want money. All my possessions are free and in the best order. Still, at fifty-five or fifty-six, the likelihood of making a very great addition to one's capital in half a year is an immense consideration. . . . I repeat the phrase, because there should be something large to set against the objections.

I dine with Forster to-day, to talk it over. I have no doubt he will urge most of your objections and particularly the last, though the American friends and correspondents he has, have undoubtedly staggered him more than I ever knew him to be staggered on the money question. Be assured that no one can present any argument to me which will weigh more heartily with me than your kind words, and that whatever comes of my present state of abeyance, I shall never forget your letter or cease to be grateful for it. Ever, my dear Wills, faithfully yours.

GAD'S HILL PLACE, HIGHAM BY ROCHESTER, KENT, Mr. W. H.
Sunday, Thirteenth June, 1867. Wills.

MY DEAR WILLS,

I have read the first three numbers of Wilkie's story * this morning, and have gone minutely through the plot of the rest to the last line. It gives a series of "narratives," but it is a very curious story, wild, and yet domestic, with excellent character in it, and great mystery. It is prepared with extraordinary care, and has every chance of being a hit. It is in many respects much better than anything he has done.

I have an impression that it was not Silvester who tried Eliza Fenning, but Knowles. One can hardly suppose Thornbury to make such a mistake, but I wish you would look into the Annual Register. I have added a final paragraph about the unfairness of the judge, whoever he was. I distinctly recollect to have read of his "putting down" of Eliza Fenning's father when the old man made some miserable suggestion in his daughter's behalf (this is not noticed by Thornbury), and he also stopped some suggestion that a knife thrust into a loaf adulterated with alum would present the appearance that these knives presented. But I may have got both these points from looking up some pamphlets in Upcott's collection which I once had.

Your account of your journey reminds me of one of the latest American stories, how a traveller by stage-coach said to the driver: "Did you ever see a snail, sir?" "Yes, sir." "Where did you meet him, sir?" "I *didn't* meet him, sir!" "Wa'al, sir, I think you did, if you'll excuse me, for I'm damned if you ever overtook him." Ever faithfully.

GAD'S HILL, *Thursday, Fourth July*, 1867. Mrs.
Henderson.

MY DEAR MRS. HENDERSON,

I was more shocked than surprised by the receipt of your mother's announcement of our poor dear Marguerite's death. When I heard of the consultation, and recalled what had preceded it and what I have seen here, my hopes were very slight.

* The Moonstone.

Your letter did not reach me until last night, and thus I could not avoid remaining here to-day, to keep an American appointment of unusual importance. You and your mother both know, I think, that I had a great affection for Marguerite, that we had many dear remembrances together, and that her self-reliance and composed perseverance had awakened my highest admiration in later times. No one could have stood by her grave to-day with a better knowledge of all that was great and good in her than I have, or with a more loving remembrance of her through all her phases since she first came to London a pretty timid girl.

I do not trouble your mother by writing to her separately. It is a sad, sad task to write at all. God help us!

Faithfully yours.

Miss
Hogarth.

ADELPHI HOTEL, LIVERPOOL,
Friday Night, Second August, 1867.

MY DEAREST GEORGY,

I cannot get a boot on—wear a slipper on my left foot, and consequently am here under difficulties. My foot is occasionally painful, but not very. I don't think it worth while consulting anybody about it as yet. I make out so many reasons against supposing it to be gouty, that I really do not think it is.

Dolby begs me to send all manner of apologetic messages for his going to America. He is very cheerful and hopeful, but evidently feels the separation from his wife and child very much. His sister * was at Euston Square this morning, looking very well. Sainton too, very light and jovial.

With the view of keeping myself and my foot quiet, I think I will not come to Gad's Hill until Monday. If I don't appear before, send basket to Gravesend to meet me, leaving town by the 12.10 on Monday. This is important, as I couldn't walk a quarter of a mile to-night for five hundred pounds.

Madame
Sainton
Dolby.

26, WELLINGTON STREET, STRAND, W.C.,
Wednesday, Seventh August, 1867.

MY DEAR MADAME SAINTON,

Don't think me a traitor for not writing to you to report how I left your brother on board the *Java*. I have been laid up with erysipelas in the foot, and my attitude has been so constrained that I could write but few letters.

He was in the best spirits possible under the circumstances, and looked ruddy and well. He was as nicely and neatly lodged as a person on board ship *can* be, and had a very cheerful and

* Madame Sainton Dolby.

modest gentleman for his travelling companion. Probably you have heard from Queenstown that eating and drinking (and being violently shaken by the screw) are the standard amusements of the *Java*. I tremble to think of his circumference when he lands in the United States!

With kind regards to Mr. Sainton, believe me always,

Very faithfully yours.

GAD'S HILL, *Monday, Second September*, 1867.   Mr. W. H
                                                 Wills.
MY DEAR WILLS,

Like you, I was shocked when this new discovery burst upon me on Friday, though, unlike you, I never could believe in ——, solely (I think) because, often as I have tried him, I never found him standing by my desk when I was writing a letter without his trying to read it.

I fear there is no doubt that since ——'s discharge, he (——) has stolen money at the readings. A case of an abstracted shilling seems to have been clearly brought home to him by Chappell's people, and they know very well what *that* means. I supposed a very clear keeping off from Anne's husband (whom I recommended for employment to Chappell) to have been referable only to ——; but now I see how hopeless and unjust it would be to expect belief from him with two such cases within his knowledge.

But don't let the thing spoil your holiday. If we try to do our duty by people we employ, by exacting their proper service from them on the one hand, and treating them with all possible consistency, gentleness, and consideration on the other, we know that we do right. Their doing wrong cannot change our doing right, and that should be enough for us.

So I have given *my* feathers a shake, and am all right again. Give *your* feathers a shake, and take a cheery flutter into the air of Hertfordshire.

Great reports from Dolby and also from Fields! But I keep myself quite calm, and hold my decision in abeyance until I shall have book, chapter, and verse before me.

Sydney has passed as a lieutenant, and appeared at home yesterday, all of a sudden, with the consequent golden garniture on his sleeve, which I, God forgive me, stared at without the least idea that it meant promotion.

I am glad you see a certain unlikeness to anything in the American story. Upon myself it has made the strangest impression of reality and originality!! And I feel as if I had read something (by somebody else), which I should never get out of my mind!!! The main idea of the narrator's position towards the other people was the idea that I _had_ for my next novel in A. Y. R. But it is very curious that I did not in the least see how to begin his state of mind until I walked into Hoghton Towers one bright April day.   Faithfully ever.

Mr. F. D. Finlay.*

GAD'S HILL PLACE, HIGHAM BY ROCHESTER, KENT, _Tuesday, Third September,_ 1867.

This is to certify that the undersigned victim of a periodical paragraph-disease, which usually breaks out once in every seven years (proceeding to England by the overland route to India and per Cunard line to America, where it strikes the base of the Rocky Mountains, and, rebounding to Europe, perishes on the steppes of Russia), is _not_ in a "critical state of health," and has _not_ consulted "eminent surgeons," and never was better in his life, and is _not_ recommended to proceed to the United States for "cessation from literary labour," and has not had so much as a headache for twenty years.

CHARLES DICKENS.

Third September, 1867.

Mr. James T. Fields.

MY DEAR FIELDS,†

Your cheering letter of the Twenty-first of August arrived here this morning. A thousand thanks for it. I begin to think (nautically) that I "head west'ard."

The other day I received a letter from Mr. ——, of New York (who came over in the winning yacht, and described the voyage in _The Times_), saying that he would much like to see me. I made an appointment in London, and observed that when he _did_ see me he was obviously astonished. While I was sensible that the magnificence of my appearance would fully account for his being overcome, I nevertheless angled for the cause of his surprise. He then told me that there was a paragraph going round the papers to the effect that I was "in a critical state of health." I asked him if he was sure it wasn't "cricketing" state of health. To which he replied, Quite. I then asked him down here to dinner, and he was again staggered by finding me in sporting training; also much amused.

Yesterday's and to-day's post bring me this unaccountable paragraph from hosts of uneasy friends, with the enormous and wonderful addition that "eminent surgeons" are sending me to

* Contradicting a newspaper report of his being "in a critical state of health."
† This and all other Letters to Mr. J. T. Fields were printed in Mr. Fields' "In and Out of Doors with Charles Dickens."

America for "cessation from literary labour"!!! So I have written a quiet line to *The Times*, certifying to my own state of health, and have also begged Dixon to do the like in *The Athenæum*. I mention the matter to you, in order that you may contradict, from me, if the nonsense should reach America unaccompanied by the truth. But I suppose that *The New York Herald* will probably have got the letter from Mr. ——— aforesaid . . .

Charles Reade and Wilkie Collins are here; and the joke of the time is to feel my pulse when I appear at table, and also to inveigle innocent messengers to come over to the summer-house, where I write (the place is quite changed since you were here, and a tunnel under the highroad connects this shrubbery with the front garden), to ask, with their compliments, how I find myself *now*.

If I come to America this next November, even you can hardly imagine with what interest I shall try Copperfield on an American audience, or, if they give me their heart, how freely and fully I shall give them mine.

I cannot thank you enough for your invaluable help to Dolby. He writes that at every turn and moment the sense and knowledge and tact of Mr. Osgood are inestimable to him.

Ever, my dear Fields, faithfully yours.

"ALL THE YEAR ROUND" OFFICE,
Monday, Sixteenth September, 1867.

M. Charles Fechter.

MY DEAR FECHTER,

Going over the prompt-book carefully, I see one change in your part to which (on Lytton's behalf) I positively object, as I am quite certain he would not consent to it. It is highly injudicious besides, as striking out the best known line in the play.

Turn to your part in Act III., the speech beginning

Pauline, *by pride*
Angels have fallen ere thy time: by pride———

You have made a passage farther on stand:

Then did I seek to rise
Out of my mean estate. Thy bright image, etc.

I must stipulate for your restoring it thus:

Then did I seek to rise
Out of the prison of my mean estate;
And, with such jewels as the exploring mind
Brings from the caves of knowledge, buy my ransom
From those twin jailers of the daring heart—
Low birth and iron fortune. Thy bright image, etc. etc.

The last figure has been again and again quoted; is identified with the play; is fine in itself; and above all, I KNOW that Lytton would not let it go. In writing to him to-day, fully explaining the changes in detail, and saying that I disapprove of nothing else, I have told him that I notice this change and that I immediately let you know that it must not be made.

(There will not be a man in the house from any newspaper who would not detect mutilations in that speech, moreover.)

Ever.

Lord
Lytton.

"ALL THE YEAR ROUND OFFICE,"
Tuesday, Seventeenth September, 1867.

MY DEAR LYTTON,

I am happy to tell you that the play was admirably done last night, and made a marked impression. Pauline is weak, but so carefully trained and fitted into the picture as to be never disagreeable, and sometimes (as in the last scene) very pathetic. Fechter has played nothing nearly so well as Claude since he played in Paris in the "Dame aux Camélias," or in London as Ruy Blas. He played the fourth act as finely as Macready, and the first much better. The dress and bearing in the fifth act are quite new, and quite excellent.

Of the Scenic arrangements, the most noticeable are :—the picturesque struggle of the cottage between the taste of an artist, and the domestic means of poverty (expressed to the eye with infinite tact) ;—the view of Lyons (Act v. Scene 1), with a foreground of quay wall which the officers are leaning on, waiting for the general ;—and the last scene—a suite of rooms giving on a conservatory at the back, through which the moon is shining. You are to understand that all these scenic appliances are subdued to the Piece, instead of the Piece being sacrificed to them ; and that every group and situation has to be considered, not only with a reference to each by itself, but to the whole story.

Beauséant's speaking the original contents of the letter was a decided point, and the immense house was quite breathless when the Tempter and the Tempted stood confronted as he made the proposal.

There was obviously great interest in seeing a Frenchman play the part. The scene between Claude and Gaspar (the small part very well done) was very closely watched for the same reason, and was loudly applauded. I cannot say too much of the brightness, intelligence, picturesqueness, and care of Fechter's impersonation throughout. There was a remarkable delicacy in his gradually drooping down on his way home with his bride, until he fell upon the table, a crushed heap of shame and remorse, while his mother told Pauline the story. His gradual recovery of himself as he formed better resolutions was equally well-expressed; and his being at last upright again and rushing enthusiastically to join the army, brought the house down.

I wish you could have been there. He never spoke English half so well as he spoke your English; and the audience heard it with the finest sympathy and respect. I felt that I should have been very proud indeed to have been the writer of the Play.

Ever affectionately.

Monday, Thirtieth September, 1867. Miss Hogarth.

MY DEAREST GEORGY,

The telegram is despatched to Boston: "Yes. Go ahead." After a very anxious consultation with Forster, and careful heed of what is to be said for and against, I have made up my mind to see it out. I do not expect as much money as the calculators estimate, but I cannot set the hope of a large sum of money aside.

I am so nervous with travelling and anxiety to decide something, that I can hardly write. But I send you these few words as my dearest and best friend.

Ever your affectionate.

OFFICE OF "ALL THE YEAR ROUND," Miss Dickens.
No. 26, WELLINGTON STREET, STRAND, LONDON, W.C.,
Monday, Thirtieth September, 1867.

MY DEAREST MAMIE,

You will have had my telegram that I go to America. After a long discussion with Forster, and consideration of what is to be said on both sides, I have decided to go through with it. I doubt the profit being as great as the calculation makes it, but the prospect is sufficiently alluring to turn the scale on the American side.

Love to all.

We have telegraphed "Yes" to Boston.

I begin to feel myself drawn towards America, as Darnay, in the "Tale of Two Cities," was attracted to the Loadstone Rock, Paris.

Ever your affectionate Father.

Mr. James
T. Fields.

* *October*, 1867.

MY DEAR FIELDS,

I hope the telegraph clerks did not mutilate out of recognition or reasonable guess the words I added to Dolby's last telegram to Boston. "*Tribune* London correspondent totally false." Not only is there not a word of truth in the pretended conversation, but it is so absurdly unlike me that I cannot suppose it to be even invented by anyone who ever heard me exchange a word with mortal creature. For twenty years I am perfectly certain that I have never made any other allusion to the republication of my books in America than the good-humoured remark, "that if there had been international copyright between England and the States, I should have been a man of very large fortune, instead of a man of moderate savings, always supporting a very expensive public position." Nor have I ever been such a fool as to charge the absence of international copyright upon individuals. Nor have I ever been so ungenerous as to disguise or suppress the fact that I have received handsome sums for advance sheets. When I was in the States, I said what I had to say on the question, and there an end. I am absolutely certain that I have never since expressed myself, even with soreness, on the subject. Reverting to the preposterous fabrication of the London correspondent, the statement that I ever talked about "these fellows" who republished my books or pretended to know (what I don't know at this instant) who made how much out of them, or ever talked of their sending me "conscience money," is as grossly and completely false as the statement that I ever said anything to the effect that I could not be expected to have an interest in the American people. And nothing can by any possibility be falser than that. Again and again in these pages ("All the Year Round") I have expressed my interest in them. You will see it in the last preface to "American Notes." Every American who has ever spoken with me in London, Paris, or where not, knows whether I have frankly said, "You could have no better introduction to me than your country." And for years and years when I have been asked about reading in America, my invariable reply has been, "I have so many friends there, and constantly receive so many earnest letters from personally unknown readers there, that, but for domestic reasons, I would go to-morrow." I think I must, in the confidential intercourse between you and me, have written you to this effect more than once.

* A ridiculous paragraph in the papers following close on the public announcement that Charles Dickens was coming to America in November, drew from him this letter to Mr. Fields, dated early in October.

The statement of the London correspondent from beginning to end is false. It is false in the letter and false in the spirit. He may have been misinformed, and the statement may not have originated with him. With whomsoever it originated, it never originated with me, and consequently is false. More than enough about it.

As I hope to see you so soon, my dear Fields, and as I am busily at work on the Christmas number, I will not make this a longer letter than I can help. I thank you most heartily for your proffered hospitality, and need not tell you that if I went to any friend's house in America, I would go to yours. But the readings are very hard work, and I think I cannot do better than observe the rule on that side of the Atlantic which I observe on this, of never, under such circumstances, going to a friend's house, but always staying at a hotel. I am able to observe it here, by being consistent and never breaking it. If I am equally consistent there, I can (I hope) offend no one.

Ever, my dear Fields,
Heartily and affectionately yours.

GAD'S HILL, *Saturday, Fifth October*, 1867.

Mr. Walter Thornbury.

MY DEAR THORNBURY,

Behold the best of my judgment on your questions.*
Susan Hopley and Jonathan Bradford? No. Too well known.
London Strikes and Spitalfields Cutters? Yes.
Fighting FitzGerald? Never mind him.
Duel of Lord Mohun and Duke of Hamilton? Ye-e-es.
Irish Abductions? I think not.
Brunswick Theatre? More Yes than No.
Theatrical Farewells? Yes.
Bow-Street Runners (as compared with Modern Detectives)? Yes.
Vauxhall and Ranelagh in the Last Century? Most decidedly. Don't forget Miss Burney.
Smugglers? No. Overdone.
Lacenaire? No. Ditto.
Madame Laffarge? No. Ditto.
Fashionable Life Last Century? Most decidedly yes.
Debates on the Slave Trade? Yes, generally. But beware of the Pirates, as we did them in the beginning of "Household Words."

Certainly I acquit you of all blame in the Bedford case. But one cannot do otherwise than sympathise with a son who is reason-

* As to subjects for articles in "All the Year Round."

ably tender of his father's memory. And no amount of private correspondence, we must remember, reaches the readers of a printed and published statement.

I told you some time ago that I believed the arsenic in Eliza Fenning's case to have been administered by the apprentice. I never was more convinced of anything in my life than of the girl's innocence, and I want words in which to express my indignation at the muddle-headed story of that parsonic blunderer whose audacity and conceit distorted some words that fell from her in the last days of her baiting.

Ever faithfully yours.

Lord
Lytton.

GAD'S HILL PLACE, HIGHAM BY ROCHESTER, KENT,
Monday, Fourteenth October, 1867.

MY DEAR LYTTON,

I am truly delighted to find that you are so well pleased with Fechter in "The Lady of Lyons." It was a labour of love with him, and I hold him in very high regard.

Don't give way to laziness, and *do* proceed with that play. There never was a time when a good new play was more wanted, or had a better opening for itself. Fechter is a thorough artist, and what he may sometimes want in personal force is compensated by the admirable whole he can make of a play, and his perfect understanding of its presentation as a picture to the eye and mind.

Ever affectionately yours.

Mr. William
Charles
Kent.

26, WELLINGTON STREET,
Saturday, Nineteenth October, 1867.

MY DEAR KENT,

In the midst of the great trouble you are taking in the cause of your undersigned affectionate friend, I hope the reading of the enclosed may be a sort of small godsend. Of course it is very strictly private. The printers are not yet trusted with the name, but the name will be, "No Thoroughfare." I have done the greater part of it; may you find it interesting !

My solicitor, a man of some mark and well known, is anxious to be on the Committee :

Frederic Ouvry, Esq.,
66, Lincoln's Inn Fields.

Ever affectionately yours.

P.S.—My sailor son !

I forgot him ! !

Coming up from Portsmouth for the dinner ! !

Der—er—oo not cur—ur—urse me, I implore.

Penitently.

GAD'S HILL,
Wednesday, Twenty-third October, 1867.

MY DEAR MRS. POWER,

I have a sad pleasure in the knowledge that our dear Marguerite so remembered her old friend, and I shall preserve the token of her remembrance with loving care. The sight of it has brought back many old days.

With kind remembrance to Mrs. Henderson,

Believe me always, very faithfully yours.

"ALL THE YEAR ROUND" OFFICE,
Friday, Twenty-fifth October, 1867.

MY DEAR LYTTON,

I have read the Play * with great attention, interest, and admiration; and I need not say to *you* that the art of it—the fine construction—the exquisite nicety of the touches—with which it is wrought out—have been a study to me in the pursuit of which I have had extraordinary relish.

Taking the Play as it stands, I have nothing whatever to add to your notes and memoranda of the points to be touched again, except that I have a little uneasiness in that burst of anger and inflexibility consequent upon having been deceived, coming out of Hegio. I see the kind of actor who *must* play Hegio, and I see that the audience will not believe in his doing anything so serious. (I suppose it would be impossible to get this effect out of the mother—or through the mother's influence, instead of out of the godfather of Hegiopolis?)

Now, as to the classical ground and manners of the Play. I suppose the objection to the Greek dress to be already—as Defoe would write it—"gotten over" by your suggestion. I suppose the dress not to be conventionally associated with stilts and boredom, but to be new to the public eye and very picturesque. Grant all that;—the names remain. Now, not only used such names to be inseparable in the public mind from stately weariness, but of late days they have become inseparable in the same public mind from silly puns upon the names, and from Burlesque. You do not know (I hope, at least, for my friend's sake) what the Strand Theatre is. A Greek name and a break-down nigger dance, have become inseparable there. I do not mean to say that your genius may not be too powerful for such associations; but I do most positively mean to say that you would lose half the play in overcoming them. At the best you would have to contend against them through the

* The Play referred to is founded on the "Captives" of Plautus, and is entitled "The Captives." It has never been acted or published.

first three acts. The old tendency to become frozen on classical ground would be in the best part of the audience; the new tendency to titter on such ground would be in the worst part. And instead of starting fair with the audience, it is my conviction that you would start with them against you and would have to win them over.

Furthermore, with reference to your note to me on this head, you take up a position with reference to poor dear Talfourd's "Ion" which I altogether dispute. It never was a popular play, I say. It derived a certain amount of out-of-door's popularity from the circumstances under which, and the man by whom, it was written. But I say that it never was a popular play on the Stage, and never made out a case of attraction there.

As to changing the ground to·Russia, let me ask you, did you ever see the "Nouvelles Russes" of Nicolas Gogol, translated into French by Louis Viardot? There is a story among them called "Tarass Boulla," in which, as it seems to me, all the conditions you want for such transplantation are to be found. So changed, you would have the popular sympathy with the Slave or Serf, or Prisoner of War, from the first. But I do not think it is to be got, save at great hazard, and with lamentable waste of force on the ground the Play now occupies.

I shall keep this note until to-morrow to correct my conviction if I can see the least reason for correcting it; but I feel very confident indeed that I cannot be shaken in it.

Saturday.

I have thought it over again, and have gone over the play again with an imaginary stage and actors before me, and I am still of the same mind.

Believe me, ever affectionately yours.

Mr. J. L.
Toole.

GAD'S HILL PLACE, HIGHAM BY ROCHESTER, KENT,
Saturday, Second November, 1867.

MY DEAR MR. TOOLE,

I heartily thank you for your elegant token of remembrance, and for your earnest letter. Both have afforded me real pleasure, and the first-named shall go with me on my journey.

Let me take this opportunity of saying that on receipt of your letter concerning to-day's dinner, I immediately forwarded your request to the honorary secretary. I hope you will understand that I could not, in delicacy, otherwise take part in the matter.

Again thanking you most cordially,

Believe me, always faithfully yours.

26, WELLINGTON STREET,
Sunday, Third November, 1867.

MY DEAR WILLS,

If you were to write me many such warm-hearted letters as you send this morning, my heart would fail me! There is nothing that so breaks down my determination, or shows me what an iron force I put upon myself, and how weak it is, as a touch of true affection from a tried friend.

All that you so earnestly say about the goodwill and devotion of all engaged, I perceived and deeply felt last night. It moved me even more than the demonstration itself, though I do suppose it was the most brilliant ever seen. When I got up to speak, but for taking a desperate hold of myself, I should have lost my sight and voice and sat down again.

God bless you, my dear fellow. I am ever and ever,

Your affectionate.

OFFICE OF "ALL THE YEAR ROUND"
Tuesday, Fifth November, 1867.

MY DEAR MRS. WATSON,

A thousand thanks for your kind letter, and many congratulations on your having successfully attained a dignity which I never allow to be mentioned in my presence. Charley's children are instructed from their tenderest months only to know me as "Wenerables," which they sincerely believe to be my name, and a kind of title that I have received from a grateful country.

Alas! I cannot have the pleasure of seeing you before I presently go to Liverpool. Every moment of my time is pre-occupied. But I send you my sincere love, and am always truthful to the dear old days, and the memory of one of the dearest friends I ever loved.

Affectionately yours.

ABOARD THE "CUBA," QUEENSTOWN HARBOUR,
Sunday, Tenth November, 1867.

MY DEAREST MAMIE,

We arrived here at seven this morning, and shall probably remain awaiting our mail, until four or five this afternoon. The weather in the passage here was delightful, and we had scarcely any motion beyond that of the screw.

We are nearly but not quite full of passengers. At table I sit next the captain, on his right, on the outside of the table and close to the door. My little cabin is big enough for everything but getting up in and going to bed in. As it has a good window which I can leave open all night, and a door which I can set open too, it suits my chief requirements of it—plenty of air—admirably. On a writing-slab in it, which pulls out when wanted, I now write in a majestic manner.

Many of the passengers are American, and I am already on the best terms with nearly all the ship.

We began our voyage yesterday a very little while after you left us, which was a great relief. The wind is S.E. this morning, and if it would keep so we should go along nobly. My dearest love to your aunt, and also to Katie and all the rest. I am in very good health, thank God, and as well as possible.

Miss
Hogarth.

ABOARD THE "CUBA," FIVE DAYS OUT,
Wednesday, Thirteenth November, 1867.

MY DEAREST GEORGY,

As I wrote to Mamie last, I now write to you, or mean to do it, if the motion of the ship will let me.

We are very nearly halfway to-day. The weather was favourable for us until yesterday morning, when we got a head-wind which still stands by us. We have rolled and pitched, of course; but on the whole have been wonderfully well off. I have had headache and have felt faint once or twice, *but have not been sick at all.* My spacious cabin is very noisy at night, as the most important working of the ship goes on outside my window and over my head; but it is very airy, and if the weather be bad and I can't open the window, I can open the door all night. If the weather be fine (as it is now), I can open both door and window, and write between them. Last night, I got a foot-bath under the dignified circumstances of sitting on a camp-stool in my cabin, and having the bath (and my feet) in the passage outside. The officers' quarters are close to me, and, as I know them all, I get reports of the weather and the way we are making when the watch is changed, and I am (as I usually am) lying awake. The motion of the screw is at its slightest vibration in my particular part of the ship. The silent captain, reported gruff, is a very good fellow and an honest fellow. Kelly has been ill all the time, and not of the slightest use, and is ill now. Scott always cheerful, and useful, and ready; a better servant for the kind of work there never can have been. Young Lowndes has been fearfully sick until mid-day yesterday. His cabin is pitch dark, and full of blackbeetles. He shares mine until nine o'clock at night, when Scott carries him off to bed. He also dines with me in my magnificent chamber. This passage in winter time cannot be said to be an enjoyable excursion, but I certainly am making it under the best circumstances.

So much for my news, except that I have been constantly

reading, and find that "Pierra" that Mrs. Hogge sent me by Katie to be a very remarkable book, not only for its grim and horrible story, but for its suggestion of wheels within wheels, and sad human mysteries. Baker's second book not nearly so good as his first, but his first anticipated it.

Saturday, Sixteenth.

Last Thursday afternoon a heavy gale of wind sprang up and blew hard until dark, when it seemed to lull. But it then came on again with great violence, and blew tremendously all night. The noise, and the rolling and plunging of the ship, were awful. Nobody on board could get any sleep, and numbers of passengers were rolled out of their berths. Having a side-board to mine to keep me in, like a baby, I lay still. But it was a dismal night indeed, and it was curious to see the change it had made in the faces of all the passengers yesterday. It cannot be denied that these winter crossings are very trying and startling; while the personal discomfort of not being able to wash, and the miseries of getting up and going to bed, with what small means there are all sliding, and sloping, and slopping about, are really in their way distressing.

This forenoon we made Cape Race, and are now running along at full speed with the land beside us. Kelly still useless, and positively declining to show on deck. Scott, with an eight-day-old moustache, more super-like than ever. My foot (I hope from walking on the boarded deck) in a very shy condition to-day, and rather painful. I shaved this morning for the first time since Liverpool; dodging at the glass, very much like Fechter's imitation of ———. The white cat that came off with us in the tender a general favourite. She belongs to the daughter of a Southerner, returning with his wife and family from a two-years' tour in Europe.

Sunday, Seventeenth.

At four o'clock this morning we got into bad weather again, and the state of things at breakfast-time was unutterably miserable. Nearly all the passengers in their berths—no possibility of standing on deck—sickness and groans—impracticable to pass a cup of tea from one pair of hands to another. It has slightly moderated since (between two and three in the afternoon I write), and the sun is shining, but the rolling of the ship surpasses all imagination or description.

I write with great difficulty, wedged up in a corner, and having my heels on the paper as often as the pen. Kelly worse than ever, and Scott better than ever.

My desk and I have just arisen from the floor.

PARKER HOUSE, BOSTON,
Thursday, Twenty-first November, 1867.

I arrived here on Tuesday night, after a very slow passage from Halifax against head-winds. All the tickets for the first four readings here (all yet announced) were sold immediately on their being issued.

You know that I begin on the Second of December with "Carol" and "Trial"? Shall be heartily glad to begin to count the readings off.

This is an immense hotel, with all manner of white marble public passages and public rooms. I live in a corner high up, and have a hot and cold bath in my bedroom (communicating with the sitting-room), and comforts not in existence when I was here before. The cost of living is enormous, but happily we can afford it. I dine to-day with Longfellow, Emerson, Holmes, and Agassiz. Longfellow was here yesterday. Perfectly white in hair and beard, but a remarkably handsome and notable-looking man. The city has increased enormously in five-and-twenty years. It has grown more mercantile—is like Leeds mixed with Preston, and flavoured with New Brighton; but for smoke and fog you substitute an exquisitely bright light air. I found my rooms beautifully decorated (by Mrs. Fields) with choice flowers, and set off by a number of good books. I am not much persecuted by people in general, as Dolby has happily made up his mind that the less I am exhibited for nothing the better. So our men sit outside the room door and wrestle with mankind.

We had speech-making and singing in the saloon of the *Cuba* after the last dinner of the voyage. I think I have acquired a high reputation from drawing out the captain, and getting him to take the second in "All's Well," and likewise in "There's not in the wide world" (your parent taking first), than from anything previously known of me on these shores. I hope the effect of these achievements may not dim the lustre of the readings. We also sang (with a Chicago lady, and a strong-minded woman from I don't know where) "Auld Lang Syne," with a tender melancholy, expressive of having all four been united from our cradles. The more dismal we were, the more delighted the company were. Once (when we paddled i' the burn) the captain took a little cruise round the compass on his own account, touching at the "Canadian Boat Song," and taking in supplies at "Jubilate," "Seas between us braid ha' roared," and roared like the seas themselves. Finally, I proposed the ladies in a speech that convulsed the stewards, and we closed with a brilliant success. Hillard has just been in and sent his love "to those dear girls." He has grown much older.

He is now District Attorney of the State of Massachusetts, which is a very good office. Best love to your aunt and Katie, and Charley and all his house, and all friends.

PARKER HOUSE, BOSTON, *Monday, Twenty-fifth November,* 1867.

Miss Hogarth.

I cannot remember to whom I wrote last, but it will not much matter if I make a mistake ; this being generally to report myself so well, that I am constantly chafing at not having begun to-night instead of this night week.

Dolby is over at New York, where we are at our wits' end how to keep tickets out of the hands of speculators. Morgan is staying with me ; came yesterday to breakfast, and goes home to-morrow. Fields and Mrs. Fields also dined yesterday. She is a very nice woman, with a rare relish for humour and a most contagious laugh. The Bostonians having been duly informed that I wish to be quiet, really leave me as much so as I should be in Manchester or Liverpool. This I cannot expect to last elsewhere ; but it is a most welcome relief here, as I have all the readings to get up. The people are perfectly kind and perfectly agreeable. If I stop to look in at a shop-window, a score of passers-by stop ; and after I begin to read, I cannot expect in the natural course of things to get off so easily. But I every day take from seven to ten miles in peace.

It is sad to see Longfellow's house (the house in which his wife was burnt) with his young daughters in it, and the shadow of that terrible story. The young undergraduates of Cambridge (he is a professor there) have made a representation to him that they are five hundred strong, and cannot get one ticket. I don't know what is to be done for them ; I suppose I must read there somehow. We are all in the clouds until I shall have broken ground in New York, as to where readings will be possible, and where impossible.

Agassiz is one of the most natural and jovial of men. I go out a-visiting as little as I can, but still have to dine, and what is worse, sup pretty often. Socially, I am (as I was here before) wonderfully reminded of Edinburgh when I had many friends in it.

Your account and Mamie's of the return journey to London gave me great pleasure. I was delighted with your report of Wilkie, and not surprised by Chappell's coming out gallantly.

My anxiety to get to work is greater than I can express, because time seems to be making no movement towards home until I shall be reading hard. Then I shall begin to count and count and count the upward steps to May.

If ever you should be in a position to advise a traveller going on a sea voyage, remember that there is some mysterious service done to the bilious system when it is shaken, by baked apples. Noticing that they were produced on board the *Cuba*, every day at lunch and dinner, I thought I would make the experiment of always eating them freely. I am confident that they did wonders, not only at the time, but in stopping the imaginary pitching and rolling after the voyage is over, from which many good amateur sailors suffer. I have hardly had the sensation at all, except in washing of a morning. At that time I still hold on with one knee to the washing-stand, and could swear that it rolls from left to right. The *Cuba* does not return until Wednesday, the Fourth December. You may suppose that every officer on board is coming on Monday, and that Dolby has provided extra stools for them.

Mr. Charles
Dickens.

PARKER HOUSE, BOSTON, U.S.,
Saturday, Thirtieth November, 1867.

MY DEAR CHARLEY,

You will have heard before now how fortunate I was on my voyage, and how I was not sick for a moment. These screws are tremendous ships for carrying on, and for rolling, and their vibration is rather distressing. But my little cabin, being for'ard of the machinery, was in the best part of the vessel, and I had as much air in it, night and day, as I chose. The saloon being kept absolutely without air, I mostly dined in my own den, in spite of my being allotted the post of honour on the right hand of the captain.

The tickets for the first four readings here (the only readings announced) were all sold immediately. The tickets for the first four readings in New York (the only readings announced there also) were on sale yesterday, and were all sold in a few hours. Engagements of any kind and every kind I steadily refuse, being resolved to take what is to be taken myself. Dolby is nearly worked off his legs; nothing can exceed his energy and good humour, and he is extremely popular everywhere. My great desire is to avoid much travelling, and to try to get the people to come to me, instead of my going to them. If I can effect this to any moderate extent, I shall be saved a great deal of knocking about.

As they don't seem (Americans who have heard me on their travels excepted) to have the least idea here of what the readings are like, and as they are accustomed to mere readings out of a book, I am inclined to think the excitement will increase when I shall have begun. Everybody is very kind and considerate, and I have a number of old friends here, at the Bar and connected with the University.   I am now negotiating to bring out the dramatic version of "No Thoroughfare" at New York.   It is quite upon the cards that it may turn up trumps.

I was interrupted in that place by a call from my old secretary in the States, Mr. Putnam.   It was quite affecting to see his delight in meeting his old master again.   And when I told him that Anne was married, and that I had (unacknowledged) grandchildren, he laughed and cried together.   I suppose you don't remember Longfellow, though he remembers you in a black velvet frock very well.   He is now white-haired and white-bearded, but remarkably handsome.   He still lives in his old house, where his beautiful wife was burnt to death. I dined with him the other day, and could not get the terrific scene out of my imagination.   She was in a blaze in an instant, rushed into his arms with a wild cry, and never spoke afterwards.

My love to Bessie, and to Mekitty, and all the babbies.

Ever, my dear Charley, your affectionate Father.

Tuesday, Third December, 1867.

Success last night beyond description or exaggeration.   The whole city is quite frantic about it to-day, and it is impossible that prospects could be more brilliant.

PARKER HOUSE, BOSTON,   Miss
Sunday, First December, 1867.   Dickens.

I received yours of the Eighteenth November, yesterday. As I left Halifax in the *Cuba* that very day, you probably saw us telegraphed in *The Times* on the Nineteenth.

I think you had best in future (unless I give you intimation to the contrary) address your letters to me, at the Westminster Hotel, Irving Place, New York City.   It is a more central position than this, and we are likely to be much more there than here.   I am going to set up a brougham in New York, and keep my rooms at that hotel.

They are said to be a very quiet audience here, appreciative but not demonstrative.   I shall try to change their character a little.

I have been going on very well. A horrible custom obtains in these parts of asking you to dinner somewhere at half-past two, and to supper somewhere else about eight.   I have run this gauntlet more than once, and its effect is, that there is no day for any useful purpose, and that the length of the evening is multiplied by a hundred.   Yesterday I dined with a club at half-past two, and came back here at half-past eight with a general impression that it was at least two o'clock in the morning. Two days before I dined with Longfellow at half-past two, and came back at eight, supposing it to be midnight. To-day we have a state dinner-party in our rooms at six, Mr. and Mrs. Fields, and Mr. and Mrs. Bigelow. (He is a friend of Forster's, and was American Minister in Paris.) There are no negro waiters here, all the servants are Irish—willing, but not able. The dinners and wines are very good. I keep our own rooms well ventilated by opening the windows, but no window is ever opened in the halls or passages, and they are so overheated by a great furnace, that they make me faint and sick. The air is like that of a pre-Adamite ironing-day in full blast. Your respected parent is immensely popular in Boston society, and its cordiality and unaffected heartiness are charming. I wish I could carry it with me.

The leading New York papers have sent men over for to-morrow night with instructions to telegraph columns of descriptions. Great excitement and expectation everywhere. Fields says he has looked forward to it so long that he knows he will die at five minutes to eight.

At the New York barriers, where the tickets are on sale and the people ranged as at the Paris theatres, speculators went up and down offering "twenty dollars for anybody's place." The money was in no case accepted. One man sold two tickets for the second, third, and fourth night "for one ticket for the first, fifty dollars" (about seven pounds ten shillings) "and a brandy cocktail," which is an iced bitter drink. The weather has been rather muggy and languid until yesterday, when there was the coldest wind blowing that I ever felt. In the night it froze very hard, and to-day the sky is beautiful.

Tuesday, Third December.

Most magnificent reception last night, and most signal and complete success. Nothing could be more triumphant. The people will hear of nothing else and talk of nothing else. Nothing that was ever done here, they all agree, evoked any approach to such enthusiasm. I was quite as cool and quick as if I were reading at Greenwich, and went at it accordingly. My love to Mr. and Mrs. Hulkes and the boy, and to Mr. and Mrs. Malleson.*

M. Charles Fechter.

PARKER HOUSE, BOSTON,
Third December, 1867.

MY DEAR FECHTER,

I have been very uneasy about you, seeing in the paper that you were taken ill on the stage. But a letter from Georgy

* The nearest neighbours at Higham, and intimate friends.

this morning reassures me by giving me a splendid account of your triumphant last night at the Lyceum.

I hope to bring out our Play* with Wallack in New York, and to have it played in many other parts of the States. I have sent to Wilkie for models, etc. If I waited for time to do more than write you my love, I should miss the mail to-morrow. Take my love, then, my dear fellow, and believe me ever

Your affectionate.

BOSTON, *Wednesday, Fourth December*, 1867.   Miss Hogarth.

MY DEAREST GEORGY,

I find that by going off to the *Cuba* myself this morning I can send you the enclosed for Mary Boyle (I don't know how to address her), whose usual flower for my button-hole was produced in the most extraordinary manner here last Monday night! All well and prosperous.

BOSTON, *Fourth December*, 1867.   Miss Mary Boyle.

MY DEAR MEERY,

You can have no idea of the glow of pleasure and amazement with which I saw your remembrance of me lying on my dressing-table here last Monday night. Whosoever undertook that commission accomplished it to a miracle. But you must go away four thousand miles, and have such a token conveyed to *you*, before you can quite appreciate the feeling of receiving it. Ten thousand loving thanks.

Immense success here, and unbounded enthusiasm. My largest expectations far surpassed.

Ever your affectionate

Jo.

WESTMINSTER HOTEL, IRVING PLACE, NEW YORK CITY,   Miss Dickens.
Wednesday, Eleventh December, 1867.

MY DEAREST MAMIE,

Dolby sends you a few papers by this post. You will see from their tone what a success it is.

We are now selling (at the hall) the tickets for the four readings of next week. At nine o'clock this morning there were two thousand people in waiting, and they had begun to assemble in the bitter cold as early as two o'clock. All night long Dolby and our man have been stamping tickets (immediately over my head, by-the-bye, and keeping me awake). This hotel is quite as quiet as Mivart's, in Brook Street. It is not very much larger. There are American hotels close by, with five hundred bedrooms, and I

* "No Thoroughfare."

don't know how many boarders ; but this is conducted on what is
called " the European principle," and is an admirable mixture of a
first-class French and English house.　I keep a very smart carriage
and pair ; and if you were to behold me driving out, furred up to
the moustache, with furs on the coach-boy and on the driver, and
with an immense white, red, and yellow striped rug for a covering,
you would suppose me to be of Hungarian or Polish nationality.

Dolby sends his kindest regards.　He is just come in from our
ticket sales, and has put such an immense untidy heap of paper
money on the table that it looks like a family wash.　He hardly
ever dines, and is always tearing about at unreasonable hours.

My best love to your aunt (to whom I will write next), and to
Katie, and to both the Charleys, and all the Christmas circle, not
forgetting Chorley, to whom give my special remembrance.　You
may get this by Christmas Day.　*We* shall have to keep it travelling from Boston here.

Miss
Hogarth.

WESTMINSTER HOTEL, IRVING PLACE, NEW YORK CITY,
Monday, Sixteenth December, 1867.

We have been snowed up here, and the communication
with Boston is still very much retarded.　Thus we have received
no letters by the Cunard steamer that came in last Wednesday,
and are in a grim state of mind on that subject.

Last night I was getting into bed just at twelve o'clock, when
Dolby came to my door to inform me that the house was on fire
(I had previously smelt fire for two hours).　I got Scott up
directly, told him to pack the books and clothes for the readings
first, dressed, and pocketed my jewels and papers, while Dolby
stuffed himself out with money.　Meanwhile the police and fire-
men were in the house, endeavouring to find where the fire was.
For some time it baffled their endeavours, but at last, bursting
out through some stairs, they cut the stairs away, and traced it to
its source in a certain fire-grate.　By this time the hose was laid
all through the house from a great tank on the roof, and everybody
turned out to help.　It was the oddest sight, and people had put
the strangest things on !　After a little chopping and cutting with
axes and handing about of water, the fire was confined to a dining-
room in which it had originated, and then everybody talked to
everybody else, the ladies being particularly loquacious and cheerful.
And so we got to bed again at about two.

The excitement of the readings continues unabated.　They are
a wonderfully fine audience, even better than Edinburgh, and
almost, if not quite, as good as Paris.

Dolby continues to be the most unpopular man in America

(mainly because he can't get four thousand people into a room that holds two thousand), and is reviled in print daily. Yesterday morning a newspaper proclaims of him: "Surely it is time that the pudding-headed Dolby retired into the native gloom from which he has emerged." He takes it very coolly, and does his best. Mrs. Morgan sent me, the other night, I suppose the finest and costliest basket of flowers ever seen, made of white camellias, yellow roses, pink roses, and I don't know what else. It is a yard and a half round at its smallest part.

BOSTON, *Sunday, Twenty-second December*, 1867.　Miss Hogarth.

Coming here from New York last night (after a detestable journey), I was delighted to find your letter of the sixth. I read it at my ten-o'clock dinner with the greatest interest and pleasure, and then we talked of home till we went to bed.

When we got here last Saturday night, we found that Mrs. Fields had not only garnished the rooms with flowers, but also with holly (with real red berries) and festoons of moss dependent from the looking-glasses and picture frames. She is one of the dearest little women in the world. The homely Christmas look of the place quite affected us. Yesterday we dined at her house, and there was a plum-pudding, brought on blazing, and not to be surpassed in any house in England. There is a certain Captain Dolliver, belonging to the Boston Custom House, who came off in the little steamer that brought me ashore from the *Cuba*. He took it into his head that he would have a piece of English mistle-toe brought out in this week's Cunard, which should be laid upon my breakfast-table. And there it was this morning. In such affectionate touches as this, these New England people are especially amiable.

As a general rule, you may lay it down that whatever you see about me in the papers is not true. But although my voyage out was of that highly hilarious description that you first made known to me, you may *generally* lend a more believing ear to the Philadelphia correspondent of *The Times*. I don't know him, but I know the source from which he derives his information, and it is a very respectable one.

Did I tell you in a former letter from here, to tell Anne, with her old master's love, that I had seen Putnam, my old secretary? Grey, and with several front teeth out, but I would have known him anywhere. He is coming to "Copperfield" to-night, accompanied by his wife and daughter, and is in the seventh heaven at having his tickets given him.

Our hotel in New York was on fire *again* the other night.

But fires in this country are quite matters of course. There was a large one there at four this morning, and I don't think a single night has passed, since I have been under the protection of the Eagle,* but I have heard the fire-bells dolefully clanging all over the city.

My love to all, and to Mrs. Hulkes and the boy. By-the-bye, when we left New York for this place, Dolby called my amazed attention to the circumstance that Scott was leaning his head against the side of the carriage and weeping bitterly. I asked him what was the matter, and he replied: "The owdacious treatment of the luggage, which was more outrageous than a man could bear." I told him not to make a fool of himself; but they do knock it about cruelly. I think every trunk we have is already broken.

I must leave off, as I am going out for a walk in a bright sunlight and a complete break-up of the frost and snow. I am much better than I have been during the last week, but have a cold.

Miss
Dickens.

WESTMINSTER HOTEL, IRVING PLACE, NEW YORK CITY,
Thursday, Twenty-sixth December, 1867.

I got your aunt's last letter at Boston yesterday, Christmas Day morning, when I was starting at eleven o'clock to come back to this place. I wanted it very much, for I had a frightful cold (English colds are nothing to those of this country), and was exceedingly depressed and miserable. Not that I had any reason but illness for being so, since the Bostonians had been quite astounding in their demonstrations. I never saw anything like them on Christmas Eve. But it is a bad country to be unwell and travelling in; you are one of say a hundred people in a heated car, with a great stove in it, and all the little windows closed, and the hurrying and banging about are indescribable. The atmosphere is detestable, and the motion often all but intolerable. However, we got our dinner here at eight o'clock, and plucked up a little, and I made some hot gin punch to drink a merry Christmas to all at home in. But it must be confessed that we were both very dull. I have been in bed all day until two o'clock, and here I am now (at three o'clock) a little better. But I am not fit to read, and I must read to-night. After watching the general character pretty closely, I became quite sure that Dolby was wrong on the length of the stay and the number of readings we had proposed in this place. I am quite certain that it is one of the national peculiarities that what they want must be difficult of attainment. I therefore a few days ago made a *coup d'état*, and altered the

* "Eagle" Fire Insurance Office.

whole scheme. There has been a great storm here for a few days, and the streets, though wet, are becoming passable again. Dolby and Osgood are out in it to-day on a variety of business, and left in grave and solemn state. Scott and the gasman are stricken with dumb concern, not having received one single letter from home since they left. What their wives can have done with the letters they take it for granted they have written is the stormy speculation at the door of my hall dressing-room every night.

If I do not send a letter to Katie by this mail, it will be because I shall probably be obliged to go across the water to Brooklyn to-morrow to see a church, in which it is proposed that I shall read ! ! ! Horrible visions of being put in the pulpit already beset me. And whether the audience will be in pews is another consideration which greatly disturbs my mind. No paper ever comes out without a leader on Dolby, who of course reads them all, and never can understand why I don't, in which he is called all the bad names in (and not in) the language.

We always call him P. H. Dolby now, in consequence of one of these graceful specimens of literature describing him as the "pudding-headed."

I fear that when we travel he will have to be always before me, so that I may not see him six times in as many weeks. However, I shall have done a fourth of the whole this very next week !

Friday.

I managed to read last night, but it was as much as I could do. To-day I am so very unwell, that I have sent for a doctor ; he has just been, and is in doubt whether I shall not have to stop reading for a while.

WESTMINSTER HOTEL, IRVING PLACE, NEW YORK,   Miss
Monday, Thirtieth December, 1867.   Dickens.

I am getting all right again. I have not been well, been very low, and have been obliged to have a doctor ; a very agreeable fellow indeed, who soon turned out to be an old friend of Olliffe's.* He has set me on my legs and taken his leave "professionally," though he means to give me a call now and then.

No news here. All going on in the regular way. I read in that church I told you of, about the middle of January. It is wonderfully seated for two thousand people, and is as easy to speak in as if they were two hundred. The people are seated in pews, and we let the pews. I stand on a small platform from

* Dr. Fordyce Barker.

which the pulpit will be removed for the occasion!! I emerge from the vestry!!! On Friday next I shall have read a fourth of my whole list, besides having had twelve days' holiday when I first came out. So please God I shall soon get to the half, and so begin to work hopefully round.

I suppose you were at the Adelphi on Thursday night last. Nothing is being played here scarcely that is not founded on my books—"Cricket," "Oliver Twist," "Our Mutual Friend," and I don't know what else, every night. I can't get down Broadway for my own portrait; and yet I live almost as quietly in this hotel, as if I were at the office, and go in and out by a side door just as I might there.

I shall be curious to know who were at Gad's Hill on Christmas Day, and how you (as they say in this country) "got along." It is exceedingly cold here again, after two or three quite spring days.

Ever your affectionate Father.

1868.

NARRATIVE.

CHARLES DICKENS remained in America through the winter, returning home from New York in the *Russia*, on the Nineteenth of April. His letters show how entirely he gave himself up to the business of the readings, how severely his health suffered from the climate, and from the perpetual travelling and hard work, and yet how he was able to battle through to the end. These letters are also full of allusions to the many kind and dear friends who contributed so largely to the pleasure of this American visit, and whose love and attention gave a touch of *home* to his private life, and left such affection and gratitude in his heart as he could never forget. Many of these friends paid visits to Gad's Hill; the first to come during this summer being Mr. Longfellow, his daughters, and Mr. Appleton, brother-in-law of Mr. Longfellow, and Mr. and Mrs. Charles Eliot Norton, of Cambridge.

For the future, there were to be no more Christmas numbers of "All the Year Round." Observing the extent to which they were now copied in all directions, Charles Dickens supposed them likely to become tiresome to the public, and so determined that in his journal they should be discontinued.

While still in America, he made an agreement with the Messrs. Chappell to give a series of farewell readings in England, to commence in the autumn of this year. So, in October, Charles Dickens started off again for a tour in the provinces. He had for some time been planning, by way of a novelty for this series, a reading from the murder in "Oliver Twist," but finding it very horrible, he was fearful of trying its effect for the first time on a public audience. It was therefore resolved, that a trial of it should be made to a limited private audience in St. James's Hall, on the evening of the Eighteenth of November. This trial proved eminently successful, and "The Murder from Oliver Twist" became one of the most popular of his selections. But the physical exertion it involved was far greater than that of any of his previous readings, and added immensely to the excitement and exhaustion which they caused him.

One of the first letters of the year from America is addressed to Mr. Samuel Cartwright, of surgical and artistic reputation, and greatly esteemed by Charles Dickens, both in his professional capacity and as a private friend.

The letter written to Mrs. Cattermole, in May, tells of the illness of Mr. George Cattermole. This dear old friend, so associated with Charles Dickens and his works, died soon afterwards, and the letter to his widow shows that Charles Dickens was exerting himself in her behalf.

We make use of the very short note addressed to Mr. John Everett Millais, R.A.,* because it is the only one he has been able to find for us.

Mr. Serle, a dramatic author, was acting-manager of Covent Garden Theatre in 1838, when his acquaintance with Charles Dickens first began. The letter to Mr. Serle is in answer to some questions as to the subject of the extension of copyright to the United States.

The play of "No Thoroughfare" having been translated into French under the title of "L'Abîme," Charles Dickens went over to Paris to be present at the first night of its production.

On the Twenty-sixth of September, his youngest son, Edward Bulwer Lytton (the "Plorn" so often mentioned), started for Australia, to join his brother Alfred Tennyson, who was already established there. It will be seen by his own words how deeply and how sadly Charles Dickens felt this parting. In October of this year, his son Henry Fielding entered Trinity Hall, Cambridge, as an undergraduate.

Mr. J. C. Parkinson, to whom a letter is addressed, was at that time holding a Government appointment, and contributing largely to journalism and periodical literature.

* Now Sir John Millais, Bart.

Miss
Hogarth.

WESTMINSTER HOTEL, IRVING PLACE, NEW YORK,
Friday, Third January, 1868.

MY DEAREST GEORGY,

To-night, I read out the first quarter of my list. It seems impossible to devise any scheme for getting the tickets into the people's hands without the intervention of speculators. The people *will not* help themselves; and, of course, the speculators and all other such prowlers throw as great obstacles in Dolby's way (an Englishman's) as they possibly can. He may be a little injudicious into the bargain. Last night, for instance, he met one of the "ushers" (who show people to their seats) coming in with Kelly. It is against orders that anyone employed in front should go out during the readings, and he took this man to task in the British manner. Instantly the free and independent usher put on his hat and walked off. Seeing which, all the other free and independent ushers (some twenty in number) put on *their* hats and walked off, leaving us absolutely devoid and destitute of a staff for to-night. One has since been improvised; but it was a small matter to raise a stir and ill will about, especially as one of our men was equally in fault.

We have a regular clerk, a Bostonian whose name is Wild. He, Osgood, Dolby, Kelly, Scott, George the gasman, and perhaps a boy or two, constitute my body-guard. It seems a large number of people, but the business cannot be done with fewer. The speculators buying the front seats to sell at a premium (and we have found instances of this being done by merchants in good position!), and the public perpetually pitching into Dolby for selling them back seats, the result is that they won't have the back seats, send back their tickets, write and print volumes on the subject, and deter others from coming.

Tell Plorn, with my love, that I think he will find himself much interested at that college,* and that it is very likely he may make some acquaintances there that will hereafter be pleasant and useful to him. Sir Sydney Dacres is the best of friends. I have a letter from Mrs. Hulkes by this post, wherein the boy encloses a violet, now lying on the table before me. Let her know that it arrived safely, and retaining its colour. I took it for granted that Mary would have asked Chorley for Christmas Day, and am very glad she ultimately did so. I am sorry that Harry lost his prize, but believe it was not his fault. Let *him* know *that*, with my love. I would have written to him by this mail in answer to his, but for other occupation. Did I tell you that my landlord made me a drink (brandy, rum, and snow the principal ingredients) called a

* The Agricultural College, Cirencester.

"Rocky Mountain sneezer"? Or that the favourite drink before you get up is an "eye-opener"? Or that Roberts (second landlord), no sooner saw me on the night of the first fire, than, with his property blazing, he insisted on taking me down into a roomful of hot smoke to drink brandy and water with him? We have not been on fire again, by-the-bye, more than once.

There has been another fall of snow, succeeded by a heavy thaw. I have laid down my sledge, and taken up my carriage again, in consequence. I am nearly all right, but cannot get rid of an intolerable cold in the head. No more news.

PARKER HOUSE, BOSTON, U.S.,   Miss
Fourth January, 1868.   Hogarth.

I write to you by this opportunity, though I really have nothing to tell you. The work is hard and the climate is hard. We made a tremendous hit last night with "Nickleby" and "Boots," which the Bostonians certainly on the whole appreciate more than "Copperfield"! Dolby's business at night is a mere nothing, for these people are so accustomed to take care of themselves, that one of these immense audiences will fall into their places with an ease amazing to a frequenter of St. James's Hall. And the certainty with which they are all in, before I go on, is a very acceptable mark of respect. I must add, too, that although there is a conventional familiarity in the use of one's name in the newspapers as "Dickens," "Charlie," and what not, I do not in the least see that familiarity in the writers themselves. An inscrutable tone obtains in journalism, which a stranger cannot understand. If I say in common courtesy to one of them, when Dolby introduces, "I am much obliged to you for your interest in me," or so forth, he seems quite shocked, and has a bearing of perfect modesty and propriety. I am rather inclined to think that they suppose their printed tone to be the public's love of smartness, but it is immensely difficult to make out. All I can as yet make out is, that my perfect freedom from bondage, and at any moment to go on or leave off, or otherwise do as I like, is the only safe position to occupy.

Again; there are two apparently irreconcilable contrasts here. Down below in this hotel every night are the bar loungers, dram drinkers, drunkards, swaggerers, loafers, that one might find in a Boucicault play. Within half an hour is Cambridge, where a delightful domestic life—simple, self-respectful, cordial, and affectionate—is seen in an admirable aspect. All New England is primitive and puritanical. All about and around it is a puddle of mixed human mud, with no such quality in it. Perhaps I may in time sift out some tolerably intelligible whole, but I certainly have not done so yet. It is a good sign, may be, that it all seems immensely more difficult to understand than it was when I was here before.

Felton left two daughters. I have only seen the eldest, a very sensible, frank, pleasant girl of eight-and-twenty, perhaps, rather like him in the face. A striking-looking daughter of Hawthorn's (who is also dead) came into my room last night. The day has slipped on to three o'clock, hence this sudden break off.

Ever affectionately.

Mr. W.
Wilkie
Collins.

WESTMINSTER HOTEL, NEW YORK,
Sunday, Twelfth January, 1868.

MY DEAR WILKIE,

First, of the play.* I am truly delighted to learn that it made so great a success, and I hope I may yet see it on the Adelphi boards. You have had a world of trouble and work with it, but I hope will be repaid in some degree by the pleasure of a triumph. Even for the alteration at the end of the fourth act (of which you tell me in your letter received yesterday), I was fully prepared, for I COULD NOT see the original effect in the reading of the play, and COULD NOT make it go. I agree with Webster in thinking it best that Obenreizer should die on the stage; but no doubt that point is disposed of. In reading the play before the representation, I felt that it was too long, and that there was a good deal of unnecessary explanation. Those points are, no doubt, disposed of too by this time.

We shall do nothing with it on this side. Pirates are producing their own wretched versions in all directions, thus (as Wills would say) anticipating and glutting "the market." I registered our play as the property of Ticknor and Fields, American citizens. But, besides that the law on the point is extremely doubtful, the manager of the Museum Theatre, Boston, instantly announced his version. (You may suppose what it is and how it is done, when I tell you that it was playing within ten days of the arrival out of the Christmas number.) Thereupon Ticknor and Fields gave him notice that he mustn't play it. Unto which he replied, that he meant to play it and would play it. Of course he knew very well that if an injunction were applied for against him, there would be an immediate howl against my persecution of an innocent, and he played it. Then the noble host of pirates rushed in, and it is being done, in some mangled form or other, everywhere.

* "No Thoroughfare."

It touches me to read what you write of your poor mother. But, of course, at her age, each winter counts heavily. Do give her my love, and tell her that I asked you about her.

Being in Boston last Sunday, I took it into my head to go over the medical school, and survey the holes and corners in which that extraordinary murder was done by Webster. There was the furnace—stinking horribly, as if the dismembered pieces were still inside it—and there are all the grim spouts, and sinks, and chemical appliances, and what not. At dinner, afterwards, Longfellow told me a terrific story. He dined with Webster within a year of the murder, one of a party of ten or twelve. As they sat at their wine, Webster suddenly ordered the lights to be turned out, and a bowl of some burning mineral to be placed on the table, that the guests might see how ghostly it made them look. As each man stared at all the rest in the weird light, all were horrified to see Webster *with a rope round his neck*, holding it up, over the bowl, with his head jerked on one side, and his tongue lolled out representing a man being hanged !

Poking into his life and character, I find (what I would have staked my head upon) that he was always a cruel man.

My dear Wilkie, yours ever affectionately.

WESTMINSTER HOTEL, NEW YORK,
Sunday, Twelfth January, 1868.

Miss Hogarth.

MY DEAREST GEORGY,

As I am off to Philadelphia this evening, I may as well post my letter here. I have scarcely a word of news. My cold steadily refuses to leave me; but otherwise I am as right as one can hope to be under this heavy work. My New York readings are over (except four farewell nights in April), and I look forward to the relief of being out of my hardest hall. Last Friday night, though it was only "Nickleby" and "Boots," I was again dead beat at the end, and was once more laid upon a sofa. But the faintness went off after a little while. We have now cold, bright, frosty weather, without snow—the best weather for me.

Having been in great trepidation about the play, I am correspondingly elated by the belief that it really *is* a success. No doubt the unnecessary explanations will have been taken out, and the flatness of the last act fetched up. At some points I could have done wonders to it, in the way of screwing it up sharply and picturesquely, if I could have rehearsed it. Your account of the first night interested me immensely, but I was afraid to open the letter until Dolby rushed in with the opened *Times*.

On Wednesday I come back here for my four church readings

at Brooklyn. Each evening an enormous ferry-boat will convey
me and my state carriage (not to mention half-a-dozen waggons,
and any number of people, and a few score of horses) across the
river, and will bring me back again. The sale of tickets there
was an amazing scene. The noble army of speculators are now
furnished (this is literally true, and I am quite serious), each man
with a straw mattress, a little bag of bread and meat, two blankets,
and a bottle of whiskey. With this outfit *they lie down in line
on the pavement* the whole night before the tickets are sold,
generally taking up their positions at about ten. It being severely
cold at Brooklyn, they made an immense bonfire in the street—a
narrow street of wooden houses !—which the police turned out to
extinguish. A general fight then took place, out of which the
people farthest off in the line rushed bleeding when they saw a
chance of displacing others near the door, and put their mattresses
in those places, and then held on by the iron rails. At eight in
the morning Dolby appeared with the tickets in a portmanteau.
He was immediately saluted with a roar of "Halloa, Dolby ! So
Charley has let you have the carriage, has he, Dolby ! How is
he, Dolby ? Don't drop the tickets, Dolby. Look alive, Dolby ! "
etc. etc. etc., in the midst of which he proceeded to business, and
concluded (as usual) by giving universal dissatisfaction.

We have an excellent gasman, who is well up to that department. We have enlarged the large staff by another clerk, yet
even now the preparation of such an immense number of new
tickets constantly, and the keeping and checking of the accounts,
keep them hard at it. And they get so oddly divided ! Kelly is
at Philadelphia, another man at Baltimore, two others are stamping tickets at the top of this house, another is cruising over New
England, and Osgood will come on duty to-morrow (when Dolby
starts off) to pick me up after the reading, and take me to the
hotel, and mount guard over me, and bring me back here. You
see that even such wretched domesticity as Dolby and self by a
fireside is broken up under these conditions.

Dolby has been twice poisoned, and Osgood once. Morgan's
sharpness has discovered the cause. When the snow is deep upon
the ground, and the partridges cannot get their usual food, they eat
something (I don't know what, if anybody does) which does not
poison *them,* but which poisons the people who eat them. The
symptoms, which last some twelve hours, are violent sickness, cold perspiration, and the formation of some detestable mucus in the stomach.
You may infer that partridges have been banished from our bill of
fare. The appearance of our sufferers was lamentable in the extreme.

Did I tell you that the severity of the weather, and the heat of the intolerable furnaces, dry the hair and break the nails of strangers? There is not a complete nail in the whole British suite, and my hair cracks again when I brush it. (I am losing my hair with great rapidity, and what I don't lose is getting very gray.)

I think this is all my poor stock of intelligence. By-the-bye, on the last Sunday in the old year, I lost my old year's pocket-book, "which," as Mr. Pepys would add, "do trouble me mightily."

PHILADELPHIA, Monday, Thirteenth January, 1868. Miss Dickens.

MY DEAREST MAMIE,

I write you this note, a day later than your aunt's, not because I have anything to add to the little I have told her, but because you may like to have it.

We arrived here last night towards twelve o'clock, more than an hour after our time. This is one of the immense American hotels (it is called the Continental); but I find myself just as quiet here as elsewhere. Everything is very good indeed, the waiter is German, and the greater part of the house servants seem to be coloured people. The town is very clean, and the day is as blue and bright as a fine Italian day. But it freezes very hard. Mr. and Mrs. Barney Williams, with a couple of servants, and a pretty little child-daughter, were in the train each night, and I talked with them a good deal. They are reported to have made an enormous fortune by acting among the Californian gold-diggers. My cold is no better, for the cars are so intolerably hot, that I was often obliged to go and stand upon the break outside, and then the frosty air was biting indeed. The great man of this place is one Mr. Childs, a newspaper proprietor, who was waiting for me at the station (always called depôt here) with his carriage.

I was very much interested in the home accounts of Christmas Day. I think I have already mentioned that we were in very low spirits on that day. I began to be unwell with my cold that morning, and a long day's travel did not mend the matter. We scarcely spoke (except when we ate our lunch), and sat dolefully staring out of window. I had a few affectionate words from Chorley, dated from my room, on Christmas morning, and will write him, probably by this mail, a brief acknowledgment. I find it necessary (so oppressed am I with this American catarrh, as they call it) to dine at three o'clock instead of four, that I may have more time to get voice, so that the days are short and letter-writing is not easy.

If I could only get to the point of being able to hold my head up and dispense with my pocket-handkerchief for five minutes, I should be all right.

Mr. Charles
Dickens.

WESTMINSTER HOTEL, IRVING PLACE, NEW YORK,
Wednesday, Fifteenth January, 1868.

MY DEAR CHARLEY,

Finding your letter here this afternoon on my return from Philadelphia (where I have been reading two nights), I take advantage of a spare half-hour in which to answer it at once, though it will not leave here until Saturday. I had previously heard of the play, and had *The Times.* It was a great relief and delight to me, for I had no confidence in its success. Fechter must be very fine, and I should greatly like to see him play the part.

I have not been very well generally, and am oppressed (and I begin to think that I probably shall be until I leave) by a true American cold, which I hope, for the comfort of human nature, may be peculiar to only one of the four quarters of the world. The work, too, is very severe. But I am going on at the same tremendous rate everywhere. "Doctor Marigold" made a great hit here, and is looked forward to at Boston with especial interest. I go to Boston for another fortnight, on end, the twenty-fourth of February. The railway journeys distress me greatly. I get out into the open air (upon the break), and it snows and blows, and the train bumps, and the steam flies at me, until I am driven in again.

I will not pass my original bound of eighty-four readings in all. My mind was made up as to that long ago. It will be quite enough. What with travelling, and getting ready for reading, and reading, the days are pretty fully occupied. Not the less so because I rest very indifferently at night.

The people are exceedingly kind and considerate, and desire to be most hospitable besides. But I cannot accept hospitality, and never go out, except at Boston, or I should not be fit for the labour. When Dolby leaves me, Osgood, a partner in Ticknor and Fields' publishing firm, has to go into the hall from the platform-door every night, and see how the public are seating themselves. It is very odd to see how hard he finds it to look a couple of thousand people in the face, on which head, by-the-bye, I notice the papers to take "Mr. Dickens' extraordinary composure" (their great phrase) rather ill, and on the whole *to imply* that it would be taken as a suitable compliment if I would stagger on to the platform and instantly drop, overpowered by the spectacle before me.

Dinner is announced (by Scott, with a stiff neck and a sore throat), and I must break off with love to Bessie and the incipient Venerableses. You will be glad to hear of your distinguished parent that Philadelphia has discovered that "he is not like the descriptions we have read of him at the little red desk. He is not at all foppish in appearance. He wears a heavy moustache and a Vandyke beard, and looks like a well-to-do Philadelphian gentleman."

Ever, my dear Charley, your affectionate Father.

P.S.—Your paper is remarkably good. There is not the least doubt that you can write constantly for A. Y. R. I am very pleased with it.

WESTMINSTER HOTEL, NEW YORK,
Tuesday, Twenty-first January, 1868.

Miss Hogarth.

MY DEAREST GEORGY,

I finished my church to-night. It is Mrs. Stowe's brother's, and a most wonderful place to speak in. We had it enormously full last night ("Marigold" and "Trial"), but it scarcely required an effort; Mr. Ward Beecher (Mrs. Stowe's brother's name) being present in his pew. I sent to invite him to come round before he left; and I found him to be an unostentatious, straightforward, and agreeable fellow.

My cold sticks to me, and I can scarcely exaggerate what I sometimes undergo from sleeplessness. The day before yesterday I could get no rest until morning, and could not get up before twelve. This morning the same. I rarely take any breakfast but an egg and a cup of tea, not even toast or bread-and-butter. My dinner at three, and a little quail or some such light thing when I come home at night, is my daily fare. At the Hall I have established the custom of taking an egg beaten up in sherry before going in, and another between the parts. I think that pulls me up; at all events, I have since had no return of faintness.

As the men work very hard, and always with their hearts cheerfully in the business, I cram them into and outside of the carriage, to bring them back from Brooklyn with me. The other night, Scott (with a portmanteau across his knees and a wideawake hat low down upon his nose) told me that he had presented himself for admission in the circus (as good as Franconi's, by-the-bye), and had been refused. "The only theayter," he said in a melancholy way, "as I was ever in my life turned from the door of." Says Kelly: "There must have been some mistake, Scott, because George and me went, and we said, 'Mr. Dickens' staff,' and they passed us to the best seats in the house. Go again, Scott." "No, I thank you, Kelly," says Scott, more melancholy than before, "I'm not a-going to put myself in the position of being refused again. It's the only theayter as I was ever turned from the door

of, and it shan't be done twice.   But it's a beastly country!"
"Scott," interposed Majesty, "don't you express your opinions
about the country."   "No, sir," says Scott, "I never do, please,
sir, but when you are turned from the door of the only theayter
you was ever turned from, sir, and when the beasts in railway cars
spits tobacco over your boots, you (privately) find yourself in a
beastly country."

I expect shortly to get myself snowed up on some railway or
other, for it is snowing hard now, and I begin to move to-morrow.
There is so much floating ice in the river that we are obliged to
leave a pretty wide margin of time for getting over the ferry to
read.

Miss Dickens.

PHILADELPHIA, *Thursday, Twenty-third January,* 1868.

When I wrote to your aunt by the last mail, I accidentally
omitted to touch upon the question of helping Anne.   So I will
begin in this present writing with reference to her sad position.
I think it will be best for you to be guided by an exact knowledge
of her *wants.*   Try to ascertain from herself what means she has,
whether her sick husband gets what he ought to have, whether she
is pinched in the articles of necessary clothing, bedding, or the like
of that; add to this intelligence your own observation of the state
of things about her, and supply what she most wants, and help her
where you find the greatest need.   The question, in the case of so
old and faithful a servant, is not one of so much or so little money
on my side, but how *most efficiently* to ease her mind and help *her.*
To do this at once kindly and sensibly is the only consideration by
which you have to be guided.   Take *carte blanche* from me for all
the rest.

My Washington week is the first week in February, beginning
on Monday, third.   The tickets are sold, and the President is
coming, and the chief members of the Cabinet, and the leaders of
parties, and so forth, are coming; and, as the Holly Tree Boots
says: "That's where it is, don't you see!"

We are not a bit too soon here, for the whole country is
beginning to be stirred and shaken by the presidential election,
and trade is exceedingly depressed, and will be more so.   Fanny
Kemble lives near this place, but had gone away a day before my
first visit here.   *She* is going to read in February or March.   Du
Chaillu has been lecturing out West about the gorilla, and has
been to see me; I saw the Cunard steamer *Persia* out in the
stream, yesterday, beautifully smart, her flags flying, all her steam
up, and she only waiting for her mails to slip away.   She gave me
a horrible touch of home-sickness.

When the First of March arrives, and I can say "next month,"

I shall begin to grow brighter. A fortnight's reading in Boston, too, will help me on gaily, I hope (the work so far off tells). It is impossible for two people to be more affectionately attached to a third, I really believe, than Fields and his wife are to me; and they are a landmark in the prospect.

BALTIMORE, *Wednesday, Twenty-ninth January,* 1868.　Miss
　　　　　　　　　　　　　　　　　　　　　　　　　　　Hogarth
As I have an hour to spare, before starting to Philadelphia, I begin my letter this morning. It has been snowing hard for four-and-twenty hours, though this place is as far south as Valentia in Spain.

They are a bright responsive people here, and very pleasant to read to. I have rarely seen so many fine faces in an audience. I read here in a charming little opera-house built by a society of Germans, quite a delightful place for the purpose. I stand on the stage, with a drop-curtain down, and my screen before it. The whole scene is very pretty and complete, and the audience have a "ring" in them that sounds in the ear. Distances and travelling have obliged us to reduce the list of readings by two, leaving eighty-two in all. Of course we afterwards discovered that we had finally settled the list on a Friday! I shall be halfway through it at Washington, of course, on a Friday also, and my birthday!

Dolby and Osgood, who do the most ridiculous things to keep me in spirits (I am often very heavy, and rarely sleep much), have decided to have a walking-match at Boston, on Saturday, Twenty-ninth February. Beginning this design in joke, they have become tremendously in earnest, and Dolby has actually sent home (much to his opponent's terror) for a pair of seamless socks to walk in. Our men are hugely excited on the subject, and continually make bets on "the men." Fields and I are to walk out six miles, and "the men" are to turn and walk round us. Neither of them has the least idea what twelve miles at a pace is. Being requested by both to give them "a breather" yesterday, I gave them a stiff one of five miles over a bad road in the snow, half the distance uphill. I took them at a pace of four miles and a half an hour, and you never beheld such objects as they were when we got back; both smoking like factories, and both obliged to change everything before they could come to dinner. They have the absurdest ideas of what are tests of walking power, and continually get up in the maddest manner and see *how high they can kick* the wall! The wainscot here, in one place, is scored all over with their pencil-marks. To see them doing this—Dolby, a big man, and Osgood, a very little one, is ridiculous beyond description.

　　＊　　　　＊　　　　＊　　　　＊　　　　＊　　　＊　 . . .

BALTIMORE, *Wednesday, Twenty-ninth January,* 1868.

MY DEAR CARTWRIGHT,

As I promised to report myself to you from this side of the Atlantic, and as I have some leisure this morning, I am going to lighten my conscience by keeping my word.

I am going on at a great pace and with immense success. Next week, at Washington, I shall, please God, have got through half my readings. The remaining half are all arranged, and they will carry me into the third week of April. It is very hard work, but it is brilliantly paid. The changes that I find in the country generally (this place is the least changed of any I have yet seen) exceed my utmost expectations. I had been in New York a couple of days before I began to recognise it at all; and the handsomest part of Boston was a black swamp when I saw it five-and-twenty years ago. Considerable advances, too, have been made socially.

One of the most comical spectacles I have ever seen in my life was "church," with a heavy sea on, in the saloon of the Cunard steamer coming out. The officiating minister, an extremely modest young man, was brought in between two big stewards, exactly as if he were coming up to the scratch in a prize-fight. The ship was rolling and pitching so, that the two big stewards had to stop and watch their opportunity of making a dart at the reading-desk with their reverend charge, during which pause he held on, now by one steward and now by the other, with the feeblest expression of countenance and no legs whatever. At length they made a dart at the wrong moment, and one steward was immediately beheld alone in the extreme perspective, while the other and the reverend gentleman *held on by the mast* in the middle of the saloon—which the latter embraced with both arms, as if it were his wife. All this time the congregation was breaking up into sects and sliding away; every sect (as in nature) pounding the other sect. And when at last the reverend gentleman had been tumbled into his place, the desk (a loose one, put upon the dining-table) deserted from the church bodily, and went over to the purser. The scene was so extraordinarily ridiculous, and was made so much more so by the exemplary gravity of all concerned in it, that I was obliged to leave before the service began.

This is one of the places where Butler carried it with so high a hand in the war, and where the ladies used to spit when they passed a Northern soldier. It still wears, I fancy, a look of sullen remembrance. (The ladies are remarkably handsome, with an Eastern look upon them, dress with a strong sense of colour, and make a brilliant audience.) The ghost of slavery haunts the houses; and the old, untidy, incapable, lounging, shambling black serves you as a free man. Free of course he ought to be; but the stupendous absurdity of making him a voter glares out of every roll of his eye, stretch of his mouth, and bump of his head. I have a strong impression that the race must fade out of the States very fast. It never can hold its own against a striving, restless, shifty people. In the penitentiary here, the other day, in a room full of all blacks (too dull to be taught any of the work in hand), was one young brooding fellow, very like a black rhinoceros. He sat glowering at life, as if it were just endurable at dinner time, until four of his fellows began to sing, most unmelodiously, a part song. He then set up a dismal howl, and pounded his face on a form. I took him to have been rendered quite desperate by having learnt anything. I send my kind regard to Mrs. Cartwright, and sincerely hope that she and you have no new family distresses or anxieties. I am always, my dear Cartwright,

Cordially yours.

PHILADELPHIA, *Friday, Thirty-first January*, 1868.   Miss Dickens.

MY DEAREST MAMIE,

From a letter Wilkie has written to me, it seems there can be no doubt that the "No Thoroughfare" drama is a real, genuine, and great success. It is drawing immensely, and seems to "go" with great effect and applause.

"Doctor Marigold" here last night (for the first time) was an immense success, and all Philadelphia is going to rush at once for tickets for the two Philadelphian farewells the week after next. The tickets are to be sold to-morrow, and great excitement is anticipated in the streets. Dolby not being here, a clerk will sell, and will probably wish himself dead before he has done with it.

It appears to me that Chorley writes to you on the legacy question because he wishes you to understand that there is no danger of his changing his mind, and at the bottom I descry an honest desire to pledge himself as strongly as possible. You may receive it in that better spirit, or I am much mistaken. I am now going out in a sleigh (and four) with unconceivable dignity and grandeur.

Third February, 1868.

*Articles of Agreement entered into at Baltimore, in the United States of America, this Third day of February in the year

* It was at Baltimore that Charles Dickens first conceived the idea of a walking-match, which should take place on his return to Boston, and he drew up a set of humorous "articles."

of our Lord one thousand eight hundred and sixty-eight, between George Dolby, British subject, *alias* the Man of Ross, and James R. Osgood, American citizen, *alias* the Boston Bantam.

Whereas, some Bounce having arisen between the above men in reference to feats of pedestrianism and agility, they have agreed to settle their differences and prove who is the better man, by means of a walking-match for two hats a side and the glory of their respective countries; and whereas they agree that the said match shall come off, whatsoever the weather, on the Mill Dam Road outside Boston, on Saturday, the twenty-ninth day of this present month; and whereas they agree that the personal attendants on themselves during the whole walk, and also the umpires and starters and declarers of victory in the match shall be James T. Fields of Boston, known in sporting circles as Massachusetts Jemmy, and Charles Dickens of Falstaff's Gad's Hill, whose surprising performances (without the least variation) on that truly national instrument, the American catarrh, have won for him the well-merited title of the Gad's Hill Gasper:

1. The men are to be started, on the day appointed, by Massachusetts Jemmy and The Gasper.

2. Jemmy and The Gasper are, on some previous day, to walk out at the rate of not less than four miles an hour by The Gasper's watch, for one hour and a half. At the expiration of that one hour and a half they are to carefully note the place at which they halt. On the match's coming off they are to station themselves in the middle of the road, at that precise point, and the men (keeping clear of them and of each other) are to turn round them, right shoulder inward, and walk back to the starting-point. The man declared by them to pass the starting-point first is to be the victor and the winner of the match.

3. No jostling or fouling allowed.

4. All cautions or orders issued to the men by the umpires, starters, and declarers of victory to be considered final and admitting of no appeal.

5. A sporting narrative of the match to be written by The Gasper within one week after its coming off, and the same to be duly printed (at the expense of the subscribers to these articles) on a broadside. The said broadside to be framed and glazed, and one copy of the same to be carefully preserved by each of the subscribers to these articles.

6. The men to show on the evening of the day of walking at six o'clock precisely, at the Parker House, Boston, when and where a dinner will be given them by The Gasper. The Gasper to occupy the chair, faced by Massachusetts Jemmy. The latter promptly

and formally to invite, as soon as may be after the date of these
presents, the following guests to honour the said dinner with their
presence; that is to say [here follow the names of a few of his
friends, whom he wished to be invited].

Now, lastly. In token of their accepting the trusts and offices
by these articles conferred upon them, these articles are solemnly
and formally signed by Massachusetts Jemmy and by the Gad's
Hill Gasper, as well as by the men themselves.

Signed by the Man of Ross, otherwise George Dolby.

Signed by the Boston Bantam, otherwise James R. Osgood.

Signed by Massachusetts Jemmy, otherwise James T. Fields.

Signed by the Gad's Hill Gasper, otherwise Charles Dickens.

WASHINGTON, *Tuesday, Fourth February,* 1868.   Miss
Dickens.

MY DEAREST MAMIE,

I began here last night with great success. The audience
was a superior one, composed of the foremost public men and their
families. At the end of the "Carol" they gave a great break
out, and applauded, I really believe, for five minutes. Immense
enthusiasm.

A devoted adherent in this place (an Englishman) had represented to Dolby that if I were taken to an hotel here it would be
impossible to secure me a minute's rest, and he undertook to get
one Wheleker, a German, who keeps a little Vérey's, to furnish his
private dining-rooms for the illustrious traveller's reception.
Accordingly here we are, on the first and second floor of a small
house, with no one else in it but our people, a French waiter, and
a very good French cuisine. Perfectly private, in the city of all
the world (I should say) where the hotels are intolerable, and
privacy the least possible, and quite comfortable. "Wheleker's
Restaurant" is our rather undignified address for the present week.

I dined (against my rules) with Charles Sumner on Sunday, he
having been an old friend of mine. Mr. Secretary Staunton (War
Minister) was there. He is a man of very remarkable memory,
and famous for his acquaintance with the minutest details of my
books. Give him any passage anywhere, and he will instantly cap
it and go on with the context. He was commander-in-chief of all
the Northern forces concentrated here, and never went to sleep at
night without first reading something from my books, which were
always with him. I put him through a pretty severe examination,
but he was better up than I was.

The gas was very defective indeed last night, and I began with
a small speech, to the effect that I must trust to the brightness of
their faces for the illumination of mine; this was taken greatly.

In the "Carol," a most ridiculous incident occurred all of a sudden. I saw a dog look out from among the seats in the central aisle, and look very intently at me. The general attention being fixed on me, I don't think anybody saw the dog; but I felt so sure of his turning up again and barking, that I kept my eye wandering about in search of him. He was a very comic dog, and it was well for me that I was reading a very comic part of the book. But when he bounced out into the centre aisle again, in an entirely new place (still looking intently at me) and tried the effect of a bark upon my proceedings, I was seized with such a paroxysm of laughter, that it 'communicated itself to the audience, and we roared at one another loud and long.

The President has sent to me twice, and I am going to see him to-morrow. He has a whole row for his family every night. Dolby rejoined his chief yesterday morning, and will probably remain in the august presence until Sunday night. He and Osgood, "training for the match," are ludicrous beyond belief. I saw them just now coming up a street, each trying to pass the other, and immediately fled. Since I have been writing this, they have burst in at the door and sat down on the floor to blow. Dolby is now writing at a neighbouring table, with his bald head smoking as if he were on fire. Kelly (his great adherent) asked me, when he was last away, whether it was quite fair that I should take Mr. Osgood out for "breathers" when Mr. Dolby had no such advantage. I begin to expect that half Boston will turn out on the twenty-ninth to see the match. In which case it will be unspeakably droll.

*   *   *   *   *

Mr. Charles Lanman.

WASHINGTON, *Fifth February,* 1868.

MY DEAR SIR,

Allow me to thank you most cordially for your kind letter, and for its accompanying books. I have a particular love for books of travel, and shall wander into the "Wilds of America" with great interest. I have also received your charming Sketch* with great pleasure and admiration. Let me thank you for it heartily. As a beautiful suggestion of nature associated with this country, it shall have a quiet place on the walls of my house as long as I live.

Your reference to my dear friend Washington Irving renews the vivid impressions reawakened in my mind at Baltimore the other day. I saw his fine face for the last time in that city. He came there from New York to pass a day or two with me before I went westward, and they were made among the most memorable

* "Autumnal Foliage in America."

of my life by his delightful fancy and genial humour. Some unknown admirer of his books and mine sent to the hotel a most enormous mint julep, wreathed with flowers. We sat, one on either side of it, with great solemnity, but the solemnity was of very short duration. It was quite an enchanted julep, and carried us among innumerable people and places that we both knew. The julep held out far into the night, and my memory never saw him afterward otherwise than as bending over it, with his straw, with an attempted gravity (after some anecdote, involving some wonderfully droll and delicate observation of character), and then, as his eyes caught mine, melting into that captivating laugh of his which was the brightest and best I have ever heard.

Dear Sir, with many thanks, faithfully yours.

WASHINGTON, *my Birthday*, 1868.   Miss
(*And my cold worse than ever.*)   Hogarth.

MY DEAREST GEORGY,

This will be but a short letter, as I have been to see the President this morning, and have little time before the post goes. He had sent a gentleman to me, most courteously begging me to make my own appointment, and I did so. A man of very remarkable appearance indeed, of tremendous firmness of purpose. Not to be turned or trifled with.

As I mention my cold's being so bad, I will add that I have never had anything the matter with me since I came here *but* the cold. It is now in my throat, and slightly on my chest. It occasions me great discomfort, and you would suppose, seeing me in the morning, that I could not possibly read at night. But I have always come up to the scratch, have not yet missed one night, and have gradually got used to that. I had got much the better of it; but the dressing-room at the hall here is singularly cold and draughty, and so I have slid back again.

The papers here having written about this being my birthday, the most exquisite flowers came pouring in at breakfast time from all sorts of people. The room is covered with them, made up into beautiful bouquets, and arranged in all manner of green baskets. Probably I shall find plenty more at the hall to-night. This is considered the dullest and most apathetic place in America. *My* audiences have been superb.

I mentioned the dog on the first night here. Next night I thought I heard (in "Copperfield") a suddenly suppressed bark. It happened in this wise: Osgood, standing just within the door, felt his leg touched, and looking down beheld the dog staring intently at me, and evidently just about to bark. In a transport of presence of mind and fury, he instantly caught him up in both hands and threw him over his own head out into the entry, where the check-takers received him like a game at ball. Last night he came again *with another dog;* but our people were so sharply on the look-out for him that he didn't get in. He had evidently promised to pass the other dog free.

Miss
Dickens.

BALTIMORE, U.S.,
Tuesday, Eleventh February, 1868.

The weather has been desperately severe, and my cold quite as bad as ever. I couldn't help laughing at myself on my birthday at Washington. It was observed as much as though I were a little boy. Flowers and garlands (of the most exquisite kind) bloomed all over the room ; letters radiant with good wishes poured in ; a shirt pin, a handsome silver travelling bottle, a set of gold shirt studs, and a set of gold sleeve links were on the dinner table. After "Boots," at night, the whole audience rose and remained (Secretaries of State, President's family, Judges of Supreme Court, and so forth) standing and cheering until I went back to the table and made them a little speech. On the same august day of the year I was received by the President, a man with a very remarkable and determined face. Each of us looked at each other very hard, and each of us managed the interview (I think) to the satisfaction of the other. In the outer room was sitting a certain sunburnt General Blair, with many evidences of the war upon him. He got up to shake hands with me, and then I found he had been out in the prairie with me five-and-twenty years ago. That afternoon my "catarrh" was in such a state that Charles Sumner, coming in at five o'clock and finding me covered with mustard poultice, and apparently voiceless, turned to Dolby and said: "Surely, Mr. Dolby, it is impossible that he can read to-night." Says Dolby : "Sir, I have told the dear Chief so four times to-day, and I have been very anxious. But you have no idea how he will change when he gets to the little table." After five minutes of the little table, I was not (for the time) even hoarse. The frequent experience of this return of force when it is wanted saves me a vast amount of anxiety.

Think of my dreaming of Mrs. Bouncer each night ! ! !

*   *   *   *   *

Mr. Henry
Fielding
Dickens.

BALTIMORE, U.S., *Tuesday, Eleventh February,* 1868.

MY DEAR HARRY,

I should have written to you before now, but for constant and arduous occupation.

In reference to the cricket club's not being what it might be, I agree with you in the main. There are some things to be considered, however, which you have hardly taken into account. The first thing to be avoided is, the slightest appearance of patronage (one of the curses of England). The second thing to be avoided is, the deprival of the men of their just right to manage their own affairs. I would rather have no club at all, than have either of these great mistakes made. The way out of them is this : Call the men together, and explain to them that the club might be larger, richer, and better. Say that you think that more of the neighbouring gentlemen could be got to be playing members. That you submit to them that it would be better to have a captain who could correspond with them, and talk to them, and in some sort manage them ; and that, being perfectly acquainted with the game, and having long played it at a great public school, you propose yourself as captain, for the foregoing reasons. That you propose to them to make the subscription of the gentlemen members at least double that of the working men, for no other reason than that the gentlemen can afford it better ; but that both classes of members shall have exactly the same right of voting equally in all that concerns the club. Say that you have consulted me upon the matter, and that I am of these opinions, and am ready to become chairman of the club, and to preside at their meetings, and to overlook its business affairs, and to give it five pounds a year, payable at the commencement of each season. Then, having brought them to this point, draw up the club's rules and regulations, amending them where they want amendment.

Discreetly done, I see no difficulty in this. But it can only be honourably and hopefully done by having the men together. And I would not have them at The Falstaff, but in the hall or dining-room—the servants' hall, an excellent place. Whatever you do, let the men ratify ; and let them feel their little importance, and at once perceive how much better the business begins to be done.

I am very glad to hear of the success of your reading, and still more glad that you went at it in downright earnest. I should never have made my success in life if I had been shy of taking pains, or if I had not bestowed upon the least thing I have ever undertaken exactly the same attention and care that I have bestowed upon the greatest. Do everything at your best. It was but this last year that I set to and learned every word of my readings ; and from ten years ago to last night, I have never read to an audience but I have watched for an opportunity of striking out something better somewhere. Look at such of my manuscripts as are in the library at Gad's, and think of the patient hours devoted year after year to single lines.

*   *   *   *   *

The weather is very severe here, and the work is very hard. Dolby, having been violently pitched into by the Mayor of Newhaven (a town at which I am to read next week), has gone bodily this morning with defiant written instructions from me to inform the said mayor that, if he fail to make out his case, he (Dolby) is to return all the money taken, and to tell him that I will not set foot in his jurisdiction; whereupon the Newhaven people will probably fall upon the mayor in his turn, and lead him a pleasant life.   Ever, my dear Harry, your affectionate Father.

Miss
Hogarth.

PHILADELPHIA, *Thursday, Thirteenth February*, 1868.
MY DEAREST GEORGY,

Nothing will induce the people to believe in the farewells. At Baltimore on Tuesday night (a very brilliant night indeed), they asked as they came out : "When will Mr. Dickens read here again?" "Never." "Nonsense! Not come back, after such houses as these? Come. Say when he'll read again." Just the same here. We could as soon persuade them that I am the President, as that I am going to read here for the last time to-morrow night.

There is a child of the Barney Williams's in this house—a little girl—to whom I presented a black doll when I was here last. I have seen her eye at the keyhole since I began writing this, and I think she and the doll are outside still. "When you sent it up to me by the coloured boy," she said after receiving it (coloured boy is the term for black waiter), "I gave such a cream that ma came running in and creamed too, 'cos she fort I'd hurt myself. But I creamed a cream of joy." She had a friend to play with her that day, and brought the friend with her, to my infinite confusion. A friend all stockings, and much too tall, who sat on the sofa very far back, with her stockings sticking stiffly out in front of her, and glared at me and never spake word. Dolby found us confronted in a sort of fascination, like serpent and bird.

The same.

NEW YORK,
Monday, Seventeenth February, 1868.

"True American" still sticking to me. But I am always ready for my work, and therefore don't much mind. Dolby and the Mayor of Newhaven alternately embrace and exchange mortal defiances. In writing out some advertisements towards midnight last night, he made a very good mistake. "The reading will be comprised within two *minutes*, and the audience are earnestly entreated to be seated ten *hours* before its commencement."

The weather has been finer lately, but the streets are in a horrible condition, through half-melted snow, and it is now snowing again. The walking-match (next Saturday week) is already in the Boston papers! I suppose half Boston will turn out on the occasion. As a sure way of not being conspicuous, "the men" are going to walk in flannel! They are in a mingled state of comicality and gravity about it that is highly ridiculous. Yesterday being a bright cool day, I took Dolby for a "buster" of eight miles. As everybody here knows me, the spectacle of our splitting up the fashionable avenue (the only way out of town) excited the greatest amazement. No doubt *that* will be in the papers to-morrow. I give a gorgeous banquet to eighteen (ladies and gentlemen) after the match. Mr. and Mrs. Fields, Do. Ticknor, Longfellow and his daughter, Lowell, Holmes and his wife, etc. etc. Sporting speeches to be made, and the stakes (four hats) to be handed over to the winner.

My ship will not be the *Cuba* after all. She is to go into dock, and the *Russia* (a larger ship, and the latest built for the Cunard line) is to take her place.

*   *   *   *   *

WASHINGTON, *Twenty-fourth February*, 1868. M. Charles Fechter.

MY DEAR FECHTER,
     Your letter reached me here yesterday.

My dear fellow, consider yourself my representative. Whatever you do, or desire to do, about the play, I fully authorise beforehand. Tell Webster, with my regard, that I think his proposal honest and fair; that I think it, in a word, like himself; and that I have perfect confidence in his good faith and liberality.

As to making money of the play in the United States here, Boucicault has filled Wilkie's head with golden dreams that have *nothing* in them. He makes no account of the fact that, wherever I go, the theatres (with my name in big letters) instantly begin playing versions of my books, and that the moment the Christmas number came over here they pirated and played "No Thoroughfare." Now, I have enquired into the law, and am extremely doubtful whether I *could* have prevented this. Why should they pay for the piece as you act it, when they have no actors, and when all they want is my name, and they can get that for nothing?

Wilkie has uniformly written of you enthusiastically. In a letter I had from him, dated the Tenth of January, he described your conception and execution of the part in the most glowing terms. "Here Fechter is magnificent." "Here his superb playing brings the house down." "I should call even his exit in the

2 x

last act one of the subtlest and finest things he does in the piece." "You can hardly imagine what he gets out of the part, or what he makes of his passionate love for Marguerite." These expressions, and many others like them, crowded his letter.

I never did so want to see a character played on the stage as I want to see you play Obenreizer. As the play was going when I last heard of it, I have some hopes that I MAY see it yet. Please God, your Adelphi dressing-room will be irradiated with the noble presence of "Never Wrong" (if you are acting), about the evening of Monday, the Fourth of May!

I am doing enormous business. It is a wearying life, away from all I love, but I hope that the time will soon begin to spin away. Among the many changes that I find here is the comfortable change that the people are in general extremely considerate, and very observant of my privacy. Generally, they are very good audiences indeed. They do not (I think) perceive touches of art to *be* art; but they are responsive to the broad results of such touches. "Doctor Marigold" is a great favourite, and they laugh so unrestrainedly at "The Trial" from "Pickwick" (which you never heard), that it has grown about half as long again as it used to be.

If I could send you a "brandy cocktail" by post I would. It is a highly meritorious dram, which I hope to present to you at Gad's. My New York landlord made me a "Rocky Mountain sneezer," which appeared to me to be compounded of all the spirits ever heard of in the world, with bitters, lemon, sugar, and snow. You can only make a true "sneezer" when the snow is lying on the ground.

There, my dear boy, my paper is out, and I am going to read "Copperfield." Count always on my fidelity and true attachment, and look out, as I have already said, for a distinguished visitor about Monday, the Fourth of May.

> Ever, my dear Fechter,
> Your cordial and affectionate Friend.

Miss
Dickens.

BOSTON, *Tuesday, Twenty-fifth February,* 1868.

MY DEAREST MAMIE,

It is so very difficult to know, by any exercise of common sense, what turn or height the political excitement may take next, and it may so easily, and so soon, swallow up all other things, that I think I shall suppress my next week's readings here (by good fortune not yet announced) and watch the course of events. Dolby's sudden desponding under these circumstances is so acute, that it is actually swelling his head as I glance at him in the glass while writing.

The catarrh is no better and no worse. The weather is intensely cold. Mrs. Fields is more delightful than ever, and Fields more hospitable. My room is always radiant with brilliant flowers of their sending. I don't know whether I told you that the walking-match is to celebrate the extinction of February, and the coming of the day when I can say "next month."

BOSTON, *Thursday, Twenty-seventh February*, 1868.   Miss Hogarth.

I have very little news to give you in return for your budget. The walking-match is to come off on Saturday, and Fields and I went over the ground yesterday to measure the miles. We went at a tremendous pace. The condition of the ground is something indescribable, from half-melted snow, running water, and sheets and blocks of ice. The two performers have not the faintest notion of the weight of the task they have undertaken.

In the first excitement of the presidential impeachment, our houses instantly went down. Nothing in this country lasts long, and I think the public may be heartily tired of the President's name by the Ninth of March, when I read at a considerable distance from here. So behold me with a whole week's holiday in view! The Boston audiences have come to regard the readings and the reader as their peculiar property; and you would be at once amused and pleased if you could see the curious way in which they seem to plume themselves on both. They have taken to applauding too whenever they laugh or cry, and the result is very inspiriting. I shall remain here until Saturday, the Seventh, but shall not read here, after to-morrow night, until the First of April, when I begin my Boston farewells, six in number.

Friday, Twenty-eighth.

It has been snowing all night, and the city is in a miserable condition. We had a fine house last night for "Carol" and "Trial," and such an enthusiastic one that they persisted in a call after the "Carol," and, while I was out, covered the little table with flowers. There is a lull in the excitement about the President, but the articles of impeachment are to be produced this afternoon, and then it may set in again. Osgood came into camp last night from selling in remote places, and reports that at Rochester and Buffalo (both places near the frontier), Canada people bought tickets, who had struggled across the frozen river and clambered over all sorts of obstructions to get them. Some of these halls turn out to be smaller than represented, but I have no doubt, to use an American expression, that we shall "get along."

To-morrow fortnight we purpose being at the Falls of Niagara, and then we shall turn back and really begin to wind up. I have got to know the "Carol" so well that I can't remember it, and occasionally go dodging about in the wildest manner to pick up lost pieces. They took it so tremendously last night that I was stopped every five minutes. One poor young girl in mourning burst into a passion of grief about Tiny Tim, and was taken out. This is all my news.

Each of the pedestrians is endeavouring to persuade the other to take something unwholesome before starting.

Miss
Dickens.

BOSTON, *Monday, Second March*, 1868.

A heavy gale of wind and a snowstorm oblige me to write suddenly for the Cunard steamer a day earlier than usual. The railroad between this and New York will probably be stopped somewhere. After all the hard weather we have had, this is the worst day we have seen.

The walking-match came off on Saturday, over tremendously difficult ground, against a biting wind, and through deep snow-wreaths. It was so cold, too, that our hair, beards, eyelashes, eyebrows, were frozen hard, and hung with icicles. The course was thirteen miles. They were close together at the turning-point, when Osgood went ahead at a splitting pace and with extraordinary endurance, and won by half a mile. Dolby did very well indeed, and begs that he may not be despised. In the evening I gave a very splendid dinner. Eighteen covers, most magnificent flowers, and such table decoration as was never seen in these parts. The whole thing was a great success, and everybody was delighted.

My holiday-making is simply thorough resting, except on Wednesday, when I dine with Longfellow. We are not quite determined whether Mrs. Fields did not desert our colours, by coming on the ground in a carriage, and having *bread soaked in brandy* put into the winning man's mouth as he steamed along. She pleaded that she would have done as much for Dolby, if *he* had been ahead, so we are inclined to forgive her. As she had done so much for me in the way of flowers, I thought I would show her a sight in that line at the dinner. You never saw anything like it. Two immense crowns; the base of the choicest exotics; and the loops, oval masses of violets. In the centre of the table an immense basket, overflowing with enormous bell-mouthed lilies; all round the table a bright green border of wreathed creeper, with clustering roses at intervals; a rose for every button-hole, and a bouquet for every lady. They made an exhibition of the table before dinner to numbers of people.

P. H. has just come in with a newspaper, containing a reference (in good taste !) to the walking-match. He posts it to you by this post.

It is telegraphed that the storm prevails over an immense extent of country, and is just the same at Chicago as here. I hope it may prove a wind-up. We are getting sick of the sound of sleigh-bells even.

Your account of Anne has greatly interested me.

*　　　*　　　*　　　*　　　*

SYRACUSE, U.S. OF AMERICA,   M. Charles
Sunday Night, Eighth March, 1868.   Fechter.

MY DEAR FECHTER,

I am here in a most wonderful out-of-the-world place, which looks as if it had begun to be built yesterday, and were going to be imperfectly knocked together with a nail or two the day after to-morrow. I am in the worst inn that ever was seen, and outside is a thaw that places the whole country under water. I have looked out of window for the people, and I can't find any people. I have tried all the wines in the house, and there are only two wines, for which you pay six shillings a bottle, or fifteen, according as you feel disposed to change the name of the thing you ask for. (The article never changes.) The bill of fare is "in French," and the principal article (the carte is printed) is "Paettie de shay." I asked the Irish waiter what this dish was, and he said: "It was the name the steward giv' to oyster patties—the Frinch name." These are the drinks you are to wash it down with: "Mooseux," "Abasinthe," "Curacco," "Marschine," "Annise," and "Margeaux"!

I am growing very home-sick, and very anxious for the Twenty-second of April; on which day, please God, I embark for home. I am beginning to be tired, and have been depressed all the time (except when reading) and have lost my appetite. I cannot tell you—but you know, and therefore why should I !—how overjoyed I shall be to see you again, my dear boy, and how sorely I miss a dear friend, and how sorely I miss all art, in these parts. No disparagement to the country, which has a great future in reserve, or to its people, who are very kind to me.

I mean to take my leave of readings in the autumn and winter, in a final series in England with Chappell. This will come into the way of literary work for a time, for, after I have rested—don't laugh—it is a grim reality—I shall have to turn my mind to—

ha! ha! ha!—to—ha! ha! ha! (more sepulchrally than before)—the—the Christmas Number!!! I feel as if I had murdered a Christmas number years ago (perhaps I did!) and its ghost perpetually haunted me. Nevertheless in some blessed rest at Gad's, we will talk over stage matters, and all matters, in an even way, and see what we can make of them, please God. Be sure that I shall not be in London one evening, after disembarking, without coming round to the theatre to embrace you, my dear fellow.

I have had an American cold (the worst in the world) since Christmas Day. I read four times a week, with the most tremendous energy I can bring to bear upon it. I travel about pretty heavily. I read in all sorts of places—churches, theatres, concert rooms, lecture halls. Every night I read I am described (mostly by people who have not the faintest notion of observing) from the sole of my boot to where the topmost hair of my head ought to be but is not. Sometimes I am described as being "evidently nervous;" sometimes it is rather taken ill that "Mr. Dickens is so extraordinarily composed." My eyes are blue, red, grey, white, green, brown, black, hazel, violet, and rainbow-coloured. I am like "a well-to-do American gentleman," and the Emperor of the French, with an occasional touch of the Emperor of China, and a deterioration from the attributes of our famous townsman, Rufus W. B. D. Dodge Grumsher Pickville. I say all sorts of things that I never said, go to all sorts of places that I never saw or heard of, and have done all manner of things (in some previous state of existence I suppose) that have quite escaped my memory. You ask your friend to describe what he is about. This is what he is about, every day and hour of his American life.

Ever, my dear Fechter,
Your most affectionate and hearty Friend.

P.S.—Don't let Madame Fechter, or Marie, or Paul forget me!

Miss
Hogarth.

SYRACUSE, *Sunday, Eighth March*, 1868.

MY DEAREST GEORGY,

This is a very grim place in a heavy thaw, and a most depressing one. The hotel also is surprisingly bad, quite a triumph in that way. We stood out for an hour in the melting snow, and came in again, having to change completely. Then we sat down by the stove (no fireplace), and there we are now. We were so afraid to go to bed last night, the rooms were so close and sour, that we played whist, double dummy, till we couldn't bear each other any longer. We had an old buffalo for supper, and an old pig for breakfast, and we are going to have I don't know what for dinner at six. In the public rooms downstairs, a number of men (speechless) are sitting in rocking-chairs, with their feet against the window-frames, staring out at window and spitting dolefully at intervals. Scott is in tears, and George the gasman is suborning people to go and clean the hall, which is a marvel of dirt.

We were at Albany the night before last and yesterday morning; a very pretty town, where I am to read on the eighteenth and nineteenth. This day week we hope to wash out this establishment with the Falls of Niagara. And there is my news, except that your *last letters* to me in America must be posted by the Cunard steamer, which will sail from Liverpool on *Saturday, the Fourth of April*. These I shall be safe to get before embarking.

I send a note to Katie (addressed to Mamie) by this mail.

BUFFALO, *Thursday, Twelfth March*, 1868.   Miss Hogarth.

      I hope this may be in time for next Saturday's mail; but this is a long way from New York, and rivers are swollen with melted snow, and travelling is unusually slow.

Just now (two o'clock in the afternoon) I received your sad news of the death of poor Chauncey.* It naturally goes to my heart. It is not a light thing to lose such a friend, and I truly loved him. In the first unreasonable train of feeling, I dwelt more than I should have thought possible on my being unable to attend his funeral. I know how little this really matters; but I know he would have wished me to be there with real honest tears for his memory, and I feel it very much. I never, never, never was better loved by man than I was by him, I am sure. Poor dear fellow, good affectionate gentle creature.

It is difficult for me to write more just now. The news is a real shock at such a distance, and I must read to-night, and I must compose my mind. Let Mekitty know that I received her violets with great pleasure, and that I sent her my best love and my best thanks.

On the Twenty-fifth of February I read "Copperfield" and "Bob" at Boston. Either on that very day, or very close upon it, I was describing his (Townshend's) house to Fields, and telling him about the great Danby picture that he should see when he came to London.

    *   *   *   *   *

* Mr. Chauncey Hare Townshend. He was one of the dearest friends of Charles Dickens and a very constant correspondent; but no letters addressed to him are in existence.

Mr. W. C.
Macready.

SPRINGFIELD, MASS.,
Saturday, Twenty-first March, 1868.

MY DEAREST MACREADY,

What with perpetual reading and travelling, and what with one of the severest winters ever known, your coals of fire received by the last mail did not burn my head so much as they might have done under less excusatory circumstances. But they scorched it too!

You would find the general aspect of America and Americans decidedly much improved. You would find immeasurably greater consideration and respect for your privacy than of old. You would find a steady change for the better everywhere, except (oddly enough) in the railroads generally, which seem to have stood still, while everything else has moved. But there is an exception westward. There the express trains have now a very delightful carriage called a " drawing-room car," literally a series of little private drawing-rooms, with sofas and a table in each, opening out of a little corridor. In each, too, is a large plate-glass window, with which you can do as you like. As you pay extra for this luxury, it may be regarded as the first move towards two classes of passengers. When the railroad straight away to San Francisco (in six days) shall be opened through, it will not only have these drawing-rooms, but sleeping-rooms too; a bell in every little apartment, communicating with a steward's pantry, a restaurant, a staff of servants, marble washing-stands, and a barber's shop! I looked into one of these cars a day or two ago, and it was very ingeniously arranged and quite complete.

I left Niagara last Sunday, and travelled on to Albany, through three hundred miles of flood, villages deserted, bridges broken, fences drifting away, nothing but tearing water, floating ice, and absolute wreck and ruin. The train gave in altogether at Utica, and the passengers were let loose there for the night. As I was due at Albany, a very active superintendent of works did all he could to " get Mr. Dickens along," and in the morning we resumed our journey through the water, with a hundred men in seven-league boots pushing the ice from before us with long poles. How we got to Albany I can't say, but we got there somehow, just in time for a triumphal " Carol " and " Trial." All the tickets had been sold, and we found the Albanians in a state of great excitement. You may imagine what the flood was when I tell you that we took the passengers out of two trains that had their fires put out by the water four-and-twenty hours before, and cattle from trucks that had been in the water I don't know how long, but so long that the sheep had begun to eat each other! It was a horrible spectacle, and the haggard human misery of their faces was quite a new study. There was a fine breath of spring in the air concurrently with the great thaw; but lo and behold! last night it began to snow again with a strong wind, and to-day a snowdrift covers this place with all the desolation of winter once more. I never was so tired of the sight of snow.

I have seen all our Boston friends, except Curtis. Ticknor is dead. The rest are very little changed, except that Longfellow has a perfectly white flowing beard and long white hair. But he does not otherwise look old, and is infinitely handsomer than he was. I have been constantly with them all, and they have always talked much of you. It is the established joke that Boston is "my native place," and we hold all sorts of hearty foregatherings. They all come to every reading, and are always in a most delightful state of enthusiasm. They gave me a parting dinner at the club, on the Thursday before Good Friday. To pass from Boston personal to New York theatrical, I will mention here that one of the proprietors of my New York hotel is one of the proprietors of Niblo's, and the most active. Consequently I have seen the "Black Crook" and the "White Fawn," in majesty, from an armchair in the first entrance, P.S., more than once. Of these astonishing dramas, I beg to report (seriously) that I have found no human creature "behind" who has the slightest idea what they are about (upon my honour, my dearest Macready!), and that having some amiable small talk with a neat little Spanish woman, who is the *première danseuse*, I asked her, in joke, to let me measure her skirt with my dress glove. Holding the glove by the tip of the forefinger, I found the skirt to be just three gloves long, and yet its length was much in excess of the skirts of two hundred other ladies, whom the carpenters were at that moment getting into their places for a transformation scene, on revolving columns, on wires and "travellers" in iron cradles, up in the flies, down in the cellars, on every description of float that Wilmot, gone distracted, could imagine!

I am delighted to hear of Benvenuta's marriage, and I think her husband a very lucky man. Johnnie has my profound sympathy under his examinatorial woes. The noble boy will give me Gavazzi revised and enlarged, I expect, when I next come to Cheltenham. I will give you and Mrs. Macready all my American experiences when you come to London, or, better still, to Gad's. Meanwhile I send my hearty love to all, not forgetting dear Katie.

Niagara is not at all spoiled by a very dizzy-looking suspension bridge. Is to have another still nearer to the Horse-shoe opened in July. My last sight of that scene (last Sunday) was thus: We went up to the rapids above the Horse-shoe—say two miles from it—and through the great cloud of spray. Everything in the magnificent valley—buildings, forest, high banks, air, water, everything—was *made of rainbow*. Turner's most imaginative drawing in his finest day has nothing in it so ethereal, so gorgeous in fancy, so celestial. We said to one another (Dolby and I), "Let it evermore remain so," and shut our eyes and came away.

God bless you and all dear to you, my dear old Friend!

     I am ever your affectionate and loving.

Miss Dickens.

PORTLAND, *Sunday, Twenty-ninth March,* 1868.

MY DEAREST MAMIE,

     I should have written to you by the last mail, but I really was too unwell to do it. The writing day was last Friday, when I ought to have left Boston for New Bedford (fifty-five miles) before eleven in the morning. But I was so exhausted that I could not be got up, and had to take my chance of an evening's train producing me in time to read, which it just did. With the return of snow, nine days ago, the "true American" (which had lulled) came back as bad as ever. I have coughed from two or three in the morning until five or six, and have been absolutely sleepless. I have had no appetite besides, and no taste. Last night here I took some laudanum, and it is the only thing that has done me good. But the life in this climate is so very hard. When I did manage to get from Boston to New Bedford, I read with my utmost force and vigour. Next morning, well or ill, I must turn out at seven to get back to Boston on my way here.

I dine at Boston at three, and at five must come on here (a hundred and thirty miles or so), for to-morrow night; there being no Sunday train. To-morrow night I read here in a very large place, and Tuesday morning at six I must start again to get back to Boston once more. But after to-morrow night, I have only the Boston and New York farewells, thank God! I am most grateful to think that when we came to devise the details of the tour, I foresaw that it could never be done, as Dolby and Osgood proposed, by one unassisted man, as if he were a machine. If I had not cut out the work, and cut out Canada, I could never have gone there, I am quite sure. Even as it is, I have just now written to Dolby (who is in New York), to see my doctor there, and ask him to send me some composing medicine that I can take at night, inasmuch as without sleep I cannot get through. However sympathetic and devoted the people are about me, they *can not* be got to comprehend that one's being able to do the two hours with spirit when the time comes round, may be co-existent with the consciousness of great depression and fatigue. I don't mind saying all this, now that the labour is so nearly over. You shall have a brighter account of me, please God, when I close this at Boston.

Monday, Thirtieth March.

Without any artificial aid, I got a splendid night's rest last night, and consequently am very much freshened up to-day. Yesterday I had a fine walk by the sea, and to-day I have had another on the heights overlooking it.

Boston, *Tuesday, Thirty-first.*

I have safely arrived here, just in time to add a line to that effect, and get this off by to-morrow's English mail from New York. Everything triumphant last night, except no sleep again. I am much mistaken if the political crisis do not damage the farewells by almost one half.

I hope that I am certainly better altogether.

My room well decorated with flowers, of course, and Mr. and Mrs. Fields coming to dinner. They are the most devoted of friends, and never in the way and never out of it.

Boston, *Wednesday, April First*, 1868.　Miss Hogarth.

I received your letter here, last night. My New York doctor has prescribed for me promptly, and I hope I am better. I am certainly no worse. We shall do (to the best of my belief) *very well* with the farewells here and at New York, but not greatly. Everything is at a standstill, pending the impeachment and the next presidential election. I forgot whether I told you that the New York press are going to give me a public dinner, on Saturday, the eighteenth.

I hear (but not from himself) that Wills has had a bad fall in hunting, and is, or has been, laid up. I am supposed, I take it, not to know this until I hear it from himself.

Thursday.

My notion of the farewells is pretty certain now to turn out right. It is not at all probable that we shall do anything enormous. Every pulpit in Massachusetts will resound to violent politics to-day and to-night. You remember the Hutchinson family? I have had a grateful letter from John Hutchinson. He speaks of "my sister Abby" as living in New York. The immediate object of his note is to invite me to the marriage of his daughter, twenty-one years of age.

You will see by the evidence of this piece of paper that I am using up my stationery. Scott has just been making anxious calculations as to our powers of holding out in the articles of tooth-powder, etc. The calculations encourage him to believe that we shall just hold out, and no more. I think I am still better to-day than I was yesterday; but I am far from strong, and have no appetite. To see me at my little table at night, you would think me the freshest of the fresh. And this is the marvel of Fields' life.

I don't forget that this is Forster's birthday.

Friday afternoon, Third.

Catarrh worse than ever! And we don't know (at four) whether I can read to-night or must stop. Otherwise all well.

Miss
Dickens.

Boston, *Tuesday, Seventh April,* 1868.

I not only read last Friday, when I was doubtful of being able to do so, but read as I never did before, and astonished the audience quite as much as myself. You never saw or heard such a scene of excitement.

Longfellow and all the Cambridge men urged me to give in. I have been very near doing so, but feel stronger to-day. I cannot tell whether the catarrh may have done me any lasting injury in the lungs or other breathing organs, until I shall have rested and got home. I hope and believe not. Consider the weather. There have been two snowstorms since I wrote last, and to-day the town is blotted out in a ceaseless whirl of snow and wind.

I cannot eat (to anything like the ordinary extent), and have established this system: At seven in the morning, in bed, a tumbler of new cream and two tablespoonsful of rum. At twelve, a sherry cobbler and a biscuit. At three (dinner time), a pint of champagne. At five minutes to eight, an egg beaten up with a glass of sherry. Between the parts, the strongest beef tea that can be made, drunk hot. At a quarter-past ten, soup, and anything to drink that I can fancy. I don't eat more than half a pound of solid food in the whole four-and-twenty hours, if so much.

If I hold out, as I hope to do, I shall be greatly pressed in leaving here and getting over to New York before next Saturday's mail from there. Do not, therefore, *if all be well,* expect to hear from me by Saturday's mail, but look for my last letter from America by the mail of the following Wednesday, the fifteenth. *Be sure* that you shall hear, however, by Saturday's mail, if I should knock up as to reading. I am tremendously "beat," but I feel really and unaffectedly so much stronger to-day, both in my body and hopes, that I am much encouraged. I have a fancy that I turned my worst time last night.

Dolby is as tender as a woman and as watchful as a doctor. He never leaves me during the reading now, but sits at the side of the platform and keeps his eye upon me all the time. Ditto George, the gasman, steadiest and most reliable man I ever employed. I am the more hopeful of my not having to relinquish a reading, because last night was "Copperfield" and "Bob"— by a quarter of an hour the longest, and, in consideration of the storm, by very much the most trying. Yet I was far fresher afterwards than I have been these three weeks.

Here ends my report. The personal affection of the people in this place is charming to the last.

Ever your affectionate Father.

ABOARD THE "RUSSIA," BOUND FOR LIVERPOOL,
Sunday, Twenty-sixth April, 1868.

Mr. James T. Fields.

MY DEAR FIELDS,

In order that you may have the earliest intelligence of me, I begin this note to-day in my small cabin, purposing (if it should prove practicable) to post it at Queenstown for the return steamer.

We are already past the Banks of Newfoundland, although our course was seventy miles to the south, with the view of avoiding ice seen by Judkins in the *Scotia* on his passage out to New York. The *Russia* is a magnificent ship, and has dashed along bravely. We had made more than thirteen hundred and odd miles at noon to-day. The wind, after being a little capricious, rather threatens at the present time to turn against us, but our run is already eighty miles ahead of the *Russia's* last run in this direction—a very fast one. . . . To all whom it may concern, report the *Russia* in the highest terms. She rolls more easily than the other Cunard Screws, is kept in perfect order, and is most carefully looked after in all departments. We have had nothing approaching to heavy weather, still one can speak to the trim of the ship. Her captain, a gentleman; bright, polite, good-natured, and vigilant. . . .

As to me, I am greatly better, I hope. I have got on my right boot to-day for the first time; the "true American" seems to be turning faithless at last; and I made a Gad's Hill breakfast this morning, as a further advance on having otherwise eaten and drunk all day ever since Wednesday.

You will see Anthony Trollope, I daresay. What was my amazement to see him with these eyes come aboard in the mail tender just before we started! He had come out in the *Scotia* just in time to dash off again in said tender to shake hands with me, knowing me to be aboard here. It was most heartily done. He is on a special mission of convention with the United States post-office.

We have been picturing your movements, and have duly checked off your journey home, and have talked about you continually. But I have thought about you both, even much, much more. You will never know how I loved you both; or what you have been to me in America, and will always be to me everything; or how fervently I thank you.

All the working of the ship seems to be done on my forehead. It is scrubbed and holystoned (my head—not the deck) at three every morning. It is scraped and swabbed all day. Eight pairs of heavy boots are now clattering on it, getting the ship under sail again. Legions of ropes'-ends are flopped upon it as I write.

Thursday, Thirtieth.

Soon after I left off as above we had a gale of wind which blew all night. For a few hours on the evening side of midnight there was no getting from this cabin of mine to the saloon, or *vice versâ*, so heavily did the sea break over the decks. The ship, however, made nothing of it, and we were all right again by Monday afternoon. Except for a few hours yesterday (when we had a very light head-wind), the weather has been constantly favourable, and we are now bowling away at a great rate, with a fresh breeze filling all our sails. We expect to be at Queenstown between midnight and three in the morning.

I hope, my dear Fields, you may find this legible, but I rather doubt it, for there is motion enough on the ship to render writing to a landsman, however accustomed to pen and ink, rather a difficult achievement. Besides which, I slide away gracefully from the paper, whenever I want to be particularly expressive. . . .

——, sitting opposite to me at breakfast, always has the following items: A large dish of porridge into which he casts slices of butter and a quantity of sugar. Two cups of tea. A steak. Irish stew. Chutnee and marmalade. Another deputation of two has solicited a reading to-night. Illustrious novelist has unconditionally and absolutely declined. More love, and more to that, from your ever affectionate friend.

The Hon.
Mrs.
Watson.

GAD'S HILL PLACE, *Monday, Eleventh May*, 1868.

MY DEAR MRS. WATSON,

I am delighted to have your letter. It comes to me like a faithful voice from dear old Rockingham, and awakens many memories.

The work in America has been so very hard, and the winter there has been so excessively severe, that I really have been very unwell for some months. But I had not been at sea three days on the passage home when I became myself again.

If you will arrange with Mary Boyle any time for coming here, we shall be charmed to see you, and I will adapt my arrangements accordingly. I make this suggestion because she generally comes here early in the summer season. But if you will propose yourself *anyhow*, giving me a margin of a few days in case of my being pre-engaged for this day or that, we will (as my American friends say) "fix it."

What with travelling, reading night after night, and speech-making day after day, I feel the peace of the country beyond all expression. On board ship coming home, a "deputation" (two in number, of whom only one could get into my cabin, while the other looked in at my window) came to ask me to read to the passengers that evening in the saloon. I respectfully replied that sooner than do it, I would assault the captain, and be put in irons.

Ever affectionately yours.

"ALL THE YEAR ROUND" OFFICE,   Mr. James
Fifteenth May, 1868.   T. Fields.

MY DEAR FIELDS,

I have found it so extremely difficult to write about America (though never so briefly) without appearing to blow trumpets on the one hand, or to be inconsistent with my avowed determination *not* to write about it on the other, that I have taken the simple course enclosed. The number will be published on the Sixth of June. It appears to me to be the most modest and manly course, and to derive some graceful significance from its title.

Thank my dear Mrs. Fields from me for her delightful letter received on the sixteenth. I will write to her very soon, and tell her about the dogs. I would write by this post, but that Wills' absence (in Sussex, and getting no better there as yet) so overwhelms me with business that I can scarcely get through it.

Miss me? Ah, my dear fellow, but how do I miss *you!* We talk about you both at Gad's Hill every day of our lives. And I never see the place looking very pretty indeed, or hear the birds sing all day long and the nightingales all night, without restlessly wishing that you were both there.

With best love, and truest and most enduring regard, ever, my dear Fields,

Your most affectionate.

Everything here looks lovely, and I find it (you will be surprised to hear) really a pretty place ! I have seen "No Thoroughfare" twice. Excellent things in it, but it drags to my thinking. It is, however, a great success in the country, and is now getting up with great force in Paris. Fechter is ill, and was ordered off to Brighton yesterday. Otherwise, thank God, I find everything well and thriving. You and my dear Mrs. Fields are constantly in my mind. Procter greatly better.

Mrs. George
Cattermole.

GAD'S HILL PLACE, HIGHAM BY ROCHESTER, KENT,
Saturday, Sixteenth May, 1868.

MY DEAR MRS. CATTERMOLE,

On my return from America just now, I accidentally heard that George had been ill. My sister-in-law had heard it from Forster, but vaguely. Until I received your letter of Wednesday's date, I had no idea that he had been very ill; and should have been greatly shocked by knowing it, were it not for the hopeful and bright assurance you give me that he is greatly better.

My old affection for him has never cooled. The last time he dined with me, I asked him to come again that day ten years, for I was perfectly certain (this was my small joke) that I should not set eyes upon him sooner. The time being fully up, I hope that you will remind him, with my love, that he is due. His hand is upon these walls here, as I should like him to see for himself, and *you* to see for *yourself*, and in this hope I shall pursue his complete recovery.

I heartily sympathise with you in your terrible anxiety, and in your vast relief; and, with many thanks for your letter, am ever, my dear Mrs. Cattermole,

Affectionately yours.

M. Charles
Fechter.

OFFICE OF "ALL THE YEAR ROUND,"
Friday, Twenty-second May, 1868.

MY DEAR FECHTER,

I have an idea about the bedroom act, which I should certainly have suggested if I had been at our "repetitions" here.* I want it done *to the sound of the Waterfall*. I want the sound of the Waterfall louder and softer as the wind rises and falls, to be spoken through—like the music. I want the Waterfall *listened to when spoken of, and not looked out at*. The mystery and gloom of the scene would be greatly helped by this, and it would be new and picturesquely fanciful.

* The Play of "No Thoroughfare" was produced at the Adelphi Theatre, under the management of Mr. Webster.

I am very anxious to hear from you how the piece seems to go,* and how the artists, who are to act it, seem to understand their parts. Pray tell me, too, when you write, how you found Madame Fechter, and give all our loves to all.

Ever heartily yours.

GAD'S HILL, HIGHAM BY ROCHESTER, KENT, *Twenty-fifth May,* 1868.   Mrs. James T. Fields.

MY DEAR MRS. FIELDS,

As you ask me about the dogs, I begin with them. When I came down first, I came to Gravesend, five miles off. The two Newfoundland dogs, coming to meet me with the usual carriage and the usual driver, and beholding me coming in my usual dress out at the usual door, it struck me that their recollection of my having been absent for any unusual time was at once cancelled. They behaved (they are both young dogs) exactly in their usual manner; coming behind the basket phaeton as we trotted along, and lifting their heads to have their ears pulled—a special attention which they receive from no one else. But when I drove into the stable-yard, Linda (the St. Bernard) was greatly excited; weeping profusely, and throwing herself on her back that she might caress my foot with her great fore-paws. Mamie's little dog, too, Mrs. Bouncer, barked in the greatest agitation on being called down and asked by Mamie, "Who is this?" and tore round and round me, like the dog in the Faust outlines. You must know that all the farmers turned out on the road in their market-chaises to say, "Welcome home, sir!" and that all the houses along the road were dressed with flags; and that our servants, to cut out the rest, had dressed this house so that every brick of it was hidden. They had asked Mamie's permission to "ring the alarm-bell" (!) when master drove up, but Mamie, having some slight idea that that compliment might awaken master's sense of the ludicrous, had recommended bell abstinence. But on Sunday the village choir (which includes the bell-ringers) made amends. After some unusually brief pious reflections in the crowns of their hats at the end of the sermon, the ringers bolted out, and rang like mad until I got home. There had been a conspiracy among the villagers to take the horse out, if I had come to our own station, and draw me here. Mamie and Georgy had got wind of it and warned me.

Divers birds sing here all day, and the nightingales all night. The place is lovely, and in perfect order. I have put five mirrors in the Swiss châlet (where I write) and they reflect and refract in

* Mr. Fechter was, at this time, superintending the production of a French version of "No Thoroughfare," in Paris. It was called "L'Abîme."

2 Y

all kinds of ways the leaves that are quivering at the windows, and the great fields of waving corn, and the sail-dotted river. My room is up among the branches of the trees; and the birds and the butterflies fly in and out, and the green branches shoot in, at the open windows, and the lights and shadows of the clouds come and go with the rest of the company. The scent of the flowers, and indeed of everything that is growing for miles and miles, is most delicious.

Dolby (who sends a world of messages) found his wife much better than he expected, and the children (wonderful to relate!) perfect. The little girl winds up her prayers every night with a special commendation to Heaven of me and the pony—as if I must mount him to get there! I dine with Dolby (I was going to write "him," but found it would look as if I were going to dine with the pony) at Greenwich this very day, and if your ears do not burn from six to nine this evening, then the Atlantic is a non-conductor.

It is time I should explain the otherwise inexplicable enclosure. Will you tell Fields, with my love (I suppose he hasn't used *all* the pens yet?), that I think there is in Tremont Street a set of my books, sent out by Chapman, not arrived when I departed. Such set of the immortal works of our illustrious, etc., is designed for the gentleman to whom the enclosure is addressed. If T., F. and Co., will kindly forward the set (carriage paid) with the enclosure to ——'s address, I will invoke new blessings on their heads, and will get Dolby's little daughter to mention them nightly.

"No Thoroughfare" is very shortly coming out in Paris, where it is now in active rehearsal. It is still playing here, but without Fechter, who has been very ill. The doctor's dismissal of him to Paris, however, and his getting better there, enables him to get up the play there. He and Wilkie missed so many pieces of stage-effect here, that, unless I am quite satisfied with his report, I shall go over and try my stage-managerial hand at the Vaudeville Theatre.

Ever, my dear Mrs. Fields,
Your most affectionate friend.

Mr.
Alexander
Ireland.

THE ATHENÆUM, *Saturday, Thirtieth May,* 1868.
DEAR MR. IRELAND,

Many thanks for the book * you have kindly lent me. My interest in its subject is scarcely less than your own, and the

---

* The volume referred to is a "List of the Writings of William Hazlitt and Leigh Hunt, chronologically arranged, with Notes, descriptive, critical, and explanatory, etc."

book has afforded me great pleasure. I hope it will prove a very useful tribute to Hazlitt and Hunt (in extending the general knowledge of their writings), as well as a deservedly hearty and loving one.

You gratify me much by your appreciation of my desire to promote the kindest feelings between England and America. But the writer of the generous article in *The Manchester Examiner* is quite mistaken in supposing that I intend to write a book on the United States. The fact is exactly the reverse, or I could not have spoken without some appearance of having a purpose to serve.

Very faithfully yours.

GAD'S HILL, *Wednesday, Tenth June*, 1868. Mr. W. C. Macready.

MY DEAREST MACREADY,

Since my return from America, I have been so overwhelmed with business that I have not had time even to write to you. You may imagine what six months of arrear are to dispose of; added to this, Wills has received a concussion of the brain (from an accident in the hunting-field), and is sent away by the doctors, and strictly prohibited from even writing a note. Consequently all the business and money details of "All the Year Round" devolve upon me. And I have had to get them up, for I have never had experience of them. Then I am suddenly entreated to go to Paris, to look after the French version of "No Thoroughfare" on the stage. And I go, and come back, leaving it a great success.

I hope Mrs. Macready and you have not abandoned the idea of coming here? The expression of this hope is the principal, if not the only, object of this present note. May the amiable secretary vouchsafe a satisfactory reply!

The undersigned is in his usual brilliant condition, and indeed greatly disappointed them at home here, by coming back "so brown and looking so well." Katie, Mary, and Georgina expected a wreck, and were, at first, much mortified. But they are getting over it now.

Ever, my dearest Macready,
Your most affectionate.

GAD'S HILL PLACE, Mr. James T. Fields.
Tuesday, Seventh July, 1868.

MY DEAR FIELDS,

I have delayed writing to you (and Mrs. Fields, to whom my love) until I should have seen Longfellow. When he was in London the first time he came and went without reporting himself, and left me in a state of unspeakable discomfiture. Indeed, I should not have believed in his having been here at all, if Mrs. Procter had not told me of his calling to see Procter. However, on his return he wrote to me from the Langham Hotel, and I went up to town to see him, and to make an appointment for his coming here. He, the girls, and Appleton, came down last Saturday night and stayed until Monday forenoon. I showed them all the neighbouring country that could be shown in so short a time, and they finished off with a tour of inspection of the kitchens, pantry, wine-cellar, pickles, sauces, servants' sitting-room, general household stores, and even the Cellar Book, of this illustrious establishment. Forster and Kent (the latter wrote certain verses to Longfellow, which have been published in *The Times*, and which I sent to D——) came down for a day, and I hope we all had a really " good time." I turned out a couple of postilions in the old red jacket of the old red royal Dover road, for our ride; and it was like a holiday ride in England fifty years ago. Of course we went to look at the old houses in Rochester, and the old cathedral, and the old castle, and the house for the six poor travellers who, " not being rogues or proctors, shall have lodging, entertainment, and four pence each."

Nothing can surpass the respect paid to Longfellow here, from the Queen downward. He is everywhere received and courted, and finds (as I told him he would, when we talked of it in Boston) the working-men at least as well acquainted with his books as the classes socially above them. . . .

Last Thursday I attended, as sponsor, the christening of Dolby's son and heir—a most jolly baby, who held on tight by the rector's left whisker while the service was performed. What time, too, his little sister, connecting me with the pony, trotted up and down the centre aisle, noisily driving herself as that celebrated animal, so that it went very hard with the sponsorial dignity.

I am delighted to find you both so well pleased with the Blind Book scheme.* I said nothing of it to you when we were together, though I had made up my mind, because I wanted to come upon you with that little burst from a distance. It seemed something like meeting again when I remitted the money and thought of your talking of it.

The dryness of the weather is amazing. All the ponds and surface-wells about here are waterless, and the poor people suffer greatly. The people of this village have only one spring to resort

---

* A copy of " The Old Curiosity Shop," in raised letters for the use of the Blind, had been printed by Charles Dickens' order at the " Perkins Institution for the Blind " in Boston, and presented by him to that institution in this year.

to, and it is a couple of miles from many cottages. I do not let the great dogs swim in the canal, because the people have to drink of it. But when they get into the Medway it is hard to get them out again. The other day Bumble (the son, Newfoundland dog) got into difficulties among some floating timber, and became frightened. Don (the father) was standing by me, shaking off the wet and looking on carelessly, when all of a sudden he perceived something amiss, and went in with a bound and brought Bumble out by the ear. The scientific way in which he towed him along was charming.

Ever your loving.

GAD'S HILL PLACE, HIGHAM BY ROCHESTER, KENT, *Sunday, Nineteenth July*, 1868.

Mr. J. E. Millais, R.A.

MY DEAR MILLAIS,

I received the enclosed letter yesterday, and I have, perhaps unjustly—some vague suspicions of it. As I know how faithful and zealous you have been in all relating to poor Leech, I make no apology for asking you whether you can throw any light upon its contents.

You will be glad to hear that Charles Collins is decidedly better to-day, and is out of doors.

Believe me always, faithfully yours.

GAD'S HILL PLACE, HIGHAM BY ROCHESTER, KENT, *Tuesday, Twenty-first July*, 1868.

Mrs. Henry Austin.*

MY DEAR LETITIA,

You will have had a telegram from me to-day. I received your sad news by this morning's post.

On Thursday I have people to see and matters to attend to, which I cannot forego or depute to another. But, *between ourselves*, I must add something else: I have the greatest objection to attend a funeral in which my affections are not strongly and immediately concerned. I have no notion of a funeral as a matter of form or ceremony. And just as I should expressly prohibit the summoning to my own burial of anybody who was not very near or dear to me, so I revolt from myself appearing at that solemn rite unless the deceased were very near or dear to me. I cannot endure being dressed up by an undertaker as part of his trade show. I was not in this poor good fellow's house in his lifetime, and I feel that I have no business there when he lies dead in it. My mind is penetrated with sympathy and compassion for the young widow, but that feeling is a real thing, and my attendance

* On the death of Mr. Henry Austin, cousin and adopted child of Mr. and Mrs. Austin.

as a mourner would not be—to myself. It would be to you, I know, but it would not be to myself. I know full well that you cannot delegate to me your memories of and your associations with the deceased, and the more true and tender they are the more invincible is my objection to become a form in the midst of the most awful realities.

Believe me, ever your affectionate Brother.

Mrs. George Cattermole.

GAD'S HILL, *Wednesday, Twenty-second July,* 1868.

MY DEAR MRS. CATTERMOLE,

Of course I will sign your memorial to the Academy. If you take either of the Landseers, certainly take Edwin. But, if you would be content with Frith, I have already spoken to him, and believe that I can answer for him. Frith will be here on Saturday, and I shall be here too. I spoke to him a fortnight ago, and found him most earnest in the cause. He said he felt absolutely sure that the whole profession in its best and highest representation would do anything for George.

Ever yours affectionately.

Mr. Serle.

GAD'S HILL, *Wednesday, Twenty-ninth July,* 1868.

MY DEAR SERLE,

I do not believe there is the slightest chance of an International Copyright law being passed in America for a long time to come. Some Massachusetts men do believe in such a thing, but they fail (as I think) to take into account the prompt Western opposition.

Such an alteration as you suggest in the English law would give no copyright in America, you see. The American publisher could buy no absolute *right* of priority. Any American newspaper could (and many would, in a popular case) pirate from him as soon as they could get the matter set up. He could buy no more than he buys now when he arranges for advance sheets from England, so that there may be simultaneous publication in the two countries. And success in England is of so much importance towards the achievement of success in America, that I greatly doubt whether previous publications in America would often be worth more to an American publisher or manager than simultaneous publication. Concerning the literary man in Parliament who would undertake to bring in a Bill for such an amendment of our copyright law, with weight enough to keep his heart unbroken while he should be getting it through its various lingering miseries, all I can say is —I decidedly don't know him.

Believe me always, faithfully yours.

Friday, Thirty-first July, 1868.   Mr. W. H. Wills.

MY DEAR WILLS,

I am very unwilling to abandon the Christmas number, though even in the case of my little Christmas books (which were immensely profitable) I let the idea go when I thought it was wearing out. Ever since I came home, I have hammered at it more or less, and have been uneasy about it. I have begun something which is very droll, but it manifestly shapes itself towards a book, and could not in the least admit of even that shadowy approach to a congruous whole on the part of other contributors which they have ever achieved at the best. I have begun something else (aboard the American mail-steamer); but I don't like it, because the stories must come limping in after the old fashion, though, of course, what I *have* done will be good for A. Y. R. In short, I have cast about with the greatest of pains and patience, and I have been wholly unable to find what I want.

And yet I cannot quite make up my mind to give in without another fight for it. I offered one hundred pounds reward at Gad's to anybody who could suggest a notion to satisfy me. Charles Collins suggested one yesterday morning, in which there is *something*, though not much. I will turn it over and over, and try a few more starts on my own account. Finally, I swear I will not give it up until August is out. Vow registered.

I am clear that a number by "various writers" would not do. If we have not the usual sort of number, we must call the current number for that date the Christmas number, and make it as good as possible.

I sit in the Châlet,* like Mariana in the Moated Grange, and to as much purpose.

I am buying the freehold of the meadow at Gad's, and of an adjoining arable field, so that I shall now have about eight-and-twenty freehold acres in a ring-fence. No more now.

I made up a very good number yesterday. You will see in it a very short article that I have called "Now!" which is a highly remarkable piece of description. It is done by a new man, from whom I have accepted another article; but he will never do anything so good again.

Ever affectionately.

---

* A model of a Swiss châlet (a present from M. Charles Fechter), used by Charles Dickens as a summer writing-room.

Mr. Rusden.   *Twenty-fourth August,* 1868.

MY DEAR SIR,

I should have written to you much sooner, but that I have been home from the United States barely three months, and have since been a little uncertain as to the precise time and way of sending my youngest son out to join his brother Alfred.

It is now settled that he shall come out in the ship *Sussex*. Of this I apprise Alfred by this mail. . . . I cannot sufficiently thank you for your kindness to Alfred. I am certain that a becoming sense of it and desire to deserve it, has done him great good.

Your report of him is an unspeakable comfort to me, and I most heartily assure you of my gratitude and friendship.

In the midst of your colonial seethings and heavings, I suppose you have some leisure to consult equally the hopeful prophets and the dismal prophets who are all wiser than any of the rest of us as to things at home here. My own strong impression is that whatsoever change the new Reform Bill may effect will be very gradual indeed and quite wholesome.

Numbers of the middle class who seldom or never voted before will vote now, and the greater part of the new voters will in the main be wiser as to their electoral responsibilities and more seriously desirous to discharge them for the common good than the bumptious singers of "Rule Britannia," "Our dear old Church of England," and all the rest of it.

If I can ever do anything for any accredited friend of yours coming to the old country, command me. I shall be truly glad of any opportunity of testifying that I do not use a mere form of words in signing myself,   Cordially yours.

M. De Cerjat.

GAD'S HILL PLACE, HIGHAM BY ROCHESTER, KENT,
Wednesday, Twenty-sixth August, 1868.

MY DEAR CERJAT,

I was happy to receive your esteemed letter a few days ago.

The severity of the winter in America (which was quite exceptional even in that rigorous climate), combined with the hard work I had to do, tried me a good deal. Neuralgia and colds beset me, either by turns or both together, and I had often much to do to get through at night. But the sea voyage home again did wonders in restoring me, and I have been very well indeed, though a little fatigued, ever since. I am now preparing for a final reading campaign in England, Scotland, and Ireland. It will begin on the

Sixth of October, and will probably last, with short occasional intermissions, until June.

The great subject in England for the moment is the horrible accident to the Irish mail-train. It is now supposed that the petroleum (known to be a powerful anæsthetic) rendered the unfortunate people who were burnt almost instantly insensible to any sensation. My escape in the Staplehurst accident of three years ago is not to be obliterated from my nervous system. To this hour I have sudden vague rushes of terror, even when riding in a hansom cab, which are perfectly unreasonable but quite insurmountable. I used to make nothing of driving a pair of horses habitually through the most crowded parts of London. I cannot now drive, with comfort to myself, on the country roads here; and I doubt if I could ride at all in the saddle. My reading secretary and companion knows so well when one of these odd momentary seizures comes upon me in a railway carriage, that he instantly produces a dram of brandy, which rallies the blood to the heart and generally prevails. I forget whether I ever told you that my watch (a chronometer) has never gone exactly since the accident? So the Irish catastrophe naturally revives the dreadful things I saw that day.

The only other news here you know as well as I; to wit, that the country is going to be ruined, and that the Church is going to be ruined, and that both have become so used to being ruined, that they will go on perfectly well.

*   *   *   *   *

Office of "All the Year Round,"
No. 26, Wellington Street, Strand, London, W.C.,
Saturday, Twenty-sixth September, 1868.

Miss Dickens.

My dearest Mamie,

I will add a line to this at the Athenæum, after seeing Plorn off, to tell you how he went away.

Athenæum, Quarter to Six.

I can honestly report that he went away, poor dear fellow, as well as could possibly be expected. He was pale, and had been crying, and (Harry said) had broken down in the railway carriage after leaving Higham station; but only for a short time.

Just before the train started he cried a good deal, but not painfully. (Tell dear Georgy that I bought him his cigars.) These are hard, hard things, but they might have to be done without means or influence, and then they would be far harder. God bless him!   Your affectionate Father.

Mr. F. D.
Finlay.*

GAD'S HILL PLACE, HIGHAM BY ROCHESTER, KENT,
Sunday, Fourth October, 1868.

MY DEAR FINLAY,

I am much obliged to you in all friendship and sincerity for your letter. I have a great respect for your father-in-law and his paper, and I am much attached to the Edinburgh people. You may suppose, therefore, that if my mind were not fully made up on the parliamentary question, I should waver now.

But my conviction that I am more useful and more happy as I am than I could ever be in Parliament is not to be shaken. I considered it some weeks ago, when I had a stirring proposal from the Birmingham people, and I then set it up on a rock for ever and a day.

Do tell Mr. Russel that I truly feel this mark of confidence, and that I hope to acknowledge it in person in Edinburgh before Christmas. There is no man in Scotland from whom I should consider this suggestion a greater honour.

Ever yours.

M. Charles
Fechter.

*   *   *   *   *

Poor Plorn is gone to Australia. It was a hard parting at the last. He seemed to me to become once more my youngest and favourite little child as the day drew near, and I did not think I could have been so shaken. You were his idol to the hour of his departure, and he asked me to tell you how much he wanted to bid you good-bye.

Ever heartily.

Mr. Henry
Fielding
Dickens.

ADELPHI HOTEL, LIVERPOOL,
Thursday, Fifteenth October, 1868.

MY DEAR HARRY,

I have your letter here this morning.

Now, observe attentively. We must have no shadow of debt. Square up everything whatsoever that it has been necessary to buy. Let not a farthing be outstanding on any account, when we begin with your allowance. Be particular in the minutest detail.

I wish to have no secret from you in the relations we are to establish together, and I therefore send you Joe Chitty's † letter bodily. Reading it, you will know exactly what I know, and will understand that I treat you with perfect confidence. It appears to me that an allowance of two hundred and fifty pounds a year

* Reply to a proposal made through Mr. Alexander Russel, then editor of *The Scotsman*, that he should allow himself to be put forward as a candidate for the representation of Edinburgh.

† Now Mr. Justice Chitty.

will be handsome for all your wants, if I send you your wines. I mean this to include your tailor's bills as well as every other expense; and I strongly recommend you to buy nothing in Cambridge, and to take credit for nothing but the clothes with which your tailor provides you. As soon as you have got your furniture accounts in, let us wipe all those preliminary expenses clean out, and I will then send you your first quarter.

You know how hard I work for what I get, and I think you know that I never had money help from any human creature after I was a child. You know that you are one of many heavy charges on me, and that I trust to your so exercising your abilities and improving the advantages of your past expensive education, as soon to diminish *this* charge. I say no more on that head.

Whatever you do, above all other things keep out of debt and confide in me. If ever you find yourself on the verge of any perplexity or difficulty, come to me. You will never find me hard with you while you are manly and truthful.

As your brothers have gone away one by one, I have written to each of them what I am now going to write to you. You know that you have never been hampered with religious forms of restraint, and that with mere unmeaning forms I have no sympathy. But I most strongly and affectionately impress upon you the priceless value of the New Testament, and the study of that book as the one unfailing guide in life. Deeply respecting it, and bowing down before the character of our Saviour, as separated from the vain constructions and inventions of men, you cannot go very wrong, and will always preserve at heart a true spirit of veneration and humility. Similarly I impress upon you the habit of saying a Christian prayer every night and morning. These things have stood by me all through my life, and remember that I tried to render the New Testament intelligible to you and lovable by you when you were a mere baby.

And so God bless you. Ever your affectionate Father.

KENNEDY'S HOTEL, EDINBURGH,
Sunday, Sixth December, 1868.

Mrs. F. Lehmann.

MY DEAR MRS. LEHMANN,

I hope you will see Nancy with the light of a great audience upon her some time between this and May; always supposing that she should not prove too weird and woeful for the general public.

You know the aspect of this city on a Sunday, and how gay and bright it is. The merry music of the blithe bells, the waving flags, the prettily-decorated houses with their draperies of various colours, and the radiant countenances at the windows and in the streets, how charming they are! The usual preparations are making for the band in the open air, in the afternoon; and the usual pretty children (selected for that purpose) are at this moment hanging garlands round the Scott monument, preparatory to the innocent Sunday dance round that edifice, with which the diversions invariably close. It is pleasant to think that these customs were themselves of the early Christians, those early birds who *didn't* catch the worm—and nothing else—and choke their young with it.   Faithfully yours always.

Mr. W.
Wilkie
Collins.

KENNEDY'S HOTEL, EDINBURGH,
Tuesday, Eighth December, 1868.

MY DEAR WILKIE,

I am hard at it here as usual, though with an audience so finely perceptive that the labour is much diminished. I have got together in a very short space the conclusion of "Oliver Twist" that you suggested, and am trying it daily with the object of rising from that blank state of horror into a fierce and passionate rush for the end. As yet I cannot make a certain effect of it; but when I shall have gone over it as many score of times as over the rest of that reading, perhaps I may strike one out.

I agree with you about the reading perfectly. In No. 3 you will see an exact account of some places I visited at Ratcliffe. There are two little instances in it of something comic rising up in the midst of the direst misery, that struck me very humorously at the time.

As I have determined not to do the "Oliver Murder" until after the Fifth of January, when I shall ascertain its effect on a great audience, it is curious to notice how the shadow of its coming affects the Scotch mind. There was such a disposition to hold back for it here (until I return to finish in February) that we had next to no "let" when we arrived. It all came with a rush yesterday. They gave me a most magnificent welcome back from America last night.

I am perpetually counting the weeks before me to be "read" through, and am perpetually longing for the end of them; and yet I sometimes wonder whether I shall miss something when they are over.

It is a very, very bad day here, very dark and very wet. I am sitting at a side window looking up the length of Princes Street, watching the mist change over the Castle and murdering Nancy by turns.   Ever affectionately.

P.S.—I have read the whole of Fitzgerald's "Zero," and the idea is exceedingly well wrought out.

KENNEDY'S HOTEL, EDINBURGH,
Saturday, Twelfth December, 1868.

Miss
Hogarth.

MY DEAREST GEORGY,

I send another *Scotsman* by this post, because it is really a good newspaper, well written, and well managed. We had an immense house here last night, and a very large turn-away.

It blew appallingly here the night before last, but the wind has since shifted northward, and it is now bright and cold. The *Star of Hope,* that picked up those shipwrecked people in the boat, came into Leith yesterday, and was received with tremendous cheers. Her captain must be a good man and a noble fellow.

Forgery of my name is becoming popular. You sent me, this morning, a letter from Russell Sturgis, answering a supposed letter of mine (presented by "Miss Jefferies"), and assuring me of his readiness to give not only the ten pounds I asked for, but any contribution I wanted, towards sending that lady and her family back to Boston.

I wish you would take an opportunity of forewarning Lady Tennent that the first night's reading she will attend is an experiment quite out of the way, and that she may find it rather horrible.

The keeper of the Edinburgh Hall, a fine old soldier, presented me, on Friday night, with the finest red camellia for my button-hole that ever was seen. Nobody can imagine how he came by it, as the florists had had a considerable demand for that colour from ladies in the stalls, and could get no such thing.

The day is dark, wet, and windy. The weather is likely to be vile indeed at Glasgow, where it always rains, and where the sun is never seen through the smoke. We go over there to-morrow at ten.

*   *   *   *   *

KENNEDY'S HOTEL, EDINBURGH,
Monday, Fourteenth December, 1868.

Mr. Russell
Sturgis.

MY DEAR MR. RUSSELL STURGIS,

I am "reading" here, and shall be through this week. Consequently I am only this morning in receipt of your kind note of the tenth, forwarded from my own house.

Believe me I am as much obliged to you for your generous and ready response to my supposed letter as I should have been if I had really written it. But I know nothing whatever of it or of "Miss Jeffries," except that I have a faint impression of having recently noticed that name among my begging-letter correspondents, and of having associated it in my mind with a regular professional hand. Your caution has, I hope, disappointed this swindler. But my testimony is at your service if you should need it, and I would take any opportunity of bringing one of those vagabonds to punishment; for they are, one and all, the most heartless and worthless vagabonds on the face of the earth.

Believe me, faithfully yours.

Miss
Dickens.

CARRICK'S ROYAL HOTEL, GLASGOW,
Tuesday, Fifteenth December, 1868.

MY DEAREST MAMIE,

It occurs to me that my table at St. James's Hall might be appropriately ornamented with a little holly next Tuesday. If the two front legs were entwined with it, for instance, and a border of it ran round the top of the fringe in front, with a little sprig by way of bouquet at each corner, it would present a seasonable appearance.

If you will think of this, and will have the materials ready in a little basket, I will call for you at the office at half-past twelve on Tuesday, and take you up to the hall, where the table will be ready for you.

No news, except that we had a great crush and a wonderful audience in Edinburgh last night.

*   *   *   *   *

Mrs. James
T. Fields.

GLASGOW, *Wednesday, Sixteenth December*, 1868.

MY DEAR MRS. FIELDS,

. . . First, as you are curious about the Oliver murder, I will tell you about that trial of the same at which you *ought* to have assisted. There were about a hundred people present in all. I have changed my stage. Besides that back screen which you know so well, there are two large screens of the same colour, set off, one on either side, like the "wings" at a theatre. And besides these again, we have a quantity of curtains of the same colour, with which to close in any width of room from wall to wall. Consequently, the figure is now completely isolated, and the slightest action becomes much more important. This was used for the first time on the occasion. But behind the stage—the orchestra being very large and built for the accommodation of a numerous chorus—there was ready, on the level of the platform, a very long table, beautifully lighted, with a large staff of men ready to open oysters and set champagne-corks flying. Directly I had done, the screens being whisked off by my people, there was disclosed one of the prettiest banquets you can imagine; and when all the people came up, and the gay dresses of the ladies were lighted by those powerful lights of mine, the scene was exquisitely pretty; the hall being newly decorated, and very elegantly; and the whole looking like a great bed of flowers and diamonds.

Now, you must know that all this company were, before the wine went round, unmistakably pale, and had horror-stricken faces. Next morning Harness (Fields knows—Rev. William—did an edition of Shakespeare—old friend of the Kembles and Mrs. Siddons), writing to me about it, and saying it was "a most amazing and terrific thing," added, "but I am bound to tell you that I had an almost irresistible impulse upon me to *scream*, and that, if anyone had cried out, I am certain I should have followed." He had no idea that, on the night, Preistley, the great ladies' doctor, had taken me aside and said: "My dear Dickens, you may rely upon it that if only one woman cries out when you murder the girl, there will be a contagion of hysteria all over this place." It is impossible to soften it without spoiling it, and you may suppose that I am rather anxious to discover how it goes on the Fifth of January!!! We are afraid to announce it elsewhere, without knowing, except that I have thought it pretty safe to put it up once in Dublin. I asked Mrs. Keeley, the famous actress, who was at the experiment: "What do *you* say? Do it or not?" "Why, of course, do it," she replied. "Having got at such an effect as that, it must be done. But," rolling her large black eyes very slowly, and speaking very distinctly, "the public have been looking out for a sensation these last fifty years or so, and by Heaven they have got it!" With which words, and a long breath and a long stare, she became speechless. Again, you may suppose that I am a little anxious!

My old likening of Boston to Edinburgh has been constantly revived within these last ten days. There is a certain remarkable similarity of *tone* between the two places. The audiences are curiously. alike, except that the Edinburgh audience has a quicker sense of humour and is a little more genial. No disparagement to Boston in this, because I consider an Edinburgh audience perfect.

I trust, my dear Eugenius, that you have recognised yourself in a certain Uncommercial, and also some small reference to a name rather dear to you? As an instance of how strangely something comic springs up in the midst of the direst misery, look to a succeeding Uncommercial, called "A Small Star in the East," published to-day, by-the-bye. I have described, *with exactness*, the poor places into which I went, and how the people behaved, and what they said. I was wretched, looking on; and yet the boiler-maker and the poor man with the legs filled me with a sense of drollery not to be kept down by any pressure.

The atmosphere of this place, compounded of mists from the highlands and smoke from the town factories, is crushing my eyebrows as I write, and it rains as it never does rain anywhere else, and always does rain here. It is a dreadful place, though much improved and possessing a deal of public spirit. Improvement is beginning to knock the old town of Edinburgh about, here and there; but the Canongate and the most picturesque of the horrible courts and wynds are not to be easily spoiled, or made fit for the poor wretches who people them to live in. Edinburgh is so changed as to its notabilities, that I had the only three men left of the Wilson and Jeffrey time to dine with me there, last Saturday.

I think you will find "Fatal Zero" (by Percy Fitzgerald) a very curious analysis of a mind, as the story advances. A new beginner in "A. Y. R." (Hon. Mrs. Clifford, Kinglake's sister), who wrote a story in the series just finished, called "The Abbot's Pool," has just sent me another story. I have a strong impression that, with care, she will step into Mrs. Gaskell's vacant place. Wills is no better, and I have work enough even in that direction.

God bless the woman with the black mittens for making me laugh so this morning! I take her to be a kind of public-spirited Mrs. Sparsit, and as such take her to my bosom. God bless you both, my dear friends, in this Christmas and New Year time, and in all times, seasons, and places, and send you to Gad's Hill with the next flowers!

Ever your most affectionate.

Mr. Russell
Sturgis.

KENNEDY'S HOTEL, EDINBURGH,
Friday, Eighteenth December, 1868.

MY DEAR MR. RUSSELL STURGIS,

I return you the forged letter, and devoutly wish that I had to flog the writer in virtue of a legal sentence. I most cordially reciprocate your kind expressions in reference to our future intercourse, and shall hope to remind you of them five or six months hence, when my present labours shall have gone the way of all other earthly things. It was particularly interesting to me when I was last at Boston to recognise poor dear Felton's unaffected and genial ways in his eldest daughter, and to notice how, in tender remembrance of him, she is, as it were, Cambridge's daughter.

Believe me always, faithfully yours.

GAD'S HILL PLACE, HIGHAM BY ROCHESTER, KENT,   Mr. J. C.
Christmas Day, 1868.   Parkinson.

MY DEAR PARKINSON,

I am diffident of addressing Mr. Gladstone on the subject of your desire to be appointed to the vacant Commissionership of Inland Revenue, because, although my respect for him and confidence in him are second to those of no man in England (a bold word at this time, but a truthful one), my personal acquaintance with him is very slight. But you may make, through any of your friends, any use you please of this letter, towards the end of bringing its contents under Mr. Gladstone's notice.

In expressing my conviction that you deserve the place, and are in every way qualified for it, I found my testimony upon as accurate a knowledge of your character and abilities as anyone can possibly have acquired. In my editorship both of "Household Words" and "All the Year Round," you know very well that I have invariably offered you those subjects of political and social interest to write upon, in which integrity, exactness, a remarkable power of generalising evidence and balancing facts, and a special clearness in stating the case, were indispensable on the part of the writer. My confidence in your powers has never been misplaced, and through all our literary intercourse you have never been hasty or wrong. Whatever trust you have undertaken has been so completely discharged, that it has become my habit to read your proofs rather for my own edification than (as in other cases) for the detection of some slip here or there, or the more pithy presentation of the subject.

That your literary work has never interfered with the discharge of your official duties, I may assume to be at least as well known to your colleagues as it is to me. It is idle to say that if the post were in my gift you should have it, because you have had, for some years, most of the posts of high trust that have been at my disposal. An excellent public servant in your literary sphere of action, I should be heartily glad if you could have this new opportunity of distinguishing yourself in the same character. And this is at least unselfish in me, for I suppose I should then lose you ?

Always faithfully yours.

MY DEAREST PLORN,*   Mr. Edward
I write this note to-day because your going away is much Bulwer
upon my mind, and because I want you to have a few parting Lytton
                                                    Dickens.

* This letter has been already published by Mr. Forster in his "Life."
It was given by Charles Dickens to his youngest son on the day of his departure for Australia.

words from me to think of now and then at quiet times. I need not tell you that I love you dearly, and am very, very sorry in my heart to part with you. But this life is half made up of partings, and these pains must be borne. It is my·comfort and my sincere conviction that you are going to try the life for which you are best fitted. I think its freedom and wildness more suited to you than any experiment in a study or office would ever have been; and without that training, you could have followed no other suitable occupation.

What you have already wanted until now has been a set, steady, constant purpose. I therefore exhort you to persevere in a thorough determination to do whatever you have to do as well as you can do it. I was not so old as you are now when I first had to win my food, and do this out of this determination, and I have never slackened in it since.

Never take a mean advantage of anyone in any transaction, and never be hard upon people who are in your power. Try to do to others, as you would have them do to you, and do not be discouraged if they fail sometimes. It is much better for you that they should fail in obeying the greatest rule laid down by our Saviour, than that you should.

I put a New Testament among your books, for the very same reasons, and with the very same hopes that made me write an easy account of it for you, when you were a little child; because it is the best book that ever was or will be known in the world, and because it teaches you the best lessons by which any human creature who tries to be truthful and faithful to duty can possibly be guided. As your brothers have gone away, one by one, I have written to each such words as I am now writing to you, and have entreated them all to guide themselves by this book, putting aside the interpretations and inventions of men.

You will remember that you have never at home been wearied about religious observances or mere formalities. I have always been anxious not to weary my children with such things before they are old enough to form opinions respecting them. You will therefore understand the better that I now most solemnly impress upon you the truth and beauty of the Christian religion, as it came from Christ Himself, and the impossibility of your going far wrong if you humbly but heartily respect it.

Only one thing more on this head. The more we are in earnest as to feeling it, the less we are disposed to hold forth about it. Never abandon the wholesome practice of saying your own private prayers, night and morning. I have never abandoned it myself, and I know the comfort of it.

I hope you will always be able to say in after life, that you had a kind father. You cannot show your affection for him so well, or make him so happy, as by doing your duty.

Your affectionate Father.

1869.

NARRATIVE.

THE "Farewell Readings" in town and country were resumed immediately after the beginning of this year, and were to have been continued until the end of May. The work was even harder than it had ever been. Charles Dickens began his country tour in Ireland early in January, and read continuously in all parts of England and Scotland until the end of April. A public dinner (in commemoration of his last readings in the town) was given to him at Liverpool on the Tenth April. Besides all this severe country work, he was giving a series of readings at St. James's Hall, and reading the "Murder" from "Oliver Twist," in London and in the country, frequently four times a week. In the second week of February, a sudden and unusually violent attack of the old trouble in his foot made it imperatively necessary to postpone a reading at St. James's Hall, and to delay for a day or two his departure for Scotland. The foot continued to cause him pain and inconvenience, but, as will be seen from his letters, he generally spoke of himself as otherwise well, until he arrived at Preston, where he was to read on the Twenty-second of April. The day before this appointed reading, he wrote home of some grave symptoms which he had observed in himself, and had reported to his doctor, Mr. F. Carr Beard. That gentleman, taking alarm at what he considered "indisputable evidences of overwork," wisely resolved not to content himself with written consultations, but went down to Preston on the day appointed for the reading there, and, after seeing his patient, peremptorily stopped his work, carried him off to Liverpool, and the next day to London. There he consulted Sir Thomas Watson, who entirely corroborated Mr. Beard's opinion. And the two doctors agreed that the course of readings must be given up for this year, and that reading *combined with travelling*, must be stopped *for ever*. Charles Dickens had no alternative but to acquiesce in this verdict; but he felt it keenly, not only for himself, but for the sake of the Messrs. Chappell, who showed the most disinterested kindness and solicitude on the occasion. He at once returned home to Gad's Hill, and the rest and quiet of the country restored him, for the time, to almost his usual condition of health and spirits. But it was observed, by all who loved him, that from this time forth he never regained his old vigour and elasticity. The attack at Preston was the "beginning of the end!"

During the spring and summer of this year, he received visits from many dearly-valued American friends. In May, he stayed with his daughter and sister-in-law for two or three weeks at the St. James's Hotel, Piccadilly, having promised to be in London at the time of the arrival of Mr. and Mrs. Fields, of Boston, who visited Europe this year, accompanied by Miss Mabel Lowell (the daughter of the famous American poet). Besides these friends, Mr. and Mrs. Childs, of Philadelphia—from whom he had received the greatest kindness and hospitality, and for whom he had a hearty regard—Dr. Fordyce Barker and his son, Mr. Eytinge (an illustrator of an American edition of Charles Dickens' works), and Mr. Bayard Taylor paid visits to Gad's Hill, which were thoroughly enjoyed by Charles Dickens and his family. This last summer was a very happy one. He had the annual summer visitors and parties of his friends in the neighbourhood. He was, as usual, projecting improvements in his beloved country home; one, which he called the "crowning improvement of all," was a large conservatory, which was to be added during the absence of the family in London in the following spring.

The state of Mr. Wills' health made it necessary for him now to retire altogether from the editorship of "All the Year Round." Charles Dickens' letters express the regret which he felt at the dissolution of this long and always pleasant association. Mr. Wills' place at the office was filled by Charles Dickens' eldest son, now sole editor and proprietor of the journal.

In September Charles Dickens went to Birmingham, accompanied by his son Harry, and presided at the opening of the session of (what he calls in his letter to Mr. Arthur Ryland, "*our* Institution") the Midland Institute. He made a speech on education to the young students, and promised to go back early in the following year and distribute the prizes. In one of the letters which we give to Mr. Ryland, he speaks of himself as "being in full force again," and "going to finish his farewell readings soon after Christmas." He had obtained the sanction of Sir Thomas Watson to giving twelve readings, *in London only*, which he had fixed to take place in the beginning of the following year.

The letter to his friend Mr. Finlay, which opens the year, was in reply to a proposal for a public banquet at Belfast, projected by the Mayor of that town, and conveyed through Mr. Finlay. This gentleman was at that time proprietor of *The Northern Whig* newspaper, at Belfast.

Charles Dickens' letter this New Year to M. De Cerjat was his last. That faithful and affectionate friend died very shortly afterwards.

To Miss Mary Boyle he wrote to acknowledge a New Year's gift, which he had been much touched by receiving from her, at a time when he knew she was deeply afflicted by the sudden death of her brother, Captain Cavendish Boyle, for whom Charles Dickens had a true friendship.

While he was giving his series of London readings in the spring, he received a numerously signed circular letter from actors and actresses of the various London theatres. They were very curious about his reading of the "Oliver Twist" murder, and representing to him the impossibility of their attending an evening reading, requested him to give a morning one, for their especial benefit. We give his answer, complying with the request. And the occasion was, to him, a most gratifying and deeply interesting one.

The letter to Mr. Edmund Ollier was in answer to an invitation to be present at the inauguration of a bust of Mr. Leigh Hunt, which was to be placed over his grave at Kensal Green.

The letter to Mr. Shirley Brooks, the well-known writer, who succeeded Mr. Mark Lemon as editor of "Punch," and for whom Charles Dickens had a cordial regard, was on the subject of a memorial on behalf of Mrs. Peter Cunningham, whose husband had recently died.

Our latest letters for this year are in October. One to Mr. Charles Kent, sympathising with him on a disappointment which he had experienced in a business undertaking, and one to Mr. Macready, in which he tells him of his being in the "preliminary agonies" of a new book. The first number of "Edwin Drood" was to appear before the end of his course of readings in March; and he was at work so long beforehand with a view to sparing himself, and having some numbers ready before the publication of the first one.

THE ATHENÆUM (CLUB), *New Year's Day*, 1869. Mr. F. D. Finlay.

MY DEAR FINLAY,

First my heartfelt wishes for many prosperous and happy years. Next, as to the mayor's kind intentions. I feel really grateful to him and gratified by the whole idea, but acceptance of the distinction on my part would be impracticable. My time in Ireland is all anticipated, and I could not possibly prolong my stay, because I *must* be back in London to read on Tuesday fortnight, and then must immediately set forth for the West of England. The work is so hard, and my voice is so precious, that I fear to add an ounce to the fatigue, or I might be overweighted. The avoidance of gas and crowds when I am not in the act of *being cooked before those lights of mine*, is an essential part of the training to which (as I think you know) I strictly adhere, and although I have accepted the Liverpool invitation, I have done so as an exception ; the Liverpool people having always treated me in our public relations with a kind of personal affection.

I am sincerely anxious that the Mayor of Belfast should know how the case stands with me. If you will kindly set me straight and right, I shall be truly obliged to you.

My sister-in-law has been very unwell (though she is now much better), and is recommended a brisk change. As she is a good sailor, I mean to bring her to Ireland with me ; at which she is highly delighted.

Faithfully yours ever.

M. De Cerjat.

GAD'S HILL PLACE, HIGHAM BY ROCHESTER, KENT, *Monday, Fourth January,* 1869.

MY DEAR CERJAT,

I will answer your question first. Have I done with my farewell readings? Lord bless you, no; and I shall think myself well out of it if I get done by the end of May. I have undertaken one hundred and six, and have as yet only vanquished twenty-eight. To-morrow night I read in London for the first time the "Murder" from "Oliver Twist," which I have re-arranged for the purpose. Next day I start for Dublin and Belfast. I am just back from Scotland for a few Christmas holidays. I go back there next month; and in the meantime and afterwards go everywhere else.

Take my guarantee for it, you may be quite comfortable on the subject of papal aspirations and encroachments. The English people are in unconquerable opposition to that church. They have the animosity in the blood, derived from the history of the past, though perhaps unconsciously. But they do sincerely want to win Ireland over if they can. They know that since the Union she has been hardly used. They know that Scotland has *her* religion, and a very uncomfortable one. They know that Scotland, though intensely anti-papal, perceives it to be unjust that Ireland has not *her* religion too, and has very emphatically declared her opinion in the late elections. They know that a richly-endowed church, forced upon a people who don't belong to it, is a grievance with these people. They know that many things, but especially an artfully and schemingly managed institution like the Romish Church, thrive upon a grievance, and that Rome has thriven exceedingly upon this, and made the most of it. Lastly, the best among them know that there is a gathering cloud in the West, considerably bigger than a man's hand, under which a powerful Irish-American body, rich and active, is always drawing Ireland in that direction ; and that these are not times in which other powers would back our holding Ireland by force, unless we could make our claim good in proving fair and equal government.

Poor Townshend charged me in his will "to publish without alteration his religious opinions, which he sincerely believed would tend to the happiness of mankind." To publish them without alteration is absolutely impossible ; for they are distributed in the strangest fragments through the strangest note-books, pocket-books, slips of paper and what not, and produce a most incoherent and tautological result. I infer that he must have held some always-postponed idea of fitting them together. For these reasons I would certainly publish nothing about them, if I had any discretion in the matter. Having none, I suppose a book must be made. His pictures and rings are gone to the South Kensington Museum, and are now exhibiting there.

Charley Collins is no better and no worse. Katie looks very young and very pretty. Her sister and Miss Hogarth (my joint housekeepers) have been on duty this Christmas, and have had enough to do. My boys are now all dispersed in South America, India, and Australia, except Charley, whom I have taken on at "All the Year Round" Office, and Henry, who is an undergraduate at Trinity Hall, and I hope will make his mark there. All well.

The Thames Embankment is (faults of ugliness in detail apart) the finest public work yet done. From Westminster Bridge to near Waterloo it is now lighted up at night, and has a fine effect. They have begun to plant it with trees, and the footway (not the road) is already open to the Temple. Besides its beauty, and its usefulness in relieving the crowded streets, it will greatly quicken and deepen what is learnedly called the "scour" of the river. But the Corporation of London and some other nuisances have brought the weirs above Twickenham into a very bare and unsound condition, and they already begin to give and vanish, as the stream runs faster and stronger.

I like to read your patriarchal account of yourself among your Swiss vines and fig-trees. You wouldn't recognise Gad's Hill now; I have so changed it and bought land about it. And yet I often think that if Mary were to marry (which she won't) I should sell it and go genteelly vagabondising over the face of the earth. Then indeed I might see Lausanne again. But I don't seem in the way of it at present, for the older I get, the more I do and the harder I work.   Yours ever affectionately.

Miss Mary
Boyle.

OFFICE OF "ALL THE YEAR ROUND,"
Wednesday, Sixth January, 1869.

MY DEAR MARY,

I was more affected than you can easily believe, by the sight of your gift lying on my dressing-table on the morning of the new year. To be remembered in a friend's heart when it is sore is a touching thing; and that and the remembrance of the dead quite overpowered me, the one being inseparable from the other.

You may be sure that I shall attach a special interest and value to the beautiful present, and shall wear it as a kind of charm. God bless you, and may we carry the friendship through many coming years!

My preparations for a certain murder that I had to do last night have rendered me unfit for letter-writing these last few days, or you would have heard from me sooner. The crime being completely off my mind and the blood spilled, I am (like many of my fellow-criminals) in a highly edifying state to-day.

Ever believe me, your affectionate Friend.

Miss
Dickens.

TORQUAY, *Wednesday, Twenty-seventh January*, 1869.

MY DEAREST MAMIE,

This place is most beautiful, though colder now than one would expect. This hotel, an immense place, built among picturesque broken rocks out in the blue sea, is quite delicious. There are bright green trees in the garden, and new peas a foot high. Our rooms are *en suite*, all commanding the sea, and each with two very large plate-glass windows. Everything good and well served.

A *pantomime* was being done last night in the place where I am to read to-night. It is something between a theatre, a circus, a riding-school, a Methodist chapel, and a cow-house. I was so disgusted with its acoustic properties on going in to look at it, that the whole unfortunate staff have been all day, and now are, sticking up baize and carpets in it to prevent echoes.

I have rarely seen a more uncomfortable edifice than I thought it last night.

At Clifton, on Monday night, we had a contagion of fainting. And yet the place was not hot. I should think we had from a dozen to twenty ladies borne out, stiff and rigid, at various times. It became quite ridiculous.

*   *   *   *   *

OFFICE, *Wednesday, Third February,* 1869.   Mrs. F. Lehmann.

DEAR MRS. LEHMANN,

Before getting your kind note, I had written to Lehmann, explaining why I cannot allow myself any social pleasure while my farewell task is yet unfinished. The work is so very hard, that every little scrap of rest *and silence* I can pick up is precious. And even those morsels are so flavoured with "All the Year Round," that they are not quite the genuine article.

Joachim* came round to see me at the hall last night, and I told him how sorry I was to forego the pleasure of meeting him (he is a noble fellow !) at your pleasant table.

I am glad you are coming to the "Murder" on the Second of March. (The house will be prodigious.) Such little changes as I have made shall be carefully presented to your critical notice, and I hope will be crowned with your approval. But you are always such a fine audience that I have no fear on that head. I saw Chorley yesterday in his own room. A sad and solitary sight. The widowed Drake, with a certain *gin*coherence of manner, presented a blooming countenance and buxom form in the passage ; so buxom indeed that she was obliged to retire before me like a modest stopper, before I could get into the dining decanter where poor Chorley reposed.

Faithfully yours always.

P.S.—My love to Rudie.

EDINBURGH, *Friday, Twenty-sixth February,* 1869.   Miss Hogarth.

MY DEAREST GEORGY,

The foot conducts itself splendidly. We had a most enormous cram at Glasgow. Syme saw me again yesterday (before I left here for Glasgow), and repeated "Gout!" with the greatest indignation and contempt, several times. The aching is going off as the day goes on, if it be worth mentioning again. The ride from Glasgow was charming this morning ; the sun shining brilliantly, and the country looking beautiful.

I told you what the Nortons were. Mabel Lowell is a charming little thing, and very retiring in manner and expression.

We shall have a scene here to-night, no doubt. The night before last, Ballantyne, unable to get in, had a seat behind the screen, and was nearly frightened off it by the "Murder." Every

---

* Herr Joseph Joachim, the renowned violinist.

vestige of colour had left his face when I came off, and he sat staring over a glass of champagne in the wildest way. I have utterly left off *my* champagne, and, I think, with good results. Nothing during the readings but a very little weak iced brandy-and-water.

I hope you will find me greatly improved on Tuesday.

*   *   *   *   *

Miss
Dickens.

BIRMINGHAM, *Friday, Fifth March*, 1869.

MY DEAREST MAMIE,

This is to send you my best love, and to wish you many and many happy returns of to-morrow, which I miraculously remember to be your birthday.

I saw this morning a very pretty fan here. I was going to buy it as a remembrance of the occasion, when I was checked by a dim misgiving that you had a fan not long ago from Chorley. Tell me what you would like better, and consider me your debtor in that article, whatever it may be.

I have had my usual left boot on this morning, and have had an hour's walk. It was in a gale of wind and a simoom of dust, but I greatly enjoyed it. Immense enthusiasm at Wolverhampton last night over "Marigold." Scott made a most amazing ass of himself yesterday. He reported that he had left behind somewhere three books—"Boots," "Murder," and "Gamp." We immediately telegraphed to the office. Answer, no books there. As my impression was that he must have left them at St. James's Hall, we then arranged to send him up to London at seven this morning. Meanwhile (though not reproached), he wept copiously and audibly. I had asked him over and over again, was he sure he had not put them in my large black trunk? Too sure, too sure. Hadn't opened that trunk after Tuesday night's reading. He opened it to get some clothes out when I went to bed, and there the books were! He produced them with an air of injured surprise, as if we had put them there.

*   *   *   *   *

Miss
Hogarth.

QUEEN'S HOTEL, MANCHESTER,
Sunday, Seventh March, 1869.

We have had our sitting-room chimney afire this morning, and have had to turn out elsewhere to breakfast; but the chamber has since been cleaned up, and we are reinstated. Manchester is (*for* Manchester) bright and fresh.

Tell Russell that a crop of hay is to be got off the meadow this year, before the club use it. They did not make such use of it last year as reconciles me to losing another hay-crop. So they must wait until the hay is in, before they commence active operations.

Poor Olliffe! I am truly sorry to read those sad words about his suffering, and fear that the end is not far off.

We are very comfortably housed here, and certainly that immense hall is a wonderful place for its size. Without much greater expenditure of voice than usual, I a little enlarged the action last night, and Dolby (who went to all the distant points of view) reported that he could detect no difference between it and any other place. As always happens now—and did not at first—they were unanimously taken by Noah Claypole's laugh. But the go throughout was enormous. Sims Reeves was doing Henry Bertram at the theatre. It was a night of excitement for Cottonopolis.

I received from Mrs. Keeley this morning a very good photograph of poor old Bob. Yesterday I had a letter from Harry, reminding me that our intended Cambridge day is the day next after that of the boat-race. Clearly it must be changed.

*   *   *   *   *

QUEEN'S HOTEL, MANCHESTER,
Monday, Eighth March, 1869.

Mrs. Forster.

MY DEAR MRS. FORSTER,

A thousand thanks for your note, which has reached me here this afternoon. At breakfast this morning Dolby showed me the local paper with a paragraph in it recording poor dear Tennent's * death. You may imagine how shocked I was. Immediately before I left town this last time, I had an unusually affectionate letter from him, enclosing one from Forster, and proposing the friendly dinner since appointed for the twenty-fifth. I replied to him in the same spirit, and felt touched at the time by the gentle earnestness of his tone. It is remarkable that I talked of him a great deal yesterday to Dolby (who knew nothing of him), and that I reverted to him again at night before going to bed—with no reason that I know of. Dolby was strangely impressed by this, when he showed me the newspaper. Ever your affectionate.

OFFICE OF "ALL THE YEAR ROUND,"
Saturday, Thirteenth March, 1869.

Mr. Austen Henry Layard.

MY DEAR LAYARD,

Coming to town for a couple of days, from York, I find your beautiful present.† With my heartiest congratulations on your

---

* Sir James Emerson Tennent.
† Some Venetian glass champagne tumblers.

marriage, accept my most cordial thanks for a possession that I shall always prize foremost among my worldly goods; firstly, for your sake; secondly, for its own.

Not one of these glasses shall be set on table until Mrs. Layard is there, to touch with her lips the first champagne that any of them shall ever hold! This vow has been registered in solemn triumvirate at Gad's Hill.

The first week in June will about see me through my present work, I hope. I came to town hurriedly to attend poor dear Emerson Tennent's funeral. You will know how my mind went back, in the York up-train at midnight, to Mount Vesuvius and our Neapolitan supper.

I have given Mr. Hills, of Oxford Street, the letter of introduction to you that you kindly permitted. He has immense local influence, and could carry his neighbours in favour of any good design.   My dear Layard, ever cordially yours.

Miss
Florence
Olliffe.

26, WELLINGTON STREET,
Tuesday, Sixteenth March, 1869.

MY DEAR FLORENCE,*

I have received your kind note this morning, and I hasten to thank you for it, and to assure your dear mother of our most cordial sympathy with her in her great affliction, and in loving remembrance of the good man and excellent friend we have lost. The tidings of his being very ill indeed had, of course, been reported to me. For some days past I had taken up the newspaper with sad misgivings; and this morning, before I got your letter, they were realised.

I loved him truly. His wonderful gentleness and kindness, years ago, when we had sickness in our household in Paris, has never been out of my grateful remembrance. And, socially, his image is inseparable from some of the most genial and delightful friendly hours of my life. I am almost ashamed to set such recollections by the side of your mother's great bereavement and grief, but they spring out of the fulness of my heart.

May God be with her and with you all!

Ever yours affectionately.

Miss
Hogarth.

QUEEN'S HOTEL, MANCHESTER,
Saturday, Twentieth March, 1869.

MY DEAREST GEORGY,

The Theatre Royal, Liverpool, will be a charming place to read in. Ladies are to dine at the dinner, and we hear it is to be

---

* Miss Florence Olliffe (now Mrs. Hugh Bell), who wrote to announce the death of her father, Sir Joseph Olliffe.

a very grand affair. Trade is very bad *here*, and the gloom of the Preston strike seems to brood over the place. The Titiens Company have been doing wretchedly. I should have a greater sympathy with them if they were not practising in the next room now.

My love to Letitia and Harriette.*

Will you tell Mary that I have had a letter from Frith, in which he says that he will be happy to show her his pictures " any day in the first week of April " ? I have replied that she will be proud to receive his invitation. His object in writing was to relieve his mind about the " Murder," of which he cannot say enough.

> Ever affectionately.

GAD'S HILL PLACE, HIGHAM BY ROCHESTER, KENT, *Wednesday, Twenty-fourth March,* 1869.

Mr. John Clarke.

LADIES AND GENTLEMEN,

I beg to assure you that I am much gratified by the desire you do me the honour to express in your letter handed to me by Mr. John Clarke.

Before that letter reached me, I had heard of your wish, and had mentioned to Messrs. Chappell that it would be highly agreeable to me to anticipate it, if possible. They readily responded, and we agreed upon having three morning readings in London. As they are not yet publicly announced, I add a note of the days and subjects :

Saturday, First May. " Boots at the Holly-Tree Inn," and " Sikes and Nancy " from " Oliver Twist."

Saturday, Eighth May. " The Christmas Carol."

Saturday, Twenty-second May. " Sikes and Nancy " from " Oliver Twist," and " The Trial " from " Pickwick."

With the warmest interest in your art, and in its claims upon the general gratitude and respect,

> Believe me, always faithfully your Friend.

ADELPHI HOTEL, LIVERPOOL, *Sunday, Fourth April,* 1869.

Miss Hogarth.

MY DEAREST GEORGY,

By this post I send to Mary the truly affecting account of poor dear Katie Macready's death. It is as sorrowful as anything so peaceful and trustful can be !

Both my feet are very tender, and often feel as though they were in hot water. But I was wonderfully well and strong, thank God ! and had no end of voice for the two nights running in that great Birmingham hall.

* His sister-in-law, Mrs. Augustus Dickens, always a welcome visitor at Gad's Hill.

So far as I understand the dinner arrangements here, they are much too long. As to the acoustics of that hall, and the position of the tables (both as bad as bad can be), my only consolation is that, if anybody can be heard, *I* probably can be. The honorary secretary tells me that six hundred people are to dine. The mayor, being no speaker and out of health besides, hands over the toast of the evening to Lord Dufferin. The town is full of the festival. The Theatre Royal, touched up for the occasion, will look remarkably bright and well for the readings.

I hear that Anthony Trollope, Dixon, Lord Houghton, Lemon, Esquiros (of the *Revue des Deux Mondes*), and Sala are to be called upon to speak; the last for the newspaper press. All the Liverpool notabilities are to muster. And Manchester is to be represented by its mayor with due formality.

I had been this morning to look at St. George's Hall, and suggest what can be done to improve its acoustics. As usually happens in such cases, their most important arrangements are already made and unchangeable. I should not have placed the tables in the committee's way at all, and could certainly have placed the daïs to much greater advantage. So all the good I could do was to show where banners could be hung with some hope of stopping echoes. Such is my small news, soon exhausted.

It is a curious little instance of the way in which things fit together that there is a ship-of-war in the Mersey, whose flags and so forth are to be brought up to St. George's Hall for the dinner. She is the *Donegal*, of which Paynter told me he had just been captain, when he told me all about Sydney at Bath.

One of the pleasantest things I have experienced here this time, is the manner in which I am stopped in the streets by working men, who want to shake hands with me, and tell me they know my books. I never go out but this happens. Down at the docks just now, a cooper with a fearful stutter presented himself in this way. His modesty, combined with a conviction that if he were in earnest I would see it and wouldn't repel him, made up as true a piece of natural politeness as I ever saw.

*   *   *   *   *

Mr. James
T. Fields.

ADELPHI HOTEL, LIVERPOOL,
Friday, Ninth April, 1869.

MY DEAR FIELDS,

The faithful *Russia* will bring this out to you, as a sort of warrant to take you into loving custody and bring you back on her return trip.

I rather think that when the Twelfth of June shall have shaken off these shackles,* there *will* be borage on the lawn at Gad's. Your heart's desire in that matter, and in the minor particulars of Cobham Park, Rochester Castle, and Canterbury, shall be fulfilled, please God! The red jackets shall turn out again upon the turnpike-road, and picnics among the cherry-orchards and hop-gardens shall be heard of in Kent. Then, too, shall the Uncommercial resuscitate (being at present nightly murdered by Mr. W. Sikes) and uplift his voice again.

The chief officer of the *Russia* (a capital fellow) was at the Reading last night. We shall be on the borders of Wales, and probably about Hereford, when you arrive. Dolby has insane projects of getting over here to meet you; so amiably hopeful and obviously impracticable, that I encourage him to the utmost. The regular little captain of the *Russia*, Cook, is just now changed into the *Cuba*, whence arise disputes of seniority, etc. I wish he had been with you, for I liked him very much when I was his passenger. I like to think of your being in *my* ship!

My son Charley has come for the dinner, and Chappell (my Proprietor, as—isn't it Wemmick?—says) is coming to-day, and Lord Dufferin (Mrs. Norton's nephew) is to come and make *the* speech. I don't envy the feelings of my noble friend when he sees the hall. Seriously, it is less adapted to speaking than Westminster Abbey, and is as large. . . .

I hope you will see Fechter in a really clever piece by Wilkie.† Also you will see the Academy Exhibition, which will be a very good one; and also we will, please God, see everything and more, and everything else after that. I begin to doubt and fear on the subject of your having a horror of me after seeing the murder. I don't think a hand moved while I was doing it last night, or an eye looked away. And there was a fixed expression of horror of me, all over the theatre, which could not have been surpassed if I had been going to be hanged to that red velvet table. It is quite a new sensation to be execrated with that unanimity; and I hope it will remain so!

[Is it lawful—would that woman in the black gaiters, green veil, and spectacles, hold it so—to send my love to the pretty M——?]

Pack up, my dear Fields, and be quick.

Ever your most affectionate.

---

* The Readings.

† The "piece" here alluded to was called "Black and White." It was produced at the Adelphi Theatre. The outline of the plot was suggested by M. Fechter.

IMPERIAL HOTEL, BLACKPOOL,
Wednesday, Twenty-first April, 1869.

MY DEAREST GEORGY,

I send you this hasty line to let you know that I have come to this sea-beach hotel (charming) for a day's rest. I am much better than I was on Sunday, but shall want careful looking to, to get through the readings. My weakness and deadness are all *on the left side*, and if I don't look at anything I try to touch with my left hand, I don't know where it is. I am in (secret) consultation with Frank Beard; he recognises, in the exact description I have given him, indisputable evidences of overwork, which he would wish to treat immediately. So I have said: " Go in and win."

I have had a delicious walk by the sea to-day, and I sleep soundly, and have picked up amazingly in appetite. My foot is greatly better too, and I wear my own boot.

Always your affectionate.

PRESTON, *Thursday Evening, Twenty-second April*, 1869.

MY DEAREST MAMIE,

Don't be in the least alarmed. Beard has come down, and instantly echoes my impression (perfectly unknown to him), that the readings must be *stopped.* I have had symptoms that must not be disregarded. I go to Liverpool to-night with him (to get away from here), and proceed to the office to-morrow.

Your affectionate Father.

PRESTON, *Thursday, Twenty-second April*, 1869.

MY DEAR SIR,

I am finishing my Farewell Readings—to-night is the seventy-fourth out of one hundred—and have barely time to send you a line to thank you most heartily for yours of the Thirtieth January, and for your great kindness to Alfred and Edward. The latter wrote by the same mail, on behalf of both, expressing the warmest gratitude to you, and reporting himself in the stoutest heart and hope. I never can thank you sufficiently.

You will see that the new Ministry has made a decided hit with its Budget, and that in the matter of the Irish Church it has the country at its back. You will also see that the " Reform League " has dissolved itself, indisputably because it became aware that the people did not want it.

I think the general feeling in England is a desire to get the Irish Church out of the way of many social reforms, and to have it done *with* as already done *for.* I do not in the least believe myself that agrarian Ireland is to be pacified by any such means, or can have it got out of its mistaken head that the land is of right the peasantry's, and that every man who owns land has stolen it and is therefore to be shot. But that is not the question.

Cordially yours.

OFFICE OF "ALL THE YEAR ROUND," Mr. Thomas
Chappell.
Monday, Third May, 1869.

MY DEAR MR. CHAPPELL,

I am really touched by your letter. I can most truthfully assure you that your part in the inconvenience of this mishap has given me much more concern than my own; and that if I did not hope to have our London Farewells yet, I should be in a very gloomy condition on your account.

Pray do not suppose that *you* are to blame for my having done a little too much—a wild fancy indeed! The simple fact is, that the rapid railway travelling was stretched a hair's breadth too far, and that *I* ought to have foreseen it. For, on the night before the last night of our reading in America, when Dolby was cheering me with a review of the success, and the immediate prospect of the voyage home, I told him, to his astonishment: "I am too far gone, and too worn out to realise anything but my own exhaustion. Believe me, if I had to read but twice more, instead of once, I couldn't do it." We were then just beyond our recent number. And it was the travelling that I had felt throughout.

The sharp precautionary remedy of stopping instantly, was almost as instantly successful the other day. I told Dr. Watson that he had never seen me knocked out of time, and that he had no idea of the rapidity with which I should come up again.

Just as three days' repose on the Atlantic steamer made me, in my altered appearance, the amazement of the captain, so this last week has set me up, thank God, in the most wonderful manner. The sense of exhaustion seems a dream already. Of course I shall train myself carefully, nevertheless, all through the summer and autumn.

I beg to send my kind regards to Mrs. Chappell, and I shall hope to see her and you at Teddington in the long bright days. It would disappoint me indeed if a lasting friendship did not come of our business relations.

In the spring I trust I shall be able to report to you that I am ready to take my Farewells in London. Of this I am pretty certain: that I never will take them at all, unless with you on your own conditions.

With an affectionate regard for you and your brother, believe me always, Very faithfully yours.

3 A

Mr. Rusden.

"ALL THE YEAR ROUND" OFFICE,
Tuesday, Eighteenth May, 1869.

MY DEAR MR. RUSDEN,

As I daresay some exaggerated accounts of my having been very ill have reached you, I begin with the true version of the case.

I daresay I *should* have been very ill if I had not suddenly stopped my Farewell Readings when there were yet five-and-twenty remaining to be given. I was quite exhausted, and was warned by the doctors to stop (for the time) instantly. Acting on the advice, and going home into Kent for rest, I immediately began to recover, and within a fortnight was in the brilliant condition in which I can now—thank God—report myself.

I cannot thank you enough for your care of Plorn. I was quite prepared for his not settling down without a lurch or two. I still hope that he may take to colonial life. . . . In his letter to me about his leaving the station to which he got through your kindness, he expresses his gratitude to you quite as strongly as if he had made a wonderful success, and seems to have acquired no distaste for anything but the one individual of whom he wrote that betrayed letter. But knowing the boy, I want to try him fully.

You know all our public news, such as it is, at least as well as I do. Many people here (of whom I am one) do not like the look of American matters.

What I most fear is that the perpetual bluster of a party in the States will at last set the patient British back up. And if our people begin to bluster too, and there should come into existence an exasperating war-party on both sides, there will be great danger of a daily-widening breach.

The first shriek of the first engine that traverses the San Francisco Railroad from end to end will be a death-warning to the disciples of Jo Smith. The moment the Mormon bubble gets touched by neighbours it will break. Similarly, the red man's course is very nearly run. A scalped stoker is the outward and visible sign of his utter extermination. Not Quakers enough to reach from here to Jerusalem will save him by the term of a single year.

I don't know how it may be with you, but it is the fashion here to be absolutely certain that the Emperor of the French is fastened by Providence and the fates on a throne of adamant expressly constructed for him since the foundations of the universe were laid.

He knows better, and so do the police of Paris, and both powers must be grimly entertained by the resolute British belief, knowing what they have known, and doing what they have done through the last ten years. What Victor Hugo calls "the drop-curtain, behind which is constructing the great last act of the French Revolution," has been a little shaken at the bottom lately, however. One seems to see the feet of a rather large chorus getting ready.

Believe me, my dear Mr. Rusden,

Yours faithfully and much obliged.

The Lord John Russell.

GAD'S HILL PLACE, HIGHAM BY ROCHESTER, KENT,
Wednesday, Twenty-sixth May, 1869.

MY DEAR LORD RUSSELL,

I have delayed answering your kind letter, in order that you might get home before I wrote. I am happy to report myself quite well again, and I shall be charmed to come to Pembroke Lodge on any day that may be most convenient to Lady Russell and yourself after the middle of June.

You gratify me beyond expression by your reference to the Liverpool dinner. I made the allusion to you with all my heart at least, and it was most magnificently received.

My dear Lord Russell, faithfully yours.

Mr. W. H. Wills.

OFFICE OF "ALL THE YEAR ROUND,"
Thursday, Twenty-fourth June, 1869.

MY DEAR WILLS,

At a great meeting* compounded of your late "Chief," Charley, Morley, Grieve, and Telbin, your letter was read to-day, and a very sincere record of regret and thanks was placed on the books of the great institution.

Many thanks for the suggestion about the condition of churches. I am so aweary of church questions of all sorts that I am not quite clear as to tackling this. But I am turning it in my mind. I am afraid of two things: firstly, that the thing would not be picturesquely done; secondly, that a general cucumber-coolness would pervade the mind of our circulation.

Nothing new here but a speaking-pipe, a post-box, and a mouldy smell from some forgotten crypt—an extra mouldy smell, mouldier than of yore. Lillie sniffs, projects one eye into nineteen hundred and ninety-nine, and does no more.

I have been to Chadwick's, to look at a new kind of cottage he has built (very ingenious and cheap).

We were all much disappointed last Saturday afternoon by a neighbouring fire being only at a carpenter's, and not at Drury

* Of the Guild of Literature and Art.

Lane Theatre. Ellen's* child having an eye nearly poked out by a young friend, and being asked whether the young friend was not very sorry afterwards, replied : "No. *She* wasn't. *I* was."

London execrable.

> Ever affectionately yours.

Mr. Shirley Brooks.

> GAD'S HILL PLACE, HIGHAM BY ROCHESTER, KENT,
> *Tuesday, Twelfth July,* 1869.

MY DEAR BROOKS,

I have appended my sign manual to the memorial, which I think is very discreetly drawn up. I have a strong feeling of sympathy with poor Mrs. Cunningham, for I remember the pretty house she managed charmingly. She has always done her duty well, and has had hard trials. But I greatly doubt the success of the memorial, I am sorry to add.

It was hotter here yesterday on this Kentish chalk than I have felt it anywhere for many a day. Now it is overcast and raining hard, much to the satisfaction of great farmers like myself.

I am glad to infer from your companionship with the Cocked Hats, that there is no such thing as gout within several miles of you. May it keep its distance.

> Ever, my dear Brooks, faithfully yours.

Mr. W. C. Macready.

> GAD'S HILL, *Tuesday, Twentieth July,* 1869.

MY DEAREST MACREADY,

I have received your letter here to-day, and deeply feel with you and for you the affliction of poor dear Katie's loss. I was not unprepared for the sad news, but it comes in such a rush of old remembrances and withered joys that it strikes to the heart.

God bless you! Love and youth are still beside you, and in that thought I take comfort for my dear old friend.

I am happy to report myself perfectly well and flourishing.

Scarcely a day has gone by this summer in which we have not talked of you and yours. Georgina, Mary, and I continually speak of you. In the spirit we certainly are even more together than we used to be in the body in the old times. I don't know whether you have heard that Harry has taken the second scholarship (fifty pounds a year) at Trinity Hall, Cambridge. The bigwigs expect him to do a good deal there.

Charley is a very good man of business, and evinces considerable aptitude in sub-editing work.

This place is immensely improved since you were here, and really is now very pretty indeed. We are sorry that there is no

---

* The housekeeper at the office.

present prospect of your coming to see it; but I like to know of your being at the sea, and having to do—*from the beach*, as Mrs. Keeley used to say in "The Prisoner of War"—with the winds and the waves and all their freshening influences.

I dined at Greenwich a few days ago with Delane. He asked me about you with much interest. He looks as if he had never seen a printing-office, and had never been out of bed after midnight.

Ever, my dearest Macready,

Your attached and affectionate.

Office of "All the Year Round," *Thursday, Twenty-second July,* 1869.

Miss Emily Jolly.

Dear Miss Jolly,

Mr. Wills has retired from here (for rest and to recover his health), and my son, who occupies his place, brought me this morning a story* in MS., with a request that I would read it. I read it with extraordinary interest, and was greatly surprised by its uncommon merit. On asking whence it came, I found that it came from you!

You need not be told, after this, that I accept it with more than readiness. If you will allow me I will go over it with great care, and very slightly touch it here and there. I think it will require to be divided into three portions. You shall have the proofs and I will publish it immediately. I think so VERY highly of it that I will have special attention called to it in a separate advertisement. I congratulate you most sincerely and heartily on having done a very special thing. It will always stand apart in my mind from any other story I ever read. I write with its impression newly and strongly upon me, and feel absolutely sure that I am not mistaken.

Believe me, faithfully yours always.

Gad's Hill Place, Higham by Rochester, Kent, *Tuesday, Third August,* 1869.

Mr. Edmund Ollier.

My dear Mr. Ollier,

I am very sensible of the feeling of the Committee towards me; and I receive their invitation (conveyed through you) as a most acceptable mark of their consideration.

But I have a very strong objection to speech-making beside graves. I do not expect or wish my feeling in this wise to guide other men; still, it is so serious with me, and the idea of ever being the subject of such a ceremony myself is so repugnant to my soul, that I must decline to officiate. Faithfully yours always.

* The story was called "An Experience."

OFFICE OF "ALL THE YEAR ROUND,"
No. 26, WELLINGTON STREET, STRAND, LONDON, W.C.,
Tuesday, Third August, 1869.

MY DEAREST MAMIE,

I send you the second chapter of the remarkable story. The printer is late with it, and I have not had time to read it, and as I altered it considerably here and there, I have no doubt there are some verbal mistakes in it. However, they will probably express themselves.

But I offer a prize of six pairs of gloves—between you, and your aunt, and Ellen Stone, as competitors—to whomsoever will tell me what idea in this second part is mine. I don't mean an idea in language, in the turning of a sentence, in any little description of an action, or a gesture, or what not in a small way, but an idea, distinctly affecting the whole story *as I found it.* You are all to assume that I found it in the main as you read it, with one exception. If I had written it, I should have made the woman love the man at last. And I should have shadowed that possibility out, by the child's bringing them a little more together on that holiday Sunday.

But I didn't write it. So, finding that it wanted something, I put that something in. What was it?

Your affectionate Father.

GAD'S HILL PLACE, HIGHAM BY ROCHESTER, KENT,
Friday, Thirteenth August, 1869.

MY DEAR MR. RYLAND,

Many thanks for your letter.

I have very strong opinions on the subject of speechification, and hold that there is, everywhere, a vast amount too much of it. A sense of absurdity would be so strong upon me, if I got up at Birmingham to make a flourish on the advantages of education in the abstract for all sorts and conditions of men, that I should inevitably check myself and present a surprising incarnation of the soul of wit. But if I could interest myself in the practical usefulness of the particular institution; in the ways of life of the students; their examples of perseverance and determination to get on; in their numbers, their favourite studies, the number of hours they must daily give to the work that must be done for a livelihood, before they can devote themselves to the acquisition of new knowledge, and so forth, then I could interest others. This is the kind of information I want. Mere holding forth "I utterly detest, abominate, and abjure."

I fear I shall not be in London next week. But if you will

kindly send me here, at your leisure, the roughest notes of such points as I have indicated, I shall be heartily obliged to you, and will take care of their falling into shape and order in my mind. Meantime I "make a note of" Monday, Twenty-seventh September, and of writing to you touching your kind offer of hospitality, three weeks before that date. Very faithfully yours.

GAD'S HILL PLACE, HIGHAM BY ROCHESTER, KENT,   Mr. Frederic
Sunday, Twenty-second August, 1869.   Ouvry.

MY DEAR OUVRY,

I will expect a call from you at the office, on Thursday, at your own most convenient hour. I admit the soft impeachment concerning Mrs. Gamp: I likes my payments to be made reg'lar and I likewise likes my publisher to draw it mild.

Ever yours.

26, WELLINGTON STREET, LONDON,   Hon. Robert
Thursday, Second September, 1869.   Lytton.*

MY DEAR ROBERT LYTTON,

"John Acland" is most willingly accepted, and shall come into the next monthly part. I shall make bold to condense him here and there (according to my best idea of story-telling), and particularly where he makes the speech :—And with the usual fault of being too long, here and there, I think you let the story out too much—prematurely—and this I hope to prevent artfully. I thnk your title open to the same objection, and therefore propose to substitute :

THE DISAPPEARANCE
OF JOHN ACLAND.

This vill leave the reader in doubt whether he really *was* murdered, until the end.

I am sorry you do not pursue the other prose series. You can do a great deal more than you think for, with whatever you touch ; and you know where to find a firmly attached and admiring friend always ready to take the field with you, and always proud to see your plume among the feathers in the Staff.

Your account of my dear Boffin † is highly charming :—I had been troubled with a misgiving that he was good. May his shadow never be more correct !

I wish I could have you at the murder from "Oliver Twist."

I am always, my dear Robert Lytton,

Affectionately your friend.

* Afterwards the Earl of Lytton.
† "Boffin" and "Fascination Fledgeby," were nicknames given to his children by Mr Robert Lytton at this time.

Pray give my kindest regards to Fascination Fledgeby, who (I have no doubt) has by this half-a-dozen new names, feebly expressive of his great merits.

<table>
<tr><td>Mr. Arthur
Ryland.</td><td>GAD'S HILL PLACE, HIGHAM BY ROCHESTER, KENT,
Monday, Sixth September, 1869.</td></tr>
</table>

MY DEAR MR. RYLAND,

I am sorry to find—I had a foreshadowing of it some weeks ago—that I shall not be able to profit by your kind offer of hospitality when I come to Birmingham for *our* Institution. Besides having a great deal in hand just now (the title of a new book among other things), I shall have visitors from abroad here at the time, and am severely claimed by my daughter, who indeed is disloyal to Birmingham in the matter of my going away at all. Pray represent me to Mrs. Ryland as the innocent victim of circumstances, and as sacrificing pleasure to the work I have to do, and to the training under which alone I can do it without feeling it.

I am in the hope of receiving your promised notes in due course, and continue in the irreverent condition in which I last reported myself on the subject of speech-making. Now that men not only make the nights of the session hideous by what the Americans call "orating" in Parliament, but trouble the peace of the vacation by saying over again what they said there (with the addition of what they *didn't* say there, and never will have the courage to say there), I feel indeed that silence, like gold across the Atlantic, is a rarity at a premium.

Faithfully yours always.

<table>
<tr><td>Hon. Robert
Lytton.</td><td>OFFICE OF "ALL THE YEAR ROUND,"
26, WELLINGTON STREET, STRAND, LONDON,
Friday, First October, 1869.</td></tr>
</table>

MY DEAR ROBERT LYTTON,

I am assured by a correspondent that "John Acland" has been done before. Said correspondent has evidently read the story—and is almost confident in "Chambers's Journal." This is very unfortunate, but of course cannot be helped. There is always a possibility of such a malignant conjunction of stars when the story is a true one.

In the case of a good story—as this is—liable for years to be told at table—as this was—there is nothing wonderful in such a mischance. Let us shuffle the cards, as Sancho says, and begin again.

You will of course understand that I do not tell you this by way of complaint. Indeed, I should not have mentioned it at all, but as an explanation. to you of my reason for winding the story up (which I have done to-day) as expeditiously as possible. You might otherwise have thought me, on reading it as published, a little hard on Mr. Doilly. I have not had time to direct search to be made in " Chambers's ; " but as to the main part of the story having been printed somewhere, I have not the faintest doubt. And I believe my correspondent to be also right as to the where. You could not help it any more than I could, and therefore will not be troubled by it any more than I am.

The more I get of your writing, the better I shall be pleased.

Do believe me to be, as I am,

Your genuine Admirer

And affectionate Friend.

OFFICE OF "ALL THE YEAR ROUND," *Thursday, Seventh October*, 1869.

Mr. William Charles Kent.

MY DEAR KENT,

I felt that you would be deeply disappointed. I thought it better not to make the first sign while you were depressed, but my mind has been constantly with you. And not mine alone. You cannot think with what affection and sympathy you have been made the subject of our family dinner talk at Gad's Hill these last three days. Nothing could exceed the interest of my daughters and my sister-in-law; or the earnestness of their feeling about it. I have been really touched by its warm and genuine expression.

Cheer up, my dear fellow ; cheer up, for God's sake. That is, for the sake of all that is good in you and around you.

Ever your affectionate Friend.

GAD'S HILL, *Monday, Eighteenth October*, 1869.

Mr. W. C. Macready.

MY DEAREST MACREADY,

I duly received your letter nearly a fortnight ago, with the greatest interest and pleasure. Above all things I am delighted with the prospect of seeing you here next summer; a prospect which has been received with nine times nine and one more by the whole house. You will hardly know the place again, it is so changed. You are not expected to admire, but there *is* a conservatory building at this moment—be still my soul !

This leaves me in the preliminary agonies of a new book, which I hope to begin publishing (in twelve numbers, not twenty) next March. The coming readings being all in London, and being, after the first fortnight, only once a week, will divert my attention very little, I hope.

My boy Sydney is now a second lieutenant, the youngest in the Service, I believe.   He has the highest testimonials as an officer.

You may be quite sure there will be no international racing in American waters.   Oxford knows better, or I am mistaken.   The Harvard crew were a very good set of fellows, and very modest.

Ryland of Birmingham doesn't look a day older, and was full of interest in you, and asked me to remind you of him.   By-the-bye, at Elkington's I saw a pair of immense tea-urns from a railway station (Stafford), sent there to be repaired.   They were honey-combed within in all directions, and had been supplying the passengers, under the active agency of hot water, with decomposed lead, copper, and a few other deadly poisons, for heaven knows how many years !

Ever, my dearest Macready,
Your most affectionate and attached.

Mr. Rusden.   GAD'S HILL PLACE, HIGHAM BY ROCHESTER,. KENT,
Sunday, Twenty-fourth October, 1869.

MY DEAR MR. RUSDEN,

This very day a great meeting is announced to come off in London, as a demonstration in favour of a Fenian "amnesty." No doubt its numbers and importance are ridiculously over-estimated, but I believe the gathering will turn out to be big enough to be a very serious obstruction in the London streets.   I have a great doubt whether such demonstrations ought to be allowed.   They are bad as a precedent, and they unquestionably interfere with the general liberty and freedom of the subject.

Moreover, the time must come when this kind of threat and defiance will have to be forcibly stopped, and when the unreasonable toleration of it will lead to a sacrifice of life among the comparatively innocent lookers-on that might have been avoided but for a false confidence on their part, engendered in the damnable system of *laisser-aller.*   You see how right we were, you and I, in our last correspondence on this head, and how desperately unsatisfactory the condition of Ireland is, especially when considered with a reference to America.   The Government has, through Mr. Gladstone, just now spoken out boldly in reference to the desired amnesty.   (So much the better for them or they would unquestionably have gone by the board.)   Still there is an uneasy feeling abroad that Mr. Gladstone himself would grant this amnesty if he dared, and that there is a great weakness in the rest of their Irish policy.   And this feeling is very strong amongst the noisiest Irish howlers.   Meanwhile, the newspapers go on arguing Irish matters as if the Irish were a reasonable people, in which immense assumption I, for one, have not the smallest faith.

Again, I have to thank you most heartily for your kindness to my two boys. It is impossible to predict how Plorn will settle down, or come out of the effort to do so. But he has unquestionably an affectionate nature, and a certain romantic touch in him. Both of these qualities are, I hope, more impressible for good than for evil, and I trust in God for the rest.

The news of Lord Derby's death will reach you, I suppose, at about the same time as this letter. A rash, impetuous, passionate man; but a great loss for his party, as a man of mind and mark. I was staying last June with Lord Russell—six or seven years older, but (except for being rather deaf) in wonderful preservation, and brighter and more completely armed at all points than I have seen him these twenty years.

As this need not be posted till Friday, I shall leave it open for a final word or two; and am until then, and then, and always afterwards, my dear Mr. Rusden,

> Your faithful and much obliged.

Thursday, Twenty-eighth.

We have no news in England except two slight changes in the Government consequent on Layard's becoming our Minister at Madrid. He is not long married to a charming lady, and will be far better in Spain than in the House of Commons. The Ministry are now holding councils on the Irish Land Tenure question, which is the next difficulty they have to deal with, as you know. Last Sunday's meeting was a preposterous failure; still, it brought together in the streets of London all the ruffian part of the population of London, and that is a serious evil which any one of a thousand accidents might render mischievous. There is no existing law, however, to stop these assemblages, so that they keep moving while in the streets.

The Government was undoubtedly wrong when it considered it had the right to close Hyde Park; that is now universally conceded.

I write to Alfred and Plorn both by this mail. They can never say enough of your kindness when they write to me.

GAD'S HILL PLACE,
Monday, Eighth November, 1869.

Mr. Austen
Henry
Layard.

MY DEAR LAYARD,

On Friday and Saturday next I can come to you at any time after twelve that will suit your convenience. I had no idea of letting you go away without my Godspeed; but I knew how busy you must be; and kept in the background, biding my time.

I am sure you know that there is no man living more attached to you than I am. After considering the subject with the jealousy of a friend, I have a strong conviction that your change * is a good one; ill as you can be spared from the ranks of men who are in earnest here.

Ever faithfully yours.

1870.

NARRATIVE.

CHARLES DICKENS passed his last Christmas and New Year's Day at Gad's Hill in the usual way, except that he was suffering again from an attack of the foot trouble, particularly on Christmas Day, when he was quite disabled by it and unable to walk at all—able only to join the party in the evening by keeping his room all day. However, he was better in a day or two, and early in January he went to London, where he had taken the house of his friends, Mr. and Mrs. Milner Gibson, for the season.

His series of " Farewell Readings " at St. James's Hall began in January, and ended on the Sixteenth March. He was writing " Edwin Drood " also, and was, of course, constantly occupied with the work of " All the Year Round." In the beginning of January, he fulfilled his promise of paying a second visit to Birmingham and making a speech, of which he wrote in his last letter to Mr. Macready.

For his last reading he gave the " Christmas Carol " and " The Trial " from " Pickwick," and at the end of the evening he addressed a few farewell words to his audience. It was a memorable and splendid occasion. He was deeply affected by the loving enthusiasm of his greeting, and it was a real sorrow to him to give up for ever the personal association with thousands of the readers of his books. But when the pain, mingled with pleasure, of this last reading was over, he felt greatly the relief of having undisturbed time for his own quieter pursuits, and looked forward to writing the last numbers of " Edwin Drood " at Gad's Hill, where he was to return in June.

The last public appearance of any kind that he made was at the Royal Academy dinner in May. He was at the time far from well, but he made a great effort to be present and to speak, from

---

* Mr. Layard's appointment as British Minister at Madrid.

his strong desire to pay a tribute to the memory of his dear old friend Mr. Maclise, who died in April.

Her Majesty having expressed a wish, conveyed through Mr. Helps (afterwards Sir Arthur Helps), to have a personal interview with Charles Dickens, he accompanied Mr. Helps to Buckingham Palace one afternoon in March. He was most graciously and kindly received by her Majesty, and came away with a hope that the visit had been mutually agreeable. The Queen presented him with a copy of her "Journal in the Highlands," with an autograph inscription. And he had afterwards the pleasure of requesting her acceptance of a set of his books. He attended a levee held by the Prince of Wales in April, and the last time he dined out in London was at a party given by Lord Houghton for the King of the Belgians and the Prince of Wales, who had both expressed a desire to meet Charles Dickens. All through the season he had been suffering, at intervals, from the swollen foot, and on this occasion it was so bad, that up to the last moment it was very doubtful whether he could fulfil his engagement.

We have very few letters for this year, and none of any very particular interest, but we give them all, as they are *the last.*

Mr. S. L. Fildes was his "new illustrator," to whom he alludes in a note to Mr. Frith; we also give a short note to Mr. Fildes himself.

We have only one letter addressed to Mrs. Frederick (now Lady) Pollock. Both she and her husband were intimate friends of Charles Dickens—thoroughly sympathetic and artistic in their tastes.

In explanation of *the last letter,* we give an extract from a letter addressed to *The Daily News* by Mr. J. M. Makeham, soon after the death of Charles Dickens, as follows: "That the public may exactly understand the circumstances under which Charles Dickens' letter to me was written, I am bound to explain that it is in reply to a letter which I addressed to him in reference to a passage in the tenth chapter of 'Edwin Drood,' respecting which I ventured to suggest that he had, perhaps, forgotten that the figure of speech alluded to by him, in a way which, to my certain knowledge, was distasteful to some of his admirers, was drawn from a passage of Holy Writ which is greatly reverenced by a large number of his countrymen as a prophetic description of the sufferings of our Saviour."

The MS. of the little "History of the New Testament" is now in the possession of his eldest daughter. She has (together with her aunt) received many earnest entreaties, both from friends and strangers, that this history might be allowed to be published, for the benefit of other children.

These many petitions have his daughter's fullest sympathy. But she knows that her father wrote this history ONLY for his own children, that it was his particular wish that it never should be published, and she therefore holds this wish as sacred and irrevocable.

Mr. James T. Fields.

5, HYDE PARK PLACE, LONDON, W.,
Friday, Fourteenth January, 1870.

MY DEAR FIELDS,

We live here (opposite the Marble Arch) in a charming house until the First of June, and then return to Gad's. The conservatory is completed, and is a brilliant success; but an expensive one!

I should be quite ashamed of not having written to you and my dear Mrs. Fields before now, if I didn't know that you will both understand how occupied I am, and how naturally, when I put my papers away for the day, I get up and fly. I have a large room here, with three fine windows, overlooking the Park—unsurpassable for airiness and cheerfulness.

You saw the announcement of the death of poor dear Harness. The circumstances are curious. He wrote to his old friend the Dean of Battle saying he would come to visit him on that day (the day of his death). The Dean wrote back: "Come next day, instead, as we are obliged to go out to dinner, and you will be alone." Harness told his sister a little impatiently that he *must* go on the first-named day; that he had made up his mind to go, and MUST. He had been getting himself ready for dinner, and came to a part of the staircase whence two doors opened—one, upon another level passage, one, upon a flight of stone steps. He opened the wrong door, fell down the steps, injured himself very severely, and died in a few hours.

You will know—*I* don't—what Fechter's success is in America at the time of this present writing. In his farewell performances at the Princess's he acted very finely. I thought the three first acts of his Hamlet very much better than I had ever thought them before—and I always thought very highly of them. We gave him a foaming stirrup cup at Gad's Hill.

Forster (who has been ill with his bronchitis again) thinks No. 2 of the new book ("Edwin Drood") a clincher,—I mean that word (as his own expression) for *Clincher*. There is a curious interest steadily working up to No. 5, which requires a great deal of art and self-denial. I think also, apart from character and picturesqueness, that the young people are placed in a very novel situation. So I hope—at Nos. 5 and 6, the story will turn upon an interest suspended until the end.

I can't believe it, and don't, and won't, but they say Harry's twenty-first birthday is next Sunday. I have entered him at the Temple just now ; and if he don't get a fellowship at Trinity Hall when his time comes, I shall be disappointed, if in the present disappointed state of existence.

I hope you may have met with the little touch of Radicalism I gave them at Birmingham in the words of Buckle ! With pride I observe that it makes the regular political traders, of all sorts, perfectly mad. Sich was my intentions, as a grateful acknowledgment of having been misrepresented.

I think Mrs. ——'s prose very admirable ; but I don't believe it ! No, I do *not*. My conviction is that those islanders get frightfully bored by the islands, and wish they had never set eyes upon them.

Charley Collins has done a charming cover for the monthly part of the new book. At the very earnest representations of Millais (and after having seen a great number of his drawings) I am going to engage with a new man ; retaining, of course, C. C.'s cover aforesaid.* Katie has made some more capital portraits, and is always improving.

My dear Mrs. Fields, if "He" (made proud by chairs and bloated by pictures) does not give you my dear love, let us conspire against him when you find him out, and exclude him from all future confidences. Until then,

Ever affectionately yours and his.

Mr. S. L. Fildes.

OFFICE OF "ALL THE YEAR ROUND,"
Wednesday, Sixteenth January, 1870.

DEAR SIR,

I beg to thank you for the highly meritorious and interesting specimens of your art that you have had the kindness to send me. I return them herewith, after having examined them with the greatest pleasure.

I am naturally curious to see your drawing from "David Copperfield," in order that I may compare it with my own idea. In the meanwhile, I can honestly assure you that I entertain the greatest admiration for your remarkable powers.

Faithfully yours.

Mr. W. H. Wills.

5, HYDE PARK PLACE, LONDON, W.,
Sunday, Twenty-third January, 1870.

MY DEAR WILLS,

In the note I had from you about Nancy and Sikes, you seem to refer to some other note you had written me. Therefore

---

* Mr. Charles Collins was obliged to give up the illustrating of "Edwin Drood" on account of his failing health.

I think it well merely to mention that I have received no other note.

I do not wonder at your not being up to the undertaking (even if you had had no cough) under the wearing circumstances. It was a very curious scene. The actors and actresses (most of the latter looking very pretty) mustered in extraordinary force, and were a fine audience. I set myself to carrying out of themselves and their observation, those who were bent on watching how the effects were got; and I believe I succeeded. Coming back to it again, however, I feel it was madness ever to do it so continuously. My ordinary pulse is seventy-two, and it runs up under this effort to one hundred and twelve. Besides which, it takes me ten or twelve minutes to get my wind back at all; I being, in the meantime, like the man who lost the fight—in fact, his express image. Frank Beard was in attendance to make divers experiments to report to Watson; and although, as you know, he stopped it instantly when he found me at Preston, he was very much astonished by the effects of the reading on the reader.

So I hope you may be able to come and hear it before it is silent for ever. I hope, now I have got over the mornings, that I may be able to work on my book. But up to this time the great preparation required in getting the subjects up again, and the twice a week besides, have almost exclusively occupied me.

I have something the matter with my right thumb, and can't (as you see) write plainly. I sent a word to poor Robert Chambers,* and I send my love to Mrs. Wills.

Ever, my dear Wills, affectionately yours.

Lord Lytton.

5, HYDE PARK PLACE,
Monday, Fourteenth February, 1870.

MY DEAR LYTTON,

I ought to have mentioned in my hurried note to you, that my knowledge of the consultation† in question only preceded yours by certain hours; and that Longman asked me if I would make the design known to you, as he thought it might be a liberty to address you otherwise. This I did therefore.

The class of writers to whom you refer at the close of your note, have no copyright, and do not come within my case at all. I quite agree with you as to their propensities and deserts.

Indeed, I suppose in the main that there is very little difference between our opinions. I do not think the present Government

* On the death of his second wife.

† A meeting of Publishers and Authors to discuss the subject of International Copyright.

worse than another, and I think it better than another by the presence of Mr. Gladstone; but it appears to me that our system fails.   Ever yours.

> 5, HYDE PARK PLACE, W.,
> *Thursday, Seventeenth February,* 1870.   Mr. Henry Fielding Dickens.

MY DEAR HARRY,

I am extremely glad to hear that you have made a good start at the Union. Take any amount of pains about it; open your mouth well and roundly, speak to the last person visible, and give yourself time.   Ever affectionately.

> *Wednesday, Second March,* 1870.   Mr. W. C. Macready.

MY DEAREST MACREADY,

This is to wish you and yours all happiness and prosperity at the well-remembered anniversary* to-morrow. You may be sure that loves and happy returns will not be forgotten at *our* table.

I have been getting on very well with my book, and we are having immense audiences at St. James's Hall. Mary has been celebrating the first glimpses of spring by having the measles. She got over the disorder very easily, but a weakness remains behind. Katie is blooming. Georgina is in perfect order, and all send you their very best loves. It gave me true pleasure to have your sympathy with me in the second little speech at Birmingham. I was determined that my Radicalism should not be called in question. The electric wires are not very exact in their reporting, but at all events the sense was there.

I am ever, my dearest Macready,

Your most affectionate.

> 5, HYDE PARK PLACE,
> *Monday, Fourteenth March,* 1870.   Mr. Frederic Chapman.

DEAR FREDERIC CHAPMAN,

Mr. Fildes has been with me this morning, and without complaining of —— or expressing himself otherwise than as being obliged to him for his care of No. 1, represents that there is a brother-student of his, a wood-engraver, perfectly acquainted with his style and well understanding his meaning, who would render him better.

I have replied to him that there can be no doubt that he has a claim beyond dispute to our employing whomsoever he knows will present him in his best aspect. Therefore, we must make the change; the rather because the fellow-student in question has engraved Mr. Fildes' most successful drawings hitherto.

Faithfully yours.

* Mr. Macready's birthday on 3rd March.

3 B

Mr. William
Charles
Kent.

5, HYDE PARK PLACE., W,
Saturday, Twenty-sixth March, 1870.

MY DEAR KENT,

I received both copies of *The Sun*, with the tenderest pleasure and gratification.

Everything that I can let you have in aid of the proposed record* (which, *of course*, would be far more agreeable to me if done by you than by any other hand) shall be at your service. Dolby has all the figures relating to America, and you shall have for reference the books from which I read. They are afterwards going into Forster's collection.†

Ever affectionately.

Mr. Henry
Fielding
Dickens.

5, HYDE PARK PLACE, W.,
Tuesday, Twenty-ninth March, 1870.

MY DEAR HARRY,

Your next Tuesday's subject is a very good one. I would not lose the point that narrow-minded fanatics, who decry the theatre and defame its artists, are absolutely the advocates of depraved and barbarous amusements. For wherever a good drama and a well-regulated theatre decline, some distorted form of theatrical entertainment will infallibly arise in their place. In one of the last chapters of "Hard Times," Mr. Sleary says something to the effect: "People will be entertained thomehow, thquire. Make the betht of uth, and not the wortht."

Ever affectionately.

Mr. W. P.
Frith, R.A.

5, HYDE PARK PLACE, W.,
Saturday, Sixteenth April, 1870.

MY DEAR FRITH,

I shall be happy to go on Wednesday evening, if convenient.

You please me with what you say of my new illustrator, of whom I have great hopes.

Faithfully yours ever.

Mr. Charles
Mackay.

OFFICE OF "ALL THE YEAR ROUND,"
Thursday, Twenty-first April, 1870.

MY DEAR MACKAY,

I have placed "God's Acre." The prose paper, "The False Friend," has lingered, because it seems to me that the idea

---

* Of the Readings. The intention was carried out. Mr. Kent's book, "Charles Dickens as a Reader," was published in 1872.

† No doubt Charles Dickens intended to add the Reading Books to the legacy of his MSS. to Mr. Forster. But he did not do so, therefore the "Readings" are *not* a part of the "Forster Collection" at the South Kensington Museum.

is to be found in an introduced story of mine called "The Baron of Grogzwig"* in "Pickwick."

Be pleasant with the Scottish people in handling Johnson, because I love them.

Ever faithfully.

Monday Morning, Twenty-fifth April, 1870.   Mr. William Charles Kent.

MY DEAR KENT,

I received your book† with the greatest pleasure, and heartily thank you for it. It is a volume of a highly prepossessing appearance, and a most friendly look. I felt as if I should have taken to it at sight; even (a very large even) though I had known nothing of its contents, or of its author!

For the last week I have been most perseveringly and ding-dong-doggedly at work, making headway but slowly. The spring always has a restless influence over me; and I weary, at any season, of this London dining-out beyond expression; and I yearn for the country again. This is my excuse for not having written to you sooner. Besides which, I had a baseless conviction that I should see you at the office last Thursday. Not having done so, I fear you must be worse, or no better? If you *can* let me have a report of yourself, pray do.

Believe me ever,

Affectionately yours.

5, HYDE PARK PLACE, W.,   Mrs. Frederick *Monday, Second May,* 1870.   Pollock.

MY DEAR MRS. POLLOCK,

Pray tell the illustrious Philip van Artevelde,‡ that I will deal with the nefarious case in question if I can. I am a little doubtful of the practicability of doing so, and frisking outside the bounds of the law of libel. I have that high opinion of the law of England generally, which one is likely to derive from the impression that it puts all the honest men under the diabolical hoofs of all the scoundrels. It makes me cautious of doing right; an admirable instance of its wisdom!

I was very sorry to have gone astray from you that Sunday; but as the earlier disciples entertained angels unawares, so the latter often meet them haphazard.

Your description of Lafont's acting is the complete truth in

* *His* mistake! The story of the "Baron of Grogzwig" is in "Nicholas Nickleby."

† A new collective edition of Kent's Poems," dedicated to his cousin, Colonel Kent, of the 77th Regiment.

‡ The Poet—Sir Henry Taylor.

one short sentence: Nature's triumph over art; reversing the copy-book axiom! But the Lord deliver us from Plessy's mechanical ingenuousness!!

And your petitioner will ever pray.

And ever be,   Faithfully yours.

Sir John
Bowring.

GAD'S HILL, *Thursday, Fifth May,* 1870.

MY DEAR SIR JOHN,

I send you many cordial thanks for your note, and the very curious drawing accompanying it. I ought to tell you, perhaps, that the opium smoking I have described, I saw (exactly as I have described it, penny ink-bottle and all) down in Shadwell this last autumn. A couple of the Inspectors of Lodging-Houses knew the woman and took me to her as I was making a round with them to see for myself the working of Lord Shaftesbury's Bill.

Believe me, always faithfully yours.

Mrs. E. M.
Ward.

5, HYDE PARK PLACE, W.,
Wednesday, Eleventh May, 1870.

MY DEAR MRS. WARD,

I grieve to say that I am literally laid by the heels, and incapable of dining with you to-morrow. A neuralgic affection of the foot, which usually seizes me about twice a year, and which will yield to nothing but days of fomentation and horizontal rest, set in last night, and has caused me very great pain ever since, and will too clearly be no better until it has had its usual time in which to wear itself out. I send my kindest regard to Ward, and beg to be pitied.

Believe me, faithfully yours always.

Mr. J. B.
Buckstone.

Sunday, Fifteenth May, 1870.

MY DEAR BUCKSTONE,

I send a duplicate of this note to the Haymarket, in case it should miss you out of town. For a few years I have been liable, at wholly uncertain and incalculable times, to a severe attack of neuralgia in the foot, about once in the course of a year. It began in an injury to the finer muscles or nerves, occasioned by over-walking in the deep snow. When it comes on I cannot stand, and can bear no covering whatever on the sensitive place. One of these seizures is upon me now. Until it leaves me I could no more walk into St. James's Hall than I could fly in the air. I hope you will present my duty to the Prince of Wales, and assure his Royal Highness that nothing short of my being (most

* Printed in Mackenzie's "Life of Dickens."

unfortunately) disabled for the moment would have prevented my attending, as trustee of the Fund,* at the dinner, and warmly expressing my poor sense of the great and inestimable service his Royal Highness renders to a most deserving institution by so kindly commending it to the public.

Faithfully yours always.

Mr. W. J. O'Driscoll.

† GAD'S HILL PLACE, HIGHAM BY ROCHESTER, KENT,
Wednesday, Eighteenth May, 1870.

MY DEAR SIR,

　　I beg to assure you, in reply to your letter, that I have not one solitary scrap of the late Mr. Maclise's handwriting in my possession. A few years ago I destroyed an immense correspondence, expressly because I considered it had been held with me, and not with the public, and because I could not answer for its privacy being respected when I should be dead. I have since allowed no letters from friends to accumulate in my possession, and hence this disappointing answer to your request. The remarks I made at the Royal Academy dinner were reported with perfect accuracy in <i>The Times.</i>

My dear Sir, yours faithfully.

Mr. Rusden.

ATHENÆUM,
Friday Evening, Twentieth May, 1870.

MY DEAR MR. RUSDEN,

　　I received your most interesting and clear-sighted letter about Plorn just before the departure of the last mail from here to you. I did not answer then because another incoming mail was nearly due, and I expected (knowing Plorn so well) that some communication from him such as he made to you would come to me. I was not mistaken. The same arguing of the squatter question—vegetables and all—appeared. This gave me an opportunity of touching on those points by this mail, without in the least compromising you. I cannot too completely express my concurrence with your excellent idea that his correspondence with you should be regarded as confidential. Just as I could not possibly suggest a word more neatly to the point, or more thoughtfully addressed, to such a young man than your reply to his letter, I hope you will excuse my saying that it is a perfect model of tact, good sense, and good feeling. I had been struck by his persistently ignoring the possibility of his holding any other position in Australia than his present position, and had inferred from it a

---

* The General Theatrical Fund.

† Printed in the preface to "A Memoir of Daniel Maclise, R.A.," by Mr. W. Justin O'Driscoll.

homeward tendency. What is most curious to me is that he is very sensible, and yet does not seem to understand that he has qualified himself for no public examinations in the old country, and could not possibly hold his own against any competition for anything to which I could get him nominated.

But I must not trouble you about my boys as if they were yours. It is enough that I can never thank you for your goodness to them in a generous consideration of me.

I believe the truth as to France to be that a citizen Frenchman never forgives, and that Napoleon will never live down, the *coup d'état.* This makes it enormously difficult for any well-advised English newspaper to support him, and pretend not to know on what a volcano his throne is set. Informed as to his designs on the one hand, and the perpetual uneasiness of his police on the other (to say nothing of a doubtful army), *The Times* has a difficult game to play. My own impression is that if it were played too boldly for him, the old deplorable national antagonism would revive in his going down. That the wind will pass over his Imperiality on the sands of France I have not the slightest doubt. In no country on the earth, but least of all there, can you seize people in their houses on political warrants, and kill in the streets, on no warrant at all, without raising a gigantic Nemesis— not very reasonable in detail, perhaps, but none the less terrible for that.

The commonest dog or man driven mad is a much more alarming creature than the same individuality in a sober and commonplace condition.

Your friend —— —— is setting the world right generally all round (including the flattened ends, the two poles), and, as a Minister said to me the other day, "has the little one fault of omniscience."

You will probably have read before now that I am going to be everything the Queen can make me.* If my authority be worth anything believe on it that I am going to be nothing but what I am, and that that includes my being as long as I live,

　　　　　　　Your faithful and heartily obliged.

Mrs.
Bancroft.

　　　　　GAD'S HILL PLACE, HIGHAM BY ROCHESTER, KENT,
　　　　　　　　Thursday, Thirty-first May, 1870.

MY DEAR MRS. BANCROFT,†
　　　I am most heartily obliged to you for your kind note, which I received here only last night, having come here from town circuitously to get a little change of air on the road. My sense of

* An allusion to an unfounded rumour.　　　† Miss Marie Wilton.

your interest cannot be better proved than by my trying the remedy you recommend, and that I will do immediately. As I shall be in town on Thursday, my troubling you to order it would be quite unjustifiable. I will use your name in applying for it, and will report the result after a fair trial. Whether this remedy succeeds or fails as to the neuralgia, I shall always consider myself under an obligation to it for having indirectly procured me the great pleasure of receiving a communication from you; for I hope I may lay claim to being one of the most earnest and delighted of your many artistic admirers.

Believe me, faithfully yours.

ATHENÆUM CLUB,
Friday Night, Twentieth May, 1870.

Mr. Alfred Tennyson Dickens.

MY DEAR ALFRED,*

I have just time to tell you under my own hand that I invited Mr. Bear to a dinner of such guests as he would naturally like to see, and that we took to him very much, and got on with him capitally.

I am doubtful whether Plorn is taking to Australia. Can you find out his real mind? I notice that he always writes as if his present life were the be-all and the end-all of his emigration, and as if I had no idea of you two becoming proprietors, and aspiring to the first positions in the colony, without casting off the old connection.

From Mr. Bear I had the best accounts of you. I told him that they did not surprise me, for I had unbounded faith in you. For which take my love and blessing.

They will have told you all the news here, and that I am hard at work. This is not a letter so much as an assurance that I never think of you without hope and comfort.

Ever, my dear Alfred,
Your affectionate Father.

(This Letter did not reach Australia until after these two absent sons of Charles Dickens had heard, by telegraph, the news of their father's death.)

* Charles Dickens' son, Alfred Tennyson.

TWO LAST LETTERS.

Gad's Hill Place,
            Higham by Rochester, Kent.*

Mr. William
Charles
Kent.

Wednesday Eighth June 1870

My Dear Kent

Tomorrow is a very bad day for me to make a call, as, in addition to my usual office business, I have a mass of accounts to settle with Wills. But I hope I may be ready for you at 3 o'clock. If I can't be — why, then I shan't be.

You must really get rid of these Opal enjoyments. They are too overpowering:

"These violent delights have violent ends."

I think it was a father of your church who made the wise remark to a young gentleman who got up late (or stayed out late) at Verona?

Ever affectionately
CD

Mr. John M.
Makeham.

Gad's Hill Place,

Higham by Rochester, Kent.

Wednesday Eighth June 1870

Dear Sir

It would be quite
inconceivable to me — but for your
letter — that any reasonable reader
could possibly attach a scriptural
reference to a passage in a book
of mine, reproducing a much abused
social figure of speech, impressed into
all sorts of service, on all sorts of
inappropriate occasions, without the
faintest connexion of it with its
original source. I am truly
shocked to find that any reader can
make the mistake

I have always striven in my
writings to express veneration for
the life and lessons of our Saviour;
because I feel it; and because I
re-wrote that history for my
children - every one of whom
knew it from having it repeated
to them . long before they could

read, and almost as soon as they could speak.

But I have never made
proclamation of this from the house tops

Faithfully yours

Charles Dickens

John M. Makeham Esqre.

All through this spring in London, Charles Dickens had been ailing in health, and it was remarked by many friends that he had a weary look, and was "aged" and altered.   But he was generally in good spirits, and his family had no uneasiness about him, relying upon the country quiet and comparative rest at Gad's Hill to have their usual influence in restoring his health and strength.   On the Second June he attended a private play at the house of Mr. and Mrs. Freake, where his two daughters were among the actresses. The next day he went back to Gad's Hill.   His daughter Kate (whose home was there at all times when she chose, and almost always through the summer months) went down on Sunday, the Fifth June, for a day's visit, to see the "great improvement of the conservatory."   Her father laughingly assured her she had now seen "the last" improvement at Gad's Hill.   At this time he was tolerably well, but Kate remarked to her sister and aunt how strangely he was tired, and what a curious grey colour he had in his face after a very short walk on that Sunday afternoon.   However, he seemed quite himself again in the evening.   The next day his daughter returned to London, accompanied by her sister, who was to pay her a short visit.

Charles Dickens was very hard at work on the sixth number of "Edwin Drood."   On the Monday and Tuesday he was well, but he was unequal to much exercise.   His last walk was one of his greatest favourites—through Cobham Park and Wood—on the afternoon of Tuesday.

On the morning of Wednesday, the eighth (one of the lovliest days of a lovely summer), he was very well; in excellent spirits about his book, of which he said he *must* finish his number that day—the next (Thursday) being the day of his weekly visit to "All the Year Round" office.   Therefore he would write all day in the Châlet, and take no walk or drive until the evening.   In the middle of the day he came to the house for an hour's rest, and smoked a cigar in the conservatory—out of which new addition to the house he was taking the greatest personal enjoyment—and seemed perfectly well, and exceedingly cheerful and hopeful. When he came again to the house, about an hour before the time fixed for the early dinner, he seemed very tired, silent, and absorbed.   But this was so usual with him after a day of engross- ing work, that it caused no alarm or surprise to his sister-in-law —the only member of his household who happened to be at home. He wrote some letters—among them, these last letters which we give—in the library of the house, and also arranged many trifling business matters, with a view to his departure for London the next morning.   He was to be accompanied, on his return at the end of the week, by Mr. Fildes, to introduce the "new illustrator" to the neighbourhood in which many of the scenes of his last book, as of his first, were laid.

It was not until they were seated at the dinner-table that a striking change in the colour and expression of his face startled his sister-in-law, and on her asking him if he was ill, he said, "Yes, very ill; I have been very ill for the last hour." But on her expressing an intention of sending instantly for a doctor, he stopped her, and said: "No, he would go on with dinner, and go afterwards to London." And then he made an effort to struggle against the fit that was fast coming on him, and talked, but incoherently, and soon very indistinctly. It being now evident that he *was* ill, and very seriously ill, his sister-in-law begged him to come to his own room before she sent off for medical help. "Come and lie down," she entreated. "Yes, on the ground," he said, very distinctly—these were the last words he spoke—and he slid from her arm and fell upon the floor.

The servants brought a couch into the dining-room, where he was laid. A messenger was dispatched for Mr. Steele, the Rochester doctor, and with a telegram to his doctor in London, and to his daughters. This was a few minutes after six o'clock.

His daughters arrived, with Mr. Frank Beard, this same evening. His eldest son the next morning, and his son Henry and his sister Letitia in the evening of the ninth—too late, alas!

All through the night Charles Dickens never opened his eyes, or showed a sign of consciousness. In the afternoon of the ninth, Dr. Russell Reynolds arrived at Gad's Hill, having been summoned by Mr. Frank Beard to meet himself and Mr. Steele. But he could only confirm their hopeless verdict, and make his opinion known with much kind sympathy, to the family, before returning to London.

Charles Dickens remained in the same unconscious state until the evening of this day, when, at ten minutes past six, the watchers saw a shudder pass over him, heard him give a deep sigh, saw one tear roll down his cheek, and he was gone from them. And as they saw the dark shadow steal across his calm, beautiful face, not one among them—could they have been given such a power—would have recalled his sweet spirit back to earth.

As his family were aware that Charles Dickens had a wish to be buried near Gad's Hill, arrangements were made for his burial in the pretty churchyard of Shorne, a neighbouring village, of which he was very fond. But this intention was abandoned in consequence of a pressing request from the Dean and Chapter of Rochester Cathedral that his remains might be placed there. A

grave was prepared and everything arranged, when it was made
known to the family, through Dean Stanley, that there was a
general and very earnest desire that Charles Dickens should find
his resting-place in Westminster Abbey.   To such a fitting tribute
to his memory they could make no possible objection, although it
was with great regret that they relinquished the idea of laying
him in a place so closely identified with his life and his works.
His name, notwithstanding, is associated with Rochester, a tablet
to his memory having been placed by his executors on the wall of
Rochester Cathedral.

With regard to Westminster Abbey, his family only stipulated
that the funeral might be made as private as possible, and that
the words of his will, "I emphatically direct that I be buried in
an inexpensive, unostentatious, and strictly private manner,"
should be religiously adhered to.   And so they were; the solemn
service in the vast cathedral being as private as the most thoughtful
consideration could make it.

The family of Charles Dickens were deeply grateful to all in
authority who so carried out his wishes.   And more especially to
the late Dean Stanley and Lady Augusta Stanley, for the tender
sympathy shown by them to the mourners on this day, and also
on Sunday, the nineteenth, when the Dean preached his beautiful
funeral sermon.

As during his life Charles Dickens' fondness for air, light, and
gay colours amounted almost to a passion, so when he lay dead
in the home he had so dearly loved, these things were not
forgotten.

The pretty room opening into the conservatory (from which he
had never been removed since his seizure) was kept bright with
the most beautiful of all kinds of flowers, and flooded with the
summer sun :

"And nothing stirred in the room. The old, old fashion. The fashion that came in
with our first garments, and will last unchanged until our race has run its course, and the
wide firmament is rolled up like a scroll. The old, old fashion—death!

"Oh, thank God, all who see it, for that older fashion yet, of immortality!"

INDEX.

MACKAY, Mr. Charles, letter to, 788
Maclise, R.A., Mr. Daniel, 21, 27, 31, 73, 77, 79, 80, 96, 101, 134, 140, 158, 169, 344; letters to, 85, 113
Macready, Mr. Jonathan, 681
Macready, Mr. W. C., 4, 12, 21, 27, 36, 58, 85, 96, 100, 102, 132, 133, 164, 165, 180, 231, 845, 883, 489, 537, 540, 546, 619, 624; and see Letters
Macready, Miss Kate, 344, 384, 409, 491, 624, 717
Macready, Mrs., 180, 624
Macready, Miss Nina, 188
Macready, Mr. W., 142
Major, Mrs., letter to, 557
Makeham, Mr. J. M., 738; Dickens' last letter written to, 746
Malleson, Mr. and Mrs., 646
"Man about Town, The," 87
Mario, Signor, 158
Marsh, Dickens' coachman, a story of, 546
Marston, Dr. Westland, 54, 446, 447; letter to, 446
Martin, Captain, 597
Martineau, Miss, 60, 276, 286
"Martin Chuzzlewit," 85; dramatised 100, 113; a story of Mrs. Harris, 445; and see 78, 85, 87, 95, 102
Mazzini, M., 494
"Memoires du Diable, Les," 404
Mesmerism, a séance of, 486
"Message from the Sea, A," 490, 511
Meyerbeer, M., 373
Millais, R.A., Mr. J. E., 735; letter to, 693
Milnes, Mr. Monckton, 37; letter to, 42; and see Houghton, Lord
Missionaries, Dickens on, 264, 260, 591
Mistake, a common, among would-be authors, 609
Mitton, Mr. Thomas; see Letters
Molesworth, Lady, 551, 552
"Money," Dickens on Lord Lytton's play of, 234
Montague, Miss Emmeline, 343
Monuments, Dickens on, 276, 834
Moore, Mr. Tom, 157

THE END

Printed by R. & R. CLARK, LIMITED, *Edinburgh.*

LaVergne, TN USA
27 May 2010
184043LV00005B/4/A